Taking Sides: Clashing Views on Moral Issues, 15/e

Owen M. Smith
Anne Collins Smith

http://create.mheducation.com

ISBN-10: 1259873390   ISBN-13: 9781259873393

Contents

Detailed Table of Contents

Unit 1: Fundamental Issues in Morality

Issue: Is Moral Relativism Correct?
YES: Torbjörn Tännsjö, from "Moral Relativism," *Philosophical Studies* (2007)
NO: Louis P. Pojman, from "The Case Against Moral Relativism," in *The Moral Life: An Introductory Reader in Ethics and Literature,* Oxford University Press (2007)

Torbjörn Tännsjö distinguishes among several types of relativism and argues in favor of one of them, which he calls "ontological relativism." According to this view, two people may disagree radically on a moral question, and yet both may be right, because each of them inhabits a different socially-constructed moral universe. Louis Pojman carefully distinguishes what he calls the diversity thesis—that moral rules differ from society to society—from ethical relativism. The diversity thesis is a straightforward description of what are acknowledged differences in the moral beliefs and practices of various human groups. But he argues that moral relativism does not follow from this diversity.

Issue: Does Morality Need Religion?
YES: C. Stephen Layman, from "Ethics and the Kingdom of God," in *The Shape of the Good: Christian Reflections on the Foundations of Ethics,* University of Notre Dame Press (1991)
NO: John Arthur, from "Religion, Morality, and Conscience," in *Morality and Moral Controversies,* Prentice Hall (1996)

Philosopher C. Stephen Layman argues that morality makes the most sense from a theistic perspective and that a purely secular perspective is insufficient. The secular perspective, Layman asserts, does not adequately deal with secret violations, and it does not allow for the possibility of fulfillment of people's deepest needs in an afterlife. Philosopher John Arthur counters that morality is logically independent of religion, although there are historical connections. Religion, he believes, is not necessary for moral guidance or moral answers; morality is social.

Unit 2: Sex, Marriage, and Reproduction

Issue: Is Casual Sex Immoral?
YES: Meg Lovejoy, from "Explaining Why the Practice [Hooking Up] Is More Costly than Beneficial," in *Is Hooking Up Empowering for College Women? A Feminist Gramscian Perspective,* Ph.D. dissertation, Brandeis University (2012)
NO: Raja Halwani, from "Casual Sex," in *Sex from Plato to Paglia: A Philosophical Encyclopedia,* Greenwood Press (2005)

Analyzing interviews with female college students enabled Meg Lovejoy to state clearly the advantages and disadvantages of sex without commitment for young women. The disadvantages, including fear of pregnancy and STDs, reduced self-esteem, and thwarted desire for intimacy, outweigh the advantages such as immediate pleasure. Raja Halwani first discusses the difficulties involved in defining casual sex precisely. He next examines a number of objections to casual sex and concludes that casual sex need not be morally wrong because each of these objections involves factors that are not, for the most part, specifically intrinsic to casual sex.

Issue: Is Abortion Immoral?
YES: Mary Meehan, from "Why Liberals Should Defend the Unborn," *Human Life Review* (2011)
NO: Amy Borovoy, from "Beyond Choice: A New Framework for Abortion?" *Dissent* (2011)

Mary Meehan argues that the unborn are exactly the kind of vulnerable population traditionally defended by liberals. She discusses a number of factors in support of this connection, such as scientific claims about when life begins, the obligations that arise from the act of conception, the disproportionate impact of abortion on poor women and women of color, and issues relating to disability rights and the environment. Amy Borovoy argues that the traditional defense of abortion, which opposes the choice of the woman against the life of the fetus, does not effectively capture the unique experience of pregnancy, and finds inspiration for a more satisfying approach in Japanese culture, where the decision whether or not to have an abortion is contextualized in the woman's responsibility not only to her fetus but to her family.

Issue: Is It Morally Right to Prohibit Same-Sex Marriage?

YES: Helen M. Alvaré, from "Brief of Amicus Curiae Helen M. Alvaré in Support of Hollingsworth and Bipartisan Legal Advisory Group," in *Hollingsworth v. Perry, U.S. v. Windsor*, Supreme Court of the United States (2013)
NO: The American Psychological Associations et al., from "Brief of Amici Curiae in Support of Affirmance in *Hollingsworth v. Perry*," Supreme Court of the United States (2013)

Law professor Helen M. Alvaré argues that the state's interest in promoting opposite-sex marriage stems from its interest in the procreation of children by opposite-sex married couples. Moreover, Alvaré traces the decline of marriage to the loss of traditional connections among marriage, sex, and children. State recognition of same-sex marriage would further undermine these connections and thus contribute to the destabilization of marriage, with negative repercussions to society, especially among the poor. Therefore, she argues, the state has an interest in prohibiting same-sex marriage. The American Psychological Association joins together with a number of other groups to argue that the substantial benefits that accrue to married couples should not be denied to same-sex couples. Citing evidence in favor of the ability of same-sex couples to form stable, long-lasting committed relationships, they argue that denying marriage to same-sex couples unfairly stigmatizes and discriminates against them.

Issue: Is it Immoral to Clone Human Beings?

YES: Michael J. Sandel, from "The Ethical Implications of Human Cloning," *Perspectives in Biology and Medicine* (2005)
NO: John A. Robertson, from "Human Cloning and the Challenge of Regulation," *The New England Journal of Medicine* (1998)

Political philosopher Michael J. Sandel argues that much of the talk about cloning revolves around a few limited concepts (e.g., rights, autonomy, and the supposed unnaturalness of asexual reproduction) that are inadequate and fail to express what is really wrong with cloning. We need, instead, to address fundamental questions about our stance toward nature. Law professor John A. Robertson maintains that there should not be a complete ban on human cloning but that regulatory policy should be focused on ensuring that it is performed in a responsible manner.

Unit 3: Law and Society

Issue: Is Paid Organ Donation Morally Permissible?

YES: Michael B. Gill and Robert M. Sade, from "Paying for Kidneys: The Case Against Prohibition," *Kennedy Institute of Ethics Journal* (2002)
NO: Anya Adair and Stephen J. Wigmore, from "Paid Organ Donation: The Case Against," *Annals of the Royal College of Surgeons of England* (2011)

Michael B. Gill and Robert M. Sade argue that since there are no moral prohibitions against donating kidneys for transplantation or selling blood plasma, there should be no moral prohibition against selling kidneys for transplantation. They further argue that selling a kidney does not violate a person's dignity and that a system in which a person can receive payment for a kidney is not inherently exploitive. Anya Adair and Stephen J. Wigmore argue that paid organ donation as currently practiced exploits the donors. They point to specific exploitive practices, such as withholding sufficient information for the donors to give truly informed consent. Further, they argue, any attempt to repair inequities in the system is doomed to failure because of the inherent inequity; only those under severe economic constraints will ever be willing to sell their organs.

Lewis Maltby analyzes the growing trend among employers to reduce health-care costs by regulating their employees' off-duty behavior, including requiring employees not to smoke. He argues that this trend is intrusive and unfair, and links it to national anti-smoking policies, which, he also believes, intrude on people's right to do what they want in their own homes. Adrien Barton argues that ads-that try to persuade people to stop smoking may seem to act against autonomy by telling them what they should do. However, since nicotine addiction takes autonomy away, helping people not to break the addiction helps to restore that autonomy.

Mirko Bagaric and Julie Clarke remind us, first of all, that torture, although prohibited by international law, is nevertheless widely practiced. A rational examination of torture and a consideration of hypothetical (but realistic) cases show that torture is justifiable in order to prevent great harm. Torture should be regulated and carefully practiced as an information-gathering technique in extreme cases. Christopher Kutz examines the reasoning intended to justify torture in a memo produced by the Bush administration and concludes that even in extreme hypothetical cases, such reasoning is not valid because the right not to be tortured is a pre-institutional right that cannot be revoked under any circumstances.

Describing the final stages of dementia as unacceptably degrading, Norman L. Cantor argues that patients who have received a dementia diagnosis are justified in planning to allow their lives to end before reaching that stage. Daniel P. Sulmasy argues that Cantor's assumption that the world would be better off without him in a deeply demented state is mistaken, and that legalizing voluntary suicide in such cases would logically lead to nonvoluntary euthanasia in others.

Kathryn L. Tucker argues that allowing mentally competent patients who face a slow and painful death to make it swifter and painless is a beneficial alternative, and that this practice is morally different from the act of suicide committed by those who are clinically depressed. George Annas et al. argue that a "right to suicide" cannot be justified on the same grounds as the right to refuse treatment, identifying several important differences between the two. Nor can such a right be justified on the same grounds as a right to abortion. The authors make it clear that rejecting the claim that people have a right to commit suicide does not affect the right to refuse unwanted medical treatment or to have an abortion.

Alexander Abdo et al. assert that the imposition of quarantine during the Ebola epidemic was unjustified, violated human rights, and even made things worse by fueling public fears. Wendy E. Parmet acknowledges that there are times when quarantine is necessary, and that in such cases it is important to craft laws that balance the need to guard against deadly contagious diseases and the need to maintain respect for human rights.

Charlotte A. Moser et al. take the position that parents are responsible for vaccinating their children, and that parents who choose not to do so must take responsibility for the consequences, not only to their own children, but to others. Leonard F. Vernon and Christopher Kent claim that attempts to portray anti-vaccination proponents as unscientific extremists clouds important issues of informed consent and freedom of choice relating to health care that they espouse, rather than facing the ethical issues surrounding fully informed consent.

Unit 4: Humanity, Nature, and Technology

Nathan Nobis argues that utilitarianism, an ethical theory in which the moral worth of an action is determined solely by its consequences, requires us to be vegetarians and avoid the consumption of meat. According to Nobis, meat and other animal products are produced under cruel conditions, and utilitarian principles require that we should not participate in or support activities that are cruel or inflict unnecessary pain on animals. Beth K. Haile argues that the consumption of meat can be part of a life that seeks to cultivate virtue and avoid vice. Although the way in which our society produces meat for consumption is morally unacceptable, there is nothing intrinsically wrong about the consumption of meat. Once meat is produced in a morally acceptable way, a virtuous life can include the consumption of meat.

Ronald Bailey is a strong supporter of genetically modified food (GMF). He argues that it is feared by many activists, but there is no strong proof that there are any problems with it. In fact, he suggests that there are great benefits that can be provided by GMFs, especially to the world's poor and to those suffering from natural calamities. Michael W. Fox is cautious about the spread of *scientism* and the morally blind push for technological development. This scientism, when combined with an aggressive spirit of enterprise, threatens to upset the balance of nature. We may try to rearrange natural things (including plants and animals) to serve our own purposes, but Fox believes that in this way we end up alienating ourselves from the natural world.

MIT Technology Review argues that applying a utilitarian analysis makes it clear that there will be times when the best outcome of a possible crash will involve injury or even death to the occupants of the car. Studies show that people want *other* people's cars to be programmed in this way, although they are unwilling to ride in such cars themselves. Jesse Kirkpatrick argues that crash optimization is a complex and subtle task, and that what is most important is transparency: drivers need to know in advance how their car is programmed.

Elizabeth Nolan Brown predicts that people will never lose their preference for actual human companionship and will enjoy sex with robots primarily as a harmless diversion. Kathleen Richardson argues that the ability to treat sex robots as things rather than people, without regard for their feelings or dignity, will increase and worsen the lack of empathy already felt by those who treat prostitutes as things rather than people.

Nora Wenthold and Teresa A. Savage consider the overall use of service animals to be justified. They describe, however, a number of situations in which ethical treatment of service animals requires careful consideration of the animal's strengths, limitations, and well-being. Understanding and respecting the animal's nature is a crucial and sometimes overlooked ethical requirement. Randy Malamud argues that our current attitudes toward service animals spring from speciesism, an attitude that members of certain species (such as humans) have greater value or more rights than certain other species (such as nonhumans). He is especially concerned about the extension of the practice to animals such as monkeys, parrots, and dolphins, which may derive little benefit to themselves from their association with humans.

Preface

This text contains essays arranged in pro and con pairs that address controversial issues in morality and moral philosophy. Each of the issues is expressed in terms of a single question in order to draw the lines of debate more clearly.

Some of the questions included in this volume have been in the mainstream of moral philosophy for hundreds or even thousands of years and are central to the discipline. These include abstract questions about relativism and the relationship between morality and religion. Other questions relate to specific topics of contemporary concern, such as cloning, abortion, affirmative action, and the relinquishment of technology.

The authors of the selections presented here take a strong stand on a given issue and provide the best defenses of their own positions. The selections were chosen for their usefulness in defending a position and for their accessibility to students. The authors include philosophers, scientists, and social critics from a wide variety of backgrounds. Each presents us with a well-defined and closely argued answer on an issue—even if we ultimately cannot accept the answer as our own.

Each issue is accompanied by an introduction, which sets the stage for the debate, and concludes with a question about middle ground, which explores the possibility of agreement. Learning outcomes, questions for critical thinking and reflection, suggestions for further reading, and Internet resources may also be found in each issue, along with biographical information about the contributors on each side of the debate.

Taking Sides: Clashing Views on Moral Issues is a tool to encourage critical thought on important moral issues. Readers are charged with the task of developing a critical and informed view of these issues, and should not feel confined to the views expressed in the selections. Some readers may see important points on both sides of an issue and construct for themselves a new and creative approach, which may incorporate the best of both sides or provide an entirely new vantage point for understanding.

Owen M. Smith
Stephen F. Austin State University

Anne Collins Smith
Stephen F. Austin State University

Editors of This Volume

OWEN M. SMITH, Professor of Philosophy and Classical Studies at Stephen F. Austin State University, earned a PhD in Philosophy from the joint program in Classics and Philosophy at the University of Texas at Austin. His primary areas of specialization are applied ethics, philosophy of religion, and natural theology in late antiquity. His research and teaching interests include gnosticism and the application of mythological and philosophical principles to popular culture.

ANNE COLLINS SMITH, Professor of Philosophy and Classical Studies at Stephen F. Austin State University, earned a PhD in Philosophy from the joint program in Classics and Philosophy at the University of Texas at Austin. Her primary areas of specialization are medieval metaphysics, natural theology, and applied ethics. Her current research and teaching interests include the use of popular culture to exemplify philosophical problems.

The editors have also written and translated graphic novels for children and young adults.

Acknowledgments We owe a debt of thanks to Stephen Satris, the original and longtime editor of *Taking Sides: Clashing Views on Moral Issues;* without his pioneering efforts, we would have had neither the opportunity nor the honor of continuing his work. We are also grateful to Gregory Kaebnick, editor of *Taking Sides: Clashing Views on Bioethical Issues*, whose collaboration on the topics of paid organ donation, directives for patients with dementia, and physician-assisted suicide was greatly appreciated.

To our parents with gratitude for their heritage and to our son with hope for the future.

Academic Advisory Board Members

Robert Covert
Coastline Community College

Judith Wagner DeCew
Clark University

John Dufour
Central Mexico Community College

L.M. Ed monds
Arizona State University

Theodore Faulders
Santa Barbara City College

Christian Fossa-Andersen
DeVry University

Amber E. George
SUNY Cortland

Joe Givvin
Mount Mercy University

Andreas Kiryakakis
College of St. Benedict

Elizabeth Langevin
University of Phoenix

Robert Micallef
Madonna University

Jimmy Montgomery
Newberry College

Robert L. Muhlnickel
Monroe Community College

Ronald Novy
University of Central Arkansas

Andreas W. Reif
Manchester Community College

Michael Robinson
College of Western Idaho

William Rodriguez
Bethune Cookman University

Karen Scialabba
Marist College

Rafayel Seyranyan
Northern Virginia Community College

Anita Silvers
San Francisco State University

Michael Thomas
Arkansas State University

Matt Zwolinski
University of San Diego

Introduction

Making decisions about what is right and wrong, what should and shouldn't be done, is an activity that we do thousands of times every day. In fact, many of these decisions are so clear-cut, so straightforward that we are scarcely, if at all, aware that we are making them. Rarely do we seriously entertain the notion of running red lights, driving onto the sidewalk and scattering pedestrians, or even ramming the cars of drivers who annoy us. True, the legal consequences of such actions provide a deterrent to indulging in these fantasies, but legal issues are not the only reasons we exercise self-discipline and self-control. While running red lights might get us to our destinations faster, it is only *fair* that everyone take their turn. Driving onto the sidewalks might enable us to get around traffic jams, but people could get hurt that way, and it's just not *worth* hurting people to save a little time. Ramming other cars might make us feel better, but the other drivers are people too, and they deserve our *respect* even when they annoy us.

In fact, only when these types of decisions are not clear-cut do we actually have to sit down and reflect on the various options that we are facing, what factors favor each option, and what factors oppose each option, in order to figure out how to act. Even then, making a decision about how to act is not like making a simple factual determination, like how many bones there are in the typical human foot. Facts are important in making these types of decisions, but they are only incidental to the process. Rather, the central part of the decision-making process involves general ideas about the sorts of actions that are right and the sorts of actions that are wrong. These ideas, known as moral principles, are then applied in specific situations by specific people. Moreover, different people may arrive at different conclusions about how to act, even if they were placed in exactly the same situation. In fact, unlike in strictly factual disputes that have only one correct answer, it is possible to respect the decision made by another person, even though you would have made a different decision.

Identifying the reasons for disputes about the proper way to act can be difficult. Sometimes there is a difference of opinion about what the facts are. Sometimes there may be agreement about what the facts are, but a difference about what they mean or how to interpret them. More fundamentally, there may be a difference in fundamental moral principles, about the very sorts of actions that are

right and wrong. Often, a dispute arises not just from one type of difference, but from many different types of reasons. Simply identifying the reason or reasons behind the dispute may not be enough to resolve the dispute. It might be the case that some disputes about how to act can never be resolved.

Judgments about the proper way to act in a specific situation are called moral judgments. Morality is a philosophical discipline that addresses how moral judgments are made in specific situations. The investigation into the principles used in making moral judgments is known as ethics. Various philosophers have proposed ethical theories about the meaning of basic moral terms such as good and bad, right and wrong. These theories often have consequences about whether disputes about moral judgments can ever be resolved. Often, people who proceed from different ethical theories end up making different moral judgments. Oddly enough, it is not uncommon for people who proceed from different ethical theories to arrive at the same moral judgment, although they provide different justifications or rationales for their judgment. People who proceed from the same ethical theories may also arrive at different moral judgments, most often because they emphasize different moral principles in making their judgments.

So, what are you to do when faced with a difficult decision about how to act, a decision that is not clear-cut or straightforward? Since the issue is not strictly a factual issue, you will have to arrive at your own decision by careful thought. Try as best you can to imagine yourself holding each position; in this way you can identify the assumptions each position makes, work carefully through the steps justifying each position, identify the advantages and disadvantages of each position, and determine how important these advantages and disadvantages are. Moreover, you should maintain an open mind toward all the positions. Strive to assume the position of an impartial judge, who can accurately state each position and can fairly assess its strengths and weaknesses. In order to accomplish these tasks, a degree of introspection is necessary. Be aware of your own initial thoughts and feelings on the issue and be sure to identify any assumptions or preconceived ideas you may possess; these assumptions and ideas will need to be tested before making a final judgment. If you have a strong prior attachment to one position, guard against unfairly favoring this position as you consider the issue. Finally, once each position has been clearly understood and carefully considered, make a choice. Morality is a practical discipline, and judgment cannot be postponed indefinitely. However, when the time for informed judgment arrives, remember that while you must make a choice, you need not choose either of the positions presented to you. There may be another way of approaching the issue, a way of establishing common ground among the incompatible positions which allows you to escape the conflict and incorporate the best parts of each position.

The process of making moral judgments is modelled for you in each of the issues discussed in this text. A practical question is posed, and two opposed positions are presented for your careful consideration. Read through each author's arguments, reasons, and examples, and decide which have merit. The questions and issues that are raised here require careful analysis and evaluation, and you may be unsatisfied with the positions expressed in the selections. View these shortcomings as an opportunity to modify and correct these positions until they are as strong and persuasive as then can be. Then reason through the issue yourself and come to your own conclusion about the moral course of action.

Decisions about how to act not only say a lot about the sort of person you are, but also can actually determine the sort of person you come to be. This process, moreover, is never over. People who are dissatisfied with themselves can become a different sort of person by consistently making different decisions about how to act; so too those who are satisfied with the sort of person they are can start down the road of becoming dissatisfied with themselves by making different decisions. In this way, morality and moral decision making have consequences beyond any given issue. There is no final exam in morality. After all, we make decisions about what is right and wrong, what should and shouldn't be done, thousands of times every day.

"It is our choices . . . that show what we truly are, far more than our abilities."

J. K. Rowling, *Harry Potter and the Chamber of Secrets*

Owen M. Smith
Anne Collins Smith

Unit 1

Fundamental Issues in Morality

*E*ven *before confronting particular moral issues, we often encounter diverging views about morality itself. Some people assert that there is no such thing as objective morality, and thus moral conflicts cannot be resolved. Such people commonly hold the view that moral judgments are simply the expression of individual or cultural views, which vary from time to time and place to place. Other people assert that morality is the product of divine revelation, and thus without religion, there is no morality. These and other ideas are discussed in this unit.*

Selected, Edited, and with Issue Framing Material by:
Owen M. Smith, *Stephen F. Austin State University*
and
Anne Collins Smith, *Stephen F. Austin State University*

ISSUE

Is Moral Relativism Correct?

YES: Torbjörn Tännsjö, from "Moral Relativism," *Philosophical Studies* (2007)

NO: Louis P. Pojman, from "The Case Against Moral Relativism," in *The Moral Life: An Introductory Reader in Ethics and Literature*, Oxford University Press (2007)

Learning Outcomes

After reading this issue, you will be able to:

- Explain the distinction between cultural moral relativism and individual moral relativism.
- Explain the central concept and basic justification of ontological relativism.
- Explain the central concept and basic justification of moral realism.
- Formulate your own position on whether morality is relative and identify evidence supporting your position.
- Identify the main objections to your position and formulate responses to these objections.

ISSUE SUMMARY

YES: Torbjörn Tännsjö distinguishes among several types of relativism and argues in favor of one of them, which he calls "ontological relativism." According to this view, two people may disagree radically on a moral question, and yet both may be right, because each of them inhabits a different socially-constructed moral universe.

NO: Louis Pojman carefully distinguishes what he calls the diversity thesis—that moral rules differ from society to society—from ethical relativism. The diversity thesis is a straightforward description of what are acknowledged differences in the moral beliefs and practices of various human groups. But he argues that moral relativism does not follow from this diversity.

Moral realism is the view that there are objective moral standards that can be applied to all actions, no matter who performs them or in what circumstances they are performed. One important aspect of moral realism is the ability to make a definitive judgment about the morality of an action: it is either morally right or morally wrong, much like a claim about reality is either factually correct or factually incorrect.

When people are discussing conflicting moral judgments, the assertion that "morality is relative" almost inevitably comes up. Such statements are often attempts to cut the discussion short, since they undermine any objective basis for establishing which moral judgments might be correct or incorrect. Moreover, the statement "morality is relative" is frustratingly vague and incomplete. To understand what is meant by that assertion, we need to answer the question "What factor or factors is morality relative to?"

Sometimes "morality is relative" means that moral judgments are relative to various aspects of a specific situation. Something as simple as washing a car might be morally permissible under normal circumstances, but morally wrong during a drought. In other cases, "morality is relative" means that moral judgments are relative to a person's interpretation of a situation, so that people who interpret the same situation differently will make different moral judgments about the right thing to do. For example, someone who believes that washing a car will make it rain might consider it morally necessary to wash a car during a drought, while those who do not share that belief would consider the same action morally wrong. Moreover, it is entirely possible that the people making different moral judgments hold the same moral values and the difference in their moral judgments arise only from the differences in their situations or from the differences in their interpretations of the same situation, not from a genuine conflict between their values. Both the car-washer (who believes that washing the car will make it rain) as well as the non-washer (who believes that washing the car will simply waste water) value responsibility to the community and respect for the environment; they merely disagree about the best way to fulfill their shared values. Because we make moral judgments in specific contexts, these kinds of relativity are inherent in all moral reasoning. Thus, the assertion that "morality is relative" does not usually refer to these kinds of relativity.

Instead, the assertion that "morality is relative" usually means that moral judgments are relative to moral values. Such relativists hold the view that there are no objective moral standards that apply in every circumstance or situation. Instead, there are many sets of different moral standards, all of which are equally correct. There are two distinct forms of this type of relativism: cultural moral relativism, which asserts that the morality of an action is determined by the culture in which the action is performed, and individual ethical relativism, which asserts that the morality of an action is determined by the opinion of the person performing the action.

While many people initially find this approach to morality attractive, most people who have thought and written about this issue reject moral relativism. As a result, the supporters of moral relativism are in the minority. Among those, however, who think moral relativism is correct, Torbjörn Tännsjö's work—excerpted here—stands out. After briefly mentioning the view that people should be tolerant of the moral problem-solving principles of other cultures, Tännsjö distinguishes between semantic relativism and ontological relativism.

Semantic relativism corresponds fairly closely to cultural moral relativism. According to semantic relativism, people make moral judgments based solely on the moral framework established within their culture. Therefore, when a person asserts that an action is morally right or morally wrong, he or she is really asserting that the action is morally permissible or morally impermissible within his or her culture. Accordingly, specific moral judgments may be both correct and incorrect, that is, they may be correct according to the principles of one culture and incorrect according to the principles of another culture. Tännsjö explicitly rejects this form of relativism.

Rather, Tännsjö argues in favor of a kind of relativism that he calls ontological relativism. Ontological relativism is akin to individual moral relativism. According to this view, each of us inhabits a separate moral universe, which we construct from the moral framework of the societies in which we live. Each person, therefore, makes moral judgments from the perspective of his or her own moral universe. Ontological relativism differs from semantic relativism, according to Tännsjö, because in ontological relativism moral judgments cannot be both correct and incorrect, they must be either correct or incorrect. They are correct if they correspond to the principles I have established in my moral universe; they are incorrect if they do not corrrepond to the principles I have established in my universe. People who make moral judgments that conflict with my moral judgments are not just different, they are wrong. It is true that people who inhabit different moral universes can make different moral judgments, but within the moral universe of each person, there is only one correct set of moral principles, and hence only one moral judgment can be correct in that universe.

In contrast, Louis Pojman argues that commonly held forms of relativism such as cultural moral relativism and individual moral relativism are incorrect. After examining the underlying principles of these positions, he offers a detailed critique of them by dissecting the premises that appear to support them. Pojman also undermines these positions by using a type of argument known as *reductio ad absurdum*. In this type of argument, he points out the absurd consequences of following the underlying principles of these forms of relativism to their logical conclusion. Finally, he asserts that what appear to be differences in moral principles between cultures may simply be differences in the way that moral principles are applied depending on particular elements or interpretations of given situations, which leaves open the possibility that different cultures can share common moral principles.

YES ⬅

Torbjörn Tännsjö

Moral Relativism

Introduction

Moral relativism comes in many varieties. One is a substantial moral doctrine, according to which we ought to respect other cultures, and allow them to solve moral problems as they see fit. I will say nothing about this kind of moral relativism in the present context.

Other kinds of relativism are metaethical doctrines. According to these doctrines, there are more than one way correctly to answer a moral question. At least this is how I am going to use the term 'relativism' in the present context. This means that I do not count expressivism and emotivism and prescriptivism as relativist doctrines. According to expressivism, emotivism, or prescriptivism, there is no moral truth. According to these doctrines, there exist no moral facts. I prefer to classify these doctrines as nihilist. Relativism is the doctrine that there exists more than one truth about some moral cases. . . .

In the present context I will focus on metaethical forms of moral relativism and set nihilism to one side. Moral (metaethical) relativism, in turn, comes in at least three forms.

One kind of moral (metaethical) relativism is semantic (or 'indexical') moral relativism, according to which, when we pass moral judgements, we make an implicit reference to some system of morality (our own). According to this kind of moral relativism, when I say that a certain action is right, my statement is elliptic. What I am really saying is that, according to some (adequate) moral framework or system S, to which I adhere, for example the one prevailing in my culture, this action is permitted.[1] I will reject this kind of relativism.

According to another kind of (metaethical) moral relativism, which we may call epistemic, it is possible that, when one person (belonging to one culture) makes a certain moral judgement, such as that this action is right, and another person (belong[ing] to another culture) makes the judgement that the very same action is wrong, they may have just as good reasons for their respective judgements; it is even possible that, were they fully informed about all the facts, equally imaginative, and so forth, they would still hold on to their respective (conflicting) judgements. They are each fully justified in their belief in conflicting judgements.[2] I will comment on this form of moral relativism in passing.

Finally, however, there is a third kind of (metaethical) moral relativism we could call ontological, according to which, when two persons pass conflicting moral verdicts on a certain action, they may both be right. Neither of them make judgements with any implicit reference to any system of norms. They both use their moral vocabulary in an absolute sense. An objectivist non-natural moral analysis (in the style of G.E. Moore or Henry Sidgwick) of what they say gives a correct representation of what they are doing. And yet, for all that, they pass conflicting judgements. The explanation why they can both, in an absolute sense, be 'right' in their judgements, is that they inhabit different moral (socially constructed) universes. So while it is true in the first person's moral universe that a certain action is right, it is true in the second person's moral universe that the very same action is wrong. I intend to explain and defend this version of ontological moral relativism.

Moral Universes

How Are We to Think of Moral Universes?

A moral universe consists of a system of common sense morality. We may compare common sense morality to grammar. And we should remember that it is possible to distinguish between descriptive and regulative grammar. In descriptive grammar we observe how language is actually used. We formulate hypotheses, and we try to find general answers to questions about language use. But we may also discuss a language from a regulative point of view. We may try to answer questions such as: is it correct to use certain words in a certain order? We may want to articulate general principles also in regulative grammar. However, these principles are not descriptive of the language in question. Rather, they answer the question: what makes a certain way of using language a proper or correct one? They provide reasons for answers to this question.

In regulative grammar we take for granted that there are facts of the matter. There are right and wrong ways of using language. These are facts. These facts do not exist independently of us, of course. We may think of them as social constructions, i.e. as constituted by us. If we were to speak differently, then different facts would obtain. And yet, for all that, these facts are in a sense objective. We may be ignorant about them. By sound argument we may be set straight with respect to them. . . .

It is worth observing that there are two different kinds of answers to the question what 'makes' a certain use of language a proper or correct one. One (regulative) kind of answer does indeed stipulate a reason for a judgement about the case: it is wrong to put the words in a certain order because, in the language in question, the noun phrase must precede the verb phrase. This is the kind of reason stated in a principle or rule of regulative grammar. However, the same question, i.e. the question what 'makes' a certain use of language a proper or correct one, can also be understood as an ontological question about what constitutes right and wrong in a language. And then the answer must be along the following lines: the correctness of a certain way of using the words is constituted by the fact that this is how the words are actually used in the linguistic community in question. But this is not the end of the matter. It is also crucial how experts on grammar assess this way of using words. If they condone this way of using the words, this contributes to this way's being a proper one. And, of course, one reason why the experts condone a certain way of using the words is that this is how the words are being used. But it is also true, to some extent, at least, that the fact that this way of using the words is condoned by the experts contributes to the explanation of why the words are used this way.

In a similar vein we may think of (conventional common sense) morality (in a society). Conventional common sense morality is learnt by children in a manner similar to how they learn their mother tongue. They learn that it is right or wrong to perform certain actions. Why is it right or wrong to perform a certain action? Once again there exist two ways of understanding and answering the question. A certain rule can be given, providing a reason to perform, or not perform, the action in question. Or, the question may be understood as an ontological question as to what constitutes right and wrong action. Once again, the answer to the latter (ontological) question has something to do with both how people actually behave, but also with how moral experts, or even people in general, tend to judge this kind of behaviour. These facts, in turn, may have, and certainly must have, some kind of natural explanation, for example one in terms of evolutionary biology.

Socially constituted moral norms seem to come to us in the form of a moral universe. This means that we think of them, ideally, at any rate, as complete. We demand of the norms making up our moral universe that, in principle, they answer all moral questions (even though the answers may be hard to come by for us) in an unambiguous way. And the set of answers to these questions is the moral universe (a set of moral facts). . . .

In general, if we want to find out about what constitutes right and wrong action in a certain society, we should focus more on how people justify their actions than on what they do. A crucial feature of morality is that we can use the morality a person explicitly adheres to when we want to criticise his or her actions, once they are at variance with this morality. But, at the same time, if everybody tend to perform a certain action, condemned by common sense morality, this may mean that, at the end of the day, this action is actually condoned by common sense morality. Common sense morality is in much way a malleable and changing entity. . . .

How are we to distinguish moral (socially constituted) facts from other kinds of (socially constituted) facts, such as facts concerning etiquette, the existing legal situation, and so forth?

I suppose one distinguishing fact is that moral facts are more basic. Moral considerations seem to override other kinds of consideration. In fact, only moral considerations provide us with, in Kant's sense, categorical norms. Even if, linguistically speaking, it is proper to put a comment in one way and improper to put it in another way, this does not mean that one ought to put it in the proper way. In a similar vein, even if a certain action is legally prescribed, economically advantageous, and so forth, this does not as such mean that we ought to perform it. This fact may be hidden, to some extent, by the fact that we may believe that we have a moral obligation to obey the law. Some may even believe that we have a moral obligation to use language properly. However, without such obligations taken for granted, law and regulative grammar lack categorical normative force.

Moreover, to be accepted as a 'morality' a normative outlook must not be too idiosyncratic, i.e., it has to [be] shared to some extent, it has to be supported by a kind of common sense.

It is a moot question to what extent, within an existing common sense morality, we can really find principles explaining all actual cases of right- and wrongdoing. This problem has a clear parallel within grammar. However, even if, in the final analysis, experts must take up a rather 'particularistic' view, and concede that they find no deterministic principles capable of explaining all cases of right- or wrong-doing (or proper or improper grammar), we all tend to believe that, in many cases, there are correct answers to these questions. Even if we cannot tell for certain why this is so, we know that it is wrong to perform certain actions (or we know that certain grammatical constructions are ill formed). . . .

It would perhaps be far-fetched to claim that, just as there are different languages, there are completely different moralities (in different societies).[3] However, I think it safe to claim at least that, just as there are somewhat different dialects or even idiolects existing within a linguistic community, there are somewhat different moralities existing in different societies.

Here is a possible example. In most (all) actual societies (with their corresponding moral universes) women are in many respects treated worse than men. However, while in some societies such unequal treatment can be defended on the ground that, by treating women worse than men, all get what they deserve, such a defence is not possible in another society (with another and different moral universe, where the value of women and men is constituted as equal).

Or, should we adopt some constraint to do with the content of a moral universe and claim that the former universe is not moral? This is something we do when we pass moral judgements, of course. If we feel that men and women are of equal worth we may hesitate to speak of the view that men are more valuable than women as a 'moral' one. We will speak of it as immoral. However, when pursuing metaethics, it might be a good idea not to include any requirement that a socially constituted system of norms should have any content in particular in order to count as a 'moral' universe. The crucial thing is that the norms composing it have an overriding nature and are not too idiosyncratic.

All this means that while, from the perspective of one existing common sense morality (society), an action may be right, it may yet, for all that, be wrong, when judged from the perspective of another existing common sense morality. . . .

Back to Semantic Relativism?

But does not all this mean that we are back to a semantic relativism of a naturalistic, indexical kind? Is the claim made above not just that, when a person in one society asserts that a certain action is right, what this person is saying is that, from the perspective of the set of moral rules operative in his or her society, this action is right?

No, this is not the proper way of understanding the claim. Note that we have distinguished between descriptive and regulative grammar; in a similar vein we ought to distinguish between descriptive and normative ethics. So, when a person asserts that a certain action is right, this assertion is indeed normative. The assertion is that the action in question is right, period. The analysis of the assertion is non-naturalist. No implicit reference to the system of norms is made; an objective claim, with reference to socially constituted moral facts, is being made. We may say that this assertion is true in the moral universe in question if and only if the action in question is right. The explanation of why it is right, simpliciter can be given, however, with reference to (the content of, not the existence of) principles in this system of morality – to the extent that moral principles can be formulated within this system of morality. The claim as such makes no reference to the existence of these principles. It is normative and categorical and objective and allows of non-naturalistic analysis.

What are we to say about a situation where two persons from different cultures make conflicting judgements about a certain action?

Well, in order for this scenario to be possible, at least one of the systems must have a general scope. If both systems restrict their judgements to actions within their respective societies, no conflict will emerge. However, while this policy of live and let live is comparatively common in a linguistic context (especially between different languages but also, to some extent, between different dialects), this kind of moral relativism (with such a restricted scope) is rare. We tend to judge, from the point of view of our own morality, the manners of others. This is rendered possible by the fact that two different moral universes may share (a part of) the one and only existing actual empirical universe. If a certain concrete action is part of both moral universes, it may be right in one of the universes while wrong in the other universe. And, as I have stressed above, if we conceive of ourselves as inhabiting a moral universe, there will be a drive towards completeness. We want answers to all moral questions, also those arising in alien cultures.

Suppose the two persons are actually making conflicting moral judgements about the very same action. Let us suppose, for example, that while one person asserts that a certain action, such as the circumcision performed on a young woman in the society to which this person belongs ought to take place, another person, belonging to another society, asserts that this very same action ought not to take place, how are we to understand their conflict?

This is indeed a conflict. So we should avoid interpreting the judgements as elliptical, with an implicit reference to each person's own system of norms (somehow corrected). They are both to be taken as issuing categorical judgements about the very same action. And these judgements are indeed, we may assume, true in each moral universe. And they are 'objective' in the sense that they may be true, irrespective of whether anyone knows about this. But does not this mean that they cannot be contradictory?

I believe we should say that these people do not, strictly speaking, contradict each other. And this is due to the fact that their respective judgements differ in meaning. In saying so, we assume a moderate amount if externalism about meaning, of course. Each person, in each universe, refers to a simple property, but the properties differ between universes. One judgement is true in virtue of facts obtaining in one universe; the other is true in virtue of facts obtaining in the other universe. People inhabiting different moral universes may agree, of course, that it is true (in their universe) that a certain action is right, if and only if this action is right, but this, seemingly identical truth condition, has different meaning in different moral universes. We cannot analyse this meaning in any natural terms. In each universe, the notion of obligation is simple and not definable in any non-moral terms. However, even if the truth-conditions of each judgement are in a way inscrutable, they differ. And this means that these persons do not contradict each other after all. The reason is that they have constituted to themselves different moral universes. They need not themselves be aware of this, of course. Each may think that there is one true morality (theirs).[4] . . .

What has now been said seems to imply that we face a kind of semantic relativism after all. And in a way we do. However, this is a new and subtler form of semantic relativism (as compared to the traditional variety described in the opening paragraph) since, taking norms to be categorical, it is compatible with the fact that the judgements in question are in conflict.

How are we to conceive of this conflict? Well, even if the judgements are logically compatible, they, and not only those who issue them, are in conflict in a practical sense. This practical conflict is rendered possible by the fact that these normative judgements have not only truth-conditions, but satisfaction conditions as well. The claim that the woman in question ought to be circumcised is satisfied if, and only if, the women is actually circumcised. And note that this satisfaction-condition is the same in all moral universes (since it is not cast in moral terms).

The normative claims that the circumcision ought to take place, and that it ought not to take place are, therefore, even if logically consistent (because issued from different moral universes using the word 'ought' in different ways), still incompatible. There is no way to satisfy both these claims.

This practical inconsistency explains why persons belonging to different moral universes, making moral judgements that are, from a strict logical point of view, consistent, may feel a need to sort out their conflicts. Even if they need not feel any intellectual drive to do so, they may well, for practical reasons, find it urgent to reach an agreement. . . .

Moral Explanation

Furthermore, while it is hard to see how we could offer moral explanations, if semantic relativism of the naturalistic, indexical, variety were true, this is something we can do on the (objectivist) version of relativism here defended. If 'This is wrong' means that, according to a certain (adequate,) framework or system of norms S, this is not permitted, then there seems to be no way of explaining what it is that makes the action in question wrong. There may be a causal explanation why the action has come to be prohibited, but there is no possibility of finding any moral explanation of its wrongness. However, on the version of relativism here defended, we may easily find a moral explanation of why the action in question is wrong, provided the moral universe is rich enough to provide such an explanation. We may say, for example, that it is wrong since it means that an innocent person is harmed (provided it is wrong to harm innocent persons in the universe in question). But this fact cannot explain why, according to S, it is not permitted. The (social) fact that it is not permitted by S, if it can be explained at all, must be explained in terms that seem to be morally irrelevant. The explanation might be, for example, that the action in question is condemned in the system because the system condemning these kinds of actions have had a certain function, explaining why it has been selected, and so forth. Such an explanation is interesting from a sociological point of view but irrelevant from a moral point of view. . . .

Logical Relations between Moral Judgements

According to the kind of moral absolutism here defined, there are indeed moral judgements, capable of being true or false. It is true that the meaning of words such as 'right' and 'wrong' tend to vary between different moral universes, but within each moral universe there exist true and false moral judgements. This means that we can conceive of logical relations in terms of truth. A moral argument is valid if, and only if, necessarily, . . . the premises of the argument are true, then the conclusion of the argument is true as well. To obtain the right moral implications we need to clarify the normative terminology, of course. But this can easily be done, for example in the following manner. A particular action is right if and only if it is not wrong. And an action is obligatory if and only if it is wrong not to perform it. Since rightness, wrongness and obligatoriness are, even if socially constituted, yet objective and genuine properties of particular actions we need only standard first-order predicate logic to get our deontic logic off the ground. . . .

When we take our moral judgements to be true or false, we may conceive of moral inconsistencies in the 'ordinary' way. Two inconsistent norms cannot both be true. And we will thus, in our pursuit for truth, have an incentive to get rid also of moral inconsistencies. When we think of moral facts as constitutive of a moral 'universe', it becomes imperative that all moral truth can be combined into one single and true (consistent) conjunction describing this universe. And our well-known epistemic goal of believing a proposition if it is true, and of not believing it if it is false, applies to our moral beliefs just as well as to other aspects of our belief system. . . .

Moral Relativism and Moral Realism

It should be noted that if moral ontological relativism, of the kind here described, is true, then epistemic moral relativism is trivially true. It is obvious that, if conflicting moral judgements, made by people living in different moral universes, may be true, then each advocate of each one of the conflicting views may have equally good reasons to support his or her favoured position. But what should a 'transcendental' moral realist of Moore's or Sidgwick's brand say about the view just outlined?

It is true that most philosophers who have advocated some kind of social constructivist view of ethics have been 'nihilists', in the sense that they have denied that there are any moral facts, existing independent of our thinking and acting.[5] Social constructivism has been resorted to by them as a kind of ersatz realism. However, this does not mean that social constructivism is inconsistent with strong moral realism. Indeed, I think it would be foolhardy of a 'transcendental' moral realist, who believes that there are objective moral reasons

and facts existing independently of us to deny that different (conventional) moral universes of the kind here described exist as well. Moral realists should be prepared to accept that, when some people pass moral verdicts on actions, they express their views from the perspective of the conventional morality into which they have been socialised. So normative ontological relativism is made true by the existence of this kind of socially constituted or constructed conventional morality. However, a moral realist, who believes that there exist moral facts independently of our conceptualisation or actions, should be expected to want to add to this picture that, once the existing different moral universes have been described, there is a way of transcending them all. One more question remains to be asked and answered: which one, if any among competing moral claims, is the uniquely correct one? They must be supposed to ask for reasons that are not only categorical and objective but also such that they are in no way of our making.

When the moral realist of Moore's or Sidgwick's variety poses this question, using the standard moral terminology in the way he or she does, it is quite possible that the question cannot be answered with reference to any principles designed to rationalise any actual conventional morality. And, more importantly, the answer to the question, if such an answer exists, cannot be taken to be constituted by us. On the contrary, it is assumed that the answer is 'out there', to be found, in the same way that answers to questions posed by physicists are thought to be 'out there' to be found.

Suppose the moral realist is right about this. Let us suppose that the moral realist is right in insisting that, when different conventional moralities have been identified, there is one more question to be asked and to be answered: which one (if any one) of two competing moral claims is the correct one?[6] What does this mean?

Well, it is obvious that the moral realist is here using the moral vocabulary in a slightly different sense from the senses used in the two competing conventional moral universes. But it is no coincidence that all the parties to this controversy translate the relevant words into 'right' and 'wrong' in their own terminology. For even if these terms, when they occur in different moral universes, take on a somewhat different meaning, they all share an important function. They are all categorical and they do all guide choices. . . .

What does all this mean for how we should understand the moral conversation between a moral realist and a person who has never contemplated this 'further' question about absolute rightness, merely passing moral judgements from his or her conventional moral universe?

The obvious answer is that we should understand this difference of opinion in a way similar to how we understood the conflict between people belonging to different (conventional) moral universes. The moral realist and the person issuing moral judgements from the perspective of a particular conventional moral universe pass moral judgements that are logically consistent (because they have different truth-conditions); however, these judgements are, since they are categorical and normative, and therefore without implicit reference to any moral universe, truly conflicting. In many cases these persons will find that there is no way of satisfying the moral demands put forward by the other party. So there will be a drive somehow to solve the conflict.

Conclusion

Global ontological relativism is a self-defeating position, or so I would be prepared to argue. However, the existence of many different conventional moral systems or moral 'universes' prepares the way for a more restricted kind of moral ontological relativism. I have argued that such moral ontological relativism is true. Here Nelson Goodman's daring metaphor of 'world-making' is indeed appropriate.

It is noteworthy that even a moral realist who believes that there exists one uniquely true morality 'out there', to be found by us, may concede that moral ontological relativism of the kind here described is true. The moral realist need not reject relativism, but only add a realistic element to the picture.

Notes

1. This version of relativism is famously defended (in several places) by David Wong and Gilbert Harman. It should be noted that Harman doesn't put forward his theory as a claim about what we actually mean by a word like 'right'; rather, if we want to understand the use of 'right' in moral context as contributing to claims that have truth-values, then this is how we should understand these uses.

2. I know of no philosopher who has actually defended this (indeed quite defensible) position.

3. Some moral relativists may be prepared to make this claim, but I find it exaggerated; in general, relativists tend to exaggerate the degree to which different moral communities hold on to different basic moral positions. It seems to me that much apparent moral disagreement can be explained away as depending on different empirical beliefs.

4. This is true of semantic, indexical kinds of relativism as well, of course. Neither Harman nor Wong need to insist that it is obvious to speakers referring to different frameworks or systems, that this is what they are actually doing.

5. For example, this seems to me to be a correct diagnosis of John McDowell. See for example his 'Non-Cognitivism and Rule-Following', in Steven H. Holtzman and Christopher M. Leich (eds.), Wittgenstein: to Follow a Rule, London: Routledge & Kegan Paul, 1981.

6. Note that even if the moral realist is right about this, there may be no way of finding out the answer to this question. If this is not possible, a kind of strong moral epistemic relativism seems to emerge. On this version of epistemic relativism a unique moral truth exits, so two conflicting moral opinions cannot both be right. And yet, for all that, two people may have equally and perfectly good reasons to believe in their favoured solution to the moral problem.

TORBJÖRN TÄNNSJÖ has been the Kristian Claëson Professor of Practical Philosophy at Stockholm University since 2002; he is also Director at the Stockholm University Stockholm Centre for Health Care Ethics, a cooperation between Stockholm University (SU), Karolinska Instistute (KI), and the Royal Institute of Technology (KTH). He is also an Affiliated Professor of Medical Ethics at Karolinska Institute. He has written and edited a number of important books in the field of ethics and has published over a hundred articles.

Louis P. Pojman   ➡ **NO**

The Case Against Moral Relativism

"Who's to Judge What's Right or Wrong?"

> Like many people, I have always been instinc-
> tively a moral relativist. As far back as I can
> remember . . . it has always seemed to be obvious
> that the dictates of morality arise from some sort
> of convention or understanding among people,
> that different people arrive at different under-
> standings, and that there are no basic moral
> demands that apply to everyone. This seemed
> so obvious to me I assumed it was everyone's
> instinctive view, or at least everyone who gave
> the matter any thought in this day and age.
>
> —Gilbert Harman[1]

> Ethical relativism is the doctrine that the moral
> rightness and wrongness of actions vary from
> society to society and that there are not abso-
> lute universal moral standards on all men at all
> times. Accordingly, it holds that whether or not
> it is right for an individual to act in a certain way
> depends on or is relative to the society to which
> he belongs.
>
> —John Ladd[2]

Gilbert Harman's intuitions about the self-evidence
of ethical relativism contrast strikingly with Plato's or
Kant's equal certainty about the truth of objectivism,
the doctrine that universally valid or true ethical principles exist. . . . "Two things fill the soul with ever new
and increasing wonder and reverence the oftener and
more fervently reflection ponders on it: the starry heav-
ens above and the moral law within," wrote Kant. On
the basis of polls taken in my ethics and introduction
to philosophy classes in recent years, Harman's views
may signal a shift in contemporary society's moral
understanding. The polls show a two-to-one ratio in
favor of moral relativism over moral absolutism, with
fewer than five percent of the respondents recognizing

that a third position between these two polar opposites
might exist. Of course, I'm not suggesting that all of
these students had a clear understanding of what relativism entails, for many who said they were relativists
also contended in the same polls that abortion except
to save the mother's life is always wrong, that capital
punishment is always wrong, or that suicide is never
morally permissible. . . .

1. An Analysis of Relativism

Let us examine the theses contained in John Ladd's suc-
cinct statement on ethical (conventional) relativism that
appears at the beginning of this essay. If we analyze it, we
derive the following argument:

1. Moral rightness and wrongness of actions vary
   from society to society, so there are no universal
   moral standards held by all societies.
2. Whether or not it is right for individuals to act
   in a certain way depends on (or is relative to) the
   society to which they belong.
3. Therefore, there are no absolute or objective moral
   standards that apply to all people everywhere.

1. The first thesis, which may be called the *diversity
thesis*, is simply a description that acknowledges the fact
that moral rules differ from society to society. The Spartans
of ancient Greece and the Dobu of New Guinea believe
that stealing is morally right, but we believe it is wrong.
The Roman father had the power of life and death . . . over
his children, whereas we condemn parents for abusing
their children. A tribe in East Africa once threw deformed
infants to the hippopotamuses, and in ancient Greece
and Rome infants were regularly exposed, while we abhor
infanticide. Ruth Benedict describes a tribe in Melanesia
that views cooperation and kindness as vices, whereas we
see them as virtues. While in ancient Greece, Rome, China
and Korea parricide was condemned as "the most execra-
ble of crimes," among Northern Indians aged persons,
persons who were no longer capable of walking, were left
alone to starve. Among the California Gallinomero, when

fathers became feeble, a burden to their sons, "the poor old wretch is not infrequently thrown down on his back and securely held while a stick is placed across his throat, and two of them seat themselves on the ends of it until he ceases to breathe."[3] Sexual practices vary over time and place. Some cultures permit homosexual behavior, while others condemn it. Some cultures practice polygamy, while others view it as immoral. Some cultures condone while others condemn premarital sex. Some cultures accept cannibalism, while the very idea revolts us. Some West African tribes perform clitoridectomies on girls, whereas we deplore such practices. Cultural relativism is well documented, and "custom is the king o'er all." There may or may not be moral principles that are held in common by every society, but if there are any, they seem to be few at best. Certainly it would be very difficult to derive any single "true" morality by observing various societies' moral standards.

2. The second thesis, the *dependency thesis,* asserts that individual acts are right or wrong depending on the nature of the society from which they emanate. Morality does not occur in a vacuum, and what is considered morally right or wrong must be seen in a context that depends on the goals, wants, beliefs, history, and environment of the society in question. As William G. Sumner says,

> We learn the morals as unconsciously as we learn to walk and hear and breathe, and [we] never know any reason why the [morals] are what they are. The justification of them is that when we wake to consciousness of life we find them facts which already hold us in the bonds of tradition, custom, and habit.[4]

Trying to see things from an independent, noncultural point of view would be like taking out our eyes in order to examine their contours and qualities. There is no "innocent eye." We are simply culturally determined beings.

We could, of course, distinguish between a weak and a strong thesis of dependency, for the nonrelativist can accept a certain degree of relativity in the way moral principles are *applied* in various cultures, depending on beliefs, history, and environment. For example, Jewish men express reverence for God by covering their heads when entering places of worship, whereas Christian men uncover their heads when entering places of worship. Westerners shake hands upon greeting each other, whereas Hindus place their hands together and point them toward the person to be greeted. Both sides adhere to principles of reverence and respect but apply them differently. But the ethical relativist must maintain a stronger thesis, one that insists that the moral principles themselves are products of the cultures and may vary from society to society." The ethical relativist contends that even beyond environmental factors and differences in beliefs, a fundamental disagreement exists among societies. . . .

In a sense we all live in radically different worlds. But the relativist wants to go further and maintain that there is something conventional about *any* morality, so that every morality really depends on a level of social acceptance. Not only do various societies adhere to different moral systems, but the very same society could (and often does) change its moral views over place and time. For example, the majority of people in the southern United States now view slavery as immoral, whereas one hundred and forty years ago they did not. Our society's views on divorce, sexuality, abortion, and assisted suicide have changed somewhat as well—and they are still changing.

3. The conclusion that there are no absolute or objective moral standards binding on all people follows from the first two propositions. Combining cultural relativism (*the diversity thesis*) with *the dependency thesis* yields ethical relativism in its classic form. If there are different moral principles from culture to culture and if all morality is rooted in culture, then it follows that there are no universal moral principles that are valid (or true) for all cultures and peoples at all times.

2. Subjectivism

Some people think that this conclusion is still too tame, and they maintain that morality is dependent not on the society but rather on the individual. As my students sometimes maintain, "Morality is in the eye of the beholder." They treat morality like taste or aesthetic judgments—person relative. This form of moral subjectivism has the sorry consequence that it makes morality a very useless concept, for, on its premises, little or no interpersonal criticism or judgment is logically possible. Suppose that you are repulsed by observing John torturing a child. You cannot condemn him if one of his principles is "torture little children for the fun of it." The only basis for judging him wrong might be that he was a hypocrite who condemned others for torturing. But suppose that another of his principles is that hypocrisy is morally permissible (for him); thus we cannot condemn him for condemning others for doing what he does.

On the basis of subjectivism Adolf Hitler and the serial murderer Ted Bundy could be considered as moral as Gandhi, so long as each lived by his own standards, whatever those might be. . . .

Notions of good and bad, or right and wrong, cease to have interpersonal evaluative meaning. We might be revulsed by the views of Ted Bundy, but that is just a matter of taste. A student might not like it when her teacher gives her an F on a test paper, while he gives another student an A for a similar paper, but there is no way to criticize him for injustice, because justice is not one of his chosen principles.

Absurd consequences follow from subjectivism. If it is correct, then morality reduces to aesthetic tastes about which there can be neither argument nor interpersonal judgment. Although many students say they espouse subjectivism, there is evidence that it conflicts with other of their moral views. They typically condemn Hitler as an evil man for his genocidal policies. A contradiction seems to exist between subjectivism and the very concept of morality, which it is supposed to characterize, for morality has to do with *proper* resolution of interpersonal conflict and the amelioration of the human predicament. . . . Whatever else it does, morality has a minimal aim of preventing a Hobbesian state of nature . . . , wherein life is "solitary, poor, nasty, brutish, and short. But if so, subjectivism is no help at all, for it rests neither on social agreement of principle (as the conventionalist maintains) nor on an objectively independent set of norms that bind all people for the common good. If there were only one person on earth, there would be no occasion for morality, because there wouldn't be any interpersonal conflicts to resolve or others whose suffering he or she would have a duty to ameliorate. Subjectivism implicitly assumes something of this solipsism, an atomism in which isolated individuals make up separate universes.

Subjectivism treats individuals like billiard balls on a societal pool table where they meet only in radical collisions, each aimed at his or her own goal and striving to do in the others before they themselves are done in. This atomistic view of personality is belied by the facts that we develop in families and mutually dependent communities in which we share a common language, common institutions, and similar rituals and habits, and that we often feel one another's joys and sorrows. As the poet John Donne wrote, "No man is an island, entire of itself; every man is a piece of the continent."

Radical individualistic ethical relativism is incoherent. If so, it follows that the only plausible view of ethical relativism must be one that grounds morality in the group or culture. This form is called *conventionalism*.

3. Conventionalism

Conventional ethical relativism, the view that there are no objective moral principles but that all valid moral principles are justified (or are made true) by virtue of their cultural acceptance, recognizes the social nature

of morality. That is precisely its power and virtue. It does not seem subject to the same absurd consequences which plague subjectivism. Recognizing the importance of our social environment in generating customs and beliefs, many people suppose that ethical relativism is the correct metaethical theory. Furthermore, they are drawn to it for its liberal philosophical stance. It seems to be an enlightened response to the sin of ethnocentricity, and it seems to entail or strongly imply an attitude of tolerance toward other cultures. Anthropologist Ruth Benedict says, that in recognizing ethical relativity, "We shall arrive at a more realistic social faith, accepting as grounds of hope and as new bases for tolerance the coexisting and equally valid patterns of life which mankind has created for itself from the raw materials of existence."[5] The most famous of those holding this position is the anthropologist Melville Herskovits, who argues even more explicitly than Benedict that ethical relativism entails intercultural tolerance.

1. If morality is relative to its culture, then there is no independent basis for criticizing the morality of any other culture but one's own.
2. If there is no independent way of criticizing any other culture, we ought to be tolerant of the moralities of other cultures.
3. Morality is relative to its culture. Therefore,
4. We ought to be tolerant of the moralities of other cultures.[6]

Tolerance is certainly a virtue, but is this a good argument for it? I think not. If morality simply is relative to each culture, then if the culture in question does not have a principle of tolerance, its members have no obligation to be tolerant. Herskovits seems to be treating the *principle of tolerance* as the one exception to his relativism. He seems to be treating it as an absolute moral principle. But from a relativistic point of view there is no more reason to be tolerant than to be intolerant and neither stance is objectively morally better than the other.

Not only do relativists fail to offer a basis for criticizing those who are intolerant, but they cannot rationally criticize anyone who espouses what they might regard as a heinous principle. If, as seems to be the case, valid criticism supposes an objective or impartial standard, relativists cannot morally criticize anyone outside their own culture. Adolf Hitler's genocidal actions, so long as they are culturally accepted, are as morally legitimate as Mother Teresa's works of mercy. If Conventional Relativism is accepted, racism, genocide of unpopular minorities, oppression of the poor, slavery, and even the advocacy of war for its own sake are as equally moral as their opposites. And if a subculture decided that starting a nuclear war was somehow morally acceptable, we could not morally criticize these people. Any actual morality, whatever its content, is as valid as every other, and more valid than ideal moralities—since the latter aren't adhered to by any culture.

There are other disturbing consequences of ethical relativism. It seems to entail that reformers are always (morally) wrong since they go against the tide of cultural standards. William Wilberforce was wrong in the eighteenth century to oppose slavery; the British were immoral in opposing suttee in India (the burning of widows, which is now illegal in India). The early Christians were wrong in refusing to serve in the Roman army or to bow down to Caesar, since the majority in the Roman Empire believed that these two acts were moral duties. In fact, Jesus himself was immoral in breaking the law of His day by healing on the Sabbath day and by advocating the principles of the Sermon on the Mount, since it is clear that few in His time (or in ours) accepted them.

Yet we normally feel just the opposite, that the reformer is a courageous innovator who is right, who has the truth, against the mindless majority. Sometimes the individual must stand alone with the truth, risking social censure and persecution. . . . Yet if relativism is correct, the opposite is necessarily the case. Truth is with the crowd and error with the individual. . . .

There is an even more basic problem with the notion that morality is dependent on cultural acceptance for its validity. The problem is that the notion of a *culture* or *society* is notoriously difficult to define. This is especially so in a pluralistic society like our own where the notion seems to be vague with unclear boundary lines. One person may belong to several societies (subcultures) with different value emphases and arrangements of principles. A person may belong to the nation as a single society with certain values of patriotism, honor, courage, laws (including some which are controversial but have majority acceptance, such as the current law on abortion). But he or she may also belong to a church which opposes some of the laws of the State. He may also be an integral member of a socially mixed community where different principles hold sway, and he may belong to clubs and a family where still other rules are adhered to. Relativism would seem to tell us that where he is a member of societies with conflicting moralities he must be judged both wrong and not-wrong whatever he does. For example, if Mary is a U.S. citizen and a member of the Roman Catholic Church, she is wrong (qua Catholic) if she chooses to have an abortion and not-wrong (qua citizen of the U.S.A.) if she acts against the teaching of the Church on abortion. As a member of a racist university fraternity, KKK, John has no obligation to treat his fellow Black student as an equal, but as a member of the university community itself (where the principle of equal rights is accepted) he does have the obligation; but as a member of the surrounding community (which may reject the principle of equal rights) he again has no such obligation; but then again as a member of the nation at large (which accepts the principle) he is obligated to treat his fellow with respect. What is the morally right thing for John to do? The question no longer makes much sense in this moral Babel. It has lost its action-guiding function.

Perhaps the relativist would adhere to a principle which says that in such cases the individual may choose which group to belong to as primary. If Mary chooses to have an abortion, she is choosing to belong to the general society relative to that principle. And John must likewise choose among groups. The trouble with this option is that it seems to lead back to counter-intuitive results. If Murder Mike of Murder, Incorporated, feels like killing Bank President Ortcutt and wants to feel good about it, he identifies with the Murder, Incorporated society rather than the general public morality. Does this justify the killing? In fact, couldn't one justify anything simply by forming a small subculture that approved of it? Ted Bundy would be morally pure in raping and killing innocents simply by virtue of forming a little coterie. How large must the group be in order to be a legitimate subculture or society? Does it need ten or fifteen people? How about just three? Come to think about it, why can't my burglary partner and I found our own society with a morality of its own? Of course, if my partner dies, I could still claim that I was acting from an originally social set of norms. But why can't I dispense with the interpersonal agreements altogether and invent my own morality—since morality, on this view, is only an invention anyway? Conventionalist relativism seems to reduce to subjectivism. And subjectivism leads, as we have seen, to moral solipsism, to the demise of morality altogether. . . .

. . . I don't think you can stop the move from conventionalism to subjectivism. The essential force of the validity of the chosen moral principle is that it is dependent on choice. The conventionalist holds that it is the choice of the group, but why should I accept the group's silly choice, when my own is better (for me)? Why should anyone give such august authority to a culture of society? If this is all morality comes to, why not reject it altogether—even though one might want to adhere to its directives when others are looking in order to escape sanctions?

4. A Critique of Ethical Relativism

However, while we may fear the demise of morality, as we have known it, this in itself may not be a good reason for rejecting relativism. That is, for judging it false. Alas, truth may not always be edifying. But the consequences of this position are sufficiently alarming to prompt us to look carefully for some weakness in the relativist's argument. So let us examine the premises and conclusion listed at the beginning of this essay as the three theses of relativism.

1. *The Diversity Thesis.* What is considered morally right and wrong varies from society to society, so that there are no moral principles accepted by all societies.
2. *The Dependency Thesis.* All moral principles derive their validity from cultural acceptance.
3. *Ethical Relativism.* Therefore, there are no universally valid moral principles, objective standards which apply to all people everywhere and at all times.

Does any one of these seem problematic? Let us consider the first thesis, the diversity thesis, which we have also called cultural relativism. Perhaps there is not as much diversity as anthropologists like Sumner and Benedict suppose. One can also see great similarities between the moral codes of various cultures. E. O. Wilson has identified over a score of common features,[7] and before him Clyde Kluckhohn has noted much significant common ground between cultures.

> Every culture has a concept of murder, distinguishing this from execution, killing in war, and other "justifiable homicides." The notions of incest and other regulations upon sexual behavior, the prohibitions upon untruth under defined circumstances, of restitution and reciprocity, of mutual obligations between parents and children—these and many other moral concepts are altogether universal.[8]

Colin Turnbull's description of the sadistic, semidisplaced, disintegrating Ik in Northern Uganda supports the view that a people without principles of kindness, loyalty, and cooperation will degenerate into a Hobbesian state of nature.[9] But he has also produced evidence that underneath the surface of this dying society, there is a deeper moral code from a time when the tribe flourished, which occasionally surfaces and shows its nobler face.

On the other hand, there is enormous cultural diversity and many societies have radically different moral codes. Cultural relativism seems to be a fact, but, even if it is, it does not by itself establish the truth of ethical relativism. Cultural diversity in itself is neutral between theories. For the objectivist could concede complete cultural relativism, but still defend a form of universalism; for he or she could argue that some cultures simply lack correct moral principles.

On the other hand, a denial of complete cultural relativism (i.e., an admission of some universal principles) does not disprove ethical relativism. For even if we did find one or more universal principles, this would not prove that they had any objective status. We could still *imagine* a culture that was an exception to the rule and be unable to criticize it. So the first premise doesn't by itself imply ethical relativism and its denial doesn't disprove ethical relativism.

We turn to the crucial second thesis, the dependency thesis. Morality does not occur in a vacuum, but rather what is considered morally right or wrong must be seen in a context, depending on the goals, wants, beliefs, history, and environment of the society in question. We distinguished a weak and a strong thesis of dependency. The weak thesis says that the application of principles depends on the particular cultural predicament, whereas the strong thesis affirms that the principles themselves depend on that predicament. The nonrelativist can accept a certain relativity in the way moral principles are *applied* in various cultures, depending on beliefs, history, and environment. For example, a raw environment with scarce natural resources may justify the Eskimos' brand of euthanasia to the objectivist, who in another environment would consistently reject that practice. The members of a tribe in the Sudan throw their deformed children into the river because of their belief that such infants *belong* to the hippopotamus, the god of the river. We believe that they have a false belief about this, but the point is that the same principles of respect for property and respect for human life are operative in these contrary practices. They differ with us only in belief, not in substantive moral principle. This is an illustration of how nonmoral beliefs (e.g., deformed children belong to the hippopotamus) when applied to common moral principles (e.g., give to each his due) generate different actions in different cultures. In our own culture the difference in the nonmoral belief about the status of a fetus generates opposite moral prescriptions. The major difference between pro-choicers and pro-lifers is not whether we should kill persons but whether fetuses are really persons. It is a debate about the facts of the matter, not the principle of killing innocent persons.

So the fact that moral principles are weakly dependent doesn't show that ethical relativism is valid. In spite of this weak dependency on nonmoral factors, there could still be a set of general moral norms applicable to all cultures and even recognized in most, which are disregarded at a culture's own expense.

What the relativist needs is a strong thesis of dependency, that somehow all principles are essentially cultural inventions. But why should we choose to view morality this way? Is there anything to recommend the strong thesis over the weak thesis of dependency? The relativist may argue that in fact we don't have an obvious impartial standard from which to judge. "Who's to say which culture is right and which is wrong?" But this seems to be dubious. We can reason and perform thought experiments in order to make a case for one system over another. We may not be able to know with certainty that our moral beliefs are closer to the truth than those of another culture or those of others within our own culture, but we may be *justified* in believing that they are. If we can be closer to the truth regarding factual or scientific matters, why can't we be closer to the truth on moral matters? Why can't a culture be simply confused or wrong about its moral perceptions? Why can't we say that the society like the Ik which sees nothing wrong with enjoying watching its own children fall into fires is less moral in that regard than the culture that cherishes children and grants them protection and equal rights? To take such a stand is not to commit the fallacy of ethnocentricism, for we are seeking to derive principles through critical reason, not simply uncritical acceptance of one's own mores.

Many relativists embrace relativism as a default position. Objectivism makes no sense to them. I think this is Ladd and Harman's position, as the latter's quotation at the beginning of this article seems to indicate. Objectivism has insuperable problems, so the answer must be relativism. . . .

In conclusion I have argued (1) that cultural relativism (the fact that there are cultural differences regarding moral principles) does not entail ethical relativism (the thesis that there are no objectively valid universal moral principles) [and] (2) that the dependency thesis (that

morality derives its legitimacy from individual cultural acceptance) is mistaken. . . .

So "Who's to judge what's right or wrong?" We are. We are to do so on the basis of the best reasoning we can bring forth, and with sympathy and understanding.[10]

Notes

1. Gilbert Harman, "Is There a Single True Morality?" in *Morality, Reason and Truth*, eds. David Copp and David Zimmerman (Rowman & Allenheld, 1984).
2. John Ladd, *Ethical Relativism* (Wadsworth, 1973).
3. Reported by the anthropologist Powers, *Tribes of California*, p. 178. Quoted in E. Westermarck, *Origin and Development of Moral Ideals* (London, 1906), p. 386. This work is a mine of examples of cultural diversity.
4. W. G. Sumner, *Folkways* (Ginn & Co., 1906), p. 76.
5. Ruth Benedict, *Patterns of Culture* (New American Library, 1934), p, 257.
6. Melville Herskovits, *Cultural Relativism* (Random House, 1972).
7. E. O. Wilson, *On Human Nature* (Bantam Books, 1979), pp. 22–23.
8. Clyde Kluckhohn, "Ethical Relativity: Sic et Non," *Journal of Philosophy*, LII (1955).
9. Colin Turnbull, *The Mountain People* (New York: Simon & Schuster, 1972).
10. Bruce Russell, Morton Winston, Edward Sherline, and an anonymous reviewer made important criticisms on earlier versions of this article, issuing in this revision.

Louis P. Pojman (1935–2005) was a prolific American philosopher who published (as editor or author) over 30 books and wrote more than 100 articles. His writing extends widely and embraces many areas of philosophy, but Pojman is best remembered as a writer on ethical, social, and political issues. He was particularly concerned to make ideas clear to nonphilosophers.

EXPLORING THE ISSUE

Is Moral Relativism Correct?

Critical Thinking and Reflection

1. How can disagreements about right and wrong between people within the same culture be solved: (a) within a framework of moral relativism and (b) within framework of moral realism?
2. How can disagreements about right and wrong between people from different cultures be resolved: (a) within a framework of moral relativism and (b) within a framework of moral realism?
3. Both Pojman and Tännsjö criticize cultural moral relativism (also known as semantic relativism). How are these criticisms similar? How are they different? Are these criticisms consistent with one another?
4. Find an example of an action that is considered morally right in one culture and morally wrong in another culture. How might the different moral judgments be explained without cultural moral relativism? Do you find these explanations persuasive?
5. As a result of the rapid development of communication technology, such as the Internet, differences among societies are decreasing and a more uniform international culture is developing. If this process continues, then a single society might be influencing the construction of each person's individual reality, thereby introducing a uniformity among these realities. In this case, could this uniformity result in the development of a universal, and hence quasi-objective, moral standard by which to judge actions?

Is There Common Ground?

It seems unlikely that an author who defends ethical relativism would also be sympathetic to moral realism. The objective moral standards described by Tännsjö within the framework of ontological relativism are objective only from the perspective of a specific person's socially constructed reality. There need be no objective moral standards beyond these individual realities that apply to the socially constructed realities of every single person. However, Tännsjö wraps up his article by saying that his position is entirely consistent with the possibility that objective moral standards do exist, although it would be a challenge for a person to "break out" of his/her own reality in order to discover such a universal moral standard.

While Pojman's objectivist system allows no room for moral relativism, he nonetheless allows for what he calls "a certain relativity" in the application of moral principles to form judgments. He can thus provide a sympathetic account of how societies that appear to have radically different ethical views may in fact share common norms with other cultures. Rather than stating that these cultures are simply mistaken about objective moral standards, Pojman asserts that they may hold different beliefs that account for the different ways in which these common norms are expressed.

Additional Resources

Maria Baghramian, *Relativism* (Routledge, 2004)

Michael C. Brannigan, *Ethics Across Cultures* (McGraw-Hill, 2005)

Neil Levy, *Moral Relativism: A Short Introduction* (One-World Publications, 2002)

Paul K. Moser and Thomas L. Carson, eds., *Moral Relativism: A Reader* (Oxford University Press, 2000)

Internet References . . .

Ethics Updates: Introduction to Moral Theory

http://ethics.sandiego.edu/theories/Intro/index.asp

Internet Encyclopedia of Philosophy: Moral Philosophy

www.iep.utm.edu/moral-re/

Online Guide to Ethics and Moral Philosophy: Ethical Relativism

http://caae.phil.cmu.edu/cavalier/
80130/part2/sect6.html

Selected, Edited, and with Issue Framing Material by:
Owen M. Smith, *Stephen F. Austin State University*
and
Anne Collins Smith, *Stephen F. Austin State University*

ISSUE

Does Morality Need Religion?

YES: C. Stephen Layman, from "Ethics and the Kingdom of God.," in *The Shape of the Good: Christian Reflections on the Foundations of Ethics*, University of Notre Dame Press (1991)

NO: John Arthur, from "Religion, Morality, and Conscience," in *Morality and Moral Controversies*, Prentice Hall (1996)

Learning Outcomes

After reading this issue, you will be able to:

- Describe the reasons people give for choosing to behave morally.
- Discuss each author's position on the relationship between religion and morality.
- Formulate your own position on whether morality needs religion and identify evidence supporting your position.
- Identify the main objections to your position and formulate responses to these objections.

ISSUE SUMMARY

YES: Philosopher C. Stephen Layman argues that morality makes the most sense from a theistic perspective and that a purely secular perspective is insufficient. The secular perspective, Layman asserts, does not adequately deal with secret violations, and it does not allow for the possibility of fulfillment of people's deepest needs in an afterlife.

NO: Philosopher John Arthur counters that morality is logically independent of religion, although there are historical connections. Religion, he believes, is not necessary for moral guidance or moral answers; morality is social.

There is a widespread feeling that morality and religion are connected. One view is that religion provides a ground for morality, so without religion there is no morality. Thus, a falling away from religion implies a falling away from morality.

Such thoughts have troubled many people. The Russian novelist Dostoyevsky (1821–1881) wrote, "If there is no God, then everything is permitted." Many Americans today also believe that religious faith is important. They often maintain that even if doctrines and dogmas cannot be known for certain, religion nevertheless leads to morality and good behavior. President Dwight D. Eisenhower is reputed to have said that everyone should have a religious

faith but that it did not matter what that faith was. And many daily newspapers throughout the country advise their readers to attend the church or synagogue of their choice. Apparently, the main reason why people think it is important to subscribe to a religion is that only in this way will one be able to attain morality. If there is no God, then everything is permitted and there is moral chaos. Moral chaos can be played out in societies and, on a smaller scale, within the minds of individuals. Thus, if you do not believe in God, then you will confront moral chaos; you will be liable to permit (and permit yourself to do) anything, and you will have no moral bearings at all.

Such a view seems to face several problems, however. For example, what are we to say of the morally good atheist or of the morally good but completely nonreligious person? A true follower of the view that morality derives from religion might reply that we are simply begging the question if we believe that such people *could* be morally good. Such people might do things that are morally right and thus might *seem* good, the reply would go, but they would not be acting for the right reason (obedience to God). Such people would not have the same anchor or root for their seemingly moral attitudes that religious persons do.

Another problem for the view that links morality with religion comes from the following considerations: If you hold this view, what do you say of devoutly religious people who belong to religious traditions and who support moralities that are different from your own? If morality is indeed derived from religion, if different people are thus led to follow different moralities, and if the original religions are not themselves subject to judgment, then it is understandable how different people arrive at different moral views. But the views will still be different and perhaps even incompatible. If so, the statement that morality derives from religion must mean that one can derive *a* morality from *a* religion (and not that one derives morality itself from religion). The problem is that by allowing this variation among religions and moralities back into the picture, we seem to allow moral chaos back in, too.

The view that what God commands is good, what God prohibits is evil, and without divine commands and prohibitions nothing is either good or bad in itself is called the *divine command theory*, or the *divine imperative view*. This view resists the recognition of any source of good or evil that is not tied to criteria or standards of God's own creation. Such a recognition is thought to go against the idea of God's omnipotence. A moral law that applied to God but was not of God's own creation would seem to limit God in a way in which he cannot be limited. But, on the other hand, this line of thought (that no moral law outside of God's own making should apply to him) seems contrary to the orthodox Christian view that God is good. For if good means something in accordance with God's will, then when we say that God is good, we are only saying that he acts in accordance with his own will—and this just does not seem to be enough.

In the following selections, C. Stephen Layman argues that a religious perspective makes better sense of moral commitment than a secular perspective. Indeed, in his view, it is not even clear that a secular individual who followed the dictates of morality would be rational. John Arthur asserts that morality does not need a religious foundation at all and that morality is social.

YES ↵

C. Stephen Layman

Ethics and the Kingdom of God

Why build a theory of ethics on the assumption that there is a God? Why not simply endorse a view of ethics along . . . secular lines . . . ? I shall respond to these questions in [two] stages. First, I contrast the secular and religious perspectives on morality. Second, I explain why I think the moral life makes more sense from the point of view of theism [belief in God] than from that of atheism. . . .

❧

As I conceive it, the modern secular perspective on morality involves at least two elements. First, there is no afterlife; each individual human life ends at death. It follows that the only goods available to an individual are those he or she can obtain this side of death.[1]

Second, on the secular view, moral value is an *emergent* phenomenon. That is, moral value is "a feature of certain effects though it is not a feature of their causes" (as wetness is a feature of H_2O, but not of hydrogen or oxygen).[2] Thus, the typical contemporary secular view has it that moral value emerges only with the arrival of very complex nervous systems (viz., human brains), late in the evolutionary process. There is no Mind "behind the scenes" on the secular view, no intelligent Creator concerned with the affairs of human existence. As one advocate of the secular view puts it, "Ethics, though not consciously created [either by humans or by God], is a product of social life which has the function of promoting values common to the members of society."[3]

By way of contrast, the religious point of view (in my use of the phrase) includes a belief in God and in life after death. God is defined as an eternal being who is almighty and perfectly morally good. Thus, from the religious point of view, morality is not an emergent phenomenon, for God's goodness has always been in existence, and is not the product of nonmoral causes. Moreover, from the religious point of view, there are goods available after death.

Specifically, there awaits the satisfaction of improved relations with God and with redeemed creatures.

It is important to note that, from the religious perspective, *the existence of God and life after death* are not independent hypotheses. If God exists, then at least two lines of reasoning lend support to the idea that death is not final. While I cannot here scrutinize these lines of reasoning, I believe it will be useful to sketch them.[4] (1) It has often been noted that we humans seem unable to find complete fulfillment in the present life. Even those having abundant material possessions and living in the happiest of circumstances find themselves, upon reflection, profoundly unsatisfied. . . . [I]f this earthly life is the whole story, it appears that our deepest longings will remain unfulfilled. But if God is good, He surely will not leave our deepest longings unfulfilled provided He is able to fulfill them—at least to the extent that we are willing to accept His gracious aid. So, since our innermost yearnings are not satisfied in this life, it is likely that they will be satisfied after death.

(2) Human history has been one long story of injustice, of the oppression of the poor and weak by the rich and powerful. The lives of relatively good people are often miserable, while the wicked prosper. Now, if God exists, He is able to correct such injustices, though He does not correct all of them in the present life. But if God is also good, He will not leave such injustices forever unrectified. It thus appears that He will rectify matters at some point after death. This will involve benefits for some in the afterlife—it may involve penalties for others. (However, the . . . possibility of post-mortem punishment does not necessarily imply the possibility of hell as *standardly conceived*.)

We might sum up the main difference between the secular and religious views by saying that the only goods available from a secular perspective are *earthly* goods. Earthly goods include such things as physical health, friendship, pleasure, self-esteem, knowledge, enjoyable activities, an adequate standard of living, etc. The religious or theistic perspective recognizes these earthly goods *as*

Layman, C. Stephen. From *The Shape of the Good: Christian Reflections on the Foundations of Ethics.* Copyright 1991 by the University of Notre Dame Press, Notre Dame, IN 46556.

good, but it insists that there are non-earthly or *transcendent* goods. These are goods available only if God exists and there is life after death for humans. Transcendent goods include harmonious relations with God prior to death as well as the joys of the afterlife—right relations with both God and redeemed creatures.

❧

[One secular] defense of the virtues amounts to showing that society cannot function well unless individuals have moral virtue. If we ask, "Why should we as individuals care about society?", the answer will presumably be along the following lines: "Individuals cannot flourish apart from a well-functioning society, *so morality pays for the individual.*"

This defense of morality raises two questions we must now consider. First, is it misguided to defend morality by an appeal to self-interest? Many people feel that morality and self-interest are fundamentally at odds: "If you perform an act because you see that it is in your interest to do so, then you aren't doing the right thing *just because it's right.* A successful defense of morality must be a defense of duty for duty's sake. Thus, the appeal to self-interest is completely misguided." Second, *does* morality really pay for the individual? More particularly, does morality always pay in terms of earthly goods? Let us take these questions up in turn.

(1) Do we desert the moral point of view if we defend morality on the grounds that it pays? Consider an analogy with etiquette. Why should one bother with etiquette? Should one do the well-mannered thing simply for its own sake? Do we keep our elbows off the table or refrain from belching just because these things are "proper"?

To answer this question we must distinguish between the *justification of an institution* and *the justification of a particular act within that institution.* (By 'institution' I refer to any system of activities specified by rules.) This distinction can be illustrated in the case of the game (institution) of baseball. If we ask a player why he performs a particular act during a game, he will probably give an answer such as, "To put my opponent out" or "To get a home run." These answers obviously would not be relevant if the question were, "Why play baseball at all?" Relevant answers to this second question would name some advantage for the individual player, e.g., "Baseball is fun" or "It's good exercise." Thus, a justification of the institution of baseball (e.g., "It's good exercise") is quite different from a justification of a particular act within the institution (e.g., "To get a home run").

Now let's apply this distinction to our question about etiquette. If our question concerns the justification of a particular act within the institution of etiquette, then the answer may reasonably be, in effect, "This is what's proper. This is what the rules of etiquette prescribe." . . .

But plainly there are deeper questions we can ask about etiquette. Who hasn't wondered, at times, what the point of the institution of etiquette is? Why do we have these quirky rules, some of which seem to make little sense? When these more fundamental questions concerning the entire institution of etiquette are being asked, it makes no sense to urge etiquette for etiquette's sake. What is needed is a description of the human *ends* the institution fulfills—ends which play a justificatory role similar to fun or good exercise in the case of baseball. And it is not difficult to identify some of these ends. For example, the rules of etiquette seem designed, in part, to facilitate social interaction; things just go more smoothly if there are agreed upon ways of greeting, eating, conversing, etc.

If anyone asks, "Why should I as an individual bother about etiquette?", an initial reply might be: "Because if you frequently violate the rules of etiquette, people will shun you." If anyone wonders why he should care about being shunned, we will presumably reply that good social relations are essential to human flourishing, and hence that a person is jeopardizing his own best interests if he places no value at all on etiquette. Thus, in the end, a defense of the institution of etiquette seems to involve the claim that the institution of etiquette *pays* for those who participate in it; it would not be illuminating to answer the question, "Why bother about etiquette?" by saying that etiquette is to be valued for its own sake.

Now, just as we distinguish between justifying the institution of etiquette (or baseball) and justifying a particular act within the institution, so we must distinguish between justifying the institution of morality and justifying a particular act within the institution. When choosing a particular course of action we may simply want to know what's right. But a more ultimate question also cries out for an answer: "What is the point of the institution of morality, anyway? Why should one bother with it?" It is natural to respond by saying that society cannot function well without morality, and individuals cannot flourish apart from a well-functioning society. In short, defending the institution of morality involves claiming that morality pays for the individual in the long run. It seems obscurantist to preach duty for duty's sake, once the more fundamental question about the point of the institution of morality has been raised.

But if morality is defended on the grounds that it pays, doesn't this distort moral motivation? Won't it mean that we no longer do things because they are right, but rather because they are in our self-interest? No. We must bear in mind our distinction between the reasons that justify a particular act within an institution and the reasons that justify the institution itself. A baseball player performs a given act in order to get on base or put an opponent out; he does not calculate whether this particular swing of the bat (or throw of the ball) is fun or good exercise. A well-mannered person is not constantly calculating whether a given act will improve her relations with others, she simply does "the proper thing." Similarly, even if we defend morality on the grounds that it pays, it does not follow that the motive for each moral act becomes, "It will pay" for we are not constantly thinking of the philosophical issues concerning the justification of the entire system of morality; for the most part we simply do things because they are right, honest, fair, loving, etc. Nevertheless, our willingness to plunge wholeheartedly into "the moral game" is apt to be vitiated should it become clear to us that the game does not pay.

At this point it appears that the institution of morality is justified only if it pays for the individuals who participate in it. For if being moral does not pay for individuals, it is difficult to see why they should bother with it. The appeal to duty for duty's sake is irrelevant when we are asking for a justification of the institution of morality itself.

(2) But we must now ask, "Does morality in fact pay?" There are at least four reasons for supposing that morality does not pay from a *secular* perspective. (a) One problem for the secular view arises from the fact that the moral point of view involves a concern for *all* human beings—or at least for all humans affected by one's actions. Thus, within Christian theology, the parable of the good Samaritan is well known for its expansion of the category of "my neighbor." But human societies seem able to get along well without extending full moral concern to all outsiders; this is the essence of tribal morality. Thus, explorers in the 1700s found that the Sioux Indians followed a strict code in dealing with each other, but regarded themselves as free to steal horses from the Crow. Later on, American whites repeatedly broke treaties with the American Indians in a way that would not have been possible had the Indians been regarded as equals. It is no exaggeration to say that throughout much of human history tribal morality has been the morality humans lived by.

And so, while one must agree . . . that the virtues are necessary for the existence of society, it is not clear that this amounts to anything more than a defense of tribal morality. . . . From a purely secular point of view, it is unclear why the scope of moral concern must extend beyond one's society—or, more precisely, why one's concern must extend to groups of people outside of one's society *who are powerless and stand in the way of things one's society wants*. Why should the members of a modern industrial state extend full moral consideration to a tiny Amazonian tribe? . . .

(b) A second problem for secular views concerns the possibility of secret violations of moral rules. What becomes of conscientiousness when one can break the rules in secret, without anyone knowing? After all, if I can break the rules in secret, I will not cause any social disharmony. Of course, there can be no breaking of the rules in secret if there is a God of the Christian type, who knows every human thought as well as every human act. But there are cases in which it is extraordinarily unlikely that any *humans* will discover one's rule breaking. Hence, from a secular perspective, there are cases in which secret violations of morality are possible.

Consider the following case. Suppose A has borrowed some money from B, but A discovers that B has made a mistake in his records. Because of the mistake, B believes that A has already paid the money back. B even goes out of his way to thank A for prompt payment on the loan. Let us further suppose that B is quite wealthy, and hence not in need of the money. Is it in A's interest to pay the money back? Not paying the money back would be morally wrong; but would it be irrational, from a secular point of view? Not necessarily. Granted, it might be irrational in some cases, e.g., if A would have intense guilt feelings should he fail to repay the loan. But suppose A will not feel guilty because he really needs the money (and knows that B does not need it), and because he understands that secret violations belong to a special and rare category of action. Then, from a secular point of view, it is doubtful that paying the loan would be in A's interest.

The point is not that theists never cheat or lie. Unfortunately they do. The point is rather that secret violations of morality arguably pay off from a secular point of view. And so, once again, it seems that there is a "game" that pays off better (in terms of earthly goods) than the relatively idealistic morality endorsed by the great ethicists, viz., one allowing secret "violations."

(c) Even supposing that morality pays for some people, does it pay for *everyone* on the secular view? Can't there be well-functioning societies in which some of the members are "moral freeloaders"? In fact, don't all actual societies have members who maintain an appearance of decency, but are in fact highly manipulative of others? How would one show, on secular grounds, that it is in the interest of these persons to be moral? Furthermore, according to psychiatrists, some people are highly amoral, virtually without feelings of guilt or shame. Yet in numerous cases these amoral types appear to be happy.

These "successful egoists" are often intelligent, charming, and able to evade legal penalties for their unconventional behavior.[5] How could one show, on secular grounds, that it is in the interests of such successful egoists to be moral? They seem to find their amoral lives amply rewarding.

(d) Another problem from the secular perspective stems from the fact that in some cases morality demands that one risk death. Since death cuts one off from all earthly goods, what sense does it make to be moral (in a given case) if the risk of death is high?

This point must be stated with care. In many cases it makes sense, from a secular point of view, to risk one's life. For example, it makes sense if the risk is small and the earthly good to be gained is great; after all, one risks one's life driving to work. Or again, risking one's life makes sense from a secular point of view if failing to do so will probably lead to profound and enduring earthly unhappiness. Thus, a woman might take an enormous risk to save her child from an attacker. She might believe that she would be "unable to live with herself" afterward if she stood by and let the attacker kill or maim her child. Similarly, a man might be willing to die for his country, because he could not bear the dishonor resulting from a failure to act courageously.

But failing to risk one's life does not always lead to profound and enduring earthly unhappiness. Many soldiers play it safe in battle when risk taking is essential for victory; they may judge that victory is not worth the personal risks. And many subjects of ruthless tyrants entirely avoid the risks involved in resistance and reform. Though it may be unpleasant for such persons to find themselves regarded as cowards, this unpleasantness does not necessarily lead to profound and enduring earthly unhappiness. It seems strained to claim that what is commonly regarded as moral courage always pays in terms of earthly goods.

At this point it appears that the institution of morality cannot be justified from a secular point of view. For, as we have seen, the institution of morality is justified only if it pays (in the long run) for the individuals who participate in it. But if by "morality" we mean the relatively idealistic code urged on us by the great moralists, it appears that the institution of morality does not pay, according to the secular point of view. This is not to say that no moral code could pay off in terms of earthly goods; a tribal morality of some sort might pay for most people, especially if it were to include conventions which skirt the problems inherent in my "secret violation" and "risk of death" cases. But such a morality would be a far cry from the morality most of us actually endorse.

Defenders of secular morality may claim that these difficulties evaporate if we look at morality from an evolutionary point of view. The survival of the species depends on the sacrifice of individuals in some cases, and the end of morality is the survival of the species. Hence, it is not surprising that being highly moral will not always pay off for individuals.

This answer is confused for two reasons. First, even if morality does have survival value for the species, we have seen that this does not by itself justify the individual's involvement in the institution of morality. In fact, it does not justify such involvement if what is best for the species is not what is best for the individual member of the species. And I have been arguing that, from a secular point of view, the interests of the species and the individual diverge.

Second, while evolution might explain why humans *feel* obligated to make sacrifices, it is wholly unable to account for genuine moral obligation. If we did not feel obligated to make sacrifices for others, it might be that the species would have died out long ago. So, moral *feelings* may have survival value. However, *feeling obligated* is not the same thing as *being obligated*. . . . Thus, to show that moral feelings have survival value is not to show that there are any actual moral obligations at all. . . . The point is, the evolutionary picture does not require the existence of real obligations; it demands only the existence of moral feelings or beliefs. Moral feelings or beliefs would motivate action even if there were in actuality no moral obligations. For example, the belief that human life is sacred may very well have survival value even if human life is not sacred. Moral obligation, as opposed to moral feeling, is thus an unnecessary postulate from the standpoint of evolution.

At this point defenders of the secular view typically make one of two moves: (i) They claim that even if morality does not pay, there remain moral truths which we must live up to; or (ii) they may claim that morality pays in subtle ways which we have so far overlooked. Let us take these claims up in turn.

(i) It may be claimed that moral obligation is just a fact of life, woven into the structure of reality. Morality may not always pay, but certain moral standards remain true, e.g., "Lying is wrong" or "Human life is sacred." These are not made true by evolution or God, but are necessary truths, independent of concrete existence, like "1 + 1 = 2" or "There are no triangular circles."

There are at least three difficulties with this suggestion. First, assuming that there are such necessary truths about morality, why should we care about them or pay them any attention? We may grant that an act is correct from the moral point of view and yet wonder whether we have good reason to participate in the institution of morality. So, even if we grant that various statements of the form "One ought to do *X*" are necessarily true, this does not show that the institution of morality pays off. It just says that morality is a "game" whose rules are necessary truths. . . . To defend the institution of morality simply on the grounds that certain moral statements are necessarily true is to urge duty for duty's sake. And . . . this is not an acceptable defense of the institution of morality.

Second, the idea that some moral truths are necessary comports poorly with the usual secular account. As Mavrodes points out, necessary moral truths seem to be what Plato had in mind when he spoke about the Form of the Good. And Plato's view, though not contradicted by modern science, receives no support from it either. Plato's Form of the Good is not an emergent phenomenon, but is rather woven into the very structure of reality, independently of physical processes such as evolution. So, Plato's view is incompatible with the typically modern secular view that moral value is an emergent phenomenon, coming into existence with the arrival of the human nervous system. For this reason, Plato's views have "often been taken to be congenial . . . to a religious understanding of the world."[6]

Third, it is very doubtful that there are any necessary truths of the form "One ought to do *X*." We have seen that the institution of morality stands unjustified if participation in it does not pay (in the long run) for individuals. And why should we suppose that there are *any* necessary moral truths if the institution of morality is unjustified? . . . [S]tatements of the form "One ought to do *X*" are not *necessary* truths, though they may be true *if* certain conditions are met. . . . Hence, if there are any necessary moral truths, they appear to be conditional (if-then) in form: If certain conditions exist, one ought to do *X*. Among the conditions, as we have seen, is the condition that doing *X* pays for the individual in the long run. So, it is very doubtful that there are any necessary moral truths of the form "One ought to do *X*."[7] The upshot is that morality is partly grounded in those features of reality which guarantee that morality pays; and the secular view lacks the metaphysical resources for making such a guarantee. . . .

(ii) But some have claimed that, if we look closely at human psychology, we can see that morality does pay *in terms of earthly goods*. For example, Plato suggested that only a highly moral person could have harmony between the various elements of his soul (such as reason and desire). Others have claimed that being highly moral is the only means to inner satisfaction. We humans are just so constituted that violations of morality never leave us with a net gain. Sure, we may gain earthly goods of one sort or another by lying, stealing, etc., but these are always outweighed by inner discord or a sense of dissatisfaction with ourselves.

There are several problems with this. First, some may doubt that moral virtue is the best route to inner peace. After all, one may experience profound inner discord when one has done what is right. It can be especially upsetting to stand up for what is right when doing so is unpopular; indeed, many people avoid "making waves" precisely because it upsets their inner peace. . . .

Second, how good is the evidence that inner peace *always* outweighs the benefits achievable through unethical action? Perhaps guilt feelings and inner discord are a reasonable price to pay for certain earthly goods. If a cowardly act enables me to stay alive, or a dishonest act makes me wealthy, I may judge that my gains are worth the accompanying guilt feelings. A quiet conscience is not everything.

Third, if inner discord or a sense of dissatisfaction stems from a feeling of having done wrong, why not reassess my standards? Therapists are familiar with the phenomenon of false guilt. For example, a married woman may feel guilty for having sex with her spouse. The cure will involve enabling the patient to view sex as a legitimate means of expressing affection. The point is that just because I feel a certain type of act is wrong, it does not follow that the only route to inner peace is to avoid the action. I also have the option of revising my standards, which may enable me to pursue self-interested goals in a less inhibited fashion. Why drag along any unnecessary moral baggage? How could it be shown, on secular grounds, that it is in my interest to maintain the more idealistic standards endorsed by the great moralists? Certainly, some people have much less idealistic standards than others, and yet seem no less happy.

By way of contrast with the secular view, it is not difficult to see how morality might pay if there is a God of the Christian type. First, God loves all humans and wants all included in his kingdom. So, a tribal morality would violate his demands, and to violate his demands is to strain one's most important personal relationship. Second, there are no secret violations of morality if God exists. Since God is omniscient, willful wrongdoing of any sort will estrange the wrongdoer from God. Third, while earthly society may be able to function pretty well even though there exists a small number of "moral freeloaders," the freeloaders themselves are certainly not attaining harmonious relations with God. Accordingly, their ultimate fulfillment is in jeopardy. Fourth, death is the end of earthly life, but it is not the end of conscious existence, according to Christianity. Therefore, death does not end one's opportunity for personal fulfillment; indeed, if God is perfectly good and omnipotent, we can only assume that the afterlife will result in the fulfillment of our deepest needs—unless we willfully reject God's efforts to supply those needs.

So, it seems to me that the moral life makes more sense from a theistic perspective than from a secular perspective. Of course, I do not claim that I have proved the existence of God, and a full discussion of this metaphysical issue would take us too far from matters at hand.[8] But if I have shown that the moral life makes more sense from a theistic perspective than from a secular one, then I have provided an important piece of evidence in favor of the rationality of belief in God. Moreover, I believe that I have turned back one objection to the Christian teleological view, namely, the allegation that theism is unnecessary metaphysical baggage.

Notes

1. It can be argued that, even from a secular perspective, some benefits and harms are available after death. For example, vindicating the reputation of a deceased person may be seen as benefiting that person. See, for example, Thomas Nagel, *Mortal Questions* (London: Cambridge University Press, 1979), pp. 1–10. But even if we grant that these are goods for the deceased, it is obvious that, from the secular point of view, such postmortem goods cannot be consciously enjoyed by the deceased. They are not available in the sense that he will never take pleasure in them.

2. George Mavrodes, "Religion and the Queerness of Morality," in *Rationality, Religious Belief, and Moral Commitment,* ed. Robert Audi and William J. Wainwright (Ithaca, N.Y.: Cornell University Press, 1986), p. 223.

3. Peter Singer, *Practical Ethics* (London: Cambridge University Press, 1970), p. 209.

4. For an excellent discussion of arguments for immortality, see William J. Wainwright, *Philosophy of Religion* (Belmont, Calif.: Wadsworth, 1988), pp. 99–111.

5. My source for these claims about "happy psychopaths" is Singer, *Practical Ethics*, pp. 214–216. Singer in turn is drawing from Hervey Cleckley, *The Mask of Sanity,* (*An Attempt to Clarify Some Issues About the So-Called Psychopathic Personality*), 5th ed. (St. Louis, Mo.: E. S. Cleckley, 1988).

6. Mavrodes, "Religion and the Queerness of Morality," p. 224. I am borrowing from Mavrodes throughout this paragraph.

7. Those acquainted with modal logic may have a question here. By a principle of modal logic, if p is a necessary truth and p necessarily implies q, then q is a necessary truth. So, if it is necessarily true that "certain conditions are met" and necessarily true that "If they are met, one ought to X," then, "One ought to do X" is a necessary truth. But I assume it is not *necessarily true* that "certain conditions are met." In my judgment it would be most implausible to suppose, e.g., that "Morality pays for humans" is a necessary truth.

8. Two fine discussions of moral arguments for theism are Robert Merrihew Adams, "Moral Arguments for Theistic Belief," in *Rationality and Religious Belief,* ed. C. F. Delaney (Notre Dame, Ind.: University of Notre Dame Press, 1979), pp. 116–140, and J. L. Mackie, *The Miracle of Theism* (Oxford: Oxford University Press, 1982), pp. 102–118.

C. Stephen Layman is a Professor of Philosophy at Seattle Pacific University. He has published in logic, metaphysics, and the philosophy of religion. His books include *The Shape of the Good* (University of Notre Dame Press, 1991), *The Power of Logic,* 3rd ed. (McGraw-Hill, 2005), and *Letters to a Doubting Thomas: A Case for the Existence of God* (Oxford University Press, 2007).

John Arthur   ➡ **NO**

Religion, Morality, and Conscience

My first and prime concern in this paper is to explore the connections, if any, between morality and religion. I will argue that in fact religion is not necessary for morality. Yet despite the lack of any logical or other necessary connection, I will claim, there remain important respects in which the two are related. In the concluding section I will discuss the notion of moral conscience, and then look briefly at the various respects in which morality is "social" and the implications of that idea for moral education. First, however, I want to say something about the subjects: just what are we referring to when we speak of morality and of religion?

Morality and Religion

A useful way to approach the first question—the nature of morality—is to ask what it would mean for a society to exist without a social moral code. How would such people think and behave? What would that society look like? First, it seems clear that such people would never feel guilt or resentment. For example, the notions that I ought to remember my parents' anniversary, that he has a moral responsibility to help care for his children after the divorce, that she has a right to equal pay for equal work, and that discrimination on the basis of race is unfair would be absent in such a society. Notions of duty, rights, and obligations would not be present, except perhaps in the legal sense; concepts of justice and fairness would also be foreign to these people. In short, people would have no tendency to evaluate or criticize the behavior of others, nor to feel remorse about their own behavior. Children would not be taught to be ashamed when they steal or hurt others, nor would they be allowed to complain when others treat them badly. (People might, however, feel regret at a decision that didn't turn out as they had hoped; but that would only be because their expectations were frustrated, not because they feel guilty.)

Such a society lacks a moral code. What, then, of religion? Is it possible that a people lacking a morality would nonetheless have religious beliefs? It seems clear that it is possible. Suppose every day these same people file into their place of worship to pay homage to God (they may believe in many gods or in one all-powerful creator of heaven and earth). Often they can be heard praying to God for help in dealing with their problems and thanking Him for their good fortune. Frequently they give sacrifices to God, sometimes in the form of money spent to build beautiful temples and churches, other times by performing actions they believe God would approve such as helping those in need. These practices might also be institutionalized, in the sense that certain people are assigned important leadership roles. Specific texts might also be taken as authoritative, indicating the ways God has acted in history and His role in their lives or the lives of their ancestors.

To have a moral code, then, is to tend to evaluate (perhaps without even expressing it) the behavior of others and to feel guilt at certain actions when we perform them. Religion, on the other hand, involves beliefs in supernatural power(s) that created and perhaps also control nature, the tendency to worship and pray to those supernatural forces or beings, and the presence of organizational structures and authoritative texts. The practices of morality and religion are thus importantly different. One involves our attitudes toward various forms of behavior (lying and killing, for example), typically expressed using the notions of rules, rights, and obligations. The other, religion, typically involves prayer, worship, beliefs about the supernatural, institutional forms and authoritative texts.

We come, then, to the central question: What is the connection, if any, between a society's moral code and its religious practices and beliefs? Many people have felt that morality is in some way dependent on religion or religious truths. But what sort of "dependence" might there be? In what follows I distinguish various ways in which one might claim that religion is necessary for morality, arguing against those who claim morality depends in some way on religion. I will also suggest, however, some other important ways in which the two are related, concluding with a brief discussion of conscience and moral education.

Religious Motivation and Guidance

One possible role that religion might play in morality relates to motives people have. Religion, it is often said, is necessary so that people will DO right. Typically, the argument begins with the important point that doing what is right often has costs: refusing to shoplift or cheat can mean people go without some good or fail a test; returning a billfold means they don't get the contents. Religion is therefore said to be necessary in that it provides motivation to do the right thing. God rewards those who follow His commands by providing for them a place in heaven or by insuring that they prosper and are happy on earth. He also punishes those who violate the moral law. Others emphasize less self-interested ways in which religious motives may encourage people to act rightly. Since God is the creator of the universe and has ordained that His plan should be followed, they point out, it is important to live one's life in accord with this divinely ordained plan. Only by living a moral life, it is said, can people live in harmony with the larger, divinely created order.

The first claim, then, is that religion is necessary to provide moral motivation. The problem with that argument, however, is that religious motives are far from the only ones people have. For most of us, a decision to do the right thing (if that is our decision) is made for a variety of reasons: "What if I get caught? What if somebody sees me—what will he or she think? How will I feel afterwards? Will I regret it?" Or maybe the thought of cheating just doesn't arise. We were raised to be a decent person, and that's what we are—period. Behaving fairly and treating others well is more important than whatever we might gain from stealing or cheating, let alone seriously harming another person. So it seems clear that many motives for doing the right thing have nothing whatsoever to do with religion. Most of us, in fact, do worry about getting caught, being blamed, and being looked down on by others. We also may do what is right just because it's right, or because we don't want to hurt others or embarrass family and friends. To say that we need religion to act morally is mistaken; indeed it seems to me that many of us, when it really gets down to it, don't give much of a thought to religion when making moral decisions. All those other reasons are the ones which we tend to consider, or else we just don't consider cheating and stealing at all. So far, then, there seems to be no reason to suppose that people can't be moral yet irreligious at the same time.

A second argument that is available for those who think religion is necessary to morality, however, focuses on moral guidance and knowledge rather than on people's motives. However much people may want to do the right thing, according to this view, we cannot ever know for certain what is right without the guidance of religious teaching. Human understanding is simply inadequate to this difficult and controversial task; morality involves immensely complex problems, and so we must consult religious revelation for help.

Again, however, this argument fails. First, consider how much we would need to know about religion and revelation in order for religion to provide moral guidance. Besides being sure that there is a God, we'd also have to think about which of the many religions is true. How can anybody be sure his or her religion is the right one? But even if we assume the Judeo-Christian God is the real one, we still need to find out just what it is He wants us to do, which means we must think about revelation.

Revelation comes in at least two forms, and not even all Christians agree on which is the best way to understand revelation. Some hold that revelation occurs when God tells us what he wants by providing us with His words: The Ten Commandments are an example. Many even believe, as evangelist Billy Graham once said, that the entire *Bible* was written by God using 39 secretaries. Others, however, doubt that the "word of God" refers literally to the words God has spoken, but believe instead that the *Bible* is an historical document, written by human beings, of the events or occasions in which God revealed Himself. It is an especially important document, of course, but nothing more than that. So on this second view revelation is not understood as *statements* made by God but rather as His *acts* such as leading His people from Egypt, testing Job, and sending His son as an example of the ideal life. The *Bible* is not itself revelation, it's the historical account of revelatory actions.

If we are to use revelation as a moral guide, then, we must first know what is to count as revelation—words given us by God, historical events, or both? But even supposing that we could somehow answer those questions, the problems of relying on revelation are still not over since we still must interpret that revelation. Some feel, for example, that the *Bible* justifies various forms of killing, including war and capital punishment, on the basis of such statements as "An eye for an eye." Others, emphasizing such sayings as "Judge not lest ye be judged" and "Thou shalt not kill," believe the *Bible* demands absolute pacifism. How are we to know which interpretation is correct? It is likely, of course, that the answer people give to such religious questions will be influenced in part at least by their own moral beliefs: if capital punishment is thought to be unjust, for example, then an interpreter will seek to read the *Bible* in a way that is consistent with that moral truth. That is not, however, a happy conclusion for those wishing to rest morality on revelation, for it means that their understanding of what God has revealed is itself dependent on their prior moral views. Rather than revelation serving as a guide for morality, morality is serving as a guide for how we interpret revelation.

So my general conclusion is that far from providing a short-cut to moral understanding, looking to revelation for guidance often creates more questions and problems. It seems wiser under the circumstances to address complex moral problems like abortion, capital punishment, and affirmative action directly, considering the pros and cons of each side, rather than to seek answers through the much more controversial and difficult route of revelation.

The Divine Command Theory

It may seem, however, that we have still not really gotten to the heart of the matter. Even if religion is not necessary for moral motivation or guidance, it is often claimed, religion is necessary in another more fundamental sense. According to this view, religion is necessary for morality because without God there could BE no right or wrong. God, in other words, provides the foundation or bedrock on which morality is grounded. This idea was expressed by Bishop R. C. Mortimer:

> "God made us and all the world. Because of that He has an absolute claim on our obedience. . . . From [this] it follows that a thing is not right simply because we think it is. It is right because God commands it."[1]

What Bishop Mortimer has in mind can be seen by comparing moral rules with legal ones. Legal statutes, we know, are created by legislatures; if the state assembly of New York had not passed a law limiting speed people can travel, then there would be no such legal obligation. Without the statutory enactments, such a law simply would not exist. Mortimer's view, the *divine command theory*, would mean that God has the same sort of relation to moral law as legislature has to statutes it enacts: without God's commands there would be no moral rules, just as without a legislature there would be no statutes.

Defenders of the divine command theory often add to this a further claim, that only by assuming God sits at the foundation of morality can we explain the objective

difference between right and wrong. This point was forcefully argued by F. C. Copleston in a 1948 British Broadcasting Corporation radio debate with Bertrand Russell.

Copleston: . . . The validity of such an interpretation of man's conduct depends on the recognition of God's existence, obviously. . . . Let's take a look at the Commandant of the [Nazi] concentration camp at Belsen. That appears to you as undesirable and evil and to me too. To Adolf Hitler we suppose it appeared as something good and desirable. I suppose you'd have to admit that for Hitler it was good and for you it is evil.

Russell: No, I shouldn't go so far as that. I mean, I think people can make mistakes in that as they can in other things. If you have jaundice you see things yellow that are not yellow. You're making a mistake.

Copleston: Yes, one can make mistakes, but can you make a mistake if it's simply a question of reference to a feeling or emotion? Surely Hitler would be the only possible judge of what appealed to his emotions.

Russell: . . . You can say various things about that; among others, that if that sort of thing makes that sort of appeal to Hitler's emotions, then Hitler makes quite a different appeal to my emotions.

Copleston: Granted. But there's no objective criterion outside feeling then for condemning the conduct of the Commandant of Belsen, in your view. . . . The human being's idea of the content of the moral law depends certainly to a large extent on education and environment, and a man has to use his reason in assessing the validity of the actual moral ideas of his social group. But the possibility of criticizing the accepted moral code presupposes that there is an objective standard, that there is an ideal moral order, which imposes itself. . . . It implies the existence of a real foundation of God.[2]

Against those who, like Bertrand Russell, seek to ground morality in feelings and attitudes, Copleston argues that there must be a more solid foundation if we are to be able to claim truly that the Nazis were evil. God, according to Copleston, is able to provide the objective basis for the distinction, which we all know to exist, between right and wrong. Without divine commands at the root of human obligations, we would have no real reason for condemning the behavior of anybody, even Nazis. Morality, Copleston thinks, would then be nothing more than an expression of personal feeling.

To begin assessing the divine command theory, let's first consider this last point. Is it really true that only the commands of God can provide an objective basis for moral judgments? Certainly many philosophers have felt that morality rests on its own perfectly sound footing, be it reason, human nature, or natural sentiments. It seems wrong to conclude, automatically, that morality cannot rest on anything but religion. And it is also possible that morality doesn't have any foundation or basis at all, so that its claims should be ignored in favor of whatever serves our own self-interest.

In addition to these problems with Copleston's argument, the divine command theory faces other problems as well. First, we would need to say much more about the relationship between morality and divine commands. Certainly the expressions "is commanded by God" and "is morally required" do not *mean* the same thing. People and even whole societies can use moral concepts without understanding them to make any reference to God. And while it is true that God (or any other moral being for that matter) would tend to want others to do the right thing, this hardly shows that being right and being commanded by God are the same thing. Parents want their children to do the right thing, too, but that doesn't mean parents, or anybody else, can make a thing right just by commanding it!

I think that, in fact, theists should reject the divine command theory. One reason is what it implies. Suppose we were to grant (just for the sake of argument) that the divine command theory is correct, so that actions are right just because they are commanded by God. The same, of course, can be said about those deeds that we believe are wrong. If God hadn't commanded us not to do them, they would not be wrong.

But now notice this consequence of the divine command theory. Since God is all-powerful, and since right is determined solely by His commands, is it not possible that He might change the rules and make what we now think of as wrong into right? It would seem that according to the divine command theory the answer is "yes": it is theoretically possible that tomorrow God would decree that virtues such as kindness and courage have become vices while actions that show cruelty and cowardice will henceforth be the right actions. (Recall the analogy with a legislature and the power it has to change law.) So now rather than it being right for people to help each other out and prevent innocent people from suffering unnecessarily, it would be right (God having changed His mind) to create as much pain among innocent children as we possibly can! To adopt the divine command theory therefore commits its advocate to the seemingly absurd position that even the greatest atrocities might be not only acceptable but morally required if God were to command them.

Plato made a similar point in the dialogue *Euthyphro*. Socrates is asking Euthyphro what it is that makes the virtue of holiness a virtue, just as we have been asking what makes kindness and courage virtues. Euthyphro has suggested that holiness is just whatever all the gods love.

Socrates: Well, then, Euthyphro, what do we say about holiness? Is it not loved by all the gods, according to your definition?

Euthyphro: Yes.

Socrates: Because it is holy, or for some other reason?

Euthyphro: No, because it is holy.

Socrates: Then it is loved by the gods because it is holy: it is not holy because it is loved by them?

Euthyphro: It seems so.

Socrates: . . . Then holiness is not what is pleasing to the gods, and what is pleasing to the gods is not holy as you say, Euthyphro. They are different things.

Euthyphro: And why, Socrates?

Socrates: Because we are agreed that the gods love holiness because it is holy: and that it is not holy because they love it.[3]

This raises an interesting question: Why, having claimed at first that virtues are merely what is loved (or commanded) by the gods, would Euthyphro so quickly contradict this and agree that the gods love holiness *because* it's holy, rather than the reverse? One likely possibility is that Euthyphro believes that whenever the gods love something they do so with good reason, not without justification and arbitrarily. To deny this, and say that it is merely the gods' love that makes holiness a virtue, would mean that the gods have no basis for their attitudes, that they are arbitrary in what they love. Yet—and this is the crucial point—it's far from clear that a religious person would want to say that God is arbitrary in that way. If we say that it is simply God's loving something that makes it right, then what sense would it make to say God wants us to do right? All that could mean, it seems, is that God wants us to do what He wants us to do; He would have no reason for wanting it. Similarly "God is good" would mean little more than "God does what He pleases." The divine command theory therefore leads us to the results that God is morally arbitrary, and that His wishing us to do good or even God's being just mean nothing more than that God does what He does and wants whatever He wants. Religious people who reject that consequence would also, I am suggesting, have reason to reject the divine command theory itself, seeking a different understanding of morality.

This now raises another problem, however. If God approves kindness because it is a virtue and hates the Nazis because they were evil, then it seems that God discovers morality rather than inventing it. So haven't we then identified a limitation on God's power, since He now, being a good God, must love kindness and command us not to be cruel? Without the divine command theory, in other words, what is left of God's omnipotence?

But why, we may ask, is such a limitation on God unacceptable? It is not at all clear that God really can do anything at all. Can God, for example, destroy Himself? Or make a rock so heavy that He cannot lift it? Or create a universe which was never created by Him? Many have thought that God cannot do these things, but also that His inability to do them does not constitute a serious limitation on His power since these are things that cannot be done at all: to do them would violate the laws of logic. Christianity's most influential theologian, Thomas Aquinas, wrote in this regard that "whatever implies contradiction does not come within the scope of divine omnipotence, because it cannot have the aspect of possibility. Hence it is more appropriate to say that such things cannot be done than that God cannot do them."[4]

How, then, ought we to understand God's relationship to morality if we reject the divine command theory? Can religious people consistently maintain their faith in God the Creator and yet deny that what is right is right because He commands it? I think the answer to this is "yes." Making cruelty good is not like making a universe that wasn't made, of course. It's a moral limit on God rather than a logical one. But why suppose that God's limits are only logical?

One final point about this. Even if we agree that God loves justice or kindness because of their nature, not arbitrarily, there still remains a sense in which God could change morality even having rejected the divine command theory. That's because if we assume, plausibly I think, that morality depends in part on how we reason, what we desire and need, and the circumstances in which we find ourselves, then morality will still be under God's control since God could have constructed us or our environment very differently. Suppose, for instance, that he created us so that we couldn't be hurt by others or didn't care about freedom. Or perhaps our natural environment were created differently, so that all we have to do is ask and anything we want is given to us. If God had created either nature or us that way, then it seems likely our morality might also be different in important ways from the one we now think correct.

In that sense, then, morality depends on God whether or not one supports the divine command theory.

"Morality Is Social"

I have argued here that religion is not necessary in providing moral motivation or guidance, and against the divine command theory's claim that God is necessary for there to be morality at all. In this last section, I want first to look briefly at how religion and morality sometimes *do* influence each other. Then I will consider the development of moral conscience and the important ways in which morality might correctly be thought to be "social."

Nothing I have said so far means that morality and religion are independent of each other. But in what ways are they related, assuming I am correct in claiming morality does not *depend* on religion? First, of course, we should note the historical influence religions have had on the development of morality as well as on politics and law. Many of the important leaders of the abolitionist and civil rights movements were religious leaders, as are many current members of the pro-life movement. The relationship is not, however, one-sided: morality has also influenced religion, as the current debate within the Catholic church over the role of women, abortion, and other social issues shows. In reality, then, it seems clear that the practices of morality and religion have historically each exerted an influence on the other.

But just as the two have shaped each other historically, so, too, do they interact at the personal level. I have already suggested how people's understanding of revelation, for instance, is often shaped by morality as they seek the best interpretations of revealed texts. Whether trying to understand a work of art, a legal statute, or a religious text, interpreters regularly seek to understand them in the best light—to make them as good as they can be, which requires that they bring moral judgment to the task of religious interpretation and understanding.

The relationship can go the other direction as well, however, as people's moral views are shaped by their religious training and beliefs. These relationships between morality and religion are often complex, hidden even from ourselves, but it does seem clear that our views on important moral issues, from sexual morality and war to welfare and capital punishment, are often influenced by our religious outlook. So not only are religious and moral practices and understandings historically linked, but for many religious people the relationship extends to the personal level—to their understanding of moral obligations as well as their sense of who they are and their vision of who they wish to be.

Morality, then, is influenced by religion (as is religion by morality), but morality's social character extends deeper even than that, I want to argue. First, of course, we possess a socially acquired language within which we think about our various choices and the alternatives we ought to follow, including whether a possible course of action is the right thing to do. Second, morality is social in that it governs relationships among people, defining our responsibilities to others and theirs to us. Morality provides the standards we rely on in gauging our interactions with family, lovers, friends, fellow citizens, and even strangers. Third, morality is social in the sense that we are, in fact, subject to criticism by others for our actions. We discuss with others what we should do, and often hear from them concerning whether our decisions were acceptable. Blame and praise are a central feature of morality.

While not disputing any of this, John Dewey has stressed another, less obvious aspect of morality's social character. Consider then the following comments regarding the origins of morality and conscience in an article he titled "Morality Is Social":

In language and imagination we rehearse the responses of others just as we dramatically enact other consequences. We foreknow how others will act, and the foreknowledge is the beginning of judgment passed on action. We know *with* them; there is conscience. An assembly is formed within our breast which discusses and appraises proposed and performed acts. The community without becomes a forum and tribunal within, a judgment-seat of charges, assessments and exculpations. Our thoughts of our own actions are saturated with the ideas that others entertain about them. . . . Explicit recognition of this fact is a prerequisite of improvement in moral education. . . . Reflection is morally indispensable.[5]

To appreciate fully the role of society in shaping morality and influencing people's sense of responsibility, Dewey is arguing, requires appreciating the fact that to think from the moral point of view, as opposed to the selfish one, for instance, means rejecting our private, subjective perspective in favor of the view of others, envisioning how they might respond to various choices we might make. Far from being private and unrelated to others, moral conscience is in that sense "public." To consider a decision from the moral perspective, says Dewey, requires that we envision an "assembly of others" that is "formed within our breast." In that way, our moral conscience cannot be sharply distinguished from our nature as social beings since conscience invariably brings with it, or constitutes, the perspective of the other. "Is this right?" and "What would this look like were I to have to defend it to others?" are not entirely separable questions.[6]

It is important not to confuse Dewey's point here, however. He is *not* saying that what is right is finally to be determined by the reactions of actually existing other people, or even by the reaction of society as a whole. What is right or fair can never be finally decided by a vote, and might not meet the approval of any specific others. But what then might Dewey mean in speaking of such an "assembly of others" as the basis of morality? The answer is that rather than actual people or groups, the assembly Dewey envisions is hypothetical or "ideal." The "community without" is thus transformed into a "forum and tribunal within, a judgment seat of charges, assessments and exculpations." So it is through the powers of our imagination that we can meet our moral responsibilities and exercise moral judgment, using these powers to determine what morality requires by imagining the reaction of Dewey's "assembly of others."

Morality is therefore *inherently* social, in a variety of ways. It depends on socially learned language, is learned from interactions with others, and governs our interactions with others in society. But it also demands, as Dewey put it, that we know "with" others, envisioning for ourselves what their points of view would require along with our own. Conscience demands we occupy the positions of others.

Viewed in this light, God would play a role in a religious person's moral reflection and conscience since it is unlikely a religious person would wish to exclude God from the "forum and tribunal" that constitutes conscience. Rather, for the religious person conscience would almost certainly include the imagined reaction of God along with the reactions of others who might be affected by the action. Other people are also important, however, since it is often an open question just what God's reaction would be; revelation's meaning, as I have argued, is subject to interpretation. So it seems that for a religious person morality and God's will cannot be separated, though the connection between them is not the one envisioned by defenders of the divine command theory.

Which leads to my final point, about moral education. If Dewey is correct, then it seems clear there is an important sense in which morality not only can be taught but must be. Besides early moral training, moral thinking depends on our ability to imagine others' reactions and to imaginatively put ourselves into their shoes. "What would somebody (including, perhaps, God) think if this got out?" expresses more than a concern with being embarrassed or punished; it is also the voice of conscience and indeed of morality itself. But that would mean, thinking of education, that listening to others, reading about what others think and do, and reflecting within ourselves about our actions and whether we could defend them to others are part of the practice of morality itself. Morality cannot exist without the broader, social perspective introduced by others, and this social nature ties it, in that way, with education and with public discussion, both actual and imagined. "Private" moral reflection taking place independent of the social world would be no moral reflection at all; and moral education is not only possible, but essential.

Notes

1. R. C. Mortimer, *Christian Ethics* (London: Hutchinson's University Library, 1950), pp. 7–8.
2. This debate was broadcast on the "Third Program" of the British Broadcasting Corporation in 1948.
3. Plato, *Euthyphro*, tr. H. N. Fowler (Cambridge, MA: Harvard University Press, 1947).
4. Thomas Aquinas, *Summa Theologica*, Part I, Q.25, Art. 3.
5. John Dewey, "Morality Is Social" in *The Moral Writings of John Dewey*, revised edition, ed. James Gouinlock (Amherst, NY: Prometheus Books, 1994), pp. 182–184.
6. Obligations to animals raise an interesting problem for this conception of morality. Is it wrong to torture animals only because other *people* could be expected to disapprove? Or is it that the animal itself would disapprove? Or, perhaps, duties to animals rest on sympathy and compassion while human moral relations are more like Dewey describes, resting on morality's inherently social nature and on the dictates of conscience viewed as an assembly of others?

JOHN ARTHUR (1946–2007) created and served as Director of the Institute for Philosophy, Politics, and Law at Binghamton University. He published three books: *Words That Bind: Judicial Review and the Grounds of Modern Constitutional Practice* (Westview Press, 1995), *The Unfinished Constitution: Philosophy and Constitutional Practice* (1989), and *Race, Equality, and the Burdens of History* (Cambridge University Press, 2007). He was also the editor or co-editor of more than 8 other books and authored over 25 articles addressing issues of public concern.

EXPLORING THE ISSUE

Does Morality Need Religion?

Critical Thinking and Reflection

1. In what sense can we say that it "pays" to behave morally in today's society? Can you think of any additional examples in which acting morally means acting against your own self-interest? In such cases, should people behave morally? Why or why not?
2. Do you think that religion is needed to provide a motivation to do the right thing? What other possible motivations do people have to do the right thing?
3. The problem raised by Plato and mentioned by Arthur with regard to Divine Command theory is an important one: is something good because God commands it, or does God command it because it is good? How would you resolve this question?

Is There Common Ground?

Layman's argument that the secular viewpoint provides inadequate grounds for morality conflicts directly with Arthur's argument that morality does not depend on religion. Arthur does, however, discuss ways in which morality and religion are related, while Layman attempts to describe hypothetical, if incomplete, secular justifications for morality.

A position that neither philosopher explicitly addresses that might bring them into some agreement is the view known as *etiamsi daremus* (Latin for "even if we should grant"). This is a view held by many theistic philosophers that even if we should grant that there is no God, we would still be able to derive moral principles by which to lead our lives from observation and analysis of human nature and the world around us. Natural law ethics, for example, has an *etiamsi daremus* basis; although it is a system of ethics often followed by believers, it does not rely on religious belief for its foundation. Natural law provides an ethics that is consistent with ethics derived from religious faith, and that can be accounted for within a theistic metaphysical system as being "built into" the

way God created the world. In such a system, Layman could find a morality with an ultimate theistic basis, while Arthur could find a morality that does not require religious belief.

Additional Resources

E. M. Adams, *Religion and Cultural Freedom* (Temple University Press, 1993)

Paul Chamberlain, *Can We Be Good Without God? A Conversation About Truth, Morality, Culture, and a Few Other Things That Matter* (InterVarsity Press, 1996)

Richard J. Mouw, *The God Who Commands: A Study in Divine Command Ethics* (University of Notre Dame Press, 1990)

D. Z. Phillips, ed., *Religion and Morality* (St. Martin's Press, 1996)

Glenn Tinder, "Can We Be Good Without God? On the Political Meaning of Christianity," *The Atlantic Monthly* (December 1989)

Internet References . . .

Council for Secular Humanism

www.secularhumanism.org/

Ontario Consultants on Religious Tolerance: Ethics and Morality

www.religioustolerance.org/morality.htm

Philosophy Links: Philosophy of Religion

http://users.ox.ac.uk/~worc0337/phil_topics_religion.html

Society of Christian Philosophers

www.societyofchristianphilosophers.com/

Unit 2

UNIT

Sex, Marriage, and Reproduction

*S*exuality *is an important, powerful dimension of being human. It is therefore important to have an understanding of the moral permissibility or impermissibility of certain types of sexual activity. The role of government in sexual matters also becomes a matter for moral judgment, as people must decide which types of marriage should be recognized and encouraged by the state. Finally, medical and technological advances raise a host of moral questions about reproductive matters. The issues in this section do not question the morality of sexual activity itself, but they do raise questions about the moral judgments we should make about controversial topics involving human sexuality.*

Selected, Edited, and with Issue Framing Material by:
Owen M. Smith, *Stephen F. Austin State University*
and
Anne Collins Smith, *Stephen F. Austin State University*

ISSUE

Is Casual Sex Immoral?

YES: Meg Lovejoy, from "Explaining Why the Practice [Hooking Up] Is More Costly than Beneficial," in *Is Hooking Up Empowering for College Women? A Feminist Gramscian Perspective*, Ph.D. dissertation, Brandeis University (2012)

NO: Raja Halwani, from "Casual Sex," in Sex *from Plato to Paglia: A Philosophical Encyclopedia*, Greenwood Press (2005)

Learning Outcomes

After reading this issue, you will be able to:

- Discuss the difficulties involved in defining "casual sex" and offer a provisional definition of this term.
- Identify and assess the importance of the positive (favorable) consequences of sex outside of a committed relationship.
- Identify and assess the importance of the negative (unfavorable) consequences of sex outside of a committed relationship, especially with regard to the dynamics of social marketization and systemic gender inequality that currently characterize our society.
- Apply consequentialist ethical principles to formulate and defend a position on the morality of sex outside of a committed relationship.
- Apply deontological ethical principles to formulate and defend a position on the morality of sex outside of a committed relationship.

ISSUE SUMMARY

YES: Analyzing interviews with female college students enabled Meg Lovejoy to state clearly the advantages and disadvantages of sex without commitment for young women. The disadvantages, including fear of pregnancy and STD's, reduced self-esteem, and thwarted desire for intimacy, outweigh the advantages such as immediate pleasure.

NO: Raja Halwani first discusses the difficulties involved in defining casual sex precisely. He next examines a number of objections to casual sex, and concludes that casual sex need not be morally wrong because each of these objections involves factors that are not, for the most part, specifically intrinsic to casual sex.

For many people, sex and morality are interconnected. Yet, with the exception of specialized issues such as sexual harassment, most contemporary moral philosophers have very little to say about sexual morality. This silence may, in part, be due to the view that many traditional views about sex are outdated and have little relevance to the world in which we now live.

During the ancient and medieval period, moral philosophy was integrated into a larger framework of philosophical theories about the structure of reality and the role of humans within that structure. Ancient Greek philosophers developed elaborate metaphysical theories, which were in turn adapted by medieval philosophers and theologians. According to these theories, humans were different from animals, and in general from the rest of the natural world, because they were rational and were thus thought to have an immaterial or spiritual dimension that was not possessed by other purely material beings. The special metaphysical or supernatural status of humans had consequences for the moral assessment of sexual actions. To the extent that the certain sexual actions, like casual sex, failed to express, or even undermined, the immaterial or spiritual dimension of humanity, they were morally wrong.

Belief in an immaterial or spiritual dimension to humanity, however, has waned in recent decades, and it is now more common to view humans as purely material beings that form part of the natural world, without any special metaphysical or supernatural status. The view that humans are purely material beings, like animals, has had an influence on contemporary attitudes toward sexual activity. Sexual desires are now considered to be simply a part of our physical nature, like our eating preferences. This view, however, does not automatically mean that it is morally right to indulge these sexual desires, such as an urge for casual sex. After all, we have natural desires to eat certain foods, but that does not mean that eating these foods is good for us. We cannot simply eat whatever we feel like whenever we want to; we must curb our desires and use our reason to choose the correct foods from a nutritional standpoint. Traditionalists take a similar approach to natural sexual desires.

It is not moral to indulge in all our sexual desires. Rather, we must exercise self-control regarding our sexual urges, and use our reason to determine when, and with whom, sexual activity is appropriate. Of course, some modernists disagree, arguing that the analogy between eating and sexual activity is flawed in many ways, not least because eating habits were only minimally affected by cultural attitudes, whereas cultural attitudes greatly affected sexual practices.

Today, we are left with a mixed view toward sexual activity, composed of elements drawn from ancient, medieval, and modern thought. It is clear that we cannot disregard modern views about human sexuality and simply return to a traditional approach to sexual morality. However, the precise role that modern views should play in sexual morality is not yet clear.

In the following selections, Steven Rhoads argues that our contemporary culture's support for casual sex has had significant negative repercussions, especially for young women. Raja Halwani, on the other hand, argues that casual sex itself is not morally problematic; rather, the immorality of certain casual sexual acts stems from factors other than its casualness.

YES ↵

Meg Lovejoy

Explaining Why the Practice [Hooking Up] Is More Costly than Beneficial

To understand why hooking up is more costly than beneficial it is necessary to understand why the costs are so high and why the benefits are not as significant as the costs. Essentially this can be explained as follows: the socially marketized nature of the practice, in combination with systemic gender inequality, produced many serious and consequential costs while social marketization yielded benefits which tended to be superficial and transitory in nature.

Why the Costs of Hooking Up are So Substantial

The dynamics of social marketization and systemic gender inequality in combination explain why the costs of hooking up were so significant. First, the practice can be viewed as costly due to its socially marketized nature. Specifically, three socially marketized characteristics of the practice, sexual deregulation, sexual individualism and sexual commodification were key in explaining the largely negative consequences of the practice. In particular, sexual deregulation and individualism produced *anomic* conditions and dynamics that yielded numerous costs for women; and sexual commodification contributed to several costs, most notable among them, self-sexualization and women's sexualization in the hookup culture. Secondly, systemic gender inequality as an important context of hooking up was also a primary facilitator of costs in the practice. Systemic gender inequality, manifesting as gendered sexual scripts, women's preference for relational sex, and women's sexual vulnerability, contributed to a number of primary objective costs for women in the hookup which in turn created a multitude of secondary costs. . . .

Social Marketization: Anomie

Anomic conditions and dynamics, following Durkheim (1951 [1897]), are those in which dashed expectations, moral anxiety, normative confusion, or destructive behavior are caused by unclear or weak social norms/rules. In other words, anomie results when society has exerted too little influence over individuals for the common good. My research illustrates how the sexually deregulated and sexually individualistic (socially marketized) character of hooking up produced various *anomic* conditions and dynamics that are painful and disruptive to women's social, sexual, romantic and emotional lives. In the following discussion I detail the variety of ways in which social marketization produced anomie in the hookup culture and its ensuing costs for women.

First, sexual deregulation often produced the romance gap or an unrequited desire for romantic intimacy or relationship with the hookup partner. . . . This dynamic occurred because of the contradiction between the hookups context of sexual intimacy, which tended to foster feelings of emotional and romantic intimacy in women, and it's extremely weak intimacy norms, which discouraged partner expectations of romantic intimacy and commitment. The romance gap led to a host of costs, some of which could be substantial such as various forms of *romantic discontent* (romantic hurt and disappointment, romantic cynicism, suppression of romantic feelings), *sexual alienation* (sexual and emotional disconnection, feeling sexually used), and *social disruption* (social awkwardness, damaged or broken social relationships), and *emotional distress* (regrets, self-blame, diminished confidence, depression).

Second, sexual deregulation generated the intimacy gap which involved an experience of having become too sexual given the level of emotional and romantic intimacy a woman felt for her hookup partner. This dynamic occurred in part because of the dissonance between women's preference for sex embedded in some type of emotional or romantic intimacy, and the hookup's weak intimacy norms that discouraged partner expectations of the same. The intimacy gap was common and generated a large number of substantial costs, including various forms of *sexual alienation* (sexual and emotional disconnection, sexual and emotional discomfort, little sexual pleasure/sexual dissatisfaction, feeling sexually used), *emotional distress* (shame, regrets, self-blame, diminished confidence), and *social disruption* (social awkwardness, damaged or broken social relationships).

Third, sexual deregulation and individualism together produce partner exploitation and mistreatment in the hookup. While weak or insufficient pro-social norms in the deregulated relationship of the hookup discouraged partner mutual accountability and investment, individualistic norms encouraged partners to prioritize sexual self-interest over sexual mutuality. As I have documented, this led to a range of negative social behaviors ranging from the insensitive to the exploitative (i.e., romantic exploitation, sexual rumor-spreading) to the anti-social (i.e., sexual victimization). Partner exploitation and mistreatment produce some of the most substantial and wide-ranging costs of the hookup and include the following: forms of *sexual alienation* (feeling sexually used/violated, negative sexual reputation, little sexual pleasure, sexual dissatisfaction, sexual compliance, sexual & emotional discomfort), *social disruption* (social awkwardness, damaged, broken social relationships), *Romantic discontent* (romantic cynicism), *compromised ethics* (diminished ethical integrity), *emotional distress* (shame, guilt, fear, embarrassment, anger and betrayal, jealousy, regrets, self-blame, diminished confidence, depression).

Fourth, sexual deregulation often generated romantic ambiguity, the difficulty of discerning whether a hookup relationship had become romantic or not; it also produced social ambiguity, the awkwardness of redefining a friendship that had become sexual but not romantic after a hookup. These dynamics occurred for two reasons. First, the hookups lack of expectations for romantic intimacy often clashed with women's perception of hooking up as an appropriate, and indeed, as the only vehicle in the dating culture for developing romantic relationships. Second, the hookup's weak norms concerning partner communication about the meaning and status of the relationship meant that explicit communication about the status of the relationship typically did not occur. Together, these dynamics generated normative confusion resulting in the following costs: *romantic discontent* (romantic confusion, romantic cynicism, romantic suppression), *emotional distress* (anger and betrayal), *social disruption* (social awkwardness, damaged social relationships).

Finally, alcohol as a tool of sexual deregulation produced anomic outcomes previously mentioned, the intimacy gap and sexual victimization. Alcohol use fostered the intimacy gap because it diminished women's inhibitions concerning the perceived disconnect between physical and emotional intimacy and impaired their judgment about their ability to tolerate this disjuncture. At the same time, alcohol fueled sexual victimization because it reduced men's and women's internal checks on risky and damaging actions.[1] Normative alcohol use also generated additional anomic outcomes, the attraction gap, and certain sexually self-destructive behaviors. The attraction gap involved women hooking up with partners to whom they were not sufficiently physically attracted. Alcohol use facilitated this dynamic by removing women's sexual inhibitions and diminishing their judgment about choice of hookup partners. The attraction gap led to the following types of costs: *sexual alienation* (sexual and emotional disconnection, sexual dissatisfaction/lack of pleasure), *social disruption* (social awkwardness), *emotional conflict and distress* (embarrassment, regret).

Lastly, alcohol use fueled two sexually self-destructive behaviors, namely sexual health risk-taking and sexual compliance. Sexual health risk-taking involved women neglecting to use condoms in hookup sex thereby putting themselves at risk for STD's and potentially unwanted pregnancy (if they were not taking birth control).[2] . . . Sexual compliance involves women's consent to unwanted sex. In both cases, alcohol impaired women's ability to adequately protect themselves from risky or unwanted sexual situations. Sexual health risk-taking and sexual compliance resulted in . . . the costs mentioned above. . . . In all of the above ways, alcohol use not only reflected sexual deregulation by the individual women and men who drank.

But also by the larger campus culture and society that tolerated and even encouraged excessive college drinking. Hence, one can say that weak campus and societal norms around drinking promoted the anomic conditions and behaviors discussed above.

In sum, hooking up can be considered an anomic practice because of its sexually deregulated and individualistic (socially marketized) nature. Following from this, the anomic conditions and dynamics the practice generated can be viewed as one of the primary reasons that the practice is so costly.

. . .

Social Marketization: Sexual Commodification

The costliness of hooking up can also be explained in terms of its sexually commodified character. . . . Sexual commodification is a dynamic facilitated by hooking up which promotes an instrumentalized view of one's partner as a sexual object to be acquired and used or consumed in the pursuit of one's own gratification. Here I argue that sexual commodification contributed to processes of women's sexualization, their sexual compliance, and feeling sexually used in the practice.

First the dynamic of sexual commodification in the hookup tended to promote women's self-sexualization and hypersexualization in the hookup culture. It did so by foregrounding the purely physical aspects of sex and the sexual appeal of partners, while short-circuiting its social and emotional dimensions. This dynamic tended to promote a sexualizing view of the partner in which their appearance and sexual attractiveness or appeal was assessed as their primary value. Given that women are already the targets of intensive societal sexualization through the media and their gendered socialization, women likely tended to be more consistently and exclusively assessed through the lens of appearance than men, and therefore were more likely to be sexualized and self-sexualize in the practice than men. Indeed, I found that the sexually commodified nature of the practice reinforced women's self-objectification by enabling them to seek affirmation for their sexual appeal through the number and quality (i.e., social status) of hookup partners they could attract. The dynamic of sexual commodification which profoundly promotes sexual objectification may also explain findings from other research which suggests that women are hypersexualized in the hookup culture. Recall the national study by Freitas which found a widespread popularity of college theme parties (typical vehicles for the hookup culture) on many campuses in which women were regularly cast as sluts and whores or sexualized subordinates to men's roles of power. The sexually commodified nature of the practice may promote such intensive sexualization of women in the hookup culture through its concentrated focus on sexuality as physical appeal.

A second dimension of sexual commodification further reinforced women's self-sexualization in hooking up while sometimes also facilitating their sexual compliance. . . . Some women used sex in the hookup as a kind of currency in exchange for sexual validation or social status as a heterodesirable woman. That is, they hooked up for the primary purpose of gaining sexual affirmation, and sometimes they were willing to engage in unwanted sex in order to achieve this end. Sexual commodification may explain this dynamic because it facilitated a view of the hookup as an instrumental relationship in which one's partner, and even the sexual act itself is viewed as a means to an end. Such an instrumentalized perspective appears to have facilitated some women's use of the hookup as a means to achieving sexual validation or social status even when they were not attracted to their hookup partner or interested in engaging in a suggested sexual act. Therefore, this form of sexual commodification both facilitated women's self-sexualization in the hookup

and could also produce sexual compliance in the process. Sexual compliance led to many costs. . . .

Finally, the sexually commodified nature of hooking up often led to women feeling sexually used in the practice. . . . Feeling sexually used is the subjective dimension of the socially marketized dynamic of social commodification in which one or both partners use each other as sexual objects of consumption to gratify their needs. Women often experienced the subjective feeling of being used when their partner had treated them in an exploitative, hurtful or insensitive manner which revealed the typically transactional nature of the relationship in a stark manner. These forms of exploitation and mistreatment ranged from sexual victimization (the ultimate sexual violation) to a partner only calling a woman for sex at three o' clock in the morning when he was drunk.

Overall, social marketization working through anomie and sexual commodification produced a large number of substantial costs for women; these processes help to explain why hooking up as a practice was so *intrinsically* costly.

Systemic Gender Inequality

Gender inequality also contributed to making hooking up a mostly costly practice for women in fundamentally systemic ways. . . . In the romantic and sexual realm, systemic gendered costs – that is, costs which are largely borne by women and produced by system-wide social relations of male domination – largely are generated by culture because it predominantly shapes interactions between individual men and women. Likewise, with respect to hooking up, my research shows how the overall costliness of the practice for women is fostered by a gendered culture (and to a lesser extent gendered structures), in which women are subordinate. Such a gendered culture forms the context for hooking up and therefore is also a potent source of costs for women. Gendered sexual scripts and women's preference for relational sex, both elements of this culture, contributed to a number of primary objective costs for women in the hookup which in turn created a multitude of secondary costs. . . .

The traditional sexual script which largely guided the sexual rules of the hookup, generated many costs for women in the practice. Researchers have observed that because of the double standard women are under much closer scrutiny for their sexual behavior in the hookup culture than men. As a consequence of this scrutiny, and the ongoing sexist expectation that women's femininity and sexual virtue is enhanced by limiting their sexuality particularly outside of marriage and monogamy, women could potentially receive a negative sexual reputation for participating in the hookup culture in a perceived gender deviant manner. While the rules for "over the line" sexual behavior were vague, generally participants feared receiving a negative sexual reputation if their sexual behavior was perceived as too assertive, frequent or indiscriminate. A negative sexual reputation usually originated in a hookup partner's sexual rumor-spreading, and sometimes women could receive a reputation simply because they were the unlucky recipient of rumors by a partner bent on sexual revenge or the desire to brag to his buddies. Therefore the double standard gave men much power in the hookup culture. Not only did they have the power to judge women's sexuality and spread rumors about them, they were also free of the fear of acquiring a negative sexual reputation themselves. In fact, because men's masculinity is heightened by being sexual according to the double standard, their active participation in the hookup culture could potentially enhance their sexual reputations. I found that sexual rumor-spreading and the acquisition of a negative sexual reputation generated major costs for women as follows: *emotional distress* (shame, embarrassment, social hurt and rejection, anger and betrayal, loss of confidence, depression) and *social disruption* (damaged or ruptured social relationships).

The Traditional Sexual Script (in conjunction with women's vulnerability in sex) also may have facilitated the sexual victimization of women in the hookup. The notion of male sexual initiative constructs men's sexual drive as overpowering. From this perspective, it is men's right to remove women's sexual restrictions in order to meet their sexual needs, a gender construction which may legitimate sexual victimization of women in a variety of contexts including the hookup. Sexual victimization in the hookup was common and led to a host of costs including, *sexual alienation* (feeling sexually used or violated, sexual and emotional disconnection, sexual and emotional discomfort, sexual compliance), *emotional distress* (shame, embarrassment, fear, anger and betrayal, self-blame, diminished confidence, depression), and *social disruption* (social awkwardness, damaged or broken social relationships).

The Traditional Sexual Script's double standard as well as its construction of women's sexuality as naturally more relational, together likely strongly shaped women's preference for relational sex (a preference which was itself varied in character and degree). However, . . . this preference may also be shaped by other factors such as women's greater vulnerability in sex relative to men due to systemic gender inequality which may contribute to their perception of relational sex as a less risky form of intimacy.[4] However, whatever its origins, women's well-documented preference for relational sex made them more vulnerable to experiencing the anomic dynamics and costs of both the romance and intimacy gaps. For these same reasons,

women were also more vulnerable to romantic exploitation by men who could play on their desire for greater romantic intimacy in the hookup to achieve their sexual ends. Romantic exploitation resulted in the following costs: *romantic discontent* (romantic hurt and disappointment, romantic confusion, romantic cynicism), *sexual alienation* (feeling sexually used), *emotional distress* (anger and betrayal, regrets, diminished confidence), *social disruption* (damaged social relationships). . . .

The Traditional Sexual Script and the Contemporary Sexual Script together were primary influences on women's sexual compliance in the hookup. The Traditional Sexual Script motivated women to sexually please their partners or to accept unwanted sex in the hopes that it would promote romantic intimacy with a hookup partner they desired to date. The Contemporary Sexual Script motivated women to become involved in unwanted sex (or sometimes even to initiate it) in order to feel "hot," "sexually daring" or to project an image of being comfortable with casual sex or to avoid being perceived as a "sexual prude." . . .

In addition, the Contemporary Sexual Script's prescriptions for women to look and act "hot" or hyper-sexualized motivated many of them to hookup as a means of seeking out sexual attention from men in a manner celebrated by the script; that is by, demonstrating their willingness to display their sexuality and sexual availability to men in a seemingly empowered or autonomous manner. This dynamic facilitated women's self-sexualization in the hookup which, as just described, was a particularly compatible vehicle for women to demonstrate their sex appeal in accordance with the contemporary script. According to my research, self-sexualization could facilitate sexual dissatisfaction and sexually compulsive/addictive behavior. The latter occurred when women who were lacking in confidence used the hookup in a compulsive or addictive manner to seek male sexual affirmation, which they sought as a proxy for their desire for greater self-esteem. Other research has found that self-sexualization leads to a multitude of serious costs for women, such as body shame and dissatisfaction, eating disorders, low self-esteem, and depression, and diminished sexual health, and cognitive functioning. . . .

Finally, some of the costliness of the practice for women may be attributed to women's greater vulnerability in sex which is a function of structural, cultural, and physiological factors combined. Women are more physiologically susceptible to acquiring STDs, . . . and are more vulnerable to the physiological and social costs of pregnancy. . . . In addition, women are more at risk for sexual victimization due to their greater vulnerability in sex relative to men. This vulnerability is produced by gendered culture, structures, and physiology. Gendered physiological factors (i.e., women's lesser size and physical strength as a group, relative to men) make women more vulnerable to physical and sexual violence by men. However, gendered culture and structures construct men's use of sexual pressure (and even force) as normal and legitimate in several key ways, thereby greatly magnifying this vulnerability. Culturally, the societal-wide devaluation of women and of women's sexuality in combination with the traditional sexual script (described earlier), place women at greater risk for sexual violence or harm in heterosexual contexts. In addition, structural factors make women more vulnerable to sexual victimization than men because a range of social institutions reinforce and reproduce men's dominance, thereby legitimating and enabling their power over women. . . .

Social Marketization and Systemic Gender Inequality Create Gendered Costs Synergistically

Systemic gender inequality and social marketization appear to be synergistic in creating costs for women; the former heightening the negative consequences of the latter, hence making the costs more likely to be borne by women. As sexual deregulation and individualism free hook up partners from sexual and romantic constraints, systemic gender inequality determines which partners (women) are less well socialized and otherwise supported by the culture to appreciate, exploit, and manage this anomic sexual state, and thereby are more likely to incur its substantial costs. Because of their preference for relational sex, greater sexual vulnerability, and gendered sexual scripts, women are likely to be the more romantically, emotionally, and sexually vulnerable party in the hookup interaction, and hence are more likely to experience related problems. For the same reasons, they are less able or willing to make use of the practice in exploitative ways that can benefit them. Conversely, social marketization heightens the negative consequences of systemic gender inequality for women in two ways. First, sexual deregulation intensifies the enactment of the traditional male hegemonic sexual script, thereby heightening the constraints on women's power and agency in hooking up. This is because the lack of partner intimacy and familiarity in the hookup reduced women's comfort in challenging the dominance of the traditional sexual script and in pursuing alternative but more egalitarian personal or cultural sexual scripts. Secondly, the sexually commodified nature of the practice (which promoted partner objectification) particularly accentuates women's sexualization in hooking up because of women's prevailing societal status

as sexual objects – a status created by systemic gender inequality.

. . .

Why the Benefits Were Not As Significant As the Costs

Finally, while the socially marketized nature of hooking up largely explained why the practice was so costly, it can also illuminate why the benefits of hooking up are not as significant as the costs. Briefly, the sexually consumeristic character of the practice – its orientation towards instant gratification, sexual novelty, and sexual materialism – tended to produce benefits that were correspondingly transitory, superficial or otherwise limited in value from the perspective of women's health and well-being. These non-substantial benefits included (but were not limited to) fun and enjoyment geared towards immediate pleasures, such as sexual validation, thrills, instant feelings of power or empowerment, temporary intimacy, and more. While these benefits were often appealing and compelling to women, some were intrinsically costly themselves (e.g., sexual validation) or ethically unsound (e.g., instant power through romantic exploitation), and therefore proved to be a dubious gamble when weighed against the significant costs that women risked in hooking up.

Conclusions

The research on the costs and benefits of hooking up has been seriously hindered by its narrow, fragmented and at times, one-sided and ideologically driven approach to the topic. Mine is the first study to comprehensively and systematically assess the consequences of hooking up by methodically evaluating the broad range of negative and positive outcomes of the practice and weighing their relative significance for women's health and psychological, social, and sexual well-being. In brief, I found that hooking up is largely costly to women because the costs outweighed the benefits and were significantly more numerous and consequential than the benefits. Notably, some of the more substantial costs of hooking up could entail serious long-term harm to women. While the benefits of hooking up motivated women to participate, they tended to be superficial and fleeting in nature and could sometimes be costly in and of themselves; or alternatively (and to a lesser extent), they were substantial but not reliably achieved through the practice. Therefore, hooking up appears to be a largely costly practice for women.

. . .

Notes

1 Specifically, . . . it heightened men's sexual aggressiveness/expectancy and diminished women's judgment about and ability to resist undesirable or potentially harmful sexual situations.

2 Sexual health risk-taking could also involve a hookup partner not disclosing their disease status to their partner and thereby endangering the health of their partner, but since this was not mentioned by any of my participants as a behavior that they engaged in personally I do not include it here.

3 . . . Such a preference may also reflect an intrinsic desire for sexuality and intimacy to be joined (to varying degrees) which is either gender-specific (to women) or a gender non-specific manifestation of a fundamentally human desire for intimacy. Alternatively, men and women's different sexual preferences may largely be shaped by culture. The explanation for this preference is beyond the scope of my research.

Meg Lovejoy is a researcher at the Institutes on Assets and Social Policy at Brandeis University with expertise on social inequalities, the life course, and qualitative methodology. She has co-led or contributed to the design and analysis of a variety of projects focusing on the impact of race, class, and gender inequalities on the well-being of women and families across the life course, and is currently co-authoring a book about the long-term work and family consequences of taking a career break for professional women.

Raja Halwani   **NO**

Casual Sex

Casual sex is often characterized as sex for the sake of sexual pleasure itself, rather than, say, for procreation, and is often contrasted with sex that expresses **love** or is done in a loving context. It involves **sexual desire** alone rather than sexual desire *and* love. Men, generally, engage in casual sex, or would like to, more than women—excluding female sex workers (for an evolutionary account of this difference, see Buss). When gay men engage in it, they often keep it impersonal, especially when otherwise involved in (nonmonogamous) relationships (Blumstein and Schwartz, 295–97). Types of casual sex include one-night stands, orgiastic and "swinging" sex, anonymous encounters in bathhouses and the backrooms of bars (usually between gay men), encounters in Internet chat rooms (**cybersex**), and **prostitution**. Casual sex admits of both conceptual and normative questions. I start with the conceptual. It might seem easy to define "casual sex," but it is not. This, however, does not mean that "there is no such thing as a casual . . . sexual act" (Anscombe, 24).

No definition that relies only on behavioral criteria will work. Such a definition might capture some sexual acts that are casual, such as orgies, sex with animals (**bestiality**), and sex with human corpses (necrophilia), but it would not capture the difference between two couples, one that engages in oral sex casually and the other noncasually. There might be no behavioral differences between them. Beliefs or other mental states must figure in the definition.

One might define "casual sex" as "sexual activity for the sake of sexual pleasure only." It is not sex intended for procreation or the communication of love but solely for pleasure, as in recreational sex. This will not do. We can describe sex for pleasure as recreational if it occurs between two people in a loving relationship, but here it is not casual. Anthony Ellis defines "casual sex" as sex between partners who have no deep or substantial relationship (157). This definition does not specify the type of prior relationship that exists between the parties: that they are strangers, acquaintances, or friends. This is good because not only strangers engage in casual sex. Acquaintances sometimes do, and friends. But the definition fails. Suppose both parties believe that their sex will lead to a committed relationship. Even in the presence of these beliefs, the sexual act, on Ellis's definition, would still be casual. But it is plausible that the presence of these beliefs renders their sex not (fully) casual. It is likely a mark of casual sex that it be done without any beliefs that it be anything more than a sexual encounter.

Let us try this definition: "Casual sex is sexual activity engaged in with the understanding or belief that it will not lead to emotional commitments." One good thing about this definition is that it includes only "negative" mental states as necessary for sex to be casual. The inclusion of "positive" states leads to counterintuitive results. For example, suppose the positive intention "for the sake of sexual pleasure" is necessary. This yields the result that **sexual activity** between a prostitute and her client is not casual, because prostitutes typically are not motivated to engage in sex for their own pleasure. Thus, the motives and intentions of the parties must be left open: We should stipulate only that the parties understand that there is no future commitment.

"Understanding" is important. Suppose Monica has sex with Bill, hoping or desiring that it will lead to a love relationship. However, Monica understands that Bill has no such hope and that he does not desire to be in a relationship with her. Thus, Monica realizes that Bill is about to engage in casual sex, yet nevertheless hopes, against the odds, that it will lead somewhere. Despite her hopes, the sex between them is casual, for both realize that it is engaged in only for the sake of sex. Thus, while mental states are crucial for defining casual sex, we must carefully choose which ones to include. Certain hopes and desires should not factor into the definition.

This definition faces problems. First, must both parties involved have the above understanding? What if one person understands that the sexual encounter will not lead to a future commitment, while the other does not, or believes the opposite? Indeed, how would we describe a sexual encounter in which the parties, or at least one, have no beliefs one way or the other? Should we require that the parties *have* the belief that their sex will not lead to any commitment or that the parties have *no* belief that there will be a commitment? If the former, how strong must the belief be? Should the parties believe that their sex *will not*, or *probably* will not, lead to a commitment? Further, must these beliefs be genuine or veridical, or could they be self-deceptive or false? And how should we describe sex occurring between a person and an entity that cannot have beliefs: an animal, an inflated doll, a cadaver? Perhaps these sexual acts are not casual; at least the latter two are cases of **masturbation**, and masturbation might not be casual sex, due to the absence of a partner. But sex with an animal could not be dismissed so easily.

Second, the definition does not reflect the understanding of most people that casual sex involves one important positive motive, the desire for sexual pleasure. The definition does not mention this motive. However, there are many motives for casual sex, and thus most people's understanding might be mistaken. Third, the definition applies to a sexual act, **rape**, that might be, strictly speaking, casual, yet is not the first case that comes to mind when we think of casual sex. Marital and **date rape** (perhaps) aside, the rapist does not think of himself as forcing sex on a person while believing that this will lead to a committed relationship. Even if rape is casual sex because of this fact, this is not the way we usually think of rape or of casual sex. Fourth, it is worthwhile to reconsider whether it is necessary that a definition of "casual sex" refers to mental states. If the parties to a casual encounter do believe it will lead to an emotional commitment, but it does not, that failure would seem to be sufficient to describe their sex as casual.

Thus, the above definition does not capture *exactly* what we mean by "casual sex." Perhaps "casual sex" is too vague for precise analysis, and pinning down a definition might come at the cost of jettisoning some of our intuitions about it. There is, of course, the danger of confusing the concept of casual sex with promiscuity. Any definition of promiscuity must assert that it is sexual activity with different partners over time (Frederick Elliston [1944–1987], 225–26). Because casual sex does not entail multiple partners (a single one-night stand in a person's life might be casual), it is not the same as promiscuity. It might even be that promiscuity does not entail casual sex. Suppose one has sex with many partners while believing that this is the best way to secure a committed relationship. This person's sexual behavior is promiscuous, but because of the intention we would not necessarily describe it as casual. (Benatar [193–94] equates promiscuity and casual sex, but this is because he defines promiscuity as sex lacking romantic or emotional significance instead of in terms of sex with multiple partners.)

I turn, now, to normative issues. These can arise along three logically different axes: the moral versus the immoral, the sexually pleasurable versus the not pleasurable, and the normal versus the perverted.

Sometimes casual sex is morally wrong for reasons having nothing to do with its being casual. If two married people engage in casual sex (with persons other than their spouses), each also commits **adultery**. Insofar as adultery is wrong, their casual sex is wrong as adultery. Casual sex might also be wrong because it involves deception or coercion. If Tom falsely promises Nicole **marriage** if Nicole were to have sex with him, Nicole's **consent** is not genuine because it relies on false information. Tom has deceived her, and the ensuing sex would be morally wrong. If Sally tells the destitute Mark, who does not desire Sally, that she will not evict him and his children from their apartment if he were to have sex with her, the ensuing sex would be coerced and hence wrong (see Mappes, 180–83). Again, it is not wrong just because it is casual. Casual sex might also be wrong due to a lack of adequate communication. Suppose Edna and Skinner are about to have sex. Edna does not desire that it be more than casual but is unsure of Skinner's intentions. It might even be uncommon that the parties, excited by desire, know each other's intentions. If there is a moral obligation to disclose one's intentions, failure to do so would make casual sex wrong—although not because it is casual. Note that unclarity about intentions might be gendered; women, more than men, often use sexual encounters as preludes to relationships (Blumstein and Schwartz, 297).

Even if casual sex involves no deception or coercion, is not adulterous, and the parties clearly communicate their intentions, it still might be wrong in virtue of its consequences (an "external" reason for its wrongfulness), that is, harm to the parties involved and harm to other people. Two possible bad consequences of casual sex are contracting disease and unwanted pregnancy. These are consequences to the parties to the sexual act, but they might also affect other persons and society in general. Anthony Ellis claims that these effects are not morally relevant because they are "medical problems" (166). This is not exactly true. Some **sexually transmitted diseases** (e.g., HIV [human immunodeficiency virus]) present serious moral problems. Unwanted pregnancies also change one's life drastically, as pregnant teenage girls know. The parties to the sexual act should, morally and pragmatically, take precautions against disease and pregnancy. But that casual sex that leads to unwanted pregnancy or disease might be morally wrong does not show that casual sex itself is wrong.

It is not obvious what other bad consequences casual sex has. One possibility is that insofar as society applies a double standard to men and women, women who accept casual sex are seen as cheap ("sluts"), while men are not (Blumstein and Schwartz, 297). Such negative views about women might be a form of harm (for example, a blow to their "reputation"). However, the double standard is only a contingent and perhaps disappearing feature of our society. This may be why casual sex does not always cause negative judgments. Many female college students who engage in casual sex are not viewed negatively and so escape the double standard. Further, whether some people's judging a woman a "slut" harms her depends on how it affects her psychologically: Some woman can brush it off easily or even laugh at it. Moreover, the argument does not tell against casual sex between men.

Another possibility was suggested by **G.E.M. Anscombe** (1919–2001) in claiming that casual sex makes one "shallow" (24), perhaps by making practitioners incapable of forming meaningful, loving relationships (see Kristjansson). However, this argument applies primarily to promiscuous sex, not casual sex. It is difficult to see why a few casual sexual events in one's life would make one incapable of forming loving relationships. Further, the argument depends on the assumption that love relationships are crucial in a person's leading a good life. This might not be true. It seems that one can, logically and psychologically, lead a good life without such relationships (though perhaps not without **friendship;** Halwani, chaps. 2, 3). Indeed, **Albert Ellis** argues that "personality growth"—an increase in enlightened self-interest, self-acceptance, tolerance, flexibility, and acceptance of ambiguity and uncertainty—is "abetted and enhanced by sexual adventuring" (95). Casual sex, as a form of "sexual adventuring," might have these benefits. However, whether healthy or successful sexual adventuring *presupposes* these admirable personality traits, instead of enhancing them, is unclear. Further, the list of traits praised by Ellis is obviously value-laden and might not be fully accepted by other psychologists.

Casual sex might also be morally wrong for "internal" reasons. Some motives could make a casual sex act morally wrong. Having a one-night stand with a monk to humiliate him afterward about his lax virtue is wrong, since it is done out of the vicious intention to demean. Having sex with a teenage girl or a married woman to blackmail her is also wrong. But such motives are not part of casual sex itself. Some motives are, of course, good. A nurse or a friend might masturbate a willing quadruple amputee to orgasm out of kindness. Most casual sex is not done from such motives. Tpically, it is done for sexual pleasure. What needs to be shown, to make the moral case against casual sex, is that the motive to achieve sexual pleasure is morally bad. Perhaps this motive leads one to neglect the needs of one's partner. If this refers to the partner's needs outside the context of the sexual act, then further argument must be provided to explain why this is morally objectionable; for in most of our dealings with people, we do not consider all their other needs. If, however, the needs are sexual and pertain to the casual sex event itself, the argument is likely unsound. It involves misunderstanding what a person typically feels in casual sex. He or she does not usually want another to be a passive body but wants full sexual interaction with that person. This usually takes the form of tending to the partner's sexual needs, even if partly for one's own sake (Goldman, 268–71; Soble, "Sexual Use," 229–32). Prostitution might be an exception, casual sex in which the client does not typically go out of his way to please the prostitute.

The crucial accusation on the grounds of base motives might be that sexual desire leads one to treat one's partner as less than fully human; desire focuses on one aspect of a person, his or her body, and on the sexual organs in particular. This is the accusation of **sexual objectification.** Note that to claim that casual sex is objectifyingly immoral need not turn on issues of motive. Casual sex might be objectifyingly immoral even if done out of non-lustful motives, as when a prostitute engages in sex with a client for the money. **Immanuel Kant** (1724–1804) claimed that whenever we sexually desire another, we do not desire the person as such but only his or her sexual parts (*Lectures*, 162–68). This leads to a problem: On this account of sexual desire, it is difficult for sexuality to satisfy Kant's Second Formulation of the Categorical Imperative: "Act in such a way that you treat humanity, whether in your own person or in the person of any other, always at the same time as an end and never simply as a means" (*Grounding*, Ak 4:429). Casual sex, from a Kantian perspective, involves one person's not only treating another as an object but also treating oneself the same way. Kant thought the only time that sexual activity was permissible, despite its objectification, was when it occurs within marriage.

In contemporary discussions of objectification (unlike Kant's), the focus is not on the agent's objectifying himself in the sexual act but on the agent's objectifying the other. Prostitution, **pornography**, and casual sex have been judged immoral because they involve objectification, that is, treating a person as an object. This is wrong because persons are not, or not *just,* objects. The main problem with objectification is that it reduces a person to the status of something less than human, like an animal or inanimate object. But we are not animals or objects, since we possess something special—rationality, inherent worth, dignity, autonomy, or an immaterial and eternal soul. But here we must be cautious. These attributions are not empirical in any straightforward way. For we find many humans to be irrational, lacking worth, or undignified. The claim that humans have a special ontological and hence moral status needs cogent defense. If it is false, casual sex would not be objectifying, because it could not reduce us to something we are not or fail to respect a status we do not have (see Soble, *Pornography,* chap. 2).

The second normative issue concerns the nonmoral goodness of casual sex. Is casual sex pleasurable? It might seem that a positive answer to this question is obvious, for people find a large, indefinite number of people desirable. Sexual activity is, under certain "normal" conditions, enjoyable. However, this does not mean that casual sex is always pleasurable. Just because the prospect of sex is exciting, it need not turn out satisfying and pleasurable. One might want to distinguish the pleasure that regular sexual partners experience and the pleasure that casual sex partners experience (see Moulton, 538–39; Soble, *Sexual Investigations,* 87–89). The sexuality of regular partners might be routine, but the parties know what to expect and can count on some satisfaction. Casual sex partners, however, do not know what to expect. While they might approach the encounter with anticipatory excitement (and indeed experience the pleasure of making contact with a new person), the ensuing sex might not be as satisfying as imagined: The partners do not know how to satisfy each other's particular needs or desires. Nevertheless, some types of casual sex might have higher probabilities of yielding satisfaction. Two examples are anonymous sex and sex within purely sexual relationships (say, between "fuck buddies")—the former because the expectations are minimal to begin with, the latter because the expectations are known. Note that **Sigmund Freud** (1856–1939) once speculated that both men (183) and women (186), for different psychological reasons, had some difficulty achieving full sexual satisfaction with their spouses, someone they loved. Men, in particular, often find casual sexual encounters more satisfying than sexual activity with their beloved and loving wives. This division between the sexual and the affectionate psychological currents implies a sexual problem with or disadvantage of marriage and long-term relationships (which, of course, may still offer other benefits). What Kant thought was terribly morally suspicious about sexuality Freud identifies as an important factor in satisfaction.

The third normative issue about casual sex concerns psychological normality and **sexual perversion**. There are some types of casual sex that might qualify as also being perverted, just like some casual sex is adulterous, harmful, and so forth. *If* shoe or panty fetishism is perverted, then any coupled casual sex involving gratification with shoes or panties will be perverted, but not because it is casual. A more interesting question is whether casual sex might be psychologically abnormal, even when it is morally permissible or pleasurable (or even *because* it is pleasurable). If the natural or normal way that sexual desire and activity progress is by aiming at or culminating in love (see **Roger Scruton**, chaps. 4, 10), then casual sex, perhaps by definition, would not be normal. However, given that we very often experience sexual desire directed at various people without love entering the scene at all (not even unconsciously), it seems that the very common event of casual sex is perfectly within the bounds of the psychologically normal. It is implausible to analyze the sexually normal so that many people turn out to be abnormal or perverted. Perhaps the philosopher who argues that casual sex is abnormal is not, after all, offering a psychological thesis but is telling us how he or she would *like* things to be (Primoratz, chap. 3).

Casual sex is difficult to define. We know that it has much to do with the lack of an emotional or loving commitment and much to do with seeking pleasure for its own sake. Other than that, a plausible definition immune to counterexamples is elusive. Casual sex does not seem to be morally wrong as such. The one plausible case to be made revolves around objectification. But there is room for dissent, and if casual sex is faulted for being objectifying, much else in the sexual domain must also be faulted. It might even be that some casual sex is "an act of charity which proclaims the glory of God" (Williams, 81–82).

References

Anscombe, G.E.M. "Contraception and Chastity." *The Human World,* no. 7 (1972), 9–30; Benatar, David. "Two Views of Sexual Ethics: Promiscuity, Pedophilia, and Rape." *Public Affairs Quarterly* 16:3 (2002), 191–201; Blumstein, Philip, and Pepper Schwartz. *American Couples: Money, Work, Sex.* New York: Morrow, 1983; Buss, David M. "Casual Sex." In *The Evolution of Desire: Strategies of Human Mating.* New York: Basic Books, 1994, 73–96; Ellis, Albert. "Sexual Adventuring and Personality Growth." In Herbert A. Otto, ed., *The New Sexuality.* Palo Alto, Calif.: Science and Behavior Books, 1971, 94–109; Ellis, Anthony. "Casual Sex." *International Journal of Moral and Social Studies* 1:2 (1986), 157–69; Elliston, Frederick. "In Defense of Promiscuity." In Robert Baker and Frederick Elliston, eds., *Philosophy and Sex,* 1st ed. Buffalo, N.Y.: Prometheus, 1975, 223–43; Freud, Sigmund. (1912) "On the Universal

Tendency to Debasement in the Sphere of Love." In James Strachey, ed. and trans., *The Standard Edition of the Complete Psychological Works of Sigmund Freud*, vol. 11. London: Hogarth Press, 1953–1974, 177–90; Goldman, Alan. "Plain Sex." *Philosophy and Public Affairs* 6:3 (1977),267–87; Halwani, Raja. *Virtuous Liaisons: Care, Love, Sex, and Virtue Ethics*. Chicago, Ill.: Open Court, 2003; Kant, Immanuel. (1785) *Grounding for the Metaphysics of Morals*. Trans. James Ellington. Indianapolis, Ind.: Hackett, 1993; Kant, Immanuel. (ca. 1780) *Lectures on Ethics*. Trans. Louis Infield. New York: Harper and Row, 1963; Kristjansson, Kristjan. "Casual Sex Revisited." *Journal of Social Philosophy* 29:2 (1998), 97–108; Mappes, Thomas A. "Sexual Morality and the Concept of Using Another Person." In Thomas A. Mappes and Jane S. Zembaty, eds., *Social Ethics: Morality and Social Policy*, 6th ed. Boston, Mass.: McGraw-Hill, 2002, 170–83; Moulton, Janice. "Sexual Behavior: Another Position." *Journal of Philosophy* 73:16 (1976), 537–46; Primoratz, Igor. *Ethics and Sex*. New York: Routledge, 1999; Scruton, Roger. *Sexual Desire: A Moral Philosophy of the Erotic*. New York: Free Press, 1986; Soble, Alan. *Pornography, Sex, and Feminism*. Amherst, N.Y.: Prometheus, 2002; Soble, Alan. *Sexual Investigations*. New York: New York University Press, 1996; Soble, Alan. "Sexual Use and What to Do about It: Internalist and Externalist Sexual Ethics." In Alan Soble, ed., *The Philosophy* of Sex, 4th ed. Lanham, Md.: Rowman and Littlefield, 2002, 225–58; Williams, Harry Abbott. "Theology and Self-Awareness." In A. R. Vidler, ed., *Soundings: Essays Concerning Christian Understanding*. Cambridge: Cambridge University Press, 1963,67–101.

Raja Halwani is a Professor of Philosophy at the School of the Art Institute of Chicago. His publications include the books *Philosophy of Love, Sex, and Marriage: An Introduction* and *Virtuous Liaisons: Care, Love, Sex, and Virtue Ethics*.

EXPLORING THE ISSUE

Is Casual Sex Immoral?

Critical Thinking and Reflection

1. How is casual sex different from sex in a committed relationship? In what ways do you think it might be better? In what ways do you think it might be worse?
2. Are there negative consequences of casual sex that affect primarily men? If so, what are they and how strongly do they influence your assessment of the morality of casual sex?
3. In your opinion, are the negative consequences of casual sex are incidental to this type of sexual activity or are they inherent? Why do you hold this view?
4. In what way(s) do people engaged in casual sex objectify themselves? In what way(s) do they objectify their partners? Do you think it is always wrong to treat a human being merely as an object, rather than as a person? Why or why not?
5. Do you think that social changes regarding gender expectations, especially with regard to sexual activity by women, will significantly affect the morality of casual sex? If so, how?

Is There Common Ground?

It is clear that Halwani and Lovejoy arrive at fundamentally different conclusions regarding the immorality of casual sex. For Halwani, casual sex is only incidentally immoral, and so the morality of casual sex depends on the circumstances under which specific examples of this sexual activity occurs. Lovejoy, in contrast, considers casual sex to be inherently immoral.

Although the two authors arrive at different conclusions, they use similar analytical methods. Both Halwani and Lovejoy use the principles of consequentialist ethics to determine the morality of casual sex. Each acknowledges positive (beneficial) consequences of this form of sexual activity, including the pleasure of sexual gratification. Each acknowledges its negative (harmful) consequences, including unwanted pregnancy, the spread of sexually transmitted infections (STIs), and damage to the social standing of those who participate in casual sex, especially women. It is primarily in their identification of the consequences of casual sex (especially the number and type of negative consequences) and in their assessment of the importance of these consequences that they differ.

In assessing the morality of casual sex, both Halwani and Lovejoy also make use of the principles of deontological ethics, primarily its focus on the intrinsic value of human beings. Each is concerned about the moral implications of objectifying human beings, and thereby failing to acknowledge their value as persons. Each also recognizes

that there are two forms of objectification operative in casual sexual activity: objectification of one's partner as well as objectification of oneself. Halwani, in fact, finds opposition to casual sex on deontological grounds more plausible than the consequentialist objections to this form of sexual activity. For Lovejoy, the deontological difficulties with casual sex confirm and reinforce the consequentialist grounds for opposing this form of sexual activity.

Finally, both Halwani and Lovejoy acknowledge that men tend to view casual sex differently than women, with the result that women bear a disproportionate amount both of the negative consequences and the objectification involved with this form of sexual activity. However, whether or not societal changes will mitigate these problems is yet another point on which they disagree.

Additional Resources

Thomas A. Mappes, "Sexual Morality and the Concept of Using Another Person," in Thomas A. Mappes and Jane S. Zembaty, eds., Social Ethics: Morality and Social Policy, 8th edition. (Boston: McGraw-Hill, 2011).

Alan Soble, The Philosophy of Sex and Love (Saint Paul, Minnesota: Paragon House, 2008).

John Marhsall Townsend, What Women Want–What Men Want: Why the Sexes Still See Love and Commitment so Differently (Oxford University Press, 1998).

Internet References . . .

The Internet Encyclopedia of Philosophy: Philosophy of Sexuality

http://www.iep.utm.edu/sexualit/

The Society for the Philosophy of Sex and Love: Resources

http://philosophyofsexandlove.wordpress.com/resources/

Women's History Sourcebook

http://www.fordham.edu/halsall/women/womensbook.asp

Selected, Edited, and with Issue Framing Material by:
Owen M. Smith, *Stephen F. Austin State University*
and
Anne Collins Smith, *Stephen F. Austin State University*

ISSUE

Is Abortion Immoral?

YES: **Mary Meehan**, from "Why Liberals Should Defend the Unborn," *Human Life Review* (2011)

NO: **Amy Borovoy**, from "Beyond Choice: A New Framework for Abortion?" *Dissent* (2011)

Learning Outcomes
After reading this issue, you will be able to:
• Explain the stages of development in a normal human pregnancy and identify common reasons why a spontaneous abortion (miscarriage) might terminate a pregnancy.
• Explain the difference between a legal judgment about the permissibility of induced abortion and a moral judgment about the permissibility of induced abortion.
• Explain the importance of the concept of personhood to both legal and moral judgments about the permissibility of induced abortion.
• Formulate your own position on abortion and identify evidence supporting your position
• Identify the main objections to your position and formulate responses to these objections.

ISSUE SUMMARY

YES: Meehan argues that the unborn are exactly the kind of vulnerable population traditionally defended by liberals. She discusses a number of factors in support of this connection, such as scientific claims about when life begins, the obligations that arise from the act of conception, the disproportionate impact of abortion on poor women and women of color, and issues relating to disability rights and the environment.

NO: Borovoy argues that the traditional defense of abortion, which opposes the choice of the woman against the life of the fetus, does not effectively capture the unique experience of pregnancy, and finds inspiration for a more satisfying approach in Japanese culture, where the decision whether or not to have an abortion is contextualized in the woman's responsibility not only to her fetus but to her family.

Abortion is a divisive topic, and discussions concerning abortion can easily become polarized. Rational discourse about this topic, then, should begin by establishing a neutral set of facts about pregnancy and abortion based on scientific and medical research. Moral principles can then be applied to these facts to reach moral judgments about the circumstances, if any, under which abortion may be moral.

The life of a human being begins when the reproductive cell from a female (the ovum or egg) unites with the reproductive cell from a male (the spermatozoon or sperm). Each type of reproductive cell has 23 chromosomes, and once mature, these cells have a very brief life span. Reproductive cells cannot divide and have no potential to develop to a rational being. The fusion of the two reproductive cells forms a fertilized ovum or zygote with 46 chromosomes, which then begins to divide and has the potential to develop into a rational being. The fertilization of the ovum normally occurs in one of the female's fallopian tubes; during the course of the pregnancy, the zygote travels through the fallopian tube, enters the female's uterus, and implants itself in the uterine wall. The implanted zygote, now generally referred to as an embryo, continues to develop, along with a placenta and umbilical cord, which nourish and protect it. Once the basic structural plan of the embryo is complete, the developing organism is called a fetus, a designation it retains until birth.

From fertilization of the ovum until the birth of the fetus, the human pregnancy lasts an average of 38 weeks (266 days). The precise date of the fertilization of the ovum can be difficult to determine, and so the length of the human pregnancy is usually measured from the first day of the woman's last menstrual period. Since fertilization typically takes place about 2 weeks after this date, the length of a human pregnancy is normally considered to be 40 weeks (280 days). This period is traditionally divided into three approximately equal periods, known as trimesters. The first trimester consists of the period from the fertilization of the ovum to the twelfth week of development, during which the developing organism is called first a zygote and then an embryo. The second trimester consists of the period from the thirteenth week to the twenty-fifth week of development, during which the developing organism is known as a fetus. The final stages of fetal development occur during the third trimester, which covers the period from the twenty-sixth week of fetal development until birth.

During the course of a normal human pregnancy, the developing organism passes a number of significant milestones. While still a zygote, the developing organism may split into two or more groups of cells. These groups may then refuse into a single zygote or continue separate development; in the latter case, the multiple organisms become identical siblings. It is possible for a woman's reproductive tract to contain more than one zygote, each resulting from the fusion of separate pairs of reproductive cells. If the development of the zygotes proceeds in parallel, the developing organisms become fraternal multiples. Occasionally, however, two separate zygotes will fuse into a single being, known as a chimera, with two distinct sets of genetic material. At a certain stage of development, however, the zygote loses the ability to split and refuse, leaving a single organism to continue its development. The embryo becomes sufficiently developed to generate brain waves and a heartbeat during the first trimester, after about six weeks of development. Spontaneous movement of the fetus can first be felt at about 14 or 15 weeks of development; this event is traditionally known as the quickening of the fetus. The age at which the fetus attains viability, or the ability to live independently of the

woman's body (albeit with assistance), depends on many factors, including the current state of medical technology. Infants have survived birth as early as the second trimester, during the twentieth week of pregnancy after 18 weeks of fetal development.

Human pregnancy is a complex process, and many events can occur that cause the death of the developing organism and terminate the pregnancy. The zygote may never implant itself in the lining of the uterus and die as it passes out of the woman's body. This event is far from infrequent; research involving assisted reproduction technologies such as *in vitro* fertilization has yielded estimates that 30–70 percent of all zygotes fail to implant themselves in the uterus. Alternately, the zygote may implant itself somewhere other than in the uterus, resulting in an ectopic pregnancy; the developing organism is not normally able to proceed to term in an ectopic pregnancy, and the condition can cause potentially fatal blood loss in the woman if the pregnancy is not terminated. Chromosomal abnormalities may halt the development of the organism and cause its death. Problems with the woman's reproductive system may also prevent a pregnancy from proceeding to term and result in the death of the developing organism. The rate at which these events occur is difficult to measure, since the death of the organism can occur while it is still a zygote, before the woman even suspects she is pregnant. If the death of the developing organism occurs before the twentieth week of pregnancy, the termination of the pregnancy is known as a spontaneous abortion or miscarriage. According to some estimates, as many as half of all pregnancies end in spontaneous abortion. About 15 percent of all recognized pregnancies end in spontaneous abortion, usually within the first trimester. It is relatively uncommon for pregnancies that have lasted 20 weeks or more to terminate on their own; such events are termed late miscarriages. The termination of pregnancy at any stage by artificial methods that are intended to cause the death of the developing organism is generally termed induced abortion.

In order to address the issue of abortion clearly, it is important to distinguish between moral judgments and legal judgments. A moral judgment is a conclusion about the morality of an action that is reached by applying a moral rule of behavior (moral standard) to a specific set of circumstances. In contrast, a legal judgment is a conclusion about the legality of an action that is reached by applying a law (legal standard) to a specific set of circumstances. Since moral rules of behavior do not have the same status as laws, moral judgments are not the same as legal judgments. The distinction between moral judgments and legal judgments is central to the issue of abortion because the assertion that abortion is legal is not the same thing as the assertion that abortion is moral.

In its landmark 1973 ruling in *Roe v. Wade*, the Supreme Court ruled that a human being comes to have the legal status of a person only upon birth. Therefore, developing human beings such as fetuses does not have the legal rights and protections according to persons, be they natural persons such as human beings or artificial entities such as corporations that have been legally granted this status. As a consequence, while the state has a legitimate interest in protecting the potentiality of human life, laws restricting induced abortion in the early stages of pregnancy, coinciding approximately with the first trimester, is an unconstitutional restriction upon the freedom of the pregnant woman. In later stages of pregnancy, coinciding approximately with the second and third trimesters, the state may protect its interest in the woman's health by appropriate regulation of induced abortions. However, once the fetus achieves viability, the state may regulate or prohibit induced abortions "except where it is necessary, in appropriate medical judgment, for the preservation of the life or health of the mother" (410 U.S. 113, 93 S. Ct. 705 [1973]). In a companion decision, *Doe v. Bolton*, the Supreme Court made it clear that the medical grounds warranting the induced termination of a pregnancy, even after the fetus becomes viable, are at the complete discretion of the woman and her physician, effectively permitting induced abortion on demand at any time during pregnancy. In subsequent decades, various states have attempted to exercise their authority to regulate induced abortion and, subject to certain restrictions, even prohibit the practice, with varying degrees of success.

Traditional arguments about the morality of abortion also turn on the issue of the personhood of a zygote, embryo, or fetus. According to most philosophers, persons may not ethically be treated in the same way as nonpersons. In particular, they must be recognized as having intrinsic value, and so cannot morally be treated merely as means to another person's end. If these entities are persons in the ethical sense, most induced abortions would be morally impermissible. If not, the moral status of induced abortions is relatively unproblematic, save for the moral obligations to protect the welfare of the woman and to treat the unborn human being in humane fashion, like any sentient, non-personal entity such as an animal.

In the following selections, Mary Meehan constructs an argument based on liberal principles to support a pro-life position. She focuses on the liberal tradition of protecting the most vulnerable members of society, which, she argues, should include the unborn. Amy Borovoy finds traditional arguments that attempt to justify abortion on the basis of a woman's right to choose unsatisfactory, and looks beyond Western culture to gain a more holistic understanding of the issues that underlie the decision whether to have an abortion.

YES ↵

Mary Meehan

Why Liberals Should Defend the Unborn

Why does the warm heart of liberalism turn to ice on the subject of unborn children? Why do so many liberals support abortion and *Roe v. Wade*? These are not easy questions to answer, given liberal convictions that should instead lead them to oppose abortion. As someone with an early background in antiwar politics, and who lived through the legalization of abortion, I will suggest reasons why so many liberals support it. Then I will offer many reasons why they should, instead, defend the unborn. Most of those reasons should also appeal to radicals and libertarians. I hope that all will consider my case, both in their personal lives and in thinking about public policy.

Whatever Happened to the Joy of Life?

In 1973, when the U.S. Supreme Court issued its decision in *Roe v. Wade,* liberals still revered the Court for its defense of civil rights and civil liberties in the 1950s and 1960s. They trusted the Court, and especially the three liberal justices who bore much responsibility for *Roe:* William Brennan, William O. Douglas, and Thurgood Marshall. They also had faith in the American Civil Liberties Union, which supported legal abortion. Led astray by institutions and people they relied on, many liberals did not follow their own better instincts. Nor did they do the hard thinking they should have done on a matter of life or death. . . .

There is a great need to engage liberals intellectually—and press them hard—on the ways that abortion breaks faith with basic liberal principles and traditions. We need the kind of robust dialogue and debate that should have occurred decades ago.

Back to Basics

Liberals respect science, and science confirms that a new human life begins at fertilization.[1] Each of us started as a tiny embryo: the President of the United States, every justice of the Supreme Court, every member of Congress, the window-washer on a skyscraper, the teacher in the classroom, the lawyer in the courtroom, the farmer in the fields, the truck driver on the highways. We should think about our own humble origins, rather than disdain the tiny size of the newest humans. That tiny size is deceptive, for the embryo is a *"self-assembler"*[2] who grows by leaps and bounds. We should view the complexity and rapid development of human embryos with awe and respect.

Defending those who cannot defend themselves has long been the pride of the left. When no one else would do it, liberals and radicals stood up for the little guys and the little gals: day laborers and domestic workers, abused children, African Americans and other minorities, elderly patients with dementia, the poor, the unloved and unwanted, the down-and-outers. The unborn are the most defenseless members of the human community. Others can cry out for help, and some can defend themselves, but unborn children cannot. To abandon them is to abandon the heart and honor of the left. . . .

Another liberal tradition, much neglected now, is optimism about the future and the possibility of progress. A gloomy and pessimistic view of life never characterized liberals at their best. Nor did they view children as liabilities, or as predestined for bad outcomes by poverty or disability. Instead, liberals saw children as a sign of hope. And progressives used to be the can-do people of our politics. They used to say, "Let's change conditions that keep people down. *Right now!*" The anti-slavery movement, early feminism, the labor movement, and the civil rights movement did not begin in pessimism and despair—and certainly did not end there. Liberals and radicals *belong* on the side of life. . . .

The right to life underlies and sustains every other right we have. To destroy human beings at the beginning of their lives is to destroy, with just one blow, all of their rights and liberties. Deprived of their entire future, the aborted unborn will never exercise the rights to free speech or a free press. They will never organize, vote, or run for office. They will never pursue or enjoy happiness. Civil libertarians who support abortion are profoundly

Meehan, Mary. From *Human Life Review,* Summer 2011, pp. 15, 17–22, 23, 25–30. Copyright ©2011 by Mary Meehan. Reprinted by permission of the author.

wrong and are actually attacking their own principles. By undermining the right to life at its beginning, they endanger that right—and all other rights—for humans of all ages and conditions. Thus, within a dozen years of *Roe v. Wade,* many Americans supported the denial of lifesaving surgery for handicapped newborns. *Roe* also emboldened advocates of euthanasia for adults.

It is a mistake to argue that abortion must be legal because some disagree about when each human life begins. The scientific evidence for fertilization as the starting point is overwhelming. It is reactionary to appeal, as some abortion advocates do, to the mistaken embryology of Aristotle or medieval philosophers in order to promote doubt on the matter. In his *Roe v. Wade* opinion, Justice Harry Blackmun acknowledged that briefs in the case had outlined "at length and in detail the well-known facts of fetal development." Then he proceeded to ignore those facts, saying the Court "need not resolve the difficult question of when life begins." Yet that question had been resolved by science long before Blackmun wrote.[3] All the Court had to do was take judicial notice of a fact already known and accepted. Liberals, given their respect for science, should be dismayed by the Court's failure on this key point.

Intellectual Chaos

Some liberals claim that one can be a human being without being a person and that we have a right to kill "non-persons." They fail to realize what a heavy burden of proof they must meet here, especially since they cannot even agree among themselves on when personhood begins. (Some favor weeks after fertilization, while others say months later, or even at birth.) Restating a classic ethical case in the plural: Hunters notice movement in a thicket, but don't know whether it is caused by a deer or another human being. If they shoot without determining the facts, and kill a human, they are guilty of homicide. Many abortion supporters say they cannot find out, yet they are willing to shoot anyway.

Libertarians for Life founder Doris Gordon comments: "Abortion choicers try to get around the intellectual chaos on their side by saying, 'Let the woman decide.' If one is free to decide whether another is a person, then whoever is strongest will do the deciding, and we all had better be thinking about our own prospects." She also notes: "No sperm or ovum can grow up and debate abortion; they are not 'programmed' to do so. What sets the *person* aside from the *non-person* is the root capacity for reason and choice. If this capacity is not in a being's nature, the being cannot develop it. We had this capacity on Day One, because it came with our human nature."[4]

One could even contend that it is worse to kill human beings before, rather than after, they develop the potential their nature gives them. At least the rest of us have the chance to use our potential. Whether we use it well or poorly, we have our day in the sun. As a recent March for Life sign asked: "You got a chance/Why can't they?" And if we discriminate against others on the basis of intellectual ability, we reject the principle of equal rights. We establish two classes of humanity—those who have rights and those who do not. That dangerous precedent places many other people at risk: newborn babies, stroke survivors, people who are retarded or demented, accident survivors who have severe brain injuries. Liberals should ponder the words of the late Dr. Bernard Nathanson, who said that our era keeps "defining personhood upward so that fewer and fewer of us make the cut." He warned that "everything, including your life, my friend, is up for discussion."[5]

"All I Can Believe in Is Life"

The right to life is a bedrock right for secular people as well as religious believers. Perhaps non-believers should defend life even more ardently than believers do. Existence on earth should be more precious, not less, to those who believe it's the only one we have. Nat Hentoff, the noted author and civil libertarian, said that "it's a lot easier for an atheist—at least, this atheist—to be against abortion because all I have is life, this life. All I can believe in is life." As Hentoff and others realize, attacking the right to life of a whole class of humans undermines that right—and thus all other rights—for everyone else as well. Non-believers also can rely on the Golden Rule, "Do unto others as you would have them do unto you," which has been honored through the centuries by both religious and secular people. Bernard Nathanson, once an abortion doctor, was an atheist when he joined the pro-life side. He described the Golden Rule as "a statement of innate human wisdom" and applied it to abortion. "Looked at this way," he said, "the 'sanctity of life' is not a theological but a secular concept, which should be perfectly acceptable to my fellow atheists." A group called SecularProLife.org notes that the "human right to life is affirmed in the Declaration of Independence, the fourteenth amendment of the United States Constitution, and many other human rights documents. . . . You don't have to be religious to join one of today's most important human rights movements![6]

Religious people have done most of the organizing and speaking against abortion, and those opposed to them claim that they are trying to impose their religious beliefs on others. Yet most great movements for social change in American history, although separately justifiable on secular grounds, have been deeply rooted in the religious community. Quakers and evangelical Protestants led the anti-slavery movement.[7] "Labor priests" were important to the rise of the labor movement. Quakers, Mennonites, mainline Protestants, Catholics, and Jews have provided much leadership for the peace movement. Religious people have been deeply involved in efforts to abolish the death penalty. Dr. Martin Luther King, Jr., and other ministers made the African American churches the backbone of the civil rights movement in the 1950s and 1960s. No one suggests that civil rights laws passed in that era are invalid because their advocates had religious motivation for their work. There should not be a different standard today for the religious motivation of many pro-lifers. The right to life is not the private property of any church. It is a universal human right.

Don't Shove Her Out in Mid-flight!

Abortion is an escape from an obligation that parents owe their children. By bringing a child into existence, Doris Gordon notes, the parents place her in a state of dependence with a need for care. "Liberals believe we have enforceable obligations toward strangers, including other people's children. Why not our own?" she asks. She says that conceiving and then aborting one's child "could be compared to capturing someone, placing her on one's airplane, and then shoving her out in mid-flight without a parachute."[8]

Roe v. Wade does not acknowledge the obligation of parents to protect from harm the human beings they bring into existence. It ignores the father's obligation. It treats the mother as having no responsibility for the child before birth, yet virtually total responsibility if she decides against abortion. "Maternity, or additional offspring, may force upon the woman a distressful life and future. . . . Mental and physical health may be taxed by child care," the *Roe* justices declared. Nothing there about the father's joint responsibility for children and child care. If the justices were determined to act as a legislature rather than a court, they at least should have called for *more* male responsibility, not less.

They were remarkably negative toward parenting and children, referring to "the distress, for all concerned, associated with the unwanted child."[9] As the late Hispanic activist Grace Olivarez once said, 'Those with power in our society cannot be allowed to 'want' and 'unwant' people at will. . . . I believe that, in a society that permits the life

of even one individual (born or unborn) to be dependent on whether that life is 'wanted' or not, all its citizens stand in danger."[10] The *Roe* justices also ignored the preamble to the Constitution, which speaks of securing "the blessings of liberty to ourselves and our posterity." Posterity means *all* descendants. Our Founders were deeply concerned about posterity, and they did not make deadly distinctions between wanted and unwanted children, nor between born children and "fetuses." General George Washington, when perplexed about a problem during the American Revolution, said that what Congress wanted him to do, "I know no more than the child unborn and beg to be instructed."[11] This was just ten years before Washington presided over our Constitutional Convention.

"We Created a Monster"

The *Roe* justices should have upheld the right to life guaranteed by the Constitution's Fifth and Fourteenth Amendments: that no person may be deprived of "life, liberty, or property, without due process of law." Instead, *Roe* pushed local and federal governments into defending abortion clinics with police, federal court injunctions, and federal marshals. That is governmental action to deprive unborn human beings of their lives. So is the subsidy of abortion that many states provide. The governments involved do not hold trials to give due process to the unborn. After all, of what crime could they be accused? The crime of existing?

The *Roe* justices dealt briefly and unconvincingly with the Fourteenth Amendment, claiming that its use of "person" does not cover the unborn. This is where they established a legal policy of two classes of humanity. Under the 1857 *Dred Scott* decision, African American slaves were the non-citizens of our Constitution, but the *Dred Scott* majority at least called them a "class of persons." Southern state laws offered slaves some protection. Although those laws were often ignored in practice, a few whites were sentenced to death for killing slaves.[12] Under *Roe*, however, unborn children are non-persons, lacking even the right not to be killed.

Roe places women in an adversarial position toward their own children and, in a real sense, toward themselves. This is what Joan Appleton faced when she saw women go through emotional trauma over abortion. As head nurse of an abortion clinic in Virginia, Appleton was a committed feminist who saw her clinic work as a chance to help other women. Although she counseled women carefully, she saw many go through emotional ordeals over abortion. She said some came back to her, months or even years later, as "psychological wrecks." This and other evidence led her to conclude: "We created a monster, and now we don't know what to do with it." Like Dr. Nathanson, Appleton joined the pro-life side.[13]

When young men face a draft in wartime, this forces them to start adult life by deciding whether to kill other human beings. There is never a good time to make such a decision, but the volatile teen years are an especially bad time. Now young women face the same decision in their teens, often under strong pressure from others to destroy their own children. This sets them up for psychological problems. Dr. David Fergusson, a New Zealand professor, has led major studies of abortion's psychological effects on a group of young New Zealand women. In 2006 he and his colleagues reported that those who had abortions had higher rates of depression, anxiety, and thoughts of suicide than other women in the group. The rates were especially high for those who were 15 to 18 years old. Fergusson, who described himself as pro-choice and "an atheist and a rationalist," acknowledged on a television program that he was surprised by results of his study. Another Fergusson-led study in 2008 found that women in the group who had abortions "had rates of mental health problems that were about 30% higher than rates of disorder in other women."[14]

Pro-Life Feminists, Then and Now

But what about the argument that women need abortion availability in order to have true equality with men? This was not the view of American feminists of the 1800s such as Susan B. Anthony, Elizabeth Cady Stanton, and Elizabeth Blackwell. Writer Mary Krane Derr and her colleagues show that early feminists thought men—through unreasonable sexual demands, abandonment, or outright coercion—bore the greatest responsibility for abortion. But they also show that those feminists did not condone abortion or see it as a good for women. Nor did they say it should be legalized. . . .

The early feminists thought equality, both within marriage and in society, was the best preventive of abortion. Today's pro-life feminists carry on that tradition when they say we should change society to accommodate mothers, rather than vice-versa. Serrin Foster, president of Feminists for Life of America, works hard to spread this view around the country and on Capitol Hill. She is keenly aware of economic pressures that push women toward abortion. She knew that such pressures resulted in abortion for Kate Michelman, former president of NARAL Pro-Choice America. That knowledge, Foster said, "inspired me personally to work for child-support enforcement" when Congress debated welfare reform some years ago.[15] Her group works to make college life easier for women who are pregnant and students who are caring for small children.

The Feminists for Life have a can-do approach, and they are willing to work with people on all sides of the abortion issue to make life better for women and their children. . . .

Why should we worship at the shrine of choice? "Abortion" is a terrible word, and a terrible reality, so we should not be surprised that its advocates prefer to say "freedom of choice," "pro-choice," and "the choice issue." Yet the glory of humanity does not consist in making choices as such, but in making them wisely and well and in a way that avoids harming other people. We should not fear being called "anti-choice" when we support laws that are needed to prevent great harm to others, especially when that harm will end their lives. Ginny Desmond Billinger, a pro-life feminist, once wrote an essay called "Confessions of an Anti-Choice Fanatic." She was anti-choice not only on abortion , but also on spousal and child abuse, drunk driving, unsafe disposal of hazardous wastes, and more.[16] A little reflection shows that liberals are anti-choice on many issues. They should add abortion to the list. . . .

Targeting Poor Children and Minorities

Anyone concerned about civil rights should be alarmed by abortion as lethal discrimination against poor people and ethnic minorities. Eugenicists long have targeted both groups for population control. The 1956 membership list of the American Eugenics Society could have been called *Who's Who in Population Control*. It included sociologist Kingsley Davis, ethicist Joseph Hetcher, biologist Bentley Glass, birth-control leader Margaret Sanger, physician Alan Guttmacher, and other movers and shakers in public policy. Some of them later suggested coercive population control, and many supported abortion as a quick way to reduce birthrates. Most were white males who didn't care about adverse health effects on women of the early birth control pill, IUDs, and surgical abortion. They were not worried about women's health or about ethics; they just wanted to get the numbers down. Some had major influence on the legalization of abortion.[17]

But where eugenicists of the 1920s were blunt about their disdain for the poor, their heirs of the 1970s presented abortion as a *good* for poor women. In 1971 Dr. Guttmacher (by then the president of Planned Parenthood) wrote Governor Nelson Rockefeller of New York to support Medicaid funding of abortion for poor women. Guttmacher said a recent cut-back of such funding was "grossly discriminatory against the least privileged citizens of this State." He asked, "What are such poor souls to do in the future?" Then he added, as abortion advocates often did—and many still do—an economic argument for eliminating poor children: "To save a few million dollars now the State must pay far more eventually for prenatal care and delivery and the eighteen-year annual upkeep of children likely to become financial burdens of the State."[18]

Planned Parenthood leaders fought hard in Congress and the federal courts for subsidized abortion. When they lost at the federal level, they fought and often won in state courts. Naive liberals did much to aid those fights. So did the American Civil Liberties Union. Aryeh Neier, who was the ACLU executive director in 1970–78, later referred to "whites who were eager to eliminate or limit the number of welfare mother babies out of an anti-black feeling" and acknowledged that "I dealt with some supporters of abortion who are very much in favor of abortion for exactly that reason." Interviewed by one of his law students at New York University, Prof. Neier said two foundations, one in Pittsburgh and one in Missouri, supported abortion efforts because of such racist views. "I don't regard it as dirty money," he said, "so long as people don't try to impose conditions on what you can do with the money.... So as long as they don't try to impose restrictions, I will always take the money."[19]

The abortion rate for poor women is far higher than the rate for middle-class and upper-class women. In the year 2000, the abortion rate for African American women was nearly four times that for white women, according to a survey report by—ironically—the Alan Guttmacher Institute. The authors estimated that of all pregnancies among black women in 2000, 43 percent led to abortion.[20] Civil rights activist Dick Gregory was right, many years earlier, when he called abortion "a death sentence upon us." The late Fannie Lou Hamer, a great civil rights activist in Mississippi, shared his view.[21] Many African American women have suffered bitter regret and depression as a result of abortion. Pamela Carr had one when she was just 17 and headed toward college. "The anguish and guilt I felt were unbelievable," she wrote later in *Ebony*. "I became deeply depressed. . . . Over time I was able to forgive myself and go on with my life, but always with the knowledge that I had swept away a part of my future which could never be recovered." Her question about the unborn: "How many more of them have to die before we realize that abortion is not a solution but another, more troubling, problem plaguing our community?" Arlene Campbell had a legal abortion that nearly killed her: "Depression became a major part of my daily existence. . . . I now speak of life, but for many years all I could think of was death."[22]

Disability Rights for the Unborn

Abortion also involves lethal discrimination against children with disabilities. Some writers suggest that a "new eugenics" produced prenatal testing and abortion of the handicapped unborn. Actually, it was the same old eugenics that for decades supported compulsory sterilization of the "feebleminded." After the Nazi era, though, U.S. eugenics leaders realized they had to be more subtle. Frederick Osborn, the shrewd chief of the American Eugenics Society, was co-founder and first administrator of the Population Council. He used the Council to advance all of his eugenic interests. In addition to other population-control programs, the Council funded medical-genetics fellowships for students who were recommended by a committee of Osborn's eugenics society. His society also promoted heredity counseling, which it called "the opening wedge in the public acceptance of eugenic principles."[23]

Osborn supported the new American Society of Human Genetics (ASHG), which other eugenicists had started, and served as that group's vice president in 1958. Many other ASHG leaders and members were deeply involved in developing or advocating prenatal testing for fetal handicaps such as Down Syndrome and spina bifida. But prenatal testing would have meant little had abortion remained illegal. Big money took care of that problem: In 1962 a project to develop a Model Penal Code for the states, funded by the Rockefeller Foundation, proposed the legalization of abortion for fetal disability and other hard cases.[24] Several states followed its advice; then *Roe* made special exceptions unnecessary.

It is tragic that the disability rights movement was still getting off the ground in the 1970s. Had it become a major force decades earlier, eugenics might not have developed into such a powerful monster. But the disability rights movement came of age after *Roe v. Wade*, and it includes both people who support *Roe* and people who oppose abortion and are appalled by its use as a tool of eugenics. Joseph P. Shapiro, who authored a history of the movement, said it has dealt with abortion "largely by keeping its distance."[25]

Liberals usually side with people who have disabilities, insisting that they have equal rights. That's where liberals and disability rights activists should be on the issue of eugenic abortion. They should remind everyone that most of us have one or more disabilities, ranging from poor eyesight to severe problems, and that we will have more as we grow older. As disability rights activist Mary Jane Owen has said, "developing a few glitches, developing impairments, is *not* the end of the joy of life," and "we can enjoy life learning new functions and new ways of being."[26]

Protect the Children, and "Live Lightly on the Earth"

Liberals should realize, too, that abortion harms children who are not aborted, but hear about abortion when they are very young. One psychiatrist reported, "I have had children who suffer from night terrors and who fear to fall asleep because they overheard their parents discussing an abortion they had or planned to have. These children fear they may be gotten rid of the next time they make their parents angry."[27] Drs. Philip G. Ney and Marie A. Peeters-Ney wrote that some children suffer from "survivor guilt" because they know that one or more siblings were aborted. Children who know their parents considered aborting *them,* the doctors suggested, tend to be fearful and over-eager to please. And the Neys quoted someone who had cancer at the age of twelve: "My mother told me she was going for prenatal diagnosis to make sure the baby was alright [sic]. I knew what would happen if the baby wasn't. One night I thought perhaps if I did not get better the doctors would get rid of me too. I never trusted my mother after that. In actual fact I never trusted anybody after that."[28]

Abortion also goes against the harmony with nature that environmentalists celebrate and encourage. Childbirth, after all, is the natural way to end a pregnancy. Why, then, do so many environmentalists promote abortion? Many do so because they see all human beings—except, perhaps, themselves and those they love—as threats to the natural environment. They assume that the fewer people there are, the less pollution and resource exhaustion we will have. Some of their messages make people feel guilty to be alive or to have children. Yet environmentalists over look what seems to be a perverse result of population control: The fewer people there are, the more *things* each person wants. Despite today's norm of two children per family, American houses are larger than ever before. Many tiny families rattle around in mini-castles—and drive huge, gas-guzzling vans and SUVs. Where a family used to have one television, many now have one per bedroom, plus others scattered around the home. Has all of this led to greater happiness? That seems doubtful, given how hard people work to buy all their stuff, to take care of it, and then to buy even bigger houses to store it all. "Live lightly on the earth" is a splendid environmental slogan, and that is where our emphasis should be. Instead of eliminating people, we should return to simpler and less stressful lifestyles.

Liberals, like most Americans, tend to acquire too much stuff. They also have inherited much ideological debris from recent generations of the left. Neither kind of junk makes them happy. If they discard both, they will have plenty of room for children and for life. Then they might, like Lucinda Matlock, shout to the wooded hills and sing to the green valleys.

Notes

1. In the case of identical twins, a second human life begins when the first embryo divides. Triplets and higher multiples can be identical, fraternal, or a combination. See Keith L. Moore and others, *Before We Are Born,* 7th ed. (Philadelphia: Saunders/Elsevier , 2008), 2 & 88–90.
2. John Walker, "Power and Act: Notes Towards Engaging in a Discussion of One of the Underlying Questions in the Abortion Debate," *International Journal of Sociology and Social Policy* 19, nos. 3/4 (1999), 54–64, 57 (available at www.141.org; go to "Library").
3. *Roe v. Wade,* 410 U.S. 113 at 156 & 159 (1973); Alan Frank Guttmacher with Ellery Rand, *Life in the Making* (New York: Viking , 1933), 3; and George W. Comer, *Ourselves Unborn: An Embryologist's Essay on Man* (New Haven: Yale, 1944; reprint, Hamden, Conn.: Archon Books/Shoe String Press, 1972), 1. Comer wrote, "When a man is born, he is already nine months old."
4. Doris Gordon, "Abortion and Rights: Applying Libertarian Principles Correctly," *International Journal of Sociology and Social Policy* 19, nos. 3/4 (1999), 97–127, 112 & 111. This is the best, richest, and clearest philosophical article on abortion that I have ever read. It is available on the Libertarians for Life website, www.141.org (go to "Library").
5. "March for Life 2011 Photos," www.meehanreports.com, accessed 28 March 2011; and Bernard Nathanson, *The Hand of God* (Washington: Regnery, 1996), 4 & 5.
6. Nat Hentoff, "You Don't Have to Believe in God to Be Prolife," *U.S. Catholic,* March 1989, 28–30, 28; and Bernard N . Nathanson with Richard N. Ostling, *Aborting America* (Garden City, N.Y.: Doubleday, 1979), 227. (Nathanson eventually joined the Catholic Church.) See, also: "Is Abortion a Religious Issue?" www.secularprolife.org (under "Publications"), accessed 30 March 2011.
7. On evangelicals' role in the anti-slavery movement, see Benjamin P. Thomas, *Theodore Weld,*

Crusader for Freedom (New Brunswick, N.J.: Rutgers, 1950); Henry Mayer, *All on Fire: William Lloyd Garrison and the Abolition of Slavery* (New York: St. Martin's, 1998); and Bertram Wyatt-Brown, *Lewis Tappan and the Evangelical War Against Slavery* (Cleveland: Case Western Reserve, 1969).

8. Doris Gordon, telephone conversation with the author, 15 April 2011; and Gordon (n. 11), 120.

9. *Roe v. Wade* (n. 10) at 153.

10. "Separate Statement of Grace Olivarez" in U.S. Commission on Population Growth and the American Future, *Population and the American Future* (Washington: U.S. Government Printing Office, 1972), 160–64, 161 & 163.

11. George Washington to Benjamin Harrison, 19 Aug. 1777, in John C. Fitzpatrick, ed., *The Writings of George Washington* (Washington: U.S. Government Printing Office, 1931–44), vol. 9, 95–96.

12. *Roe v. Wade* (n. 10) at 156–59; *Dred Scott v. Sandford*, 60 U.S. (19 Howard) 393 at 403, 404, 407, 409, 411 & 422 (1857); and Kenneth M. Stampp, *The Peculiar Institution* (New York: Knopf, 1956), 217–24.

13. Joan Appleton, Remarks at "Meet the Abortion Providers" conference, 3 April 1993, sponsored by the Pro-Life Action League, Chicago, Ill., audio recording.

14. David M. Fergusson and others, "Abortion in Young Women and Subsequent Mental Health," *Journal of Child Psychology and Psychiatry* 47, no. 1 (2006), 16–24, 19; Australian Broadcasting Corporation, "Higher Risk of Mental Health Problems After Abortion: Report," transcript of 3 Jan. 2006 broadcast; and David M. Fergusson and others, "Abortion and Mental Health Disorders: Evidence from a 30-Year Longitudinal Study," *British Journal of Psychiatry* (2008), 444–51, 449.

15. Serrin Foster, interview by author, 22 Jan. 1998, Washington, D.C., transcript.

16. Ginny Desmond Billinger, "Confessions of an Anti-Choice Fanatic," in Gail Grenier Sweet, ed., *Pro-Life Feminism: Different Voices* (Toronto: Life Cycle Books, 1985), 77–78.

17. American Eugenics Society, "Membership List, 1956," *Eugenics Quarterly* 3, no. 4 (Dec. 1956), 243–52 (Margaret Sanger listed under her married name of Margaret Sanger Slee, 249); Meehan, "The Road to Abortion" (n. 3); and Rebecca Messall, "The Long Road of Eugenics: From Rockefeller to *Roe v. Wade*," *Human Life Review* 30, no. 4 (Fall 2004), 33–74.

18. Alan F. Guttmacher to Nelson Rockefeller, 12 April 1971 [mimeographed copy distributed to media], Alan Frank Guttmacher Papers, HMS c155, box 4, f. 45, Harvard Medical Library in the Francis A. Countway Library of Medicine, Boston, Mass.

19. Aryeh Neier, interview with Thomas J. Balch, 3 Nov. 1979, in Balch's "Convincing the Courts on Abortion," a paper for Prof. Neier's "Litigation and Public Policy" course [New York University School of Law], Fall 1979, appendix, 12–13. See, also, Mary Meehan, "ACLU *v.* Unborn Children," *Human Life Review* 27, no. 2 (Spring 2001), 49–73.

20. Rachel K. Jones and others, "Patterns in the Socioeconomic Characteristics of Women Obtaining Abortions in 2000–2001," *Perspectives on Sexual and Reproductive Health* 34, no. 5 (Sept.–Oct. 2002), 226–35, 228.

21. Barry Farrell, "Running with Dick Gregory," *Ramparts*, Aug.–Sept. 1975, 26 ff., 54; and Kay Mills, *This Little Light of Mine: The Life of Fannie Lou Hamer* (New York: Dutton/Penguin, 1993), 260–61 & 274.

22. Pamela Carr, "Which Way Black America? Anti-Abortion," *Ebony* 44, no. 12 (Oct. 1989), 134 ff., 138; and Arlene Campbell, "A Shattered Life," *Black Americans for Life* newsletter, Washington, D.C., Spring 2005 [3].

23. American Eugenics Society, *Five-Year Report of the Officers: 1953–1957* (New York, n.d.), 9–11, 10.

24. Mary Meehan, "The Triumph of Eugenics in Prenatal Testing," *Human Life Review* 35, no. 3 (Summer 2009), 28–40, 33–36.

25. Joseph P. Shapiro, *No Pity* (New York: Times Books/Random House, 1993), 278.

26. Mary Jane Owen, telephone interview by author, 31 July 1992, transcript.

27. Edward J. Sheridan, interview by John G. Gatewood, *Georgetown University Right to Life Journal* 2 (Fall 1981), 1–5, 1.

28. Philip G. Ney and Marie A. Peeters-Ney, *Abortion Survivors* (Victoria, B.C., Canada: Pioneer Publishing, 1998), 26–27 & 33.

MARY MEEHAN is a writer and speaker who links a consistent pro-life ethic to a number of issues, including stances against war and the death penalty as well as suicide prevention strategies.

Amy Borovoy

Beyond Choice: A New Framework for Abortion?

Every year I teach a class called "Mind, Body, and Bioethics in Japan" to a group of Princeton undergraduates made up of students drawn to ethical dilemmas—aspiring doctors, scientists, and lawyers. The class departs from typical approaches to bioethics. Instead of attempting to arrive logically at the "right" or "best" answer to the human dilemmas posed by modern medicine, we take an anthropological approach, asking how the dilemmas themselves are shaped by and understood through the context of culture.

The unit focusing on pregnancy, prenatal care, and attitudes toward abortion and human life, in particular, provokes some of the most passionate discussion. The topic is fraught in any context, but given the polarized politics of "life" vs. "choice" to which U.S. students have been exposed, Japan reveals intriguing contradictions. Japanese obstetricians do not practice aggressive prenatal screening; women are encouraged to accept the baby that is born, and fetal selection for birth abnormalities or sex is regarded as unethical. A fetus is humanized—so much so that obstetricians routinely hail their clients as "Mom," even from the early stages of the pregnancy. At the same time, terminating a pregnancy is accepted as a morally sound means of preventing a situation in which a child would go uncared for. Small statues commemorating the unborn at Buddhist temples mark an institutionalized space in which women mourn their aborted fetuses.

Teaching the class has sharpened my feelings that there is something missing from the traditional "pro-choice" stance on abortion. The position is an heir of *Roe v. Wade*'s legal framework of the right to privacy and, also, of 1960s and 1970s liberal feminism, with its emphasis on women's autonomy. When I started teaching, I had no children. Now, as a parent, even though I support the right to abortion, when I see T-shirts on college campuses emblazoned with "My body, my choice," I feel that they are glib and vaguely irresponsible, an attitude I know I share with others who also support abortion

rights. Successful campaigns against legitimating abortion primarily in terms of "choice" and "rights" have led to such bipartisan initiatives as the Prevention First Act, the Pregnant Women Support Act, and the Reducing the Need for Abortion and Supporting Parents Act. Many Democrats have backed away from aggressive promotion of "rights" and "choice." Barack Obama's 2010 reassertion of Bill Clinton's statement that we should make abortion "safe, legal, and rare" reflects a liberal attempt to recognize the moral dimension of the problem while holding on to a "right" that in many places in the United States is a "right" in name only.

Meanwhile, anthropologists and sociologists who study reproductive health care on the ground, in clinics, note how the discourse of "choice" offers little space to recognize the conflicted feelings often associated with terminating a pregnancy on the part of women, abortion rights advocates, and even health care practitioners themselves. Jeannie Ludlow, in a powerful essay entitled, "Sometimes, It's a Child *and* a Choice," has written about women's attachments to what the majority refer to as their "baby," despite their decision to terminate the pregnancy, and about committed abortion providers' private confusion about the status of the fetus. Most women seeking abortions must balance demanding work schedules while caring for other dependents. Some 61 percent of American women getting abortions today are already mothers of one or more children; 69 percent are economically disadvantaged. Only 18 percent of women obtaining abortions are teenagers. Concern about their ability to adequately care for an additional child is central to their decision.

The Japanese example offers a window into the particularities of the American debate and the limits of each position. As here, the fetus is humanized in many contexts, and yet abortion is ethically acceptable. Even second trimester abortions are legal in Japan. The question of when life begins, central to U.S. abortion politics, is less important to the Japanese ethical framework. The focus is neither on the rights of the mother nor on the

Borovoy, Amy. From *Dissent*, Fall 2011, pp. 73–79. Copyright ©2011 by Foundation for Study of Independent Ideas, Inc. Reprinted by permission of University of Pennsylvania Press. www.dissentmagazine.org

personhood of the fetus, but rather on the social life of the child, the welfare of the family, and the question of the social good more broadly. Although teenage abortion rates are rising, the majority of women seeking abortions are in their thirties and forties. The strong sense that these are decisions made by parents out of concern for family welfare undercuts the logic of opposing abortion based on the fetus's humanity alone. In Japan, as elsewhere, a mother is trusted to make the decision about the fate of her fetus not because she has freedom of "choice" but rather because she is its trusted caregiver; a parent alone can provide her child with an appropriate environment. Japanese parents do live with deep psychic tensions between the acceptance of the humanity of the fetus and the pervasive practice of abortion. This tension is easily exploited by Buddhist sects harboring marginal views, and images of the innocent, child-like fetuses make their appearance in comics and other forms of popular culture that treat the issue of abortion and women's inner conflict. Still, the logic is that child rearing and a mother's health (both physical and emotional) are central to producing a good society, and that children respond to the resources and care they receive. This notion of abortion as a social necessity differs from the notion of abortion as a "right" and deemphasizes the dividing lines between "life" and "choice."

Japanese school textbooks treat the issue of birth control and abortion in required courses on home economics. A common middle-school textbook explains the procedure under a section entitled, "Deciding when and when not to give birth." It begins by stating that "as an individual human being, a child has the right to be raised in an appropriate environment." The passage suggests that a parent should be concerned foremost with appropriate upbringing and socialization of a child, and should thus practice birth control rigorously. While the textbook reassures its readers that abortion as a last resort is safe and legal, it cautions that such a measure constitutes "the termination of a life that one has cultivated," and also that "the hardship for a woman, physically and emotionally, is large." Thus, while the passage explicitly imagines the fetus as a life, the ethical focus is not on the fetus but rather on a mother's welfare and the future child's environment. The entire section appears in a chapter on "Childrearing."

As such stories suggest, family has hardly been regarded as a "private sphere" in modern Japan. The status of abortion as a family matter must be seen in the context of social policy that has historically regarded strong families as integral to a successful society. In fact, the history of abortion is closely entwined with platforms for social betterment—producing a "planned family," a strong society, and powerful nation. Infanticide was a common practice throughout the seventeenth and eighteenth centuries in many parts of Japan for reasons of poverty and food shortage. In prosperous areas, such "weeding" (*mabiki,* as it was called) was carried out by midwives at the behest of the family with the objective of creating "small, healthy, and economically productive families"—while the state looked away. Abortion was banned at the turn of the century in order to encourage population growth and fuel Japan's imperial ambitions.

Despite citizens' activism toward legalization in the 1920s and 1930s, the government did not officially legalize abortion until 1948, in the context of postwar devastation and starvation, out of concern for population control. At the height of the eugenic policies that influenced the industrialized world, the bill emphasized the priority of population quality, permitting abortion if there was evidence of a hereditary condition that might be transmitted to a child and compelling sterilization in certain instances. The law, the National Eugenic Protection Law (*Nihon Yūsei Hogo-Hō*), included a list of specific hereditary conditions that legitimized abortion. In the context of the postwar baby boom, many women began to take advantage of the law, and a clause was added permitting abortion for reasons of economic hardship.

After decades of opposition by human rights activists, the eugenic clause was eventually deleted in a 1996 law, which was re-titled, "The Maternal Body Protection Law" (*Botai Hogo Hō*). The economic necessity clause remains (in addition to rape, incest, or possible harm to the mother), and is the primary legal recourse for abortion. Abortion as a means of fetal selection is undoubtedly still practiced under the cloak of economic need, but it is regarded warily by obstetricians and families alike.

Still, family continues to be the primary prism through which decisions to terminate a pregnancy are viewed. The anthropologist Margaret Lock, who has studied Japanese attitudes toward fetal selection and new reproductive technologies, suggests that the ethical question of whether to terminate a problematic pregnancy hinges foremost on its consequences for family life. One mother whom she interviewed, who was raising a child with Down Syndrome, expressed the view that terminating a first pregnancy for reasons of the discovery of a chromosomal abnormality would be "selfish." However, terminating a second abnormal pregnancy that could jeopardize family life and the quality of parenting for the first child would more likely be regarded as acceptable. Japanese obstetricians have steadfastly declined to conduct proactive prenatal testing, even tests that are considered routine in the United States. Instead they direct their focus to the mother's behavior and the "environment" she creates for her fetus. As eugenic practices have come to be regarded as taboo among obstetricians, what has replaced them is a strong commitment to the power of motherhood, which is thought to begin with pregnancy. A recent ethnography of prenatal care by Israeli anthropologist Tsipy Ivry demonstrates the burden but also the pride that such practices confer on Japanese women. Ivry's book, *Embodying Culture*, draws a striking contrast with Israel, where concern for birth outcomes results in more aggressive prenatal testing, trivializing the mother and the pregnancy itself as an influence on the baby.

During Japan's decades of rapid economic growth in the sixties, seventies, and eighties, the government, together with Japanese enterprise, subsidized middle-class women to stay at home, protecting the family wage system through mutual corporate shareholding and bank loans for companies that buffered employees from economic volatility. The middle-class housewives of this era, while economically dependent on their husbands, enjoyed a good deal of economic stability and social security and regarded the work of raising children as socially important, skilled labor. Suzanne Vogel, one of the first Western scholars of the Japanese family, remarked that one rarely hears a Japanese woman refer to herself as "just a housewife."

In some ways, the family values that have defined the discourse on pregnancy and abortion have recently come to dissuade women from having children—an irony that is visible in other "family friendly" nations, such as Italy, Spain, and South Korea. Ideals concerning motherhood are so high that it is difficult to combine them with women's advancement in the labor force, and economic instability has made the single wage-earner model less viable for many. While it is tempting to see the low fertility rate as evidence of "women's liberation" or a rebellion from traditional roles, there is evidence, in Japan at least, that it marks a continuing conservatism in what constitutes an ideal child-rearing environment.

Japan stands out, for example, for its low incidence of children born out of wedlock—despite the conditions of urbanization and rising rates of education for women that made illegitimacy more common in other industrialized nations. In Japan, more than half of all premarital pregnancies to women aged fifteen to twenty-nine between the years 2000 and 2004 were aborted; 38 percent of pregnancies to this age group ended up as marital births. Only 4 percent led to non-marital births. (In the United States, almost 50 percent of non-maritally conceived children result in nonmarital births.) Oxford University sociologist

Ekaterina Hertog interviewed sixty-eight women from the small population of women in their thirties and forties who decided to give birth outside of marriage. All emphasized the difficulty of their decision. Her recent book, *Tough Choices*, demonstrates the preference among women to raising children within a dual-parent household, preferably with a primary wage-earner. Single motherhood almost always compels Japanese women to work outside the home. Japanese social support for single mothers is not generous, though it is somewhat more expansive than in the United States, and the women whom Hertog interviewed told her that having a father and breadwinner in the house allows women to be more present mothers—although such a father may be remote from the daily goings-on of family life. For many women in such circumstances, abortion is deemed the "responsible" choice, despite the often powerful desire to have a child.

Japan's entrenched division of labor and conservative ideals about family are hardly enviable, and we might argue that Japan's liberal policy around abortion helps to reinforce those ideals. Although Japan was one of the first nations to permit legal abortion, the law was passed from on high and reflects less concern with women's "choice" or sexual freedom than with producing appropriate mothers and children, as some feminists have pointed out.

There are other reasons not to envy Japan. Japanese women have a high abortion rate. Abortion has continued to be the predominant form of birth control in Japan well after the invention and legalization of birth control medication in many other industrialized countries. A revealing study by political scientist Tiana Norgren showed how a cluster of professional groups with a vested interest in defending access to abortion (midwives, ob-gyns, and even feminists who worried about the pill's health effects) obstructed the legalization of the birth control pill until 1999—more than forty years after Food and Drug Administration approval of the first pill in the United States. Given the political and economic conflicts in the country, there is no cause to celebrate the normalcy of abortion.

Still, to the extent that termination of pregnancy is inevitable in some cases, can we not find something useful in the ability to cast this decision in terms of its consequences for social stability and care for others? And should we not envy this society's recognition and value of the dignity and importance of parenting? Japanese attitudes toward pregnancy are fully entwined with an appreciation for the importance of parenthood, an ideal celebrated in popular U.S. culture but disdained in social and economic policy and at the workplace. Can we not find here a way around the discourse that currently pits a woman's "choice" against the sanctity of a fetus's "life"?

In regarding abortion as an aspect of social welfare, health, and family, Japan is not unusual among social democracies. Germany, the United Kingdom, Switzerland, Canada, and many of the East European post-socialist societies harbor similar politics and trade-offs. In Germany, abortion has been legally sanctioned as a matter of "protection"—the responsibility of the welfare state to care for German families. The 1994 law that went into effect after German unification legalized women's rights to terminate a pregnancy within the first trimester; it linked this with state-funded abortions for women on welfare and promises to increase state support for kindergartens and other aid for childcare. In essence, the German courts weighed the potential hardship of the mother against their emphasis on the sanctity of human life. While the state requires counseling which must be "pro-life oriented but outcome-open," the law defines its responsibility as being to "help not punish" the pregnant woman.

In Canada, just across the U.S. border, law and court deliberations on abortion led to allowing abortion largely as a matter of universal provision of health care (with health defined as emotional, physical, or psychological). Although some Canadian pro-choice feminists have expressed envy of the protection of abortion as a woman's private right in the United States, there is a reluctance to regard the matter of abortion as a "private" matter. Abortions are financed by public insurance in Canada—a provision that was excluded from *Roe v. Wade* and remains one of the most contentious issues in U.S. social policy. As William Saletan and others have noted, *Roe v. Wade*'s protection of abortion through women's right to privacy set the stage for the retrenchment of abortion services across the country; states may not interfere with a woman's right to an early abortion, but they are under no legal responsibility to provide them.

What makes the German and Canadian legislation stand out in contrast to *Roe v. Wade*, is their focus on protection. German law, like West European law more broadly, emphasizes public health and humanitarian justifications for the practice of abortion: the social costs of unwanted pregnancy, health risks to women, the psychic toll of raising unwanted children, and the state's positive obligation to protect women. In contrast, *Roe v. Wade* defined the right to first-trimester abortion primarily in terms of negative liberty—the right of the individual to decide for herself whether abortion is appropriate; it deliberately and explicitly excluded the possibility of the state's consideration for women's broader social circumstances.

These comparisons help us frame a bigger picture: nations that see abortion in terms of social welfare are paternalistic, "nannying," and often socially conservative, viewing motherhood as women's primary role. Concerns for "quality" of population and family values are sometimes uncomfortably close to concerns for social homogeneity, elitism, and what could potentially become intolerance. A woman's right to a first-trimester abortion on any grounds in the United States is envied by many women around the world. But, as many other commentators on the debate in the United States have asked, to what extent are we protecting women's "freedom," "choice," or "autonomy" when we focus on abortion as a right in the absence of other social protections for women and families: subsidized day care, job security, a family wage, quality public education, and universal health care?

Roe v. Wade created the possibility for women to have control over their lives and choices. But the discourse of "choice" alone has not provided a sustaining moral framework for handling the necessity of abortion, which will always be a final recourse. What is needed is a framework that can simultaneously be compatible with liberal and feminist values.

In fact, the inadequacy of our current categories has been known for some time. In the early 1980s, in a study widely known among anthropologists, Faye D. Ginsburg (*Contested Lives: The Abortion Debate in an American Community*) listened to women in Fargo, North Dakota, after the opening of the controversial Fargo Women's Health Center. The pro-life activists remembered their mothers' suffering in raising children they could not afford; the pro-choice activists described what they called their "Midwestern feminism," rooted in responsibility to kin, community, and a larger social order. Both saw reproductive decision-making as an opportunity to affirm the importance of family and nurturance in the context of a society that they perceived as increasingly committed to rationalism and personal fulfillment.

Yet it is surprising how little the current discourse on either side of the abortion debate is connected to family and social welfare (although in the United States, too, the promotion of birth control was linked to eugenic concerns through the mid-twentieth century). It is a pattern that differentiates American feminism from many industrial democracies, as Eastern Europeanist Kristen Ghodsee and I have noted in an unpublished essay, "Is Individual Liberation Good for Women?" arguing that feminism in the social democracies and post-socialist East Europe has emphasized a better life for women through securing social and economic security, even at the cost of individual liberties.

Perhaps the hesitation to address abortion rights in the context of family is also because the Left has had to respond to an increasingly extremist Right. The conservative judges who dissented in *Roe v. Wade* worried that the decision disempowered individual states from wrestling with the "relative importance of the continued existence and development of the fetus . . . against a spectrum of possible impacts on the mothers." These judges recognized the need to balance competing needs within the family. However, the humanization of the fetus in today's political environment feels threatening rather than considerate, as conservatives push to use ultrasound images to change the minds of women who seek to terminate their pregnancies. And then there are cases of women who have been prosecuted for unhealthy practices such as smoking or other drug abuse while pregnant.

How can liberals include a concern for family in their discourse, so as not to cede this issue to the Right? Some thinkers, such as the communitarian moral philosopher Michael J. Sandel, have suggested that liberals must take a position on the life of the fetus; they can no longer ignore the issue. Feminist provocateur Naomi Wolf wrote in the *New Republic* several years ago that liberals must recognize abortion's inhumanity. Others, such as the moral philosopher Judith Jarvis Thompson, have made the case that even if we grant the humanity of the fetus, a woman is still not ethically obliged to keep it. All these interventions are helpful. But what I am suggesting here is slightly different; it is a greater focus on the dignity and importance of parenthood.

From a medical standpoint, some have begun to question whether obstetrical practices that are rooted in the view of the fetus as autonomous constitute "best practices." In a recent issue of *Obstetrics and Gynecology*, a group of medical sociologists, philosophers, and ethicists founded by Anne D. Lyerly and Maggie Little, who focus on the issue of risk in obstetrical practice, expressed concern with obstetrical practices that are rooted in the view of the fetus as autonomous. They explore, for instance, how obstetricians should ethically balance a mother's need for antidepressants or asthma medications against the small likelihood of risk to the fetus. Should not physicians take into account the indisputable truth that the welfare and empowerment of the mother are also related to the outcome of the pregnancy?

As pundits, politicians, physicians, and others grapple for some vocabulary to enter into this new terrain, popular culture is already moving out in front. The 2007 film *Juno*, for example, captured pregnancy in a way that was startlingly fresh, highlighting the inadequacy of the standard "pro-choice" rhetoric, while remaining firmly in the liberal camp. *Juno* plays with all the tropes of "pro-life" and

"pro-choice" discourse, tossing them aside like so many clichés. Upon learning that she is pregnant from a sexual encounter with her high school boyfriend, Juno, a slacker-type who lives with her father and step mother, dutifully phones a clinic she finds in the yellow pages ("Women Now"), telling them in dead-pan fashion that she wishes to "procure a hasty abortion." (She reassures her boyfriend that she intends to "nip it in the bud.") In front of the clinic, Juno finds her high-school friend Su-Chin, carrying placards and chanting perfunctorily, "All babies want to get born!" Juno shrugs off her friend and proceeds into the clinic. In the end, however, she is unable to go through with the procedure. She leaves the clinic and, after deliberating with another friend, instead decides to seek a family to adopt the baby, consulting the classifieds in the local paper. Amid the advertisements, Juno finds an elegant, loving, stable young couple who, she decides, will be the perfect parents, and, in what follows, Juno cultivates a deep attachment to the new parents.

Through her connection to them, Juno experiences many parent-like moments, sharing images of the ultrasound, imagining names, and visiting the home during the daytime to bond over music and horror films with the husband. In one scene, Juno and the husband begin to dance, listening to oldies, and, as Juno rests her head on the husband's shoulder, her pregnant stomach protruding between them, one senses that Juno has fallen in love with him—but less as an object of erotic desire and more as the father of her imagined child. In another scene, Juno encounters the wife at a shopping mall and beams as the prospective mother is able to feel the baby kick.

Through this romantic fantasy, the movie offers a different approach to the politics of pregnancy. Liberals can be moved by Juno's decision to carry the baby to term, because it is rooted in something different from the inherent personhood of the fetus ("the right to life"). At the same time, Juno's "choice" is not constructed in terms of autonomy or freedom but rather in the context of Juno's growing relationships to others: the new mother Juno chooses to adopt the baby; Juno's old-fashioned working-class dad, who, despite what he might consider a source of "shame," supports her decision; and, in particular, one of the film's heroes, Juno's imperfect stepmother, a hard-bitten woman who becomes Juno's champion and caregiver during her pregnancy, but who doesn't hesitate to remind Juno of the sacrifices she has made to help raise her and her sister. The handsome husband of the young couple (the prospective father) who, through Juno, clings to his fantasy of remaining young and unburdened is the one figure regarded with disdain. What Juno's pregnancy affirms is neither the autonomy of fetus or woman but the value of committed social relationships, the desire to make a social contribution, and the struggle to care for those one is responsible for.

Policy analysts, moral philosophers, and social scientists—all have expressed dissatisfaction with the stale terms of the debate on abortion and the fetus. As the debate unfolds, encumbered by the language of autonomy and rights that both sides marshal to make their case, it is worth remembering that the United States looks unusual in the context of other industrial democracies, and that elsewhere it is more intuitive for liberals as well as conservatives to see pregnancy—and abortion—in terms of family.

AMY BOROVOY is an Associate Professor of East Asian Studies at Princeton University. Her research focuses on Japanese culture, including issues of public health and women's roles; she has published a number of articles as well as a book, *The Too-Good Wife: Alcohol, Codependency, and the Politics of Nurturance in Postwar Japan* (University of California Press, 2005).

EXPLORING THE ISSUE

Is Abortion Immoral?

Critical Thinking and Reflection

1. Proponents of legalized abortion typically prefer the term "pro-choice" rather than "pro-abortion." Based on the arguments presented by Borovoy in favor of abortion, which term do you think is more accurate? Explain your answer.
2. Opponents of legalized abortion typically prefer the term "pro-life" rather than "anti-abortion." Based on the arguments presented by Meehan against abortion, which term do you think is more accurate? Explain your answer.
3. Because human pregnancy is a complex process, many factors must be considered in determining whether a zygote, embryo, or fetus should be accorded the moral status of a person. Which factors about human pregnancy are morally relevant to this determination? Do these factors support or undermine the assertion that an unborn human should be morally regarded as a person? Explain your answer.
4. What alternative solutions can be found to the problems that typically lead women to consider abortion?
5. What impact would the development of a safe, reliable, easily accessible method for transferring a human embryo from one uterus to another (either natural or artificial) have on the morality of abortion? Explain your answer.

Is There Common Ground?

Meehan and Borovoy are both dissatisfied with the traditional positions usually staked out by conservatives and liberals in the abortion debate. Meehan believes that a genuinely pro-life attitude has much in common with liberal rather than conservative values. Her position is in agreement with ideas expressed by groups such as Feminists for Life, who contend that it is essential to resolve the problems that lead women to consider abortion, such as employers and schools that are hostile to the needs of pregnant workers and students.

Borovoy is part of a movement within feminism to situate the abortion decision not within an opposition between the interests of the woman and the embryo or fetus, but within the special relationship that a woman has with her embryo or fetus. Some contemporary feminists claim that this relationship entails both rights and responsibilities, including the right—or even the responsibility—to abort under certain circumstances. While this position is still squarely in the pro-choice camp, it assigns a much greater value to the unborn child than traditional pro-choice arguments that compare an embryo or fetus to a mere clump of cells to be removed, or to an unrelated intruder to be evicted.

Additional Resources

David Boonin, *A Defense of Abortion* (Cambridge University Press, 2002)

Anne Hendershott, *The Politics of Abortion* (Encounter Books, 2006)

Louis Pojman and Francis J. Beckwith, *The Abortion Controversy: 25 Years after Roe vs. Wade, a Reader* (Wadsworth, 1998)

Laurie J. Schrage, *Abortion & Social Responsibility: Depolarizing the Debate* (Oxford University Press, 2003)

Internet References . . .

Ethics Updates: Internet Resources on Abortion

http://ethics.sandiego.edu/Applied/Abortion/index.asp

Feminists for Life

www.feministsforlife.org

NARAL Pro Choice America

www.naral.org

National Right to Life

www.nrlc.org/

Selected, Edited, and with Issue Framing Material by:
Owen M. Smith, *Stephen F. Austin State University*
and
Anne Collins Smith, *Stephen F. Austin State University*

ISSUE

Is It Morally Right to Prohibit Same-Sex Marriage?

YES: Helen M. Alvaré, from "Brief of Amicus Curiae Helen M. Alvaré in Support of Hollingsworth and Bipartisan Legal Advisory Group" in *Hollingsworth v. Perry, U.S. v. Windsor,* Supreme Court of the United States (2013)

NO: The American Psychological Association et al., from "Brief of Amici Curiae in Support of Affirmance" in *Hollingsworth v. Perry*, Supreme Court of the United States (2013)

Learning Outcomes

After reading this issue, you will be able to:

- Understand social changes with regard to marriage over the past century.
- Describe the role of government in defining marriage and determining/restricting the eligibility of certain people to enter into a marriage.
- Formulate your own position on same-sex marriage and identify evidence supporting your position.
- Identify the main objections to your position and formulate responses to these objections.

ISSUE SUMMARY

YES: Law professor Helen Alvaré argues that the state's interest in promoting opposite-sex marriage stems from its interest in the procreation of children by opposite-sex married couples. Moreover, Alvaré traces the decline of marriage to the loss of traditional connections among marriage, sex, and children. State recognition of same-sex marriage would further undermine these connections and thus contribute to the destabilization of marriage, with negative repercussions to society, especially among the poor. Therefore, she argues, the state has an interest in prohibiting same-sex marriage.

NO: The American Psychological Association joins together with a number of other groups to argue that the substantial benefits that accrue to married couples should not be denied to same-sex couples. Citing evidence in favor of the ability of same-sex couples to form stable, long-lasting, committed relationships, they argue that denying marriage to same-sex couples unfairly stigmatizes and discriminates against them.

In the United States, individual states and Native American jurisdictions have the authority to determine eligibility requirements for marriage licenses. Until recently, eligibility for marriage was either explicitly or presumptively restricted to opposite-sex couples. Over the last several decades, the movement to broaden these eligibility requirements to include same-sex couples has achieved significant success, both in terms of legislative initiatives establishing the right of same-sex couples to marry and legal challenges to laws that prohibit same-sex marriage. Currently, approximately one-third of the population of the United States lives in areas that permit same-sex couples to marry. Furthermore, when the Supreme Court declared a key provision of the Defense of Marriage Act (DOMA) unconstitutional in 2013, the federal government was required to recognize same-sex married couples as spouses for purposes of all federal laws.

Eligibility for marriage confers important practical advantages upon a couple. The government of the United States offers its citizens a vast array of incentives to marry, including tax advantages, access to a spouse's Social Security and veteran's benefits, health care decision-making privileges, family leave, and laws designed to protect spouses' interests in case of separation or divorce. These benefits have long been available to heterosexual couples, and access to these benefits by same-sex couples is a principal goal of those who wish to gain legal recognition of/for same-sex marriage.

Nevertheless, for many same-sex couples, the right to marry is fundamentally an issue of fairness, not benefits. In their view, there are no relevant differences between people who desire to marry members of their own sex and people who desire to marry members of the opposite sex. In the absence of relevant differences between the two groups, they argue, the two groups should have the same rights and privileges, including the right to marry the spouse of their choice. Denying them this right, they insist, is unfair and immoral.

Opponents of the legalization of same-sex marriages typically seek to frame the debate carefully. The morality (and legality) of same-sex marriages, they insist, is distinct from issues concerning homosexual orientation and homosexual activity. They do not deny that same-sex couples and opposite-sex couples are being treated differently under the law. Rather, they point to differences between same-sex couples and opposite-sex couples and assert that these differences are relevant to the issue of whether same-sex marriage is moral and should receive government approval.

Helen Alvaré is an opponent of the legalization of same-sex marriage. She first addresses the basis for governmental interest in marriage. Since the state would cease to exist unless current citizens reproduced and brought new generations of citizens into existence, she argues, the state has a legitimate interest in promoting marriages in which children can be produced. Opposite-sex couples are able to procreate and contribute directly to the next generation of citizens, while same-sex couples are not. For this reason, the state has a legitimate interest in promoting the marriage of opposite-sex couples, not same-sex couples.

While this argument may provide support for governmental recognition of opposite-sex marriage, it is neutral toward governmental recognition of same-sex marriage; there may be reasons other than the production of new citizens that justify bestowing the right to marry on same-sex couples. Therefore, Alvaré offers an additional argument that the state actually has an interest in opposing same-sex marriage. Alvaré observes that our society has, over the past several decades, experienced a decrease in the stability of marriage and the nuclear family: fewer people are getting married and staying married, and more children are being born out of wedlock. Moreover, this decrease is not spread evenly across society; it is disproportionately found among the poor. The combination of poverty and single parenthood is associated with a multitude of problems both for the poor themselves and for society as a whole, not the least of which is a greater probability of poverty and single parenthood in subsequent generations. Alvaré traces the destabilization of marriage to the delinking of marriage, sex, and procreation, which were formerly closely connected to one another in our society. She argues that sanctioning same-sex marriage will contribute to this delinking, thereby worsening the decline of marriage and, as a consequence, the plight of the poorest members of society. In order to promote the welfare of its poorest citizens, she concludes, the state should prohibit same-sex marriage.

In January, 2013, the American Psychological Association (APA), together with other organizations, filed a brief with the U.S. Supreme Court supporting the legality of same-sex marriage. This brief begins with an explanation by the APA regarding scientific research; it is especially important to note the APA does not reject studies simply because they disagree with the conclusion. Based on the research they have examined, the APA makes two key assertions: (1) same-sex couples are capable of forming stable, long-lasting relationships similar to those formed by opposite-sex couples, and (2) children raised by same-sex parents in stable, committed relationships are as healthy and well-adjusted as children raised by opposite-sex parents. Moreover, they point to research conducted among opposite-sex couples showing that those who are married are generally happier and healthier than unmarried opposite-sex couples who live together. Thus, there appear to be significant psychological and physical health benefits of marriage. If same-sex couples are not allowed to marry, the APA argues, they will be deprived of these benefits. Since this deprivation is not justified by any research findings, the APA concludes that it can only be based on unfair discrimination.

YES ↵

Helen M. Alvaré

Brief of Amicus Curiae Helen M. Alvaré in Support of Hollingsworth and Bipartisan Legal Advisory Group

I. The State Has at Least a Legitimate, But More Likely a Compelling, Interest in Singling Out Opposite-Sex Marriage for Protection, Sufficient to Satisfy the Equal Protection Clause

Plaintiffs[1] in these cases claim that the Equal Protection Clause of the Fourteenth Amendment prohibits states from defining marriage as the union of a man and a woman. In addition to the many contrary arguments asserted by the *Hollingsworth* Petitioners, this *amicus* adds that this Court should recognize that states have governmental interests sufficient to justify their recognizing opposite-sex but not same-sex partnerships as "marriages."

States are constitutionally permitted in legislation to classify people into groups that "possess distinguishing characteristics relevant to interests the State has the authority to implement."[2]

Even more relevant to the question of same-sex marriage, this Court has affirmed the constitutionality of state classifications where recognizing or benefitting one group "promotes a legitimate governmental purpose, and the addition of other groups would not."[3]

As described in Section III below, recognizing same-sex marriage as the institution defined by Plaintiffs—as an adult-centered, emotion-based accomplishment—would not only fail to promote the government's substantial interest in opposite-sex marriages, but contradict that interest in ways likely to harm the segment of society already suffering the most from a retreat from marriage.

In *Perry*, the Ninth Circuit held that California's Proposition 8 "operates with no apparent purpose but to impose on gays and lesbians . . . a majority's private disapproval of them and their relationships."[4] The district court concluded similarly, partially relying on the fact that "California, like every other state, has never required that individuals entering a marriage be willing or able to procreate."[5] Yet the lack of a pre-marital "procreation test" does not undermine the legitimacy of the state's classifying couples as same-sex or opposite-sex, and offering marriage only to the latter.

This Court has repeatedly stated that "[t]he rationality commanded by the Equal Protection Clause does not require States to match . . . distinctions and the legitimate interests they serve with razorlike precision"[6] or "mathematical nicety."[7] Rather, classifications that neither involve fundamental rights nor suspect classifications are "accorded a strong presumption of validity."[8] For such classifications, the government is not required to "actually articulate at any time the purpose or rationale supporting its classification,"[9] and a court should uphold it against an Equal Protection challenge "if there is any reasonably conceivable state of facts that could provide a rational basis for the classification."[10]

Moreover, even if intermediate scrutiny applies (as for gender-based classifications) an exact fit is not required. Intermediate scrutiny mandates only a "substantial relation" between the classification and the underlying objective, not a perfect fit.[11] "None of our gender-based classification equal protection cases have required that the statute . . . be capable of achieving its ultimate objective in every instance."[12]

In *Perry*, the voters of the State of California drew a distinction between same-sex and opposite-sex couples that is rationally and substantially related to California's interests in preserving the link between sex, marriage, and procreation. In *Windsor*, Congress made the same calculation in enacting the Defense of Marriage Act. No same-sex couples can procreate; the vast majority of opposite-sex couples can and do. According to the Census Bureau, by the age of 44, over 80% of married couples have children in the household. This figure does not even include couples whose children are older or have moved away from home.[13]

Given the invasions of privacy that would certainly be involved in ascertaining couples' procreative willingness and capacities prior to marriage, the possibility of unintended pregnancies, and couples' changing intentions, it would be impossible for states, effectively, to determine the procreative potential of any particular opposite-sex couple. Drawing a line between same-sex and opposite-sex couples is rationally related to the state's interests in maintaining in the public mind the links between sex, marriage, and children.

II. This Court Has Regularly and Frequently Recognized with Approval the Importance of States' Interests in the Procreative Aspects of Opposite-Sex Marriage. While It Has Also Recognized That Marriage Serves Adults' Interests in Happiness and Stability, the Court Has Not Isolated These from the Procreative Aspects of Marriage

Supreme Court decisions from the early nineteenth to the late twentieth century have repeatedly recognized, with approval, states' interests in the procreative features of marriage: childbirth and childrearing by the adults who conceived them, and the contribution of that childrearing to a stable democratic society.

The Court has written a great deal on the nature of the states' interests in the context of evaluating state laws affecting entry into or exit from marriage, or concerning parental rights and obligations. Typically, these statements recognize that states are vitally interested in marriage because of the advantages not only to adults but also to children and to the larger society. Children replenish communities, and communities benefit when children are reared by their biological parents because parents best assist children to grow to become well-functioning citizens. The Court does not give special attention to adults' interests nor accord them extra weight. Nor are the interests of some children vaulted over the interests of all children generally.

The material below considers the various manners in which this Court has, in the past, discoursed approvingly about marriage and parenting as expressing states'

interwoven interests in the flourishing of adults, children, and society.

A. States have substantial interest in the birth of children.

While it is difficult to disentangle completely the Court's language recognizing a legitimate state interest in the very birth of children from the state's interest in the healthy *formation* of children within marriage, still it is possible to discern it.

In the case refusing to allow polygamy on the grounds of the Free Exercise Clause, *Reynolds v. United States*, this Court explained states' interests in regulating marriage with the simple declaration: "Upon [marriage] society may be said to be built."[14] Nearly 100 years later in *Loving v. Virginia*, striking down a state's anti-miscegenation law, the Court referred to marriage as "fundamental to our very existence and survival," necessarily endorsing the role of marriage in propagating society through childbearing.[15]

Even in cases where *only* marriage or childbearing was at issue, but not both, the Court has referred to "marriage and childbirth" together in the same phrase, nearly axiomatically. The following cases illustrate:

- In *Meyer v. Nebraska*, which vindicated parents' constitutional right to have their children instructed in a foreign language, this Court referred not merely to parents' rights to care for children but to citizens' rights "to marry, establish a home and bring up children."[16]
- In *Skinner v. Oklahoma ex rel. Williamson*, concerning a law punishing certain classifications of felons with forced sterilization, the Court opined: "Marriage and procreation are fundamental to the very existence and survival of the race."[17]
- In *Zablocki v. Redhail*, which struck down a Wisconsin law restricting marriage for certain child support debtors, the Court wrote: "[I]t would make little sense to recognize a right of privacy with respect to other matters of family life and not with respect to the decision to enter the relationship that is the foundation of the family in our society."[18] As in *Loving*, *Zablocki* reiterated that marriage is "fundamental to our very existence and survival,"[19] and recognized, additionally the right to "deci[de] to marry and raise the child in a traditional family setting."[20]
- The 1977 opinion in *Moore v. City of East Cleveland*, announcing a blood-and-marriage-related family's constitutional right to co-reside, nonetheless referenced the procreative aspect of family life stating: "the institution of the family is deeply rooted in this Nation's history and tradition. It

is through the family that we inculcate and pass down many of our most cherished values, moral and cultural."[21]

- Similarly, in *Parham v. J.R.*, a case treating parents' rights to direct their children's health care, the Court stated: "Our jurisprudence historically has reflected Western civilization concepts of the family as a unit with broad parental authority over minor children."[22]

B. States have substantial interest in the way marriage socializes children.

A second prominent theme in this Court's prior cases touching upon marriage is the unique importance of the marital family for forming and educating citizens for the continuation of a free, democratic society.

Preliminarily, in cases in which natural parents' interests in directing children's upbringing have conflicted with the claims of another, this Court has approvingly noted the importance of the bond between parents and their natural children. This is found in its observations that states presume that biological parents' "natural bonds of affection" lead them to make decisions for their children that are in the children's best interests. Statements in this vein have been made in *Parham v. J.R.* ("historically [the law] has recognized that natural bonds of affection lead parents to act in the best interests of their children"[23]), in *Smith v. Organization of Foster Families for Equality & Reform* (families' "blood relationship" forms part of the "importance of the familial relationship, to the individuals involved and to the society"[24]), and in the "grandparents' rights" case of *Troxel v. Granville* ("there is a presumption that fit parents act in the best interests of their children"[25]). . . .

Reflecting upon states' continual interest in marriage legislation, in a case concerning the affordability of divorce process, Justice Black's dissenting opinion (objecting to the expansion of the contents of the federal Due Process Clause) in *Boddie v. Connecticut,* asserted that: "The States provide for the stability of their social order, for the good morals of all their citizens and for the needs of children from broken homes. The States, therefore, have particular interests in the kinds of laws regulating their citizens when they enter into, maintain and dissolve marriages."[26]

In the 1977 case in which this Court refused to extend equal parental rights to foster parents, the court wrote about the relationships between family life and the common good stating: "Thus the importance of the familial relationship, to the individuals involved and to the society, stems from the emotional attachments that derive from the intimacy of daily association, and from

the role it plays in 'promot[ing] a way of life' through the instruction of children, as well as from the fact of blood relationship."[27]

As recently as 1983, in the single father's rights case, *Lehr v. Robertson,* the Court referenced the social purposes of the family quite explicitly in terms of states' legitimate interest in maintaining the link between marriage and procreation. Refusing to treat an unmarried father identically to a married father with respect to rights concerning the child, the Court wrote: "marriage has played a critical role . . . in developing the decentralized structure of our democratic society. In recognition of that role, and as part of their general overarching concern for serving the best interests of children, state laws almost universally express an appropriate preference for the formal family."[28]

In summary, it is fair to conclude, upon a review of this Court's family law jurisprudence, that states' interests in the procreational aspects of marriage have been both recognized by this Court and affirmed to be not only legitimate, but essential.

C. The view of marriage advocated by Plaintiffs in *Perry* and *Windsor* ignores children and society.

Undoubtedly the state also values adults' interests in marriage: adult happiness, mutual commitment, increased stability, and social esteem. Yet a view of marriage that focuses solely on these adult-centric interests is incomplete and denies the Court's decisions affirming the states' interests in procreation and healthy childrearing by stably linked, biological parents. It also risks institutionalizing, in law and culture, a notion of marriage that is at the core of an alarming "retreat from marriage" among disadvantaged Americans. (See, *infra,* Section III.)

Same-sex marriage proponents take great pains to excise references to children when quoting this Court's family law opinions. In their Complaint and Trial Memorandum in *Perry,* for example, Plaintiffs reference from *Loving v. Virginia* only the language about marriage as a "basic civil right" of adults, or a "vital personal right essential to the orderly pursuit of happiness by free men," leaving out *Loving's* immediately adjoining reference to marriage as the fount of society.[29] Plaintiffs similarly quote *Cleveland Board of Education v. La Fleur*[30] without noting that the freedom at issue there was a married teacher's "deciding to bear a child."[31]

Perhaps the most egregious example of Plaintiffs' selectively quoting from this Court's opinions addressing the meaning of marriage is their misuse of *Turner v. Safley,* the case in which this Court held that certain prisoners were required to have access to state-recognized marriage.[32] Plaintiffs cite *Turner* for the proposition that civil marriage is an "'expression . . . of emotional support and public commitment,'" and "an exercise in spiritual unity, and a fulfillment of one's self."[33] The district court's Findings of Fact and Conclusions of Law does likewise, selectively quoting only the adult-related aspects of this Court's statements about the meaning of marriage and excising references to procreation.[34]

However, *Turner* explicitly acknowledged, in two ways, both the adults' *and* the procreative interests in marriage. . . . *Turner* concluded that adults' interests were only "elements" or "an aspect" of marriage,[35] and that marriage had other "incidents" that prisoners would eventually realize, referring specifically to consummation, *i.e.* heterosexual intercourse with a spouse.[36] . . .

In reality, proponents of same-sex marriage ask this Court to insist that every state enact and convey a *new* understanding of marriage. This new understanding would signify that what the state values about sexually intimate couples is their emotional happiness and willingness to commit to one another, exclusively, for a long time.[37] In the case of same-sex couples, marriage would additionally connote that the state and society are sorry for past discrimination and stigmatizing of gays and lesbians.[38] However, this understanding completely disregards the procreative aspects of marriage which this Court has recognized as essential. At the same time, it paints a picture of marriage closely associated with a retreat from marriage among the most vulnerable Americans.

Notably, proponents of same-sex marriage acknowledge the power of marriage laws to affect citizens' perceptions and behavior. Indeed, a change of perceptions and behaviors is precisely what the Plaintiffs sought in bringing suit,[39] and what the courts below attempted to achieve in upholding the Plaintiffs' claims.[40] Plaintiffs specifically urge that marriage *not* be understood to imply procreation. . . .

Importantly, same-sex marriage proponents' attempt to redefine "marriage" to excise childbearing, and childrearing comes at a time in history when new empirical data shows that childbearing and childrearing in marriage is threatened—a threat disproportionately visited upon the most vulnerable populations. (See Section III.) States have responded to the data. In fact, over the past 20 years, the legislatures in all 50 states have introduced bills to reform their marriage and divorce laws precisely to better account for children's interests in their parents' marriages.[41] The federal government has done the same, particularly via the marriage-promotion sections of the landmark "welfare reform" law passed in 1996 by bipartisan majorities,

and signed into law by President Clinton.[42] Furthermore, Presidents Bush and Obama, in particular, have promoted extensive federal efforts on behalf of marriage and fatherhood.[43]

In sum, the Court should reaffirm its many prior statements supporting the interests of states in childbearing, childrearing, and social stability that are advanced by opposite-sex marriages. It should resist Plaintiffs' effort to redefine marriage. That states and the federal government may have ignored children's interests too much in the past, is not a reason why states may not choose, and are not choosing today, to legislate to better account for both children's and society's robustly and empirically supported interests in marriage.

III. Redefining Marriage in a Way That De-links Sex, Marriage and Children Can Harm the Most Vulnerable Americans and Exacerbate the "Marriage Gap," Which Is Responsible for Increasing Levels of Social Inequality in America

The disappearing of children's interests in marriage, both at law and in culture, and the vaulting of adults' emotional and status interests, are, today, associated with a great deal of harm, particularly among the most vulnerable Americans. This, in turn, has led to a growing gap between the more and less privileged in the United States, threatening our social fabric. Recognizing same-sex marriage would confirm and exacerbate these trends. Consequently, states legitimately may wish to reconfirm their commitment to opposite-sex marriage on the grounds of its procreative aspects, and refuse to grant marriage recognition to same-sex couples. Speaking quite generally, law and culture before the 1960s normatively held together sex, marriage, and children. Obviously, this was not true in the life of every citizen or family, but social and legal norms widely reflected it. In the ensuing decades, however, these links deteriorated substantially.

First, the link between sex and children weakened with the introduction of more advanced birth control technology and abortion, both of which came to fore in the 1960s and were announced to be constitutional rights by this Court in the 1960s and 1970s. Then, the link between marriage and children was substantially weakened by the passage of no-fault divorce laws during the 1970s. The transcripts of debates concerning the uniform no-fault divorce law reveal the degree to which children's interests were minimized in favor of adult interests, sometimes with mistaken beliefs about children's resiliency and sometimes on the false assertion that most failing marriages were acrimonious such that divorce would benefit, not harm children.[44]

New reproductive technologies further separated children from marriage and sex from children. Since the creation of the first "test tube baby" in 1978, which spawned a billion dollar industry in the United States, neither the federal government nor any states have passed meaningful restraints on such practices. There are today, still, almost no laws affecting who may access these technologies or obtain "donor" sperm, oocytes, or embryos.[45] This persists despite troubling indications that "donor children" experience an enhanced risk of physical or psychological difficulties.[46]

Interwoven with these developments is the declining stigma of nonmarital sex, and even nonmarital pregnancies and births, which further separate sex from marriage, but not always from children.

The effects of these legal and social developments are not evenly distributed across all segments of the population. In fact, a robust and growing literature indicates that more privileged Americans—*i.e.* non-Hispanic Whites, and Americans with a college education—are economically and educationally pulling away from other social classes to an alarming degree.[47] In the words of prominent sociologists W. Bradford Wilcox and Andrew J. Cherlin:

> In the affluent neighborhoods where many college-educated American [s] live, marriage is alive and well and stable families are the rule . . . . [T]he divorce rate in this group has declined to levels not seen since the early 1970s. In contrast, marriage and family stability have been in decline in the kinds of neighborhoods that we used to call working class . . . . More . . . of them are having children in brittle cohabiting unions. . . . [T]he risk of divorce remains high. . . . The national retreat from marriage, which started in low-income communities in the 1960s and 1970s, has now moved into Middle America.[48]

By the numbers, Americans with no more than a high school degree, African Americans, and some groups of Hispanic Americans cohabit more, marry less often, divorce more, have lower marital quality, and have more nonmarital births than those possessing a college degree, sometimes by very large margins. The situation for those with less than a high school degree is even more dire. A few comparisons portray the situation.

- Among Americans with a college degree or more, the nonmarital birth rate is a mere 6%. Among those with only a high school degree, the rate is 44%, and among those without a high school degree, the rate is 54%.[49]
- Poor men and women are only half as likely to marry as those with incomes at three or more times the poverty level.[50]
- The children of these less-privileged groups are far less likely to be living with both their mother and their father, more likely to have a nonmarital pregnancy, and less likely to graduate college or to obtain adequate employment as an adult.[51] . . .

What best explains these trends among the disadvantaged are changes in norms regarding the relationships between sexual activity, births and marriage. Among these, researchers note legal changes emphasizing parenthood but not marriage (*e.g.* strengthened child support enforcement laws), and emphasizing individual rights as distinguished from marriage. They also point to the declining stigma of nonmarital sex, particularly among the lesser educated, and the availability of the pill for separating sex and children.[52] Professor Cherlin writes that law and culture made other ways of living, as distinguished from marriage, not only more acceptable, but also more practically feasible.[53]

Among the lesser privileged, stable employment for the man and a love relationship are the precursors for marriage. The disadvantaged are far less concerned than the more privileged about having children without marriage. To them, marriage is not about children, and children do not necessarily indicate the wisdom of marrying.

And there is further evidence that this trend away from linking children's well-being to a stable home with both a mother and a father is becoming characteristic not only of the disadvantaged, but also of the "millennial generation" as well.[54] Professor Cherlin confirms that among young adults who are not necessarily poor, the idea of "soulmate" marriage is spreading. Never-married Millennial report at a rate of 94% that "when you marry, your [sic] want your spouse to be your soul mate, first and foremost." They hope for a "super relationship," an "intensely private, spiritualized union, combining sexual fidelity, romantic love, emotional intimacy, and togetherness."[55] . . .

Professor Cherlin points to an emphasis on emotional satisfaction and romantic love and an "ethic of expressive individualism that emerged around the 1960s." There is a focus on bonds of sentiment, and the emotional satisfaction of spouses becomes an important criterion for marital success.[56] Professor Cherlin continues, stating that in the later 20th century, "an even more individualistic perspective on the rewards of marriage took root." It was about the "development of their own sense of self and the expression of their feelings, as opposed to the satisfaction they gained through building a family and playing the roles of spouse and parent. The result was a transition from the companionate marriage to what we might call the individualized marriage."[57]. . .

Notwithstanding these troubling trends, Professor Wax concludes that a "strong marriage norm" is an opportunity to "shape the habits of mind necessary to live up to its prescriptions, while also reducing the need for individuals to perform the complicated calculations necessary to chart their own course."[58] Of course, individuals' decisions will be influenced by individual characteristics and circumstances, but "nonetheless, by replacing a complex personal calculus with simple prudential imperatives, a strong expectation of marriage will make it easier . . . for individuals to muster the restraint necessary to act on long-term thinking."[59]

A strong prescription in favor of marriage as the gateway to adult responsibilities and to caring for the next generation would therefore again likely influence behavior in favor of bearing and rearing children by stably linked, biological parents, ready and able to prepare children for responsible citizenship. Simple rules and norms "place less of a burden on the deliberative capacities and will of ordinary individuals." If, however, individuals are left to guide sexual and reproductive choices in a culture of individualism, "people faced with a menu of options engage in a personal calculus of choice. Many will default to a local [short-term, personal gain] perspective."[60]

The "retreat from marriage" and marital childbearing affects not only individuals and their communities. There is evidence that its problematic effects are being felt even at the national level. Largely as a consequence of changes to family structure, including the inter-generational effects of the absence or breakdown of marriage, there is a growing income and wealth gap in the United States among the least educated, the moderately educated, and the college educated. According to a leading study of this phenomenon, family structure changes accounted for 50% to 100% of the increase in child poverty during the 1980s, and for 41% of the increase in inequality between all Americans between 1976 and 2000.[61] The National Marriage Project even suggests that "it is not too far-fetched to imagine that the United States could be heading toward a 21st century version of a traditional Latin American model of family life, where only a comparatively small oligarchy enjoys a stable married and family life."[62]

In conclusion, marriage historian John Witte Jr. has observed that:

> The new social science data present older prudential insights about marriage with more statistical precision. They present ancient avuncular observations about marital benefits with more inductive generalization. They reduce common Western observations about marital health into more precise and measurable categories. These new social science data thus offer something of a neutral apologetic for marriage.[63]

The notion of marriage that same-sex advocates are describing, and demanding from this Court and from every state, closely resembles the adult-centric view of marriage associated with the "retreat from marriage" among disadvantaged Americans. It would intrinsically and overtly separate sex and children from marriage, for every marriage and every couple and every child. It promotes a meaning of marriage that empties it of the procreative interests understood and embraced by this Court (and every prior generation). Rather, as redefined by Plaintiffs, marriage would merely become a reparation, a symbolic capstone, and a personal reward, not a gateway to adult responsibilities, including childbearing, childrearing, and the inculcating of civic virtues in the next generation for the benefit of the larger society.

Of course, it is not solely the fault of same-sex marriage proponents that we have come to a "tipping point" regarding marriage in the United States, where if the procreational aspects of marriage are not explicitly preserved and highlighted, additional harm will come upon vulnerable Americans and our social fabric itself. The historic institution of marriage was already weakened, likely emboldening same-sex marriage advocates to believe that a redefinition of marriage was only a step, not a leap away. But in its essence, and in the arguments used to promote it, same-sex marriage would be the *coup de grâce* to the procreative meanings and social roles of marriage. It is hoped that the necessary movement for equality and non-discrimination for gays and lesbians will choose a new path, and leave marriage to serve the crucial purposes it is needed to serve.

Conclusion

For the foregoing reasons, the Court should reverse the judgments in both these cases.

Notes

1. For simplicity, *amicus* refers to all proponents of same-sex marriage in *Perry, Hollingsworth,* and *Windsor* as "Plaintiffs."

2. *Bd. of Trs. of the Univ. of Ala. v. Garrett,* 531 U.S. 356, 366 (2001) (quotation marks omitted).

3. *Johnson v. Robison,* 415 U.S. 361, 383 (1974).

4. *Perry v. Brown,* 671 F.3d 1052, 1095 (9th Cir. 2012).

5. *Perry v. Schwarzenegger,* No. 3:09-2292-VRW (N.D. Cal.), Findings of Fact and Conclusions of Law 60, ECF No. 708 [hereinafter Findings of Fact; docket entries for court documents electronically filed under No. 3:09-2292-VRW shall be referred to only by their names and ECF numbers].

6. *Kimel v. Fla. Bd. of Regents,* 528 U.S. 62, 63–64 (2000) (age discrimination action brought by university employees).

7. *Dandridge v. Williams,* 397 U.S. 471, 485 (1970) (quoting *Lindsley v. Natural Carbonic Gas Co.,* 220 U.S. 61, 78 (1911)).

8. *Heller v. Doe,* 509 U.S. 312, 319 (1993).

9. *Id.* at 320 (quoting *Nordlinger v. Hahn,* 505 U.S. 1, 15 (1992)).

10. *Id.* (quoting *Federal Commc'ns Comm'n v. Beach Commc'ns, Inc.,* 508 U.S. 307, 313 (1993)).

11. *See Califano v. Webster,* 430 U.S. 313, 318 (1977) (per curiam) (upholding statute providing higher Social Security benefits for women than men because "women *on the average* received lower retirement benefits than men;" *id.* n.5 (emphasis added)).

12. *Tuan Anh Nguyen v. Immigration and Naturalization Serv.,* 533 US. 53, 70 (2001); *see Metro Broad., Inc. v. Federal Commc'ns Comm'n,* 497 U.S. 547, 579, 582–83 (1990), overruled on other grounds, *Adarand Constructors, Inc. v. Peña,* 515 U.S. 200, 227 (1995) (holding that classification need not be accurate "in every case" if, "in the aggregate," it advances the objective).

13. U.S. Census Bureau, *Family Households with Own Children Under Age 18 by Type of Family, 2000 and 2010, and by Age of Householder, 2010,* The 2012 Statistical Abstract: The National Data Book, Table 65, http://www.census.gov/compendia/statab/2012/tables/12s0065.pdf (last visited Jan. 24, 2013).

14. 98 U.S. 145, 165 (1879).

15. 388 U.S. 1, 12(1967).

16. 262 U.S. 390, 399 (1923).

17. 361 U.S. 535, 541 (1942).

18. 434 U.S. 374, 386 (1978).

19. *Id.* at 383.

20. *Id.* at 386.

21. 431 U.S. 494, 503–04 (1977).

22. 442 U.S. 584, 602 (1979).

23. *Id.* at 602.

24. 431 U.S. 816, 844 (1977).

25. 530 U.S. 57, 68 (2000).

26. 401 U.S. 371, 389 (1971) (Black, J., dissenting).

27. *Org. of Foster Families,* 431 U.S. at 844 (citation omitted).

28. 463 U.S. 248, 257 (1983).

29. Compl. for Declaratory, Injunctive, or other Relief 1, E.C.F. No 1 [hereinafter Compl.]; Pls.' & Pl.-Intervenor's Trial Mem. 3, ECF. No. 281 [hereinafter Trial Mem.]. As noted, *Loving* concludes that marriage and family are "fundamental to our very existence and survival." 388 U.S. at 12.

30. Trial Mem. 3–4, ECF. No. 281 (quoting *Cleveland Bd. of Educ. v. LaFleur,* 414 U.S. 632, 639 (1974) ("personal choice in matters of marriage and family life")).

31. 414 U.S. at 640.

32. 482 U.S. 78 (1987).

33. Trial Mem. 6, ECF No. 281 (citing *Turner v. Safley,* 482 U.S. 78, 95–96).

34. See Findings of Fact 110, ECF No. 708. This approach of Plaintiffs and the courts below is not unique. The plaintiffs in the Massachusetts same-sex marriage case similarly affirmed the ability of the law to affect social perceptions, and requested same-sex marriage recognition in order to attain "social recognition and security" for themselves and their daughter. *Goodridge v. Dep't of Pub. Health,* No. 01–1647 (Superior Court, Cnty. of Suffolk, MA (Aug. 2001), Mem. in Supp. of Pls.' Mot. for Summ. J. 1). They stated that marriage recognition would take away a social "badge of inferiority" and instead "instantly" communicate "their relationship . . . to third parties." *Id.* at 19. And the Massachusetts Supreme Court, like Judge Walker and the Ninth Circuit below, excised children from *Zablocki* and *Loving* and *Skinner* and misused *Turner* similarly. *See Goodridge v. Dep't of Pub. Health,* 798 N.E.2d 941, 970 (Mass. 2003).

35. 482 U.S. at 95–96.

36. *See id.* at 96.

37. *See* Compl. 2, 7, ECF No. 1; Findings of Fact 67, ECF No. 708; *Perry v. Brown,* 671 F.3d 1052, 1078 (9th Cir. 2012). The *Goodridge* court and well-known same-sex marriage advocates urge a similar meaning for marriage. *See Goodridge,* 798 N.E.2d at 948 (Marriage is the "exclusive commitment of two individuals to each other."); *see, e.g.,* Andrew Sullivan, *Here Comes the Groom: A (Conservative) Case for Gay Marriage,* New Republic (Aug. 28, 1989, 1:00 AM), http://www.tnr.com/article/79054/here-comes-the-groom# (describing marriage as a "deeper and

harder-to-extract-yourself from commitment to another human being"); *Talking about Marriage Equality with Your Friends and Family,* Human Rights Campaign, www.hrc.org/resources/entry/talking-about-marriage-equality-with-your-friends-and-family (last visited Jan. 24, 2013) (describing marriage as "the highest possible commitment that can be made between two adults").

38. Several times in Plaintiffs' Complaint in *Perry,* they refer to the theme of "gay and lesbian individuals['] . . . long and painful history of societal and government-sponsored discrimination," or to "stigma." Compl. 1, 4, 7–8, ECF No. 1.

39. *See, e.g.,* Compl. 9–10, ECF No. 1 (asserting that recognition of same-sex marriage would produce the result of "hav[ing] society accord their unions and their families the same respect and dignity of opposite-sex unions and families"); Compl. 8, ECF No. 1 (ameliorate the "stigmatizing" gays and lesbians experience and affect their "stature" in the community).

40. *See* Findings of Fact 86–87, ECF No. 708 (marriage recognition would convey that gays and lesbians partake of the "most socially valued form of relationship"); *Perry v. Brown,* 671 F.3d 1052, 1078 (9th Cir. 2012) (suggesting that the state's designation of a relationship as a "marriage," by itself "expresses validation, by the state and the community," and is "a symbol. . . of something profoundly important").

41. *See, e.g.,* Lynn D. Wardle, *Divorce Reform at the Turn of the Millennium: Certainties and Possibilities,* 33 Fam. L.Q. 783, 790 (1999); Karen Gardiner et al., *State Policies to Promote Marriage: Preliminary Report,* The Lewin Group (Mar. 2002).

42. The Personal Responsibility and Work Opportunity Reconciliation Act of 1996, Pub. L. No. 104–193 (1996).

43. *See* Helen M. Alvaré, *Curbing Its Enthusiasm: U.S. Federal Policy and the Unitary Family,* 2 Int'l J. Jurisprudence Fam. 107, 121–24 (2011).

44. *See* Helen M. Alvaré, *The Turn Toward the Self in Marriage: Same-Sex Marriage and Its Predecessors in Family Law,* 16 Stan. L. & Pol'y Rev. 101, 137–53 (2005).

45. *See* The President's Council on Bioethics, *Reproduction and Responsibility: The Regulation of New Biotechnologies* 8–12 (2003).

46. *See Elizabeth* Marquardt et al., *My Daddy's Name Is Donor: A New Study of Young Adults Conceived through Sperm Donation,* Commission on Parenthood's Future (2010); Jennifer J. Kurinczuk & Carol Bower, *Birth defects in infants conceived by intracytoplasmic sperm injection: an alternative explanation,* 315 Brit. Med. J. 1260 (1997).

47. *See, e.g., The Decline of Marriage and Rise of New Families,* Pew Research Center (Nov. 18, 2010), http://www.pewsocialtrends.org/2010/11/18/the-decline-of-marriage-and-rise-of-newfamilies/; Richard Fry, No *Reversal in Decline of Marriage,* Pew Research Center (Nov. 20, 2012), http://www.pewsocialtrends.org/2012/11/20/no-reversal-in-decline-of-marriage/; Pamela J. Smock & Wendy D Manning, *Living Together Unmarried in the United States: Demographic Perspectives and Implications for Family Policy,* 26 Law & Pol'y 87 (2004); The National Marriage Project and the Institute for American Values, *When Marriage Disappears: The Retreat from Marriage in Middle America,* State of Our Unions (2010), http://stateofourunions.org/2010/when-marriage-disappears.php (last visited Jan. 24, 2013).

48. W. Bradford Wilcox & Andrew J. Cherlin, *The Marginalization of Marriage in Middle America,* Brookings, Aug. 10, 2011, at 2.

49. *Id.*

50. Kathryn Edin & Joanna M. Reed, *Why Don't They Just Get Married? Barriers to Marriage among the Disadvantaged,* The Future of Children, Fall 15(2)2005, at 117–18.

51. Wilcox & Cherlin, *supra,* at 6; The National Marriage Project, *supra,* at 10–11,17 (citing Ron Haskins & Isabel Sawhill, *Creating an Opportunity Society* (2009); Nicholas H. Wolfinger, *Understanding the Divorce Cycle: The Children of Divorce in Their Own Marriages* (2005)).

52. Wilcox & Cherlin, *supra,* at 3–4.

53. Andrew J. Cherlin, *American Marriage in the Early Twenty-First Century,* The Future of Children, Fall 15(2) 2005, at 41.

54. *See* Wendy Wang & Paul Taylor, *For Millennials, Parenthood Trumps Marriage,* Pew Research Center, 2 (Mar. 9, 2011), http://www.pewsocial-trends.org/2011/03/09/for-millennialsparenthood-trumps-marriage/ (on the question of a child's need for two, married parents, 51% of Millennials disagreed in 2008, compared to 39% of Generation Xers in 1997).

55. Andrew J. Cherlin, *The Deinstitutionalization of American Marriage,* 66 J. of Marriage & Fam. 848, 856 (2004).

56. Cherlin, *The Deinstitutionalization of American Marriage, supra,* at 851.

57. *Id.* at 852.

58. *Id.*

59. *Id.*

60. *Id.* at 61.

61. Molly A. Martin, *Family Structure and Income Inequality in Families with Children, 1976–2000,* 43 Demography 421, 423–24, 440 (2006).

62. The National Marriage Project and the Institute for American Values, *supra*, at 17.
63. John Witte, Jr., *The Goods and Goals of Marriage*, 76 Notre Dame L. Rev. 1019, 1070 (2001).

Bibliography

Cases

Adarand Constructors, Inc. v. Peña, 515 U.S. 200 (1995)

Bd. of Trs. of the Univ. of Ala. v. Garrett, 531 U.S. 356 (2001)

Boddie v. Connecticut, 401 U.S. 371 (1971)

Butler v. Wilson, 415 U.S. 953 (1974)

Califano v. Webster, 430 U.S. 313 (1977)

Cleveland Bd. of Educ. v. LaFleur, 414 U.S. 632 (1974)

Dandridge v. Williams, 397 U.S. 471 (1970)

Federal Commc'ns Comm'n v. Beach Commc'ns, Inc., 508 U.S. 307 (1993)

Goodridge v. Dep't of Pub. Health, 798 N.E.2d 941 (Mass. 2003)

Heller v. Doe, 509 U.S. 312 (1993)

Johnson v. Robison, 415 U.S. 361 (1974)

Johnson v. Rockefeller, 365 F. Supp. 377 (S.D.N.Y. 1973)

Kimel v. Fla. Bd. of Regents, 528 U.S. 62 (2000)

Lehr v. Roberston, 463 U.S. 248 (1983)

Lindsley v. Natural Carbonic Gas Co., 220 U.S. 61 (1911)

Loving v. Virginia, 388 U.S. 1 (1967)

Maynard v. Hill, 125 U.S. 190 (1888)

Metro Broad., Inc. v. Federal Commc'ns Comm'n, 497 U.S. 547 (1990)

Meyer v. Nebraska, 262 U.S. 390 (1923)

Moore v. City of East Cleveland, 431 U.S. 494 (1977)

Murphy v. Ramsey, 114 U.S. 15 (1885)

Nordlinger v. Hahn, 505 U.S. 1 (1992)

Parham v. J.R., 442 U.S. 584 (1979)

Perry v. Brown, 671 F.3d 1052 (9th Cir. 2012)

Prince v. Massachusetts, 321 U.S. 158 (1944)

Reynolds v. United States, 98 U.S. 145 (1879)

Skinner v. Oklahoma ex rel. Williamson, 361 U.S. 535 (1942)

Smith v. Org. of Foster Families for Equal. & Reform, 431 U.S. 816 (1977)

Troxel v. Granville, 530 U.S. 57 (2000)

Tuan Anh Nguyen v. Immigration and Naturalization Serv., 533 US. 53 (2001)

Turner v. Safley, 482 U.S. 78 (1987)

Zablocki v. Redhail, 434 U.S. 374 (1978)

Statutes

The Personal Responsibility and Work Opportunity Reconciliation Act of 1996, Pub. L. No. 104–193 (1996).

Other Authorities

Amy L. Wax, *Diverging family structure and "rational" behavior: the decline in marriage as a disorder of choice*, in Research Handbook on the Economics of Family Law (Lloyd R. Cohen & Joshua D. Wright, eds., 2011)

Andrew J. Cherlin, *The Deinstitutionalization of American Marriage*, 66 J. of Marriage & Fam. 848 (2004)

Andrew Sullivan, *Here Comes the Groom: A (Conservative) Case for Gay Marriage*, New Republic (Aug. 28, 1989, 1:00 AM), http://www.tnr.com/article/79054/here-comes-the-groom# (describing marriage as a "deeper and harder-to-extract-yourself from commitment to another human being")

Elizabeth Marquardt et al., *My Daddy's Name Is Donor: A New Study of Young Adults Conceived through Sperm Donation*, Commission on Parenthood's Future (2010)

Garry J. Gates, *Family Focus on . . . LGBT Families: Family Formation and Raising Children among Same-Sex Couples*, National Council on Family Relations Report, Issue FF51, 2011

Helen M. Alvaré, *Curbing Its Enthusiasm: U.S. Federal Policy and the Unitary Family*, 2 Int'l J. Jurisprudence Fam. 107 (2011)

Helen M. Alvaré, *The Turn Toward the Self in Marriage: Same-Sex Marriage and Its Predecessors in Family Law*, 16 Stan. L. & Pol'y Rev. 101 (2005)

Jennifer J. Kurinczuk & Carol Bower, *Birth Defects in Infants Conceived by Intracytoplasmic Sperm Injection: an Alternative Explanation*, 315 Brit. Med. J. 1260 (1997)

John Witte, Jr., *Response to Mark Strasser, in Marriage and Same-Sex Unions* (Lynn Wardle et al., eds., 2003)

John Witte, Jr., *The Goods and Goals of Marriage*, 76 Notre Dame L. Rev. 1019 (2001)

Karen Gardiner et al., *State Policies to Promote Marriage: Preliminary Report,* The Lewin Group (Mar. 2002)

Kathryn Edin & Joanna M. Reed, *Why Don't They Just Get Married? Barriers to Marriage among the Disadvantaged,* The Future of Children, Fall 15(2) 2005

Lynn D. Wardle, *Divorce Reform at the Turn of the Millennium: Certainties and Possibilities,* 33 Fam. L.Q. 783 (1999)

Mark Regnerus, *How Different Are the Adult Children of Parents Who Have Same-Sex Relationships? Findings from the New Family Structures Study,* 41 Soc. Sci. Research 752 (2012)

Molly A. Martin, *Family Structure and Income Inequality in Families with Children, 1976–2000,* 43 Demography 421 (2006)

Nicholas H. Wolfinger, *Understanding the Divorce Cycle: The Children of Divorce in Their Own Marriages* (2005)

Pamela J. Smock & Wendy D. Manning, *Living Together Unmarried in the United States: Demographic Perspectives and Implications for Family Policy,* 26 Law & Policy 87 (2004)

Pamela J. Smock, *The Wax and Wane of Marriage: Prospects for Marriage in the 21st Century,* 66 J. of Marriage & Fam. 966 (2004)

Ron Haskins & Isabel Sawhill, *Creating an Opportunity Society* (2009)

Talking about Marriage Equality with Your Friends and Family, Human Rights Campaign, www.hrc.org/resources/entry/talking-about-marriage-equality-with-your-friends-and-family (last visited Jan. 24, 2013)

The National Marriage Project and the Institute for American Values, *When Marriage Disappears: The Retreat from Marriage in Middle America,* State of Our Unions (2010), http://stateofourunions.org/2010/when-marriage-disappears

The President's Council on Bioethics, *Reproduction and Responsibility: The Regulation of New Biotechnologies* (2003)

U.S. Census Bureau, *Family Households with Own Children Under Age 18 by Type of Family, 2000 and 2010, and by Age of Householder, 2010,* The 2012 Statistical Abstract: The National Data Book, Table 65, http://www.census.gov/compendia/statab/2012/tables/12s0065.pdf (last visited Jan. 24, 2013)

W. Bradford Wilcox & Andrew J. Cherlin, *The Marginalization of Marriage in Middle America,* Brookings, Aug. 10, 2011

Wendy Wang & Paul Taylor, For *Millennials, Parenthood Trumps Marriage,* Pew Research Center (Mar. 9, 2011), http://www.pewsocialtrends.org/2011/03/09/formillennials-parenthood-trumps-marriage/

HELEN M. ALVARÉ is a Professor of Law at George Mason University School of Law, where she teaches Family Law, Law and Religion, and Property Law. She has published in law reviews and other academic journals on matters concerning marriage, parenting, non-marital households, abortion and the First Amendment religion clauses.

The American Psychological Association et al.    **NO**

Brief of Amici Curiae in Support of Affirmance in *Hollingsworth v. Perry*

Introduction and Summary

As the Ninth Circuit noted, "Proposition 8 had one effect," to "strip[] same-sex couples" of "the right to obtain and use the designation of 'marriage.'" Perry v. Brown, 671 F.3d 1052, 1063 (9th Cir. 2012). By so doing, the initiative withholds from gay men and lesbian women an important symbol of "state legitimization and societal recognition." Id. Some proponents of the initiative claim that this exclusion merely reflects meaningful differences between same-sex and heterosexual relationships, or between the parenting abilities of same-sex and heterosexual couples. The scientific research does not justify those claims.

Rather, scientific evidence strongly supports the conclusion that homosexuality is a normal expression of human sexuality; that most gay, lesbian, and bisexual adults do not experience their sexual orientation as a choice; that gay and lesbian people form stable, committed relationships that are equivalent to heterosexual relationships in essential respects; and that same-sex couples are no less fit than heterosexual parents to raise children and their children are no less psychologically healthy and well-adjusted than children of heterosexual parents. In short, the claim that official recognition of marriage for same-sex couples undermines the institution of marriage and harms their children is inconsistent with the scientific evidence.

The body of research presented below demonstrates that the discrimination effected by Proposition 8 unfairly stigmatizes same-sex couples.

Argument

I. The Scientific Evidence Presented in This Brief

Representing the leading associations of psychological, psychiatric, medical, and social work professionals, Amici have sought in this brief to present an accurate and responsible summary of the current state of scientific and professional knowledge concerning sexual orientation and families relevant to this case.

In drawing conclusions, Amici rely on the best empirical research available, focusing on general patterns rather than any single study. Before citing a study herein, Amici have critically evaluated its methodology, including the reliability and validity of the measures and tests it employed, and the quality of its data-collection procedures and statistical analyses.

Scientific research is a cumulative process and no empirical study is perfect in its design and execution. Even well-executed studies may be limited in their implications and the generalizability of their findings.[1] Accordingly, Amici base their conclusions as much as possible on general patterns rather than any single study.

All scientific studies can be constructively criticized, and scientists continually try to identify ways to improve and refine their own work and that of their colleagues. Thus, many studies cited herein discuss their limitations and provide suggestions for further research. This is consistent with the scientific method and does not impeach the overall conclusions.

Most of the studies and literature reviews cited herein have been peer-reviewed and published in reputable academic journals. In addition, other academic books, book chapters, and technical reports, which typically are not subject to the same peer-review standards as journal articles, are included when they report research employing rigorous methods, are authored by well-established researchers, and accurately reflect professional consensus about the current state of knowledge. Amici have made a good faith effort to include all relevant studies and have not excluded any study because of its findings.

Supreme Court of the United States, January 2013.

I. Homosexuality Is a Normal Expression of Human Sexuality, Is Generally Not Chosen, and Is Highly Resistant to Change

Sexual orientation refers to an enduring disposition to experience sexual, affectional, and/or romantic attractions to one or both sexes. It also encompasses an individual's sense of personal and social identity based on those attractions, on behaviors expressing those attractions, and on membership in a community of others who share those attractions and behaviors.[2] Although sexual orientation ranges along a continuum from exclusively heterosexual to exclusively homosexual, it is usually discussed in three categories: heterosexual (having sexual and romantic attraction primarily or exclusively to members of the other sex), homosexual (having sexual and romantic attraction primarily or exclusively to members of one's own sex), and bisexual (having a significant degree of sexual and romantic attraction to both sexes).

Although homosexuality was classified as a mental disorder when the American Psychiatric Association published the first Diagnostic and Statistical Manual of Mental Disorders in 1952, only five years later a study sponsored by the National Institute of Mental Health found no evidence to support the classification.[3] On the basis of that study and others demonstrating that the original classification reflected social stigma rather than science,[4] the American Psychiatric Association declassified homosexuality as a mental disorder in 1973. In 1974, the American Psychological Association adopted a policy reflecting the same conclusion. For decades, then, the consensus of mental health professionals and researchers has been that homosexuality and bisexuality are normal expressions of human sexuality and pose no inherent obstacle to leading a happy, healthy, and productive life, and that gay and lesbian people function well in the full array of social institutions and interpersonal relationships.[5]

Most gay men and lesbians do not experience their sexual orientation as resulting from a voluntary choice. In a U.S. national probability sample of 662 self-identified lesbian, gay, and bisexual adults, 88% of gay men and 68% of lesbians reported feeling they had no choice at all about their sexual orientation, while another 7% of gay men and 15% of lesbians reported only a small amount of choice. Only 5% of gay men and 16% of lesbians felt they had a fair amount or a great deal of choice.[6]

Several amici supporting Proposition 8 challenge the conclusion that for most people sexual orientation is not a matter of choice, but they offer no credible scientific support for their position.[7] Moreover, although some groups and individuals have offered clinical interventions that purport to change sexual orientation from homosexual to heterosexual—sometimes called "conversion" therapies—these interventions have not been shown to be effective or safe. A review of the scientific literature by an American Psychological Association task force concluded that sexual orientation change efforts are unlikely to succeed and indeed can be harmful.[8]

All major national mental health organizations—including Amici—have adopted policy statements cautioning the profession and the public about treatments that purport to change sexual orientation.[9]

II. Sexual Orientation and Relationships

Sexual orientation is commonly discussed as a characteristic of the individual, like biological sex or age. This perspective is incomplete because sexual orientation necessarily involves relationships with other people. Sexual acts and romantic attractions are categorized as homosexual or heterosexual according to the biological sex of the individuals involved in them, relative to each other. Indeed, it is only by acting with another person—or desiring to act—that individuals express their heterosexuality, homosexuality, or bisexuality. Thus, sexual orientation is integrally linked to the intimate personal relationships that human beings form with others to meet their deeply felt needs for love, attachment, and intimacy. One's sexual orientation defines the universe of persons with whom one is likely to find the satisfying and fulfilling relationships that, for many individuals, comprise an essential component of personal identity.

A. Gay Men and Lesbian Women Form Stable, Committed Relationships That Are Equivalent to Heterosexual Relationships in Essential Respects

Like heterosexuals, most gay and lesbian people want to form stable, long-lasting relationships,[10] and many of them do: numerous studies using nonprobability samples of gay and lesbian people have found that the vast majority of participants have been in a committed relationship at some point in their lives, that large proportions are currently in such a relationship (40–70% of gay men and 45–80% of lesbian women), and that many of those couples have been together 10 or more years.[11] Survey data from probability samples support these findings.[12] Data from the 2010 US Census show that same-sex couples headed more than 600,000 US households and more than 90,000 in California.[13]

Empirical research demonstrates that the psychological and social aspects of committed relationships between same-sex partners largely resemble those of heterosexual partnerships. Like heterosexual couples, same-sex couples form deep emotional attachments and commitments. Heterosexual and same-sex couples alike face similar issues concerning intimacy, love, equity, loyalty, and stability, and they go through similar processes to address those issues.[14] Empirical research also shows that gay and lesbian couples have levels of relationship satisfaction similar to or higher than those of heterosexual couples.[15]

B. The Institution of Marriage Offers Social, Psychological, and Health Benefits That Are Denied to Same-Sex Couples

Marriage as a social institution has a profound effect on the lives of the individuals who inhabit it. The sociologist Emile Durkheim observed that marriage helps to protect the individual from "anomy," or social disruption and breakdowns of norms.[16] Twentieth-century sociologists advised that marriage creates order[17] and "provides a strong positive sense of identity, self-worth, and mastery."[18] Empirical research demonstrates that marriage has distinct benefits that extend beyond the material necessities of life.[19] These intangible elements of the marital relationship have important implications for the physical and psychological health of married individuals and for the relationship itself.

Because marriage rights have been granted to same-sex couples only recently and only in a few jurisdictions, no empirical studies have yet been published that compare married same-sex couples to unmarried same-sex couples, or those in civil unions. Based on their scientific and clinical expertise, Amici believe it is appropriate to extrapolate from the empirical research literature for heterosexual couples—with qualifications as necessary—to anticipate the likely effects of marriage for same-sex couples.[20]

Married men and women generally experience better physical and mental health than their unmarried counterparts.[21] These health benefits do not appear to result simply from being in an intimate relationship, for most studies have found that married heterosexual individuals generally manifest greater well-being than those of comparable cohabiting couples.[22] Of course, marital status alone does not guarantee greater health or happiness. People who are unhappy in marriage often manifest lower levels of well-being than the unmarried, and marital discord and dissatisfaction is often associated with negative health effects.[23] Nevertheless, satisfied married couples consistently manifest higher levels of happiness, psychological well-being, and physical health than the unmarried.

Being married also is a source of stability and commitment. Marital commitment is a function not only of attractive forces (i.e., rewarding features of the partner or

relationship) but also of external forces that serve as constraints on dissolving the relationship. Barriers to terminating a marriage include feelings of obligation to one's family members; moral and religious values; legal restrictions; financial concerns; and the anticipated disapproval of others.[24] In the absence of adequate rewards, the existence of barriers alone is not sufficient to sustain a marriage in the long term. Perceiving one's intimate relationship primarily in terms of rewards, rather than barriers to dissolution, is likely to be associated with greater relationship satisfaction.[25] Nonetheless, perceived barriers are negatively correlated with divorce and thus the presence of barriers may increase partners' motivation to seek solutions for problems, rather than rushing to dissolve a salvageable relationship.[26]

Lacking access to legal marriage, the primary motivation for same-sex couples to remain together derives mainly from the rewards associated with the relationship rather than from formal barriers to separation.[27] Given this fact, and the legal and prejudicial obstacles that same-sex partners face, the prevalence and durability of same-sex relationships are striking.

Amici emphasize that the abilities of gay and lesbian persons as parents and the positive outcomes for their children are not areas where credible scientific researchers disagree.[28] Thus, after careful scrutiny of decades of research, the American Psychological Association concluded in 2004 that (a) "there is no scientific evidence that parenting effectiveness is related to parental sexual orientation: Lesbian and gay parents are as likely as heterosexual parents to provide supportive and healthy environments for their children" and (b) that "research has shown that the adjustment, development, and psychological well-being of children are unrelated to parental sexual orientation and that the children of lesbian and gay parents are as likely as those of heterosexual parents to flourish." Am. Psychol. Ass'n, Resolution on Sexual Orientation, Parents, and Children (2004), available at http://www.apa.org/about/governance/council/policy/parenting.pdf.

Similarly, the American Academy of Pediatrics has recently adopted a policy statement which states: "Scientific evidence affirms that children have similar developmental and emotional needs, and receive similar parenting, whether they are raised by parents of the same or different genders. If a child has 2 living and capable parents who choose to create a permanent bond by way of civil marriage, it is in the best interests of their child(ren) that legal and social institutions allow and support them to do so, irrespective of their sexual orientation." Am. Acad. of Pediatrics, Committee on Psychosocial Aspects of Child and Family Health, Policy Statement: Promoting the

Well-Being of Children Whose Parents Are Gay or Lesbian, 131 Pediatrics (forthcoming 2013).

NASW has similarly determined that "[t]he most striking feature of the research on lesbian mothers, gay fathers, and their children is the absence of pathological findings. The second most striking feature is how similar the groups of gay and lesbian parents and their children are to heterosexual parents and their children that were included in the studies." Nat'l Ass'n of Soc. Workers, Policy Statement: Lesbian, Gay, and Bisexual Issues, in Social Work Speaks 193, 194 (4th ed. 1997). See also Nat'l Ass'n of Soc. Workers, Policy Statement: Family Planning and Reproductive Choice, in Social Work Speaks 129, 132 (9th ed. 2012).

The American Psychoanalytic Association has likewise determined that "[t]here is no credible evidence that shows that a parent's sexual orientation or gender identity will adversely affect the development of the child." Am. Psychoanalytic Ass'n, Position Statement: Parenting (2012), available at http://www.apsa.org/about_apsaa/position_statements/parenting.aspx.

In adopting an official Position Statement in support of legal recognition of same-sex civil marriage, the American Psychiatric Association observed that "no research has shown that the children raised by lesbians and gay men are less well adjusted than those reared within heterosexual relationships." Am. Psychiatric Ass'n, Position Statement: Support of Legal Recognition of Same-Sex Civil Marriage (2005), available at http://www.psych.org/Departments/EDU/Library/APAOfficialDocumentsandRelated/PositionStatements/200502.aspx.

Finally, the American Medical Association likewise has adopted a policy supporting legislative and other reforms to allow adoption by same sex partners.[29]

III. Denying the Status of Marriage to Same-Sex Couples Stigmatizes Them

The foregoing shows that the beliefs about gay men and lesbian women advanced to support Proposition 8—about their capacity for committed, long lasting relationships, and their ability to raise healthy well-adjusted children—are contradicted by the scientific evidence and instead reflect an unreasoned antipathy towards an identifiable minority. In depriving gay men and lesbian women of membership in an important social institution, Proposition 8 conveys the state's judgment that committed intimate relationships between people of the same sex are inferior to heterosexual relationships. This is the essence of stigma.

A stigmatized condition or status is negatively valued by society, defines a person's social identity, and thus

disadvantages that person.[30] A classic work in this area characterized stigma as "an undesired differentness."[31] It can be manifested both in social institutions, such as the law, and in individual behaviors. Laws that accord majority and minority groups differing status highlight the perceived "differentness" of the minority and thereby tend to legitimize prejudicial attitudes and individual acts against the disfavored group, including ostracism, harassment, discrimination, and violence. Large numbers of lesbian, gay, and bisexual people experience such acts of prejudice because of their sexual orientation.[32]

Proposition 8 is an instance of institutional stigma. It conveys the government's judgment that, in the realm of intimate relationships, a legally united same-sex couple is inherently less deserving of society's full recognition than are heterosexual couples. As the Ninth Circuit correctly recognized, Proposition 8 "lessen[s] the status and human dignity of gays and lesbians in California." Perry, 671 F.3d at 1063. By devaluing and delegitimizing the relationships that constitute the very core of a homosexual orientation, Proposition 8 compounds and perpetuates the stigma historically attached to homosexuality. This Court has repeatedly recognized the unconstitutional nature of stigmatizing legislation based on stereotypic classifications. See Heckler v. Mathews, 465 U.S. 728, 739–40 (1984) ("[A]s we have repeatedly emphasized, discrimination itself, by perpetuating 'archaic and stereotypic notions' or by stigmatizing members of the disfavored group as 'innately inferior' and therefore as less worthy participants in the political community* * * can cause serious non-economic injuries to those persons who are personally denied equal treatment solely because of their membership in a disfavored group.") (footnote and citations omitted).

Conclusion

The judgment below should be affirmed.

Notes

1. For example, to confidently describe the prevalence or frequency with which a phenomenon occurs in the population at large, it is necessary to collect data from a "probability" or "representative" sample. A probability sample consists of individuals selected from the study population through a process that gives each member of the population a calculable chance of being included. Nonprobability samples do not give all members of the study population a chance of being included—such as, for example, a study of voters that relies on volunteers who

phone in to a telephone number advertised in a newspaper. Case studies and nonprobability samples can be used to document the existence of a phenomenon in the study population. For studies of groups that constitute a relatively small proportion of the population, obtaining a probability sample can be extremely expensive or otherwise not feasible. Consequently, researchers studying such groups may rely on nonprobability samples. If they wish to compare members of the smaller group with members of the majority group (e.g., lesbian mothers with heterosexual mothers), they may recruit nonprobability samples of both groups that are matched on relevant characteristics (e.g., educational level, age, income). Regardless of the sampling method used, greater confidence can be placed in findings that have been replicated by others using different samples.

2. See A.R. D'Augelli, Sexual Orientation, in 7 Am. Psychol. Ass'n, Encyclopedia of Psychology 260 (A.E. Kazdin ed., 2000); G.M. Herek, Homosexuality, in 2 The Corsini Encyclopedia of Psychology 774–76 (I.B. Weiner & W.E. Craighead eds., 4th ed. 2010); Institute of Medicine, The Health of Lesbian, Gay, Bisexual, and Transgender People: Building a Foundation for Better Understanding (2011).

3. E. Hooker, The Adjustment of the Male Overt Homosexual, 21 J. Projective Techs. 18 (1957).

4. B.F. Riess, Psychological Tests in Homosexuality, in Homosexual Behavior: A Modern Reappraisal 296 (J. Marmor ed., 1980); J.C. Gonsiorek, The Empirical Basis for the Demise of the Illness Model of Homosexuality, in Homosexuality: Research Implications for Public Policy 115 (J.C. Gonsiorek & J.D. Weinrich eds., 1991).

5. See, e.g., Am. Psychiatric Ass'n, Position Statement: Homosexuality and Civil Rights (1973), in 131 Am. J. Psychiatry 497 (1974); Am. Psychol. Ass'n, Minutes of the Annual Meeting of the Council of Representatives, 30 Am. Psychologist 620, 633 (1975).

6. G. Herek et al., Demographic, Psychological, and Social Characteristics of Self-Identified Lesbian, Gay, and Bisexual Adults in a US Probability Sample, 7 Sexuality Res. & Soc. Pol'y 176 (2010). See also G. Herek et al., Internalized Stigma Among Sexual Minority Adults: Insights From a Social Psychological Perspective, 56 J. Counseling Psychol. 32 (2009).

7. See Amicus Br. of Liberty Counsel, at 35; Amicus Br. of Parents and Friends of Ex-Gays and Gays, passim; Amicus Br. of Family Research Council, at 27–28; Amicus Br. of Dr. Paul McHugh, at 14–28.

8. Am. Psychol. Ass'n, Report of the American Psychological Association Task Force on Appropriate Therapeutic Responses to Sexual Orientation (2009); see also Am. Psychol. Ass'n, Resolution on Appropriate Affirmative Responses to Sexual Orientation Distress and Change Efforts (2009), both available at http://www.apa.org/pi/lgbt/resources /sexual-orientation.aspx.

9. See Am. Psychol. Ass'n, Resolution, supra note 9; Am. Psychiatric Ass'n, Position Statement: Psychiatric Treatment and Sexual Orientation (1998), available at http://www.psych.org/Departments/ EDU/Library/APAOfficialDocumentsandRelated/ PositionStatements/199820.aspx; Am. Ass'n for Marriage & Fam. Therapy, Reparative/Conversion Therapy (2009), available at http://www.aamft. org/iMIS15/AAMFT/MFT_Resources/Content/ Resources/Position_On_Couples.aspx; Am. Med. Ass'n, Policy H-160.991, Health Care Needs of the Homosexual Population, available at http://www. ama-assn.org/ama/pub/about-ama/our-people/ member-groups-sections/glbt-advisory-committee/ama-policy-regarding-sexual-orientation. page; Nat'l Ass'n of Soc. Workers, Position Statement: "Reparative" and "Conversion" Therapies for Lesbians and Gay Men (2000), available at http:// www.naswdc.org/diversity/lgb/reparative.asp; Am. Psychoanalytic Ass'n, Position Statement: Attempts to Change Sexual Orientation, Gender Identity, or Gender Expression (2012), available at http://www.apsa.org/about_apsaa/position_statements/attempts_to_change_sexual_orientation. aspx; B.L. Frankowski, Sexual Orientation and Adolescents, 113 Pediatrics 1827 (2004).

10. In a 2005 U.S. national probability sample of 662 self-identified lesbian, gay, and bisexual adults, of those who were currently in a relationship, 78% of the gay men and 87% of the lesbian women said they would marry their partner if it was legal, and, of those not currently in a relationship, 34% of gay men and 46% of lesbian women said that they would like to marry someday. Herek et al., Demographic, supra note 7. See also Henry J. Kaiser Fam. Found., Inside-OUT: A Report on the Experiences of Lesbians, Gays and Bisexuals in America and the Public's Views on Issues and Policies Related to Sexual Orientation 31 (2001), available at http://www.kff.org/kaiserpolls/upload/ New-Surveys-on-Experiences-of-Lesbians-Gays-and-Bisexuals-and-the-Public-s-Views-Related-to-Sexual-Orientation-Report.pdf; A.R. D'Augelli et al., Lesbian and Gay Youth's Aspirations for Marriage and Raising Children, 1 J. LGBT Issues Counseling 77 (2007).

11. See A.W. Fingerhut & L.A. Peplau, Same-Sex Romantic Relationships, in Handbook of Psychology and Sexual Orientation 165 (C.J. Patterson & A.R.

D'Augelli eds., 2013); L.A. Peplau & A.W. Fingerhut, The Close Relationships of Lesbians and Gay Men, 58 Ann. Rev. Psychol. 405 (2007); L.A. Peplau & N. Ghavami, Gay, Lesbian, and Bisexual Relationships, in Encyclopedia of Human Relationships (H.T. Reis & S. Sprecher eds., 2009).

12. Herek et al., Demographic, supra note 7; T.C. Mills et al., Health-Related Characteristics of Men Who Have Sex with Men: A Comparison of Those Living in "Gay Ghettos" with Those Living Elsewhere, 91 Am. J. Pub. Health 980, 982 (Table 1) (2001); S.D. Cochran et al., Prevalence of Mental Disorders, Psychological Distress, and Mental Services Use Among Lesbian, Gay, and Bisexual Adults in the United States, 71 J. Consulting & Clinical Psychol. 53, 56 (2003); Henry J. Kaiser Fam. Found., supra note 11.

13. Same-Sex Unmarried Partner or Spouse Households by Sex of Householder by Presence of Own Children: 2010 Census and 2010 American Community Survey, available at http://www.census.gov/hhes/samesex/files/supp-table-AFF.xls.

14. L.A. Kurdek, Change in Relationship Quality for Partners from Lesbian, Gay Male, and Heterosexual Couples, 22 J. Fam. Psychol. 701 (2008); L.A. Kurdek, Are Gay and Lesbian Cohabiting Couples Really Different from Heterosexual Married Couples?, 66 J. Marriage & Fam. 880 (2004); G.I. Roisman et al., Adult Romantic Relationships as Contexts for Human Development: A Multimethod Comparison of Same-Sex Couples with Opposite-Sex Dating, Engaged, and Married Dyads, 44 Developmental Psychol. 91 (2008); see generally L.A. Kurdek, What Do We Know About Gay and Lesbian Couples?, 14 Current Directions Psychol. Sci. 251 (2005); Peplau & Fingerhut, supra note 12; Peplau & Ghavami, supra note 12.

15. K.F. Balsam et al., Three-Year Follow-Up of Same-Sex Couples Who Had Civil Unions in Vermont, Same-Sex Couples Not in Civil Unions, and Heterosexual Married Couples, 44 Developmental Psychol. 102 (2008); Kurdek, Change in Relationship Quality, supra note 15; L.A. Peplau & K.P. Beals, The Family Lives of Lesbians and Gay Men, in Handbook of Family Communication 233, 236 (A.L. Vangelisti ed., 2004).

16. E. Durkheim, Suicide: A Study in Sociology 259 (J.A. Spaulding & G. Simpson trans., Glencoe, Ill.: Free Press 1951) (original work published 1897).

17. P. Berger & H. Kellner, Marriage and the Construction of Reality: An Exercise in the Microsociology of Knowledge, 12 Diogenes 1 (1964).

18. W.R. Gove et al., The Effect of Marriage on the Well-Being of Adults: A Theoretical Analysis, 11 J. Fam. Issues 4, 16 (1990).

19. See S. Stack & J.R. Eshleman, Marital Status and Happiness: A 17-Nation Study, 60 J. Marriage & Fam. 527 (1998); R.P.D. Burton, Global Integrative Meaning as a Mediating Factor in the Relationship Between Social Roles and Psychological Distress, 39 J. Health & Soc. Behav. 201 (1998); Gove et al., supra note 19, at 5.

20. Researchers recognize that comparisons between married and unmarried heterosexual couples are complicated by the possibility that observed differences might be due to self-selection. After extensive study, however, researchers have concluded that benefits associated with marriage result largely from the institution itself rather than self-selection. See, e.g., Gove et al., supra note 19, at 10; J.E. Murray, Marital Protection and Marital Selection: Evidence from a Historical-Prospective Sample of American Men, 37 Demography 511 (2000). It is reasonable to expect that same-sex couples who choose to marry, like their heterosexual counterparts, will benefit from the institution of marriage itself.

21. See N.J. Johnson et al., Marital Status and Mortality: The National Longitudinal Mortality Study, 10 Annals Epidemiology 224 (2000); C.E. Ross et al., The Impact of the Family on Health: The Decade in Review, 52 J. Marriage & Fam. 1059 (1990); R.W. Simon, Revisiting the Relationships Among Gender, Marital Status, and Mental Health, 107 Am. J. Soc. 1065 (2002).

22. See supra note 20; see also S.L. Brown, The Effect of Union Type on Psychological Well-Being: Depression Among Cohabitors Versus Marrieds, 41 J. Health & Soc. Behav. 241 (2000). But see, e.g., C.E. Ross, Reconceptualizing Marital Status as a Continuum of Social Attachment, 57 J. Marriage & Fam. 129 (1995) (failing to detect significant differences in depression between married heterosexuals and comparable cohabiting heterosexual couples).

23. See W.R. Gove et al., Does Marriage Have Positive Effects on the Psychological Well-Being of the Individual?, 24 J. Health & Soc. Behav. 122 (1983); K. Williams, Has the Future of Marriage Arrived? A Contemporary Examination of Gender, Marriage, and Psychological Well-Being, 44 J. Health & Soc. Behav. 470 (2003); J.K. Kiecolt-Glaser & T.L. Newton, Marriage and Health: His and Hers, 127 Psychol. Bull. 472 (2001).

24. See G. Levinger, Marital Cohesiveness and Dissolution: An Integrative Review, 27 J. Marriage & Fam. 19 (1965); J.M. Adams & W.H. Jones, The Conceptualization of Marital Commitment: An Integrative Analysis, 72 J. Personality & Soc. Psychol. 1177 (1997).

25. See, e.g., D. Previti & P.R. Amato, Why Stay Married? Rewards, Barriers, and Marital Stability, 65 J. Marriage & Fam. 561 (2003).

26. See T.B. Heaton & S.L. Albrecht, Stable Unhappy Marriages, 53 J. Marriage & Fam. 747 (1991); L.K. White & A. Booth, Divorce Over the Life Course: The Role of Marital Happiness, 12 J. Fam. Issues 5 (1991).

27. L.A. Kurdek, Relationship Outcomes and Their Predictors: Longitudinal Evidence from Heterosexual Married, Gay Cohabiting, and Lesbian Cohabiting Couples, 60 J. Marriage & Fam. 553 (1998).

28. One unreplicated 1996 Australian study purports to show deficits in lesbian and gay parents and their children. See S. Sarantakos, Children in Three Contexts: Family, Education and Social Development, 21 Child. Australia 23 (1996). But the anomalous Sarantakos results are likely the result of multiple methodological problems, especially confounding the effects of parental sexual orientation with the effects of parental divorce, which is known to correlate with poor adjustment and academic performance. See, e.g., Amato, supra note 34. Some commentators have cited publications by Paul Cameron, but his work has been repeatedly discredited for bias and inaccuracy. See G.M. Herek, Bad Science in the Service of Stigma: A Critique of the Cameron Group's Survey Studies, in Stigma and Sexual Orientation: Understanding Prejudice Against Lesbians, Gay Men, and Bisexuals 223 (G.M. Herek ed., 1998); Baker v. Wade, 106 F.R.D. 526, 536 (N.D. Tex. 1985) (ruling that Cameron made "misrepresentations" to the court).

29. See Am. Med. Ass'n, Policy H-60.940, Partner Co-Adoption, available at http://www.ama-assn.org/ama/pub/about-ama/our-people/member-groups-sections/glbt-advisory-committee/ama-policy-regarding-sexual-orientation.page.

30. See E. Goffman, Stigma: Notes on the Management of Spoiled Identity (1963); B.G. Link & J.C. Phelan, Conceptualizing Stigma, 27 Ann. Rev. Soc. 363 (2001); J. Crocker et al., Social Stigma, in 2 The Handbook of Social Psychology 504 (D.T. Gilbert et al. eds., 4th ed. 1998); Am. Med. Ass'n, Policy H- 65.973, Health Care Disparities in Same-Sex Partner Households, available at http://www.ama-assn.org/ama/pub/about-ama/our-people/member-groups-sections/glbt-advisory-committee/ama-policy-regarding-sexual-orientation.page (recognizing that "exclusion from civil marriage contributes to health care disparities affecting same-sex households").

31. Goffman, supra note 65, at 5.

32. A national survey of a representative sample of gay, lesbian, and bisexual adults found that 21% of them had been the target of a physical assault or property crime since age 18 because of their sexual orientation. Thirty-eight percent of gay men had been the target of assault or property crime because of their sexual orientation. Eighteen percent of gay men and 16% of lesbians reported they had experienced discrimination in housing or employment. G.M. Herek, Hate Crimes and Stigma-Related Experiences Among Sexual Minority Adults in the United States: Prevalence Estimates from a National Probability Sample, 24 J. Interpersonal Violence 54 (2009); see also G.M. Herek et al., Psychological Sequelae of Hate-Crime Victimization Among Lesbian, Gay, and Bisexual Adults, 67 J. Consulting & Clinical Psychol. 945, 948 (1999); M.V.L. Badgett, Money, Myths, and Change: The Economic Lives of Lesbians and Gay Men (2001).

THE AMERICAN PSYCHOLOGICAL ASSOCIATION is the largest scientific and professional organization representing psychology in the United States. They are joined in this brief by the American Medical Association, the American Academy of Pediatrics, the California Medical Association, the American Psychiatric Association, the American Psychoanalytic Association, the American Association for Marriage and Family Therapy, the National Association of Social Workers and its California chapter, and the California Psychological Association.

EXPLORING THE ISSUE

Is It Morally Right to Prohibit Same-Sex Marriage?

Critical Thinking and Reflection

1. Do you believe that the morality of homosexual activity is relevant to governmental recognition of same-sex marriage? Why or why not?
2. The debate over same-sex marriage is often framed in terms of the competing interests of the individual, who wishes to exercise the freedom to choose a spouse, and the state, which seeks to promote the welfare of its citizens. How would you balance these interests? Do these interests really conflict?
3. What actions, if any, do you recommend the government take to reduce the negative impact of single parenthood on society? Do these actions include a specific governmental policy regarding marriage, either same-sex marriage or opposite-sex marriage? Why or why not?
4. How might the arguments in favor of same-sex marriage be extended to polygamy or other non-traditional forms of marriage? Should the government recognize or prohibit these forms of marriage?

Is There Common Ground?

The authors draw different conclusions regarding same-sex marriage in part because their arguments emphasize different issues. It would be interesting to reflect on each author's attitude toward the central issues raised by the other. What would Alvaré say about discrimination against homosexuals? What would the APA say about the desirability of linking marriage, sex, and procreation? There could well be agreement between the authors on the legitimacy of these interests, even if this agreement does not result in a consensus on same-sex marriage.

One position that neither author addresses is the belief that government should not be involved in marriage at all. Proponents of this view focus on the distinction between a civil union and a marriage. They assert that the state should authorize civil unions for both opposite-sex and same-sex couples who desire the advantages of a publicly recognized relationship. Couples who further desire that their union be called a marriage would be free to have their relationship blessed by the faith community of their choice. In this way, same-sex couples would have the freedom to marry in any amenable faith community and the state would protect its interests by providing incentives for couples to remain in long-term stable relationships.

Another argument that may have the potential to create common ground on the issue of same-sex marriage has to do with the interests of society in fostering stable households. While same-sex couples do not procreate directly, recent developments in reproductive technology, such as surrogate pregnancy and in-vitro fertilization, can enable them to become parents; they can also offer two-parent homes to children in need of foster care or adoption. Offering same-sex couples the option of long term, publicly recognized relationships can help the state address its interest in the generation of new citizens. Moreover, by permitting same-sex couples to marry, the state might help restore, rather than threaten, the stability of marriage and thereby promote the welfare of its poorest citizens.

Additional Resources

Geroge Chauncey, *Why Marriage? The History Shaping Today's Debate over Gay Equality* (Basic Books, 2004)

David Moats, *Civil War: A Battle for Gay Marriage* (Harcourt, 2004)

The TFP Committee on American Issues, *Defending a Higher Law: Why We Must Resist Same-Sex "Marriage" and the Homosexual Movement* (The American Society for the Defense of Tradition, Family and Property, 2004)

Evan Wolfson, *Why Marriage Matters: America, Equality, and Gay People's Right to Marry* (Simon & Schuster, 2004)

Internet References . . .

Ethics Updates: Sexual Orientation

http://ethics.sandiego.edu/Applied/
SexualOrientation/index.asp

Should Gay Marriage Be Legal?

http://gaymarriage.procon.org/

The Pew Research Center: Gay Marriage and Homosexuality

www.pewresearch.org/topics/gay-marriage
-and-homosexuality/

Selected, Edited, and with Issue Framing Material by:
Owen M. Smith, *Stephen F. Austin State University*
and
Anne Collins Smith, *Stephen F. Austin State University*

ISSUE

Is it Immoral to Clone Human Beings?

YES: **Michael J. Sandel**, from "The Ethical Implications of Human Cloning," *Perspectives in Biology and Medicine* (2005)

NO: **John A. Robertson**, from "Human Cloning and the Challenge of Regulation," *The New England Journal of Medicine* (1998)

Learning Outcomes

After reading this issue, you will be able to:

- Explain the benefits that may be provided by new developments in human cloning.
- Explain the dangers that may be posed by new developments in human cloning.
- Formulate your own position on human cloning and identify evidence supporting your position.
- Identify the main objections to your position and formulate responses to these objections.

ISSUE SUMMARY

YES: Political philosopher Michael J. Sandel argues that much of the talk about cloning revolves around a few limited concepts (e.g., rights, autonomy, and the supposed unnaturalness of asexual reproduction) that are inadequate and fail to express what is really wrong with cloning. We need, instead, to address fundamental questions about our stance toward nature.

NO: Law professor John A. Robertson maintains that there should not be a complete ban on human cloning but that regulatory policy should be focused on ensuring that it is performed in a responsible manner.

The issue of human cloning requires careful consideration. Each person is believed to be uniquely valuable. Also, many prefer to differentiate humans from animals. If it is accepted that the same technology that allows for the cloning of sheep can also be applied to the cloning of humans, both of these ideas are brought into question. In light of animal cloning, the existence of humans seems to be based on the very same biological processes that exist in sheep and other animals. And if there can be such a thing as human cloning, what happens to the idea that we are all unique? What happens to the idea that we all have our individual lives to lead, and that each person is responsible for his or her own choices?

Moreover, cloning can change ideas about reproduction. In cloning, no male is required. Consider the case of Dolly, the sheep cloned from the cell of an adult ewe. An egg cell, taken from a female sheep, had its nucleus removed; this was replaced with the nucleus of a cell taken from another female sheep. Then the result was implanted and grew in the uterus of a third female sheep, who eventually gave birth to Dolly. Normally, a newborn has genetic input from both the father's side and the mother's side, with the mother supplying the egg cell. But the original egg cell that was used in Dolly's case contributed almost nothing in this regard. The nucleus from the cell of the other sheep contained virtually all of the genetic input for Dolly.

Identical twins are familiar cases of human beings who, like clones, share a common genetic input. When environmental factors connected with identical twins are closely the same, and when they have similar clothes, haircut, etc., they can be difficult to tell apart. But when the environmental factors that impinge on their lives are quite different—as in the case of twins separated at birth—the twins can be quite different in obvious physical ways.

Physical aspects such as height have both genetic and environmental inputs; two people with the same genetic input can have quite different heights if environmental conditions (e.g., their diets) are different.

In some ways, clones are like identical twins, but in many cases there would be far less resemblance between clones than between identical twins, since they would be subject to very different environmental factors. Being conceived and born at different times—perhaps years or even decades apart from each other—they may have radically different environmental input.

Human cloning can be seen as beneficial. Cloning may provide another way for people to utilize technological assistance in reproduction. For example, a couple who could not have children naturally might consider a range of options, including cloning. Some maintain that is a relatively innocent use of human cloning, and can benefit those who are infertile.

Some object to cloning by citing other possible scenarios. Suppose a person wanted numerous clones of himself or herself. Suppose a sports star desired a clone who would then be expected to achieve greatness in sports. Suppose parents wanted a replacement for a child that they had lost, or want a child who could serve as a bone marrow or organ donor. These cases may give some pause, since the motivation for cloning appears to be questionable.

To counter this argument, it is stated that proper regulation would prevent these types of scenarios from occurring. Instead, cloning would be performed only under the correct circumstances, and would promote individual happiness.

In the following selections, Michael Sandel argues that there is something deeply wrong with human cloning. What is wrong goes beyond questions of rights, autonomy, and cloning's supposed "unnaturalness." It involves our fundamental attitudes toward nature and human existence. John A. Robertson counters that human cloning, if properly regulated, need not and would not be sinister. Properly regulated, human cloning should be permitted.

YES ↵

Michael J. Sandel

The Ethical Implications of Human Cloning

In this essay, I will consider the ethics of reproductive and therapeutic cloning. But I want also to advance a more general claim: that the cloning issue, and related debates about genetic engineering, will change the way philosophers think about their subject. Much of the debate about cloning and genetic engineering is conducted in the familiar language of autonomy, consent, and individual rights. Defenders of "liberal eugenics" argue that parents should be free to enhance the genetic traits of their children for the sake of improving their life prospects (Agar 1999; Buchanan et al. 2000; Dworkin 2000). Ronald Dworkin, for example argues that there is nothing wrong with the ambition "to make the lives of future generations of human beings longer and more full of talent and hence achievement." In fact, he maintains, the principle of ethical individualism makes such efforts obligatory (Dworkin 2000, p. 452). Many opponents of cloning and genetic engineering also invoke the language of autonomy and rights. For example, Jurgen Habermas (2003) worries that even favorable genetic enhancements may impair the autonomy and individuality of children by pointing them toward particular life choices, hence violating their right to choose their life plans for themselves.

But talk of autonomy and rights does not address the deepest questions posed by cloning. In order to grapple with the ethical implications of cloning and genetic engineering, we need to confront questions largely lost from view in the modern world—questions about the moral status of nature and about the proper stance of human beings toward the given world. Since questions such as these verge on theology, or at least involve a certain view of the best way for human beings to live their lives, modern philosophers and political theorists tend to shrink from them. But our new powers of biotechnology make these questions unavoidable.

In the United States today, no federal law prohibits human cloning, either for purposes of reproduction or for purposes of biomedical research. This is not because most people favor reproductive cloning. To the contrary, public opinion and almost all elected officials oppose it. But there is strong disagreement about whether to permit cloning for biomedical research. And the opponents of cloning for biomedical research have so far been unwilling to support a separate ban on reproductive cloning, as Britain has enacted. Because of this stalemate, no federal ban on cloning has been enacted.

The Ethics of Reproductive Cloning

I turn first to the ethics of reproductive cloning, and then to cloning for biomedical research. The case for banning human reproductive cloning is not difficult to make, at least for now. Most scientists agree that it is unsafe and likely to lead to serious abnormalities and birth defects. But suppose that, one day, producing a baby through cloning were no more risky than natural reproduction. Many believe—and I agree—that it would still be ethically objectionable. But it is not easy to say why.

The autonomy argument against cloning is not persuasive, for it wrongly implies that, absent a genetically designing parent, children can choose their physical characteristics for themselves. But none of us has a right to choose our genetic inheritance. The alternative to a cloned or genetically enhanced child is not an autonomous one, but a child at the mercy of the genetic lottery.

Some argue that cloning is wrong because it departs from natural, sexual procreation (Kass and Wilson 1998). But this objection also fails to reach the heart of the matter. What makes reproductive cloning morally troubling is that its primary purpose is to create children of a certain kind. In this respect, it is similar to other forms of genetic engineering by which parents seek to choose the traits of their children—sex, eye color, perhaps one day even their intellectual attributes, athletic prowess, and musical ability. Although a few eccentric narcissists might aspire to create genetic replicas of themselves, the real market for designer children lies elsewhere, in the desire

Sandel, Michael J. As seen in *Perspectives in Biology and Medicine*, Spring 2005, pp. 241–247. Original to *Jahrbuch für Wissenschaft und Ethik 8* (December 2003), pp. 5–10. Copyright ©2003 by Walter de Gruyter GmbH. Reprinted by permission.

of parents to produce children with genetic traits superior to their own.

The desire to control the genetic characteristics of one's offspring points to the heart of the ethical issue. The moral problem with reproductive cloning lies not in its asexual character, but in its assault on the understanding of children as gifts rather than possessions, or projects of our will, or vehicles for our happiness.

It might be replied that cloning and genetic engineering are in principle no different from other ways in which parents go to great lengths to produce children of a certain kind, or "designer children." But rather than giving us reason to embrace cloning, this observation may give us reason to worry about existing practices of childrearing.

What is most troubling about human cloning and bioengineering is not that they represent a radical departure, but that they carry to full expression troubling tendencies already present in our culture, especially in the way we regard and treat children. We have already traveled some distance down the path of regarding children as vehicles for our own ambitions or fulfillment. Consider the chilling discrepancy in sex ratios in China, South Korea, and parts of India, where boys now outnumber girls by up to 30% (Eberstadt 2002). But think also of the enormous pressure parents put on children in the United States and many other Western societies to qualify for admission to the best schools—not only at the university level, but even, in Manhattan at least, at the preschool level. Sometimes, the drive to produce successful children begins even earlier. The Harvard college newspaper recently carried an advertisement from a couple seeking an egg donor. They did not want just any egg donor. The ad specified that the donor should be attractive, athletic, at least 5 feet, 10 inches tall, and with a college entrance exam score of 1400 or above. For an egg from a donor meeting these stringent qualifications, the couple was offering a payment of $50,000 (Kolata 1999).

The notion that the project of mastery and choice is subject to certain limits is at odds with the spirit of contemporary liberalism. That is why many who are uneasy with human cloning try to cast their objections in the language of autonomy and rights, arguing that choosing the traits of one's children, by cloning or otherwise, violates their rights. The European Assembly has maintained, for example, that human cloning is wrong because it is a violation of human rights. But the language of rights misses the point. The problem is not that parents usurp the autonomy of the child they design:

it is not as if the child could otherwise choose her gender, height, and eye color for herself. The problem lies in the hubris of the designing parents, in their drive to master the mystery of birth. Even if this hubris does not make parents tyrants to their children, it disfigures the relation of parent and child. It deprives the parents of the humility and enlarged human sympathies that an openness to the unbidden "otherness" of our progeny can cultivate.

Like the autonomy objection, the argument that focuses on the asexual character of reproductive cloning misses the point. Understood simply as a departure from sexual procreation, cloning would not represent a serious threat. Sex will survive perfectly well on its own—without the help of federal legislation. By contrast, the sense of life as a gift we cannot summon or control is fragile and vulnerable. In the face of the Promethean drive to mastery that animates modern societies, an appreciation of the giftedness of life is in constant need of support.

The Ethics of Cloning for Biomedical Research

I turn now to the ethics of cloning for biomedical research. It is here that the greatest disagreement prevails. The U.S. Senate is split between those who want to ban all cloning and those who want to ban reproductive cloning but not cloning for stem cell research and regenerative medicine. (For the American debate on cloning, see President's Council 2002.) As in the case of reproductive cloning, the concepts of autonomy and rights cannot by themselves resolve the moral question. In order to assess the moral permissibility of cloning for stem cell research, we need to determine the moral status of the early embryo. If the six-day, pre-implantation embryo (or blastocyst) is morally equivalent to a person, then it is wrong to extract stem cells from it, even for the sake of curing devastating diseases such as Parkinson's, Alzheimer's, or diabetes. If the embryo is a person, then not only should all therapeutic cloning be banned, so also should all embryonic stem cell research.

Before turning to the moral status of the embryo, I would like to consider one influential argument against cloning for biomedical research that stops short of opposing embryonic stem cell research as such. Some opponents of research cloning, troubled by the deliberate creation of embryos for research, support embryonic stem cell research, provided it uses "spare" embryos left over from fertility clinics (Sandel 2002). Since in vitro fertilization (IVF) clinics (at least in the United States) create many more fertilized eggs than are ultimately implanted, some argue that there is nothing wrong with using those spares for research: if excess embryos would be discarded anyway, why not use them (with donor consent) for potentially life-saving research?

This seems to be a sensible distinction. But on closer examination, it does not hold up. The distinction fails because it begs the question whether the "spare" embryos should be created in the first place. If it is immoral to create and sacrifice embryos for the sake of curing or treating devastating diseases, why isn't it also objectionable to create and discard spare IVF embryos in the course of treating infertility? Or, to look at the argument from the opposite end, if the creation and sacrifice of embryos in IVF is morally acceptable, why isn't the creation and sacrifice of embryos for stem cell research also acceptable? After all, both practices serve worthy ends, and curing diseases such as Parkinson's is at least as important as enabling infertile couples to have genetically related children.

Of course, bioethics is not only about ends, but also about means. Those who oppose creating embryos for research argue that doing so is exploitative and fails to accord embryos the respect they are due. But the same argument could be made against fertility treatments that create excess embryos bound for destruction. In fact, a recent study found that some 400,000 frozen embryos are languishing in American fertility clinics, with another 52,000 in the United Kingdom and 71,000 in Australia (Wade 2003).

If my argument is correct, it shows only that stem cell research on IVF spares and on embryos created for research (whether natural or cloned) are morally on a par. This conclusion can be accepted by people who hold very different views about the moral status of the embryo. If cloning for stem cell research violates the respect the embryo is due, then so does stem cell research on IVF spares, and so does any version of IVF that creates and discards excess embryos. If, morally speaking, these practices stand or fall together, it remains to ask whether they stand or fall. And that depends on the moral status of the embryo.

The Moral Status of the Embryo

There are three possible ways of conceiving the moral status of the embryo: as a thing, as a person, or as something in between. To regard an embryo as a mere thing, open to any use we may desire or devise, is, it seems to me, to miss its significance as nascent human life. One need not regard an embryo as a full human person in order to believe that it is due a certain respect. Personhood is not the only warrant for respect: we consider it a failure of respect when a thoughtless

hiker carves his initials in an ancient sequoia, not because we regard the sequoia as a person, but because we consider it a natural wonder worthy of appreciation and awe—modes of regard inconsistent with treating it as a billboard or defacing it for the sake of petty vanity. To respect the old growth forest does not mean that no tree may ever be felled or harvested for human purposes. Respecting the forest may be consistent with using it. But the purposes should be weighty and appropriate to the wondrous nature of the thing.

One way to oppose a degrading, objectifying stance toward nascent human life is to attribute full personhood to the embryo. I will call this the "equal moral status" view. One way of assessing this view is to play out its full implications, in order to assess their plausibility. Consider the following hypothetical: a fire breaks out in a fertility clinic, and you have time to save either a five-year-old girl or a tray of 10 embryos. Would it be wrong to save the girl?[1]

A further implication of the equal moral status view is that harvesting stem cells from a six-day-old blastocyst is as morally abhorrent as harvesting organs from a baby. But is it? If so, the penalty provided in the proposed U.S. anti-cloning legislation—a $1 million fine and 10 years in prison—is woefully inadequate. If embryonic stem cell research is morally equivalent to yanking organs from babies, it should be treated as a grisly form of murder, and the scientist who performs it should face life imprisonment or the death penalty.

A further source of difficulty for the equal moral status view lies in the fact that, in natural pregnancies, at least half of all embryos either fail to implant or are otherwise lost. It might be replied that a high rate of infant mortality does not justify infanticide. But the way we respond to the natural loss of embryos or even early miscarriages suggests that we do not regard these events as the moral or religious equivalent of infant mortality. Otherwise, wouldn't we carry out the same burial rituals for the loss of an embryo that we observe for the death of a child?

The conviction that the embryo is a person derives support not only from certain religious doctrines but also from the Kantian assumption that the moral universe is divided in binary terms: everything is either a person, worthy of respect, or a thing, open to use. But this dualism is overdrawn.

The way to combat the instrumentalizing impulse of modern technology and commerce is not to insist on an all-or-nothing ethic of respect for persons that consigns the rest of life to a utilitarian calculus. Such an ethic risks turning every moral question into a battle over the bounds of personhood. We would do better to cultivate a more expansive appreciation of life as a gift that commands our reverence and restricts our use. Human cloning to create designer babies is the ultimate expression of the hubris that marks the loss of reverence for life as a gift. But stem cell research to cure debilitating disease, using six-day-old blastocysts, cloned or uncloned, is a noble exercise of our human ingenuity to promote healing and to play our part in repairing the given world.

Those who warn of slippery slopes, embryo farms, and the commodification of ova and zygotes are right to worry but wrong to assume that cloning for biomedical research necessarily opens us to these dangers. Rather than ban stem cell cloning and other forms of embryo research, we should allow it to proceed subject to regulations that embody the moral restraint appropriate to the mystery of the first stirrings of human life. Such regulations should include licensing requirements for embryo research projects and fertility clinics, restrictions on the commodification of eggs and sperm, and measures to prevent proprietary interests from monopolizing access to stem cell lines. This approach, it seems to me, offers the best hope of avoiding the wanton use of nascent human life and making these biomedical advances a blessing for health rather than an episode in the erosion of our human sensibilities.

Note

1. I am indebted to George Annas for this hypothetical (see Annas 1989).

References

Agar, N. 1999. Liberal eugenics. In *Bioethics,* ed. H. Kuhse and P. Singer. Oxford: Blackwell.

Annas, G. J. 1989. A French homunculus in a Tennessee court. *Hastings Cent Rep* 19(6): 20–22.

Buchanan, A., et al. 2000. *From chance to choice: Genetics and justice.* Cambridge: Cambridge Univ. Press.

Dworkin, R. 2000. Playing God: Genes, clones, and luck. In *Sovereign virtue: The theory and practice of equality,* 427–52. Cambridge: Harvard Univ. Press.

Eberstadt, N. 2002. Testimony to President's Council on Bioethics, Oct. 17. . . .

Habermas, J. 2003. *The future of human nature.* Cambridge, UK: Polity Press.

Kass, L. R., and J. Q. Wilson. 1998. *The ethics of human cloning.* Washington, DC: AEI Press.

Kolata, G. 1999. $50,000 offered to tall, smart egg donor. *NY Times,* March 3.

President's Council on Bioethics. 2002. *Human cloning and human dignity: The report of the President's Council on Bioethics.* Washington, DC: President's Council on Bioethics. Repr. New York: Public Affairs, 2002. . . .

Sandel, M. J. 2002. The anti-cloning conundrum. *NY Times,* May 28.

Wade, N. 2003. Clinics hold more embryos than had been thought. *NY Times,* May 9.

Michael J. Sandel is the Anne T. and Robert M. Bass Professor of Government at Harvard University, where he has taught political philosophy since 1980. He is the author of *Liberalism and the Limits of Justice* (Cambridge University Press, 1982, 2nd edition, 1997; translated into eight foreign languages), *Democracy's Discontent: America in Search of a Public Philosophy* (Harvard University Press, 1996), *Public Philosophy: Essays on Morality in Politics* (Harvard University Press, 2005), *The Case Against Perfection: Ethics in the Age of Genetic Engineering* (Harvard University Press, 2007), and *Justice: What's the Right Thing to Do?* (Farrar, Straus and Giroux, 2009).

John A. Robertson

→ **NO**

Human Cloning and the Challenge of Regulation

The birth of Dolly, the sheep cloned from a mammary cell of an adult ewe, has initiated a public debate about human cloning. Although cloning of humans may never be clinically feasible, discussion of the ethical, legal, and social issues raised is important. Cloning is just one of several techniques potentially available to select, control, or alter the genome of offspring.[1-3] The development of such technology poses an important social challenge: how to ensure that the technology is used to enhance, rather than limit, individual freedom and welfare.

A key ethical question is whether a responsible couple, interested in rearing healthy offspring biologically related to them, might ethically choose to use cloning (or other genetic-selection techniques) for that purpose. The answer should take into account the benefits sought through the use of the techniques and any potential harm to offspring or to other interests.

The most likely uses of cloning would be far removed from the bizarre or horrific scenarios that initially dominated media coverage.[4] Theoretically, cloning would enable rich or powerful persons to clone themselves several times over, and commercial entrepreneurs might hire women to bear clones of sports or entertainment celebrities to be sold to others to rear. But current reproductive techniques can also be abused, and existing laws against selling children would apply to those created by cloning.

There is no reason to think that the ability to clone humans will cause many people to turn to cloning when other methods of reproduction would enable them to have healthy children. Cloning a human being by somatic-cell nuclear transfer, for example, would require a consenting person as a source of DNA, eggs to be enucleated and then fused with the DNA, a woman who would carry and deliver the child, and a person or couple to raise the child. Given this reality, cloning is most likely to be sought by couples who, because of infertility, a high risk of severe genetic disease, or other factors, cannot or do not wish to conceive a child.

Several plausible scenarios can be imagined. Rather than use sperm, egg, or embryo from anonymous donors, couples who are infertile as a result of gametic insufficiency might choose to clone one of the partners. If the husband were the source of the DNA and the wife provided the egg that received the nuclear transfer and then gestated the fetus, they would have a child biologically related to each of them and would not need to rely on anonymous gamete or embryo donation. Of course, many infertile couples might still prefer gamete or embryo donation or adoption. But there is nothing inherently wrong in wishing to be biologically related to one's children, even when this goal cannot be achieved through sexual reproduction.

A second plausible application would be for a couple at high risk of having offspring with a genetic disease.[5] Couples in this situation must now choose whether to risk the birth of an affected child, to undergo prenatal or preimplantation diagnosis and abortion or the discarding of embryos, to accept gamete donation, to seek adoption, or to remain childless. If cloning were available, however, some couples, in line with prevailing concepts of kinship, family, and parenting, might strongly prefer to clone one of themselves or another family member. Alternatively, if they already had a healthy child, they might choose to use cloning to create a later-born twin of that child. In the more distant future, it is even possible that the child whose DNA was replicated would not have been born healthy but would have been made healthy by gene therapy after birth.

A third application relates to obtaining tissue or organs for transplantation. A child who needed an organ or tissue transplant might lack a medically suitable donor. Couples in this situation have sometimes conceived a child coitally in the hope that he or she would have the correct tissue type to serve, for example, as a bone marrow donor for an older sibling.[6, 7] If the child's disease was not genetic, a couple might prefer to clone the affected child to be sure that the tissue would match.

It might eventually be possible to procure suitable tissue or organs by cloning the source DNA only to the point at which stem cells or other material might be obtained for transplantation, thus avoiding the need to bring a child into the world for the sake of obtaining tissue.[8] Cloning a person's cells up to the embryo stage might provide a source of stem cells or tissue for the person cloned. Cloning might also be used to enable a couple to clone a dead or dying child so as to have that child live on in some closely related form, to obtain sufficient numbers of embryos for transfer and pregnancy, or to eliminate mitochondrial disease.[5]

Most, if not all, of the potential uses of cloning are controversial, usually because of the explicit copying of the genome. As the National Bioethics Advisory Commission noted, in addition to concern about physical safety and eugenics, somatic-cell cloning raises issues of the individuality, autonomy, objectification, and kinship of the resulting children.[5] In other instances, such as the production of embryos to serve as tissue banks, the ethical issue is the sacrifice of embryos created solely for that purpose.

Given the wide leeway now granted couples to use assisted reproduction and prenatal genetic selection in forming families, cloning should not be rejected in all circumstances as unethical or illegitimate. The manipulation of embryos and the use of gamete donors and surrogates are increasingly common. Most fetuses conceived in the United States and Western Europe are now screened for genetic or chromosomal anomalies. Before conception, screening to identify carriers of genetic diseases is widespread.[9] Such practices also deviate from conventional notions of reproduction, kinship, and medical treatment of infertility, yet they are widely accepted.

Despite the similarity of cloning to current practices, however, the dissimilarities should not be overlooked. The aim of most other forms of assisted reproduction is the birth of a child who is a descendant of at least one member of the couple, not an identical twin. Most genetic selection acts negatively to identify and screen out unwanted traits such as genetic disease, not positively to choose or replicate the genome as in somatic-cell cloning.[3] It is not clear, however, why a child's relation to his or her rearing parents must always be that of sexually reproduced descendant when such a relationship is not possible because of infertility or other factors. Indeed, in gamete donation and adoption, although sexual reproduction is involved, a full descendant

relation between the child and both rearing parents is lacking. Nor should the difference between negative and positive means of selecting children determine the ethical or social acceptability of cloning or other techniques. In both situations, a deliberate choice is made so that a child is born with one genome rather than another or is not born at all.

Is cloning sufficiently similar to current assisted-reproduction and genetic-selection practices to be treated similarly as a presumptively protected exercise of family or reproductive liberty?[10] Couples who request cloning in the situations I have described are seeking to rear healthy children with whom they will have a genetic or biologic tie, just as couples who conceive their children sexually do. Whether described as "replication" or as "reproduction," the resort to cloning is similar enough in purpose and effects to other reproduction and genetic-selection practices that it should be treated similarly. Therefore, a couple should be free to choose cloning unless there are compelling reasons for thinking that this would create harm that the other procedures would not cause.[10]

The concern of the National Bioethics Advisory Commission about the welfare of the clone reflects two types of fear. The first is that a child with the same nuclear DNA as another person, who is thus that person's later-born identical twin, will be so severely harmed by the identity of nuclear DNA between them that it is morally preferable, if not obligatory, that the child not be born at all.[5] In this case the fear is that the later-born twin will lack individuality or the freedom to create his or her own identity because of confusion or expectations caused by having the same DNA as another person.[5, 11]

This claim does not withstand the close scrutiny that should precede interference with a couple's freedom to bear and rear biologically related children.[10] Having the same genome as another person is not in itself harmful, as widespread experience with monozygotic twins shows. Being a twin does not deny either twin his or her individuality or freedom, and twins often have a special intimacy or closeness that few non-twin siblings can experience.[12] There is no reason to think that being a later-born identical twin resulting from cloning would change the overall assessment of being a twin.

Differences in mitochondria and the uterine and childhood environment will undercut problems of similarity and minimize the risk of overidentification with the first twin. A clone of Smith may look like Smith, but he or she will not be Smith and will lack many of Smith's phenotypic characteristics. The effects of having similar DNA will also depend on the length of time before the second twin is born, on whether the twins are raised together, on whether they are informed that they are genetic twins, on whether other people are so informed, on the beliefs that the rearing parents have about genetic influence on behavior, and on other factors. Having a previously born twin might in some circumstances also prove to be a source of support or intimacy for the later-born child.

The risk that parents or the child will overly identify the child with the DNA source also seems surmountable. Would the child invariably be expected to match the phenotypic characteristics of the DNA source, thus denying the second twin an "open future" and the freedom to develop his or her own identity?[5, 11, 13] In response to this question, one must ask whether couples who choose to clone offspring are more likely to want a child who is a mere replica of the DNA source or a child who is unique and valued for more than his or her genes. Couples may use cloning in order to ensure that the biologic child they rear is healthy, to maintain a family connection in the face of gametic infertility, or to obtain matched tissue for transplantation and yet still be responsibly committed to the welfare of their child, including his or her separate identity and interests and right to develop as he or she chooses.

The second type of fear is that parents who choose their child's genome through somatic-cell cloning will view the child as a commodity or an object to serve their own ends.[5] We do not view children born through coital or assisted reproduction as "mere means" just because people reproduce in order to have company in old age, to fulfill what they see as God's will, to prove their virility, to have heirs, to save a relationship, or to serve other selfish purposes.[14] What counts is how a child is treated after birth. Self-interested motives for having children do not prevent parents from loving children for themselves once they are born.

The use of cloning to form families in the situations I have described, though closely related to current assisted-reproduction and genetic-selection practices, does offer unique variations. The novelty of the relation—cloning in lieu of sperm donation, for example, produces a later-born identical twin raised by the older twin and his spouse—will create special psychological and social challenges. Can these challenges be successfully met, so that cloning produces net good for families and society? Given the largely positive experience with assisted-reproduction techniques that initially appeared frightening, cautious optimism is justified. We should be able to develop procedures and guidelines for cloning that will allow us to obtain its benefits while minimizing its problems and dangers.

In the light of these considerations, I would argue that a ban on privately funded cloning research is unjustified and likely to hamper important types of research.[8]

A permanent ban on the cloning of human beings, as advocated by the Council of Europe and proposed in Congress, is also unjustified.[15, 16] A more limited ban—whether for 5 years, as proposed by the National Bioethics Advisory Commission and enacted in California, or for 10 years, as in the bill of Senator Dianne Feinstein (D-Calif.) and Senator Edward M. Kennedy (D-Mass.) that is now before Congress—is also open to question.[5, 17, 18] Given the early state of cloning science and the widely shared view that the transfer of cloned embryos to the uterus before the safety and efficacy of the procedure has been established is unethical, few responsible physicians are likely to offer human cloning in the near future.[5] Nor are profit-motivated entrepreneurs, such as Richard Seed, likely to have many customers for their cloning services until the safety of the procedure is demonstrated.[19] A ban on human cloning for a limited period would thus serve largely symbolic purposes. Symbolic legislation, however, often has substantial costs.[20, 21] A government-imposed prohibition on privately funded cloning, even for a limited period, should not be enacted unless there is a compelling need. Such a need has not been demonstrated.

Rather than seek to prohibit all uses of human cloning, we should focus our attention on ensuring that cloning is done well. No physician or couple should embark on cloning without careful thought about the novel relational issues and child-rearing responsibilities that will ensue. We need regulations or guidelines to ensure safety and efficacy, fully informed consent and counseling for the couple, the consent of any person who may provide DNA, guarantees of parental rights and duties, and a limit on the number of clones from any single source.[10] It may also be important to restrict cloning to situations where there is a strong likelihood that the couple or individual initiating the procedure will also rear the resulting child. This principle will encourage a stable parenting situation and minimize the chance that cloning entrepreneurs will create clones to be sold to others.[22] As our experience grows, some restrictions on who may serve as a source of DNA for cloning (for example, a ban on cloning one's parents) may also be defensible.[10]

Cloning is important because it is the first of several positive means of genetic selection that may be sought by families seeking to have and rear healthy, biologically related offspring. In the future, mitochondrial transplantation, germ-line gene therapy, genetic enhancement, and other forms of prenatal genetic alteration may be possible.[3, 23, 24] With each new technique, as with cloning, the key question will be whether it serves important health, reproductive, or family needs and whether its benefits outweigh any likely harm. Cloning illustrates the principle that when legitimate uses of a technique are likely, regulatory policy should avoid prohibition and focus on ensuring that the technique is used responsibly for the good of those directly involved. As genetic knowledge continues to grow, the challenge of regulation will occupy us for some time to come.

References

1. Silver LM. Remaking Eden: cloning and beyond in a brave new world. New York: Avon Books, 1997.
2. Walters L, Palmer JG. The ethics of human gene therapy. New York: Oxford University Press, 1997.
3. Robertson JA. Genetic selection of offspring characteristics. Boston Univ Law Rev 1996;76:421–82.
4. Begley S. Can we clone humans? Newsweek. March 10, 1997:53–60.
5. Cloning human beings: report and recommendations of the National Bioethics Advisory Commission. Rockville, Md.: National Bioethics Advisory Commission, June 1997.
6. Robertson JA. Children of choice: freedom and the new reproductive technologies. Princeton, N.J.: Princeton University Press, 1994.
7. Kearney W, Caplan AL. Parity for the donation of bone marrow: ethical and policy considerations. In: Blank RH, Bonnicksen AL, eds. Emerging issues in biomedical policy: an annual review. Vol. 1. New York: Columbia University Press, 1992:262–85.
8. Kassirer JP, Rosenthal NA. Should human cloning research be off limits? N Engl J Med 1998;338:905–6.
9. Holtzman NA. Proceed with caution: predicting genetic risks in the recombinant DNA era. Baltimore: Johns Hopkins University Press, 1989.
10. Robertson JA. Liberty, identity, and human cloning. Texas Law Rev 1998; 77:1371–456.
11. Davis DS. What's wrong with cloning? Jurimetrics 1997;38:83–9.
12. Segal NL. Behavioral aspects of intergenerational human cloning: what twins tell us. Jurimetrics 1997;38:57–68.
13. Jonas H. Philosophical essays: from ancient creed to technological man. Englewood Cliffs, N.J.: Prentice-Hall, 1974:161.
14. Heyd D. Genethics: moral issues in the creation of people. Berkeley: University of California Press, 1992.
15. Council of Europe. Draft additional protocol to the Convention on Human Rights and Biomedicine on the prohibition of cloning human beings with explanatory report and Parliamentary Assembly opinion (adopted September 22, 1997). XXXVI International Legal Materials 1415 (1997).
16. Human Cloning Prohibition Act, H.R. 923, S. 1601 (March 5, 1997).
17. Act of Oct. 4, 1997, ch. 688, 1997 Cal. Legis. Serv. 3790 (West, WESTLAW through 1997 Sess.).
18. Prohibition on Cloning of Human Beings Act, S. 1602, 105th Cong. (1998).
19. Stolberg SG. A small spark ignites debate on laws on cloning humans. New York Times. January 19, 1998:A1.
20. Gusfield J. Symbolic crusade: status politics and the American temperance movement. Urbana: University of Illinois Press, 1963.
21. Wolf SM. Ban cloning? Why NBAC is wrong. Hastings Cent Rep 1997;27(5):12.
22. Wilson JQ. The paradox of cloning. The Weekly Standard. May 26, 1997:23–7.
23. Zhang J, Grifo J, Blaszczyk A, et al. In vitro maturation of human preovulatory oocytes reconstructed by germinal vesicle transfer. Fertil Steril 1997; 68:Suppl:S1. abstract.
24. Bonnicksen AL. Transplanting nuclei between human eggs: implications for germ-line genetics. Politics and the Life Sciences. March 1998:3–10.

JOHN A. ROBERTSON holds the Vinson and Elkins Chair at The University of Texas School of Law at Austin. He has written and lectured widely on law and bioethical issues. He is the author of two books in bioethics: *The Rights of the Critically Ill* (1983) and *Children of Choice: Freedom and the New Reproductive Technologies* (1994), and numerous articles on reproductive rights, genetics, organ transplantation, and human experimentation. He has served on or been a consultant to many national bioethics advisory bodies, and is currently Chair of the Ethics Committee of the American Society for Reproductive Medicine.

EXPLORING THE ISSUE

Is it Immoral to Clone Human Beings?

Critical Thinking and Reflection

1. What, according to Sandel, is the true difficulty with the concept of "designer children" (and indeed, with our contemporary attitude toward children in general)? How is this difficulty related to the morality of human reproductive cloning?
2. How does the moral status of a human embryo affect the morality of human reproductive cloning? How does it affect the morality of human cloning for biomedical research? Can the answers to these two questions be different? Why or why not?
3. Explain whether human reproductive cloning is morally permissible in each of the following situations: (a) infertile couples; (b) couples at high risk for having offspring with a genetic disease; (c) parents of a child in need of a compatible tissue donor. Are there any other cases in which you think that human reproductive cloning is permissible?
4. How is human reproductive cloning different from current methods of assisted reproduction and genetic selection? What is the moral significance, if any, of these differences?

Is There Common Ground?

As much as Sandel and Robertson disagree, neither would think it advisable for human cloning to proceed in a totally free and unregulated way. In addition to the difficulties they raise, others have also come to light.

One problem that might seem small at first, but is actually quite serious, is that we do not have a good way of assimilating the new ideas of cloning into our vocabulary and thought. For example, since a clone's genes come from a single original person, we may speak of the single original person as the clone's sole parent—or as the clone's identical twin. The parents of the original person are genetically the parents of the clone, which means that people can have children in this sense when they are very old or even after their death. Meanwhile, the woman who gives birth to the clone is not the clone's genetic mother, since her egg has its nuclear material entirely replaced by that of the original person.

Some say that the fact that cloning doesn't fit into our normal system for making sense of family relationships is due to the fact that cloning upsets the system in a fundamental way. But others say that the fact that our traditional vocabulary is inadequate to the system shows only that we are unprepared for this new situation, not that human cloning should be totally banned.

Additional Resources

Cloning Human Beings: Report and Recommendations of the National Bioethics Advisory Commission (Gem Publications, 1998)

Michael C. Brannigan, ed., *Ethical Issues in Human Cloning: Cross-Disciplinary Perspectives* (Seven Bridges Press, 2000)

Leon R. Kass, *Human Cloning and Human Dignity: The Report of the President's Council on Bioethics* (Public Affairs, 2002)

Aaron D. Levine, *Cloning: A Beginner's Guide* (Oneworld Publications, 2007)

Ian Wilmut and Roger Highfield, *After Dolly: The Promise and Perils of Cloning* (2007)

Internet References . . .

Ethics Updates: Bioethics, Cloning, and Reproductive Technologies

http://ethics.sandiego.edu/Applied/Bioethics/index.asp

The American Medical Association: Human Cloning

www.ama-assn.org//ama/pub/physician-resources/
medical-science/genetics-molecular-medicine/
related-policy-topics/stem-cell-research/
human-cloning.page

The Center for Ethics in Science and Technology

www.ethicscenter.net/

Unit 3

Law and Society

Aristotle famously asserted that humans are social animals. The social dimension of being human requires that we have rules that govern our behavior and interpersonal interactions. The issues addressed in this section have strongly divided our own society and challenge existing social institutions and practices.

Selected, Edited, and with Issue Framing Material by:
Owen M. Smith, *Stephen F. Austin State University*
and
Anne Collins Smith, *Stephen F. Austin State University*

ISSUE

Is Paid Organ Donation Morally Permissible?

YES: Michael B. Gill and Robert M. Sade, from "Paying for Kidneys: The Case Against Prohibition," *Kennedy Institute of Ethics Journal* (2002)

NO: Anya Adair and Stephen J. Wigmore, from "Paid Organ Donation: The Case Against," *Annals of the Royal College of Surgeons of England* (2011)

Learning Outcomes

After reading this issue, you will be able to:

- Understand the basic medical issues involved in kidney transplantation.
- Explain the potential impact of paid organ donation on the supply of organs available for transplantation.
- Explain the relevance of the concept of human dignity to paid organ donation.
- Formulate your own position on paid organ donation and identify evidence supporting your position.
- Identify the main objections to your position and formulate responses to these objections.

ISSUE SUMMARY

YES: Michael B. Gill and Robert M. Sade argue that since there are no moral prohibitions against donating kidneys for transplantation or selling blood plasma, there should be no moral prohibition against selling kidneys for transplantation. They further argue that selling a kidney does not violate a person's dignity and that a system in which a person can receive payment for a kidney is not inherently exploitive.

NO: Anya Adair and Stephen J. Wigmore argue that paid organ donation as currently practiced exploits the donors. They point to specific exploitive practices, such as withholding sufficient information for the donors to give truly informed consent. Further, they argue, any attempt to repair inequities in the system is doomed to failure because of the inherent inequity; only those under severe economic constraints will ever be willing to sell their organs.

An informed moral judgment about the sale of human organs for transplantation must be based on accurate medical information. In order to facilitate discussion of this issue, we will focus on one type of organ transplantation, the transplantation of kidneys to prevent or relieve kidney failure.

Kidneys function to remove waste and excess water from the blood, which are then excreted as urine. Humans are normally born with two kidneys, but as long as kidney function is stable, humans need only one kidney to survive. Serious health problems will arise when, owing to injury or disease, kidney function falls below a certain threshold, usually 20 percent of full kidney function. If kidney function ceases and waste products are allowed to build up in the blood, death will inevitably result. Fortunately, there are therapies to treat kidney failure. In a process known as dialysis, waste products are artificially removed from the body. The most common form of dialysis is hemodialysis, in which blood is removed from the body and passed through a machine that removes waste products; the cleansed blood is then returned to the body. Patients undergoing hemodialysis must usually go to a dialysis center three times per week for the procedure, which typically requires three or four hours to complete. Another form of dialysis does not require patients to visit a dialysis center. In peritoneal dialysis, a fluid that absorbs waste products is introduced into the body and then drained away; patients can learn to perform this procedure on themselves, although in continuous ambulatory peritoneal dialysis (CAPD), the most common form of peritoneal dialysis, patients must change the fluid four times per day.

Dialysis is an effective, although burdensome method for treating kidney failure. For many patients, kidney transplantation is a preferable solution because it cures the underlying problem and eliminates the need for dialysis. In a kidney transplant, a kidney is taken from a donor and surgically implanted in a patient who suffers or is about to suffer kidney failure; waste products and excess water are then removed from the patient by the new kidney. There must be a good tissue match between the donated kidney and the recipient, and recipients of kidney transplants are required to take medication for the rest of their lives to prevent their immune system from attacking and destroying the transplanted organ. Typically, kidneys used in transplantation are taken from anonymous donors who have recently died, although transplants from living donors known to the recipient are becoming more frequent.

Kidney transplantation is a common, relatively safe procedure both for the recipient and for a living donor, although there are always risks associated with major surgery. Moreover, most kidney transplants are successful, with more than 90 percent of transplanted kidneys functioning a year after the transplant surgery. In order to qualify for a transplant, a person must contact a transplant center and be evaluated by a transplant team. Patients who qualify for transplant surgery are placed on a waiting list, which in the United States is maintained by the United Network for Organ Sharing (UNOS). The number of patients on the waiting list vastly outstrips the supply of kidneys from deceased donors. When a donated organ becomes available, transplantation surgery can cost thousands of dollars, including organ procurement fees, physicians' fees, hospital and laboratory fees, and medications. In general, the costs of donating a kidney are borne not by the donor, but by the transplant center and the recipient. Since the passage of the National Organ Transplant Act

(NOTA) in 1984, it has been a federal offense to buy or sell human organs for transplantation in the United States, punishable by imprisonment for up to five years, a fine of $50,000, or both.

There are two primary moral considerations associated with the proposal to permit organ donors to receive compensation for their organs, one practical and the other theoretical. The first concerns the impact of this proposal on the availability of organs for transplant. Given the benefits of organ transplantation in general, and kidney transplantation in particular, proposals that increase the number of organs available for transplant have a moral advantage over proposals that only maintain or even decrease this number. Consequently, the inadequate supply of human organs for transplant is a factor discussed by both of the selections below.

The second consideration deals with human dignity. Philosophers have traditionally distinguished between two types of value: instrumental value and intrinsic value. Instrumental value is the value that a thing possesses as a means to an end. The value of an ordinary lead pencil is primarily instrumental—it enables a person to write words or make a sketch, and when it is too worn down to perform these tasks, it is discarded. Intrinsic value is the value that a thing possesses in and of itself. The value of a novel or a drawing is primarily intrinsic—it does nothing, but is worth having just to read or look at. It is possible for a thing to possess both instrumental value and intrinsic value. Since college graduates frequently earn more than those without college degrees, a college education may be considered to have instrumental value. But for many, the knowledge and skills learned in college have a value apart from the earning potential they confer on a college graduate. Thus, a college education may be considered to have intrinsic value as well as instrumental value.

The relevance of this distinction to the issue of payment for human organs involves the type of value that should be accorded to the human beings who donate the organs. Regarded simply as the source of organs for transplant, donors can be considered as having instrumental value. However, human beings are commonly regarded as also having intrinsic value, and an action that does not acknowledge this intrinsic value is regarded as an immoral affront to human dignity. Stealing an organ from an unwilling donor reduces the donor to a thing possessed merely of instrumental value, and so the theft of an organ is not compatible with human dignity.

Accepting an organ given freely by a donor recognizes the donor as a thing possessed of intrinsic value, worthy of praise for an act of generosity and courage, and so the uncompensated donation of an organ is compatible with human dignity. When payment for a donated organ is considered, however, the issue becomes more complex. Does paying for an organ acknowledge or deny the intrinsic value of the donor? Does it uphold or undermine human dignity? Answers to these questions are provided by the authors of both articles excerpted below.

In the first of these two selections, Michael B. Gill and Robert M. Sade argue that the United States should permit kidney donors to be paid for their organs. Since people are more likely to perform an act if they get paid for it, Gill and Sade argue that this policy would increase the available supply of kidneys. Moreover, since it is considered morally acceptable to donate a kidney and to sell body tissues such as plasma, they argue that it should be morally acceptable to sell a kidney. They explicitly address

the topic of human dignity and conclude that payment for organ donation is compatible with the intrinsic value of human beings. They also address concerns that offering payment for organs will unfairly exploit the poor.

Anya Adair and Stephen J. Wigmore, in contrast, argue against all forms of buying and selling organs. They describe the corruption that has arisen in countries where paid organ donation is permitted. In such places, paid organ donors, who are usually poor and vulnerable, often receive insufficient preoperative information and suffer from inadequate postoperative care. Thus, in the authors' view, the practice of paid organ donation is inherently so exploitative that it necessarily treats the organ donors as merely instrumentally valuable and is therefore irredeemably immoral.

YES ⤶   Michael B. Gill and Robert M. Sade

Paying for Kidneys: The Case Against Prohibition

Our society places a high priority on value pluralism and individual autonomy. With few constraints, people make personal decisions regarding what they wish to buy and sell based on their own values. There are laws prohibiting certain kinds of trade; these laws are generally aimed at preventing commercial interactions that are associated with serious harms. Payment to living organ donors has been perceived to be just such a harmful transaction.[1]

. . .

We believe that possible harms arising from allowing payment for organs have been overstated, and that healthy people should be allowed to sell one of their kidneys while they are alive—that kidney sales by living people ought to be legal. In what follows, we will present the case for the legalization of live kidney sales and answer objections to it. We confine our discussion to kidneys because the kidney is a paired organ that can be removed safely with little impact on the health of the donor. Kidney transplantation, moreover, is by far the most common of all transplants, and the discrepancy between kidney supply and need is the greatest. (Our argument does, however, bear on the sale of parts of other, nonpaired, organs, as we discuss in the section entitled "The *Prima Facie* Case for Kidney Sales.")

In presenting our case, we start by making several important preliminary points. We then present an initial argument for allowing healthy people to sell one of their kidneys. This initial argument is not conclusive in itself, but we think that it constitutes a powerful *prima facie* or presumptive case for not prohibiting kidney sales. Next we address the view that kidney sales are intrinsically wrong. Finally, we address the objection that kidney sales are wrong because paying for organs is exploitative. We hope to show that there are very good reasons for overturning the prohibition on payment for kidneys, and that neither the "intrinsically wrong" objections nor the worries about exploitation withstand careful scrutiny.

Preliminary Points

First, we are arguing for the claim that it ought to be legal for a person to *be paid* for one of his or her kidneys. We are not arguing that it ought to be legal for a potential recipient to *buy* a kidney in an open market. We propose that the buyers of kidneys be the agencies in charge of kidney procurement or transplantation; that is, we propose that such agencies should be allowed to use financial incentives to acquire kidneys. We assume that allocation of kidneys will be based on medical criteria, as in the existing allocation system for cadaveric organs. Kidneys will not be traded in an unregulated market.[2] A similar system is currently in place for blood products: a person can receive money for providing blood products, but one's chances of receiving blood are distinct from one's financial status. We further note that transplant recipients or their agents— e.g., insurance companies, Medicaid—pay for organs now, compensating the organ procurement organization that organizes the organ retrieval, the surgeon who removes the organ, the hospital where the organ is procured, and so forth. The only component of the organ procurement process not currently paid is the most critical component, the possessor of the kidney, who is *sine qua non* for organ availability.

Second, we believe the legalization of kidney sales will increase the number of kidneys that are transplanted each year and thus save the lives of people who would otherwise die. We base this belief on two views that seem to us very plausible: first, that financial incentives will induce some people to give up a kidney for transplantation who would otherwise not have done so; and second, that the existence of financial incentives will not decrease significantly the current level of live kidney donations. The first view seems to us to follow from the basic idea that people are more likely to do something if they are going to get paid for it. The second view seems to us to follow from the fact that a very large majority of live kidney donations occur between family members and the idea that the motivation of a sister who donates a kidney to a brother, or a parent who donates a kidney to a child, will not be altered by the existence of financial incentives. Although we think these views are plausible, we acknowledge that there is no clear evidence that they are true. If subsequent research were to establish that the legalization of kidney sales would lead to a decrease in the number of kidneys that are transplanted each year, some of the arguments we make would be substantially weakened.[3]

Third, we are arguing for allowing payment to living kidney donors, but many of the kidneys available for transplantation come from cadavers.We believe that payment for cadaveric organs also ought to be legalized, but we will not discuss that issue here. If we successfully make the case for allowing payment to living donors, the case for payment for cadaveric kidneys should follow easily.

The *Prima Facie* Case for Kidney Sales

With these preliminary points in mind, we will proceed to the initial argument for permitting payment for kidneys.[4] This argument is based on two claims: the "good donor claim" and the "sale of tissue claim."

The good donor claim contends that it is and ought to be legal for a living person to donate one of his or her kidneys to someone else who needs a kidney in order to survive. These donations typically consist of someone giving a kidney to a sibling, spouse, or child, but there are also cases of individuals donating to strangers. Such donations account for about half of all kidney transplants.[5] Our society, moreover, does not simply *allow* such live kidney donations. Rather, we actively praise and encourage them.[6] We typically take them to be morally unproblematic cases of saving a human life.

The sale of tissue claim contends that it is and ought to be legal for living persons to sell parts of their bodies. We can sell such tissues as hair, sperm, and eggs, but the body parts we focus on here are blood products. A kidney is more like blood products than other tissues because both are physical necessities: people need them in order to survive. Our proposed kidney sales are more like the sale of blood products in that both involve the market only in acquisition and not in allocation: the current system pays people for plasma while continuing to distribute blood products without regard to patients' economic status, just as we propose for kidneys. We do not typically praise people who sell their plasma as we do people who

donate a kidney to save the life of a sibling. At the same time, most people do not brand commercial blood banks as moral abominations. We generally take them to be an acceptable means of acquiring a resource that is needed to save lives.[7] It is doubtful, for instance, that there would be widespread support for the abolition of payment for plasma if the result were a reduction in supply so severe that thousands of people died every year for lack of blood products.

If both the good donor claim and the sale of tissue claim are true, we have at least an initial argument, or *prima facie* grounds, for holding that payment for kidneys ought to be legal. The good donor claim implies that it ought to be legal for a living person to decide to transfer one of his or her kidneys to someone else, while the sale of tissue claim implies that it ought to be legal for a living person to decide to transfer part of his or her body to someone else for money. It thus seems initially plausible to hold that the two claims together imply that it ought to be legal for a living person to decide to transfer one of his or her kidneys to someone else for money.

Of course, there seems to be an obvious difference between donating a kidney and selling one: motive. Those who donate typically are motivated by benevolence or altruism, while those who sell typically are motivated by monetary self-interest.[8] The sale of tissue claim suggests, however, that this difference on its own is irrelevant to the question of whether kidney sales ought to be legal, because the sale of tissue claim establishes that it ought to be legal to transfer a body part in order to make money. If donating a kidney ought to be legal (the good donor claim), and if the only difference between donating a kidney and selling one is the motive of monetary self-interest, and if the motive of monetary self-interest does not on its own warrant legal prohibition (the sale of tissue claim), then the morally relevant part of the analogy between donating and selling should still obtain and we still have grounds for holding that selling kidneys ought to be legal.

There is also an obvious difference between selling a kidney and selling plasma: the invasiveness of the procedure. Phlebotomy for sale of plasma is simple and quick, with no lasting side effects, while parting with a kidney involves major surgery and living with only one kidney thereafter. It is very unlikely, however, that there will be any long-term ill effects from the surgery itself or from life with a single kidney.[9] Indeed, the laws allowing live kidney donations presuppose that the risk to donors is very small and thus morally acceptable. The good donor claim implies, then, that the invasiveness of the procedure of transferring a kidney is not in and of itself a sufficient reason to legally prohibit live kidney transfer. If the only difference between selling plasma and selling a kidney is the risk of the procedure, and if that risk does not constitute grounds for prohibiting live kidney transfers, then the morally relevant part of the analogy between selling plasma and selling a kidney still should obtain and we still have grounds for holding that kidney sales ought to be legal.

The point of the preceding two paragraphs is this: if we oppose the sale of kidneys because we think it is too dangerous, then we also should oppose live kidney donations. But we do not oppose live kidney donations because we realize that the risks are acceptably low and worth taking in order to save lives. So, it is inconsistent to oppose selling kidneys because of the possible dangers while at the same time endorsing the good donor claim. Similarly, if we oppose kidney sales because we think people should not sell body parts, then we should also oppose commercial blood banks. But most people do not oppose blood banks because they realize that the banks play an important role in saving lives. So, it is inconsistent to oppose selling kidneys because it involves payment while at the same time endorsing the sale of tissue claim.[10]

. . .

Many people continue to oppose kidney sales, however, and some do so directly in the face of the good donor claim and the sale of tissue claim. For them, there are two possible methods of attack. First, they can argue that there *is* a morally relevant intrinsic difference between kidney sales and both kidney donations and plasma sales, the considerations offered above notwithstanding. Second, they can argue that while there might be nothing intrinsically wrong with selling kidneys considered in isolation, the real world circumstances under which these sales would take place would inevitably lead to exploitation. In the next section, we will examine the view that selling kidneys is intrinsically wrong, and, in the subsequent section, the view that kidney sales lead to exploitation.

The Intrinsic Immorality of Selling Organs

The Kantian View

The most common reason offered for the intrinsic wrongness of paying people for kidneys is that doing so violates the dignity of human beings or is incompatible with proper respect for persons. This opposition to kidney sales is usually grounded in the second formulation of Kant's categorical imperative, which tells us that we should never treat humanity, whether in ourselves or in others,

merely as a means (Kant 1983, p. 36). But by selling a kidney, according to this Kantian reasoning, we are treating humanity in ourselves merely as a means. Mario Morelli (1999, p. 320) summarizes the position in this way:

> The question that needs to be addressed is why, on a Kantian view, selling a body part is not respecting one's humanity, whereas donating a kidney may not be objectionable, at least sometimes. The short answer is, I think, that selling oneself or part of oneself is always treating oneself as a mere means. It is treating oneself as an object with a market price, and thus a commodity. The transaction, the selling, is done for the receipt of the money to be obtained. One's humanity, one's body, is being treated only as a means and not as an end in itself. It is not simply the giving up of a body part that is objectionable: it is giving it up for the reason of monetary gain. However, there are forms of alienation of the body, such as donation of a kidney to save another's life, that would not violate the principle. . . . One is not using oneself as a mere means if one donates a kidney for such beneficent purposes.

In the Kantian view, then, to sell one's kidney is to violate a duty to oneself; it is to violate the duty not to treat the humanity in oneself merely as a means (see Chadwick 1989, pp. 131–34; Kass 1992, p. 73). . . .

The Flaws in the Kantian View

There are two problems with this approach. First, even if selling a kidney does violate a Kantian duty to oneself, this still would not justify a legal prohibition on kidney sales; second, it is doubtful that selling a kidney does violate a Kantian duty to oneself.

Even if selling a kidney does violate a Kantian duty to oneself, it is still far from clear that we are justified in having laws and public policies against payment for kidneys. We generally do not use the law to enforce duties to oneself, and the Kantian opponents of kidney sales have not explained why we should use the law to enforce a duty to oneself in this particular case (see Dworkin 1994, pp. 155–61; Radcliffe-Richards 1996, pp. 384–87). . . .

But that is not the worst of it for the Kantian opposition to selling kidneys. The worst of it is that there is no good reason to think that selling a kidney violates the Kantian sense of autonomy.[11]

Kant says that we ought not to treat humanity in ourselves merely as a means. But my kidney is not my humanity. Humanity—what gives us dignity and intrinsic value—is our ability to make rational decisions (see

Hill 1992, pp. 38–41), and a person can continue to make rational decisions with only one kidney. Thus, Cohen's distinction between essential and nonessential parts does not help her case, for a person can function perfectly well with a single kidney and so a second kidney cannot be essential to personhood. Selling a kidney does not destroy or even seriously compromise what Kant says is intrinsically valuable and dignified (see Nelson 1991, p. 69).

The problem with the Kantian opposition shows up clearly when we consider the claim by Morelli (1999, pp. 318–24) and Cohen (1999, pp. 292–95) that kidney sales are immoral because they violate "bodily integrity." If we take "bodily integrity" in its most literal sense, then selling a kidney clearly violates it. But such literal violations occur whenever a person sells or donates plasma or gives a kidney to a relative, so opponents must not be claiming that it is wrong to engage in any activity that breaks the surface of the flesh and extracts a part of the body. What, then, is the sense in which selling a kidney violates "bodily integrity" but selling other body parts does not? As Morelli (1999, p. 321) tries to explain it,

> . . . a reasonably strong case can be made for the value of bodily integrity in terms of the Kantian principle of respect for the persons, insofar as human persons are embodied. After all, it is undeniable that our existence as rational and autonomous beings and the exercise of our powers of rationality and autonomy are dependent to a considerable extent on our physical well-being. . . . [But] what we do to or with our bodies can . . . constitute or contribute to the impairment of our capacities for rationality and autonomy.

The underlying moral idea is that it violates one's humanity to engage in activities that "impair" one's "rationality and autonomy." That is why suicide and excessive drug use are wrong. There is, however, no reason to believe that selling a kidney impairs one's rationality and autonomy in any significant respect. The medical data provide no evidence that individuals who have given away a kidney suffer any grave limitations or restrictions on their future decision making.

The reason that even a Kantian should accept kidney sales stands out sharply when we contrast that activity with suicide and selling oneself into slavery. Suicide and selling oneself into slavery clearly violate the Kantian duty to oneself. They violate this duty by destroying one's humanity through annihilation of the ability to make rational decisions. But while death and slavery are incompatible with rational decision making, selling a kidney is not. A kidney seller may be incapacitated while recovering

from surgery, but many acceptable activities (such as contracted labor and military service) involve giving up decision making in the short term for long-term benefit. Nor are the kidney seller's future options significantly limited: there are few, if any, intellectual side effects or physical sequelae. And the fact that two athletes (Sean Elliot and Pete Chilcutt) have played in the National Basketball Association with only one kidney makes it difficult to argue that having one kidney compromises the normal range of physical activity.

There is, moreover, an additional problem facing those who would try to find Kantian grounds for opposing kidney sales while allowing kidney donations. Kant argued that the moral status of an action was based entirely on the motive behind it. A person who sells a kidney, however, may have motives that do much better on the Kantian scale than those of a person who donates a kidney. A living donor, for instance, could be motivated entirely by illogical guilt and an irrationally low estimation of self-worth, or by an emotional need for grateful adoration, or by a desire to indebt and manipulate someone else. A kidney seller, by contrast, may be motivated by the idea that he ought to save someone else's life if it is in his power and that he ought to earn the money necessary to pay for his child's education. Needless to say, we do not mean to cast aspersions on the motives of those who donate their kidneys, nor to suggest that all those who sell their kidneys will have morally admirable motives. We mean merely to highlight another way in which Kantian moral theory fails to justify both the practice of kidney donation and the prohibition on kidney sales. Kant's moral theory, concerned as it is with motive, has its place in the first-person deliberations of moral agents; it is ill-equipped to draw the third-person legal distinctions that the opponents of kidney sales want to maintain. . . .

Exploitation

Much of the opposition to payment for kidneys is based not simply on Kantian duties to self but on the real-world circumstances in which such a practice would occur. A market in kidneys, it is said, will inevitably be exploitative, and for this reason it should be prohibited.[12] Some of the worries about exploitation are fueled by stories in the popular press of the international black market in kidneys. Such stories typically involve desperately poor people from underdeveloped countries selling their kidneys to wealthy individuals from developed countries. The wealthy individuals pay very large sums for an uncertain product; the poor people receive their payment and are hastily returned to their desperate lives, with poor medical follow-up and without one of their kidneys (see Finkel 2001, pp. 28–31).

The international black market in kidneys is worthy of moral condemnation, and the popular press has been right to expose it. But the horrible stories do not constitute justification for a blanket rejection of payment for kidneys in this country because there are two crucial differences between the international black market and the legal domestic program we propose.

First, in our proposal the medical setting in which legal kidney transfer would take place is that of contemporary transplantation, safe and medically sophisticated. Screening would select only potential kidney sellers whose kidneys are suitable for transfer and whose medical condition predicts minimal risk. Follow-up care would be scrupulous. Sellers would receive exactly the same medical attention and treatment that living kidney donors now receive in this country. The people to whom the kidneys are transferred will also receive the same medical attention and treatment that kidney recipients currently receive.

Second, the domestic program we propose involves money only in the acquisition of kidneys, unlike the international black market. Allocation of kidneys would be based on medical criteria, as it is today. No private individual would be able to buy a kidney outside the system. Poor individuals will have just as much chance of receiving one of the kidneys.

Disproportionate Burden

These two differences between an international black market and a legal domestic program will not, however, alter everyone's belief that payment for kidneys is exploitative. The problem, as some will continue to believe, is that even if the *benefits* are spread evenly across the economic spectrum, the *burdens* will still fall disproportionately on the poor. For it is the poor who will sell, not the rich, and there has to be something deeply morally wrong with a proposal that results in the neediest parting with a kidney while the fortunate do not.

Though this objection seems solid, the reasoning behind it is vague. When the ideas underlying the objection are clarified, it turns out to be much less substantive than it initially appears.

There are two ways of understanding the objection. First, one can hold that kidney sales are morally unacceptable no matter who does the selling and that the proposal to legalize such sales is especially pernicious because the poor will be disproportionately affected. Second, one can

hold that kidney sales *per se* are morally unobjectionable, but that we know in the real world the sellers will be disproportionately poor, and this economic disproportionality makes the proposal morally unacceptable. We will examine these two versions of the objection in order.

If payment for kidneys were morally unacceptable no matter who did the selling, then it would be especially offensive that the sellers are disproportionately poor; an activity that victimizes everyone it touches is made worse when those affected are especially vulnerable. The problem with this objection, however, is that it assumes without argument that such payments are morally unacceptable and thus ought to be illegal, when the moral and legal status of kidney sales is just what is under dispute. The objection thus begs the question. Of course, many people believe there are independent reasons for thinking that paying for kidneys is immoral and ought to be illegal, regardless of who receives the payment. But they have to articulate and defend those reasons before they can legitimately claim that economic factors will make matters worse. Pointing out that most kidney sellers will be poor will not on its own strengthen a weak argument for the intrinsic wrongness of allowing kidney sales.

The second way of understanding the objection contends that paying for kidneys might not be intrinsically wrong, but such sales ought not be allowed because the resulting situation in which the poor sell and the rich do not would be morally unacceptable. Some people might be drawn to this objection by a concern for equality, believing that it is morally unacceptable to implement any policy that widens the gap between rich and poor. An egalitarian principle of this sort requires argument, but even if we grant for the moment the essential importance of equality, it still does not speak against paying for kidneys. If paying for kidneys is legalized, the ratio of poor people with only one kidney to rich people with only one kidney probably will increase. The kind of equality that matters to egalitarians, however, concerns not the presence of one kidney versus two but economic and political power. There is no reason to think that allowing payment for kidneys will worsen the economic or political status of kidney sellers in particular or of poor people in general. To equate the selling of a kidney with being worse off is to beg the question once again.

It might seem more promising to cast this objection in terms of consent and coercion. No one should give up a kidney without freely consenting to do so. According to this objection, however, the people who sell their kidneys will be so desperate that their decision to sell will be neither reasonable nor rational and therefore should not be counted as instances of free consent. Poverty will, in effect, coerce people into selling their kidneys, and it is clearly immoral to take advantage of others' poverty in this way. The fact that we can find people desperate enough for money to do something they would not otherwise do is no justification for allowing them to do it (Abouna et al. 1990, p. 166).

In this view, the amount of money involved is what vitiates true consent to sell a kidney.[13] This concern about money could come in two guises. One could claim that paying for kidneys will be coercively exploitative because the sellers will be paid too little money, or one could claim that paying for kidneys will be coercively exploitative because the sellers will be paid too much.

Those who hold that the payment will be too low point to the international black market, where payment for a kidney is often five thousand dollars or less (see Finkel 2001, pp. 28–31). Considering the surgery the sellers must undergo, this is taken to be a relative pittance, and certainly not enough to alter in any serious and long-lasting way the dire circumstances that force people to sell their kidneys in the first place. In this view, selling a kidney for five thousand dollars is so manifestly unreasonable that anyone who agrees to do it must be too desperate to give truly informed consent.

One way of responding to this concern is to mandate that kidney sellers receive a much higher sum. Some may object, however, that if the sum is too high, it will unfairly manipulate people into making irrational decisions. Large sums of money can tempt people to do what is wrong to do (Sells 1991, p. 20).[14]

Clearly, though, the concern that people will be paid too little or too much for a kidney is not fatal to the case for payment. There are two ways to view this element of the exploitation issue. First, there is a certain amount of money that is universally too much to pay for a kidney, and a certain amount that is too little. Second, there is no objective way to decide universally the question of the monetary value of a kidney. In the first case, a universally nonexploitative payment can be established by setting the fee so that sellers are reasonably compensated without being unduly tempted to abandon their principles. We are not arguing that kidney sales be left entirely up to an unregulated market, so we do not rule out the idea that the price could be adjusted to ensure fairness and consent. The second case holds that personal values and circumstances make it impossible to set a single dollar amount for a kidney that would be reasonable and nonexploitative for all potential sellers of kidneys. Personal needs and values, regional economy, and numerous other factors will create wide variations in the payment level at which

a person will choose to part with a kidney. The best one can do, such a position suggests, is to set the price of a kidney at a level that would persuade a sufficient number of sellers to relieve the kidney shortage (Barnett, Blair, and Kaserman 1992, pp. 373–74).

These solutions, however, will leave unsatisfied some of those who believe selling kidneys to be coercively exploitative. The decision to sell a kidney, these people will argue, is always unreasonable or irrational, no matter what the price, and so no one can ever truly and freely consent to do it. There is something crucially wrong with the decision to sell a kidney, regardless of whether one is paid one thousand dollars or one million. But to hold that it is irrational or unreasonable to sell a kidney no matter what the price is to revert once again to the view that selling a kidney is intrinsically wrong. It is asserting that kidney sales would be wrong even if practiced by people across the economic spectrum and abandoning the idea that what would make kidney sales wrong is that only poor people will sell. Now many people do believe that it would be wrong to allow kidney sales no matter who engages in them. As we have argued above, however, that belief requires justification, and until that justification is provided, the fact that poor people would be more likely than rich people to sell their kidneys does not on its own constitute a moral objection to the legalization of kidney sales.

Moreover, the good donor claim makes it very difficult to show that it will always be irrational or unreasonable to sell a kidney, no matter who does the selling. If it can be rational and reasonable for a person to decide to donate a kidney to a relative or to a stranger, it is difficult to imagine why it must always be irrational and unreasonable to sell a kidney. It seems plausible that a live seller can gain from the sale something intangible that is equal in value to what a live donor gains. Indeed, it is quite plausible that a living seller can gain exactly what a living donor gains—the satisfaction of saving a life, or of significantly improving the life prospects of another—*plus* a financial reward. If it is rational or reasonable for a living person to donate a kidney, then it seems that it would also be rational or reasonable for a living person to sell a kidney when the seller receives from the transaction the same benefit as the donor plus more.

Perhaps some opponents will continue to maintain that the mere fact that only the poor will sell is clear evidence of the coercively exploitative nature of paying for kidneys, the considerations above notwithstanding. Such opponents might base their argument on the idea that an act that no wealthy person would ever agree to must have some essentially rebarbative quality that always makes it wrong to inflict on the poor. The opposition might, in other words, hold this principle: if the only people who will agree to X are poor, then X must be an activity to which no one can truly and freely consent.

The problem with this principle is that it is inconsistent with many of the jobs that employ a large percentage of our population. A wealthy person rarely will choose to clean toilets for a living, or to pick strawberries. But this does not prove that it is immoral to allow people to do these jobs. Of course we should be concerned about the wages and conditions of custodians and field hands. But the solution is to take measures to ensure fair wages and tolerable conditions, not to ban public toilets and commercially grown strawberries. Similarly, if we are concerned about the price and safety of kidney sales and removal, then the answer is not to ban them but to make them as fair and safe as possible.

Can the surgical procedure associated with kidney sales ever truly be safe? We think it can be. There are risks, to be sure, but they can be minimized so that the procedure will pose less of a threat to the seller than do many jobs and activities that our society currently allows. Live kidney donation is now not merely allowed but actively encouraged precisely because these risks can be minimized. In our proposal, potential sellers will be screened and monitored just as carefully as potential donors are, so that the risks to the former should be no greater than the risks to the latter. . . .

Conclusion

Undoubtedly, many people will continue to oppose kidney sales, regardless of the arguments we have offered. Many people will continue to find the sale of a kidney repugnant, a feeling that rational argumentation alone may be incapable of dislodging (Kass 1992, pp. 84–85). But we should not let this feeling of repugnance hold hostage our moral thinking. For a great many things we now hold in the highest esteem—including organ transplantation itself—occasioned strong repugnance in times past.

Still, it is there in our psyche and hard to shake—the sense that there is something unsavory, something sharply distasteful, about paying perfectly healthy individuals to submit to a major operation and to live thereafter without one of their internal organs. The mind flinches at the thought of what such individuals will endure for money. This reaction, however, may be the result of restricted vision, for there is another part of the story, another image that we must attend to before we can honestly say that we are responding to the matter in its entirety. The other part of the story is the people waiting for kidneys—the people who will live if they receive a kidney or die, or at least suffer

needlessly, if they do not. A complete emotional response requires that we frame in our mind an image of these sick people, as well as of their families and friends, that is just as vivid as our image of the healthy kidney sellers.

When we complete the picture, we may find that our feelings of repugnance begin to soften, and perhaps to dissipate. Such imaginative exercises should not substitute for rational moral arguments, but they may help pave the way for a fair consideration of those arguments.

Notes

1. We intentionally use the term "donor" to refer to those selling as well as those freely giving organs and tissues, in keeping with the common usage of the term with respect to other paid givers of biological materials, such as commercial blood donors, donors to sperm banks, and human egg donors.

2. This is an example of what Margaret Jane Radin (1987, p. 1919) has helpfully labeled "incomplete commodification."

3. In the early 1970s, Titmuss (1971) and Singer (1973) argued that the existence of financial incentives for blood products would decrease the amount of blood products overall, and some people might believe that the same argument can be extended to financial incentives for kidneys, leading to the conclusion that payment for kidneys will decrease the overall number of kidneys available for transplant. Singer and Titmuss's criticisms of payment for blood products are consequentialist—they argue that such payment is wrong because it would reduce the amount of blood for people who needed it. We believe, first of all, that their consequentialist arguments against payment for blood products have turned out to be inconclusive at best—that the available evidence does not support the conclusion that payment for blood products has reduced blood supply in the United States. And we believe, secondly, that because live kidney donations are usually between family members, there is a significant difference between blood and kidneys that makes it illegitimate to transfer Titmuss and Singer's conclusions to the kidney debate. We do, however, remain open to the possibility that future evidence may vitiate our belief that payment for kidneys will increase supplies. For discussion of Titmuss and Singer in relation to kidney sales, see Campbell (1992, pp. 41–42); Cherry (2000, pp. 340–41); and Harvey (1999, p. 119).

4. Similar arguments occur in Radcliffe-Richards (1996, pp. 375–416); Nelson (1991, pp. 63–78);

Tilney (1998, p. 1950); and Dworkin (1994, pp. 155–61). See also Brecher (1990, pp. 120–23).

5. As Laura Meckler (2001) reports, "Organ donations from the living jumped by 16 percent last year, the largest increase on record, as the waiting list for transplants grew much faster than donations from people who had died. More than 5,500 people gave a kidney or, less commonly, a piece of the liver, accounting for nearly half the nation's donors in 2000, said the Department of Health and Human Services. . . . The number of living donors has been growing more quickly than the number of cadaveric donors for a decade, but the gap was particularly striking in 2000. While the number of living donors jumped 16.5 percent, donations from the dead edged up by just 2.7 percent. At this rate, living donors will outnumber cadaveric donors within a year or two."

6. The New England Medical Center currently has a program to encourage organ donation. As Jay Lindsay (2001) reports, "Susan Stephens helped her 13-year-old son get a kidney transplant by giving up one of her own—to a stranger in Greece. A new kidney exchange program at the New England Medical Center allowed Stephens to donate her kidney, which wasn't a match for her son. In exchange, her son, Corey, was moved to the top of the kidney waiting list. Corey received his new kidney last month, after his mother's donation reduced a possible 18-month wait to a few weeks. Meanwhile, Stephens' kidney ended six years on a dialysis machine for Evangelos Natsinas, 36, of the Greek village Palamas. Doctors say the program will increase the critically small organ donor pool, while allowing willing donors to help loved ones, regardless of whether their organs match. So far, the program only includes kidneys."

7. As we point out in note 3, some people (Titmuss, Singer, and others) have opposed commercial blood banks. Does that opposition constitute a threat to our position? It depends upon the reasons for the opposition. If one's reasons for opposing such blood banks are (like Singer's) consequentialist—i.e., if the only reason one has for opposing blood banks is that one thinks they will lead to lower blood supplies—then one is committed to opposing the legalization of kidney sales only if legalization will lead to fewer kidneys for transplant. But this purely consequentialist reasoning may also commit one to *supporting* the legalization of kidney sales if legalization will lead to more kidneys for transplant (although the pure consequentialist would consider other effects of legalization as well; we address some of these other possible effects in our discussion of exploitation,

slippery slopes, and commodification). If one's reasons for opposing commercial blood banks are nonconsequentialist—if one thinks there is something wrong with blood banks distinct from how they affect the blood supply—then those reasons have to be defended and evaluated on their own merits. (We evaluate the Kantian class of nonconsequentialist reasons in our discussion of the objection that selling kidneys is intrinsically wrong.)

8. As we note later in the article, the difference between the motivations of a donor and a seller may not be as clear and simple as opponents of kidney sales suggest, for a donor could have selfish motives and a seller could have altruistic ones. But even if we grant for the moment that all donors will be altruistic and all sellers will be selfish, the argument presented here still seems to constitute a strong initial case for kidney sales.

9. As Andrews (1996, p. 32; in part citing Caplan (1985)) writes, "Physicians have adopted an odd view of risks to organ donors. Transplants surgeons traditionally have maintained that removing a kidney from a live donor presents minimal health risks. 'However,' Arthur Caplan points out, 'when the proposal was made to buy and sell kidneys what had historically been deemed "minimal risks" suddenly escalated into intolerable dangers when profit became an obvious motive?'" Or, as Tilney (1998, p. 1950) puts it, "The risk involved in nephrectomy is not in itself high, and most people regard it as acceptable for living related donors. . . . [T]he exchange of money cannot in itself turn an acceptable risk into an unacceptable one . . . ."

10. Some might try to counter the initial argument for kidney sales by employing an analogy to prostitution. Prostitution, they may say, consists of an act that is morally acceptable when money is not involved but morally unacceptable when money is involved. One can, of course, hold that prostitution is morally unacceptable while also holding that many other acts that involve money are morally acceptable. The example of prostitution, then, shows that the fact that a particular activity, A, is acceptable when money is not involved, and the fact that other activities are acceptable when money is involved, do not together imply that activity A is acceptable when money is involved. But if the prostitution analogy is going to bolster opposition to payment for kidneys, we have to know first of all why prostitution is wrong. Now there are two ways in which prostitution could be wrong: because it has unacceptable consequences, or because it is wrong in itself. If prostitution is wrong because of its consequences, the analogy between prostitution

and kidney sales will support opposition to the latter only if it can be shown that kidney sales have unacceptable consequences similar to those of prostitution. We will address consequentialist arguments of this sort later in the article in the section on exploitation and commodification. What of the other possibility, that prostitution is wrong in itself, distinct from its consequences? Does this argument establish that payment for kidneys is wrong? On its own, it does not. For the bare claim that prostitution is intrinsically wrong does not show that payment for kidneys is wrong as well. What we need is an explanation of the wrongness of prostitution that enables us to draw an analogy to payment for kidneys. It is not enough for opponents of kidney sales simply to point to the prohibition on prostitution; they also must show that the features of prostitution that make it wrong are shared by kidney sales. They have not done this, to our knowledge. In addition to prostitution, we have been asked at various points about a number of other things that are legal to give but not to sell. One example is selling oneself into slavery; we explain the crucial disanalogy between selling a kidney and selling oneself into slavery in our discussion of the Kantian objection below. Two other examples are buying one's way out of the military draft and selling one's body for medical experiments, both of which we discuss below in our section on the additional flaws in the exploitation argument. Our general rejoinder to all these putative counterexamples is this: our argument does not depend on the absolutist claim that everything that it is legal to give should also be legal to sell. Our view, rather, is that the fact that something is legal to give constitutes *prima facie* grounds for thinking that it should be legal to sell—that the burden of proof falls on those who would argue that something should be legal to *give* but not legal to *sell*. In the parts of this paper that follow our *prima facie* case, we address attempts to meet that burden of proof with regard to kidney transfer and try to explain why we think those attempts fail.

11. Kant himself seems to have been opposed to the selling of any body part. Even the selling of one's hair, he says, "is not entirely free from blame" (Kant 1983, p. 84). As we argue in this section, however, it is difficult to see how such opposition follows from Kant's fundamental moral principle of respect for humanity. It is worth noting, as well, that the circumstances of kidney transplantation could hardly have been anticipated by Kant, and so one must proceed with great caution when trying to draw moral conclusions about kidney transplantation (not simply from Kant's fundamental moral principles but also) from his specific judgments of practices particular to his day, such as his condemnation of one's submitting "oneself to castration in order to gain an easier livelihood as a singer" (Kant 1983, p. 84).

12. This kind of argument is made by Morelli (1999, p. 323); Chadwick (1989, pp. 137–38); Essig (1993, p. 65); and Sells (1993). This kind of argument is criticized by Andrews (1986); Cherry (2000); Harvey (1990); and Radcliffe-Richards (1996, pp. 378–84).

13. For criticism of this claim, see Radcliffe-Richards (1986, pp. 380–84); Cherry (2000, pp. 345–49); Tadd (1991, p. 97); and Nelson (1991, p. 74–75).

14. Faden and Beauchamp (1986, p. 340) criticize the idea that an offer can be coercive because it is irresistibly attractive. We agree with Faden and Beauchamp's view that the prospect of financial reward cannot in and of itself constitute coercion.

References

Abouna, G. M.; Sabawi, M. M.; Kumar, M. S. A.; and Samhan, M. 1991. The Negative Impact of Paid Organ Donation. In *Organ Replacement Therapy: Ethics, Justice, Commerce: First Joint Meeting of ESOT and EDTA/ERA, Munich, December 1990*, ed. W. Land and J. B. Dossetor, pp. 164–72. New York: Springer-Verlag.

Andrews, Lori B. 1986. My Body, My Property. *Hastings Center Report* 16 (5): 28–38.

Barnett, Andrew H.; Blair, Roger D.; and Kaserman, David L. 1992. Improving Organ Donation: Compensation Versus Markets. *Inquiry* 29: 372–78.

Brecher, Bob. 1990. The Kidney Trade: Or, the Customer Is Always Wrong. *Journal of Medical Ethics* 16:120–23.

Campbell, Courtney S. 1992. Body, Self, and the Property Paradigm. *Hastings Center Report* 22 (5): 34–42.

Caplan, Arthur L. 1985. Blood Sweat, Tears, and Profits: The Ethics of the Sale and Use of Patient Derived Materials in Biomedicine. *Clinical Research* 33: 448–451.

Chadwick, Ruth E. 1989. The Market for Bodily Parts: Kant and Duties to Oneself. *Journal of Applied Philosophy* 6: 129–39.

Cherry, Mark J. 2000. Is a Market in Human Organs Necessarily Exploitative? *Public Affairs Quarterly* 14: 337–60.

Cohen, Cynthia B. 1999. Selling Bits and Pieces of Humans to Make Babies. *Journal of Medicine and Philosophy* 24: 288–306.

Dworkin, Gerald. 1994. Markets and Morals: The Case of Organ Sales. In *Morality, Harm and the Law*, ed. Gerald Dworkin, pp. 155–61. Boulder, CO: Westview Press.

Essig, Beth. 1993. Legal Aspects of the Sale of Organs. *Mount Sinai Journal of Medicine* 60: 64–65.

Faden, Ruth R., and Beauchamp, Tom L., in collaboration with Nancy M. P. King. 1986. *A History and Theory of Informed Consent*. New York: Oxford University Press.

Finkel, Michael. 2001. This Little Kidney Went to Market. *New York Times Magazine* (27 May): 26–59 passim.

Harvey, J. 1990. Paying Organ Donors. *Journal of Medical Ethics* 16: 117–19.

Hill, Thomas E. 1992. *Dignity and Practical Reason in Kant's Moral Theory*. Ithaca: Cornell University Press.

Kant, Immanuel 1983. *Ethical Philosophy: The Complete Texts of Grounding for the Metaphysics of Morals, and Metaphysical Principles of Virtue, Part II of The Metaphysics of Morals*, trans. James W. Ellington. Indianapolis: Hackett Publishing.

Kass, Leon R. 1992. Organs for Sale? Propriety, Property, and the Price of Progress. *Public Interest* 107 (Spring): 72–85.

Lindsay, Jay. 2001. Program Allows Donors to Indirectly Donate Organs to Loved Ones. The Associated Press State & Local Wire, filed 11 April. Available on Lexis-Nexis Wire Service Reports.

Meckler, Laura. 2001. Living Organ Donations Jump in 2000. Associated Press Online, posted 16 April. Available on Lexis-Nexis Wire Service Reports.

Morelli, Mario. 1999. Commerce in Organs: A Kantian Critique. *Journal of Social Philosophy* 30: 315–24.

Nelson, Mark T. 1991. The Morality of a Free Market for Transplant Organs. *Public Affairs Quarterly* 5: 63–78.

Radcliffe-Richards, Janet. 1996. Nephrarious Goings On. *Journal of Medicine and Philosophy* 21: 375–416.

Radin, Margaret Jane. 1987. Market-Inalienability. *Harvard Law Review* 100: 1849–1937.

Sells, R. A. 1991. Voluntarism of Consent. In *Organ Replacement Therapy: Ethics, Justice, Commerce: First Joint Meeting of ESOT and EDTA/ERA, Munich, December 1990*, ed. W Land and J. B. Dossetor, pp. 18-24. New York: Springer-Verlag.

_____. 1993. Resolving the Conflict in Traditional Ethics Which Arises from Our Demand for Organs. *Transplantation Proceedings* 25: 2983–84.

Singer, Peter. 1973. Altruism and Commerce: A Defense of Titmuss Against Arrow. *Philosophy and Public Affairs 2:* 312-20.

Tadd, G. V. 1991. The Market for Bodily Parts: A Response to Chadwick. *Journal of Applied Philosophy* 8: 95–102.

Tilney, Nicholas. 1998. The Case for Allowing Kidney Sales. *Lancet* 351: 1950–51.

Titmuss, Richard M. 1971. *The Gift Relationship: From Human Blood to Social Policy*. New York: Pantheon Books.

MICHAEL B. GILL is an associate professor of philosophy at the University of Arizona. He has published numerous articles in the areas of history of ethics, medical ethics, and contemporary meta-ethics, as well as the book *The British Moralists on Human Nature and the Birth of Secular Ethics* (Cambridge University Press, 2006).

ROBERT M. SADE is a professor of surgery at the Medical University of South Carolina, where he also serves as director of Institute of Human Values in Health Care and the Clinical Research Ethics Program of the South Carolina Clinical and Translational Research Institute, and the Head of the Bioethics Section of the Division of Cardiothoracic Surgery. He has organized nearly 20 conferences and has edited over 15 special issues of peer-reviewed journals on medical/surgical and bioethical topics.

Anya Adair and Stephen J. Wigmore

Paid Organ Donation: The Case Against

Paid organ donation is an emotive subject in the transplant community. Part of the reason for this is that in many countries, including the UK, the notion of organ donation as a 'gift' is highly valued. The difference between a gift and a commodity is clearly understood and applies equally to living as well as deceased organ donation. In the UK, legislation prohibits commercial dealings in human material for transplantation (Human Tissue act 2004 (England and Northern Ireland)[1] and 2006 (Scotland)[2]).

In other countries such legal protection does not exist and in 2004 the World Health organization (WHO) urged members 'to take measures to protect the poorest and vulnerable groups from transplant tourism and the sale of tissues and organs'.[3] Paid donation and transplant tourism are inseparably intertwined. Further debate at a summit in 2008 by the Transplantation Society and the International Society of Nephrology led to the Declaration of Istanbul on Organ Trafficking and Transplant Tourism stating: 'Organ trafficking and transplant tourism violate the principles of equity, justice and respect for human dignity and should be prohibited. Transplant commercialism targets impoverished and otherwise vulnerable donors leading to inequity and injustice'.[4]

To understand the issue of paid donation it is necessary to understand the drivers for it. There is a global shortage of organs available for transplantation. This gap between demand and supply has prompted many people in the west with organ failure to seek transplants overseas, often in developing countries.[5,6] Frequently these individuals do not ask questions about how that organ was obtained.[7] The process is further fuelled by unscrupulous health professionals and brokers seeing the potential for financial gain and taking advantage of both the desperate recipient and the vulnerable seller. It is a sad indictment of the human condition that wherever there is a market, people will strive to find a profit margin even when this results in human exploitation.

This problem is often compounded by the lack of a suitable healthcare infrastructure to provide a viable transplant programme in these countries. This may be due both to economic limitations and to the inability to establish a deceased donor programme because of cultural, social and religious barriers. In such healthcare systems the focus then turns to living donation provided by unregulated private clinics.[6,7] In the west the spirit of the Hippocratic oath, primum non nocere or 'first do no harm' is embraced and the emphasis of care rests on protecting the interests of the donor. Paid donation does not support this interest. This shift in balance of responsibility to the paying recipient is disturbing and unethical.

To understand this fully let us look at the demographic of the donor. Donors are poor, with most living below the poverty line. Most are illiterate and in low-paid manual jobs, their sole reason for donating not borne of altruism but to pay off debt.[7,8] In Pakistan many individuals donate kidneys to release themselves from bonded slavery but have insufficient capital to make a new life and often return to debt (Rizvi, personal communication). We find it difficult to relate to concepts such as the entrapment represented by bonded slavery but how would our society view individuals in our own country driven to donate a kidney to pay off credit card debt, college fees or to satisfy a drug problem?

Sadly for the majority of donors, selling a kidney does not result in the significant economic benefit of which they dreamed. Often it is associated with a decline in general health. Many fall back into debt, often compounded by the inability to work following donation due to ill health.[8] Supporters of paid donation argue that a person should have the basic right to choose the fate of his or her organs. In the setting of paid donation, informed consent is often of dubious quality, with the risks of surgery often not being properly explained or understood. Furthermore, many individuals are pressured to donate by family members, with the outcome of any 'balanced discussions' about wishing to proceed with organ donation predetermined.[8]

In the UK, our society believes that we have a responsibility to protect individuals from harm. This principal applies even when harm may be self-inflicted. That is why we have motorcycle helmet and seatbelt laws. Why should this state-brokered paternalism be overturned to allow paid donation?

Perhaps the problem lies not in the principle of paid donation but in its organisation and regulation? Some individuals believe that it is possible to create an ethical market in live organs that would possess regulations and safeguards against exploitation of the seller and provide justice and equity to the recipient. Harris *et al* suggest a 'monopsony' where only one buyer exists for the products of several sellers. This purchaser would be responsible for ensuring equitable distribution of all organs purchased. The purchaser would also be responsible for tissue typing and screening for infection. In the UK they suggest the NHS would be an appropriate buyer.[9] In China attempts have been made to implement some form of government control over the selling of organs. Here permission is given to certain hospitals by the provincial health authorities, allowing them to offer organ transplants to foreign visitors, with punishment to those institutions that offer the service illegally.[10,11]

Such systems are proposed to attempt to remove the need for an underground and illegal black market in organs. We would argue that however paid donation is dressed up, the buying and selling of human organs and tissues can never be made ethical because it will always penalise the weakest. Financial gradients are inherently exploitative, with the poorest in society being the ones who come forward as sellers every time.[12] We would further argue that the system can never be adequately regulated to prevent exploitation of the poor and where financial motivation drives the decisions of the health professionals this will also undermine the care of the recipient, with financial gain taking precedence over patient care.

References

Human Tissue Act 2004. http://www.legislation.gov.uk/ukpga/2004/30/contents (cited February 2011).

Human Tissue (Scotland) Act 2006. http://www.legislation.gov.uk/asp/2006/4/contents (cited February 2011).

World Health Assembly. WHA57.18. *Human organ and tissue transplantation.*

WHA; 22 May 2004; Geneva, Switzerland. http://www.who.int/transplantation/en/A57_R18-en.pdf (cited February 2011).

International Summit on Transplant Tourism and Organ Trafficking. The Declaration of Istanbul on Organ Trafficking and Transplant Tourism. *Clin J Am Soc Nephrol* 2008; **3**: 1,227–231.

Shimazono Y. The state of the international organ trade: a provisional picture based on integration of available information. *Bull World Health Organ* 2007; **85**: 955–962.

Rizvi AH, Naqvi AS, Zafar NM, Ahmed E. Regulated compensated donation in Pakistan and Iran. *Curr Opin Organ Transplant* 2009, **14**: 124–128.

Rothman DJ, Rose E, Awaya T et al. The Bellagio Task Force report on transplantation, bodily integrity, and the International Traffic in Organs. *Transplant Proc* 1997; **29**: 2,739–745.

Goyal M, Mehta RL, Schneiderman LJ, Sehgal AR. Economic and health consequences of selling a kidney in India. *JAMA* 2002; **288**: 1,589–93.

Harris J, Erin C. An ethically defensible market in organs. *BMJ* 2002; **325**: 114–115.

Szustek A. China Cracking Down on Organ Transplants for Tourists. *Finding Dulcinea*; 2009. http://www.findingdulcinea.com/news/health/2009/feb/China-Cracking-Down-on-Organ-Transplants-for-Tourists.html (cited February 2011).

Delmonico FL. The implications of Istanbul Declaration on organ trafficking and transplant tourism. *Curr Opin Organ Transplant* 2009, **14**: 116–119.

Wigmore SJ, Lumsdaine JA, Forsythe JL. Ethical market in organs. Defending the indefensible? *BMJ* 2002; **325**: 835.

Anya Adair is a Consultant Transplant and Hepatobiliary Surgeon, and Honorary Clinical Senior Lecturer at the University of Edinburgh. Her current clinical practice involves liver, kidney and pancreas transplantation and hepatobiliary and pancreatic surgery. She has published on many aspects of organ transplantation.

Stephen J. Wigmore is Acting Head of the Department of Surgery, Professor of Transplantation Surgery, and Honorary Consultant Surgeon at the University of Edinburgh. He currently serves as Chair of the Research Committee of the Royal College of Surgeons of Edinburgh and has served as Chairman of the Ethics Committee of the British Transplantation Society. He has published on many aspects of organ transplantation.

EXPLORING THE ISSUE

Is Paid Organ Donation Morally Permissible?

Critical Thinking and Reflection

1. Would you consider donating a kidney to a family member? Would you consider donating a kidney to a stranger? Are your answers to these questions different? Why or why not?
2. Would an offer of payment increase your willingness to donate a kidney to a stranger? Why or why not?
3. Would an offer of payment for your kidney offend your human dignity? Why or why not?
4. Besides payment, can you think of any other ways to encourage more people to donate organs? Are these ways compatible with human dignity?

Is There Common Ground?

Whether they favor or oppose payment for human organs, all the authors in this section recognize the immense medical benefits provided by organ transplantation; all are also keenly aware that the number of people who need transplants far exceeds the number of organs available. They disagree, however, on the compatibility of paid organ donation with the human dignity of the donors.

Contemporary research may hold out a solution that will increase the number of organs available for transplant without compromising the human dignity of donors. The advent of stem cell technology and 3-D printers may soon make it possible to construct replacement organs from a patient's own cells. There would then be no need to harvest organs from recently deceased anonymous donors or induce living donors to provide organs. Unfortunately, it will be at least ten or fifteen years before this technology is developed to the level required to provide large numbers of organs for transplant. Until that time, patients will still need to wait and hope for donated organs. The debate about payment for organs may not last much longer, but it is still a critical issue for people who need organs now.

Additional Resources

Sunil Shroff, "Legal and ethical aspects of organ donation and transplantation," Indian Journal of Urology 25:3 (July-September 2009).

Mark J. Cherry, Kidney for Sale by Owner: Human Organs, Transplantation, and the Market (Georgetown University Press, 2005).

Lesley A. Sharp, Bodies, Commodities, and Biotechnologies: Death, Mourning, and Scientific Desire in the Realm of Human Organ Transfer (Columbia University Press, 2006).

Rohan J. Hardcastle, Law and the Human Body: Property Rights, Ownership and Control (Hart Publishing, 2007).

Donna Dickenson, Body Shopping: The Economy Fuelled by Flesh and Blood (Oneworld Publications, 2008).

Internet References . . .

Bioethics.net: Organ Transplant & Donation

http://www.bioethics.net/topics/organ-transplant-donation/

U.S. Department of Health and Human Services Organ Procurement and Transplantation Network

http://optn.transplant.hrsa.gov/resources/bioethics.asp?index=10

The Hastings Center: Organ Transplantation

http://www.thehastingscenter.org/Publications/BriefingBook/Detail.aspx?id=2198

Selected, Edited, and with Issue Framing Material by:
Owen M. Smith, *Stephen F. Austin State University*
and
Anne Collins Smith, *Stephen F. Austin State University*

ISSUE

Do Anti-Smoking Policies Violate Smokers' Moral Autonomy?

YES: Lewis Maltby, from "Whose Life Is It Anyway? Employer Control of Off Duty Smoking and Individual Autonomy," *William Mitchell Law Review* (2008)

NO: Adrien Barton, from "How Tobacco Health Warnings Can Foster Autonomy," *Public Health Ethics* (2013)

Learning Outcomes

After reading this issue, you will be able to:

- Distinguish between Classical Paternalism and Libertarian Paternalism.
- State the Principle of Autonomy and explain the conflict between the autonomy of smokers and the paternalism of government and private employers.
- Explain the exceptions to the Principle of Autonomy posed by minors and by people who harm others with secondhand smoke.
- Formulate your own position on the morality of anti-smoking policies and identify evidence supporting your position.
- Identify the main objections to your position on the morality of anti-smoking policies and formulate responses to these objections.

ISSUE SUMMARY

YES: Lewis Maltby analyzes the growing trend among employers to reduce health-care costs by regulating their employees' off-duty behavior, including requiring employees not to smoke. He argues that this trend is intrusive and unfair, and links it to national anti-smoking policies, which, he also believes, intrude on people's right to do what they want in their own homes.

NO: Adrien Barton argues that ads that try to persuade people to stop smoking may seem to act against autonomy by telling them what they should do. However, since nicotine addiction takes autonomy away, helping people not to break the addiction helps to restore that autonomy.

If you visit an online archive of historical advertisements, you may be astonished by early-to-mid 20th-century cigarette advertisements. As you might expect, tobacco companies attempted to create an atmosphere of glamor and sophistication associated with smoking; in this way, tobacco advertising has not changed all that much. Rather, what may surprise you is that tobacco companies also attempted to associate smoking with good health. Glossy advertisements, some with testimonials from medical professionals, claimed that smoking was beneficial to the throat and soothing to the digestion. Influenced by such misleading and inaccurate statements, many people chose to smoke, unaware of the health risks associated with smoking. Eventually, scientific research began to link tobacco use with a host of illnesses, and the purported health benefits of smoking were dropped from tobacco advertising campaigns. Finally, in 1964, the Surgeon General issued a report explicitly linking tobacco use with bronchitis, emphysema, low infant birth weight, heart disease, and lung cancer, effectively shattering the illusion that smoking would not only embellish your image, but improve your health.

Subsequent reports by Surgeons General have continued to publicize the health risks of tobacco use. Smoking tobacco is the leading cause of preventable death in the United States; the Centers for Disease Control (CDC) state that cigarette smoking causes one in five deaths annually. Even Lewis Maltby, who vigorously defends the freedom of American consumers to choose to purchase and use tobacco products, describes tobacco as "by far the most dangerous consumer substance available in America." Nevertheless, the CDC estimates that in 2012, 18.1 percent of all adults (42.1 million people) in the United States regularly smoked cigarettes; worldwide, the number of smokers is about one billion people.

While it may seem tempting, from a public health standpoint, simply to ban smoking altogether, proponents of the freedom to purchase and use tobacco products argue that such a ban would be an immoral violation of the freedom of adults to make personal choices. The foundation for this argument is the Principle of Autonomy, which states that adults should be accorded the dignity of making decisions about their conduct, even if those decisions imperil their health. Since a ban on smoking would restrict the ability of adults to make personal choices, such a ban would constitute a violation of the Principle of Autonomy, and hence would be immoral.

Proponents of strict regulation of tobacco products respond to this argument not by denying the Principle of Autonomy but by presenting a more nuanced application of this principle to the decision to use tobacco products. The Principle of Autonomy flows from the inherent dignity of human beings, which requires that they be recognized as having intrinsic value, not merely instrumental value. In other words, human beings are valuable in and of themselves, and it would be wrong to treat them as mere objects, whose value derives from their usefulness in achieving a desired goal. In the context of tobacco use, the Principle of Autonomy requires companies that manufacture and sell tobacco products to respect the intrinsic value of the consumers who purchase and consume their products, and not treat them merely as means to generate profit.

Does the inherent dignity of human beings preclude any activity that uses human beings as a means to an end? How then can tobacco companies, or any company for that matter, make a profit? The answer to these questions lies in recognizing that it is moral to treat human beings in an instrumental fashion as long as this treatment also respects their intrinsic value. In practical terms, this respect must be demonstrated by obtaining a person's voluntary, informed consent to be treated as a means to an end. Let us take each component of this requirement separately. First, human beings must give their consent to be treated as a means to an end; if no consent is obtained, this treatment does not respect their intrinsic value and is immoral. Second, they must be in possession of all relevant facts before giving their consent; if not, their consent is uninformed and morally invalid. Finally, they must give their consent freely and without coercion; if not, their consent is involuntary and morally invalid. In the absence of voluntary, informed consent, it is immoral to treat a person as a means to an end.

In the context of tobacco use, a tobacco company must demonstrate its respect for the intrinsic value of its customers by obtaining their voluntary, informed consent to purchase and consume tobacco products. Proponents of strict regulation of tobacco products acknowledge that many people do, in fact, give their consent to purchase and consume tobacco products. However, they deny that this consent is always informed and voluntary.

In the decades before the first Surgeon General's report on the adverse health effects of smoking, people did not have a full understanding of the significance of their choice to use tobacco; indeed, tobacco advertising misled consumers by promoting the health benefits of tobacco! As a result, their choice was uninformed, and therefore morally invalid. As a consequence of the Surgeon General's report, strict warning labels were required on tobacco products to address this problem. As tobacco companies expand into markets around the world, the World Health Organization wants to regulate advertising and require public health education to prevent people from making uninformed decisions about smoking. Thus, strict regulation of tobacco products may be seen as protecting, rather than violating the autonomy of the people who choose to purchase and consume tobacco products.

In addition, tobacco products contain a highly addictive substance, nicotine. Indeed, research suggests that the majority of smokers want to quit but find themselves unable to do so because of their addiction to nicotine. Once people have become addicted to nicotine, however, their addiction compels them to continue to use tobacco products. As a result, their consent to purchase and consume tobacco products becomes involuntary, and therefore morally invalid. Because tobacco products are inherently addictive, mere regulation may not be sufficient to protect the autonomy of potential tobacco consumers; an outright ban on tobacco products may be necessary.

In the following articles, Maltby argues that autonomy must be defending by allowing people to make the personal choice to assume the risks of smoking, so long as they do so in ways that do not harm others (e.g., by exposing them to secondhand smoke). In his opinion, anti-smoking restrictions that are not specifically aimed at preventing harm to nonsmokers violate the principle of autonomy.

Barton, on the other hand, supports the imposition of a particular type of anti-smoking policy, the mandatory display of health warnings about tobacco usage on cigarette packages. This position forces him to grapple with the classic conflict between the Principle of Autonomy, which protects a person's liberty to make harmful choices, and the Principle of Paternalism, which curtails a person's liberty to make harmful choices out of a concern to protect that person's well-being. The strategy employed by Barton is not to choose one principle over the other, but to embrace both principles by making a distinction between classical paternalism, which interferes with a person's liberty, and libertarian paternalism, which does not strictly interfere with a person's liberty, but permits that liberty to be influenced in a manner that induces people to make choices that enhance their well-being. By doing so, Barton claims that tobacco health warnings can enhance the health of an adult smoker while actually fostering the smoker's autonomy.

YES ↵

Lewis Maltby

Whose Life Is It Anyway? Employer Control of Off-Duty Smoking and Individual Autonomy

Henry Ford had his own private police force.[2] If you worked for Ford Motor Company, its officers could show up at your door at any hour of the day or night and search your entire home.[3] If they found anything Henry Ford disapproved of, you were fired.[4] If you were drinking, you were fired.[5] If there was someone upstairs at night that you were not married to, you were fired.[6] If you were playing cards for money, you were fired.[7] If you had books Ford did not like, you were fired.[8]

Today, we know that this was wrong. The fact that Henry Ford signed people's paychecks did not give him the right to control their private lives.

But we are in danger of slipping back into this kind of world. Many employers are beginning to take control of employees' private lives in the name of reducing health care costs.[9]

The most common example of this trend involves employers who prohibit employees from smoking in their private lives.[10] The Administrative Management Society has estimated that six percent of all employers in the United States discriminate against off-duty smokers.[11] These employers argue that smokers incur higher medical costs that adversely affect profitability.[12] This is clearly correct. While the magnitude by which smokers' medical costs exceed those of other employees has not been precisely measured, nor the amount of these higher costs that fall on a particular employer, there is no question that smokers cost their employers more money for medical care.[13]

But smoking is not the only behavior that increases medical costs. Alcohol isn't good for you.[14] Neither is junk food, red meat, too much coffee, lack of exercise, or lack of sleep.[15] Many forms of recreation have medical risks, including skiing, scuba diving, and riding motorcycles. Getting to work by bicycle may be good exercise, but it increases the risk of being hurt in a traffic accident. Even your sex life has health care cost implications. People with multiple sexual partners have a greater risk of acquiring STDs than those who are monogamous.[16] If it is acceptable for employers to ban off-duty smoking because it increases costs, it is equally acceptable for employers to control all of these other types of behavior. The more we learn about the relationships between behavior and health, the more we realize that everything we do in our private lives affects our health. If employers are permitted to control private behavior when it is related to health, virtually every aspect of our private lives is subject to employer control.

Some people argue this isn't really a slippery slope—employers wouldn't try to control other aspects of people's private lives, only smoking.[17] These people don't understand business. Employers don't ban off-duty smoking because they are anti-smoking; they ban off-duty smoking to increase the bottom line. To an employer, a dollar saved by forcing an employee to give up junk food and lose weight is just as valuable as a dollar saved by forcing an employee to quit smoking. Recent studies from the Centers for Disease Control show that obesity is rapidly overtaking smoking as the leading cause of preventable death in the United States.[18] Cost-conscious employers will soon have more incentive to regulate diet and exercise than smoking.

In fact, some employers have banned other forms of private behavior. Multi-Developers, a real estate development company, prohibits employees from skiing, riding a motorcycle, or engaging in any other risky hobby.[19] The Best Lock Corporation, in Indiana, prohibits the consumption of alcohol at any time.[20] Best Lock fired Daniel Winn after eight years of good performance because Mr. Winn went out for a few beers with some friends after work.[21] The city of Athens, Georgia, required all municipal employees to take cholesterol tests—if your cholesterol was too high, you were fired.[22]

Other employers have gone further. Lynne Gobbell lost her job at an Alabama insulation company because she had a "Kerry for President" bumper sticker on her car.[23] Glen Hiller, from West Virginia, was fired because his boss didn't like a question he asked a candidate at a political rally.[24] Laurel Allen, from New York, was fired by Wal-Mart because it disapproved of her boyfriend.[25] Kimberly Turic, from Michigan, was fired for telling her supervisor that she was considering having an abortion.[26]

Virtually all of these terminations were legal. Under American law, an employer has the right to fire an employee at any time, for any reason, unless there is a statute prohibiting a specific reason for termination.[27] A variety of federal and state laws prohibit discrimination based on race, age, gender, religion, disability, and (in some jurisdictions) sexual orientation.[28] However, in other than a handful of states,[29] there is no law against being fired because your employer disapproves of your private life.

Employment decisions should be based on how well you do your job, not on your private life. Most successful companies operate on this principle. There is no reason all companies shouldn't follow it.

Where does this leave employers who don't want to absorb the additional health care costs created by employee smoking? One option is for employers to require a higher personal contribution to the health care plan for employees who smoke.[30] There is nothing wrong with this in principle. We may all have the right to conduct our private lives as we choose, but we do not have the right to make other people take responsibility for the consequences of our behavior. If people choose to smoke, there is nothing unfair about requiring them to take financial responsibility for the health care costs this behavior creates. Employers could determine the amount by which health care costs of smokers exceed those of non-smokers and require smoking employees to contribute this amount personally.

Employers that choose this policy need to ensure that their surcharge is actuarially correct. While there is no question that smokers have higher health care costs, the actual cost differential is not entirely clear.[31] Moreover, most of the published estimates come from advocates and not from neutral experts.[32] Employers need to check their sources and consult with independent actuaries before determining the amount of the surcharge.

To be completely fair, employers should also analyze the amount of smokers' higher health care charges that the company will pay. For example, one of the largest components of smokers' health care costs is cancer treatment.[33] In many cases, smoking-related cancers occur later in life, after the person has retired, with the majority of that person's medical costs paid by Medicare.[34] Such factors should be included in calculating an employee's surcharge.

Even if actuarially correct, however, there are other concerns about surcharges. To be fair, surcharges should apply to all health-related off-duty behavior. Some non-smokers have higher health risks than some smokers. Someone who eats lunch at McDonald's seven days a week, never exercises, and drinks a six-pack of beer every day probably has greater health risks than a light smoker who does everything else right. Since the justification for the surcharge is the higher cost that the employee's behavior creates, in such cases the non-smoker should pay a higher surcharge. To be fair, a surcharge program needs to contain penalties for poor diet, lack of exercise, risky hobbies, risky sex, and anything else that affects health. This may not be unfair from the standpoint of personal responsibility, but from the perspective of individual autonomy it is "Henry Ford-light."

There are also privacy concerns implicated in such surcharges. For an employer to establish a comprehensive surcharge program, it needs comprehensive knowledge of its employees' private lives. It needs to know how much employees drink, what they eat, what they do in their spare time, and how many sexual partners they have. Do we really want to reveal this information to our employers? Employers' poor historical record of maintaining the privacy of personal information increases the level of concern about surrendering our privacy to this degree.[35]

Enforcement of surcharge programs also raises privacy issues. Many employees will misrepresent their private behavior in order to avoid penalties. To protect the integrity of the program, employers will need programs to detect such deception. One method is urine testing. Cotinine, the most common metabolite of nicotine, can be detected in smokers' urine, just as THC metabolites are detected in the urine of marijuana users.[36] Before initiating such a program, however, employers need to consider how employees will react. While Americans have generally become accustomed to one-time pre-employment urine tests, random testing of incumbent employees is relatively rare, in part because of employee resistance. Such programs could also run afoul of the Americans with Disabilities Act's prohibition of medical testing that is not job-related.[37]

Another method is to encourage employees who know another employee is secretly smoking off-duty (or secretly riding a motorcycle) to inform management. This approach, however, seems even more likely to cause conflict. What happens to the working relationship between two people when one has turned the other in for smoking or drinking off-duty?

In short, surcharge programs may well create more problems than their cost savings justify.

It might be far more productive for employers to approach employee medical costs from a helpful perspective rather than a punitive one. Very few of us are proud of our bad habits. Surveys repeatedly show that most smokers want to quit.[38] Millions of us make New Year's resolutions to eat less, go to the gym more often, and cut down on our drinking.[39] Employers could do a great deal to help us follow through on these good intentions. For example, employers could pay for smoking cessation programs for employees who want to quit.[40] They could even offer a modest incentive for employees who are successful, such as an extra vacation day or a small amount of money. Such programs are highly cost-effective.[41] The same approach could be equally effective in helping employees who want to lose weight. A more ambitious program would make medical personnel available for voluntary consultations with employees about how to improve their health. This type of program not only avoids the legal and morale problems of the punitive approach but would be perceived as an added benefit by employees.

The fact that so many employers are approaching this issue in a punitive fashion reflects that we have lost our way on smoking in the United States. Our goals should be:

1. Protecting non-smokers from second-hand smoke;
2. Keeping tobacco out of the hands of minors; and
3. Helping smokers who want to quit.

Our actual policy, however, has become eliminating smoking by any means necessary.

You can see this in our official national policy on smoking. The Healthy People Initiative, a program of the Federal Department of Health and Human Services, has a goal of cutting adult smoking in half by the year 2010.[42] Not to protect non-smokers, not to help smokers who want to quit, but to eliminate smoking, period.

This mistake is not merely verbal; it shows in actions as well. Legislation has been enacted in most states prohibiting companies from terminating employees based on off-duty smoking.[43] Such laws do not expose employees to second-hand smoke—they simply protect peoples' right to behave as they want in their own home. Employers can still restrict or ban tobacco use on company property. Anti-smoking groups consistently and vigorously opposed the enactment of these laws.[44] When challenged, they claimed that such laws give undeserved special protection to smokers.[45] But when bills were introduced protecting all forms of legal off-duty conduct, the anti-smoking establishment opposed them too.[46] The only policy consistent with the actions of the anti-smoking establishment is prohibition.

The prohibitionist mentality is not confined to tobacco regulation. Kelly Brownell of Yale University is one of the leading thinkers of the health community. She has proposed that the government create a special tax on junk food so that people will be encouraged to eat less of it.[47] According to Brownell, "the government needs to regulate food as it would a potentially dangerous drug."[48]

This is a serious error. Not only is it wrong for any of us to try to tell the rest of us how to live in our own homes, prohibition is unworkable in practice.

America has tried prohibition. In 1919 the Volstead Act prohibited the production or consumption of alcohol.[49] Alcohol production didn't stop; it merely went underground as legitimate companies were replaced by criminals like Al Capone.[50] Nor did Americans stop drinking. They just turned to illegal bars and homemade liquor. This required us to devote vast amounts of our criminal justice resources searching for underground bars and ordinary citizens brewing beer in their bathtubs. Only fourteen years later, Prohibition was universally rejected as a colossal failure and the law was repealed.[51] One definition of insanity is to keep repeating the same behavior expecting different results.

A comprehensive proposal for an alternative national policy is beyond the scope of this paper, but a good first step would be to give the Food and Drug Administration (FDA) jurisdiction over tobacco products. Tobacco is by far the most dangerous consumer substance available in America. To fail to regulate it is indefensible. We regulate air conditioners, hammocks, and even coffee mugs in the interest of public safety.[52] It is absurd not to regulate tobacco. Giving the FDA jurisdiction would also establish that tobacco is a legitimate consumer product that needs to be regulated, not prohibited.[53]

We need to follow a similar regulatory policy regarding other forms of risky behavior; one that focuses on protecting other people from the risks we choose to take.

Notes

1. Attributed to Justice Oliver Wendell Holmes.
2. See Henry Ford & Samuel Crowther, My Life and Work 128–29 (1922). Ford employed as many as fifty investigators in his "social welfare department" who looked into the private lives of Ford

Motor Company employees. Id. The Social Department was originally instituted to evaluate each employee's eligibility for a "prosperity-sharing" program. Id. at 129.

3. See Keith Sward, The Legend of Henry Ford 59 (1948).

4. Id.

5. Id.

6. Id.

7. Id.

8. Id.

9. See generally Jeremy W. Peters, Company's Smoking Ban Means Off-Hours, Too, N.Y. Times, Feb. 8, 2005, at C5.

10. See, e.g., Peters, supra note 9.

11. Nat'l Workrights Inst., Lifestyle Discrimination: Employer Control of Legal Off-Duty Employee Activities 2, http://www.workrights.org/issue life-style/ldbrief2.pdf [hereinafter NWI on Lifestyle Discrimination].

12. In 2002, the Centers for Disease Control and Prevention estimated that, on average, each adult smoker in the United States cost their employer $3391 in additional health care and productivity losses annually. Annual Smoking-Attributable Mortality, Years of Potential Life Lost, and Economic Costs—United States, 1995–1999, Apr. 12, 2002, http://www.cdc.gov/mmwr/preview/mmwrhtml/mm5114a2.htm [hereinafter CDC Report].

13. See id. The CDC, along with other individuals and organizations, has estimated the costs of smoking to employers. Id. See also Am. Cancer Soc'y, Smoking in the Workplace Costs You Money, http://www.cancer.org/downloads/COM/Smoking in the Workplace Costs You Money.pdf. However, all of these estimates have methodological problems that are beyond the scope of this article.

14. A recent study by the National Institute of Health found that how much and how often people consume alcohol independently influences the risk of death from a number of causes. Nat'l Inst. on Alcohol Abuse and Alcoholism, Quantity and Frequency of Drinking Influence Mortality Risk, http://www.niaaa.nih.gov/NewsEvents/News Releases/mortalityrisk.htm.

15. See, e.g., Rob Stein, Scientists Finding Out What Losing Sleep Does to a Body, Wash. Post, Oct. 9, 2005, at A01, available at http://www.washingtonpost.com/wp-dyn/content/article/2005/10/08/AR2005100801405.html.

16. The CDC states that "the most reliable way to avoid transmission of STDs is to abstain from sex or to be in a long-term, mutually monogamous relationship with an uninfected partner." Ctrs. for Disease Control & Prevention, Sexually Transmitted Diseases; Treatment Guidelines: 2006; Clinical Prevention Guidance, http://www.cdc.gov/std/treatment/2006/clinical.htm#clinical1.

17. See Micah Berman & Rob Crane, Mandating a Tobacco-Free Workforce; A Convergence of Business and Public Health Interests, 34 Wm. Mitchell L. Rev 1653, 1672 (2008) (arguing that tobacco use is distinguishable from other potentially hazardous activities and that "slippery slope concerns are entirely speculative"); Michele L. Tyler, Blowing Smoke: Do Smokers Have a Right? Limiting the Privacy Rights of Cigarette Smokers, 86 Geo. L.J. 783, 794–95(1998) (discussing the slippery slope doctrine and concluding that a smoking ban is unlikely to result in further invasions of other privacy rights because of economic factors); Christopher Valleau, If You're Smoking, You're Fired: How Tobacco Could Be Dangerous To More Than Just Your Health, 10 DePaul J. Health Care L. 457, 490-92 (2007) (concluding that the slippery slope doctrine fails because smoking is inherently different than other lifestyle behaviors).

18. Ali H. Mokdad et al., Actual Causes of Death in the United States, 2000, 291 J. Am. Med. Ass'n 1238–45 (Mar. 10, 2004), available at http://www.csdp.org/research/1238.pdf.

19. Zachary Schiller et al., If You Light Up on Sunday, Don't Come in on Monday, Bus. Wk., Aug. 26, 1991, at 68. Multi-Developers, Inc.'s policy prohibits employees from engaging in "'hazardous activities and pursuits including such things as skydiving, riding motorcycles, piloting private aircraft, mountain climbing, motor vehicle racing, etc." Id. To the author's knowledge, this is still the policy at Multi-Developers, Inc.

20. Best Lock Corp. v. Review Bd., 572 N.E.2d 520, 521 (Ind. Ct. App. 1991). Best Lock Corporation's tobacco, alcohol, and drug use rule (TAD Rule) states: "The use of tobacco, the use of alcohol as a beverage, or the use of drugs by an employee shall not be condoned. . . . Any employee violating this policy, at work or away from the plant, will be summarily terminated." Id.

21. See id. (Winn admitted under oath, in a proceeding involving the termination of his brother from Best Lock Corporation, that he had consumed alcohol on several social occasions while employed at Best Lock Corporation).

22. Schiller et al., supra note 19. The city of Athens, Georgia, for a short period of time, required job applicants to submit to a cholesterol test. Id. Applicants whose cholesterol levels ranked in the top 20% of all applicants were eliminated from

consideration for employment. Id. Local protests led to elimination of the policy. Id.

23. Paola Singer, Fired Over Kerry Sticker; Her Loss Is Their Gain, Newsday, Sept. 17, 2004, at A33.

24. Jessica Valdez, Frederick Company Fires Employee Who Taunted Bush, Wash. Post, Aug. 22, 2004, at C06.

25. Dottie Enrico, When Office Romance Collides With the Corporate Culture, Newsday, Aug. 1, 1993, at 70. Allen was dating a fellow employee while she was still married to her husband, although they were separated. Id.

26. Pregnancy Bias Case Costs a Hotel $89,000, Chi. Trib., Mar. 16, 1994, at M3. Turic later won a lawsuit for wrongful termination and was awarded $89,000. Id.

27. See generally 27 Am. Jur. 2d Employment Relationship § 10 (2008).

28. See, e.g., 42 U.S.C. § 2000e-2 (2000) (making it illegal for an employer to discriminate on the basis of race, color, religion, sex, or national origin); Minn. Stat. § 363A.08 subdiv. 2 (Supp. 2007) (listing sexual orientation as a class protected from employment discrimination).

29. New York, Colorado, North Dakota, and Montana offer broad protection of legal off-duty behavior. See NWI on Lifestyle Discrimination, supra note 11, at 11–13 (citing 2004 State by State Guide to Human Resources Law (John F. Buckley & Ronald M. Green eds., 2004)).

30. See Peters, supra note 9 (describing the $50 fee charged by one employer to all smokers to cover increased healthcare costs associated with smoking-related illnesses).

31. See CDC Report, supra note 12; see also Kate Fitch et al., American Legacy Foundation, Covering Smoking Cessation as a Health Benefit: A Case for Employers 11 (2007), http://www.americanlegacy.org/PDFPublications/MillimanreportALF—3.15.07.pdf (estimating that employees who suffer strokes or develop coronary artery disease can cost their employers upwards of $ 65,000 per year in medical expenses).

32. Two of the most active of these advocates are The American Cancer Society, http://www.cancer.org, and The American Legacy Foundation, http://www.americanlegacy.org.

33. See Am. Cancer Soc'y, Cancer Facts & Figures 2008, at 48-51, http://www.cancer.org/downloads/STT/2008CAFFfinalsecured.pdf.

34. See News Release, U.S. Dep't of Health & Human Servs., Medicare Will Help Beneficiaries Quit Smoking: New Proposed Coverage for Counseling as Medicare Shifts Focus to Prevention (Dec. 23, 2004), available at http://www.hhs.gov/news/press/2004pres/20041223a.html (stating that "in 1993, smoking cost the Medicare program about $ 14.2 billion, or approximately 10 percent of Medicare's total budget").

35. See, e.g., Rita Tehan, Cong. Research Serv. Report for Cong., Data Security Breaches: Context and Incident Summaries tbl. 1 (May 7, 2007), available at http://ftp.fas.org/sgp/crs/misc/RL33199.pdf.

36. Found. for Blood Research, Important Patient Information About . . . Cotinine Testing, http://www.fbr.org/publications/pamphlets/cotinine.html (last visited Apr. 10, 2008).

37. See Americans with Disabilities Act, 42 U.S.C. § 12112 (d)(4)(A) (2000). This provision of the ADA states:

A covered entity shall not require a medical examination and shall not make inquiries of an employee as to whether such employee is an individual with a disability or as to the nature or severity of the disability, unless such examination or inquiry is shown to be job-related and consistent with business necessity.
Id.

38. See, e.g., Jonathan Lynch, Survey Finds Most Smokers Want to Quit, CNN.com, July 25, 2002, http://archives.cnn.com/2002/HEALTH/07/25/cdc.smoking/index.html (citing a CDC survey that found that 70% of the 32,374 smokers surveyed responded that they wanted to quit smoking).

39. See, e.g., RIS Media.com, The Top New Year's Resolutions for 2008 and How to Keep Them (Dec. 20, 2007), http://rismedia.com/wp/2007-12-19/the-top-new-years-resolutions-for-2008-and-how-to-keep-them/.

40. See, e.g., Milt Freudenheim, Seeking Savings, Employers Help Smokers Quit, N.Y. Times, Oct. 26, 2007, at A1 (citing U.P.S. and Union Pacific Railroad as companies that offer smoking cessation programs).

41. See Free & Clear, Inc., Reducing the Burden of Smoking on Employee Health and Productivity, http://www.freeclear.com/caseforcessation/library/studies/burden.aspx?navsection=2 ("There is much evidence to support that paying for tobacco cessation treatment is the single, most cost-effective health insurance benefit for adults and is the benefit that has the greatest positive impact on health.") (citing Nat'l Bus. Group on Health, Reducing the Burden of Smoking on Employee Health and Productivity, Vol. 1, No. 5 (2003), available at http://www.businessgrouphealth.org/pdfs/issuebrief cphssmoking.pdf).

42. Healthy People 2010 Volume II, Tobacco Use, http://www.healthypeople.gov/Document/HTML/Volume2/27Tobacco.htm# Toc489766214 (last visited Apr. 6, 2008).

43. Thirty states and the District of Columbia have life-style discrimination statutes that prohibit employers from firing employees for certain legal, private activities, including smoking. These states include: Arizona, California, Colorado, Connecticut, Illinois, Indiana, Kentucky, Louisiana, Maine, Minnesota, Mississippi, Missouri, Montana, Nevada, New Hampshire, New Jersey, New Mexico, New York, North Carolina, North Dakota, Oklahoma, Oregon, Rhode Island, South Carolina, South Dakota, Tennessee, Virginia, West Virginia, Wisconsin, and Wyoming. NWI on Lifestyle Discrimination, supra note 11, at 11–13.

44. See, e.g., Samantha K. Graff, Tobacco Control Legal Consortium, There is no Constitutional Right to Smoke: 2008, at 3 (2d ed. 2008) (arguing that off-duty restrictions on smoking are not precluded by an employee's right to privacy), available at http://tobaccolawcenter.org/documents/constitutional-right.pdf.

45. See, e.g., Matthew Reilly, Florio Urged to Provide Smokers Bias Protection, Star-Ledger (Newark, N.J.), Jan. 4, 1991 (quoting Regina Carlson, executive director of the New Jersey Group Against Smoking Pollution (GASP), as stating that the passage of a bill that protects the privacy rights of smokers "would elevate drug addiction to civil rights status, along with race and sex").

46. See, e.g., Graff, supra note 44, at 5 (stating that "smoker protection laws," including laws protecting all off-duty legal conduct, are a "barrier to a smoke-free agenda").

47. Is it Time for a Fat Tax?, Psychol. Today, Sept.–Oct. 1997, at 16.

48. Id.

49. Darryl K. Brown, Democracy and Decriminalization, 86 Tex. L. Rev. 223, 238 (2007).

50. See, e.g., Chi. Historical Soc'y, History Files—Al Capone, http://www.chicagohs.org/history/capone/cpn1a.html (last visited Apr. 6, 2008).

51. See Brown, supra note 49, at 238.

52. See, e.g., 67 Fed. Reg. 36368-01 (Aug. 6, 2002) (to be codified at 10 C.F.R. pt. 430) (concerning the regulation of energy conservation standards for central air conditioners); Christopher D. Zalesky, Pharmaceutical Marketing Practices: Balancing Public Health and Law Enforcement Interests; Moving Beyond Regulation-Through-Litigation, 39 J. Health L. 235, 252 (2006) (discussing the FDA's regulation of the advertisement of prescription drugs, including the imprinting of prescription drug names on items such as coffee mugs).

53. A bipartisan group of legislators proposed legislation in February 2007 that would give the FDA regulatory power over tobacco. See Christopher Lee, New Push Grows for FDA Regulation of Tobacco, Wash. Post, Feb. 17, 2007, at A08. The Bush administration and the FDA's skepticism of such a regulatory measure appear to have stalled the movement for now. See Marc Kaufman, Decades-Long U.S. Decrease in Smoking Rates Levels Off, Wash. Post, Nov. 9, 2007, at A07.

Lewis Maltby is a president of the National Workrights Institute, a research and advocacy organization specializing in employment issues; he is also a faculty member of the Rutgers School of Management and Labor Relations. His publications include the book *Can They Do That? Reclaiming Our Fundamental Rights at Work* as well as a number of scholarly articles.

Adrien Barton

How Tobacco Health Warnings Can Foster Autonomy

Introduction

On 29 February 2012, a US federal judge ruled that regulations requiring large graphic health warnings on cigarette packaging violate free speech rights under the US Constitution. In his ruling, the judge argued that the government has other tools at its disposal to deter smoking, such as including simple factual information on the labels rather than gruesome images. Setting aside the legal issue and the problem of free speech for tobacco companies, this decision raises the question whether it is ethically acceptable to deter people from smoking with such warnings that seem to rely on irrational persuasion. This is an especially important question when considering that the World Health Organization recently identified health warnings on cigarette packages among the six key measures required to reduce smoking prevalence, while smoking remains the leading cause of preventable death in many developed countries.

I will analyze this new generation of tobacco health warnings in the context of a recent approach in political philosophy named 'libertarian paternalism' (Thaler and Sunstein, 2008). Libertarian paternalism proposes to affect people's choices by interventions interacting with their non-deliberative faculties and improving their welfare. Although Thaler and Sunstein have presented such measures as innocuous, it has been rightly pointed that they infringe on autonomy, and need therefore a careful justification on a case-by-case basis (see e.g. Hausman and Welch, 2010, or Grüne-Yanoff, 2012). I aim here at providing precisely such a justification for tobacco health warnings. The core of my argument will be that non-misleading health warning messages actually foster the autonomy of the typical addicted smokers, through both their informational and persuasive roles. This investigation will have significant consequences for the general

study of libertarian paternalism, by showing that classical paternalism and libertarian paternalism differ in some important aspect.

This article is structured the following way. First, I will sketch a short history of health warning messages on tobacco products and their efficiency and identify the area of investigation. Then, I will present libertarian paternalism. Afterwards, I will detail the informational role of health warning messages, and then their persuasive role. The next section will be central in my argumentation, investigating the multiple ways how health warning messages interact with people's autonomy, and concluding that it results in a net gain of autonomy for the typical addicted smoker. I will then raise two possible objections against this argument and show that they are misguided. Finally, a last section will complement the argument by considering two marginal cases: the non-addicted smoker and the willing addict. The conclusion will recap the argument and expose the difference it implies between libertarian paternalism and classical paternalism.

Health Warning Messages on Tobacco Products: A Short Presentation

Let us first sketch a brief history of health warning messages on cigarette packages. 1964 saw the release in the USA of the first report of the Surgeon General's Advisory Committee on Smoking and Health. Following that event, USA was the first nation to require a health warning on cigarette packages. The first warning was a small-sized text reading "Caution: Cigarette Smoking May be Hazardous to Your Health", and similar warnings were soon imposed in other countries and extended to smokeless tobacco products.

Barton, Adrien, "How Tobacco Health Warnings Can Foster Autonomy," *Public Health Ethics*, vol. 6, no. 2, July 2013, 207-219. Copyright ©2013 Oxford University Press. All rights reserved. Used with permission.

In December 2000, Canada became the first country to enforce graphic warnings on cigarette packaging. Nowadays, at least 40 nations, many in Europe, have imposed more eye-catching warnings than the original small-sized warnings, including graphic photos. In Australia, a law imposing so-called 'plain packaging' is implemented since December 2012: cigarettes are now sold in olive brown cartons with large graphic images covering 75 percent of the front of the pack and all of the back. Packs from different brands are only differentiated by the brand and product names, written in a standard format.

The efficiency of health warning messages on tobacco products has been largely investigated. To my knowledge, the most comprehensive study to date on this respect was made by Hammond (2011), who reviewed 94 articles on this topic. It concludes that prominent health warnings on the face of packages serve as a prominent source of health information for smokers and non-smokers, can increase health knowledge and perceptions of risk and can promote smoking cessation. Also, it states that comprehensive warnings are effective among youth and may help to prevent smoking initiation. Finally, it notices that pictorial health warnings that elicit strong emotional reactions are significantly more effective.[1] In 2011, Dr. Lawrence R. Deyton, Director of the FDA's Center for Tobacco Products, estimated (based on other countries' experience) that the new warning labels would prompt an additional 213,000 Americans to quit smoking in 2013, the (at-the-time) planned first full year with the graphic labels.

As one can see, the actuality of health warning messages on tobacco products is vibrant, and in need of ethical analysis that may complement and enlighten the legal and psychological investigations on the topic. This is precisely what this article will attempt to provide, by investigating how such warnings interfere with people's autonomy, and whether this is ethically acceptable or not. Cigarette being by far the most consumed tobacco product worldwide, I will concentrate on health warning messages on cigarette packs. In order to tackle this question, I will show first how imposing such warnings can be considered as a libertarian paternalistic intervention.

Health Warning Messages and Libertarian Paternalism

In order to introduce the topic of libertarian paternalism, one should first explain what a regular (that is, non-libertarian) paternalistic measure is. Elaborating on Dworkin (2010), we can say that an action toward an agent is paternalistic if it fulfills different conditions: first, it interferes with the liberty of the agent (this also includes changing the financial incentives in acquiring a product); second, it is done without his consent and third, it will improve his welfare. For example, some classical measures aiming at decreasing tobacco consumption—like imposing a special tax on tobacco goods—are instances of paternalism: they change the financial incentives in buying tobacco, they are done without the consent of the smokers and they aim (amongst other goals) at improving their health.

It should be noted that attempts to reduce people's smoking are not univocally paternalistic: they can be justified, for example, in order to reduce second-hand smoke absorption. Moreover, paternalism is not always problematic, especially when it concerns minors rather than adults. In order to strengthen my point, I will therefore focus in this article on the hardest case, namely justifying attempts to deter adults (rather than minors) from smoking through health warnings, for their own good (rather than in order to protect other people from second-hand smoke).

I will now show that health labels belong to a specific form of paternalism, namely libertarian paternalism (Thaler and Sunstein, 2008). For this, let us first notice the obvious fact that decisions are never taken by humans in a vacuum, but in an environment arranged in a certain way. The insight behind libertarian paternalism is that environments could be arranged in different ways so that people make spontaneously decisions which are better for themselves. For example, instead of arranging the pizzas and salads side-by-side in a cafeteria, the salads could be placed more prominently with the pizzas a bit further back. Such a change in the location of food items can increase or decrease the consumption of a specific food by 25% (Thaler and Sunstein, 2008). The environment within which a choice is made is named 'choice architecture'. A 'nudge' is an aspect of the choice architecture that alters people's behavior in a predictable way, without forbidding or significantly changing their economic incentives (that is, the intervention must be easy and cheap to avoid). To my knowledge, nudges have not been precisely defined yet in a non-controversial way, but at least a significant subclass of them[2] consist of interventions that influence people by interacting with their non-deliberative faculties (see Grüne-Yanoff, 2012, for a related account): simply bringing new information to people can alter their choices when being processed by their deliberative faculties, but does not count as a nudge.

There are many ways of defining 'deliberative' and 'non-deliberative' faculties in the cognitive psychology literature. What we will say will fit with several of these accounts, but we will endorse here more specifically the one proposed by Kruglanski and Gigerenzer (2011), which characterizes deliberative faculties as requiring cognitive effort and being accessible to conscious awareness. Non-deliberative faculties, on the other hand, require relatively little cognitive effort and are not accessible to awareness. In particular, as emphasized by Kruglanski and Gigerenzer (2011), deliberative faculties should not be confused with rule-based faculties (as intuitive faculties may be rule-based too), nor with 'rational' faculties (as it may be rational to use non-deliberative faculties). Here, 'faculties' should be understood as 'faculties of judgment and decision' (excluding e.g. perceptual faculties).

Let us consider again the above example of arranging the food in a cafeteria; in such a scenario, people are nudged to eat more salads and less pizzas, as this choice is not taken deliberately. Libertarian paternalism can be defined in the following way: an intervention counts as libertarian paternalistic if it nudges people to make choices that improve their welfare.

By definition, classical paternalistic measures interfere with an agent's liberty. On the contrary, libertarian paternalistic measures are not liberty-reducing[3]: they keep all choice alternatives open. That said, libertarian paternalistic measures do not come without a price. By influencing people while addressing their non-deliberative faculties, nudges may interfere with their autonomy. Therefore, libertarian paternalism involves a trade-off between autonomy and well-being.

Before going further, this concept of autonomy needs to be defined a bit further. The general idea behind autonomy is the 'capacity to live one's life according to reasons and motives that are taken as one's own and not the product of manipulative or distorting external forces' (Christman, 2011). Drawing on this account, we can dissociate two components of autonomy. First, 'the independence of one's deliberation and choice from manipulation by others' (Christman, 2011), which I will call the 'independence' component; the word 'manipulation' being negatively connoted, let us use instead the more neutral word 'persuasion', which we will define as an intervention addressing non-deliberative faculties.[4] The independence component of autonomy implies that the judgments and decisions of a perfectly autonomous agent should not be influenced in a way that addresses his non-deliberative faculties. The second component of autonomy is the 'capacity to rule oneself' (Christman, 2011) in order to aim at some goals, which I will call the 'self-ruling' component. This capacity requires in particular to be well-informed, so that following a self-chosen rule will have the desired effects. In the rest of the article, self-ruling should therefore be understood as 'informed self-ruling'.

With these distinctions in mind, we can claim that libertarian paternalistic measures that address people's non-deliberative faculties interfere with people's independence component of autonomy, and therefore raise ethical worries. Imposing health labels on tobacco products amounts to arranging the choice architecture in which someone will take the decision to smoke or not: as a matter of fact, in most cases, someone who is about to smoke will see the warning. If one can show that these labels address people's non-deliberative faculties, this will prove that they are a libertarian paternalistic intervention. I will show that this is indeed the case, by detailing the informational role and the persuasive role of these messages.

The Informational Role of Tobacco Health Warnings

In many respects, tobacco health warnings can be described as a kind of 'anti-advertising' against tobacco products. As a matter of fact, like advertising, tobacco health warnings have two functions: informing and persuading (Chapman, 1996). On one hand, they aim at informing the consumer about the risks raised by tobacco products; and on the other hand, they aim at persuading him not to buy the product. Whereas their informational role appeals to people's deliberative faculties, their persuasive role addresses their non-deliberative faculties. Let us start by detailing this informational role of health tobacco warnings.

A study led by the International Tobacco Control Policy Evaluation Project in 2009 showed that health warnings on cigarette packages were the second source of information after TV about the risks of smoking in a majority of countries. Moreover, evidence suggests that countries with pictorial warnings demonstrate fewer disparities in health knowledge across educational levels (Hammond, 2011); therefore, pictorial warnings appear to be an efficient tool in order to spread information about tobacco risks in a way that is socially just.

Tobacco companies have long considered that the initial small-letter health warnings were sufficient to inform the consumers about the hazards of smoking. However, it has been shown that large text-based warnings are associated with increased health knowledge (Hammond, 2011). This provides an important justification for the transition from small-letter warnings to large-letter ones that has been operated in many countries. Other stylistic aspects may be important too in order to fulfill this informational role. For example, contrasted colors, like black letters on a white background, have been found to increase comprehension (Hammond, 2011). To sum up, there is an important ethical justification for writing objective informational messages and also for writing them in large contrasted letters rather than in small characters.

Some other messages fulfill an important information function—although I will show later that they also raise a few ethical worries. Messages mentioning specific diseases that may be caused by tobacco belong to this category. As a matter of fact, Chapman and Lieberman (2005) noticed that it is not enough, for being adequately informed, to know that smoking increases health risks: one should also be aware of the specific diseases caused by smoking. It appears that smokers are poorly informed in this respect, even for the most well-known tobacco-related diseases. Therefore, messages like 'smoking causes gangrene' in Singapore (as well as images showing the possible extent of the diseases) fulfill an informational role. One could object that such a disease is rare (more will be said about that in the next section); however, it might be rational to decide to smoke or not to smoke on the basis of this specific information only. For example, someone could follow a simple strategy which is to decide on the basis of the worst possible outcome; it would be justified for him to decide to stop smoking when learning that smoking can cause gruesome gangrene.

The Persuasive Role of Tobacco Health Warnings

Now that the informational role of tobacco health warnings has been presented, let us turn to their persuasive role. I will not try to make an exhaustive investigation of all existing warning messages, but I will present here three possible ways for tobacco health warning messages to address non-deliberative faculties: using social mechanisms like submission to authority; using emotional persuasion and exploiting cognitive heuristics.

Authoritative Messages and Recommendation Power

A first step away from the informational role is made when authoritative commands appear on warnings, like 'Smoking is highly addictive, don't start', which exploit people's natural submission to authority. Authoritative message can take a more hidden form, related to what Grüne-Yanoff (unpublished data) has called 'recommendation power' (in the context of default choices). In a nutshell, the idea is that messages can give implicit signals about what the best action is. A good example would be the warning 'Your doctor or pharmacist can help you quit

smoking', which—despite not being commanding—suggests to smokers that they should quit. People reading this message may be inclined to follow the recommendation without deliberating about it. But recommendations can be even less direct. For example, it has been shown that viewers often equate the size of the warning with the magnitude of the risk (Hammond, 2011). However, the notion of 'magnitude' of a risk is— at least to some extent—subjective, since it depends on people's valuation of the bad consequences. Moreover, people generally evaluate risk and benefits not as two different entities but as one general compound: when one says that something is risky, it implies not only that he thinks it has some probable bad consequences but also that he thinks the benefits of this activity are not worth these bad consequences (Gregory and Mendelsohn, 1993). Therefore, a large-sized warning message may communicate implicitly that smoking is not worth its benefits. But people may have different valuations of smoking's bad consequences and benefits: some people may fear premature death more than others, some people may take a higher pleasure from smoking than others, etc. Therefore, when reading such messages, people may be pushed to take a decision independently of their values, instead of deliberating whether this is a good decision given their own values.

More simply, the fact that an originally informational message is read over and over confers upon it a strong recommendation power and makes it persuasive rather than simply informational. Being told only once that tobacco damages health is informational; being told this message 2000 times is also persuasive.

To sum up, some health labels influence people's valuations in ways that address their non-deliberative faculties. This is an instance of a general problem for libertarian paternalism identified by Rizzo and Whitman (2008): choice architects are privileged in selecting which values and preferences are promoted by the nudges they design.

Messages Using Emotional Persuasion

Some messages rely on emotional persuasion. Psychological research has shown that graphic depictions of disease appear to be the most reliable way to elicit negative emotional reactions (like fear or disgust) to health warnings, which in turn have been associated with engaging in cessation behavior[5] (Hammond, 2011). However, this cognitive process addresses non-deliberative faculties, playing on emotional reactions rather than on thoughtful deliberations.

Purely textual messages can also rely on emotional persuasion. For example, a European tobacco warning message states: 'Cigarette smoke contains benzene, nitrosamines, formaldehyde and hydrogen cyanide.' It is likely that most readers have no idea of the composition or effects of such products. But since these names evoke dangerous chemicals, people will infer (rightly) that they are dangerous and react with fear or disgust. However, the right inference is taken by non-deliberative means that may lead to false beliefs in other contexts. People without any biochemical knowledge would also presumably react with fear if a warning would inform them (falsely) that cigarettes contain L-ascorbic acid (which is the biochemical name for vitamin C): in a given context, any specific chemical name can raise fear.

Messages Exploiting Cognitive Heuristics

Other warnings rely on mechanisms that are less social or emotional, but more cognitive in nature. It has been largely documented that in situations of uncertainty, people tend to rely on cognitive shortcuts named 'heuristics', instead of using fully their deliberative faculties. When used in a context that is not appropriate, these heuristics can lead to cognitive biases—that is, deviation from the normatively correct judgments. One common heuristic on which people rely is the 'availability heuristic' (introduced by Tversky and Kahneman, 1973), which uses the ease with which examples come to mind in order to make judgments about the probability of events. For example, someone may consider that crime is frequent in his city because he has heard several times recently the TV news mentioning crimes committed there. Although this availability heuristic may sometimes be beneficial (see e.g. the work on the fluency heuristic, cf. Schooler and Hertwig, 2005), the frequencies that events come to mind are usually not accurate reflections of their actual probabilities in reality.

I have shown above that health warning messages mentioning specific diseases caused by tobacco fulfill an important informational role; however, they may also lead people to overestimate the probability of these diseases when using the availability heuristics. This could be especially worrisome when health warnings mention some rare diseases, for example the above-mentioned Singaporean warning stating 'Smoking causes gangrene'. The incidence of the corresponding disease (named Brueger's disease) is relatively low (8 to 12 per 100,000 adults in the USA, most of them due to tobacco products). Such a risk communication exploits the same kind of bias as the many advertisements for lotteries that insist on the size of the main prize, without mentioning the low probability of winning it[6]; in this respect, it is misleading.

Even messages giving correct statistics may be misleading. A warning in Canada states '85% of lung cancers are caused by smoking'. Even if this figure is accurate, many people are likely to commit what is called the 'inverse fallacy' (Villejoubert and Mandel, 2002) and confuse it with the incorrect statement '85% of smokers will get lung cancers' (the inverse fallacy consists in confusing the probability of A given B with the probability of B given A). Before putting the blame on people's poor understanding of probabilities, it must be noticed that this warning message has little relevance to inform a smoker about his risks: if lung cancer had a very low prevalence, 85% of lung cancers could be caused by smoking while the risk of getting lung cancer from smoking would be very low (as it happens, around 13% of smokers will get lung cancer—an already alarmingly high statistics). Therefore, this message invites to commit the 'inverse fallacy', since the incorrect statement '85% of smokers will get lung cancers' would be much more relevant in this context (see Sperber and Wilson, 1995, for an account of how people try to maximize relevance in communication). To sum up, although it gives the correct numbers, this warning can be seen as a misleading statistics. It is not unlike a former advertising for a French lottery that stated '100% of all winners have tried their luck'.[7]

Persuasive Role: Summary

In summary, several text warning messages rely on strategies that address non-deliberative faculties: this shows that they infringe on the independence component of autonomy, by interfering with the choice of smoking in a persuasive way; and therefore, that they can be counted as a libertarian paternalistic measure. However, it is important to dissociate two families of messages. Some of them may trigger false inferences by non-deliberative means and are therefore both persuasive and misleading; for example, 'Smoking causes gangrene' may trigger the false inference that it is likely that a smoker will get gangrene. Some others may trigger true inferences by non-deliberative means, and are therefore persuasive but not misleading; for example, the warning 'Cigarette smoke contains benzene, nitrosamines, formaldehyde and hydrogen cyanide.' may trigger the true inference that cigarettes contain dangerous chemicals. The first family of message seems more problematic, and indeed, I will show in the next section that they are. Now that these informative and persuasive roles have been carefully dissociated, I can analyze the multiple ways by which health warnings may interfere with people's autonomy and how problematic this is.

The Interference on Autonomy

In general, libertarian paternalistic interventions on an agent trade a partial autonomy loss for a gain in welfare. It may be difficult—although not necessarily impossible—to evaluate the ethicality of such interventions, as these goods (autonomy and welfare) are heterogeneous categories. It may well be that the exceptional burden of disease associated with cigarette consumption would justify some loss of autonomy (it may well even justify fully paternalistic measures like taxes on tobacco products). However, it would be more satisfying if such measures could be justified without putting in the same balance goods that belong to heterogeneous categories. This is precisely such a justification that I will attempt to provide here: I will show that although health warning messages infringe on the independence component of addicted smoker's autonomy, this is compensated by an increase in their self-ruling component of autonomy, leading to a net gain in autonomy.

For this, the interference on autonomy occasioned by health warnings needs to be investigated closely. First, I will show that the informational role of health warnings fosters people's self-ruling component of autonomy, whereas misleading health warnings infringe on this component. Second, I will argue that the persuasive role of non-misleading health warnings also fosters the self-ruling component of autonomy of the addicted smoker. Third, I will show that although health warnings infringe on the independence component of autonomy, they protect against another cause of infringement, namely the implicit advertisement in a cigarette pack's design. Fourth, I will claim that health warning messages are fully transparent, and that everyone can easily avoid them substantially.

How Health Warnings' Informational Role Fosters People's Self-Ruling Component of Autonomy

Mill (1859) already argued that 'labelling [a] drug with some word expressive of its dangerous character, may be enforced without violation of liberty', since presumably 'the buyer cannot wish not to know that the thing he possesses has poisonous qualities'. This illustrates that the informational role of tobacco health warnings fosters people's self-ruling component of autonomy: indeed, by knowing more about the risks of tobacco, a rational agent should be able to lead his life in a better-informed way (as a reminder, being well-informed is an important dimension of the self-ruling component of autonomy). Moreover, the informational role does not address people's

non-deliberative faculties, and therefore does not infringe on the independence component of autonomy.

For symmetrical reasons, insofar as misleading tobacco health warnings trigger false inferences, they make people less well informed, and therefore decrease their self-ruling component of autonomy. Therefore, misleading tobacco health warnings should be limited as much as possible (see the Conclusion section for a further discussion of this point).

How Health Warnings' Persuasive Role Fosters Addicted Smokers' Self-Ruling Component of Autonomy

Let us now turn to the persuasive role of health warnings and show that it also fosters the self-ruling component of autonomy for a typical addicted smoker[8] (when it is not misleading). For this, we need to investigate more precisely how health warnings may influence smokers' actions or desires.

Drawing on Frankfurt (1971), Goodin (1989) established a distinction between smokers' desires: they have a compulsive desire to smoke (a 'first-order' desire), but they also have a desire not to desire to smoke (since this is a desire about desires, it is called a 'second-order' desire). That is, most smokers suffer from a discrepancy between their first-order desires and their second-order desires. The typical smoker may also have a first-order desire not to smoke (or to smoke less), but tobacco addiction being strong, his first-order desire not to smoke is weaker than his first-order desire to smoke. Therefore, he smokes.

The persuasive role of health warning messages addresses people's non-deliberative faculties. It will reinforce their first-order desire not to smoke (or to smoke less) relatively directly. For example, a disgusting image of a cancerous lung will generally reinforce the first-order desire not to smoke without any need of deliberation. In some cases, this will enable this desire to be stronger than the desire to smoke, and consequently, the smoker will stop smoking (or will reduce his smoking). The self-ruling component of autonomy of the addicted smoker would then be fostered, as he now acts according to a rule (given by his second-order desire) that he has set for himself.

How Health Warnings Protect Against Another Cause of Infringement on Autonomy

I have established that the persuasive role of tobacco health warning messages addresses people's non-deliberative faculties, and thereby infringe on their independence component of autonomy. However, I will argue here that this loss is not as important as one could think.

Large and graphic health warning messages hide parts of the classical packaging that is designed by tobacco companies to attract smokers; this is of course especially true for the plain tobacco packaging format that is implemented in Australia since December 2012, which prohibit any companies' own design. As revealed in industry documents, 'the tobacco industry fully appreciates that packs are the premier site for communicating with smokers' (Chapman and Lieberman, 2005): packs' design acts as an implicit advertisement. Insofar as health warnings cover parts of the packs, they diminish the non-deliberative influence of the classical packaging's design. Therefore, they replace one source of interference with the independence component of autonomy (the tobacco company's implicit advertisement in their packaging's design) by another interference with this component (the health warning message). Arguably, the interference caused by some of the health warning messages may be stronger than the one caused by the packaging's design; but it can still be concluded that the independence component of autonomy is not decreased as much as one could think by the introduction of large health warnings.

One can even notice that some packaging formats may be considered as misleading advertisements. In particular, the design of some 'light' cigarette packs (with e.g. light colors predominating) may suggest the false idea that they are not harmful for smoking. Insofar as health warnings cover parts of the packs, they protect against this misleading implicit message. Therefore, they foster the self-ruling component of autonomy of the smoker.

Transparency and Avoidability

Let us now turn to another worry related to autonomy. Hausman and Welch (2010) have pointed that the government should inform people of efforts to shape their choices when they are engaging into libertarian paternalistic measures: people have a right to know that they are under influence. Bovens (2009) introduced a further distinction: government should not only inform people about how it will try to interfere with their agency—this is called 'type transparency'—but also inform people every time it tries to interfere with their agency—this is called 'token transparency'. As a matter of fact, people should not only know that they are under influence but they may also have a right to know when they are being influenced. Moreover, token transparency enables people who do not appreciate this type of manipulation to avoid nudges.

Knowing when he is under influence is important for an agent to direct his life, and therefore to protect his self-ruling component of autonomy.

Coming back to health warning messages on tobacco products, it should be noted that they fully satisfy both requirements of type transparency and token transparency. As a matter of fact, people not only know that the government is trying to reduce smoking prevalence through warning messages in general: they also know, every time they see a warning message, that the government is trying to reduce smoking prevalence through this specific message. However, a superficial analysis could suggest that health warning messages are very difficult to avoid despite their transparency: indeed, they act as a kind of 'portative anti-advertising', following the smoker wherever he brings his cigarette pack. But it can be objected that special cases that hide the warning messages of cigarette packs are commercialized in many countries.[9] Therefore, a smoker can avoid these warnings substantially[10] if they wish to, for an insignificant price.

In conclusion, warning messages on tobacco products are both type and token transparent, and they can be avoided substantially at a negligible cost. Therefore, they raise little worries in this respect.

Interference on Autonomy: Summary

I have shown that the informational role of health warning message protects people's self-ruling component of autonomy; this role is therefore uncontroversial. On the opposite, misleading messages are ethically not justified: the government should not communicate messages that are clearly known to trigger false inferences.

However, the persuasive role of some non-misleading messages has a more complex interaction with autonomy. On one hand, they increase typical addicted smokers' self-ruling component of autonomy (when they are not misleading); and on the other hand, they interfere with people's independence component of autonomy, by addressing non-deliberative faculties (although not as much as one could think, as they also protect against the infringement on autonomy due to the implicit advertisement in the design of the cigarette packs). In order to determine their net consequences on autonomy for the typical addicted smoker, we need to put in a balance their effects on his independence and self-ruling components of autonomy. Arguably, the second component is more important for the addicted smoker. Indeed, the independence component of autonomy is valuable mainly[11] to the extent that it protects people from interference on their authentic choices—the ones they can recognize as expressing their own selves.[12] However, the first-order desire to smoke of an addicted smoker is the effect of an unwanted addiction and does not push towards an authentic choice. Therefore, it is arguably more authentic for an addicted smoker to lead his life following his second-order desire to desire not to smoke,[13] rather than to keep his first-order desires (and the actions to which they lead) safe from any influence addressing his non-deliberative faculties. One can consequently argue that the interference with his independence component of autonomy is compensated by the increase in his self-ruling component. All in all, the persuasive role of non-misleading health warning messages would then end up fostering the autonomy of a typical addicted smoker.

Apparent Asymmetries between the Autonomy Loss Caused by Health Warning Messages and Tobacco Addiction

I will now turn to two apparent dissimilarities between the respective actions of health warning messages and tobacco addiction, which could be used to counter the conclusion that the persuasive role of health warning messages end up fostering the addicted smoker's autonomy. I will rebut these two arguments.

Tobacco Addiction and Judgments

It looks like although tobacco causes a craving in the smoker (that is, a very strong first-order desire to smoke), it does not influence his judgments: an addicted smoker seems to be free to think by himself. Indeed, many smokers know that they are addicted and recognize that smoking endangers their health. On the contrary, it could seem that health labels exercise their influence in a more insidious way: they modify the judgment of people, changing their perception of tobacco risks, by addressing their non-deliberative faculties. I will show here that the situation is not as asymmetric as one could think: tobacco also modify a smoker's judgments by addressing his non-deliberative faculties, although in a quite subtle way.

To establish this, some findings of the research literature on smokers' risk perception need to be reminded. Its results could appear paradoxical: on one hand, several studies seem to show that smokers overestimate the numerical risk of smoking (Marsh and Matheson 1983, Viscusi, 1990, McCoy et al., 1992); but on the other hand, smokers still resist the idea that these risks are personally

relevant (Chapman and Liberman, 2005). For example, smokers are prone to believe that they have a lower risk of developing a smoking-related disease than the average smoker (Hansen and Malotte, 1986; McKenna et al., 1993; Weinstein et al., 2005). Also, they overestimate their life expectancy (Schoenbaum, 1997).

These apparently paradoxical findings are generally explained by the cognitive dissonance theory. On one hand, smokers know that smoking is dangerous (and people being notoriously bad with numerical probabilities, they overestimate the numerical risk of smoking); on the other hand, they are addicted and cannot stop smoking. They can solve the conflict between their action of smoking and their belief that smoking is dangerous by holding the additional belief that, although smoking is dangerous in general, it is not too dangerous for them. For example, many smokers hold the false beliefs that exercise undoes most smoking effects, or that they are protected by some genetic factors (see Peretti-Watel et al., 2007). In a nutshell, smokers believe the practice is not too dangerous for them because they smoke, rather than smoke because they believe it to be not too dangerous for them (Pears, 1984).

Therefore, it is not true that addiction to tobacco only influences desires: by making people addicted, it also influences their judgments in a non-deliberative way and causes false beliefs. Both tobacco addiction and health labels influence judgments by addressing non-deliberative faculties.

Tobacco Addiction and Agency

Let us now turn to a second possible objection. The addiction caused by tobacco seems to be due to the natural biochemical effect of the plant, not to anyone's agency. On the other hand, health warning messages are caused by thinking agents—namely public health officials, who therefore interfere with smokers' agency. Isn't an influence due to a thinking agent ethically more problematic, in some respect, than a natural biochemical influence?

However, this view overlooks a well-known fact: employees of tobacco companies have intentionally manipulated the tobacco blend to enhance the effects of nicotine in cigarettes, thereby increasing the addiction of the smoker. Addiction to tobacco is therefore partially caused by an agentive intervention.

In summary, both addiction to cigarettes and health warning messages are (to some extent) agentive interferences and interferences with people's desires and judgments. The argument claiming for an asymmetry in these respects is therefore rebutted.

Marginal Cases: The Non-Addicted Smoker and the Willing Addict

The focus was until here on the case of the addicted smoker, by far the most frequent. However, in order to complete this account, two further special cases need to be considered. The first one is the case of the non-addicted smoker. The second one is the case of someone who actually wants to be addicted to tobacco—for example, someone who wants to follow a classical 'rockstar' lifestyle, which implies to live in the present, to not care about the future and to indulge in all the pleasures associated with this lifestyle. Such a person may want to smoke and even wants to get addicted to tobacco, since this is part of this very lifestyle.

When they are persuasive rather than informational, health warnings interfere with the independence component of autonomy of the non-addicted smoker or the willing addict; but they also infringe on their self-ruling component of autonomy, by influencing them not to smoke, despite the fact that the non-addicted smoker freely choses to smoke, and that the 'aspiring rockstar' wants to get addicted. In these both (marginal) cases, the autonomy of an agent is violated; one could therefore argue that from a strict deontological point of view, this is not acceptable.

There are two ways to answer this objection. The first one would be to adopt a moderate consequentialist point of view, and thereby justify the violation of autonomy of this small minority by an appeal to the autonomy-fostering of the greater majority of addicted smokers. Although autonomy is a central value in deontological ethical reasoning, it can also be considered as a good in consequentialist ethical reasoning. Indeed, John Stuart Mill claimed that autonomy is 'one of the elements of well-being' (cf. Christman, 2011). It is therefore not absurd to consider that a small loss of autonomy of a small minority can be compensated by a greater gain of autonomy for the overwhelming majority. The second way to answer this objection is to notice that the autonomy loss for non-addicted smokers and willing addicts can be substantially avoided, since, as it was noticed, health warnings can be easily and cheaply avoided by placing the cigarette pack or the cigarettes in another case designed to this effect.

Conclusion

The original question 'Is tobacco health warnings' interference with people's autonomy ethically justifiable in order to deter them from smoking?' can now be answered. I have first highlighted that convincing minors not to smoke, or convincing adults not to smoke with the intention of protecting their surroundings from second-hand smoke, was ethically less problematic than using health warnings in order to deter adults from smoking, for their own good. Therefore, I have focused on this harder case. I have argued that warning messages foster people's self-ruling component of autonomy in two ways: first, by fulfilling an important informational role; and second, when they are not misleading, by influencing in a non-deliberative way typical smokers' actions so that they fit with their second-order desires to desire not to smoke. Admittedly, these messages infringe on people's independence component of autonomy—but not as much as one could think, as they protect against another attack on autonomy, namely the implicit advertisement in the cigarette's packaging design. Moreover, the self-ruling component of autonomy of an addicted smoker is more important than his independence component of autonomy; therefore, health warning messages result in a net gain of autonomy for the typical addicted smoker. Thus, an ethical justification of health warnings has been provided—not only for the original small ones but also for the large-print and graphic ones, and even for the most extreme format, namely the 'plain packaging' that is implemented in Australia since December 2012.

I have also emphasized that warning messages should be designed to be as little misleading as possible—that is, they should trigger as few false inferences as possible. Some of the existing messages should therefore be corrected. It would not only be unethical to use plainly misleading statements: it could also be perceived as some kind of propaganda, which may decrease these warnings' efficiency or lead to a loss of trust in the state on the long-run.

Admittedly, when considering the ethicality of tobacco health warnings, one should also deal with other considerations than the infringement on people's autonomy. For example, health warnings—especially pictorial ones—may be very unpleasant to look at; however, this loss in well-being is arguably largely compensated by the gain in lives saved through health warning messages. Also, health warnings may contribute to the stigmatization of smokers; however, it might be argued that this compensates for long years of tobacco advertising that have tried to present the smoking lifestyle on a positive light (see Voigt, forthcoming, for a more extensive treatment of this question).

It should also be understood that the interference of health warning messages with autonomy are justified because of the specificities of tobacco products; therefore, health warning messages could not be imposed on other products without a strong, independent justification. For example, the fact that labeling tobacco products is ethically permissible does not imply that e.g. alcohol, junk food or saccharin labeling is also ethically permissible.

More generally, this article points to an important difference between regular paternalism and libertarian paternalism. Grüne-Yanoff (2012) has argued that libertarian paternalism is similar to regular paternalism and is merely 'old wine in new casks'. Although he showed successfully that the similarities between regular paternalism and libertarian paternalism are more important than what Sunstein and Thaler (2003) sometimes suggest, my argument here shows that there is nevertheless an important qualitative shift when moving from regular paternalism to libertarian paternalism: libertarian paternalism does not interfere with people's liberty,[14] but with their autonomy, and render possible some kinds of justification that would not be available to regular paternalism. For example, a full ban on smoking would be a (non-libertarian) paternalistic measure and would infringe on people's liberty to smoke; it would be difficult, in order to determine the ethicality of such a law, to balance the loss of liberty versus the gain in health and autonomy for the addicted smoker. On the contrary, health warning messages on tobacco products interfere with smokers' autonomy in order to foster (amongst other goods) this very same autonomy. Here, the loss and gains are easier to put in balance because they concern the same good: autonomy. Therefore, the case of health warnings on tobacco products illustrates that classically paternalistic and libertarian paternalistic measures differ in an important aspect. This shows how the study of a specific applied problem can shed light on a quite general and fundamental debate in ethics and political philosophy.

Notes

1. The dominant view in the literature is that health warnings are an effective tobacco-control strategy; but see e.g. Peters et al. (in press) for an alternative view.

2. Many nudges aim at triggering non-deliberative faculties, like the food arrangement mentioned above. However, as was pointed by an anonymous reviewer, some of them aim at blocking non-deliberative faculties, like mandatory cool-off periods before making an important expanse, which may enhance opportunities for deliberation. It is to my knowledge an open question whether nudges are coextensive with interventions that interact with non-deliberative faculties in some way (by either triggering them or blocking them).

3. At least, according to some classical accounts of liberty, but see e.g. Grüne-Yanoff (2012) who shows that they are not liberty-preserving according to Isaiah Berlin's (2002) account of liberty.

4. The account of what it means to 'address' non-deliberative faculties will presumably depend on the specific account of non-deliberative faculties that is chosen. A tentative definition would be that an intervention addresses non-deliberative faculties when the processing of the information conveyed by this intervention is made (at least in part) by non-deliberative faculties (and when this was intended by the person who designed the intervention).

5. The underlying cognitive mechanism has sometimes been called the 'affect heuristic' (Slovic, 2000).

6. Even if the bias in the lottery case is more significant, as it is unfortunately much more likely to get Brueger's disease when smoking than winning the first prize when playing lottery.

7. The lottery advertisement is actually less misleading than this tobacco warning message, as it is designed in a humorous way: virtually everyone reading the advertisement can realize that confusing it with the statement '100% of people who tried their luck have won' would be blatantly false.

8. Most smokers are addicted: it is estimated that 90% of smokers would like to stop smoking without success; and over 90% of attempts to quit smoking fail in the first year (Carlson and Luhrs, 1997). Moreover, most smokers are unwilling addicts—if they could smoke without being addicted, they would choose that option. Therefore, the phrase 'typical smoker' will refer to an unwillingly addicted smoker. Two marginal cases, the non-addicted smoker and the willing addict, will be considered in a later section.

9. Even if the warning message would reach the inside of the cigarette pack, it would be easy to transfer the cigarettes into a warnings-free case.

10. 'Substantially' only, because the smoker will still be exposed to the warnings every time she buys cigarettes or removes a pack from the case, as pointed by an anonymous reviewer.

11. It is an open question whether this independence component has any value in itself (that is, a value associated with its procedural dimension), beyond the value of leading to authentic choices when it does so (that is, a value associated with its non-procedural dimension). Here, I just make the reasonable assumption that even if this component has any value in itself, this value is of lesser extent than the value of leading to authentic choices.

This may differ from other standard hierarchical accounts of autonomy that do not balance the values of the two components one with another.

12. A full definition of authenticity would exceed the scope of this article, but one can adopt here the tentative following definition: an action is authentic on the condition that it would have been chosen by the agent if he would have been in the same state of knowledge as he is, with the same faculties of judgment and decision, but free of any external influence. In our present case, the addicted smoker who is influenced not to smoke (or to smoke less) by the persuasive role of tobacco health warnings is taking an authentic action (because, if he would have been free of any influence from tobacco addiction and persuasive health warnings, he would not have smoked or would have smoked less).

13. One could wonder how authentic would be the choice not to smoke for an addicted smoker who would follow his second-order desire to desire not to smoke. As a matter of fact, one could wonder whether this second-order desire may have originated in the persuasive role of health warnings; in that case, persuasive health warnings would be a kind of propaganda that changes people's second-order desires. However, the smoker would presumably hold this second-order desire even without any persuasive health warnings: indeed, before the introduction of such contemporary, persuasive health warnings, at a time when health warnings were mainly informative, a majority of smokers already wanted to stop or to reduce smoking (cf. e.g. Goodin, 1989). Therefore, if an addicted smoker would chose not to smoke, this choice would be authentic, given the account of authenticity proposed here above.

14. It does not decrease liberty in the classical sense of keeping all alternatives open; as mentioned earlier, Grüne-Yanoff (2012) argues that it does reduce liberty according to Berlin's account.

References

Berlin, I. (2002). *Liberty. Oxford*: Oxford University Press.

Bovens, L. (2009). The Ethics of Nudge. In Grüne-Yanoff, T. and Hansson, S. O. (eds), *Preference Change: Approaches from Philosophy, Economics and Psychology (Theory and Decision Library A)*. Berlin and New York: Springer, pp. 207–220.

Carlson, M. and Luhrs, C. (1997). The Ethics of Tobacco Marketing. In Burkhart, L., Friedberg, J.,

Martin, T. and Sharma, K. (eds), *Confronting Information Ethics in the New Millennium*. Boulder, Colorado: Ethica Publishing, pp. 72–78.

Chapman, S. (1996). The Ethics of Tobacco Advertising and Advertising Bans. *British Medical Bulletin*, 52, 121–131.

Chapman, S. and Lieberman, J. (2005). Ensuring Smokers Are Adequately Informed: Reflections on Consumer Rights, Manufacturer Responsibilities, and Policy Implications. *Tobacco Control*, 14(**Suppl 2**), ii8–ii13.

Christman, J. (2011). Autonomy in Moral and Political Philosophy. In Zalta, E. N. (ed.), *The Stanford Encyclopedia of Philosophy (Spring 2011 Edition)*, available from: http://plato.stanford.edu/archives/spr2011/entries/autonomy-moral/.

Dworkin, G. (2010). Paternalism. In Zalta, E. N. (ed.), *The Stanford Encyclopedia of Philosophy (Summer 2010 Edition)*, available from http://plato.stanford.edu/archives/sum2010/entries/paternalism/.

Frankfurt, H. (1971). Freedom of the Will and the Concept of a Person. *Journal of Philosophy*, 68, 5–20.

Goodin, R. E. (1989). The Ethics of Smoking. *Ethics*, 99, 575–624.

Gregory, R. and Mendelsohn, R. (1993). Perceived Risk, Dread, and Benefits. *Risk Analysis*, 13, 259–264.

Grüne-Yanoff, T. (2012). Old Wine in New Casks: Libertarian Paternalism Still Violates Liberal Principles. *Social Choice and Welfare*, 38, 635–645.

Hammond, D. (2011). Health Warning Messages on Tobacco Products: A Review. *Tobacco Control*, 20, 327–337.

Hansen, W. B. and Malotte, C. K. (1986). Perceived Personal Immunity: The Development of Beliefs About Susceptibility to the Consequences of Smoking. *Preventive Medicine*, 15, 363–372.

Hausman, D. M. and Welch, B. (2010). Debate: To Nudge or Not to Nudge. *Journal of Political Philosophy*, 18, 123–136.

Kruglanski, A. W. and Gigerenzer, G. (2011). Intuitive and Deliberate Judgments are Based on Common Principles. *Psychological Review*, 118, 97–109.

Marsh, A. and Matheson, J. (1983). *Smoking Attitudes and Behaviour*. London: Her Majesty's Stationery Office.

McCoy, S. B., Gibbons, F. X., Reis, T. J., Gerrard, M., Luus, C. A. and Sufka, A. V. (1992). Perceptions of Smoking Risk as a Function of Smoking Status. *Journal of Behavioral Medicine*, 15, 469–488.

McKenna, F. P., Warburton, D. M. and Winwood, M. (1993). Exploring the Limits of Optimism: The Case of Smokers' Decision Making. *British Journal of Psychology*, 84, 389–394.

Mill, J. S. (1859). *On Liberty. London*: Penguin Books.

Pears, D. (1984). *Motivated Irrationality*. Oxford: Clarendon Press.

Peretti-Watel, P., Halfen, S. and Grémy, I. (2007). The 'Moral Career' of Cigarette Smokers: A French Survey. *Health, Risk & Society*, 9, 259–273.

Peters, G.-J. Y., Ruiter, R. A. C. and Kok, G. (2012). Threatening Communication: A Critical Re-analysis and a Revised Meta-analytic Test of Fear Appeal Theory. *Health Psychology Review*, doi:10.1080/17437199.2012.703527.

Rizzo, M. and Whitman, D. (2008). Little Brother is Watching You: New Paternalism on the Slippery Slopes. *New York University Law and Economics Working Papers*, Paper 126, available from: http://lsr.nellco.org/nyu_lewp/126 [accessed February 26, 2013].

Schoenbaum, M. (1997). Do Smokers Understand the Mortality Effects of Smoking? Evidence from the Health and Retirement Survey. *American Journal of Public Health*, 87, 755–759.

Schooler, L. J. and Hertwig, R. (2005). How Forgetting Aids Heuristic Inference. *Psychological Review*, 112, 610–628.

Slovic, P. (2000). *The Perception of Risk*. London: Earthscan Publications.

Sperber, D. and Wilson, D. (1995). *Relevance: Communication and Cognition*. 2nd edn. Oxford: Blackwell.

Sunstein, C. R. and Thaler, R. H. (2003). Libertarian Paternalism is Not an Oxymoron. *University of Chicago Law Review*, 70, 1159–1202.

Thaler, R. H. and Sunstein, C. R. (2008). *Nudge. Improving Decisions About Health, Wealth and Happiness*. New Haven: Yale University Press.

Tversky, A. and Kahneman, D. (1973). Availability: A Heuristic for Judging Frequency and Probability. *Cognitive Psychology*, 5, 207–232.

Villejoubert, G. and Mandel, D. R. (2002). The Inverse Fallacy: An Account of Deviations from Bayes's Theorem and the Additivity Principle. *Memory & Cognition*, 30, 171–178.

Viscusi, W. K. (1990). Do Smokers Underestimate Risks? *The Journal of Political Economy*, 98, 1253–1269.

Voigt, K. (forthcoming). 'If You Smoke, You Stink.' Denormalisation Strategies for the Improvement of Health-Related Behaviours: The Case of Tobacco. In Strech, D., Hirschberg, I. and Marckmann, G. (eds), *Ethics in Public Health and Health Policy*. Amsterdam: Springer.

Weinstein, N. D., Marcus, S. E. and Moser, R. P. (2005). Smokers' Unrealistic Optimism About Their Risk'. *Tobacco Control*, 14, 55–59.

Adrien Barton is a reader in the Department of Applied Criminology and Forensic Studies at the University of Winchester. His research and writing focuses on substance use policy, and the interrelationships among drugs, alcohol, and crime. His books include *Illicit Drugs: Use and Control* and *Policymaking in the Criminal Justice System*.

EXPLORING THE ISSUE

Do Anti-smoking Policies Violate Smokers' Moral Autonomy?

Critical Thinking and Reflection

1. Explain why employers wish to prohibit risky off-duty behavior, such as smoking, by their employees. Do such restrictions impermissibly restrict the moral autonomy of employees? Why or why not?
2. Do you think that a person who is addicted to nicotine is capable of giving voluntary consent to the purchase and use of tobacco products? Why or why not? If not, does the addictiveness of nicotine provide paternalistic grounds to ban the purchase and use of tobacco products?
3. Does libertarian paternalism adequately protect a person's moral autonomy, or, like classical paternalism, does it come into direct conflict with this moral autonomy?
4. Select another aspect of life in which people are addicted or obsessed with an activity that poses significant health risks. How would you balance their moral autonomy against a paternalistic desire to protect their well-being?
5. Would you accept a position working for a company that produces, sells, or advertises tobacco products? Why or why not?

Is There Common Ground?

Despite their conflicting views on the moral permissibility of anti-smoking policies, there is a great deal of agreement between the two authors. With regard to smoking, and the use of tobacco products in general, both acknowledge that tobacco is an addictive and highly dangerous substance that poses significant health risks to its users. As a result, they agree that helping people who wish to quit smoking is a laudable goal, as is preventing harm to people who might be exposed to second-hand smoke. Moreover, they agree that a paternalistic regard for the welfare of smokers justifies regulation of tobacco use by minors, who are not fully capable of wisely exercising their autonomy.

It is the extent to which paternalistic concerns justify limitations on the autonomy of smokers that they principally disagree. Even then, both are concerned about the constraints on autonomy posed by classical paternalism, which limits a person's capacity for self-rule out of concern for that person's welfare and without that person's consent. For Maltby, contemporary society provides numerous examples of classical paternalism gone wild, especially with regard to punitive actions taken by the government and private employers to curb harmful choices; Barton too, finds the potential abuses of classical paternalism troublesome, and so he concurs with Maltby regarding the ability of consumers to make informed choices on tobacco use, free from the influence of deceptive advertisements and with accurate knowledge of the detrimental health effects of tobacco. With regard to libertarian paternalism, however, there is a fine line between influencing (nudging) a person to make healthy choices and manipulating them to act in ways that others, such as the government or private employers, think is best for them. Both authors are aware of this line, and while Barton asserts that it is possible to craft anti-smoking policies to avoid this type of manipulation, Maltby is highly suspicious of such attempts.

Additional Resources

Robert Goodin, No Smoking: The Ethical Issues, University of Chicago Press, 1990.

J. E. Katz, "Individual rights advocacy in tobacco control policies: an assessment and recommendation," Tobacco Control 14 (2005).

Thaddeus Mason Pope, "Balancing public health against individual liberty: the ethics of smoking regulations," University of Pittsburgh Law Review (2000).

C. R. Hooper and C. Agule, "Tobacco Regulation: Autonomy up in Smoke?" Journal of Medical Ethics 35:6 (2009).

Internet References . . .

Centers for Disease Control and Prevention: Smoking & Tobacco Use

http://www.cdc.gov/tobacco/index.htm

Citizens for Tobacco Rights

https://tobaccorights.com/

National Cancer Institute: Harms of Cigarette Smoking and Health Benefits of Quitting

https://www.cancer.gov/about-cancer/causes-prevention/risk/tobacco/cessation-fact-sheet

The Tobacco Institute Document Site

http://www.tobaccoinstitute.com/

Selected, Edited, and with Issue Framing Material by:
Owen M. Smith, *Stephen F. Austin State University*
and
Anne Collins Smith, *Stephen F. Austin State University*

ISSUE

Is Torture Ever Morally Justified?

YES: **Mirko Bagaric and Julie Clarke**, from "Not Enough Official Torture in the World? The Circumstances in Which Torture Is Morally Justifiable" *University of San Francisco Law Review* (2005)

NO: **Christopher Kutz**, from "Torture, Necessity, and Existential Politics," *California Law Review* (2007)

Learning Outcomes

After reading this issue, you will be able to:

- Explain the difference between a legal judgment and a moral judgment, and explain why legal judgments do not always correspond with moral judgments in a society.
- Identify significant factors that limit the acceptable use of torture, and explain how these factors should be applied in specific circumstances.
- Distinguish between institutional (legal) and pre-institutional (moral) rights, and explain why the necessity defense cannot override pre-institutional rights.
- Formulate your own position on the morality of torture and identify evidence supporting your position.
- Identify the main objections to your position and formulate responses to these objections.

ISSUE SUMMARY

YES: Bagaric and Clarke remind us, first of all, that torture, although prohibited by international law, is nevertheless widely practiced. A rational examination of torture and a consideration of hypothetical (but realistic) cases show that torture is justifiable in order to prevent great harm. Torture should be regulated and carefully practiced as an information-gathering technique in extreme cases.

NO: Christopher Kutz examines the reasoning intended to justify torture in a memo produced by the Bush administration and concludes that even in extreme hypothetical cases, such reasoning is not valid because the right not to be tortured is a pre-institutional right that cannot be revoked under any circumstances.

The morality of torture was brought to the attention of the American people in a new and urgent way because of the terror attacks on 9/11. Prior to these events, philosophers had been discussing this issue primarily in a theoretical context. Afterwards, when torture was first proposed, and then adopted by the American government as a method to combat terror attacks, the issue moved from the realm of theory to practical urgency.

In order to address this issue clearly, it is important to distinguish between moral judgments and legal judgments. A moral judgment is a conclusion about the morality of an action that is reached by applying a moral rule of behavior (moral standard) to a specific set of circumstances. In contrast, a legal judgment is a conclusion about the legality of an action that is reached by applying a law (legal standard) to a specific set of circumstances. Since moral rules of behavior do not have the same status as laws, moral judgments are not the same as legal judgments. It is true that moral judgments and legal judgments often coincide: killing someone for entertainment is regarded by most people as immoral and is illegal in most societies, while donating canned food to a food bank is regarded by most people as moral and is legal in most societies. However, moral judgments and legal judgments do not always coincide: lying about one's plans in order to avoid a social obligation, while considered immoral by many people, is usually legal, while breaking the speed limit in order to get a severely injured person to the hospital is considered moral by most people, but is technically illegal. There are many reasons why a moral judgment may not correspond with a legal judgment:

- A society may not wish to devote the extensive resources needed to investigate, prosecute, and punish all immoral actions as crimes;
- A society may reject the extensive governmental intrusion required to treat all immoral actions as crimes; and
- Laws without a basis in morality, such as driving on the right side of the road, are necessary to prevent confusion and foster efficient interactions among citizens.

The distinction between moral judgments and legal judgments is central to the issue of torture because the assertion that torture is legal is not the same thing as the assertion that torture is moral. A governmental authority, such as a legislature, attorney general, or court, may determine that torture is legal under certain circumstances, but torture is not thereby made moral. Indeed, many societal advances in the United States and around the world have occurred because conscientious people have concluded that certain actions, while legal, are nevertheless immoral or unjust, and as result of this conclusion, have chosen to challenge, and if necessary to violate, the immoral laws of their society and work for their repeal or amendment.

In examining the morality of torture, both sides frequently make use of hypothetical scenarios. Those who hold the view that torture can be morally justified construct scenarios in which a person has information that can prevent a great harm, but chooses not to divulge the information to the appropriate authorities. They advocate the use of torture, that is, the deliberate infliction of pain, to induce that person to reveal the information and thus prevent or mitigate the great harm. The moral reasoning behind such a scenario is essentially utilitarian in nature: the benefit to the persons escaping the great harm is sufficiently greater than the harm inflicted on the person being tortured as to make the torture morally justified. This argument is enhanced if the harm involves irreparable injury or death to innocent parties and the torture inflicts no lasting damage on the guilty party.

Those who hold the view that torture cannot be morally justified criticize these scenarios on several grounds. One ground concerns the reliability of the information extracted by torture. The harm suffered by the person being tortured is morally justified on utilitarian grounds only if it results in the production of reliable information that can sufficiently benefit others. If the information is not reliable, then the benefit to others may not be realized, and the harm inflicted through torture would not therefore be morally justified. Another ground for rejecting the morality of torture is based not on utilitarianism, but on a different approach to ethics called deontology. An important principle of deontology is that persons should never be treated merely as a means to an end; rather, persons should always be valued as end in themselves. According to this ethical theory, torture is fundamentally immoral because it treats the person being tortured merely as a means to gaining information. As such, torture is morally wrong, no matter how important the information is or how much harm the information can prevent.

In the first reading, Bagaric and Clarke present such a scenario and advance a utilitarian argument to support their assertion that torture is sometimes justified. They further argue that torture is already being practiced widely—although unmonitored and "underground." Their idea is to acknowledge it, endorse it to some extent, but draw lines to regulate and limit its use.

In the second reading, Christopher Kutz does not wish to condone torture at all. He argues from a deontological perspective that we must maintain our commitment to human rights even in a scenario such as the one proposed by Bagaric and Clarke. On his view, the gravest danger in the war on terror is the damage that we ourselves may do to our own most deeply held principles about human rights.

YES ↵

Mirko Bagaric and Julie Clarke

Not Enough Official Torture in the World? The Circumstances in Which Torture Is Morally Justifiable

Recent events stemming from the "war on terrorism" have highlighted the prevalence of torture, both as an interrogation technique and as a punitive measure. Torture is almost universally deplored. It is prohibited by international law and is not officially sanctioned by the domestic laws of any state. The formal prohibition against torture is absolute—there are no exceptions to it. This is not only pragmatically unrealistic, but unsound at a normative level. Despite the absolute ban on torture, it is widely used. Contrary to common belief, torture is not the preserve of despot military regimes in third world nations. For example, there are serious concerns regarding the treatment by the United States of senior Al Qaeda leader Khalid Shaikh Mohammad. There is also irrefutable evidence that the United States tortured large numbers of Iraqi prisoners, as well as strong evidence that it tortured prisoners at Guantanamo Bay prison in Cuba, where suspected Al Qaeda terrorists are held. More generally Professor Alan Dershowitz has noted, "[C]ountries all over the world violate the Geneva Accords [prohibiting torture]. They do it secretly and hypothetically, the way the French did it in Algeria."

Dershowitz has also recently argued that torture should be made lawful. His argument is based on a harm minimization rationale from the perspective of victims of torture. He said, "Of course it would be best if we didn't use torture at all, but if the United States is going to continue to torture people, we need to make the process legal and accountable." Our argument goes one step beyond this. We argue that torture is indeed morally defensible, not just pragmatically desirable. The harm minimization rationale is used to supplement our argument.

While a "civilized" community does not typically condone such conduct, this Article contends that torture is morally defensible in certain circumstances, mainly when more grave harm can be avoided by using torture as an interrogation device. The pejorative connotation associated with torture should be abolished. A dispassionate analysis of the propriety of torture indicates that it is morally justifiable. At the outset of this analytical discussion, this Article requires readers to move from the question of whether torture is *ever* defensible to the issue of the circumstances in which it is morally permissible.

Consider the following example: A terrorist network has activated a large bomb on one of hundreds of commercial planes carrying over three hundred passengers that is flying somewhere in the world at any point in time. The bomb is set to explode in thirty minutes. The leader of the terrorist organization announces this intent via a statement on the Internet. He states that the bomb was planted by one of his colleagues at one of the major airports in the world in the past few hours. No details are provided regarding the location of the plane where the bomb is located. Unbeknown to him, he was under police surveillance and is immediately apprehended by police. The terrorist leader refuses to answer any questions of the police, declaring that the passengers must die and will do so shortly.

Who in the world would deny that all possible means should be used to extract the details of the plane and the location of the bomb? The answer is not many. The passengers, their relatives and friends, and many in society would expect that all means should be used to extract the information, even if the pain and suffering imposed on the terrorist resulted in his death.

Although the above example is hypothetical and is not one that has occurred in the real world, the force of the argument cannot be dismissed on that basis. As C.L. Ten notes, "fantastic examples" that raise fundamental issues for consideration, such as whether it is proper to torture wrongdoers, play an important role in the evaluation of moral principles and theories. These examples sharpen contrasts and illuminate the logical conclusions of the respective principles to test the true strength of our commitment to the principles. Thus, fantastic examples cannot be dismissed summarily merely because they are "simply" hypothetical.

Bagaric, Mirko and Clarke, Julie. From *University of San Francisco Law Review,* vol. 39, Spring 2005, pp. 581–616. Copyright ©2005 by University of San Francisco Law Review. Reprinted by permission.

Real life is, of course, rarely this clear cut, but there are certainly scenarios approaching this degree of desperation, which raise for discussion whether it is justifiable to inflict harm on one person to reduce a greater level of harm occurring to a large number of blameless people. Ultimately, torture is simply the sharp end of conduct whereby the interests of one agent are sacrificed for the greater good. As a community, we are willing to accept this principle. Thus, although differing in degree, torture is no different in nature from conduct that we sanction in other circumstances. It should be viewed in this light.

Given this, it is illogical to insist on a blanket prohibition against torture. Therefore, the debate must turn to the circumstances when torture is morally appropriate. This is the topic of this Article.

International law defines torture as severe pain and suffering, generally used as an interrogation device or as a punitive measure. This Article focuses on the use of torture as an interrogation device and poses that the device is only permissible to prevent significant harm to others. In these circumstances, there are five variables relevant in determining whether torture is permissible and the degree of torture that is appropriate. The variables are (1) the number of lives at risk; (2) the immediacy of the harm; (3) the availability of other means to acquire the information; (4) the level of wrongdoing of the agent; and (5) the likelihood that the agent actually does possess the relevant information.

This Article analyzes the meaning of torture and the nature and scope of the legal prohibition against torture [and] examines whether torture is morally defensible. It is argued that torture is no different than other forms of morally permissible behavior and is justifiable on a utilitarian ethic. It is also argued that, on close reflection, torture is also justifiable against a backdrop of a non-consequentialist rights-based ethic, which is widely regarded as prohibiting torture in all circumstances. Thus, the Article concludes that torture is morally justifiable in rare circumstances, irrespective of which normative theory one adopts. [We] examine the circumstances in which torture is justifiable. Finally, [we] debunk the argument that torture should not be legalized because it will open the floodgates to more torture.

Torture: Reality and Legal Position

The Law on Torture

Pursuant to international law, "torture" is defined as:

> Any act by which severe pain or suffering, whether physical or mental, is intentionally inflicted on a person for such purposes as obtaining from him

or a third person information or a confession, punishing him for an act he or a third person has committed or is suspected of having committed, or intimidating or coercing him or a third person, or for any reason based on discrimination of any kind, when such pain or suffering is inflicted by or at the instigation of or with the consent or acquiescence of a public official or other person acting in an official capacity. It does not include pain or suffering arising only from, inherent in or incidental to lawful sanctions.

Torture is prohibited by a number of international documents. It is also considered to carry a special status in customary international law, that of *jus cogens*, which is a "peremptory norm" of customary international law. The significance of this is that customary international law is binding on all states, even if they have not ratified a particular treaty. At the treaty level, there are both general treaties that proscribe torture and specific treaties banning the practice.

In terms of general treaties, torture is prohibited by a number of international and regional treaties. . . .

The rigidity of the rule against torture is exemplified by the fact that it has a non-derogable status in human rights law. That is, there are no circumstances in which torture is permissible. This prohibition is made clear in Article 2(2) of the U.N. Convention Against Torture, which states, "No exceptional circumstances whatsoever, whether a state of war or a threat of war, internal political instability or any other public emergency, may be invoked as a justification of torture." Thus, the right not to be tortured is absolute. . . .

This absolute prohibition is frequently highlighted by Amnesty International and other human rights organizations. For example, Amnesty International states, "The law is unequivocal—torture is absolutely prohibited in all circumstances. . . . The right to be free from torture is absolute. It cannot be denied to anyone in any circumstances."

Torture is also prohibited as a war crime, pursuant to humanitarian law. In addition, torture is considered to be a crime against humanity when the acts are perpetrated as part of a widespread or systematic attack against a civilian population, whether or not they are committed in the course of an armed conflict.

The Reality of Torture

As with many legal precepts, the black letter law must be considered against the context of reality. As this part shows, various forms of torture are used despite the legal prohibition of it.

1. Forms of Torture

As is noted by Dershowitz, torture comes in many different forms and intensities:

> Torture is a continuum and the two extremes are on the one hand torturing someone to death—that is torturing an enemy to death so that others will know that if you are caught, you will be caused excruciating pain—that's torture as a deterrent. . . . At the other extreme, there's non-lethal torture which leaves only psychological scars. The perfect example of this is a sterilised needle inserted under the fingernail, causing unbearable pain but no possible long-term damage. These are very different phenomena. What they have in common of course is that they allow the government physically to come into contact with you in order to produce pain.

Various methods of torture have and continue to be applied in a multitude of countries. The most common methods are beating, electric shock, rape and sexual abuse, mock execution or threat of death, and prolonged solitary confinement. Other common methods include sleep and sensory deprivation, suspension of the body, "shackling interrogees in contorted painful positions" or in "painful stretching positions," and applying pressure to sensitive areas, such as the "neck, throat, genitals, chest and head."

2. The Benefits of Torture: An Effective Information Gathering Device

The main benefit of torture is that it is an excellent means of gathering information. Humans have an intense desire to avoid pain, no matter how short term, and most will comply with the demands of a torturer to avoid the pain. Often even the threat of torture alone will evoke cooperation. To this end, Dershowitz cites a recent kidnapping case in Germany in which the son of a distinguished banker was kidnapped. The eleven-year-old boy had been missing for three days. The police had in their custody a man they were convinced had perpetrated the kidnapping. The man was taken into custody after being seen collecting a ransom that was paid by the boy's family. During seven hours of interrogation the man "toyed" with police, leading them to one false location after another. After exhausting all lawful means of interrogation, the deputy commissioner of the Frankfurt police instructed his officers, in writing, that they could try to extract information "by means of the infliction of pain, under medical supervision and subject to prior warning." Ten minutes after the warning was given the suspect told the police where the boy was; unfortunately the boy was already dead, having been killed shortly after the kidnapping.

3. The Widespread Use of Torture

a. Torture Around the World Despite the contemporary abhorrence against it, dozens of countries continue to use torture. A study of 195 countries and territories by Amnesty International between 1997 and mid-2000 found reports of torture or ill-treatment by state officials in more than 150 countries and in more than seventy countries that torture or ill-treatment was reported as "widespread or persistent." It is also clear that torture is not limited to military regimes in third world nations. Amnesty International recently reported that in 2003 it had received reports of torture and ill-treatment from 132 countries, including the United States, Canada, Japan, France, Italy, Spain, and Germany. . . .

The Circumstances in Which Torture Is Acceptable

The only situation where torture is justifiable is where it is used as an information gathering technique to avert a grave risk. In such circumstances, there are five variables relevant in determining whether torture is permissible and the degree of torture that is appropriate. The variables are (1) the number of lives at risk; (2) the immediacy of the harm; (3) the availability of other means to acquire the information; (4) the level of wrongdoing of the agent; and (5) the likelihood that the agent actually does possess the relevant information. Where (1), (2), (4) and (5) rate highly and (3) is low, all forms of harm may be inflicted on the agent—even if this results in death.

The Harm to Be Prevented

The key consideration regarding the permissibility of torture is the magnitude of harm that is sought to be prevented. To this end, the appropriate measure is the number of lives that are likely to be lost if the threatened harm is not alleviated. Obviously, the more lives that are at stake, the more weight that is attributed to this variable.

Lesser forms of threatened harm will not justify torture. Logically, the right to life is the most basic and fundamental of all human rights—non-observance of it would render all other human rights devoid of meaning. Every society has some prohibition against taking life, and "the intentional taking of human life is . . . the offence which society condemns most strongly." The right to life is also enshrined in several international covenants. For example, Article 2 of the European Convention on Human Rights (which in essence mirrors Article 6 of the International Covenant on Civil and Political Rights) provides that "everyone's right to life shall be protected by law.

No one shall be deprived of his life intentionally save in the execution of a sentence of a court following his conviction of a crime for which this penalty is provided by law."

Torture violates the right to physical integrity, which is so important that it is only a threat to the right to life that can justify interference with it. Thus, torture should be confined to situations where the right to life is imperiled.

Immediacy of Harm and Other Options to Obtain Information

Torture should only be used as a last resort and hence should not be utilized where there is time to pursue other avenues of forestalling the harm. It is for this reason that torture should only be used where there is no other means to obtain the relevant information. Thus, where a terrorist has planted a bomb on a plane, torture will not be permissible where, for example, video tapes of international airports are likely to reveal the identity of the plane that has been targeted.

The Likelihood of Knowledge or Guilt

As a general rule torture should normally be confined to people that are responsible in some way for the threatened harm. This is not, however, invariably the case. People who are simply aware of the threatened harm, that is "innocent people," may in some circumstances also be subjected to torture.

Regardless of the guilt of the agent, it is most important that torture is only used against individuals who actually possess the relevant information. It will be rare that conclusive proof is available that an individual does, in fact, possess the required knowledge; for example, potential torturees will not have been through a trial process in which their guilt has been established. This is not a decisive objection, however, to the use of torture. The investigation and trial process is simply one means of distinguishing wrongdoers from the innocent. To that end, it does not seem to be a particularly effective process. There are other ways of forming such conclusions. One is by way of lie-detector tests. The latest information suggests that polygraphs are accurate about eighty to ninety per cent of the time. There has been little empirical research done to ascertain the number of innocent people who are ultimately convicted of criminal offenses. As one example, however, research carried out in the United Kingdom for the Royal Commission on Criminal Justice suggests that up to eleven percent of people who plead guilty claim

innocence. The wrongful acquittal rate would no doubt be even higher than this.

Moreover, it is important to note that even without resort to polygraphs there will be many circumstances where guilt or relevant knowledge is patently obvious. A clear example is where a person makes a relevant admission that discloses information that would only be within the knowledge of the wrongdoer. Another example occurred in the recent German kidnapping case, referred to earlier, where the man in custody had been witnessed collecting a ransom and had indicated to the police that the kidnapped boy was still alive. Where lesser forms of evidence proving guilt are available, the argument in favor of torture is lower.

The Formula

Incorporating all these considerations, the strength of the case in favor of torture can be mapped as follows:

$$\frac{W + L + P}{T \times O}$$

Where:

W = whether the agent is the wrongdoer

L = the number of lives that will be lost if the information is not provided

P = the probability that the agent has the relevant knowledge

T = the time available before the disaster will occur ("immediacy of the harm")

O = the likelihood that other inquiries will forestall the risk

W is a weighting that is attributable to whether the agent has had any direct connection with the potential catastrophe. Where the person is responsible for the incident—for example, planted or organized the bomb—more emphasis should be attached. Where the agent is innocent and has simply stumbled on the relevant information—for example, she saw the bomb being planted or overheard the plan to plant the bomb—this should be reduced by a certain amount. The prohibition against inflicting harm on the innocent is certainly strong, but it is not inviolable.

Torture should be permitted where the application of the variables exceeds a threshold level. Once beyond this level, the higher the figure the more severe the forms of torture that are permissible. There is no bright line that can be drawn concerning the point at which the "torture threshold" should be set. More precision can, however, be obtained by first ascribing unit ranges to each of the above variables (depending on their relative importance), then applying the formula to a range of hypothetical situations, and then making a judgment about the numerical point at which torture is acceptable.

There is obviously a degree of imprecision attached to this process and considerable scope for discussion and disagreement regarding the *exact* weight that should be attached to each variable. It is important to emphasize, however, that this is not an argument against our proposal. Rather it is a signal for further discussion and refinement. This is a call that we are confident other commentators will take up. The purpose of this Article is not to set in stone the full range of circumstances where torture is justifiable. Our aim is more modest—to convince readers that torture is justifiable in some circumstances and to set out the variables that are relevant to such an inquiry.

Regulation Better Than Prohibition

In addition to the moral argument for torture as an interrogation device, Dershowitz has argued that torture should be legalized for harm minimization reasons. Dershowitz has pushed for the introduction of "a torture warrant," which would place a "heavy burden on the government to demonstrate by factual evidence the necessity to administer this horrible, horrible technique of torture." He further adds:

> I think that we're much, much better off admitting what we're doing or not doing it at all. I agree with you, it will much better if we never did it. But if we're going to do it and subcontract and find ways of circumventing, it's much better to do what Israel did. They were the only country in the world ever directly to confront the issue, and it led to a supreme court decision, as you say, outlawing torture, and yet Israel has been criticized all over the world for confronting the issue directly. Candor and accountability in a democracy is very important. Hypocrisy has no place.

The obvious counter to this is the slippery slope argument. "If you start opening the door, making a little exception here, a little exception there, you've basically sent the signal that the ends justify the means," resulting in even more torture. The slippery slope argument is often invoked in relation to acts that in themselves are justified, but which have similarities with objectionable practices, and urges that in morally appraising an action we must not only consider its intrinsic features but also the likelihood of it being used as a basis for condoning similar,

but in fact relevantly different undesirable practices. The slippery slope argument in the context of torture holds that while torture might be justified in the extreme cases, legalizing it in these circumstances will invariably lead to torture in other less desperate situations.

This argument is not sound in the context of torture. First, the floodgates are already open—torture is widely used, despite the absolute legal prohibition against it. It is, in fact, arguable that it is the existence of an unrealistic absolute ban on torture that has driven torture "beneath the radar screen of accountability" and that the legalization of torture in very rare circumstances would, in fact, reduce the instances of torture because of the increased level of accountability.

Second, there is no evidence to suggest that the *lawful* violation of fundamental human interests will necessarily lead to a violation of fundamental rights where the pre-conditions for the activity are clearly delineated and controlled. Thus, in the United States the use of the death penalty has not resulted in a gradual extension of the offenses for which people may be executed or an erosion in the respect for human life. Third, promulgating the message that the "means justifies the ends [sometimes]" is not inherently undesirable. Debate can then focus on the precise means and ends that are justifiable.

Conclusion

The absolute prohibition against torture is morally unsound and pragmatically unworkable. There is a need for measured discussion regarding the merits of torture as an information gathering device. This would result in the legal use of torture in circumstances where there are a large number of lives at risk in the immediate future and there is no other means of alleviating the threat. While none of the recent high profile cases of torture appear to satisfy these criteria, it is likely that circumstances will arise in the future where torture is legitimate and desirable. A legal framework should be established to properly accommodate these situations.

Mirko Bagaric is a Professor of Law at Deakin University's School of Law in Australia; he is currently Dean and Head of the School of Law. He has published on a wide variety of social issues. His publications include books such as *How to Live: Being Happy and Dealing with Moral Dilemmas* (University Press of American, 2006) and *Future Directions in International Law and Human Rights* (Sandstone Academic Press, 2007).

Christopher Kutz

 **NO**

Torture, Necessity, and Existential Politics

> "[I]f there is something worse than accepting slavery, it consists in defending it."[1]
>
> —Bernard Williams, *Shame and Necessity*

Introduction

The Costs of Rights

Rights have costs—that is their point. The cost of rights is in the coin of foregone welfare gains. No one minds a claim to a particular right when honoring that right simultaneously enhances welfare. For example, the distinctively modern achievement for speech and conscience has been to demonstrate the consilience of rights protecting those domains with the promotion of a flourishing public and private life. As a result, claims of rights to free speech and conscience are among the most easily accepted in U.S. public life. The test of a claim of right, however, comes not when its exercise serves the public good, directly or indirectly, but when it represents a direct hit to welfare. At the level of institutional and philosophical discourse, the United States used to honor the right of individuals to be free of torture in this way. The U.S. government viewed it as justified independently of the costs or gains that might accrue from respecting it.[2] Now things are different. The current administration of George W. Bush has decided not to pay those costs. Instead, it chooses to use coercive interrogation techniques that would conventionally be thought of as straightforwardly torturous, including water-boarding, false burial, "Palestinian hanging" (where the prisoner is suspended by his arms, manacled behind his back), being left naked in a cold cell and doused with cold water, and being made to stand for forty hours while shackled to a cell floor.[3] The override of detainee rights against torture has been justified on grounds of "necessity," i.e., that the welfare cost of observing the right would be too great for the nation rationally to bear. . . .

My aim in this Essay is to take up the question of torture's justification . . . raised by the infamous (and now withdrawn) Office of Legal Counsel (OLC) memorandum of August 1, 2002, which became widely known as the "Torture memo."[4] . . .

I argue that attention to the concept of necessity as a justification for torture, and especially to the limits of that justification, reveals that we make use in legal and political thought of two very different normative concepts of rights. The first concept serves to impose limits on institutional considerations, while the second is far more sensitive to such considerations. Instances of the former are core human rights protections; instances of the latter are rights of disposition over property. Legal and philosophical arguments purporting to justify torture by reference to necessity betray a failure to grasp these distinctions.[5] . . .

[T]he heart of the paper takes up the claim of necessity in ethics, first in relation to the infamous "ticking bomb" example so often put forward to establish a principle of permissibility. The ticking bomb case is a particular example of a general problem for principle-based ("deontological," in philosophers' jargon), rather than welfare-based (or "utilitarian"), ethics, namely making sense of limits to rights claims without giving up the core of deontological theory. I distinguish here between two different, familiar and ubiquitous conceptions of rights: rights inherently sensitive to necessity claims, and those insensitive—of which, I argue, rights against torture are the primary example. . . .

I

Micro- and Macro-Necessity as a Criminal Defense to Torture

As the story is now familiar, I will summarize: In the spring of 2004, the leak of government memoranda creating a legal basis for U.S. personnel to use torture in interrogations was a shock to many outside the administration. The shock lay less in the acknowledgment that the U.S. was deploying torture than in the lawyerly *justification* of torture, particularly because, despite the erratic and frequently cruel course of actual state practice, the eradication of the moral and legal basis for torture has been one of the defining features of post-Enlightenment liberal politics. This moral and legal evolution began with the early polemics of Voltaire and Beccaria[6] and continued with the now-twenty-year-old U.N. Convention against Torture and other Cruel, Inhuman, or Degrading Treatment or Punishment, which has been ratified by sixty-five countries, including all of the most developed nations save Korea.[7] Against growing international consensus, the U.S. administration made clear in the days immediately following the terrorist attacks of September 11th that, in Vice President Dick Cheney's words, "we have to work, though, sort of the dark side."[8] With a political go-ahead, the CIA decided to use a number of formerly proscribed interrogation techniques on "high value" interrogees, notably including "water-boarding," which consists of repeated submersion in cold water to create the impression of drowning.[9] At some point, before or after the interrogations had actually begun, the CIA apparently became worried that its personnel might be subject to the harsh penalties dictated by 18 U.S.C. §§ 2340-2340A, the implementing legislation for the Convention against Torture. Section 2340A authorizes up to twenty years imprisonment for anyone who outside the U.S. "commits or attempts to commit torture," with capital punishment authorized if death results.[10] Insofar as the statutory definition of torture includes acts "specifically intended to inflict severe physical or mental pain or suffering," which pain or suffering can result from "the threat of imminent death," orders to deploy waterboarding (which by design arouses a sensation of imminent death by drowning) would clearly have focused the minds of U.S. personnel on the consequences of the Torture statute.[11]

Prompted by the CIA's request, the OLC, under the signature of Jay Bybee, provided a memorandum to the White House on August 1, 2002.[12] This memorandum, which I will call the Bybee memo, made a number of arguments toward several aims. First, it sought to reduce the potential scope of § 2340 to include only the most heinous forms of torture. Second, it sought to suggest a range of complete criminal defenses U.S. personnel could deploy if charged under the statute. Finally, it sought to establish as a principle of constitutional law that § 2340A could not constitutionally be interpreted to bind the President while exercising his war powers as Commander in Chief.[13]

After giving its restrictive definition of torture, the memo contemplates the case in which U.S. personnel may be found to have engaged in acts within the scope of the statutory prohibition, namely to have inflicted with specific intent or attempted to inflict severe physical or mental pain or suffering.[14] It then argues for the claim that "[s]tandard criminal law defenses of necessity and self-defense could justify interrogation methods needed to elicit information to prevent a direct and imminent threat to the United States and its citizens."[15] As the memo rightly describes the Model Penal Code (MPC), necessity will justify a defendant in violation of a law when he or she engages in conduct that the actor "believes to be necessary to avoid a harm or evil to himself or to another," provided that violating the norm is necessary to avoid a "harm or evil" that is "greater than that sought to be prevented by the law defining the offense charged," but only so long as there is no specific legislation or "legislative purpose" to exclude the justification.[16] Necessity justifies otherwise criminal acts against subjects who do not directly pose a threat to the actor. In its paradigm applications, for example, necessity justifies sailors jettisoning cargo to save their ship or a hiker breaking into a cabin to escape a sudden storm.[17] Necessity is, therefore, a potential justification for the situation under consideration in the memo: the decision whether to torture a subdued detainee, who may have information that may help avert a threat that may arise.

Specifically, the claim would have to be used to justify an interrogation technique believed to be the sole effective means of avoiding yet worse harms. On its face, then, necessity might provide a good fit for the interrogation practices in question. . . .

As the memo correctly states, the core of self- or other-defense lies in the defender's belief that such force is "immediately necessary" to avoid the harm posed by someone presenting a direct and imminent threat of serious bodily harm to oneself or another.[18] Necessity grounds the permission to use otherwise impermissible force.

So the argument for the justifiability of torture as a matter of criminal law must stand or fall with the force of the general necessity defense and its limitations. Let us return, then, to the general justificatory element of necessity, specifically, the "necessity" of deploying force in order to prevent a more serious harm. Taken literally, the defense is limited to cases in which the use of force is the only possible response to the threat and is sure to be an effective response to the threat. Only when the defendant's act is a necessary element of a set of conditions sufficient to avert the harm can it be said that the defendant acted as he must, in order to minimize evil. It cannot, in other words, be necessary to act when one's act will be ineffective, even if, were other conditions in place, it might have been part of a set of conditions sufficient to avert the harm.[19]

In fact, the criminal defense of "necessity" presents much softer constraints than true, logical "necessity" would indicate, in large part because it is applied relative to the actor's beliefs about the threat and its projected alternatives. Under the MPC, actors can assert the defense so long as they believe in the necessity of their acts, both regarding the likelihood of the threat and the effectiveness of the alternatives, even if in fact there is no threat, or the means chosen could not be effective. Thus, the MPC defense protects actors who believe, however unreasonably, in the necessity of their acts. However, the necessity provision also provides for liability for defendants who are reckless or negligent in either bringing about the conditions demanding their response or in assessing the necessity of the response.[20] The net result, under both common law and the MPC, is that full justification is provided only to actors who reasonably appraise the situation as calling for their violation of the law.[21] But it should be understood that the subjective extension of the defense, to the reasonable but mistaken defendant, clearly gets its justificatory force from the objective situation where, under the circumstances, the defendant performed an act necessary in fact to avert the greater evil.[22] Put otherwise, an actor's *judgment* of necessity can only be exculpatory if, when the factual premises of that judgment are true, the actor really would be justified. If necessity were instead conceived as an excuse, then any belief, however unreasonable, would be sufficient to exculpate. Since common law and the MPC are clear that only reasonable mistake fully exculpates, the underlying principle must be one of objective justification.[23]

Note the slippage in the theory of necessity—a slippage that, as we shall see, plays a role in evaluating the special case of the ticking-bomb hypothetical. The objective situation is posed timelessly, where the antecedent threat can be weighed against the future consequence of the law-breaking response. But in reality, of course, the defense must apply to conduct undertaken before the threat materializes. It is nearly always impossible to know whether the threat really would have been realized—perhaps the attacker would have suddenly run rather than shot, or a rescue ship might have appeared on the horizon, had defendants waited a few more days.[24] Furthermore, it is almost always impossible for anyone, let alone the defendant, to know in advance whether the use of force will be effective in meeting the threat. Defendants cannot perfectly anticipate the consequences of their acts, but must instead calculate the expected value of their responses in relation to the expected disvalue of the threatened harm. This is an elementary point, but, when understood, it means that in practice actual "necessity"

almost never exists. The defense must instead be read to justify the rather oxymoronic category of "probabilistic necessity": the defense justifies extralegal acts when and only when they are highly likely to avert a virtually certain threat, and it is also highly likely that there are no other options. The normative force of necessity resides in the epistemic requirement of high certainty—a requirement necessary to foreclose the possibility of defendants taking extremely low-probability gambles on high-payoff results.[25] In sum, it is a form of cost-benefit analysis that justifies criminal acts when, given only two options, good consequences outweigh the bad, restricted to some indeterminate extent by a requirement of substantial certainty as to the relevant gambles.[26] . . .

Thus, whatever might be said on behalf of the Bybee's analysis, a great deal more clearly needs to be said before it could be deemed independently convincing, let alone serve as a foundation stone for an enormously controversial change in the United States' legal conception of its duties to detainees. Yet the memo was influential, serving as the basis for the subsequent and widely disseminated Department of Defense Working Group Report, which set policy for interrogations involving military personnel around the world.[27] . . .

In short, the Bush administration has made two distinct propositions about the justifiability of torture and has supported those propositions with its actions even as it has backed away from its legal claims. Those propositions are:

> (i) Micro-necessity: a governmental actor may use torture in interrogation at least when torture is the only available and a highly likely means of avoiding a near certain threat of harm graver than that incurred by the act of torture.
>
> (ii) Macro-necessity: the President, pursuing national security or other military objectives, may authorize torture as a necessary response to a threat to national security, irrespective of statutory restrictions.

I turn now to considering these propositions as matters of ethical and political theory.

II

Necessity, Thresholds and Ticking Bombs

[T]he core philosophical notion of a right is that rights provide us with reasons to act (or not act), even when considerations about overall welfare raise morally powerful concerns about the consequences of those acts.[28]

There are always illegitimate reasons not to honor a rights claim—my selfish desires give me (illegitimate) reason to take your property or to make you an instrument of my desire. Rights claims do rule out such obviously inappropriate claims, but were their force maintained only in such cases, they would have no distinctive content. Long-run welfare-based considerations ("consequentialist" considerations, in philosophers' jargon) about the general misery of a world lived amid theft and abuse would rule those claims out of bounds as well. For claims of right to have distinctive content, for it to be more than a rule of thumb for maximizing welfare, it must apply even in the face of putatively good reasons, particularly if violating the rule would maximize social welfare.

This is a point about the philosophical concept of right, for that concept to have distinctive content. It is not a general justification of rights—a project far beyond the scope of this Essay—nor even a specification of what rights we humans may be said to have. It is simply a point about what the concept must mean, given the role it is meant to play in arguments about morals, politics, and law. But this descriptive, conceptual point has a consequence: it makes clear why a general ethical defense of micro-necessity and a deontological conception of right are incompatible. The necessity justification proposes precisely what the rights claim denies: that action may be taken when the good pays for the bad, as measured by the "cost" of the rights violation. An unconstrained micro-necessity justification consists, effectively, in the forcible conversion of a deontological ethical framework into utilitarian one. Necessity justifications ignore the concept of right.

The Necessity Defense in Criminal Law: Beyond the Bybee Memo

Criminal law protects individual rights of bodily integrity and security of possession as much as it protects aggregate social interests such as the maintenance of public order or the rendering of just deserts. Given the disparate goals of criminal law, you might think that theoretical discussions of the necessity defense would recognize the inherent limits of any basically utilitarian mode of argument applied to individual rights. On the contrary, Anglo-American criminal law theorists and treatise writers, including the authors of the MPC, are typically critical of the courts for giving the necessity defense so little force beyond its formal recognition. Theorists complain about the failure of common-law courts to extend the justification beyond its well-recognized instances (where it typically justifies regulatory violations, such as speeding en route to the hospital or very local property violations).[29] . . .

The relatively few decisions on the necessity defense meet this pattern: necessity claims usually lose, and when they win, it is for easy cases, which fall far short of the infliction of violence, let alone homicide (excluding self-defense). This statement from a recent California case, *People v. Coffman*, is typical: "It is not acceptable for a defendant to decide that it is necessary to kill an innocent person in order that he [or she] may live."[30] . . .

[T]here are no decisions in Anglo-American law, nor any documented decisions not to prosecute, in which innocents not otherwise in harm's way are assaulted or killed in order to avert harm from others.

The same appears also to be true in European jurisdictions. . . . The standard Continental examples of successful necessity defenses are, in essence, gleaning cases: squatters found justified in taking over abandoned housing, breaking and entering to shelter poor children, and in principle the theft of food (though it is generally impossible to show that theft was the only option).[31]

Necessity in Moral Philosophy

. . . Let us look now at the infamous ticking bomb. . . . In the standard story, an interrogator is faced with a terrorist who has planted a bomb that will kill many innocent citizens. Torturing the terrorist is the last, best hope for saving them. The first thing to be said, and the first thing that was said, in Henry Shue's seminal article twenty-five years ago, is that at best the ticking-bomb hypothetical is of virtually no practical significance, and at worst it is utterly corrupt in the illicit conclusions it invites.[32] The example gains its force from its stipulated perfect satisfaction of all the traditional criteria of necessity: the interrogator is certain of the threat and its attendant costs, knows that the person to be tortured is responsible for the bomb, and is reasonably certain that torturing him is the sole means of avoiding catastrophe and is likely to be effective. While under these conditions, there might be widespread consensus that torture would be justifiable, relax any of the dimensions of justification—maybe it's a hoax, maybe it's the wrong guy, maybe the interrogator has chosen to torture the terrorist's child instead, maybe the suspect will lie—and dissensus emerges immediately.

In the real world, it is most likely that some or all of the traditional criteria will be unsatisfied. Moreover, institutions and institutional actors tend to abuse the limits of their discretion and coerced confessions are demonstrably of inferior intelligence quality to detective work.[33] For all these reasons, attempts to institutionalize any principle of morally permissible torture invariably either (1) define the circumstances under which torture is permissible so *narrowly* that the requisite criteria are virtually never met; or

(2) define the circumstances under which torture is permissible so *broadly* that the torture is allowed even when it is not morally justified.[34] To the extent that the Bybee memo goes beyond the hypothetical exploration of an *ex post* defense to a charge of torture and actually lays out *ex ante* an institutional space for torture (grounded in the qualified immunity of officials relying on its legal advice), I believe it is tantamount to criminal complicity.[35]

With all these considerations against it, the persistence of the ticking-bomb hypothetical might seem hard to explain. Since the conditions under which its conclusion results never actually obtain, it might be best to treat it as a kind of ethical "singularity," a black hole that swallows up intuition and lets nothing emerge. But, in fact, the ticking-bomb example is no harmless anomaly. It persists because of a series of related mistakes in thinking about rights under pressure from welfare, and how to conceive the role of necessity in these cases. Necessity really does justify overriding some kinds of rights claims in many instances, but these are rights of a fundamentally different nature from the ones involved in the ticking-bomb example. Criminal theorists have over-generalized the appropriate normative scope of the necessity defense by confusing those rights whose abrogation the defense can legitimately justify with all rights.

Institutional versus Pre-Institutional Rights

Let us put aside, for a moment, the cases of torture and ticking bombs and shift to the law of torts and property. As controversial as a legal decision authorizing homicide or torture would be, so uncontroversial are decisions in tort cases like *Vincent v. Lake Erie Transp. Co.*, or *Ploof v. Putnam*,[36] which involved intentional trespasses upon property clearly justified as necessary under the choices of evils at hand. So clear is the force of the necessity defense in such cases that no prosecutor would consider them, and the question of justice is simply who should pay the costs. As I discussed above, criminal necessity defenses are generally found to lie in affronts to property rights, as well as to violations of regulations that impair no rights.[37] The difference might be thought simply a matter of the relatively weaker interests at play, property versus life, but I think it goes deeper than that, to the kind of right the law of property protects, versus the kind of right protected by homicide law—or, in the instant case, by § 2340 and the body of international treaty and customary law that stands behind it.[38] This is the difference between what I want to call *institutional* and *pre-institutional* rights.[39]

Institutional rights are the rights consequentialists defend: individual claims secured by a general promise that their respect will promote welfare. Pre-institutional rights, by contrast, are claims that institutions must honor, and the institutions' basic justice or legitimacy is assessed by reference to these claims. . . .

A full account of the force of the right against torture would focus on the peculiar horror of torture, the combination of suffering with the deliberate subordination of the victim's consciousness to the will of the interrogator.[40] But it would share with the peacetime right against homicide a commitment to the value of the individual life, a value that cannot be aggregated, or so our legal and moral theories have generally presumed. The scene of torture, in the imagination of those who reject it, makes the nature of this value especially clear: the interrogee is not confronted as a part of an armed host, but as an individual, already disarmed and vulnerable.[41] This is the field of basic, pre-institutional human rights. . . .

Summary

In criminal law, the defense of necessity runs out when it confronts pre-institutional rights, whose value is not the product of an instrumental calculus.[42] My point is not that we could not conceive it in these terms, nor even that we do not, since obviously some people do. My point is that the tradition of criminal law, across the civilian and Anglo-American spectrum, is remarkably fallow ground for justifying acts of violence against individuals, outside either the peculiar space of warfare, or the narrow context of immediate self-defense. While torture and other forms of intentional violence against persons occur on the battlefield as well as in the station house, such acts have received no official legal authorization beyond the awkward discussion in the Israeli Supreme Court and the Bybee memo in the United States. Criminal law theorists have commonly remarked that the near-absolute value of life shows that the law "reflects a moral uneasiness with reliance on a utilitarian calculus."[43] It would be more precise to say that the law responds in a utilitarian fashion to institutional rights and in a non-utilitarian fashion to pre-institutional rights.

III

Necessities at War: Fact versus Justification

I have so far argued that we operate across ethics, politics, and law with two distinct concepts of rights. Institutional, instrumentally justified rights—of which property rights are exemplary—are subject to override by what I have called a micro-necessity justification. But pre-institutional rights, which reflect a conception of the distinct value of individuals, are as a conceptual matter immune to micro-necessity overrides. Assertion of a necessity justification in their face simply denies their deontological status. Rights against torture are core examples of pre-institutional rights and so it follows logically that they are immune from violation justified by necessity. . . .

Perhaps it is not too overwrought to worry instead that the real existential threat comes from the evisceration of our principles in the name of security. . . .

It does no dishonor to a principled commitment against torture to recognize its limits in the hypothetical of the ticking bomb. Nor do we dishonor a general commitment to life's value by insisting that the hypothetical is imaginary, that we remain outside the state of emergency until we can no longer resist its existential claim. . . .

Conclusion

I have argued that the attempt to justify . . . torture and . . . by reference to necessity fails. It rests upon a conflation of necessity as fact with necessity as justification and on a broad and deep misunderstanding of the nature of pre-institutional rights.

The bedrock principles we have, concerning the dignity of humanity and the limits of legitimate power, are hard-won achievements of the last several centuries. Scrabbled together out of convention, claimed in the shadow of authoritarian power, they have become the marks by which we know our moral identities as both persons and nations. Threats and emergencies demand response, but that response must be grounded in a confidence in our principles' abilities to meet the demands of the world on our own terms. This confidence is equally a form of judgment: the determination that threats to our interests not be confused with threats to our existence. Far more dangerous to us, to who we are, is the threat of finding necessity in every conflict with evil and emergency in every war.

At the level of philosophical reflection, the ticking-bomb example does show something. It shows that we can *imagine* limits to even our most deeply held moral principles. But we should use this realization to strengthen our principles and their application in the world, not to abridge them. Here is how the realization of imagined limits can *strengthen* principles such as the right against torture. By their very divergence from real situations (existential necessity can exist only in a hypothetical world), imagined scenarios like the ticking-bomb example can continually remind us that we have not reached the imagined limits in reality, that we need to push our principles further and ever further, that if we relinquish our deepest precepts in an ideal world of imagined scenarios, there will surely be no hope for them in the real world we all inhabit.

Notes

1. BERNARD WILLIAMS, SHAME AND NECESSITY 111 (1993).
2. I echo here David Luban's claims in his paper, *Liberalism. Torture, and the Ticking Bomb*, in THE TORTURE DEBATE IN AMERICA 35 (Karen J. Greenberg ed., 2006) [hereinafter THE TORTURE DEBATE]. I am throughout indebted to his discussion.
3. While there is debate over whether some other well-documented techniques (mild assault, sexual humiliation, terrorization with dogs) legally constitute torture or merely "cruel, inhuman, or degrading" treatment, there is no reasonable debate whether water-boarding (whose point is to introduce fear of death), hanging, and induced hypothermia fit within the definition of torture. *See* Brian Ross and Richard Esposito, *CIA's Harsh Interrogation Techniques Described*, ABC NEWS, Nov. 18, 2005, http://abcnews.go.com/WNT/lnvestigation/story?id=1322866&page=1; Michael Hirsh and Mark Hosenball, *The Politics of Torture*, NEWSWEEK, Sept. 25, 2006, http://www.msnbc.msn.com/id/14872708/site/newsweek/; Dana Priest, *CIA Holds Terror Suspects in Secret Prisons*, WASH. POST, Nov. 2, 2005, at Al; Jane Mayer, *A Deadly Interrogation*, THE NEW YORKER, Nov. 14, 2005, at 44, *available at* http://www.newyorker.com/fact/content/articles/051114fa_fact. . . .
4. Bybee memo, *supra* note 7.
5. I discuss examples of this confusion below, in Section III.
6. Voltaire (François Marie Arouet), "Torture," DICTIONNAIRE PHILOSOPHIQUE (1764), *available at* http://www.voltaire-integral.com/Html/20/torture.htm; Cesare Beccaria, "Ch. 16: Of Torture," ON CRIMES AND PUNISHMENTS (Edward D. Ingraham trans., 1778), *available at* http://www.constitution.org/cb/crim_pun.htm.
7. Convention against Torture and other Cruel, Inhuman, or Degrading Treatment or Punishment, June 26, 1987, 1465 U.N.T.S. 85. The Convention was ratified by the U.S. on April 18, 1988.
8. Interview by Tim Russert with Richard Cheney, "Meet the Press" (Sept. 16, 2001) (transcript available at www.whitehouse.gov/vicepresident/news-speeches/speeches/vp20010916.html). As Cofer Black, former Director of CIA Counterterrorist Center, subsequently testified to Congress, "All I want to say is that there was 'before' 9/11 and 'after' 9/11. After 9/11 the gloves come off." Testimony of Cofer Black to Joint House and Senate Select Intelligence Committee, Sept. 26, 2002, *available at* http://www.fas.org/irp/congress/2002_hr/092602black.html.

9. Douglas Jehl and David Johnston, *C.I.A. Expands its Inquiry into Interrogation Tactics*, N.Y. Times, Aug. 29, 2004, at Al; Mark Danner, *Abu Ghraib: The Hidden Story*, N.Y. Rev. of Books, Oct. 7, 2004, *available at* http://www.nybooks.com/articles/l7430.

10. 18 U.S.C. § 2340A(a).

11. 18 U.S.C. § 2340(1), (2)(c).

12. Bybee memo, *supra* note 7.

13. I discuss the Bybee memos at greater length, and the specific role of the OLC lawyers, in two papers: *The Lawyers Know Sin*, in The Torture Debate, *supra* note 2, at 241-46; and *Causeless Complicity: The Case of the OLC Lawyers*, Crim. L and Phil. (forthcoming 2007).

14. Bybee memo, *supra* note 7, at 27.

15. *Id.* at 39.

16. Model Penal Code § 3.02(1), (l)(a) [hereinafter MPC]. More exactly, § 3.02(1) provides for a defense whenever a defendant believes, even unreasonably, that he or she is in a situation of necessity. Under § 3.02(2), however, reckless or negligent defendants can still be liable for crimes for which recklessness or negligence suffice for culpability. The net result approximates the position at common law, according to which only a reasonable belief as to the necessity of the act serves as a defense.

17. Model Penal Code and Commentaries § 3.02, cmt. 1, at 9–10 [hereinafter MPC Commentaries].

18. Bybee memo, *supra* note 7, at 42–43 (citing MPC § 3.04 and LaFave & Scott, *supra* note 25, at 649).

19. Logically, if "ought implies can,"—that is, one only has obligations to do what it is possible to do—then "cannot" also implies "not ought." One has no obligation, much less requirement, to do the impossible. My swimming to rescue the drowning swimmer might have been a necessary condition of his being saved, if I am the only one within range; but if I cannot swim, it is not necessary that I try.

20. MPC § 3.02(2) states:
When the actor was reckless or negligent in bringing about the situation requiring a choice of harms or evils or in appraising the necessity for his conduct, the justification afforded by this Section is unavailable in a prosecution for any offense for which recklessness or negligence, as the case may be, suffices to establish culpability.

21. *See* Wayne R. LaFave, Criminal Law § 10.1(d)(3) (4th ed. 2003).

22. The effect of rendering the justification subjective is to include both objectively unjustified but morally non-culpable actors, and to exclude coincidentally justified but morally culpable actors. The essentially objective character of the justification is evident in LaFave and Scott's treatment, and is manifest in the memo, which discusses the defense as providing a genuine justification, and not just exculpation.

23. As LaFave says,

The rationale of the necessity defense is not that a person, when faced with the pressure of circumstances of nature, lacks the mental element which the crime in question requires. Rather, it is this reason of public policy: the law ought to promote the achievement of higher values at the expense of lesser values, and sometimes the greater good for society will be accomplished by violating the literal language of the criminal law.

LaFave, *supra* note 30, at 524.

24. See the famous example of *Regina v. Dudley & Stephens*, 14 Q.B.D. 273 (1884) (upholding rejection of defense of necessity by cannibalistic sailors, in part because the sailors "might possibly have been picked up next day by a passing ship; they might possibly not have been picked up at all.") (Lord Coleridge, C.J.).

25. At common law, self-defenders are not even held to such a high standard. The majority of states do not require defenders to choose to retreat, even when they can do so in safety, and one need never retreat from a home. *See* LaFave & Scott, *supra* note 25, § 10.4(f).

26. Treatises, the MPC Commentaries, and the Bybee memo straightforwardly identify the defense as having utilitarian value. *See* MPC Commentaries, *supra* note 23, §3.02, cmt. 3; LaFave, *supra* note 30, §10.1(a); Bybee memo, *supra* note 7, at 40.

27. Working Group Report on Detainee Interrogations in the Global War on Terrorism: Assessment of Legal, Historical, Policy, and Operational Considerations (Apr. 4, 2003), *reprinted in* The Torture Papers, *supra* note 7, at 241-85. Also available at http://www.gwu.edu/~nsarchiv/NSAEBB/NSAEBB127/03.04.04.pdf.

28. This is, I think, a consensus view of what a deontological conception of rights, or of duties grounding rights, is committed to: a claim of right (or duty not to act in some way) overrides whatever instrumental (welfare-based or other) considerations militate in favor of acting contrary to the right. For its sources in the philosophical literature, see, obviously, Immanuel Kant, Groundwork of the Metaphysics of Morals Bk. II (1785) (our duties as rational agents to treat others as free and equal agents create in

them rights not to be used for our purposes, and to be aided in the pursuit of their ends); ROBERT NOZICK, ANARCHY, STATE & UTOPIA 30-34 (1977) (the function of rights is to limit, as "side constraints," the pursuit of individual or collective welfare gains); Thomas Nagel, *War and Massacre, reprinted in* MORTAL QUESTIONS 53-74 (1979) (duties to others are deontological constraints which limit the force of consequentialist justifications); SAMUEL SCHEFFLER, THE REJECTION OF CONSEQUENTIALISM 80-83 (rev. ed. 1994) (duties not to act in certain ways limit the force of consequentialist claims). . . .

29. On the potential justifiability of killing a non-threatening individual, see LaFAVE, *supra* note 30, § 10.1(a); MPC Commentaries, *supra* note 23, § 3.02, Commentary 3; GLANVILLE WILLIAMS, CRIMINAL LAW: THE GENERAL PART § 237 (2d ed. 1961); SANFORD H. KADISH, BLAME AND PUNISHMENT 122-23 (1987). George Fletcher is a rare criminal law theorist who explicitly rejects a much less restrictive necessity test. *See* GEORGE FLETCHER, RETHINKING CRIMINAL LAW § 10.4 (1978). J.C. Smith notes that if English law does permit application of the defense to cases of homicide (unclear, given the infamous *R. v. Dudley & Stephens* precedent, 14 Q.B.D. 273 (1884)) the defense does not extend past cases of killing some lest all die. SIR JOHN SMITH & BRIAN HOGAN, CRIMINAL LAW 271-74 (10th ed. 2003).

30. 34 Cal. 4th 1, 100 (2004), *cert. denied,* 544 U.S. 1063 (2005) (denying necessity defense in robbery-murder where defendant alleged co-perpetrator had threatened her life and the life of her son) (internal quotation marks omitted).

31. *Id.* at § 10.2; ROBERT, *supra* note 67, at 272.

32. Henry Shue, *Torture,* 7 PHIL. & PUB. AFF. 124, 142-43 (1978).

33. John Langbein quotes Sir James FitzJames Stephen's *A History of the Criminal Law of England,* concerning "the proclivity of the native police [in India] for torturing suspects. 'It is far pleasanter to sit comfortably in the shade rubbing red pepper in some poor devil's eyes than to go about in the sun hunting up evidence.'" John H. Langbein, *The Legal History of Torture, in* TORTURE: A COLLECTION 93, 101 (Sanford Levinson ed., 2004). Notably, Justice Frankfurter also quotes Stephen in *McNabb v. United States,* 318 U.S. 332, 343 (1943), an important coerced-confession case in which the Court asserted its inherent authority to regulate federal investigatory authority.

34. There is no way to institutionalize any principle of permissible torture without falling into the swamp of Abu Ghraibs and Bagrams, in which innocents are routinely subjected to abuse for the amusement of sadists playing "intelligence" games. On the abuses at Bagram, see Tim Golden's exposé, *In U.S. Report. Brutal Details Of 2 Afghan Inmates' Deaths,* N.Y. TIMES, May 20, 2005, at A1.

35. I defend these claims in *The Lawyers Know Sin, supra* note 19, at 241. Briefly, there exists a basis for accomplice liability for any purposefully abetted acts of assault or torture, and for purposefully abetting acts, in reckless disregard of the risks, that through recklessness or negligence led to the deaths of some of the detainees.

36. 124 N.W. 221, 222 (Minn. 1910) (holding boat operator acted justifiably, but still liable for damage to dock incurred during unconsented use during storm); 81 Vt. 471, 474-75 (1908) (plaintiff had right to compensated use of defendant's dock during storm).

37. Arguably, this is not quite right. If one accepts a right to be free from certain degrees of ex ante risk, then a speeding driver on the way to the hospital may be violating the rights of those he endangers. French criminal law explicitly treats the issue in this way, and deems it a matter of justified necessity. ROBERT, *supra* note 67, at 273-77 (citing CA Metz, 8 mars 1990, Dr. pén., 1991, comm. 49).

38. Apart from the Convention against Torture, torture is categorically prohibited by the International Covenant on Civil and Political Rights, 999 U.N.T.S. 171 (Dec. 16, 1966); by all four Geneva Conventions, through both Common Article 3 and through specific articles: Geneva Convention for the Amelioration of the Condition of the Wounded and Sick in Armed Forces in the Field, 75 U.N.T.S. 31; Geneva Convention for the Amelioration of the Condition of Wounded, Sick and Shipwrecked Members of Armed Forces at Sea, 75 U.N.T.S. 85; Geneva Convention Relative to the Treatment of Prisoners of War, 75 U.N.T.S. 135 [hereinafter GC III]; Geneva Convention Relative to the Protection of Civilian Persons in Time of War, 75 U.N.T.S. 287 [hereinafter GC IV]. All were signed 12 Aug. 1949. The rule against torture is also seen as a non-derogable, *jus cogens* norm of customary international law. *See, e.g.,* REST. (THIRD) OF FOREIGN RELATIONS LAW OF THE UNITED STATES, § 702, and Reporter's Note 5.

39. I borrow the idea of the institutional vs. pre-institutional distinction from John Rawls, though he uses it to discuss the related issue

of desert. JOHN RAWLS, THEORY OF JUSTICE § 48 (2d ed. 1999).

40. For excellent discussions, see Luban, *supra* note 2; David Sussman, *What's Wrong With Torture?*, 33 PHIL. & PUB. AFF. 1(2005).

41. Of course, from the perspective of the interrogators, it is this scene that renders the victim least human, as Hannah Arendt observed of the concentration camp inmates. HANNAH ARENDT, THE ORIGINS OF TOTALITARIANISM, 284 (1973).

42. I want to put aside the very different case of knowingly running ex ante risks of statistical deaths, even risks up to a moral certainty.

Such risks can, I think, be justified on a basis consistent with individual rights. I discuss this briefly in *Self-Defense and Political Justification*, 88 CALIF. L. REV. 751, 751-58 (2000).

43. *See, e.g.,* KADISH, *supra* note 61, at 123.

CHRISTOPHER KUTZ is a Professor of Law at University of California-Berkeley. His publications include the book *Complicity: Ethics and Law for a Collective Age* as well as articles on ethics, criminal law, and legal and political philosophy.

EXPLORING THE ISSUE

Is Torture Ever Morally Justified?

Critical Thinking and Reflection

1. Bagaric and Clarke assert that torture is already being practiced widely. If true, does this fact affect the morality of torture? Why or why not?
2. While Bagaric and Clarke argue that torture can be both moral and legal, they nevertheless advocate that limits be placed on torture. What is the moral justification for these limits? Can limits on torture address the deontological concerns raised by Kutz?
3. How useful is the formula proposed by Bagaric and Clarke for justifying torture? Can precise data ever be identified for insertion into the formula, especially in light of Kutz's discussion of real-life situations? Is precise data even needed for this formula to be useful?
4. If you were placed in a hypothetical situation like the one described by Bagaric and Clarke, would you authorize the use of torture to gain information that might prevent a terrorist attack? What considerations influence you most in making your decision? Why are these the most important considerations for you?

Is There Common Ground?

The authors of these articles agree on one fundamental issue: torture is inherently evil and repulsive. In ideal world, there would be no need for torture, and questions about the morality and legality of torture would not arise. However, we do not live in an ideal world. We live in a world where torture is a tempting method for gaining information that might eliminate threats to the social order and prevent grievous harm to innocent people.

The question, therefore, is not how best to use torture, but whether we can circumscribe the use of torture in a way that sufficiently mitigates its inherent evil. Our authors have diametrically opposed responses to this question. Kutz answers in the negative, and so concludes that torture is morally wrong, no matter how it is used. Bagaric and Clarke answer in the affirmative, and so propose limitations and regulations for the use of torture. These differences stem from a basic incompatibility in the fundamental principles of utilitarian and deontological ethics, and there appears to be no way to resolve this dispute.

Additional Resources

Philip E. Devine, "What's Wrong with Torture?" *International Philosophical Quarterly* (vol. 49, September 2009)

Karen J. Greenberg, *The Torture Debate in America* (Cambridge University Press, 2005)

Sanford Levinson, *Torture: A Collection* (Oxford University Press, 2006)

Jeff McMahan, "Torture, Morality, and Law," *Case Western Reserve Journal of International Law* (vol. 37, 2006)

Darius Rejali, *Torture and Democracy* (Princeton University Press, 2009)

Internet References . . .

Amnesty International: Torture

www.amnestyusa.org/our-work/issues/torture

Ethics Updates—Philosophers Speak Out about War, Terrorism, and Peace

http://ethics.sandiego.edu/Resources/PhilForum/Terrorism/index.asp

Political Concepts: Torture

www.politicalconcepts.org/issue1/torture/

The Stanford Encyclopedia of Philosophy: Torture

http://plato.stanford.edu/entries/torture/

Selected, Edited, and with Issue Framing Material by:
Owen M. Smith, *Stephen F. Austin State University*
and
Anne Collins Smith, *Stephen F. Austin State University*

ISSUE

Can a Person Morally Direct Caregivers to Withhold Life-saving Medical Treatment If He or She Develops Moderate Dementia?

YES: **Norman L. Cantor**, from "On Avoiding Deep Dementia," *Hastings Center Report* (2018)

NO: **Daniel P. Sulmasy**, from "An Open Letter to Norman Cantor Regarding Dementia and Physician-Assisted Suicide," *Hastings Center Report* (2018)

Learning Outcomes

After reading this issue, you will be able to:

- Identify and explain the progression of Alzheimer's disease, as well as the reasons that an early-stage Alzheimer's patient might wish not to prolong life in later stages.
- Identify and explain the Principle of Autonomy, especially in regard to the right to determine how one's life will be recalled by others.
- Identify and explain the concept of respect for basic human dignity, as it relates to caring for an Alzheimer's patient as well as valuing the lives of people with other kinds of disabilities.
- Formulate your own position on advanced directives for patients who anticipate becoming mentally incompetent and identify evidence supporting your position.
- Identify the main objections to your position and formulate responses to these objections.

ISSUE SUMMARY

YES: Describing the final stages of dementia as unacceptably degrading, Cantor argues that patients who have received a dementia diagnosis are justified in planning to allow their lives to end before reaching that stage.

NO: Sulmasy argues that Cantor's assumption that the world would be better off without him in a deeply demented state is mistaken, and that legalizing voluntary suicide in such cases would logically lead to nonvoluntary euthanasia in others.

As people age, a certain amount of occasional forgetfulness is considered normal. But when the brain begins malfunctioning to such an extent that memory loss and other cognition problems cause interference with everyday life, more serious conditions are suspected. The best known of these conditions is Alzheimer's disease, a form of progressive dementia that afflicts from 5 to 10 percent of people over the age of 65. Alzheimer's disease is always fatal and there is no known cure.

The later stages of Alzheimer's disease are especially frightening. Following a period of moderate decline, patients eventually experience severe mental impairment that prevents them from completing even simple cognitive tasks, such as counting backward from 10. Loss of memory leads patients to fail to recognize friends and family members and, combined with changes in mood and personality, lead to the impression of a loss of self. As the disease progresses toward its final stage, patients need help with daily activities such as bathing, grooming, dressing, and using the toilet, and may be unable to walk.

People in the earliest stage of dementia, who are beginning to experience forgetfulness, loss of concentration, and other mild symptoms, are still mentally competent for the most part, and able to make decisions about their own health care. Given the frightening prospect of gradually losing the memories and relationships that contribute to one's sense of self, as well as the unpleasant prospect of being eventually confined to bed in diapers in a nursing home, it is understandable that some people in this situation might not wish to prolong their lives unnecessarily once they reach a stage of serious decline.

Elsewhere in this volume, we have seen people argue both for and against the right of a terminally ill, mentally competent patient to request a physician's assistance in hastening death without pain, rather than a later death with a great deal of pain. While the question of physician-assisted suicide is still under debate, it is widely agreed that such patients have the right to reject medical treatment that would delay death. While patients in early-stage dementia are terminally ill and mentally competent, their situation is not yet such that they desire to hasten death or prevent its delay at that time. Rather, some wish to designate a time in the future at which they would prefer to reject treatments such as antibiotics or artificial nutrition so as to allow themselves to die from treatable conditions such as infection or malnutrition, rather than experience the mental and physical degradation of late-stage dementia. At that future time, however, they will no longer be mentally competent to make that decision. Thus, they must depend on others to carry out their advance directives. Such directives are relatively uncontroversial.

Cantor, in his essay, introduces complications into this kind of advance directive. He describes his own advance directive, which he has prepared in case he finds himself in the early stages of dementia. In addition to describing clear-cut rejection of medical treatments designed to prolong life, he also discusses the possibility of supporting efforts to commit suicide. For example, a competent patient can refuse to eat or drink and thereby die from dehydration, an option that Cantor finds morally acceptable, but which he would not be willing to choose while he was still mentally competent. There are, however,

incompetent patients who, while they do not need a feeding tube, are not interested in eating, or not able to eat and drink without some assistance. Cantor explains that his advance directive states that, if he reaches this state, he should not be coaxed or helped to eat and drink. It is possible that this decision by his previous competent self might cause distress to his present incompetent self; if so, sedation should be used to comfort the present self.

Another complication introduced by Cantor is his choice of the future time when he would want his directive to be implemented. Rather than waiting until the late-stage dementia described above, he wishes that his directive be implemented when he is in the moderate stage of dementia. At this point, patients have difficulty with complex cognitive tasks, but may not be suffering in any way and may still be able to derive enjoyment from some aspects of life. Nonetheless, he considers this stage of the illness to be unacceptable, and wishes that his life in this stage not be prolonged. The reason he offers for this decision is an extension of the Principle of Autonomy, which states that patients are moral agents and should be accorded the dignity of making decisions about their own treatment. Cantor argues that his right to self-determination extends to a right to determine the narrative integrity of his life by shaping the memories that his survivors have of him. He wishes them to remember him as an, intelligent, aware human being, not as someone suffering from cognitive decline.

Sulmasy's response praises Cantor for tackling such difficult issues head-on, and supports his desire not to undergo life-prolonging medical treatment in the possible future that Cantor envisions. However, Sulmasy takes issue with the notion of directing others to carry out directions that are tantamount to assisted suicide, and also asserts that Cantor undervalues his future self, giving short shrift to his own basic human dignity. Moreover, Sulmasy argues, in deciding that such a life is not worth living for himself, Cantor risks making the claim that such a life is not worth living for anyone, a position that is strongly resisted by advocates for the disabled, who should not have to contend with such challenges to their own continued existence. Indeed, argues Sulmasy, permitting patients to direct others to help them to kill themselves will put pressure on other patients to do the same so as not to become a burden to their families or to the health-care system. It is the duty of physicians to find ways to treat Alzheimer's patients, not to end their lives.

YES ↵

Norman L. Cantor

On Avoiding Deep Dementia

Absent medical breakthroughs, millions of Americans will be diagnosed in coming years with Alzheimer's, adding to the 5.3 million who already have the disease. These millions will have to cope with an affliction that entails precipitous mental decline, starting with mild memory loss, confusion, and diminished problem-solving skills, and ending with cognitive detachment from one's surroundings. The advanced stage includes nonrecognition and noncommunication with loved ones and caretakers and complete dependence on assistance in dressing, bathing, eating, mobility, and toileting. On average, the stricken person will survive four to eight years after diagnosis but may subsist as long as twenty years. On average, forty percent of the postdiagnosis survival period is in an advanced stage of cognitive dysfunction and physical dependence.[1]

Some people will confront Alzheimer's with a measure of resignation, a determination to struggle against the progressive debilitation and to extract whatever comforts and benefits they can from their remaining existence. Such people might believe that all life is sacred and worthwhile, or they may be hoping for a miracle cure to surface, or they might value whatever interactions they can salvage with their loved ones. They are entitled to pursue that resolute path.

For other people, like myself, protracted maintenance during progressive cognitive dysfunction and helplessness is an intolerably degrading prospect. The ultimate specter is an advanced stage of decline with no ability to recall either recent or distant past or to recognize loved ones or surroundings—an uncomprehending, noncommunicative status. This strong aversion to being mired in dementia is not based on prospective emotional distress or suffering. While some people with advanced dementia may experience significant anxiety, frustration, anger, or agitation, others may remain placid and indifferent to their debilitated status. My antipathy is rather to reduced cognitive function to a point that, for me, is intolerably demeaning (with or without accompanying feelings of distress). That antipathy reflects unwillingness to soil the lifetime image or memories to be left with my survivors. I care mightily about posthumous recollections of my personality, and I strive to shape my life trajectory (including a dying process) consistently with my personal vision of dignity. Another impetus for my strong aversion to deep dementia is unwillingness to be a physical, emotional, and financial burden on others, especially my family and friends, even if they would willingly assume such burdens.

The critical question for those of us seeking to avoid protracted dementia is how best to accomplish that objective. One strategy is to engineer one's own death while still mentally competent to do so (even in the stage of mild dementia).[2] The increasingly common term for this is "self-deliverance"—a fitting euphemism for suicidal conduct by a person stricken with a fatal affliction. A variety of means of self-deliverance exist. If I were to use a preemptive strategy in the face of a dementia diagnosis, I would probably choose to stop eating and drinking, a process known as voluntarily stopping eating and drinking (VSED).[3] Strict cessation of nutrition and hydration will typically result in death within fourteen days.

. . .

An alternative tactic for avoiding prolonged dementia would be to allow oneself to decline into moderate dementia—thus losing capacity to perform self-deliverance or even to make serious medical decisions—but before getting to that point to provide advance instructions rejecting prospective life-sustaining medical interventions. These advance instructions would authorize palliative but not curative measures. They would seek to facilitate a stricken person's demise (once a self-defined stage of mental debilitation has been reached) by declining even simplistic medical interventions such as antibiotics, tube feeding, blood transfusions, or anti-arrythmics. The hope would be that infection would soon occur in the urinary tract, skin, or respiratory tract and that this condition, left untreated (except for palliation), would precipitate death, or that an eating disorder would arise early on and that death would ensue pursuant to advance rejection of medical means of nutrition and hydration.

My current personal instructions define the point of intolerable cognitive decline triggering medical nonintervention as "mental deterioration to a point when I can no longer read and understand written material such as a newspaper or financial records such as a checkbook."[4] These instructions dictate allowing my demise at a point of moderate dementia when I may not be perceptibly suffering, when I may still be getting some rudimentary satisfaction from my debilitated life, and when I no longer recall the preoccupation with personally intolerable indignity that motivated my instructions. Can I expect that my advance instructions will be implemented in those circumstances? Is it lawful, and is it moral for a surrogate decision-maker and associated caregivers to allow an uncomprehending, ostensibly content but demented individual to die? My analysis herein contends that it is not only lawful and moral but also legally required to implement clear, considered advance instructions even at a stage of moderate dementia.

The Legal Foundation for Binding Instructions Hastening Death

American jurisprudence broadly recognizes the prerogative of a competent person to shape the medical fate of his or her future incompetent self. That jurisprudence started with judicial recognition that the common law gives a competent patient autonomy to decline medical services. A physician's bodily intervention without patient consent constitutes a legal wrong, the tort of battery. Toward the end of the twentieth century, the patient's autonomy prerogative was held to include even rejection of potentially life-preserving treatments, as when Jehovah's Witnesses decline blood transfusions.[5] Neither the contrary preferences of medical practitioners nor their benevolent, life-preserving intentions could override the patient's opposition to treatment.

Medico-legal jurisprudence has evolved beyond these common-law roots. The patient's underlying interests in self-determination and bodily integrity were judicially recognized as so fundamental that a patient's choice about medical intervention was deemed a constitutionally protected liberty under either the Fourteenth Amendment to the U.S. Constitution or state constitutional provisions safeguarding personal decision-making. The landmark New Jersey case *In re Quinlan*, in 1976, accorded constitutional protection to a patient's rejection of a life-sustaining respirator.[6] Other state supreme courts followed suit, including Florida's recognition of "all medical choices" as part

of fundamental liberty under its state constitution.[7] Even the U.S. Supreme Court in *Cruzan*, in 1991, assumed that personal choice about medical intervention is a fundamental aspect of protected liberty under the Fourteenth Amendment.

This same jurisprudence recognizes the prerogative of a competent person to shape his or her postcompetence medical fate. The cases establish that a patient's autonomy right to accept or reject medical intervention is not vitiated by the onset of mental incapacity. That is, if a person has articulated choices regarding future medical interventions, those preferences must be respected whether as a matter of state common law or of state or federal constitutional law. For example, the Florida Supreme Court declared that the self-determination principle of the state constitution "requires that we safeguard an individual's right to chart his or her own medical course in the event of later incapacity."[8] Under this rubric of prospective or precedent autonomy, any surrogate decision-maker on behalf of a now-incompetent patient is supposed to implement the patient's prior express wishes regarding future medical treatment. (I use the terms "precedent autonomy" and "prospective autonomy" interchangeably.) The widely accepted "substituted-judgment" standard for surrogate medical decision-making incorporates this prospective autonomy principle. Pursuant to a duty to reach the same medical decision that the now-incompetent patient would make if capable, the surrogate is required to seek and respect clearly expressed wishes.[9] Prior expressions thus serve as the means to project a once-competent patient's autonomy rights into a postcompetence setting.

. . .

The Boundaries of Prospective Autonomy

How far can advance planning go in avoiding or shortening the period in which a stricken person will be mired in deep dementia? Precedent autonomy surely includes advance rejection of a range of indisputably "medical" interventions, including cardiac resuscitation, mechanical respiration, and dialysis. A variety of other life-preserving bodily interventions are, however, more problematic.

Basic personal care. Could advance instructions, in an effort to hasten death, seek to foreclose not just life-extending medical interventions in the face of natural afflictions but also basic personal care such as providing hygiene, warmth, and food and drink? One claim might be that even bathing or turning a patient involves a tortious battery if rejected by a competent person. A further contention might be that a person can delegate advance authority to a surrogate to reject such "tortious" ministrations (in an effort to hasten infections and thus shorten the time a patient with dementia spends in unwanted limbo).

While there may not be a moral distinction between life-sustaining medical treatment and basic personal care like cleaning and clothing a person, there is a legal distinction. The prospective autonomy prerogative described above probably does not extend to touching involving personal care even if administered by medical personnel. Keep in mind that the legal framework governing a surrogate decision-maker's control of an incompetent patient with dementia holds that the surrogate's role is fiduciary. As a fiduciary obligation, it generally requires promotion of the well-being, comfort, and dignity of the incompetent ward. In the setting of a significantly debilitated person with dementia, it generally entails provision of shelter, warmth, hygiene, food, and medical care. A surrogate who unilaterally rejects any of these ministrations sustaining a nonsuffering patient would ordinarily be chargeable with unlawful neglect of the demented ward. What insulates a surrogate's otherwise neglectful conduct is a legally binding advance instruction from a previously competent patient. However, it is only the medical interventions that can (and must, given the prospective autonomy prerogative) be withheld. Instructions regarding the provision of warmth, shelter, and hygiene—basic personal care—don't fall within the currently recognized medical treatment bounds of precedent autonomy. The supporting constitutional and common-law jurisprudence recognizes that precedent autonomy may shape medical interventions, but not basic personal care.

Even if providing warmth and hygiene were classifiable as medical care when administered by health care providers, a further principle limits advance instructions seeking to foreclose such basic care. The prospective autonomy prerogative carries an implicit obligation to respect the humanity and intrinsic dignity of the person with dementia whose fate is determined by advance instructions. Under our cultural norms, keeping a patient properly covered, clean, and kempt is required by respect for the person's humanity. It is impermissibly degrading for a patient to wallow in filth or to lie naked and exposed even if dementia prevents the person from understanding the debasement being experienced. Our culture and tradition uphold a person's intrinsic dignity even if that person is unaware of or indifferent to the offense to dignity. Imposition of serious indignities cannot, therefore, be part of a surrogate's authority to uphold prospective autonomy.

. . .

Nutrition and hydration. An important issue is how these limitations on prospective autonomy—regarding basic personal care and inhumane medical handling—relate to matters of nutrition and hydration. Keep in mind that while a mildly demented person can reject in advance all sorts of life-sustaining medical interventions, the prospective autonomy prerogative does not ensure an early demise when someone with dementia is no longer competent. Medical pathologies set in capriciously, and they might not occur before years of unwanted lingering in a seriously debilitated cognitive status. A prerogative of advance control over nutrition and hydration would therefore greatly facilitate control of the timing of death at postcompetence stages of dementia.

As a result, some people seek to use advance instructions to preclude all provision of food and drink once their demented persona reaches a defined level of cognitive decline. However, as noted, a surrogate is obligated to provide basic personal care protecting the well-being of a demented ward, and that obligation generally includes provision of food and water to a person with dementia who is still willing and able to ingest and digest nourishment. At the same time, if a naturally occurring pathology disrupts a person's ingestion and digestion system, then medical intervention (such as artificial nutrition and hydration—ANH) clearly can be declined via advance instruction.

Where does this leave the hand feeding necessitated by an Alzheimer patient's increasing indifference to eating or incapacity for self-feeding? In some situations, hand feeding constitutes declinable medical intervention. For example, a still competent patient (at an early phase of affliction) has a widely acknowledged right to stop eating and drinking and precipitate death by dehydration. Despite the patient's suicidal intent, the afflicted patient is entitled to invoke self-determination and bodily integrity to reject nutrition and hydration.[10] In the context of a competent patient who is determined not to eat or drink, any overriding of the patient's wishes would involve medical intervention (ANH, possibly coupled with physical or chemical restraint) or other inhumane handling (forced feeding). A competent patient resisting hand feeding is therefore deemed to be rejecting unwanted medical intervention.

That competent patient's prerogative to stop eating and drinking is not readily transferable via advance directive. If the later, incompetent persona is accepting regular offerings of food and drink, then providing nutrition is, as noted, part of basic care (not medical treatment). No ANH is involved. Also, no inhumane handling (restraint and forced feeding) is involved, as there would be in overcoming the will of a competent patient.

While the acknowledged right to stop eating and drinking is thus confined to competent persons, prospective autonomy and advance directives still have an important role in controlling the nutritional status of a later, incompetent dementia patient. Various eating deficits and disorders occur in the course of progressive dementia. If the responses to these pathologies are properly characterized as medical treatment, as is clearly the case with artificial nutrition and hydration (tube feedings), then they are subject to prospective autonomy and control via advance instructions. For example, if dementia results in dysphagia (a serious disorder to the ingestion system), then the medical solution (often a percutaneous endoscopic gastrostomy, or PEG, tube) is subject to advance patient instructions.

The appropriate characterization of some responses to eating disorders is still an unresolved matter. Progressive dementia is frequently accompanied by the pathologies of agnosia (nonrecognition of familiar objects, including food and eating utensils) or dyspraxia (loss of motor coordination, including physical skills for eating and drinking). The common response to such pathological conditions is hand feeding. Is such hand feeding basic care, thus lying outside the scope of prospective autonomy? Or is it medical treatment subject to advance instructions?

One perspective is that hand feeding is not a medical procedure, but rather basic care commonly provided by lay persons. From this perspective, failure to provide this simplistic nutritional input in the face of agnosia or dyspraxia could be treated as punishable patient neglect.[11] Even where the feeding is undertaken by professional medical caregivers, some health care providers regard hand feeding both as basic care and as so symbolically linked to caring and compassion for helpless persons as to be deemed (ethically, if not legally) obligatory.[12]

An alternative perspective regards hand feeding in response to debilitations like agnosia and dyspraxia accompanying dementia as a part of the medical treatment program supervised by health care professionals. That is, professionals must assess the patient's nutritional needs and the consequences of various feeding techniques. They must monitor the type and texture of foods in connection with swallowing difficulties, choking, and aspiration risks. Particularly for someone in advanced dementia, continued nutrition, including hand feeding, entails potential harms or burdens, such as edema, diarrhea, and pulmonary congestion. Some commentators and medical caregivers therefore see even hand feeding as a medical issue subject to resolution in accord with the advance instructions of the person who now has dementia.[13]

This latter approach seems right to me. If progressive dementia prompts mental or physical incapacity to feed oneself, then hand feeding should be regarded as a form of medical intervention subject to advance instructions. If the patient, while still competent, defined the current stage of decline as intolerably demeaning and designated nutrition and hydration as part of the care to be withheld at this stage, then it shouldn't matter whether the nutrition is being administered by tube or by spoon.

Categorizing hand feeding in the face of agnosia and dyspraxia as medical intervention does not end the inquiry regarding the force of advance instructions. An additional constraint on prospective autonomy is that the patient's chosen course should not subject the subsequent demented persona to inhumane treatment. A relevant question then is whether the dying process following cessation of hand feeding would be so distressful or burdensome as to be deemed inhumane.

. . .

One clearly humane approach to implementation of an advance instruction to forgo hand feeding is to employ comfort feeding only (CFO).[14] Comfort feeding is limited to what the patient willingly and readily accepts. This approach ensures that a patient who becomes resistant or indifferent to hand feeding, as is common at least at an advanced stage of dementia, is not impelled to eat and is allowed to expire in accordance with an advance instruction. CFO avoids the specter of a patient seeking and being denied nutrition and hydration. End of Life Choices, a New York organization, provides a form allowing a declarant to decide whether or not comfort feeding should be offered.[15]

Comfort feeding can produce sporadic eating or drinking that protracts the dying process for a patient who wished to hasten death by rejecting hand feeding. An alternative humane approach is to provide sedation to calm any agitation or upset on the part of the now-demented patient whose prior instruction not to be hand fed is being implemented. That is what commonly occurs in the context of a competent patient exercising VSED who slips into incompetence and becomes delirious and confused. Sedation mitigates any discomfort or agitation ensuing when hand feeding is withheld. My current advance directive prescribes sedation rather than comfort feeding because I am apprehensive about CFO prolonging the duration of the unwanted demented status.

. . .

Applying Precedent Autonomy in the Context of Moderate Dementia

In my own advance directive, I reject life-sustaining medical intervention from the point "when I can no longer read and understand written material such as a newspaper or financial records such as a checkbook." While that phase is only moderate dementia, it represents an unwanted level of cognitive decline. My personal vision of intolerable indignity includes having such a substantial cognitive decline soil the life image of a vibrant, articulate figure that I have cultivated to shape my survivors' recollections. I understand that at this juncture I might not be physically or emotionally suffering and I might still be deriving some rudimentary satisfactions (from music or television, for instance) from life. And I understand that, while this defined level of cognitive decline is repulsive and degrading to my current, competent self, my future demented persona may not recall or care about my convictions concerning the indignity of mental debilitation. Can I expect that my advance instructions—to be allowed to die from treatable comorbidities like infections or eating disorders—will be implemented at this stage?

Does my constitutionally grounded prospective autonomy right apply at this stage? While the binding effect of advance instructions is increasingly recognized in both judicial and disciplinary forums,[16] no judicial precedents speak to an incompetent patient in a moderately demented state.

. . .

Some medico-legal commentators would contend that it is immoral or unethical to implement prior instructions rejecting life-sustaining medical intervention for a patient who has dementia but is not suffering, appears to be content, and no longer remembers her underlying dignity-based or altruistic concerns. Rebecca Dresser, for example, posits an overriding ethical obligation to "protect vulnerable people from harm,"[17] by which she means either a hastened death or any discomfort in the dying process following withholding of life-sustaining medical intervention pursuant to advance instructions. Her position elevates the contemporaneous well-being of the demented patient to a determinative status regardless of a patient's prior wishes. Paul Menzel adopts a variation on Dresser's theme. He urges a balancing or sliding scale test under which the positive experiential interests of the now-demented patient can prevail over the patient's prior dignity-based instructions.[18]

My analysis is that the jurisprudence of death and dying does not allow an incompetent patient's immediate well-being to overcome clear prior instructions. Surrogate decision-makers are required to implement a now-incompetent patient's chosen medical preferences even if the surrogates feel that an alternative course would be more consistent with the patient's contemporaneous best interests.[19]

. . .

In addition to the supportive legal framework, there is a solid moral foundation for permitting a competent person's considered choices about quality of life to govern future medical treatment. A person, by a lifetime of nurturing and developing a body, character, and relationships, has earned a prerogative to shape his or her life narrative—including the medical fate of a succeeding, incompetent persona. A person's determination to preserve the integrity of a life as a whole (and to shape the recollections of survivors) when threatened by prolonged dementia or other degenerative afflictions is well understood and respected.[20] As Justice John Paul Stevens explained in his dissenting opinion in *Cruzan* in 1991,

> Each of us has an interest in the kind of memories that will survive after death. To that end, individual decisions are often motivated by their impact on others. [A patient devoted to family . . .] would likely have not only a normal interest in minimizing the burden that her own illness imposes on others, but also an interest in having their memories of her filled predominantly with thoughts about her past vitality rather than her current condition.[21]

I understand that some health care providers will be repelled by my articulated determination to cut short not just immersion in advanced dementia lacking meaningful interaction with my surroundings but also moderate dementia with substantially diminished cognitive function. It cannot be easy for either health care agents or caregivers to allow a helpless, ostensibly content individual to die based on concerns about lifetime image, intolerable indignity, and altruistic values that the demented individual no longer recalls. Should I develop progressive dementia, I will need a resolute health care agent to accomplish my stated preferences for forgoing postcompetence medical intervention. Yet a basic precept of precedent autonomy is that a person's values and principles—whether grounded on religion, altruistic concern for others, or a conception of intolerable dignity—are entitled to implementation.

Note also that my instructions rejecting life-sustaining medical interventions at a stage of moderate dementia do not ignore the contemporaneous well-being and experiential interests of my future demented persona. My prerogative to shape a dying process consistent with my desired life image is constrained by limits of inhumane treatment. Palliative care is therefore expected and sought. And I abjure any steps that would cause irremediable torturous distress or suffering during a contemplated dying process. That is, I leave it to my health care agent and caregivers to consider whether withholding of medical interventions will, in any given instance, precipitate unconscionable distress that can't be mitigated by sedation or other palliative steps.

Notes

1. These statistics are drawn from "2017 Alzheimer's Disease Facts and Figures," published by the Alzheimer's Association, www.alz.org/documents_custom/2017-facts-and-figures.

2. See D. S. Davis, "Alzheimer Disease and Preemptive Suicide," *Journal of Medical Ethics* 40 (2014): 543-49.

3. N. L. Cantor, "My Plan to Avoid the Ravages of Extreme Dementia," *Bill of Health,* April 16, 2015, http://blogs.law.harvard.edu/billofhealth/2015/04/16/my-plan-to-avoid-the-ravages-of-extreme-dementia.

4. Parts of my advance directive intended to foreclose protracted dementia can be found in the sidebar. The entire version can be found in N. L. Cantor, "Changing the Paradigm of Advance Directives to Avoid Prolonged Dementia," *Bill of Health,* April 20, 2017, http://blogs.harvard.edu/billofhealth/2017/04/20/changing-the-paradigm-of-advance-directives/. For another model, see B. Gaster et al., "Advance Directives for Dementia: Meeting a Unique Challenge," *Journal of the American Medical Association* 318 (2017): 2175-76.

5. See Public Hospital v. Wons, 541 So.2d 96 (Fla. 1989); Norwood Hospital v. Munoz, 564 N.E.2d 1017 (Mass. 1991).

6. 355 A.2d 647 (N.J. 1976).

7. In re Browning, 568 So.2d 4 (Fla. 1991).

8. Browning, 568 So.2d at 12-13.

9. In re Jobes, 529 A.2d 434, 451 (N.J. 1987); In re Conroy, 486 A.2d 1209, 1229 (N.J. 1985). Substituted judgment aims to secure for incompetent patients "the same right to choose or reject treatment" as accorded to competent persons (In re Brandon, 677 N.E.2d 114, 119 [Mass. 1997]).

10. See T. M. Pope and L. E. Anderson, "VSED: A Legal Treatment at the End of Life," *Widener Law Review* 17, no. 363 (2012): 363-427; R. D. Truog and T. I. Cochrane, "Refusal of Hydration and Nutrition: Irrelevance of the 'Artificial' vs 'Natural' Distinction," *Archives of Internal Medicine* 165, no. 22 (2005): 2574-76.

11. C. A. Meier and T. Ong, "To Feed or Not to Feed? Analysis of Withholding Food and Drink in a Patient with Advanced Dementia," *Journal of Pain & Symptom Management* 50, no. 6 (2015): 887-90; C. Taylor and R. Barnet, "Hand Feeding: Moral Obligation or Elective Intervention," Catholic Health Association of the United States, 2014, at htpps://www.chausa.org.

12. F. Baumgartner, "The Ethical Requirement to Provide Hydration and Nutrition," *Archives of Internal Medicine* 166 (2006): 1324-25; Taylor and Barnet, "Hand Feeding."

13. Willingness to withhold hand feeding is most evident where the patient is perceived to be at the end stage of a dying process (see American Nurses Association, "Position Statement on Nutrition and Hydration at the End of Life," 2017, www.nursingworld.org, p. 3) or at least at an advanced stage of dementia. See J. K. Schwarz, "Alzheimer's Disease and Written Directions to Withhold Oral Feedings," *Seattle Journal for Social Justice* 15, no. 3 (2017): 740-70, at 760-63.

14. See E. J. Palecek et al., "Comfort Feeding Only: A Proposal Regarding Difficulty with Eating for Persons with Advanced Dementia," 58, no. 3 *Journal of the American Geriatric Society* (2010): 580-84; Schwarz, *Alzheimer's Disease,* 762.

15. "Advance Directive for Receiving Oral Foods and Fluids in the Event of Dementia," End of Life Choices New York, at http://www.endoflifechoicesny.org/.

16. T. M. Pope, "Legal Briefing: New Penalties for Disregarding Advance Directives and DNR Orders," *Journal of Clinical Ethics* 28, no. 1 (2017): 74-81.

17. Dresser, "Pre-emptive Suicide, Precedent Autonomy and Preclinical Alzheimer Disease," 551; Dresser, "Toward a Humane Death," 39.

18. P. T. Menzel and C. Chandler-Cramer, "Advance Directives, Dementia, and Withholding Food and Water by Mouth," *Hastings Center Report* 44, no. 3 (2014): 23-37; P. T. Menzel, "Respect for Personal Autonomy in the Justification of Death-Hastening Choices," in *Euthanasia and Assisted Suicide*, ed. M. J. Cholbi (Santa Barbara, CA: Praeger, 2017), 231-52.

19. According to *In re Browning*, where the patient's wishes are known, "the surrogate must make the medical choice that the patient . . . would have made . . . and not one that the surrogate might think is in the patient's best interests" (568 So.2d, p. 13).

20. See J. McMahan, *The Ethics of Killing: Problems at the Margins of Life* (Oxford: Oxford University Press, 2002), 498-500; B. Rich, "Prospective Autonomy and Critical Interests: A Narrative Defense of the Moral Authority of Advance Directives," *Cambridge Quarterly of Health Care Ethics* 6, no 2 (1997): 138-47.

21. Cruzan v. Director, Missouri Dept of Health, 110 S.Ct. 2841, 2892 (1990).

NORMAN L. CANTOR is a professor of Law Emeritus and Nathan Jacobs Scholar Emeritus at Rutgers University School of Law, Newark. He has widely published in legal and medical journals on the topic of the legal handling of dying medical patients and has published three books in that field.

Daniel P. Sulmasy

An Open Letter to Norman Cantor Regarding Dementia and Physician-Assisted Suicide

Dear Norm,

Thank you for sharing such a personal and heartfelt essay.[1] I have been asked by the editors to comment. Reading it inspires me to do so in a similarly heartfelt way. Although I don't know you well, I thought I'd write to you as if you were my patient. You are not my patient, so pardon me if this seems presumptuous.

You and I have been fellow travelers on the road to improve care at the end of life for a long time—you for a longer time than I.[2] I deeply admire and appreciate all your effort, your keen intellect, your careful legal scholarship, and your passion. I also appreciate your honesty—manifest especially in this latest essay. Unlike many who share your views, you're not afraid to call things as they are—using words like "suicide" and frankly describing committing suicide by means of measures like carbon monoxide poisoning or voluntarily stopping eating and drinking. You then argue that suicide is justified in the circumstances you describe rather than falling back on euphemisms that obscure the ethical issues.

I share your sense that Alzheimer disease is a terrible scourge. I've seen much of this disease over a lifetime of practice, and I deeply understand its ravages and the debility and suffering it causes. All the progress medicine has made in curing other illnesses has resulted in more people living long enough to develop dementia. If I were a physician-scientist, it's the disease for which I would most like to do the research that would lead to a cure.

But what you propose is not a good solution for the problems that Alzheimer disease poses for patients, families, and society. It will ultimately do far more harm than good. Please let me try to explain.

We should not ratify your desire to kill yourself. Most of your essay concerns finding legal justifications for various methods of ending your life should you become afflicted by Alzheimer disease. Rather than discuss your legal reasoning, I want to address this issue of "self-deliverance" (your preferred term for suicide under these circumstances)[3] head on.

I know how you feel. Many of us have been there, witnessing someone who was once a professor lying in bed, staring vacantly, no longer able to converse, no longer in control of bowel and bladder function. Reasonable people are bound to think, "I never want to end up this way. I'll kill myself first."

But we should not endorse letting you, or anyone else, act on such inclinations. We should never ratify the idea that the world is better off without you even if you come to believe it. We should mourn your loss, not precipitate it. The reason we shouldn't endorse your killing yourself is the same reason you gave in your essay about why we should not let you soil yourself—out of respect for your basic human dignity. You are valuable not only for your intellect but as a fellow human being. Should you develop a dementing illness, we should keep you warm, comfortable, and clean, treat your pain, and care for you.

You may counter by asserting that if you develop deep dementia, we will then, in a sense, already have lost you. Yet you know that's not really true. The most profound pathos we feel in seeing someone we love develop dementia comes from knowing the person who suffers from that awful disease. It will be you, or Aunt Molly, or Cousin George who is now demented, not really "someone else" and certainly not nobody. Everybody is a somebody—even a demented person. Martin Luther King had to forcefully remind us that this is what respecting dignity really means—recognizing that everybody is a somebody.[4]

You say you don't want to be a burden on others. I understand that sentiment, but we should not construct a society in which that feeling is endorsed by those who would be charged with caring for you. Even common courtesy suggests that when someone says, "I wouldn't want to be a burden," the proper response is, "Not at all." It is not respectful of human dignity to endorse anyone's belief that their illness makes them too much of a burden on the rest of us.

Anyone who sees someone with Alzheimer disease feels bad for that person. Yet your view of what it is like to be a person with Alzheimer disease is not necessarily the view of a person with the disease; that person may not know what has been lost and may even be content. Your fear is based on how you now believe you will appear to others. As a fellow human being, but especially as a physician, I have moral obligations that are less dependent on an abstraction like your precedent autonomy than on treating the actual patient before me. To sedate you rather than feed you if you say you are hungry because the person before me is not the "real" patient seems cruel, based on allegiance to a cold ideology. Ethics is best when it is a response to reality rather than to abstractions.[5]

We should not ask doctors to help you to do so. None of this is to say that we must do everything conceivable to prolong your life. We both agree that you can forgo life-sustaining treatments that you (or those who represent you) deem to be more burdensome than beneficial. Urinary tract infections need not be treated, if that accords with your wishes. When the end approaches, pneumonia can become the old person's friend. And we have good evidence that when patients with Alzheimer disease become bedbound and unable to swallow in a coordinated way, feeding tubes do not even prolong their lives.[6]

Moreover, we can do more now than in the whole history of humankind to treat your symptoms. Alzheimer disease is typically not painful, but associated conditions may be painful, and pain and other symptoms ought to be treated vigorously. Clinicians and society have obligations to work to improve palliative care and hospice for the demented among us, and to do more to help caregivers. These are the pressing issues to which we should be devoting our attention. Assisted suicide is both a distraction and a seductively inexpensive alternative to this kind of hard work.

You might disagree, but clinicians, the law, and the person on the street all recognize that there is a difference between forgoing life-sustaining treatments and killing a patient (or assisting a patient in killing himself or herself).[7] When I, as a physician, discontinue ventilator support because the patient has determined that it has become more burdensome than beneficial, I am acknowledging the limits of medicine. That is a good thing. When I act with the intention of making someone dead, or help someone to make herself dead, because I cannot otherwise cure or relieve the suffering that she has deemed unacceptable, then I have, in effect, refused to accept the limits of medicine. Medicine becomes the ultimate solution to the problem of human suffering. That is a terrible power—a power so great that it cannot help but be corrupting. It is a power no doctor should want and no wise society should grant to its healers.

Behind the closed door of the examination room, even powerful and independent persons like you become vulnerable. This is the nature of illness. Countertransference is a powerful force in the patient-physician relationship. As a physician, I know that it can make *my* feelings of helplessness in the face of incurable disease seem like *your* independent judgment; your choice to ask me to help you end your life can be an acquiescence to my judgment that your life is not worth living or is too much of a burden on others.[8] We need a firm boundary. The understanding that this option is off the table helps to establish the conditions of trust that make the healing relationship possible for you and for all patients.

We should not give this the force of law. Autonomy is a thin reed upon which to rest the massive weight of legalized medical killing. Even if your decision is genuinely substantially autonomous, free from any coercive, manipulative, or misinformed influences, you really need to think about the impact that legal sanction of the practices you describe will have on others. Once we let you make a first-person determination that your life is not worth living, then it is really not that big a step to permit third-person determinations that the lives of others are not worth living. After all, it was not fanatics but a respectable psychiatrist and a law professor who introduced the phrase *"lebensunwerten Lebens"* ("life unworthy of being lived") in 1922.[9] They first argued that "mercy killing" was justified for terminally ill persons who autonomously decided that their lives were no longer worth living, and then they extended this logic to allow others to decide this for the mentally incapacitated.

This is why people living with disabilities are so fearful of legalized assisted suicide and other forms of medically assisted killing. It is not so much that they anticipate being lined up in wheelchairs and forcibly injected (at least not in the near term). It is the assault to their dignity that comes with social sanction of the idea that lives characterized by incontinence, cognitive incapacity, and dependence on others are unworthy of life and so can be ended by direct killing. Norm, if we sanction your starving yourself to death so that you don't suffer Alzheimer disease, then we throw a question smack in the face of countless disabled persons everywhere: why are *you* still burdening yourself (and us) with your life, which is similarly unworthy of life?

Moreover, suicide is not a purely self-regarding act. We know that publicity about assisted suicide for the terminally ill can lead to copycat suicides among the mentally ill.[10] And there is emerging evidence that overall suicide rates increase in places where physician-assisted suicide is legalized for the terminally ill.[11]

Above all, your essay illustrates the disingenuousness of arguments that legalized physician-assisted suicide (PAS) is the end goal of proponents. As you well note, under current laws, patients with Alzheimer disease who want to end their lives directly face a catch-22. When someone with Alzheimer disease is still competent, it is too early in the course of the disease to qualify for PAS since the condition is not yet terminal. Yet if one waits until one is terminal, then because of the depth of the dementia, one would be disqualified by lack of decisional capacity. The whole point of your essay is to find legal ways out of that catch-22. Yet the terrain is, as you freely admit, murky. If I stop hand feeding you and sedate you, at your advance request, is that really a refusal of life-sustaining treatment? Is it assisted suicide? Or is it euthanasia? All this points out is that there will be pressure to permit third parties to make substituted judgments, interpret advance directives, and provide euthanasia for those unable to participate in assisted suicide due to dementia. This is not a psychological slippery slope; it is just logic. If the terminally ill with capacity can access PAS, then it just seems like discrimination to prevent those who lack capacity from equal access to death. Voluntary assisted suicide laws will beget nonvoluntary euthanasia.[12] Legislation to move in this direction is already brewing.[13]

We agree, Norm, that Alzheimer disease is bad. It's really bad. But the ramifications of your proposed solution are wide. And the compassionate care we are capable of providing for you, if we are wise and respectful, is probably better than you think. So, before you sign your advance directive, let's talk it over. What we really need is your intellect and energy focused on the struggle to improve care at the end of life—providing better access to hospice and palliative care, better education about forgoing life-sustaining treatments, better financial and social support for the frail elderly and their caregivers.

Please give me a call. When your time comes, we can promise to care for you without forcing you to linger. But we never want to endorse the idea that the world would be a better place without you.

With admiration and gratitude,
Your colleague,
Dan

1. N. O. Cantor, "On Avoiding Deep Dementia," *Hastings Center Report* 48, no. 4 (2018): 15-24.

2. Norman Cantor has been working on issues related to care at the end of life since the 1970s and was involved as a legal advisor to the family in the landmark Karen Ann Quinlan case. See, for example, N. L. Cantor, "A Patient's Decision to Decline Lifesaving Medical Treatment: Bodily Integrity versus the Preservation of Life," *Rutgers Law Review* 26, no. 2 (1973): 228-64.

3. Cantor, "On Avoiding Deep Dementia," 16.

4. G. Baker-Fletcher, *Somebodiness: Martin Luther King, Jr. and the Theory of Dignity* (Minneapolis, MN: Fortress Press, 1993).

5. See I. Murdoch, *Metaphysics as a Guide to Morals* (New York: Penguin, 1993).

6. D. P. Sulmasy, "Ethical Issues in Medically Assisted Nutrition and Hydration at the End of Life: Separating the Wheat from the Chaff," in *The Oxford Handbook of Ethics at the End of Life* ed. R. M. Arnold and S. Youngner (New York: Oxford University Press, 2016), 126-53.

7. D. P. Sulmasy, "Killing and Allowing to Die: Another Look," *Journal of Law, Medicine & Ethics* 26 (1998): 55-64; Washington v. Glucksberg, 117 S.Ct. 2258 (1997); Vacco v. Quill, 117 S.Ct. 2293 (1997); Morris v Brandenburg. Supreme Court of New Mexico No. S-1-SC-35478; 2016-NMSC-027; 356 P.3d 836 (2016).

8. S. H. Miles, "Physician-Assisted Suicide and the Profession's Gyrocompass," *Hastings Center Report* 25, no. 3 (1995): 17-19; F. T. Varghese and B. Kelly, "Countertransference and Assisted Suicide," *Issues in Law and Medicine* 16, no. 3 (2001): 235-58.

9. K. Binding and A. Hoche, *Die Freigabe der Vernichtung lebensunwerten Lebens: ihr Maß und ihre Form* (Leipzig, Germany: Felix Meiner Verlag, 1920; 2nd ed., 1922), available in English translation as: K. Binding and A. Hoche, "Permitting the Destruction of Unworthy Life: Its Extent and Form," *Issues in Law and Medicine* 8, no. 2 (1992): 231-65.

10. P. M. Marzuk et al., "Increase in Suicide by Asphyxiation in New York City after the Publication of Final Exit," *New England Journal of Medicine* 329 (1993): 1508-10; P. M. Marzuk, K. Tardiff, and A. C. Leon, "Increase in Fatal Suicidal Poisonings and Suffocations in the Year Final Exit Was Published: A National Study," *American Journal of Psychiatry* 151 (1994): 1813-14.

11. T. A. Boer, "Does Euthanasia Have a Dampening Effect on Suicide Rates? Recent Experiences from the Netherlands," *Journal of Ethics in Mental Health* 9, special theme issue II (2017): https://www.jemh.ca/issues/v9/theme2.html; D. A. Jones and D. Paton, "How Does Legalization of Physician-Assisted Suicide Affect Rates of Suicide?," *Southern Medical Journal* 108 (2015): 599-604.

12. D. A. Jones, "Is There a Logical Slippery Slope from Voluntary to Nonvoluntary Euthanasia?," *Kennedy Institute of Ethics Journal* 21 (2011): 379-404; N. Gorsuch, *The Future of Euthanasia and Assisted Suicide* (Princeton, NJ: Princeton University Press, 2006): 93-101; J. Keown, *Euthanasia, Ethics, and Public Policy* (Cambridge: Cambridge University Press, 2002): 70-80.

13. J. Richer, "Quebec Opens Door to Expanding End-of-Life Law to Alzheimer's Disease," *Montreal Gazette*, February 23, 2017; Oregon Senate Bill 893, 2017; M. Harbarger "Legislator's Promise to a Dying Friend," *Oregonian*, April 30, 2015.

Daniel P. Sulmasy is a senior research scholar at the Kennedy Institute of Ethics and holds a joint appointment at the Pellegrino Center for Clinical Bioethics. His research interests encompass both theoretical and empirical investigations of the ethics of end-of-life decision-making, ethics education, and spirituality in medicine. He is the author or editor of six books in these areas.

EXPLORING THE ISSUE

Can a Person Morally Direct Caregivers to Withhold Life-Saving Medical Treatment If He or She Develops Moderate Dementia?

Critical Thinking and Reflection

1. Suppose that a patient in a moderate stage of cognitive decline, who is mentally incompetent but happy and free from pain, contracts an infection. The patient has an advanced directive forbidding the use of antibiotics in this case, and will die if left untreated. Should the patient be treated for the infection? Why or why not?
2. Suppose that a patient in a moderate stage of cognitive decline, who is mentally incompetent but happy and free from pain, begins to have difficulty eating. The patient has an advanced directive forbidding the use of assisted eating in this case, and will die if not helped to eat. Is this case morally different from the case in question #1? If so, how? If not, why not?
3. Suppose that a mentally incompetent patient who has a directive as described above, explicitly states a desire to continue living, which would entail medical treatment forbidden by the directive. Which preference should be upheld: the one that the patient expressed earlier while mentally competent, or the one that the patient is expressing now?

Is There Common Ground?

The authors of the following selections appear fundamentally opposed. Cantor believes that it is his right, based on the Principle of Autonomy, to direct a kind of assisted suicide for his future self if he is stricken with dementia. Sulmasy believes, based on the notion of basic human dignity, that not only is Cantor wrong to do so for himself, but that such a decision would have far-reaching negative consequences for others.

However, Cantor and Sulmasy share many areas of agreement. They agree that Alzheimer's disease is a terrible scourge and that people recently diagnosed with Alzheimer's have reason to be concerned about a difficult and uncertain future. They also agree that the purpose of medical care is not to prolong life indefinitely, and both agree

that it is moral for a patient to reject medical treatment in order to allow natural death to occur, even if that death would be easily preventable by such treatment.

Additional Resources

Jonathan Wolff, "Dementia, death and advance directives," Health Economics, Policy, and Law 7:4, pp. 499–506.

Anne-Mei The, In death's waiting room living and dying with dementia in a multicultural society. Amsterdam: Amsterdam University Press, 2008.

Gaynor Macdonald, "Death in life or life in death? Dementia's ontological challenge," Death Studies, 42:5, p. 290.

Internet References . . .

Alzheimer's Association

    https://www.alz.org/

Center for Disease Control and Prevention: Alzheimer's Disease and Healthy Aging

https://www.cdc.gov/aging/aginginfo/alzheimers.htm

The Alzheimer Society of Ireland: Understanding Late-Stage Dementia

https://www.alzheimer.ie/Alzheimer/media/SiteMedia/ Helpline%20and%20Information%20Resources/ Info%20Pack%20PDF%27s/Understanding-late- stage-dementia_Section-A6.pdf

Selected, Edited, and with Issue Framing Material by:
Owen M. Smith, *Stephen F. Austin State University*
and
Anne Collins Smith, *Stephen F. Austin State University*

ISSUE

Is Physician-Assisted Suicide Morally Permissible?

YES: Kathryn L. Tucker, from "In the Laboratory of the States: The Progress of Glucksberg's Invitation to States to Address End-of-Life Choice," *Michigan Law Review* (2008)

NO: George Annas et al., from "Brief of Amicus Curiae Bioethics Professors in Vacco v. Quill," Supreme Court of the United States (1997)

Learning Outcomes

After reading this issue, you will be able to:

- Distinguish physician-assisted suicide from other forms of suicide.
- State the Principles of Autonomy, Nonmaleficence, and Beneficence.
- Explain how assisting someone to commit suicide may or may not conflict with the moral obligations imposed on physicians by these principles.
- Formulate your own position on physician-assisted suicide and identify evidence supporting your position.
- Identify the main objections to your position and formulate responses to these objections.

ISSUE SUMMARY

YES: Kathryn L. Tucker argues that allowing mentally competent patients who face a slow and painful death to make it swifter and painless is a beneficial alternative, and that this practice is morally different from the act of suicide committed by those who are clinically depressed.

NO: George Annas et al. argue that a "right to suicide" cannot be justified on the same grounds as the right to refuse treatment, identifying several important differences between the two. Nor can such a right be justified on the same grounds as a right to abortion. The authors make it clear that rejecting the claim that people have a right to commit suicide does not affect the right to refuse unwanted medical treatment or to have an abortion.

When end of life issues arise, especially in cases where medical intervention is ineffective in curing the patient or relieving the patient's pain and suffering, physicians face a tangled web of moral responsibilities. Because of the vulnerability of their patients, physicians are held to a rigorous set of professional obligations designed to ensure that they do not misuse their authority and abuse the extraordinary trust placed in them by their patients. In antiquity, these obligations were codified into the Hippocratic Oath, in which physicians swore to a variety of gods to follow a specific set of ethical practices. In the 20th century, various alterations were proposed to the Hippocratic Oath, and while the oath is not required of physicians who practice in the United States, the vast majority of new physicians take some form of the oath before beginning to practice medicine.

Modern versions of the Hippocratic Oath embody several important ethical principles regarding the practice of medicine. First is the Principle of Autonomy, which states that patients are moral agents and should be accorded the dignity of making decisions about their own treatment. The Principle of Autonomy flows from the recognition that a patient is a human being, with intrinsic value, and not merely an object or thing. If doctors were to impose their judgment on patients and administer treatment without consulting them or in defiance of their wishes, they would be treating their patients as mere things, objects on which to practice medicine, not human beings. Consequently, this principle requires physicians to obtain a patient's voluntary informed consent before beginning medical treatment. Even when patients are unable to give consent, as for example when an unconscious person arrives in an emergency room in need of treatment, the physician is to take only those actions that are in the patients' best interest and would reasonably be approved by the patients, were they able to given consent.

Another ethical principle governing the practice of medicine is the Principle of Nonmaleficence. This principle obligates physicians to avoid exposing their patients to the unnecessary risk of needless harm. This principle does not enjoin physicians from causing harm to their patients, since medical treatment may at times require harming a patient, as when a surgeon cuts into a patient's body to repair an injured organ. This principle only forbids physicians from performing harmful actions that are not necessary for the accomplishment of a greater good, such as curing a patient or relieving a patient's pain and suffering. Moreover, it is not necessary for a physician to cause actual harm to a patient to violate this principle. Simply exposing a patient to needless harm, for example by acting in a careless or negligent fashion, violates this principle.

A third ethical principle governing the practice of medicine is the Principle of Beneficence. This principle imposes on physicians the moral obligation to help their patients when they are able to do so. Although philosophers differ whether there is a general moral obligation to help other people (as opposed to not hurting them), a fundamental aspect of the relationship between physician and patient is the dependence of the patients on their physicians to supply the knowledge, skill, and experience they lack in diagnosing and treating their medical conditions. This dependence requires physicians not merely to avoid harming their patients unnecessarily, but to act to promote their patients' welfare. This obligation applies not merely to physicians, but to the members of all the helping professions, such as nurses, therapists, and social workers. While is difficult to circumscribe the extent of this positive duty precisely, this principle has led many physicians and health-care workers to expose themselves to injury and infection on behalf of their patients, sometimes at the cost of their own lives.

While these principles provide physicians with clear and concise guidance in the practice of medicine, the compatibility of these principles, and the moral obligations they impose on physicians, may become problematic when a patient wishes to die and requests the assistance of a physician in performing this act. A simple appeal to the Principle of Autonomy is not sufficient to resolve the problem. Physicians as well as patients are moral agents and must be accorded the dignity of choosing how to act. The mere fact that a patient desires a medical treatment does not obligate a physician to provide the treatment, although the physician may be obligated to direct the patient to a physician who will provide the treatment. An appeal to the Principle of Beneficence may suffice to justify a physician prescribing treatment to relieve the pain and suffering of a patient, but if a patient faces the prospect of an extended period of pain and suffering, especially if the patient has a terminal illness and hence no hope of recovery or cure, the welfare of the patient may well be served by ending the life the patient, and with it all pain and suffering. The Principle of Nonmaleficence is often considered the determining principle—causing the death of a patient is unambiguously an act of harming the patient, and thus would seem to be clearly prohibited by the Principle of Nonmaleficence. However, the Principle of Nonmaleficence prohibits only needless harm, and if the pain of the patient can only be ended by the patient's death, causing the death of the patient may not qualify as needless harm.

In this circumstance, the requirements imposed on a physician by the Principle of Nonmaleficence might be addressed in another way. While this principle may prohibit the physician from taking direct action to cause the death of a patient, it does not clearly enjoin a physician from assisting a patient to achieve this goal. The knowledge, skill, and experience that enable a physician to treat illnesses and injuries can also be used to cause illness, injury, and even death; the Hippocratic Oath and the principles it embodies originated precisely to prevent unscrupulous physicians from acting in this way. A physician is in an excellent position to provide advice to a person who wishes to commit suicide, for example by identifying the appropriate drugs and providing directions on how they might effectively be used to provide a painless death. Since death is the result of the patient's own actions, not those of the physician, it can be argued that a physician who assists a patient to commit suicide does not actually kill the patient, and so does not violate the Principle of Nonmaleficence. By providing this type of assistance, a physician might also be praised for respecting the autonomy of the patient and for promoting the patient's welfare by bringing an end to the patient's pain and suffering.

Care would have to be taken, however, so that the reasoning used to circumvent the Principle of Nonmaleficence is applied only in appropriate circumstances, and not to the detriment of patients or the medical profession as a whole. The strongest case for physician-assisted suicide is a terminally ill patient undergoing extensive pain and suffering. If physician-assisted suicide is permitted in this case, however, the practice of physician-assisted suicide might expand to other cases where the justification is far less clear. A person with a terminal illness, but who is not yet in pain, may seek the assistance of a physician to avoid the pain that would inevitably arise. A person who is not terminally ill, but who experiences chronic pain and suffering might also seek such help. So might a person who is not terminally ill and not in chronic pain, but who suffers discomfort or embarrassment from a physical or mental disability. Even more disturbing, a person might request physician-assisted suicide on behalf of another who is unable to make such a request or even give an opinion on the matter. A person might be pressured by family members or government officials to request physician-assisted suicide in order to avoid expensive medical bills, even though this person does not want to die. Such cases form a slippery slope in which the rationale for physician-assisted suicide can be used to attack the very principles on which the ethical practice of medicine is based. Such a slippery slope, moreover, is not merely theoretical. Cases such as these have been reported in countries where the practice of physician-assisted suicide is legal.

These issues are addressed in greater detail in the two selections excerpted for this issue. In the first, Tucker provides a defense of physical-assisted suicide, although she objects to the use of the emotionally and ethically laden term "suicide" in this context. For her, there is a vast difference between clinically depressed individuals who choose to kill themselves out of hopelessness and despair and mentally competent, terminally ill individuals choose a painless death after deliberate and rational reflection. She dismisses the specter of sick, helpless patients being pressured by families or doctors to consent to euthanasia, so often raised by opponents of this practice, by noting that in Oregon, where physical-assisted suicide has been legal under certain circumstances for a decade, vulnerable patients have not been pressured to make this choice against their will. Indeed, the very existence of a legal option for a dignified, peaceful end for their suffering has comforted even patients who ultimately do not choose to exercise this option.

In contrast, a group of bioethicists led by George Annas express their lingering concerns over the practice of physician-assissted suicide. In an amicus curiae (friend of the court) brief in a legal case involving physician-assisted suicide, they allege that this topic is rife with the conflation of key concepts, which need to be defined precisely and carefully distinguished to analyze this practice properly. In particular, the well-recognized right of a patient to choose to forego medical treatment must be distinguished from the purported right of a patient to choose physician-assisted suicide. In addition, they argue, the proposed analogy between choosing to have an abortion and choosing physician-assisted suicide suffers from too many dissimilarities to be morally or legally useful. In particular, the concept of being "terminally ill," unlike the concept of being pregnant, ultimately rests on the subjective judgment of individual physicians, and has thus been defined in widely different ways by a variety of court decisions and state legislatures. Consequently, there is no clear-cut class of people who are entitled to choose physician-assisted suicide, leading to confusion and potential abuse of this practice.

YES ⤶

Kathryn L. Tucker

In the Laboratory of the States: The Progress of Glucksberg's Invitation to States to Address End-of-Life Choice

Introduction

Invoking continued debate, the U.S. Supreme Court concluded its 1997 decision in *Washington v. Glucksberg* with these words: "Throughout the Nation, Americans are engaged in an earnest and profound debate about the morality, legality, and practicality of physician-assisted suicide. Our holding permits this debate to continue, as it should in a democratic society."[1]

The debate has indeed continued these past ten years, and there have been two particularly significant developments worthy of close examination. First, Oregon has been implementing its Death with Dignity Act[2] ("Dignity Act") since 1997. This law empowers terminally ill, mentally competent adult Oregonians to control the timing and manner of their deaths, subject to careful procedures. A fraction of dying patients confront a dying process so prolonged and marked by such extreme suffering and deterioration that, even with excellent pain and symptom management, they determine that hastening impending death is the least-bad alternative. The data show that passing this law has harmed no one and has benefited both the relatively few patients *in extremis* who make use of it, and a great many more who draw comfort from knowing this option is available.

Second, an important evolution has occurred in the terminology used to discuss the choice of a mentally competent, terminally ill patient to self-administer medications to bring about a peaceful death. It is increasingly recognized that it is inaccurate to consider this choice to be "suicide." The Dignity Act itself states that such actions "shall not, for any purpose, constitute suicide, assisted suicide, mercy killing or homicide, under the law."[3] The Oregon Department of Human Services, which reports on the implementation of the Dignity Act, rejects referring to this as "assisted suicide" or "physician assisted suicide."

From a mental health perspective, "suicide" and the choice of a dying patient to hasten impending death in a peaceful and dignified manner are starkly different.[4] The American Psychological Association has recognized that "the reasoning on which a terminally ill person (whose judgments are not impaired by mental disorders) bases a decision to end his or her life is fundamentally different from the reasoning a clinically depressed person uses to justify suicide."[5]

Many medical experts[6] and legal experts[7] have also come to recognize that the term "suicide" or "assisted suicide" is inappropriate when discussing the choice of a mentally competent, terminally ill patient to seek medications that he or she could consume to bring about a peaceful and dignified death. The term "assisted suicide" has been replaced with more accurate and value-neutral terms such as "aid in dying" or "physician-assisted dying."[8] The only active opponents of this evolution in terminology are opponents of the practice who continue to malign the choice for aid in dying by labeling it "suicide."

It is timely now, ten years after *Glucksberg*, to assess the lessons learned from the experience in Oregon, and to consider if the laboratory ought to and/or can be expanded beyond Oregon, as well as the likelihood that such expansion will occur. Part I of this Article reviews the constitutional landscape in the wake of *Glucksberg* and *Vacco v. Quill*.[9] Part II describes the Oregon statute, the legal challenges it has survived, and the record of its implementation. Finally, Part III reviews the support and opposition to aid-in-dying laws nationwide and concludes that there are substantial prospects that other states will enact laws similar to Oregon's.

I. The Constitutional Landscape

A. Where Did Glucksberg and Quill Leave Us?

In an effort to establish that competent, dying patients have the right to openly choose a humane, physician-assisted death, laws prohibiting assisted suicide in New York and Washington were challenged on federal constitutional grounds in the cases of *Vacco v. Quill*[10] and *Washington v. Glucksberg*.[11]

In these cases, patients and physicians challenged the assisted suicide laws to the extent that they prohibited doctors from providing medications to competent, dying patients that the patients could use to hasten death if they so chose.[12] Liberty and equality guaranteed by the Fourteenth Amendment of the U.S. Constitution formed the basis of the claims.[13] Two federal courts of appeals, including the Ninth Circuit sitting en banc, agreed that statutes preventing patients from exercising this option were unconstitutional.[14] The Supreme Court reversed these decisions, but left the door open to both future legislative reform and a future successful constitutional claim.[15]

The opinions, both majority and concurring, invited legislative reform. The majority did so in the passage quoted at the beginning of this Article, and Justice Souter's concurring opinion stated an explicit preference for legislative action in this area. He wrote that "[t]he Court should . . . stay its hand to allow reasonable legislative consideration,"[16] and that "the legislative process is to be preferred."[17] Similarly, Justice O'Connor's concurrence demonstrated her concern that state legislatures be given the first opportunity to address the issue: "States are presently undertaking extensive and serious evaluation of physician-assisted suicide and other related issues. . . . In such circumstances, the . . . challenging task of crafting appropriate procedures for safeguarding . . . liberty interests is entrusted to the 'laboratory' of the States . . . ."[18]

. . .

B. Aggressive Pain and Symptom Management

In *Glucksberg* and *Quill*, several members of the Court suggested that patients may have a right to aggressive pain management. In a concurring opinion joined by Justice Breyer, Justice O'Connor stated that "a patient who is suffering from a terminal illness and who is experiencing great pain has no legal barriers to obtaining medication, from qualified physicians, to alleviate that suffering, even to the point of causing unconsciousness and hastening death."[19] She further wrote that "[t]here is no dispute that dying patients . . . can obtain palliative care, even when doing so would hasten their deaths."[20]

Thus Justices O'Connor and Breyer answered a question that the parties had not actually posed, appearing to recognize a constitutional right to adequate pain medication—including the practice of terminal or palliative sedation.[21] In the years since the decisions issued, the practice has become steadily incorporated in end-of-life care, and authoritative literature in medical journals detailing the practice is burgeoning.[22] Where patients can expect good pain and symptom management, the argument that all that is really needed is simply better pain and symptom management[23] has little traction.[24]

II. The Oregon Experience: Has the Laboratory Served its Function?

A decade after the Supreme Court's invitation for legislative reform, and with a decade of experience with Oregon's landmark aid-in-dying law, what have we learned? Has the laboratory envisioned by the Court served its purpose?

. . .

B. Implementation and Its Implications

The Oregon Death with Dignity Act demonstrates that aid-in-dying laws can, and do, work well. The Dignity Act establishes tightly controlled procedures under which competent, terminally ill adults who are under the care of an attending physician may obtain a prescription for medication to allow them to control the time, place, and manner of their own impending death. The attending physician must, among other things, determine that the patient is mentally competent and an Oregon resident, and confirm the patient's diagnosis and prognosis.[25] To qualify as "terminally ill," a person must have "an incurable and irreversible disease that has been medically confirmed and will, within reasonable medical judgment, produce death within six months."[26]

The attending physician must also inform persons requesting such medication of their diagnosis and prognosis, the risks and probable results of taking the medication, and alternatives to taking their own lives, including—although not limited to—hospice care and pain relief.[27] A consulting physician must confirm the attending physician's medical opinion.[28]

Once a request from a qualifying patient has been properly documented and witnessed, and all waiting periods have expired,[29] the attending physician may prescribe, but not administer, medication to enable the patient to end his or her life in a humane and dignified manner. The Dignity Act protects physicians and pharmacists who act in compliance with its comprehensive procedures from civil or criminal sanctions and any professional disciplinary actions based on that conduct.[30]

The Dignity Act requires healthcare providers to file reports with the state documenting their actions.[31] Oregon's experience with aid in dying has therefore been extensively documented and studied. To date, the Oregon Public Health Division and Department of Human Services have issued nine annual reports that present and evaluate the state's experience with the Dignity Act.[32] Related reports and articles have also been published in leading medical journals.[33] These reports constitute the only source of reliable data regarding actual experience with legal, regulated physician-assisted dying in America.

C. The Laboratory Has Served Its Function

In invoking the laboratory of the States, the Court in *Glucksberg* contemplated that one courageous state could address this controversial issue, and other states could watch and learn. This is exactly what has happened in Oregon.

The experience in Oregon has demonstrated that a carefully drafted law does not place patients at risk.[34] In a report examining the Oregon experience to assess whether vulnerable populations were put at risk, the researchers concluded that there was no evidence supporting this concern.[35] The Oregon experience has caused even staunch opponents to admit that continued opposition to such a law can only be based on personal, moral, or religious grounds.[36]

The Oregon reports have shown the dire predictions of those initially opposed to the Dignity Act to have been unfounded. The data demonstrate that the option of physician-assisted dying has not been unwillingly forced upon those who are poor, uneducated, uninsured, or otherwise disadvantaged.[37] In fact, the studies show just the opposite. For example, the eighth annual report found that a higher level of education is strongly associated with the use of physician-assisted dying; those with a baccalaureate degree or higher were 7.9 times more likely than those without a high school diploma to choose physician-assisted dying.[38] The report found that 100% of patients opting for physician-assisted dying under the Dignity Act had either private health insurance, Medicare, or Medicaid, and 92% were enrolled in hospice care.[39] Furthermore, the reports demonstrate that use of physician-assisted dying is limited. During the first nine years in which physician-assisted dying was a legal option, only 292 Oregonians chose it.[40] And although there has been a gradual increase in the rate of those opting for physician-assisted dying, the overall rate remains low: the 38 terminally ill adults who chose this option in 2005 represented only 12 deaths

for every 10,000 Oregonians who died that year.[41] A 2000 survey of Oregon physicians found that they granted 1 in 6 requests for aid in dying, and that only 1 in 10 requests resulted in hastened death.[42] Roughly one-third of those patients who complete the process of seeking medications under the Dignity Act do not go on to consume the medications. These individuals derive comfort from having the option to control the time of death yet ultimately die of their disease without exercising that control.[43]

Outside observers, after carefully studying implementation of the aid-in dying law in Oregon, have concluded that the law poses no risk to patients. For example, a report prepared for the Vermont legislature, after thoroughly reviewing the Oregon experience, concluded that "it is quiet [sic] apparent from credible sources in and out of Oregon that the Death with Dignity Act has not had an adverse impact on end-of-life care and in all probability has enhanced the other options."[44] Leading scholars have come to conclusions such as this: "I worried about people being pressured to do this. . . . But this data confirms . . . that the policy in Oregon is working. There is no evidence of abuse or coercion, or misuse of the policy."[45]

Indeed, rather than posing a risk to patients or the medical profession, the Dignity Act has galvanized significant improvements in the care of the dying in Oregon. Oregon doctors report that since the passage of the Dignity Act, efforts have been made to improve their ability to provide adequate end-of-life care.[46] These efforts include improving their knowledge of the use of pain medications for the terminally ill, improving their ability to recognize depression and other psychiatric disorders, and more frequently referring their patients to hospice programs.[47] One survey of Oregon physicians on their efforts to improve end-of-life care since 1994 found that 30% of respondents increased their number of referrals to hospice care and 76% made efforts to increase their knowledge of pain medication.[48] A survey of hospice nurses and social workers in Oregon reveals that they observed, during a period from 1998 to 2003, an increase in physicians' knowledge of palliative care and willingness both to refer and to care for hospice patients.[49]

In addition to the improvement of end-of-life care, the legal option of aid in dying has psychological benefits for both the terminally ill and the healthy. The availability of the option of aid in dying gives the terminally ill autonomy, control, and choice, which physicians in Oregon have identified as the overwhelming motivational factor behind the decision to request assistance in dying.[50] Healthy Oregonians know that if they ever face a terminal illness, they will have control and choice over their manner of death.

The data demonstrate that, far from posing any hazard to patients or the practice of medicine, making the option of assisted dying available has galvanized improvements in end-of-life care and benefited all terminally ill Oregonians. A central argument against allowing patients access to aid in dying has been that risks would arise if the option were available.[51] Actual experience demonstrates that these risks do not, in fact, exist. And the lack of these risks undermines the argument against aid in dying.[52] This has led some major medical organizations to conclude that passage of Oregon-type aid-in-dying laws is good policy and to adopt policy supporting passage of such laws.[53]

III. Are Other States Ready for an Assisted Dying Law?

The arguments against aid in dying are unpersuasive. Once those arguments are dismissed, the question remains: given the successful experience in Oregon, can and should other states adopt laws permitting aid in dying?

A. Support and Opposition

Since 1991, when Washington voters were the first in the nation to consider the question of legalizing physician-assisted dying, the issue has been in the public eye. In early 1993, Compassion in Dying, now called Compassion & Choices, was formed as a non-profit public interest organization. This group provides direct counseling to patients confronting end-of-life decisionmaking and advocates for improved end-of-life care and expanded choices for terminally ill patients, including aid in dying. This group has been operating since 1993, advancing the public dialogue on this subject, speaking in public forums, and counseling thousands of individuals and their families in states across the nation.

Though Oregon is the only state yet to have legalized the option of physician aid in dying, support for the option is widespread nationwide. A poll released by the Pew Research Center in January 2006 found that 60% of Americans "believe a person has a moral right to end their life if they are suffering great pain and have no hope of improvement," an increase of nearly 20 percentage points since 1975, and 53% "believe a person has a moral right to end their life if suffering from an incurable disease."[54] A Harris poll published in January 2002 found that 65% of respondents supported legalization of the right to physician-assisted dying, and 61% favored implementation of a version of the Dignity Act in their own states.[55] Another group of studies found that between 63% and 90% of people with a terminal illness supported a right to physician-assisted dying and would like to have the option available

to them.[56] In California, surveys in February 2005 and February 2006 found that 70% of California residents supported the idea that "incurably ill patients have the right to ask for and get life-ending medication."[57]

Support is also strong among physicians. A national survey conducted in February 2005 found that 57% of the 1088 physicians polled believed it is ethical for a physician to assist a competent, dying patient to hasten death.[58] A 2001 survey published by the Journal of the American Medical Association found that 51% of responding physicians in Oregon supported the Dignity Act and legalization of physician-assisted dying.[59] A nationwide survey published in 2001 in the Journal of General Internal Medicine found that 45% of responding physicians believed that physician-assisted death should be legal, whereas only 34% expressed views to the contrary.[60] Some medical associations have adopted policies supporting passage of aid-in dying laws,[61] while others, recognizing the division within the medical community on the question, have opted to embrace a position of neutrality on the question of legalizing physician-assisted dying.[62] Women's health advocates also support legalization of aid in dying. For example, the National Women's Law Center and the National Women's Health Network endorsed passage of the aid-in-dying law ("AB 374")[63] proposed in California in 2007. The National Women's Law Center drew a connection to the issue of reproductive rights:

> As an organization that supports reproductive rights, the Center is committed to making sure that the religious beliefs of some individuals or entities do not impose barriers to health care quality or access. We have seen tremendous opposition to certain care at the end of life from the same forces that oppose women's right to reproductive health care. Because these two issues implicate similar interests of privacy, autonomy, bodily integrity, and respect for the patient's conscience and beliefs, we feel compelled to support AB 374. . . . This bill would place California, along with Oregon, at the forefront of efforts to respect individuals' right to consult with their doctors to make the health care decisions they deem best, and perhaps encourage other states to do the same.[64]

One might conclude that, with such strong support for legalizing aid in dying, other states would be passing laws similar to Oregon's. However, certain groups remain staunchly opposed. These include the so-called "right to life" lobby[65] and the Catholic Church.[66] In addition, a vocal segment of the disability rights community has raised arguments in opposition to passage of such laws, contending that legalization of aid in dying for competent, terminally ill patients would somehow put persons with disabilities into jeopardy. These arguments have been addressed and shown to be without foundation by a number of scholars.[67]

. . .

Conclusion

Ten years after *Glucksberg*, it is timely, prudent, and humane for other states to enact laws to empower terminally ill, mentally competent adult citizens to control the timing and manner of their deaths by enabling them to obtain medications from their physician that could be self-administered to bring about a peaceful and humane death, subject to careful procedures.

Even with excellent pain and symptom management, a fraction of dying patients confront a dying process so prolonged and marked by such extreme suffering and deterioration that they determine that hastening impending death is the least-bad alternative. Passage of aid-in-dying laws harms no one and would benefit both the relatively few patients in extremis who would make use of the option and a great many more who would draw comfort from knowing this is available should their dying process become intolerable.

Any state now considering the issue does so with a decade of data from the state of Oregon, which firmly puts to rest the concern that a legal option of aid in dying poses risk to patients or physicians. The question, finally, is simply this: is a state sufficiently compassionate to allow the choice of aid in dying to terminally ill, competent patients who are receiving state-of-the art end-of-life care but are still suffering?

Notes

1. 521 U.S. 702, 735 (1997).
2. Or. Rev. Stat. §§ 127.800-995 (2005).
3. Id. § 127.880. Since it is explicit in the law that the death of a patient under the Dignity Act does not constitute "suicide," there is no basis for a suicide exemption under an insurance policy which excludes payment of benefits in cases of "suicide."
4. E. James Lieberman, Letter to the Editor, Death with Dignity, Psychiatric News, Aug. 4, 2006, at 29.
   . . .
   Id.
5. Rhea K. Farberman, Am. Psychological Ass'n, Terminal Illness and Hastened Death Requests:

The Important Role of the Mental Health Professional, 28 Prof. Psychol.: Res. & Prac. 544, 544 (1997), quoted in Brief of Amicus Curiae Coalition of Mental Health Professionals in Support of Respondents at 17, Gonzales v. Oregon, 546 U.S. 243 (2006) (No. 04-623); see also David M. Smith & David Pollack, A Psychiatric Defense of Aid in Dying, 34 Community Mental Health J. 547 (1998).

6. The American Medical Women's Association's position statement Aid in Dying notes as follows:
   The terms "assisted suicide" and/or "physician assisted suicide" have been used in the past, including in an AMWA position statement, to refer to the choice of a mentally competent, terminally ill patient to self administer medication for the purpose of controlling time and manner of death, in cases where the patient finds the dying process intolerable. The term "suicide" is increasingly recognized as inaccurate and inappropriate in this context and we reject that term. We adopt the less emotionally charged, value-neutral, and accurate terms "Aid in Dying" or "Physician Assisted Dying".
   Position Statement, Am. Med. Women's Ass'n, Aid in Dying (Sept. 9, 2007), http://www.amwadoc.org (follow "Advocacy" hyperlink; then follow "Position Statements" hyperlink); see also Charles F. McKhann, A Time to Die: The Place for Physician Assistance (1999); Joseph B. Straton, Physician Assistance with Dying: Reframing the Debate; Restricting Access, 15 Temp. Pol. & Civ. Rts. L. Rev. 475, 475 (2006) . . .; Principles Regarding Physician-Assisted Suicide, Resolution D01, Am. Med. Student Ass'n House of Delegates (March 15, 2008) (on file with author) [hereinafter AMSA Principles] . . .; Position Statement, Am. Acad. of Hospice & Palliative Med., Physician-Assisted Death (Feb. 14, 2007), available at http://www.aahpm.org/positions/suicide.html. . . .
7. E.g., James E. Dallner & D. Scott Manning, Death with Dignity in Montana, 65 Mont. L. Rev. 309, 314-15 (2004). . . .
   Id.
8. E.g., Kevin B. O'Reilly, Oregon nixes use of term "physician-assisted suicide", Am. Med. News, Nov. 6, 2006, available at http://www.ama-assn.org/amednews/2006/11/06/prsc1106.htm. . .; Policy Statement, Am. Pub. Health Ass'n, Supporting Appropriate Language Used to Discuss End of Life Choices: Policy No. LB-06-02 (Nov. 8, 2006), available at http://www.compassionandchoices.org/pdfs/APHA_Policy.pdf. . . .

9. 521 U.S. 793 (1997).
10. Id.
11. 521 U.S. 702 (1997).
12. It should be noted that in these cases, it was assumed that these laws could reach the conduct of a physician prescribing medications for this purpose. . . .
13. These cases have been the subject of extensive commentary. A terms and connectors search for the Glucksberg cite in the Westlaw "law reviews and journals" database on March 1, 2008 yielded 1625 cites; a similar search with the Quill cite yielded 467 citations.
14. See Compassion in Dying v. Washington, 79 F.3d 790 (9th Cir. 1996) (en banc), rev'd sub nom. Glucksberg, 521 U.S. 702; Quill v. Vacco, 80 F.3d 716 (2d Cir. 1996), rev'd, 521 U.S. 793.
15. The fact that the door was plainly left ajar by the Glucksberg Court distinguishes the Glucksberg ruling from Bowers v. Hardwick, 478 U.S. 186 (1986), and the two decisions ought not be considered of a kind. But see Brian Hawkins, Note, The Glucksberg Renaissance: Substantive Due Process since Lawrence v. Texas, 105 Mich. L. Rev. 409, 411 (2006) (arguing Gluckberg's restrictive approach to due process is alive and well).
16. Glucksberg, 521 U.S. at 789 (Souter, J., concurring).
17. Id. at 788.
18. Id. at 737 (O'Connor, J., concurring) (second and third omissions in original) (citation and internal quotation marks omitted).
    . . .
19. Glucksberg, 521 U.S. at 736-37 (O'Connor, J., concurring).
20. Id. at 737-38; see also id. at 791 (Breyer, J., concurring) ("[The challenged statutes] do not prohibit doctors from providing patients with drugs sufficient to control pain despite the risk that those drugs themselves will kill."). . . .
21. Many commentators have observed that courts have recognized the constitutional right to adequate pain medication. . . .
22. E.g., Nat'l Ethics Comm., Veterans Health Admin., The Ethics of Palliative Sedation as a Therapy of Last Resort, 23 Am. J. Hospice & Palliative Med. 483, 484 (2007). . . .
23. For an example of such an argument, see Susan M. Wolf, Pragmatism in the Face of Death: The Role of Facts in the Assisted Suicide Debate, 82 Minn. L. Rev. 1063, 1100 (1998).
24. See Kathryn L. Tucker, The Chicken and the Egg: The Pursuit of Choice for a Human[e] Hastened-Death as a Catalyst for Improved End-of-Life Care; Improved End-of-Life Care

25. as a Precondition for Legalization of Assisted Dying, 60 N.Y.U. Ann. Surv. Am. L. 355, 356 (2004).
25. Id. § 127.815.
26. Id. § 127.800(12).
27. Id. § 127.800(7).
28. Id. §§ 127.800(4), .800(8), .820.
29. Id. §§ 127.840-850. The Dignity Act requires a fifteen day waiting period between the patient's initial oral request and the writing of the prescription, and a forty-eight hour waiting period between the patient's written request and the writing of the prescription. Id. § 127.850.
30. Id. § 127.885(1)-(2).
31. Id. § 127.865.
32. Or. Dep't of Human Servs., Death with Dignity Act Annual Reports, http://oregon.gov/dhs/ph/pas/ar-index.shtml (last visited Jan. 19, 2008) [hereinafter Annual Reports].
33. E.g., Margaret P. Battin et al., Legal Physician-Assisted Dying in Oregon and the Netherlands: Evidence Concerning the Impact on Patients in "Vulnerable" Groups, 33 J. Med. Ethics 591 (2007); Andrew I. Batavia, So Far So Good: Observations on the First Year of Oregon's Death With Dignity Act, 6 Psychol. Pub. Pol'y & L. 291 (2000); Arthur E. Chin et al., Legalized Physician-Assisted Suicide in Oregon-The First Year's Experience, 340 New Eng. J. Med. 577 (1999); David Orentlicher, The Implementation of Oregon's Death With Dignity Act: Reassuring, But More Data Are Needed, 6 Psychol. Pub. Pol'y & L. 489 (2000) (stating that implementation of Oregon law has so far been limited to terminally ill patients with a clear, persistent, and voluntary request for hastened death); Amy D. Sullivan et al., Legalized Physician-Assisted Suicide in Oregon-The Second Year, 342 New Eng. J. Med. 598 (2000); see also Straton, supra note 6; Timothy E. Quill & Christine K. Cassel, Professional Organizations' Position Statements on Physician-Assisted Suicide: A Case for Studied Neutrality, 138 Annals Internal Med. 208 (2003).
34. Battin et al., supra note 50. . . .
35. Battin et al., supra note 50, at 591. The American Medical Student Association took note of the Battin study and findings in reaching its own policy to support aid in dying. AMSA Principles, supra note 6. . . .
36. See Daniel E. Lee, Physician-Assisted Suicide: A Conservative Critique of Intervention, Hastings Center Rep., Jan.-Feb. 2003, at 17.
37. E.g., Ctr. for Disease Prevention & Epidemiology, Or. Health Div., Dep't of Human Res.,

Oregon's Death with Dignity Act: The First Year's Experience 7 (1999), available at http://oregon.gov/dhs/ph/pas/docs/year1.pdf. . . .

38. Office of Disease Prevention & Epidemiology, Or. Dep't of Human Servs., Eighth Annual Report on Oregon's Death with Dignity Act 12 (2006), available at http://oregon.gov/dhs/ph/pas/docs/year8.pdf [hereinafter Eighth Annual Report].

39. Id. at 23.

40. Or. Pub. Health Div., Or. Dep't of Hum. Servs., Death with Dignity Annual Reports: Year 9 - 2006 Summary (2007), http://oregon.gov/dhs/ph/pas/docs/year9.pdf [hereinafter Ninth Annual Report]. . . .

41. Eighth Annual Report, supra note 55, at 4-5.

42. Linda Ganzini et al., Physicians' Experiences with the Oregon Death with Dignity Act, 342 New Eng. J. Med. 557, 557 (2000) (finding that the availability of palliative care led some, but not all, patients to change their mind about hastened death).

43. See Annual Reports, supra note 49; Ninth Annual Report, supra note 57 (showing number of prescription recipients each year compared to number of deaths from use of prescriptions).

44. Vt. Legislative Council, Oregon's Death with Dignity Law and Euthanasia in the Netherlands: Factual Disputes § 3E (2004), available at http://www.leg.state.vt.us/reports/05Death/Death_With_Dignity_Report.htm.

45. William McCall, Assisted-suicide cases down in '04, Columbian (Vancouver, Wash.), Mar. 11, 2005, at C2 (quoting Arthur Caplan, director of the Center for Bioethics at the University of Pennsylvania School of Medicine); see also Straton, supra note 6, at 480-82.

46. U.S. Gen. Accounting Office, Report to the Honorable Ron Wyden, U.S. Senate, End-of-Life Care 17 (2007). . . .

. . . .

Id.

47. See Ganzini et al., supra note 51; see also Lee & Tolle, supra note 51, 268-69; Lawrence J. Schneiderman, Physician-Assisted Dying 293 JAMA 501, 501 (2005); Quill & Cassel, supra note 50, at 209. . . .

48. Ganzini et al., supra note 51, at 2363.

49. Elizabeth R. Goy et al., Oregon Hospice Nurses and Social Workers' Assessment of Physician Progress in Palliative Care Over the Past 5 Years, 1 Palliative & Supportive Care 215 (2004).

50. Kathy L. Cerminara & Alina Perez, Therapeutic Death: A Look at Oregon's Law, 6 Psychol. Pub. Pol'y & L. 503, 512-13 (2000) . . .; Linda

Ganzini et al., Oregon Physicians' Perceptions of Patients Who Request Assisted Suicide and Their Families, 6 J. Palliative Med. 381 (2003). . . .

51. See, e.g., Washington v. Glucksberg, 521 U.S. 702, 732 (1997) ("We have recognized . . . the real risk of subtle coercion and undue influence in end-of-life situations.").

52. See Tucker, supra note 27. . . .

53. See, e.g., AMSA Principles, supra note 6. . . .

54. News Release, Pew Research Ctr. for the People & the Press, More Americans Discussing and Planning-End-of-Life Treatment: Strong Public Support for Right to Die, at 8 (Jan. 5, 2006), available at http://people-press.org/reports/pdf/266.pdf.

55. Humphrey Taylor, 2-to-1 Majorities Continue to Support Rights to Both Euthanasia and Doctor-Assisted Suicide, Harris Poll, Jan. 9, 2002, http://www.harrisinteractive.com/harris_poll/index.asp?PID=278.

56. Andrew I. Batavia, The Relevance of Data on Physicians and Disability on the Right to Assisted Suicide: Can Empirical Studies Resolve the Issue?, 6 Psychol. Pub. Pol'y & L. 546, 553 (2000) . . ., and Brett Tindall et al., Letter to the Editor, Attitudes to Euthanasia and Assisted Suicide in a Group of Homosexual Men with Advanced HIV Disease, 6 J. Acquired Immune Deficiency Syndrome 1069, 1069 (1993)).

57. Mark DiCamillo & Mervin Field, Continued Support for Doctor-Assisted Suicide. Most Would Want Their Physician to Assist Them If They Were Incurably Ill and Wanted To Die, Field Poll (Field Research Corp., S.F., Cal.), Mar. 15, 2006, at 1, 2, available at http://www.field.com/fieldpollonline/subscribers/RLS2188.pdf.

58. Jewish Theological Seminary, Physician-Assisted Suicide Survey, http://www.jtsa.edu/x5533.xml (last visited Jan. 19, 2008).

59. Ganzini et al., supra note 51, at 2365 tbl.2.

60. Simon N. Whitney et al., Views of United States Physicians and Members of the American Medical Association House of Delegates on Physician-Assisted Suicide, 16 J. Gen. Internal Med. 290, 292-93 (2001). . . .

61. See supra note 70.

62. See, e.g., Position Statement, Am. Acad. of Hospice & Palliative Med., supra note 6.

63. California Compassionate Choices Act, Assemb. 374, 2007-08 Leg., Reg. Sess. (Cal. 2007).

64. Memorandum from Judy Waxman, Vice President of Health, Nat'l Women's Law Ctr., to Members of the Cal. State Assembly (May 15, 2007) (footnotes omitted) (on file with

author). A footnote in the memorandum's text refers readers wishing to obtain more information on the Center's Religious Restrictions Project to http://www.nwlc.org/details.cfm?id=252&section=health.

65. That this advocacy community has turned its attention to end-of-life issues was made abundantly clear in the sensationalized case involving Terri Schiavo, where so-called right to life groups sought to prevent the patient's wishes from being implemented and to force continued tube feeding on a woman who had permanently lost all cognitive function and was in a permanent vegetative state. . . .

66. In California, Catholic bishops and their political arm have been at the forefront of opposition to AB 374. Cardinal Roger Mahony led the attack, charging those who support the bill with participating in a "culture of death." See

Jim Sanders, Cardinal scolds Núñez on death aid, Sacramento Bee, Apr. 3, 2007, at A1.

67. See, e.g., Battin et al., supra note 50, at 594-95; Alicia Ouellette, Disability and the End of Life, 85 Or. L. Rev. 123 (2006); see also Lois Shepherd, Terri Schiavo: Unsettling The Settled, 37 Loy. U. Chi. L.J. 297, 320-26 (2006); Kathryn L. Tucker et al., The Sky is Not Falling: Disability and Aid-in-Dying, in End of Life Issues and Persons with Disabilities (Timothy H. Lillie & James L. Werth eds., 2007).

KATHRYN L. TUCKER, is the executive director of End of Life Liberty Project and past executive director of the Disability Rights Legal Center. Her work to protect and expand the rights of the terminally ill has put her at the forefront of nearly every advocacy effort in this arena in the United States since 1990.

George J. Annas et al.

Brief of Amicus Curiae Bioethics Professors in Vacco v. Quill

Questions Presented

Is there a difference between the constitutional right of a competent adult to refuse medical treatment, including life-sustaining medical treatment, and the right of a competent, terminally ill adult to have a physician prescribe lethal medication for the purpose of committing suicide?

Does the constitutional right of a pregnant woman to terminate a pregnancy by a physician-performed or prescribed medical procedure support a constitutional right of a competent, terminally ill adult to have a physician prescribe lethal medication for the purpose of committing suicide?

. . .

Interest of Amicus

Amicus is an ad hoc group of 50 professors who teach medical ethics to medical students and/or physicians in universities, medical schools, and clinical settings. The Amicus professors include philosophers, theologians, attorneys, and physicians of different religious backgrounds who have a major professional interest in medical ethics. The Amicus group strongly believes that permitting competent adults to refuse any medical treatment is a fundamental right consistent with medical ethics, is independent of any purported right to physician assisted suicide, and should continue to be protected by the Court. The Amicus group also strongly believes that a woman's constitutional right to decisionmaking regarding abortion in the privacy of the physician-patient relationship should continue to be protected independent of any purported right to physician assisted suicide.

. . .

Argument

I. The Right of a Competent Individual to Refuse Medical Treatment is Universally Recognized, is Deeply Rooted in the History and Traditions of the United States and has Never Before Been Equated with Suicide by an Appeals Court or a Legislature.

A. The Right of a Competent Individual to Refuse Medical Treatment is Universally Recognized and Deeply Rooted in the History and Traditions of the United States.

The major premise upon which both the Ninth Circuit Court of Appeals in *Compassion in Dying v. Washington*, 79 F.3d 790 (9th Cir. 1996), and the Second Circuit Court of Appeals in *Quill v. Vacco*, 80 F.3d 716 (2d Cir. 1996), rely to find that there is a constitutional right to physician assisted suicide is that there is no rational distinction between physician assisted suicide and the right of an individual to refuse life-saving medical treatment. This premise is not only incorrect, but threatens the well established right to refuse treatment.

The Ninth Circuit Court of Appeals mistakenly believes that the right of individuals to refuse treatment is a modern invention that was only recently bestowed upon individuals by the courts. It states, "The first major breakthrough occurred when the terminally ill were permitted to reject medical treatment." 79 F.3d at 821, citing *Satz v. Perlmutter*, 362 So. 2d 160 (Fla. Dist. Ct. App. 1978), *aff'd*, 379 So. 2d 359 (Fla. 1980). The Ninth Circuit Court of Appeals refers to the recognition of the rights of individuals both to refuse and to terminate medical treatment, as "drastic changes regarding acceptable medical

Supreme Court of the United States, January 1997.

practice . . ." 79 F.3d at 822. To reach this conclusion, the court must have believed that until the 1970's the law permitted patients to be forcibly treated. This demonstrates a profound misunderstanding of the source and application of the right to refuse treatment. It was not until 1912 "when for the first time in human history . . . a random patient with a random disease consulting a doctor chosen at random stood a better than 50-50 chance of benefiting from the encounter." Richard Harris, A Sacred Trust 5 (1966). Since medicine had little effective treatment to offer prior to this century, there was no reason to ever attempt to force treatment on patients. When the consent issue did come before courts, their decisions were clear. In 1905, for example, an Illinois court held:

> Under a free government at least, the free citizen's first and greatest right which underlies all others—the right to the inviolability of his person, in other words, his right to himself—is the subject of universal acquiescence, and this right necessarily forbids a physician . . . to violate, without permission, the bodily integrity of the patient by a major or capital operation.

Pratt v. Davis, 118 Ill. App. 161 (1905), *aff'd* 224 Ill. 300, 79 N.E. 562 (1906).

Similarly, in a 1914 New York case, Justice Brandeis wrote, "every human being of adult years and sound mind has a right to determine what shall be done with his own body . . ." *Schloendorff v. Society of New York Hospital*, 211 N.Y. 125, 129, 105 N.E. 92, 93 (1914).

The principles of bodily integrity and self-determination are so basic that they seem to need no justification. Nothing empowers the state to require a free living, competent adult to always comply with medical advice. Such a rule would convert medical advice into medical tyranny. One searches in vain to find a case in which free living competent adults are restrained against their will and forced to submit to treatment by physicians. The law is entirely in the other direction - competent adults are under no legal obligation to submit to offered treatment.

. . .

The case law throughout the United States is consistent and unequivocal: competent adults have the right to refuse any medical treatment, and the exercise of this right is not contingent on suffering from a terminal illness. In *In re Quackenbush*, 156 N.J. Super. 282, 383 A.2d 785 (1978), for example, a 72-year-old man refused to have his gangrenous legs amputated. He was not terminally ill or comatose. He could live indefinitely if he submitted to the recommended treatment but would soon die if he refused the treatment. The court found that this competent man could refuse such life saving treatment. Similarly, in *Lane v. Candura*, 6 Mass. App. Ct. 373, 376 N.E.2d 1232 (1978), the Massachusetts appeals court found that a competent 77-year-old woman could refuse a life-saving amputation of her foot. She was not terminally ill and could live indefinitely if the procedure were performed. As the court concluded, "we are all of the opinion that the operation may not be forced upon her against her will." 6 Mass. App. Ct. at 384, 376 N.E.2d at 1236.

Failure to honor this right leads to horrific consequences. William Bartling, a 70-year-old man who was suffering from five potentially fatal illnesses, was so insistent on refusing treatment that he had removed the ventilator himself on several occasions. In response, the physicians ordered his hands tied to his bed. The trial judge ruled that his ventilator could not be removed because Mr. Bartling was not terminally ill, comatose, or brain dead. Since none of these conditions are pre-requisites for treatment refusal, the California Court of Appeals reversed. It ruled that a competent adult could refuse any treatment, including life-sustaining treatment, and that the act of removing a ventilator at the patient's demand was no different legally from not attaching a ventilator in the first place. *Bartling v. Superior Court*, 163 Cal. App. 3d 186, 209 Cal. Rptr. 220 (2d Dist. 1984). No competent person should ever be forcibly treated in this country, and appellate courts have consistently confirmed this principle.

The principle of consent with its complementary right to refuse and withdraw consent is fundamental. How could it be otherwise? What power could be called upon that would permit the state to forcibly amputate the limbs of competent people? . . . In an era in which most people die in hospitals or nursing homes, this opens the possibility of all patients being forcibly subjected to an unlimited onslaught of medical interventions at the end of life. Nothing in American law permits this absent patient consent.

This Court has recognized the individual's strong interest in avoiding unwanted treatment. The Court noted, "*The forcible injection of medication* into a nonconsenting person's body represents a substantial interference with that person's liberty." *Washington v. Harper*, 494 U.S. 210 (1990) (emphasis added). In *Cruzan* the Court stated "The principle that a competent person has a constitutionally protected liberty interest in refusing *unwanted medical treatment* may be inferred from our prior decisions." *Cruzan v. Director, Missouri Dept. of Health*, 497 U.S. 261 (1990), 497 U.S. at 278 (emphasis added). Justice O'Connor, in her concurring opinion, said, "Requiring a competent adult to endure *such procedures against her will* burdens the patient's liberty, dignity and freedom to determine the course of her own treatment." 497 U.S. at 289 (emphasis added).

. . .

The right defined and protected in all the right to refuse treatment cases is the right to be free from unwanted bodily intrusions. It is not the "right to die" or to determine "the time and manner of one's own death" or to "hasten" one's death.

B. The Right to Refuse Treatment has Never been Equated with Suicide by an Appeals Court or State Legislature and is Unrelated to any Purported Right to Physician Assisted Suicide.

Both the Ninth and Second Circuit Courts of Appeals base their opinions on the finding that there is no difference between the act of refusing life-sustaining treatment and suicide. In this they are both wrong. Nonetheless, even though courts have repeatedly found that refusing treatment is not suicide, there is some language in two judicial opinions that show a confusion between refusing treatment and suicide. In *Georgetown College*, the judge states, with no analysis,

> where attempted suicide is illegal by the common law or statute, a person may not be allowed to refuse necessary medical assistance when death is likely to ensue without it. Only quibbles about the distinction between misfeasance and nonfeasance, or the specific intent necessary to be guilty of attempted suicide, could be raised against this latter conclusion.

331 F.2d at 1008-9.

This statement is startlingly incorrect. First, at the time it was made, neither the common law nor statutes made it a crime to attempt to commit suicide. Second, the distinction between misfeasance and nonfeasance is far from a quibble. Third, the issue of specific intent is a critical element to be guilty of a crime. Fourth, the judge recognized that the patient did not want to die, but rather death would be "an unwanted side effect of a religious scruple." 331 F.2d at 1009. Finally, the judge found that the patient was incompetent. Because she was not capable of making any decision, she could not attempt to commit suicide. Thus, the discussion of attempted suicide is both misinformed and irrelevant given the facts of the case.

The second case that confuses treatment refusal and suicide is strikingly similar in its lack of analysis. In *JFK Memorial Hospital v. Heston*, 58 N.J. 576, 279 A.2d 670 (1971), the New Jersey Supreme Court ordered a blood transfusion for a 22-year-old Jehovah's Witness who was injured in an accident. In its decision the court said, "It seems correct to say there is no constitutional right to choose to die. Attempted suicide was a crime at common law and was held to be a crime [in New Jersey]. It is now denounced as a disorderly persons offense." 58 N.J. at 580, 279 A.2d at 672. Once again there was no analysis, merely an assumption that refusing treatment was the same as attempting suicide. Again the person in question was unconscious and therefore could not attempt suicide.

The courts that have actually analyzed this issue have readily distinguished refusing treatment from suicide. The same court that decided *Heston* later decided *In re Quinlan*, 70 N.J. 10, 355 A.2d 647 (1976). In that case, referring to *Heston*, the New Jersey Supreme Court wrote, "we would see, however, a real distinction between the self-infliction of deadly harm and a self determination against artificial life support or radical surgery . . ." 70 N.J. at 43, 355 A.2d at 665.

In a later case the New Jersey Supreme Court addressed the issue more directly, saying:

> declining life-sustaining medical treatment may not properly be viewed as an attempt to commit suicide. Refusing medical intervention merely allows the disease to take its natural course; if death were eventually to occur, it would be the result, primarily, of the underlying disease, and not the result of a self-inflicted injury. . . . The difference is between self-infliction or self-destruction and self-determination. To the extent that our decision in [*Heston*] implies the contrary, we now overrule it.

In re Conroy, 98 N.J. 321, 350-51, 486 A.2d 1209, 1224 (1985).

All the courts that have enforced the right to refuse treatment have pointed out that the state may have compelling interests that would allow it to abridge the exercise of that right. One of the avowed countervailing state interests is the prevention of suicide. However no court has ever prevented a person from refusing treatment on the grounds that it would constitute suicide. Rather, *all* courts since *Quinlan* that have considered the issue distinguish between refusing treatment and attempting suicide. *See, e.g., Superintendent of Belchertown v. Saikewicz,* 373 Mass. 728, 370 N.E. 2d 417 (1977) ("There is no connection between the conduct here at issue [refusing life-saving treatment] and any state concern to prevent suicide."); *Satz v. Perlmutter*, 362 So. 2d 160 (Fla. Dist. Ct. App. 4th Dist. 1978) (removing respirator from competent person would not be suicide but rather death from natural causes); *Bartling v. Superior Court*, 163 Cal. App.3d 186, 209 Cal. Rptr. 220 (2d Dist. 1984); *Matter of Colyer*, 99 Wash. 2d 114, 660 P.2d 738 (1983); *Fosmire v. Nicoleau*, 75 N.Y. 2d 218, 551 N.E. 2d 77, 551 N.Y.S. 2d 876 (1990) ("merely declining medical care, even essential treatment, is not considered a suicidal act").

This makes sense when one considers the legal elements of suicide. To commit suicide one must (1) have the specific intent to die, and (2) intentionally set the death producing agent into motion. *Saikewicz*, 370 N.E.2d at 426, n.11. In all the refusing treatment cases the person refusing the treatment did not put the death producing agent into effect; death would be caused by the underlying medical condition which the person did not cause. *None* of the courts that have decided the right to refuse treatment cases have questioned the state's interest in the prevention of suicide. Rather, they all distinguish suicide from treatment refusal. The fact that a treatment refusal leads to death does not mean the patient's refusal of treatment is suicide.

The Second Circuit Court of Appeals holding is based entirely on equal protection analysis, and thus its conclusion is controlled by its finding that there is not even the most minimally rational distinction between refusing treatment and suicide. The Second Circuit Court of Appeals opinion states,

> [I]t seems clear that New York does not treat similarly circumstanced persons alike: those in the final stages of terminal illness who are on life-support systems are allowed to hasten their deaths by directing the removal of such systems; but those who are similarly situated, *except for the previous attachment of life-sustaining equipment,* are not allowed to hasten death by self administering prescribed drugs.

80 F.3d at 728-9 (emphasis added).

This statement itself demonstrates that these classes of individuals are not similarly situated. One group is on life support, the other group is not. The fact that one group is on life support demonstrates that members of this group are being subjected to an ongoing bodily intrusion. This intrusion could only have taken place with their consent and, just as they could have refused the intrusion, they can withdraw their consent at any time. The circumstance that empowers the person on life-sustaining equipment to refuse further treatment is not the terminal illness, but the now undesired bodily intrusion. One need not be terminally ill to withdraw consent from an intrusion - one need only be intruded upon. Thus the "terminally ill" person

who is not on life support is differently situated because he or she is not being subjected to an ongoing physical intrusion. Both have the same right to refuse treatment, although, as a practical matter, this right can only be exercised by one who is being treated or for whom treatment is recommended. In terms of the purported right to physician assisted suicide, the person on life support is treated identically to the person not on life support by the law: neither may have their suicide assisted by the provision of a prescription drug by their physicians (assuming that such an act by the physician is illegal at all).

Both the Second and the Ninth Circuit Courts of Appeals rely heavily on the termination of artificial nutrition and hydration cases to support the proposition that there is no difference between a physician who complies with a patient's right to refuse treatment and a physician who assists suicide. 79 F.3d at 822-823, 80 F.3d at 729. They argue that a person like Nancy Cruzan does not die of her underlying condition but rather of an independent cause, starvation. This is simply incorrect. When a person requires the administration of artificial forms of nutrition and hydration for his continued existence, this is because, by definition, he suffers from a condition that prevents him from eating and drinking in a normal fashion. In the absence of medical treatment that provides artificial nutrition and hydration, the person would die from the lack of nutrition or hydration which is itself caused by the disease or condition. Thus, terminating artificial nutrition or hydration is no different from terminating any other medical treatment including artificial respiration, kidney dialysis or chemotherapy. Termination of treatment returns the person to the status quo prior to the bodily intrusion. Subsequently, in the absence of these intrusions, the disease takes its course.

This is in stark contrast to assisted suicide. In such a case the person dies from a cause entirely external to the disease or condition from which the person suffers. If a person has cancer or AIDS, the person will not die from a barbiturate overdose, potassium chloride poisoning, or carbon monoxide poisoning unless these foreign substances are introduced into the person's body. If the substances are introduced, then death would be caused by poisoning, and not by the disease process taking its course.

The failure to distinguish real causes of death from the medical tools and techniques that may temporarily substitute for particular bodily functions is fatal to the logic of both of these opinions. If one were to accept that Nancy Cruzan "died of starvation" and not from the vegetative condition that made it impossible for her to eat or drink, one would also have to accept the conclusion that when physicians stop attempted cardiopulmonary resuscitation on a patient in cardiac arrest, what kills the patient is not the cardiac arrest but rather the physician who intentionally stops compressing the heart. Since the failure to perform cardiopulmonary resuscitation always "hastens death," under each court's logic, patients who refuse cardiopulmonary resuscitation would always be committing suicide.

Similarly, the Ninth Circuit Court of Appeals wrongly assumes that physicians who administer drugs for pain relief that could also shorten life *intend* the death of the patients. 79 F.3d at 827. This indicates that the Ninth Circuit Court of Appeals misunderstands the principle of the double effect, in which an action may have two known consequences, only one of which is intended. Thus, the conclusion that pain relief and death are equally intended by a physician who administers a pain-relieving drug that may also shorten life is false. Physicians titrate pain relieving drugs in an attempt to provide maximum effective pain relief without causing death. The principle of the double effect means that treating the patient's pain is acceptable even if the treatment may hasten death. Providing medication to control pain has always been a legitimate and lawful medical act, even if death or suicide is risked. Most invasive medical interventions carry the risk of death or disability. But if a patient dies during surgery, the surgeon is not guilty of homicide. This is because there is a real difference between an intended result and an unintended but accepted consequence of medical care where the goal is to benefit the patient. The difference between intended and unintended but foreseen consequences of medical treatment was also addressed by the first presidential bioethics commission. It concluded that the relevant moral issue:

> . . . is not really that death is forbidden as a means to relieve suffering but is sometimes acceptable if it is merely a foreseeable consequence. Rather, the moral issue is whether or not the decisionmakers have considered the full range of foreseeable effects, have knowingly accepted whatever risk of death is entailed, and have found the risk to be justified in light of the paucity and undesirability of other options.
>
> PRESIDENT'S COMMISSION FOR THE STUDY OF ETHICAL PROBLEMS IN MEDICINE AND BIO-MEDICAL AND BEHAVIORAL RESEARCH, DECIDING TO FOREGO LIFE-SUSTAINING TREATMENT 82 (1983).

. . .

The right to refuse treatment is an expression of the patient's autonomy and the right to refuse unwanted bodily invasions. Any competent adult can refuse treatment for any reason. The right of a competent person to refuse treatment has never been conditioned on having a terminal illness or any other medical status. Nor does a patient need the permission or cooperation of a physician to refuse treatment. If a person refuses treatment, the physician may not lawfully treat the person. If the patient withdraws consent to treatment, the physician must cease to treat the person.

In contrast, the purported "right" to physician assisted suicide in the instant cases is defined entirely by a physician's subjective assessment of the patient's circumstances. The person must be found to be "terminally ill" (an undefined and undefinable term), must be in a condition where death will soon occur, and must be suffering in a way a physician finds distressing enough to prescribe the desired drugs. This is unrelated to the right of all individuals to refuse treatment for their own reasons. This Court should affirm the right to refuse treatment and make clear that rejection of the purported right to assisted suicide does not in any way undermine the right to refuse treatment.

II. The Constitutional Right of Pregnant Women to Terminate a Pregnancy is Based on Facts and Constitutional Principles that do not Encompass any Asserted Constitutional Right to Physician Assistance in Suicide.

A. The Constitutional Right of a Pregnant Women to Terminate her Pregnancy is Based on her Interest in her own Life, Health, and Future.

The Ninth Circuit Court of Appeals saw no difference between the woman's interest in continuing or terminating a pregnancy, and a terminally ill person's interest in obtaining assistance in committing suicide, finding both "central to personal dignity and autonomy." 79 F.3d at 813-814. But this parallel could be drawn only by misunderstanding the fundamental basis on which the abortion cases have been decided. Constitutional protection of a women's right does not require also protecting a right to physician assisted suicide.

The Ninth Circuit Court of Appeals reached its conclusion that there is a substantive due process right to determine "the time and manner of death" almost solely on the basis of the following two sentences from the joint opinion in *Planned Parenthood v. Casey*, 505 U.S. 833, 851 (1992).

> "These matters, involving the most intimate and personal choices a person may make in a lifetime,

choices central to personal dignity and autonomy, are central to the liberty protected by the Fourteenth Amendment. At the heart of liberty is the right to define one's own concept of existence, of meaning, of the universe, and of the mystery of human life."

79 F.3d at 813.

Unlike the Ninth Circuit, however, the joint opinion in *Casey* continued its reasoning after the two sentences quoted above, saying, "These considerations begin our analysis . . . but cannot end it. . . ." 505 U.S. at 852. In *Casey*, as in earlier decisions, this Court recognized a constitutional right related to "marriage, procreation, contraception, family relationships, child rearing, and education." 505 U.S. at 851. In *Casey*, the Court reaffirmed "the right of the individual, married or single, to be free from unwarranted governmental intrusion into matters so fundamentally affecting a person as the decision to bear or beget a child." 505 U.S. at 851. This choice is so central to a woman's life, health, future, and place in society that only she should be able to make it. This is because, as the joint opinion in *Casey* explained, "abortion is a unique act . . . [T]he liberty of a woman is at stake in a sense unique to the human condition and so unique to the law. . . . The destiny of the woman must be shaped to a large extent on her own conception of her spiritual imperatives and her place in society." 505 U.S. at 852.

The reasons for protecting a woman's right to choose to continue or terminate a pregnancy simply do not apply beyond pregnant women. A woman's decision whether to have a child determines not only her future relationships with others but her own conception of herself and her role in society. Furthermore, the constitution protects the woman's right in order to ensure that women are treated fairly as free and equal participants in a democracy. ("The ability of women to participate equally in the economic and social life of the Nation has been facilitated by their ability to control their reproductive lives." 505 U.S. at 856). The woman's right is thus "implicit in the concept of ordered liberty." *Palko v. Connecticut*, 302 U.S. 319, 325 (1937).

None of these reasons apply to a person who seeks assistance in committing suicide. A decision to commit suicide does not further the goals of reproductive liberty, equality and full participation in the "economic and social life of the nation," values preserved by the Court in *Casey*. Therefore, the Second Circuit Court of Appeals was correct to reject a substantive due process right to assistance in suicide based on the abortion cases. 80 F.3d at 725.

B. Unlike Other Aspects of Personal Life That Have Been Protected From State Interference by the Constitutional Right of Privacy or Personal Liberty, the Right to Physician Assisted Suicide Is Poorly Defined and Its Exercise Cannot be Limited by Logic or Principle.

The very core of the constitutional privacy and liberty cases is that individuals have "zones of privacy" into which the government may not enter. These involve decisions that are so personal and important to the individual, and which do not affect the general public, that government simply has no role in limiting the decisions an individual might make in these areas. *Griswold v. Connecticut*, 381 U.S. 479 (1965); *Carey v. Population Services*, 431 U.S. 678 (1977); and *Eisenstadt v. Baird*, 405 U.S. 438 (1972). In *Griswold*, by outlawing the use of contraceptives, the state required married people to risk pregnancy or to refrain from marital sexual relations. *Griswold* forbade the state from invading the marital bedroom and controlling the activities that occurred there. In *Eisenstadt* and *Population Services*, the Court extended *Griswold* by properly noting that the decision whether or not to bear or beget a child is a *personal* right that is reserved to every person, and that the state has no role in that highly personal decision. Likewise, in *Roe v. Wade*, 410 U.S. 113 (1973), and its progeny, including *Casey*, the Court has continued to recognize this zone of privacy into which the state could not intrude.

What is notable about this line of cases, and the cases which supplied the conceptual foundation for them, *Loving v. Virginia*, 388 U.S. 1 (1967), *Stanley v. Georgia*, 394 U.S. 567 (1969) and *Pierce v. Society of Sisters*, 268 U.S. 510 (1925), is that they involved discrete decisions, made by members of a readily identifiable category of individuals, who did not have to justify the reasons for their decisions.

. . .

Every pregnant woman may choose whether or not to terminate her pregnancy; *every* person who engages in sexual activity may choose whether or not to use contraceptives; *every* parent may choose what type of school their child attends; *every* person may decide whom to marry regardless of race.

In its conclusion, the Ninth Circuit Court of Appeals says, "We hold that a liberty interest exists in the choice of how and when one dies, and that the provision of the Washington statute banning assisted suicide, as applied to competent, terminally ill adults who wish to hasten their deaths by obtaining medication prescribed by their doctors, violates the Due Process Clause." 79 F. 3d at 838. In stark contrast to contraception, abortion and marriage rights, the scope of the right to assisted suicide as portrayed by the Ninth Circuit Court of Appeals is not ascertainable.

Moreover, unlike the broad classes of people to whom other liberty rights apply, the "right" to suicide assistance described by Ninth Circuit Court of Appeals only applies to "terminally ill" people. Unlike pregnant women, for example, this is not an objectively definable class. Arguably, anyone who is diagnosed with an incurable, lethal disease is terminally ill. Thus, an AIDS patient with a life expectancy of five years, an 18-year-old with cystic fibrosis and a twelve year life expectancy and a cancer patient who is in the final stages of a disease, are all "terminally ill." In some places the Ninth Circuit Court of Appeals describes a terminally ill patient as one who has an "incurable and painful degenerative disease" that leads to "debilitating pain and humiliating death." 79 F.3d at 821. Elsewhere the court describes patients "wracked by pain and deprived of all pleasure." 79 F.3d at 814. Still elsewhere the court argues that a person who is "reduced at the end of his existence to a childlike state of helplessness, diapered, sedated, incontinent," has "a strong liberty interest in choosing a dignified and humane death." 79 F.3d at 814. Obviously these are people who are suffering from different conditions.

The Ninth Circuit Court of Appeals itself acknowledges that the term "terminally ill" does not constitute a "clear line of demarcation." 79 F.3d at 830. But the court draws comfort from the fact that some states in their "natural death laws" have defined terminal illness as meaning death is likely to ensue in six months. It is remarkable that the Ninth Circuit Court of Appeals creates a constitutional right for a class it cannot define in any principled way because some state legislatures have adopted an arbitrary definition (and one that applies to differently-situated people for different reasons). This is a dramatic departure from the thoughtful and precise way this Court has applied the constitutional right of privacy or liberty in other contexts.

The Ninth Circuit Court of Appeals also seems to believe that, unlike the exercise of other rights in this area, it can require people to justify their individual exercise of this right. Thus the court imperiously asserts that a forty-year-old alcoholic has no right to physician assisted suicide but does not explain why his suffering does not entitle him to the rights the court grants other suffering patients. 79 F.3d at 821. Assume that this person has struggled with his alcoholism for 20 years, has lost his job and family as a result of his drinking, and has repeatedly undergone unsuccessful treatment. Why does the court think that *it* or the *state* can determine that this person's very real, ongoing and life long suffering and humiliation do not meet the constitutional requirements for assisted

suicide, but that a cancer patient's suffering at the end of life does? No constitutional principle can distinguish these two cases.

This is not a "slippery slope" argument. The point is that if assisted suicide is a constitutionally protected right to end suffering, then neither the courts nor the states should be able to say how much suffering is enough. That is necessarily a personal judgment to be made by the individual. The very failure of the Ninth Circuit Court of Appeals to recognize this point demonstrates that the "right" to assisted suicide is not like the right to choose to terminate pregnancy or the right to use contraception, and thus is not related to the privacy and liberty rights this Court has previously recognized.

. . .

Conclusion

Amicus therefore respectfully requests this Court to:

1) Reverse the judgment of the Ninth Circuit Court of Appeals.
2) Reverse the judgment of the Second Circuit Court of Appeals.
3) Explicitly recognize that rejection of a constitutional right to physician assistance in committing suicide in no way affects the common law and constitutional right to refuse medical treatment.
4) Explicitly recognize that rejection of a right to physician assistance in committing suicide in no way affects a woman's constitutional right to determine whether or not to terminate her pregnancy.

Respectfully submitted,

George J. Annas*

Leonard H. Glantz

Wendy K. Mariner

Health Law Department

Boston University School of Public Health

80 E. Concord Street

Boston, Massachusetts 02118

(617) 638-4626

Attorneys for Amicus Curiae

12 November 1996

———

*Counsel of Record

. . .

APPENDIX

BIOETHICS PROFESSORS

George J. Annas, J.D., M.P.H.
Boston University Schools of Medicine and Public Health, Boston, MA

Paul W. Armstrong, J.D., LL.M.
University of Medicine and Dentistry of New Jersey, NJ

Bob Arnold, M.D.
University of Pittsburgh, Center for Medical Ethics, Pittsburgh, PA

Adrienne Asch, Ph.D.
Wellesley College, Wellesley, MA

Jeffrey R. Botkin, M.D., M.P.H.
Children's Hospital, Salt Lake City, UT

Jane Boyajian, B.A., D.Min
Director Emeritus, Northwest Institute of Ethics and the Life Sciences Seattle, WA

Arthur Caplan, Ph.D.
Director, Bioethics Center, University of Pennsylvania, Philadelphia, PA

Alexander M. Capron, J.D.

Director, Pacific Center for Health Policy and Ethics
University of Southern California, Los Angeles, CA

Larry R. Churchill, Ph.D.
 University of North Carolina School of Medicine, Chapel Hill, NC

Arthur R. Derse, M.D., J.D.
Medical College of Wisconsin, Milwaukee, WI

Sherman Elias, M.D.
Baylor School of Medicine, Houston, TX

Alan R. Fleischman, M.D.
Albert Einstein College of Medicine, New York, NY

Lachlan Forrow, M.D.
Harvard Medical School, Cambridge, MA

Leonard Glantz, J.D.
Boston University Schools of Medicine and Public Health, Boston, MA

Shimon Glick, M.D.
Ben Gurion University Medical School, Be'er Sheva, Israel

Kenneth W. Goodman, Ph.D.
University of Miami, Miami, FL

Jane L. Greenlaw, J.D.
University of Rochester School of Medicine, Rochester, NY

Michael A. Grodin, M.D.
Director, Law, Medicine and Ethics Program Boston University Schools of Medicine and Public Health, Boston, MA

John Collins Harvey, M.D., Ph.D.
Georgetown University Medical Center, Washington, DC

Edmund G. Howe, M.D., J.D.
Uniformed Services University of the Health Sciences, Bethesda, MD

Bruce Jennings, M.A.
Hastings Center, Briarcliff Manor, NY

Al Jonsen, Ph.D.
University of Washington School of Medicine, Seattle, WA

Jay Katz, M.D.
Yale University School of Law, New Haven, CT

George Khushf, Ph.D.
University of South Carolina, Columbia, SC

Nancy M. P. King, J.D.
University of North Carolina School of Medicine, Chapel Hill, NC

Patricia A. King, J.D.
Georgetown University Law Center, Washington, DC

Gregory L. Larkin, M.D., MSPH
University of Pittsburgh School of Medicine, Pittsburgh, PA

Bernard Lo, M.D.
Director, Program in Medical Ethics University of California San Francisco, San Francisco, CA

Wendy K. Mariner, J.D., M.P.H.
Boston University Schools of Medicine and Public Health, Boston, MA

Thomas W. Mayo, J.D.
Southern Methodist University School of Law, Dallas, TX

Ellen McGee, Ph.D.
Long Island University, Brookville, NY

Glenn McGee, Ph.D.
University of Pennsylvania, Philadelphia, PA

Steve Miles, M.D.
Center for Biomedical Ethics, Minneapolis, MN

Jonathan D. Moreno, Ph.D.
Director, Humanities in Medicine State University of New York Brooklyn, Brooklyn, NY

Robert M. Nelson, M.D., Ph.D.
Medical College of Wisconsin, Milwaukee, WI

Lois LaCivita Nixon, Ph.D.
University of South Florida College of Medicine, Tampa, FL

Robert S. Olick, M.A., J.D.
University of Iowa College of Medicine, Iowa City, IA

Lois Snyder, JD
American College of Physicians, Philadelphia, PA

Rebecca D. Pentz, Ph.D.
University of Texas Medical School, TX

Lynn Peterson, M.D.
Harvard Medical School, Cambridge, MA

Rabbi Joseph Polak
Boston University School of Public Health, Boston, MA

Stephen G. Post, Ph.D.
Case Western Reserve University School of Medicine, Cleveland, Ohio

Warren T. Reich, STD
Georgetown University Medical Center, Washington, DC

David J. Rothman, Ph.D.
Columbia College of Physicians and Surgeons, New York, NY

Mark Sheldon, Ph.D.
Indiana University School of Medicine, Gary, IN

Evelyne Shuster, Ph.D.
University of Pennsylvania, Philadelphia, PA

Daniel P. Sulmasy, OFM, M.D., Ph.D.
Georgetown University Medical Center, Washington, DC

W. D. White, Ph.D.
University of North Carolina School of Medicine, Chapel Hill, NC

Susan M. Wolf, J.D.
University of Minnesota Law School, Minneapolis, MN

Laurie Zoloth-Dorfman, Ph.D.
San Francisco State University, San Francisco, CA

GEORGE J. ANNAS is a William Fairfield Warren Distinguished Professor at Boston University and director of the Center for Health Law, Ethics & Human Rights at Boston University School of Public Health, and a member of the Department of Health Law, Policy and Management at the School of Public Health. He is also a professor at the School of Law and School of Medicine. He is author or editor of 20 books on health law and bioethics.

EXPLORING THE ISSUE

Is Physician-Assisted Suicide Morally Permissible?

Critical Thinking and Reflection

1. Under what circumstances, in your opinion, might death be a "necessary harm" in the context of the Principle of Nonmaleficence? How might it be possible to prevent these circumstances so that physician-assisted suicide is unnecessary?
2. Where in the slippery slope of cases listed in the Issue Introduction would you draw the line between morally acceptable physician-assisted suicide and immoral physician-assisted suicide? What justification can you provide for your answer? Are there any other cases in which you think physician-assisted suicide is moral? Explain your answer.
3. Is there a significant moral difference between a physician accepting a patient's refusal to undergo life-saving treament and a physician assisting a patient to commit suicide? Why or why not?
4. Is there a significant moral difference between a physician assisting a patient to commit suicide and a physician taking direct action to kill a patient? Why or why not?
5. Do you think a physician has an obligation to provide the medical treatment requested by a patient regardless of the physician's own moral view? What impact would your view have on the morality of physician-assisted suicide? What impact would your view have on the morality of other controversial medical treatments?

Is There Common Ground?

The positions taken by the authors of the articles on this issue are fundamentally opposed: Tucker considers physician-assisted death to be a beneficial option that should be made available to all terminally ill, mentally competent patients, while the team of bioethicists led by Annas disagree. Nonetheless, advocates and opponents of physician-assisted suicides do share some important ethical concerns.

In conformity with traditional principles of medical ethics, both advocates and opponents of physician-assisted suicide place a high value on patient autonomy. The primary source of conflict arises from the recognition that patient autonomy is not unlimited. Tucker argues for an interpretation of patient autonomy that is broad enough to include the ability to choose a death assissted by physicians, while Annas and his fellow ethicists argue for a more limited understanding of patient autonomy, one that encompasses the freedom to refuse unwanted medical treatment, but does not extend to requesting life-terminating procedures.

Additional Resources

James H. Ondrey, Physician-Assisted Suicide (Greenhaven Press, 2006).

Charles L. Sprung et al., "Physician-Assisted Suicide and Euthanasia," Journal of Palliative Care 33:4 (October 2018); pp. 197–203.

Ian Dowbiggin, A Merciful End: The Euthanasia Movement in Modern America (Oxford University Press, 2007).

Joris Vandenberghe, "Physician-Assisted Suicide and Psychiatric Illness," The New England Journal of Medicine 378:10 (March 2018); p. 885.

Richard Doerflinger, from "Assisted Suicide: Pro-Choice or Anti-Life?" Hastings Center Report (January/February 1989).

Internet References . . .

A General History of Euthanasia

http://www.life.org.nz/euthanasia/abouteuthanasia/
history-euthanasia1

Euthanasia and Physician Assisted Suicide

http://www.bbc.co.uk/ethics/euthanasia/

Should Euthanasia or Physician-Assisted Suicide Be Legal?

http://euthanasia.procon.org/

Selected, Edited, and with Issue Framing Material by:
Owen M. Smith, *Stephen F. Austin State University*
and
Anne Collins Smith, *Stephen F. Austin State University*

ISSUE

Is It Morally Permissible for Individuals to Break Quarantine?

YES: Alexander Abdo et al., from "Fear, Politics, and Ebola: How Quarantines Hurt the Fight Against Ebola and Violate the Constitution," ACLU Foundation and Yale Global Health Justice Partnership (2015)

NO: Wendy E. Parmet, from "Quarantine Redux: Bioterrorism, AIDS and the Curtailment of Individual Liberty in the Name of Public Health," *Health Matrix: Journal of Law-Medicine* (2003)

Learning Outcomes

After reading this issue, you will be able to:

- Identify and explain the factors that make a quarantine effective as well as the factors that make a quarantine ineffective.
- Explain the difference between egoism and altruism and then contrast the way egoists and altruists make moral judgments.
- Formulate your own position on whether it is moral to break quarantine and identify evidence supporting your position.
- Identify the main objections to your position and formulate responses to these objections.

ISSUE SUMMARY

YES: Alexander Abdo et al. assert that the imposition of quarantine during the Ebola epidemic was unjustified, violated human rights, and even made things worse by fueling public fears.

NO: Wendy E. Parmet acknowledges that there are times when quarantine is necessary, and that in such cases it is important to craft laws that balance the need to guard against deadly contagious diseases and the need to maintain respect for human rights.

Imagine awaiting the latest news reports tracking the progress of a virulent disease across the countryside toward your home, watching panicked refugees fleeing the infected regions and monitoring the rising death count. Consider the steps you might need to take to protect yourself, your family, and your friends from the deadly contagion.

The situation is both emotionally compelling and intellectually challenging. It should come as no surprise,

then, that films and television programs recounting a zombie apocalypse are popular forms of contemporary entertainment. Such works, however, are no recent phenomenon; literary records survive for most the plagues that have periodically swept through Europe, from the plague that devastated Athens during the time of Pericles (5th century B.C.E.), the widespread epidemics that swept the Roman Empire, such as the Antonine Plague (2nd century C.E.) and the Plague of Justinian (6th century C.E.), the repeated waves of the Black Death that afflicted the medieval world (beginning in the 14th century and continuing virtually uninterrupted until the 17th century), and the Spanish Influenza pandemic (1918–1920). A similar litany of epidemics can be recounted for every continent with significant human habitation. Nor are such outbreaks merely historical relics; even with the advent of antibiotics and modern medical technology, outbreaks of hemorrhagic fevers such as Ebola pose serious challenges to our own society, especially since a number of these diseases have few, if any, effective treatments and cannot, as yet, be controlled by vaccinations. The specter of bioterrorism also raises the possibility that weaponized forms of diseases, such as anthrax and smallpox, might be deployed in areas with high population densities.

What would be the proper public health response to the occurrence of such a catastrophic illness? Inevitably, the answer to this question involves the imposition of a quarantine on the affected areas. The term "quarantine" arises from the medieval Italian term quarantina, the period of 40 days during which travelers were isolated and observed for the outbreak of contagious diseases. In the context of epidemics or bioterrorism, this term has a more specific meaning. In such situations, patients who have already begun to show symptoms will have already been isolated in treatment facilities, where protocols are used to prevent the spread of the disease, especially to health-care workers. If a disease has an incubation period during which asymptomatic patients are contagious, individuals who have been exposed to the disease may be isolated from healthy populations until they show symptoms or until the incubation period had passed. This form of involuntary confinement of potential diseases carriers for the purpose of containing the spread of a disease is known as a quarantine. If the exposure to a disease organism is ongoing/continuous, such as in the case of a plague affecting a city or village, an individual may be quarantined indefinitely.

The imposition of a quarantine by public health officials is usually justified in consequentialist terms: the positive consequences of preventing the spread of a serious disease to a large population, and thereby limiting the number of people who suffer or die from the illness, exceeds the negative consequences of restricting the liberty of the people who are subject to a quarantine.

From the perspective of asymptomatic individuals who are placed under quarantine, however, a different moral conflict arises. Submission to the quarantine deprives them of personal liberty and subjects them to all the harms this deprivation entails, such as isolation from family and friends, loss of employment, loss of education, loss of access to goods and services they desire to purchase,

and even social stigma as former associates avoid them even after the quarantine has ended. As great as these harms are, however, they pale in contrast with another factor: a healthy person who has been placed in quarantine with individuals to have been exposed to a serious disease have a dramatically increased risk of contracting the disease and experiencing its attendant harms, up to and including death.

On the other hand, if quarantines are effective in curtailing the spread of a serious illness, an asymptomatic individual must also consider the benefits that accrue to the people who are spared from the disease. These benefits, moreover, are not insignificant: the Plague of Justinian was estimated to have killed about 40 percent of the people in the areas where it occurred; when the Black Death first appeared in Europe, it killed approximately 50 percent of the population; and the indigenous people of Mexico suffered a fatality rate in excess of 80 percent following European colonization. A strong case might be made to asymptomatic individuals that the primary moral consideration should be the good of those who will not contract the disease because its spread was curtailed by quarantine.

So, what moral choice should an asymptomatic individual make when placed under quarantine? This question reflects a conflict between two general approaches to moral judgments: egoism and altruism.

- The term "egoism" arises from the Latin ego, meaning "I." In making a moral judgment, an egoist considers the welfare of the self to be the only relevant moral consideration. As a result, egoists act to benefit themselves, regardless of how their actions affect others.
- The term "altruism" arises from the Latin alter, meaning "another." In making a moral judgment, an altruistic considers the welfare of everyone to be of equal moral relevance. As a result, egoists will balance the effects of an action on other people against the effects of the action on themselves.

The decision made by an asymptomatic individual to submit to quarantine or to break quarantine will depend in large measure on whether the person adopts an egoistic or an altruistic approach to morality. Egoists are far more likely to attempt to break quarantine, since this action restores their liberty and decreases their risk of infection; altruists are far more likely to submit to quarantine, since the welfare of everyone, taken together, outweighs the harms, both actual and potential, they experience themselves.

Of course, the moral choice by an asymptomatic individual subject to quarantine depends a great deal on the success of quarantines in limiting the spread of contagious disease. One of the reasons the Black Death traveled so quickly through medieval Europe was that people refused to stay in quarantined areas; as infected but asymptomatic individuals fled to plague-free areas, they brought the disease with them. Similarly, strict quarantines were credited with limiting the 2003 outbreak of SARS (Severe Acute Respiratory Syndrome) in Chinas, effectively ending the epidemic.

The routine imposition of quarantine on asymptomatic individuals has also had a negative impact on disease prevention and control. In the West African Ebola epidemic (2013–2016), asymptomatic health-care providers returning to the United States from stricken areas were routinely subjected to quarantine. Ebola, however, is only contagious when symptoms are present. This quarantine did nothing to prevent the spread of the disease, but rather imprisoned those who had chosen to treat affected individuals at significant personal risk, discouraging other health-care workers from volunteering for this hazardous duty and depriving victims of critically needed assistance.

When quarantines are imposed for reasons of public health, they must be carefully considered and tailored to the specific diseases they are designed to contain.

In its article opposing the use of quarantine, the ACLU (American Civil Liberties Union) acknowledges the theoretical possibility of designing and implementing an effective quarantine to limit the spread of contagious disease. However, in their view, the actual practice of imposing quarantines is fundamentally flawed, and therefore unjustified. In fact, the ACLU supported a successful lawsuit against the state of New Jersey by a nurse who was quarantined after returning from treating Ebola patients. Parmet, too, acknowledges that past impositions of quarantine have been flawed, and so she argues that the imposition of quarantine in future emergencies must include provisions that protect the liberty of health-care workers and their dependents from unnecessary restrictions. However, unlike the ACLU, she supports the use of quarantine, asserting that curtailing the liberty of asymptomatic individuals can be both appropriate and necessary to limit the harm caused by dangerous epidemics.

YES ⬋

Alexander Abdo et al.

FEAR, POLITICS, AND EBOLA

How Quarantines Hurt the Fight Against Ebola and Violate the Constitution

I. Introduction

The 2014–2015 Ebola epidemic was the largest and most serious such outbreak in history, resulting in more than 28,000 infections and over 11,000 deaths through August 2015.[1] In three West African countries—Guinea, Liberia, and Sierra Leone—thousands died as public health systems floundered.

Weak local health care systems meant that an adequate response to Ebola could not be mounted without help from abroad. Health care workers from around the world traveled to West Africa to administer care and coordinate public health efforts to curb the infection rate. American health care workers played an important role in the response, and U.S.-based relief organizations sent considerable staff and resources to West Africa.

In the face of any international health crisis, the unhindered participation of the global health community is critical to reducing harm and saving lives. The response of health departments within the United States, however, actually hurt the effort to combat Ebola. Public policy in the United States, motivated by misinformation and unwarranted fear, resulted in scientifically unjustified quarantines and other restrictions. These measures primarily affected returning health care workers, who deserved to be celebrated as heroes rather than treated as pariahs. This punitive response discouraged individuals from going to West Africa, diverted the resources of relief organizations, and infringed on the constitutional rights of an unknown number of Americans. Returning health care workers faced logistical nightmares and personal, psychological, and social trauma. "The hardest part of the work I did in Liberia," says Aubrey F., a nurse who volunteered with Partners In Health, "was when I returned and was stuck at home for 21 days."

> *Nearly 40 years of encounters with Ebola have shown that infected patients do not transmit the disease before symptoms appear.*

We do not know precisely how many people in the United States were quarantined. Such data is not publicly available, and despite repeated requests, state and federal officials did not provide us with this information. Remarkably, as far as we could determine, no governmental entity has even collected this data. We do know, however, that no one needed to be quarantined. Quarantine, by definition, is the separation from others of someone who *is not experiencing symptoms or showing signs of infection*. Nearly 40 years of encounters with Ebola—and an overwhelming consensus in the medical and public-health communities—have shown that infected patients do not transmit the disease before symptoms appear, and therefore quarantine was not and is not needed to prevent the spread of Ebola in the United States for anyone who is willing and able to self-monitor for symptoms. In fact, no one quarantined in the United States developed Ebola, and no one transmitted Ebola outside of a hospital setting.

Because the Ebola quarantines of 2014–2015 were not medically necessary, they violated the U.S. Constitution. A quarantine is a form of imprisonment and therefore a very significant incursion on an individual's freedom. Under the Constitution, quarantines are permitted only when the state has a compelling interest in imposing one and when such interventions are the least restrictive measures available to prevent the spread of disease. Because the Ebola quarantines were not medically necessary, they did not satisfy those criteria. Furthermore, quarantined individuals are legally entitled to due process of law, including a timely hearing before a judge or other neutral arbiter. Few of the states that imposed quarantines did this. States are also required to quarantine under humane conditions, and not all states did so.

Ebola is a serious and potentially fatal infectious disease. However, experts say the danger posed by Ebola to the U.S. population was vastly overstated. In previous decades, many Americans traveled abroad to respond to previous outbreaks of Ebola and other highly infectious diseases and returned home without facing quarantine or other restrictions on their movement, and without infecting others in the United States. The Ebola quarantines and other movement restrictions put in place throughout the nation beginning in late 2014 were motivated by fear and by politics, not by medical science.

Media outlets gain readers and viewers when they report on the next "apocalypse," while governors and other politicians may believe that an overly aggressive response to a foreign threat like Ebola makes them look strong. For example, Governor Dannel Malloy of Connecticut, running a tight race for re-election, declared a public health emergency before any case of Ebola transmission had been known to occur inside the United States. With the media and politicians stoking fears, quarantine measures were widely supported by the American public. There was little room in the political sphere or popular media for rational discussion of Ebola.

> *There was little room in the political sphere or popular media for rational discussion of Ebola.*

Aside from a handful of widely publicized cases, the human impacts of the quarantines did not receive wide attention. Although the exact number of people quarantined or otherwise restricted in their movements in the United States is unclear, a review of these incidents from media reports shows that hundreds of health care workers returning from harrowing work in West Africa were essentially confined to their homes and shunned by their communities. Children entering or returning to the United States from affected countries were separated from their parents and prevented from going to school. International medical relief organizations found it more difficult to recruit desperately needed volunteers, and found their management staff spending valuable time dealing with quarantines in the United States rather than helping manage the crisis in West Africa. Stigma against the West African community grew. Tax dollars were spent to administer and enforce quarantine orders rather than to tend to pressing public health concerns.

It is time to reflect on the missteps authorities took in responding to Ebola in the United States, and to correct them where necessary. It is critical that we do so. While a few states moderated their quarantine policies after public hysteria died down, many continue to mandate quarantine in inappropriate circumstances, and those policies will remain in place in any future outbreaks.[2] In our age of global travel and trade, new epidemics of Ebola—and diseases that from a public health standpoint are far more dangerous—will inevitably emerge and cross international borders. We need to learn from the mishandling of the U.S. Ebola epidemic that wasn't, and respond to future health scares with smart policies based on decades of scientific evidence, not reactive policies based on misinformation and political grandstanding. Punitive and scientifically baseless approaches violate the law and make us less safe.

. . .

An Overwhelming Scientific Consensus that Ebola Quarantines don't Make Sense

There is broad consensus in the scientific community that, because the risk of transmission from asymptomatic individuals infected with Ebola is so low, quarantines of asymptomatic individuals with potential Ebola exposure are unnecessary.[3]

Quarantines could be effective tools for preventing the transmission of a disease that fits—at a minimum—two biological conditions: It is often infectious before symptoms appear, and it is deadly or has other serious medical consequences.

While Ebola is highly deadly, it is not transmitted before symptoms arise and therefore does not meet the minimum criteria required to justify quarantine.

Even when a disease may fulfill these criteria, quarantines have been rarely used in recent history because of:

- The severity of these measures.
- The ethical and legal issues involved.
- The feasibility of successful implementation.
- Questions about their effectiveness.
- The adverse complications of their use on public and individual health.
- The availability of other less restrictive treatment or prevention approaches.[4]

In short, quarantine is an intervention of last resort, and requires an extensive analysis of disease-specific criteria as well as the broader considerations outlined above. Most infectious diseases fail this test, and quarantine "should not be considered a primary public health strategy in most imaginable circumstances."[5] In the United States, quarantine and other harsh measures have been deployed in the past in response to outbreaks of plague and smallpox, and "have consistently accelerated rather than slowed the spread of disease, while fomenting public distrust and, in some cases, riots."[6] The most recent use of large-scale quarantine for SARS in parts of Asia and in Canada also sparked controversy about the effectiveness of these measures.[7]

There may be extraordinary and individualized cases where a deadly disease is not infectious in the asymptomatic phase and yet quarantines would make sense, if, for example, the possibly infected individuals refused to or were unable to monitor themselves for the onset of symptoms, and less-restrictive alternatives were for some reason unworkable. Health care workers returning from the fight against Ebola in West Africa do not, however, fit into that narrow category. They have monitored themselves for symptoms, and as with Dr. Craig Spencer from MSF, contacted health authorities and agreed to be isolated when they saw that they had elevated temperatures suggesting onset of disease. They also have a major incentive to self-report at the earliest signs of disease, because early treatment can dramatically improve the chances of survival, as health care workers would well know.

Movement restrictions short of full quarantine may be justified in some circumstances—for example, it might be appropriate to ban someone who had documented exposure to the disease from boarding a cruise ship that lacks the facilities to deal with an Ebola patient, in case that person does become ill. Overall, these kinds of exceptional cases will be rare, and not a basis for large-scale quarantine or movement-restriction of health care workers and others who may have come in contact with someone with the disease.

Many different voices within the scientific community have spoken out against the Ebola quarantines. Dr. Anthony Fauci, the Director of the National Institute of Allergies and Infectious Diseases at the National Institutes of Health (NIH), is a clinician who has treated Ebola patients and been a leader in the country's response to every major infectious threat in the United States for over 30 years. Dr. Fauci has unequivocally stated that quarantines are unjustified and that monitoring of those returning from disease-affected areas is sufficient to stop any Ebola outbreaks on our shores.[8] Furthermore:

- The Infectious Disease Society of America, the Society for Healthcare Epidemiology of America, and the Association for Professionals in Infection Control and Epidemiology all unequivocally opposed the quarantine of returning health care workers in an unprecedented joint statement in October 2014.[9]
- The President of the American Medical Association has criticized the quarantines as well: "It is critical that we respect and support U.S. health professionals who are volunteering to help bring this epidemic under control in West Africa."[10]
- The AMA's Code of Medical Ethics emphasizes that decisions related to quarantine or isolation must be based on scientifically sound information.[11]

Ebola has now reached the United States twice and may very well do so again, but this is not the first deadly infectious disease to arrive here. In fact, several such cases have occurred in the past decade without inciting national panic. In 2008, a woman in Colorado was diagnosed with Marburg virus, a hemorrhagic fever virus related to Ebola, after returning from a trip to Uganda.[12] In March 2014, just as the 2013–2015 Ebola outbreak was beginning to draw international attention, a man was hospitalized in Minnesota with what turned out to be a case of Lassa Hemorrhagic Fever, a disease with many similarities to Ebola. Both patients received proper treatment under safe conditions and survived their infections. Neither case drew much media attention, let alone calls for quarantines and border closures.

Indeed, in 2014 a much less publicized Ebola outbreak occurred in the Democratic Republic of the Congo.[13] Like every previous Ebola outbreak, no travel or other restrictions were placed on health care workers or others traveling from Congo to the United States. Individuals were trusted to self-monitor and take appropriate precautions. And in neither the 2014 Congo outbreak nor any of the prior outbreaks was anyone in the United States infected with Ebola by a health care worker.

Simply put, the evidence does not support quarantines and movement restrictions for asymptomatic people who may have been exposed to the Ebola virus. What it does support is close monitoring of such people, and rigorous training of health care workers who may come into contact with an Ebola patient. But Ebola quarantines provide no public health benefits, hurt people for no reason, and harmed the fight against Ebola in West Africa. After nearly four decades of rational American responses to Ebola epidemics, the quarantines set a dangerous precedent for dealing with future public health crises, which require sound scientific evidence to guide effective policy.

Ebola quarantines waste scarce public-health resources, and impose a multitude of costs.

Ebola quarantines also waste scarce public-health resources, and impose a multitude of costs on public-health authorities and individuals alike. Many of those costs are hidden. For individuals, they can include costs associated with transportation, housing, lost wages and business opportunities, legal and administrative fees, health care delivery, and child or elder care expenses for quarantined individuals unable to perform such duties. They also squander the valuable time of public-health and law-enforcement personnel. In some cases, states station shifts of police officers outside individuals' homes for 24 hours a day during the 21-day quarantine period. In many jurisdictions, public health officials are required to pay home visits to quarantined individuals at least once a day to take their temperature and to monitor for other Ebola symptoms. All of this is expensive. Many of the economic costs of mandatory quarantine are borne by strapped state and local health departments that are already swamped with other responsibilities.[14]

It's important to recognize that quarantines also took a psychological toll on many of those affected. Dr. Dorothy Morgos, a clinical psychologist who provides mental health services to returning MSF field staff, observed that combined with the stresses of Ebola missions, quarantine "increased the risk of chronic stress and compassion fatigue," and that the lack of proper mental health support for those in quarantine hurt "relationships with family and friends, increased the sense of isolation, heightened perception of community rejection and fear, [and] brought unwanted public attention." As a result, she wrote,

> returning field staff were not able to properly process the emotional impact of the Ebola mission upon return, having to deal instead with the new challenges presented by the quarantine procedures. Field staff reported fearing returning home after an intense Ebola mission. They were isolated from the natural emotional support systems and communities, which usually act as a major mitigating/buffer factor following adverse critical exposure. Overall, the "home return process" following an Ebola mission had an unexpected long term negative impact as exhibited in reported symptoms such as delayed chronic emotional reactions, increased burn out symptoms and other related mental health issues.[15]

Bad policies not only hurt hundreds of men, women, and children across the country, but they also cut into scarce resources available for protecting members of the broader public from diseases far more likely to affect them than Ebola virus disease.

. . .

VI. Ebola Quarantines Violated the Constitution

In addition to all the other problems with the quarantines imposed in response to the panic surrounding the 2014 Ebola outbreak, they violated the U.S. Constitution. States derive the legal authority to ensure the public health from their general "police powers."[16] Like all exercises of state authority, these powers are subject to constitutional constraints.[17] Although there is little recent precedent on the constraints applicable to quarantines, courts will likely permit states to impose quarantines and other restrictions on movement, in combatting the spread of a disease, only if:

1. The state has a compelling interest in doing so.
2. The restrictions are the least restrictive measures available to prevent the spread of disease.
3. The state affords affected individuals due process of law, including a timely hearing before a neutral decisionmaker, appointed counsel if the individual cannot afford one, and adequate notice explaining the basis for the restriction and the process for challenging it.
4. The state confines the individuals, if at all, in humane conditions.

The quarantines imposed in 2014 violated these constitutional restrictions. (Remember that, by definition, quarantine is the confinement of individuals *without* any symptoms of disease; nobody disputes that those who are actually sick with Ebola need to be isolated.) Since, as explained above, quarantines of individuals not presenting symptoms of Ebola are scientifically unjustified, the states that imposed such quarantines violated individual rights. They acted not out of public health necessity, but largely in response to political pressure based on unfounded public fear.

States acted largely in response to political pressure based on unfounded public fear.

In the future, there may be outbreaks of disease that raise difficult questions about the balance between individual liberty and collective risk. This Ebola epidemic was not one of them. All of the scientific evidence points in the same direction: Ebola quarantine policies for asymptomatic individuals are not justified because quarantines of such individuals are not scientifically necessary except in extraordinary circumstances.

Particularly where politics and fear overwhelm rational decision making, it is essential that courts serve their traditional role as a check on abuse of power. In the 2014 Ebola outbreak, only one court had the opportunity to evaluate the legality of an Ebola quarantine, and it found that it was clearly beyond the power of the state to impose.[18] The court concluded that "people are acting out of fear and . . . this fear is not entirely rational."[19]

States Violated Individuals' Constitutional Rights by Imposing Quarantines and Movement Restrictions that were Scientifically Unjustified when Less Restrictive Alternatives were Available

The Fourteenth Amendment to the U.S. Constitution provides that no state may "deprive any person of life, liberty, or property without due process of law; nor deny to any person . . . the equal protection of the laws."[20] It is this provision that protects individuals against arbitrary or unreasonable state deprivations of liberty. When a state deprives an individual of certain fundamental rights, the state must satisfy the highest constitutional standard to justify its action. Under this standard, known as strict scrutiny, a state must show that its action is narrowly tailored to serve a compelling governmental interest.

In response to Ebola, states interfered with constitutionally protected liberties by subjecting individuals to quarantines or restrictions upon their movement. Those measures implicated at least three fundamental rights: the right to be free from restraint,[21] the right to travel,[22] and the right to freely associate with other individuals.[23] Moreover, some states indirectly imposed those same restrictions through coercion, by, for example, threatening individuals with quarantine orders if they did not simply consent to limit their movements.

Because state-imposed quarantines and restrictions on movement implicate fundamental rights, states must show that they serve a compelling governmental interest and that they are narrowly tailored to that interest. There is little question that preventing the spread of Ebola is a compelling governmental interest.[24] However, quarantines and other restrictions on the movements of asymptomatic individuals are not narrowly tailored to that interest, because there are a number of alternatives to quarantine that are equally effective at preventing the spread of Ebola, but that do not involve as severe a deprivation of individual liberty.[25] In other words, states may not fight Ebola "by means that broadly stifle fundamental personal liberties when the end can be more narrowly achieved."[26]

Courts do give some deference to public health authorities when the authorities ground their actions in scientific evidence.[27] But such deference is not absolute: courts will strike down a public health policy that implicates fundamental rights where the "real or substantial relation" between the means and the ends is absent.[28] Under that doctrine, courts have struck down scientifically unjustified public health measures, including quarantines. For example, one court invalidated a quarantine of an entire district in San Francisco, finding it "unreasonable, unjust, and oppressive."[29] The court relied on the affidavit of a medical professional who testified that the quarantine was "unscientific."[30] The court recognized that the quarantine was, for that reason, "not a reasonable regulation to accomplish the purposes sought."[31]

The Ebola quarantines and restrictions on movement similarly contravened sound scientific evidence. Many alternatives to quarantine would not have involved as severe a deprivation of liberty, and yet would have been equally effective in combatting the spread of the disease. These alternatives included self-monitoring, active monitoring, direct monitoring, and perhaps certain narrow and specific movement restrictions.[32] Because asymptomatic individuals cannot transmit Ebola, any or all of these less-restrictive alternatives would have prevented the spread of Ebola.

The one court to consider the legality of an Ebola quarantine of an asymptomatic individual did so under a statute requiring the state to show by clear and convincing evidence that the quarantine was "necessary."[33] The court came to the same conclusion as the public health consensus—and it did so at the height of the national panic over Ebola. When Kaci Hickox, an asymptomatic health care worker in Maine, challenged her quarantine order in court, that court held that the state had failed to prove that quarantine was necessary.[34] The court noted that it was "fully aware of the misconceptions, misinformation, bad science and bad information being spread from shore to shore in our country with respect to Ebola."[35] Instead of

Returning health care workers were well acquainted with the precautionary measures necessary to prevent the spread of Ebola.

ordering a quarantine as requested by the state, the court found that Hickox need only comply with direct active monitoring, a less-restrictive measure that would accomplish the state's public health goals.[36]

Some have argued that quarantines are justified by the possibility that returning health care workers will not comply with public health measures even after they begin to manifest symptoms of Ebola.[37] However, states may not quarantine individuals on unsubstantiated speculation that those individuals will be non-compliant. In prior cases involving the isolation of individuals with tuberculosis—which, unlike Ebola, is airborne and thus highly contagious through casual contact—courts required that the state make a particularized showing specific to the individual in question that there was a "substantial likelihood" of non-compliance.[38] The injustice of a generalized presumption of non-compliance is especially apparent in the context of the Ebola quarantines, given that the quarantine orders were directed primarily at returning health care workers who had demonstrated dedication to fighting this disease, had seen its terrible effects first-hand, and were well acquainted, as few others are, with the precautionary measures necessary to prevent its spread. Many of those health care workers had also previously volunteered in West Africa and so had already demonstrated their willingness to comply with public health authorities' orders.

States that quarantined asymptomatic individuals ignored the science of Ebola and imposed measures that deprived individuals of their fundamental liberties. As a result, the Ebola quarantines, like those at issue in the San Francisco case, were "unreasonable, unjust, and oppressive"[39] and, therefore, violated the Constitution.[40]

Some States Failed to Safeguard Individuals' Right to Due Process

When a state deprives an individual of a fundamental liberty interest, it has an affirmative duty under the Due Process Clause of the Fourteenth Amendment to initiate a hearing before a neutral decision-maker at which it justifies the deprivation.[41] That hearing must ordinarily take place before the deprivation occurs,[42] or, at the very least, *promptly* afterward.[43]

Under the Maine public health emergency statute, for example, the state must initiate a hearing within 48 hours after quarantine begins.[44] This statute was at issue in Kaci Hickox's case, during which the state sought an order permitting quarantine to continue and Ms. Hickox obtained her ruling that she need only comply with direct active monitoring.[45] This provision of the Maine statute

was the means by which Maine sought to afford Ms. Hickox her right to due process, and to ensure that the public health restrictions imposed upon her were scientifically justified.

States imposed quarantines without hearings, and placed the burden on individuals to challenge their own quarantines.

No other state that instituted a quarantine appears to have complied with this requirement of due process. The other states imposed quarantines without hearings, and placed the burden on individuals to challenge their own quarantines.[46] Due process generally requires the opposite—that, at a minimum, the state initiate a hearing before a neutral decisionmaker who is independent of the agency that is seeking to impose the quarantine.

The constitutional requirement that a state initiate a quarantine hearing has the salutary effect of increasing transparency. In Maine, there is now a publicly available record of the state's asserted justifications for quarantine. Moreover, even if the record of Ms. Hickox's hearing had been sealed, the very fact that the sealed record existed would still aid the public in determining the number of people who were quarantined by the state, which is currently impossible to determine. In all states other than Maine, by contrast, there is no publicly available record of the number of people quarantined, let alone of the states' alleged justifications for quarantine.

The Due Process Clause also requires that states afford individuals *notice* of the basis for the deprivation of their liberty.[47] This bedrock requirement ensures that individuals can meaningfully challenge the state's actions.[48] But a number of states failed to provide constitutionally adequate notice in their implementation of Ebola quarantines. For example, after returning from West Africa, one asymptomatic individual, Laura Skrip, a doctoral student in epidemiology at Yale, was told over the phone that she was under a quarantine order and could not leave her home. After she reported to public health authorities that she had never received official notice informing her of her due process rights, they finally delivered notice to her home a full five days after the start of her quarantine. As a result, Skrip remained without written notice of the basis for her quarantine (and any potential procedures to challenge it) for one-fourth of her time in quarantine.[49]

Our interviews with other individuals who were quarantined suggest that this example is representative of a larger trend in which states provided individuals with no adequate notice and no opportunity to be heard before a neutral decisionmaker when instituting Ebola quarantines.

Additionally, some states appear to have deliberately circumvented due process requirements by coercing individuals into signing "voluntary" quarantine agreements.

Lastly, states have not provided—but should consider providing—the assistance of counsel for those who are indigent to challenge the validity of a quarantine. Although courts have not ruled on whether the right to counsel is constitutionally required when a person is quarantined for public health reasons, the nature of the liberty interest at stake suggests that providing counsel is required to ensure fairness and due process.[50]

Some States Quarantined Individuals under Inhumane Conditions that Violated Constitutional Standards

When the state civilly confines an individual, it takes on an affirmative duty to provide basic services and care because the restriction on liberty renders the individual incapable of providing for him or herself.[51] How this constitutional obligation applies in the context of home quarantines is, at best, a complicated question. But at a minimum, when the state quarantines individuals in their homes, it must ensure that they have access to the necessities of life, including food, medical care, and conditions of "reasonable safety."[52]

> *When the state quarantines individuals in their homes, it must ensure that they have access to the necessities of life.*

There is reason to believe that a number of states imposed quarantines without ensuring access to basic services and care. For example, the State of Texas quarantined the partner and family members of Ebola patient Thomas Eric Duncan in apparently unsafe conditions.[53] After Duncan was taken to the hospital, the state for several days confined Duncan's partner Louise Troh, her thirteen-year-old son, and two nephews in the Texas apartment that Duncan had inhabited during his illness, including during a period when he had GI symptoms and may have been infectious.[54] Duncan's sweat-stained sheets remained in the apartment because authorities would not allow Troh

to dispose of them.[55] When a biohazard cleaning service arrived to help decontaminate the apartment, authorities turned the service away because it lacked the necessary permit to transport hazardous waste on Texas highways.[56] Because Ebola can be transmitted through contact with surfaces that were exposed to an infected individual's bodily fluids, Troh and her family members were needlessly placed at risk. In subjecting Troh and her family members to that risk, the State of Texas appears to have violated its obligation to ensure "reasonable care and safety."[57]

A related question is whether states must provide job protection when imposing Ebola quarantines or movement restrictions on individuals. Although there is no clear legal precedent requiring states to protect individuals against adverse employment action, the imposition of a quarantine in the name of public health imposes a civic obligation similar to jury duty. To the extent that returning health care workers might face job loss or other adverse consequences from being subject to an Ebola quarantine, states should enact policies to protect against such consequences and to protect public health by lowering incentives not to comply. To accomplish the same end, some states, such as New York, have said that they would compensate workers for lost wages.[58]

VIII. Recommendations

Government authorities at all levels must ensure that the public health polices they implement to address infectious diseases are based on scientific evidence and public health necessity, rather than political expediency. Any other approach is likely to be ineffective in protecting the public and to violate constitutional rights. These recommendations aim to ensure that any restrictions on individuals in the name of combating infectious diseases comport with scientific evidence, comply with constitutional requirements, and protect civil liberties, while also ensuring that government authorities can effectively address public-health concerns.

The domestic response, particularly at the state level, to the Ebola epidemic in West Africa provides a good lesson in how not to manage a public health crisis, real or perceived. We therefore recommend that, at a minimum, the following principles be followed in any future infectious disease outbreaks, actual or threatened:

1. Do not Quarantine or Restrict the Movement of Asymptomatic Individuals Who Present no Real Risk of Transmission

Such quarantines are unnecessary, unwise, and unlawful. Ebola provides a case in point. Public health experts overwhelmingly agree that quarantines of asymptomatic individuals are scientifically unjustified and counter-productive, in that they hinder efforts to control Ebola transmission. Furthermore, given the important liberty interests at stake—including an individual's ability to work, travel, and carry out daily activities—unjustified quarantines and movement restrictions are unconstitutional. The CDC should update its guidelines on Ebola to make clear that quarantines of, or movement restrictions on, asymptomatic individuals are unjustified.

2. Employ the Least Restrictive Alternatives Available to Stem Transmission of Infection

Public health authorities have a wide array of tools available to control disease transmission short of quarantine. In the case of Ebola, these tools include self-monitoring, active monitoring, and direct active monitoring. In any individual person's case, public health authorities should implement interventions that are scientifically justified for the level of risk posed by that individual and least restrictive of their liberty. In the case of asymptomatic, compliant individuals who fall into the CDC's Some Risk category for Ebola, for example, it is sufficient to require active or direct active monitoring for the 21-day period following potential Ebola exposure.

3. Provide Robust Procedural Protections

Given the serious liberty interests at stake whenever a government authority imposes movement restrictions or quarantine, it must provide robust procedural protections to enable individuals to contest those restrictions. Public health authorities must ensure that (1) each individual has timely and adequate notice of the restrictions the state seeks to impose; (2) each individual is given a hearing before a neutral decisionmaker, at which he or she can present evidence against the restrictions, with the assistance of counsel; (3) any such hearing take place before the restrictions are imposed, or, if time does not permit, as soon as possible after the restrictions are imposed; and (4) each individual be informed of, and permitted, a right to appeal the decision to a judicial body if the initial hearing was not before a court.

4. Increase Transparency

Public health authorities must be transparent about the policies and procedures they have for determining when to implement movement restrictions or quarantines in the name of controlling the transmission of disease. Public health authorities should make these policies explicit and public, and should include both the substantive criteria and the procedures they will follow in determining

individual restrictions. It is also essential to ensure that public health officials do in fact apply the written policies, and that each individual subject to a movement restriction or quarantine is given a written decision explaining the reasons for it, with reference to those policies. Finally, there should be a public record of the implementation of quarantine or other interventions used to control the spread of a disease. The fact that there is no public information on the number of people subject to quarantine or other movement restrictions in the United States during the Ebola scare is unacceptable.

5. Ensure Humane Conditions of Confinement

In those cases where a quarantine is scientifically and constitutionally justified, public health authorities must ensure that individuals are provided with adequate conditions of confinement, which include ensuring access to food, medical care, mental health support, and other necessities of life.

6. Protect Privacy

Public health authorities should avoid unnecessarily infringing on the privacy of individuals who have potentially been exposed to transmissible diseases, especially given the potential for stigmatization in communities and workplaces. For example, states should not affirmatively post signs or notices outside the homes of individuals who have been subject to public health-related restrictions. Officials should be trained in appropriate ways to protect privacy.

7. Provide Income and Job Protections

A quarantine is not a punishment, but a burden placed on behalf of society on people who, through no fault of their own, are potential disease victims. States should ensure that their laws prohibit adverse action by employers against employees unable to perform their ordinary job duties due to a quarantine or to restrictions on movement, and should provide reasonable compensation to the individual for lost income or other damages caused by the restriction.

Notes

1 World Health Organization (WHO), *Ebola Situation Reports* (Sept. 2, 2015), http://apps.who.int/ebola/ebola-situation-reports.

2 In August 2015, for example, six Birmingham, Alabama, firefighters were quarantined after coming into contact with a sick man who had

just returned from West Africa, though the authorities did not even know whether that man was positive for Ebola (he was later found not to be). Sneha Shankar, *Ebola Outbreak: Alabama Man Being Tested for Virus, 6 Firefighters, 2 Family Members Quarantined*, International Business Times, Aug. 5, 2015, http://www.ibtimes.com/ebola-outbreak-alabama-man-being-tested-virus-6-firefighters-2-family-members-2039362.

3 Jeffrey M. Drazen, M.D. et al., *Ebola and Quarantine*, 371 New Eng. J. Med. 2029 (Nov. 20, 2014), http://www.nejm.org/doi/pdf/10.1056/NEJMe1413139; Interview with VR, Interview with Daniel Bausch, Interview with LM; WHO, *Ebola Virus Disease Fact Sheet N. 103* (Aug. 2015), http://www.who.int/mediacentre/factsheets/fs103/en/; Osterholm et al., see *supra* note 30.

4 A notable exception was the 2003 SARS epidemic. J. Barbera, et al., *Large-Scale Quarantine Following Biological Terrorism in the United States: Scientific Examination, Logistic and Legal Limits, and Possible Consequences* 2711–2717, *JAMA*, 286(21).

5 *Ibid.*

6 George J. Annas, Wendy K. Mariner and Wendy E. Parmet, *Pandemic Preparedness: The Need for a Public Health—Not a Law Enforcement/National Security—Approach*, ACLU (Jan. 2008), https://www.aclu.org/sites/default/files/field_document/asset_upload_file399_33642.pdf.

7 D. Barbisch, K. L. Koenig, & F. Y. Shih, *Is There a Case for Quarantine?: Perspectives From SARS to Ebola*. Disaster Med. and Pub. Health Preparedness 1–7, Mar. 23, 2015.

8 Benjamin Bell, *Infectious Disease Specialist Dr. Anthony Fauci Rejects Mandatory Quarantine*, ABC News (Oct. 26, 2014), http://abcnews.go.com/Health/infectious-disease-specialist-dr-anthony-fauci-rejects-mandatory/story?id=26465651; NBC News, *Fauci: Returning Ebola Health Workers Shouldn't Face 'Draconian' Rules* (Oct. 26, 2014), http://www.nbcnews.com/storyline/ebola-virus-outbreak/fauci-returning-ebola-healthworkers-shouldnt-face-draconian-rules-n234141.

9 Assoc. for Prof'ls in Infection Control and Epidemiology, Joint Statement: Leading Infectious Disease Medical Societies Oppose Quarantine for Asymptomatic Health Care Personnel Traveling from West Africa (Oct. 31, 2014), http://www.apic.org/For-Media/Announcements/Article?id=4d3c286c-1ef6-4aef-95f6-85f3f020af47.

10 Alice Park, *Ebola Quarantines 'Not Grounded on Science,' Say Leading Health Groups*, Time, Oct. 27, 2014, http://time.com/3542069/ebola-quarantines-not-grounded-on-science-say-leading-health-groups/.

11 *Id.*

12 CDC, *Imported Case of Marburg Hemorrhagic Fever: Colorado, 2008*, http://www.cdc.gov/mmwr/preview/mmwrhtml/mm5849a2.htm (last visited Aug. 4, 2015).

13 CDC, *2014 Ebola Outbreak in Democratic Republic of the Congo*, http://www.cdc.gov/vhf/ebola/outbreaks/drc/2014-august.html (last visited Aug. 4, 2015).

14 Jessica Firger, *Ebola in the U.S.: Who Pays the Bills?*, CBS News (Oct. 31, 2014), http://www.cbsnews.com/news/ebola-in-the-us-whopays-the-bills/.

15 Email from MSF, Sept. 9, 2015.

16 *See, e.g., Jacobson v. Massachusetts*, 197 U.S. 11, 25 (1905) ("According to settled principles, the police power of a state must be held to embrace, at least, such reasonable regulations established directly by legislative enactment as will protect the public health and the public safety.").

17 *See, e.g., Mugler v. Kansas*, 123 U.S. 623, 661 (1887) ("There are, of necessity, limits beyond which legislation cannot rightfully go. . . . If, therefore, a statute purporting to have been enacted to protect the public health, the public morals, or the public safety, has no real or substantial relation to those objects, or is a palpable invasion of rights secured by the fundamental law, it is the duty of the courts to so adjudge, and thereby give effect to the constitution.").

18 *Hickox*, No. 2014–36 at 2 (Me. Dist. Ct. Oct. 31, 2014).

19 *Id.* at 3.

20 U.S. Const. amend. XIV.

21 *See, e.g., Jacobson*, 197 U.S. at 26 (recognizing a liberty interest in being free from restraint while acknowledging limits on that liberty in the name of public health).

22 *See, e.g., Shapiro v. Thompson*, 394 U.S. 618, 629 (1969) ("This Court long ago recognized that the nature of our Federal Union and our constitutional concepts of personal liberty unite to require that all citizens be free to travel throughout the length and breadth of our land uninhibited by statutes, rules, or regulations which unreasonably burden or restrict this movement.").

23 U.S. Const. amend. I; *see also Roberts v. U.S. Jaycees*, 468 U.S. 609, 617–18 (1984) ("Our decisions have referred to constitutionally protected 'freedom of association' in two distinct

senses. In one line of decisions, the Court has concluded that choices to enter into and maintain certain intimate human relationships must be secured against undue intrusion by the State because of the role of such relationships in safeguarding the individual freedom that is central to our constitutional scheme. . . . In another set of decisions, the Court has recognized a right to associate for the purpose of engaging in those activities protected by the First Amendment—speech, assembly, petition for the redress of grievances, and the exercise of religion.").

24 *See, e.g., Jacobson*, 197 U.S. at 25 (noting that the Court "has distinctly recognized the authority of a state to enact quarantine laws and health laws of every description.") (internal quotation marks omitted).

25 *See, e.g. id.* at 28 ("[A]n acknowledged power of a local community to protect itself against an epidemic threatening the safety of all might be exercised in particular circumstances and in reference to particular persons in such an arbitrary, unreasonable manner, or might go so far beyond what was reasonably required for the safety of the public, as to authorize or compel the courts to interfere for the protection of such persons.").

26 *Shelton v. Tucker*, 364 U.S. 479, 488 (1960); *see also Covington v. Harris*, 419 F.2d 617, 623 (D.C. Cir. 1969) ("A statute sanctioning such a drastic curtailment of the rights of citizens must be narrowly, even grudgingly, construed in order to avoid deprivations of liberty without due process of law.") (internal quotation marks omitted).

27 *See, e.g., Jacobson*, 197 U.S. 11, 28 (1905) (noting that "the court would usurp the functions of another branch of government if it adjudged, as matter of law, that the [smallpox vaccination] adopted under the sanction of the state, to protect the people at large was arbitrary, and not justified by the necessities of the case.").

28 *See id.* at 31 ("[I[f a statute purporting to have been enacted to protect the public health, the public morals, or the public safety, has no real or substantial relation to those objects, or is, beyond all question, a plain, palpable invasion of rights secured by the fundamental law, it is the duty of the courts to so adjudge, and thereby give effect to the Constitution.").

29 *Jew Ho v. Williamson*, 103 F. 10, 26 (C.C.N.D. Cal. 1900).

30 *Id.* at 21 ("[D]efendants have proceeded from erroneous theories to still more erroneous and unscientific practices and methods of dealing with the same; for, instead of quarantining the supposedly infected rooms or houses in which said deceased persons lived and died, and the persons who had been brought in contact with and been directly exposed to said disease, said defendants have quarantined, and are now maintaining a quarantine over, a large area of territory, and indiscriminately confining therein between ten and twenty thousand people, thereby exposing, and they are now exposing, to the infection of the said disease said large number of persons.") (Quoting affidavit of Dr. J. I. Stephen).

31 *Id.* at 23 ("The court cannot but see the practical question that is presented to it as to the ineffectiveness of this method of quarantine against such a disease as this. So, upon that ground, the court must hold that this quarantine is not a reasonable regulation to accomplish the purposes sought."). Although there are few recent cases squarely addressing these issues, recent lower-court cases arising in different legal contexts have found that segregation of asymptomatic individuals for tuberculosis does not meet a requirement of employing the least restrictive means. *See, e.g., Jihad v. Wright*, 929 F. Supp. 325, 330–32 (N.D. Ind. 1996) (holding that prison officials should not have removed an inmate at risk of developing active tuberculosis to a medical isolation unit because a less restrictive alternative would have been periodic testing to determine if the inmate became capable of infecting others); *Jolly v. Coughlin*, 76 F.3d 468, 479–80 (2d Cir. 1996) (finding that prisoner's confinement was not least restrictive means of protecting inmates from tuberculosis where prisoner was not contagious and could be monitored for the development of active tuberculosis).

32 *See* CDC, *Interim U.S. Guidance for Monitoring and Movement of Persons with Potential Ebola Virus Exposure* (Dec. 24, 2014), http://www.cdc.gov/vhf/ebola/exposure/monitoring-and-movement-of-persons-with-exposure.html.

33 Several other states' laws require that the government prove the need for a quarantine by "clear and convincing evidence." *See* Alaska, AS 18.15.385 (2014); Illinois, 20 Ill. Comp. Stat. § 2305/2 (2015); Minnesota, Minn. Stat. § 144.4195 (2014).

34 *Hickox*, No. 2014–36 at 2.

35 *Id.* at 3.

36 *Id.* at 2.

37 *See, e.g.,* Robert J. Vickers, *Ebola Aid Workers Can't Be Trusted,* Seattle Times, Oct. 31, 2014, http://blogs.

seattletimes.com/opinionnw/2014/10/31/ebola-aid-workers-cant-be-trusted/.

38 *City of New York v. Antoinette R.*, 630 N.Y.S.2d 1008, 1015 (N.Y. Sup. Ct. 1995) (holding, in the context of a quarantine of a TB patient for allegedly not complying with treatment, "The prerequisite for an order is that there is a substantial likelihood, based on the person's past or present behavior, that the individual cannot be relied upon to participate in or complete an appropriate prescribed course of medication or, if necessary, follow required contagion precautions for tuberculosis.").

39 *Jew Ho*, 103 F. at 26.

40 This result would hold no matter the evidentiary standard that a court applied, because the scientific consensus against blanket quarantines or movement restrictions for asymptomatic individuals is overwhelming. Nevertheless, the Constitution would require states to meet a demanding evidentiary standard—the "clear and convincing evidence" standard, which is the highest in the civil context—to justify such serious deprivations of liberty. Although no court has addressed this question in the context of Ebola restrictions, the Supreme Court has addressed it in the closely analogous context of civil commitment. *See Addington v. Texas*, 441 U.S. 418, 425 (1979) (holding that states must meet the intermediate burden of proof, "clear and convincing evidence," when civilly committing an individual with mental illness). The same standard would apply before states could effectively imprison asymptomatic individuals in their homes.

41 *See, e.g., Mathews v. Eldridge*, 429 U.S. 319, 333 (1976) ("The 'right to be heard before being condemned to suffer grievous loss of any kind, even though it may not involve the stigma and hardships of a criminal conviction, is a principle basic to our society.'" (quoting *Joint Anti-Fascist Comm. v. McGrath*, 341 U.S. 123, 168 (1951) (Frankfurter, J., concurring))).

42 *See, e.g., Goldberg v. Kelly*, 397 U.S. 254, 264 (1970) (holding that the state must provide a pre-termination evidentiary hearing when it terminates a welfare recipient's benefits because termination "may deprive an eligible recipient of the very means by which to live while he waits.").

43 *See, e.g., Mathews*, 429 U.S. at 349 ("All that is necessary is that the procedures be tailored, in light of the decision to be made, to 'the capacities and circumstances of those who are to be heard,' to insure that they are given a meaningful opportunity to present their case." (quoting *Goldberg v. Kelly*, 397 U.S. 254, 268–269 (1970))); *Nat'l Council of Resistance of Iran v. Dep't of State (NCRI)*, 251 F.3d 192, 205 (D.C. Cir. 2001) ("[[B]efore the government can constitutionally deprive a person of the protected liberty or property interest, it must afford him notice and hearing.").

44 Me. Rev. Stat. tit. 22 § 820 (2005) ("A hearing must be held before a judge of the District Court, a justice of the Superior Court or a justice of the Supreme Judicial Court as soon as reasonably possible but not later than 48 hours after the person is subject to prescribed care to determine whether the person must remain subject to prescribed care.").

45 *Hickox*, No. 2014-36 at 3.

46 *See, e.g.*, CT Gen Stat § 19a–131b (2013).

47 *See, e.g., Addington v. Texas*, 441 U.S. 418, 425 (1979), ("[C]ivil commitment for any purpose constitutes a significant deprivation of liberty that requires due process protection."); *O'Connor v. Donaldson*, 422 U.S. 563, 580 (1975) (Burger, concurring) ("There can be no doubt that involuntary commitment to a mental hospital, like involuntary confinement of an individual for any reason, is a deprivation of liberty which the State cannot accomplish without due process of law.").

48 *Vitek v. Jones*, 445 U.S. 480, 495–96 (1980); *see also id.* at 492 ("Were an ordinary citizen to be subjected involuntarily to these consequences, it is undeniable that protected liberty interests would be unconstitutionally infringed absent compliance with the procedures required by the Due Process Clause."); *Addington*, 441 U.S. 418; *O'Connor*, 422 U.S. 563.

49 Notice that is constitutionally adequate is that which "ensure[s] that the opportunity for a hearing is meaningful." *See City of West Covina v. Perkins*, 525 U.S. 234, 240 (1999). Thus, while a state is not required to provide notice of procedures that are publicly delineated in statutes and case law, it must give adequate notice of the availability of administrative procedures that are not publicly known, as well as any factual information necessary to invoke those procedures. *See Perkins*, 525 U.S. at 242–44; *see also Memphis Light, Gas & Water Div. v. Craft*, 436 U.S. 1, 13–14 (1978). The contents of the notice required will thus vary state to state.

50 In determining whether appointed counsel is required in civil proceedings, the Supreme Court has considered "the nature of the private interest that will be affected," "the comparative

risk of an erroneous deprivation of that interest with and without additional or substitute procedural safeguards," and any "asymmetry of representation." *Turner v. Rogers*, 131 S. Ct. 2507, 2510–2518 (2011) (internal quotation marks omitted). In the context of Ebola quarantines, those factors all favor the provision of counsel to individuals who cannot afford counsel on their own. Indeed, many states already recognize a right to state-appointed counsel in the context of civil commitment, and should extend that recognition to the quarantine context. *See e.g.,* Treatise on Health Care Law § 20.04 (containing information on many states' civil commitment counsel requirements. See, for example, its description of South Carolina's law: "Before the hearing, two court-appointed examiners must determine whether involuntary treatment is required and if so, the court must appoint counsel for that respondent and hold a full hearing within 15 days of the respondent's initial admission."); *see also* Christyne E. Ferris, *The Search for Due Process in Civil Commitment Hearings: How Procedural Realities Have Altered Substantive Standards,* 61 Vand. L. Rev. 959, 961–68 (2008) ("[A]lmost all states mandate assistance of counsel as a basic due process requirement of civil commitment hearings. . . . Most states also grant the right to counsel, who will be appointed if the respondent is indigent.").

51 *See, e.g., DeShaney v. Winnebago Cnty. Dep't of Soc. Servs.,* 489 U.S. 189, 199–200 (1989) ("[W]hen the State takes a person into its custody and holds him there against his will, the Constitution imposes upon it a corresponding duty to assume some responsibility for his safety and general well-being."); *Youngberg v. Romeo,* 457 U.S. 307, 317 (1982) ("When a person is institutionalized—and wholly dependent on the State . . . a duty to provide certain services and care does exist.")

52 Youngberg, *supra,* at 324 ("[T]he State concedes a duty to provide adequate food, shelter, clothing, and medical care. These are the essentials of the care that the State must provide. The State also has the unquestioned duty to provide reasonable safety for all residents and personnel within the institution.").

53 Gregg Botelho and Michael Martinez, *Frustrated Women Quarantined With Sheets, Towels Soiled by Ebola Patient,* CNN (Oct. 3, 2014, 4:40 AM), http://www.cnn.com/2014/10/02/us/texas-woman-quarantine-ebola-thomas-duncan/.

54 *Id.*

55 *Id.*

56 *Id.*

57 Youngberg, 457 U.S. at 324.

58 Matt Flegenheimer, Michael D. Shear and Michael Barbaro, Under Pressure, Cuoma Says Ebola Quarantines Can Be Spent at Home, N.Y. Times, Oct. 26, 2014, http://www.nytimes.com/2014/10/27/nyregion/ebola-quarantine.html.

Alex Abdo is a senior staff attorney at the Knight First Amendment Institute and a former senior staff attorney at the ACLU. He has been at the forefront of litigation relating to NSA surveillance, encryption, anonymous speech online, government transparency, and the post-9/11 abuse of detainees in U.S. custody.

Wendy E. Parmet

→ **NO**

Quarantine Redux: Bioterrorism, AIDS and the Curtailment of Individual Liberty in the Name of Public Health

Novel sources of death are especially frightening. In the early 1980s, the emergence of the AIDS epidemic was the source not only of suffering and loss, but also of fear, hysteria, and irrationality. It was in that heated climate that public debate turned to the questions of when and whether government may infringe upon individual liberties in order to protect public health.[1]

Although AIDS is still with us, and indeed it causes more suffering each year,[2] in the United States it is no longer the public health threat that induces the greatest fears. Bioterrorism may now claim that honor. And so *it* now provokes the old debate pitting individual liberties against the state.

. . .

In November 2001, the Center [for Law and the Public's Health at Georgetown and Johns Hopkins Universities] released a draft version of the "Model State Emergency Health Powers Act" ("Model Act") which was revised in December.[3] Many states are now considering legislation based upon the Model Act.[4]

Although the two versions of the Model Act differ significantly in many ways, both would grant governors the ability to declare a public health emergency which would then permit the imposition of isolation, quarantine, mandatory medical examinations, and other coercive measures.[5] In effect, both versions of the Model Act grant states coercive powers in order to meet the threat of bioterrorism. At the same time, the Model Act's authors attempt to mediate the perceived clash between the use of the coercive powers and individual rights. The preamble states that

the Act recognizes that a state's ability to respond to a public health emergency must respect the dignity and rights of persons. . . . The Act thus provides that, in the event of the exercise of emer-

gency powers, the civil rights, liberties, and needs of infected or exposed persons will be protected to the fullest extent possible consistent with the primary goal of controlling serious health threats.[6]

. . .

I. Legal Responses to Bioterrorism

Since ancient times, human beings have been known to use disease to injure their enemies.[7] During the middle ages, soldiers threw the bodies of plague victims over the walls of enemy cities.[8] During the French and Indian Wars, the English gave blankets exposed to smallpox to enemy Indian troops.[9]

. . .

It was in response to the urgency created by September 11 and the anthrax attacks, as well as the perception that inadequate laws undermined the nation's ability to respond to bioterrorism that the CDC commissioned the Center to draft the Model Act. According to Secretary of Health and Human Services Tommy Thompson, "[w]e need[ed] not only a strong health infrastructure and a full stockpile of medical resources, but also the legal and emergency tools to help our citizens quickly."[10] The Model Act's chief drafter, Professor Lawrence O. Gostin concurred saying that the act was needed because "[c]urrent public health laws are too highly antiquated and inadequate to ensure a strong and effective response to bioterrorism [Public health laws] tend to be highly inadequate, confusing and contradictory - even within states there's an inconsistent response.[11]

In response to this perceived need, the Model Act seeks first and foremost to clarify and rationalize public health law. . . . As the Model Act's findings state, "government must do more to protect the health, safety, and general well being of its citizens."[12]

The key provisions in the Act for providing the state with the authority to "do more" are found in Articles III, IV, and V, which enable the Governor to declare a "state of public health emergency"[13] thereby triggering "special powers."[14] Under the Model Act, the Governor may declare a "state of public health emergency" upon the occurrence of an imminent threat of an illness or health condition that:

(1) is believed to be caused by any of the following:
   (i) bioterrorism;
   (ii) the appearance of a novel or previously controlled or eradicated infectious agent or biological toxin;
   (iii) [a natural disaster;]
   (iv) [a chemical attack or accidental release; or]
   (v) [a nuclear attack or accident]; and

(2) poses a high probability of any of the following harms:
   (i) a large number of deaths in the affected population;
   (ii) a large number of serious or long-term disabilities in the affected population; or
   (iii) widespread exposure to an infectious or toxic agent that poses a significant risk of substantial future harm to a large number of people in the affected population.[15]

Importantly, the Governor may declare such a state even "'without consulting with the public health authority or other experts when the situation calls for prompt and timely action."[16] Once declared the state of emergency may continue for thirty days, whereupon the Governor (presumably again without consulting with anyone) may renew the declaration for another thirty days.[17] This process apparently can continue ad infinitum although at any time the legislature may terminate the declaration if it finds that the "illness or health condition that caused the emergency does not or no longer poses a high probability of a large number of deaths in the affected population, a large number of incidents of serious permanent or long-term disability in the affected population, or a significant risk of substantial future harm to a large number of people in the affected population."[18] Hence a state of emergency can continue without any legislative affirmation indefinitely unless a majority of the legislature votes to repeal it.[19]

Once a declaration is made, the Model Act gives the Governor and the public health agency extraordinary powers.[20] Briefly, the declaration gives the Governor authority to "[s]uspend the provisions of any regulatory statute prescribing procedures for conducting State business, or the orders, rules and regulations of any State agency, to the extent that strict compliance with the same would prevent, hinder, or delay necessary action . . . by the public health authority."[21] It would also permit the Governor to mobilize the militia into service.[22] In addition, the public health authority would be authorized to close or decontaminate facilities,[23] to require health care facilities to provide services,[24] and to require other facilities (the nature of which is undefined) to provide a wide variety of services to the state.[25]

The most interesting provisions, however, authorize the state to exert broad coercive powers over individuals, once a declaration of emergency has been made. First, the public health authority may perform physical examinations and/or tests "necessary for the diagnosis or treatment of individuals."[26] Because the Model Act does not specify what types of tests may be performed, or whether the examinations need to have anything to do with the health threat instigating the declaration, a state of emergency would presumably authorize the public health authority to perform almost any diagnostic test on anyone. Thus a public health authority acting in bad faith would have the lawful authority to use a public health threat as an excuse to perform mandatory HIV tests! Under the Act, an individual's refusal to permit this examination might justify isolation if the authority was uncertain if the individual was infected.[27]

Once a public health emergency has been declared, the public health authority would also have the power to vaccinate and treat individuals.[28] Individuals who are "unable or unwilling" to submit to these procedures "for reasons of health, religion, or conscience" may be subject to isolation and quarantine.[29] What happens to people who refuse to submit for other reasons (such as suspicion of public authorities) is not made clear.

The isolation and quarantine provisions are undoubtedly among the most central in the act.[30] Under the Model Act, isolation and/or quarantine is authorized when individuals refuse to submit to an examination, treatment or vaccination as discussed above, as well as when they are "the least restrictive means necessary to prevent the spread of a contagious or possibly contagious disease to others."[31] Again the Model Act does not require that the "contagious disease" which is the object of the isolation or quarantine be the illness that triggered the public health emergency in the first place. Thus the appearance of anthrax, a non-contagious bioterrorist agent, could theoretically trigger isolation for HIV or hepatitis if the public health authority believed that it was the "least restrictive means necessary to spread" the infection.

. . .

Concerned about the human rights and dignity of those subject to these orders, the Model Act requires the state to provide for the "needs" of individuals subject to the order, by providing them with at least "adequate food, clothing, shelter, means of communication . . . medication, and competent medical care."[32] Interestingly, the Act does not explicitly require the state to provide for the economic consequences, such as loss of wages or unemployment, that an individual may face due to an isolation or quarantine order, although this may perhaps be included as part of an individual's "needs." Likewise, the Act does not explicitly obligate the state to care for an affected individual's dependants. Moreover, the stringent immunity provisions of the Model Act would appear to foreclose the possibility of any damage remedy for the state's failure to abide by some of those provisions, as well as any compensation for any economic or other injuries that may result from inappropriate or unnecessary isolation.[33]

. . .

Three axioms that public health law is most fundamentally about the restraint of individual liberties, that it requires modernization, and that modernization can ensure the protection of individual rights while restraining those rights – animate the Model Act. The question remains: how valid are these premises?

III. The Role of Coercive Powers in Public Health Protection

There can be no doubt that the restraint of individuals, especially via quarantine and isolation, has long played an important role in public health law. During the middle ages, lepers were subject to isolation throughout Europe.[34] On these shores, quarantines against smallpox were instituted as far back as 1622.[35]

There can also be little doubt that courts have generally upheld the use of isolation and quarantine for public health goals.[36]

. . .

The ubiquity and legality of quarantine and isolation, however, do not in themselves establish that they have been or ought to be seen as the core to public health law in general or central to our efforts to confront bioterrorism or many emerging threats.[37] With respect to history, the focus on isolation and quarantine of individuals overlooks the fact that historically quarantines were probably more often instituted against cargo vessels than against individuals.[38] Indeed, in U.S. constitutional law, the police power doctrine developed significantly in contests over the government's ability to regulate commerce.[39] In the 19th century it was often business interests, not advocates for

individual rights, who challenged the authority of public health boards.[40]

These points are salient not because they question the ability of government to restrain the liberty of individuals, but because they should remind us that public health, in practice and in law, generally has had as much or more to do with regulatory efforts to shape the market than to restrain individuals. In the 19th century, after all, the great early steps taken by public health focused on the supply of clean water and wholesome foods.[41] In these instances government restrained liberty, but it was not the personal liberty of individuals to control their movement or make decisions about their own health care and bodily integrity; rather it was the liberty of businesses to sell unpasteurized milk or the liberty of taxpayers to avoid supporting a public water supply.

Certainly as the germ theory and contagionism took hold and the massive epidemics of the 19th century faded from memory, public health practitioners were more apt to see an individual who carried an infectious agent rather than filth or miasma as the source of danger. Likewise, as clinical medicine became more efficacious and more dominant, public health increasingly adopted its individualistic orientation and came to believe that identifying patients and getting them to treatment was central to its mission.[42] As a result, public health advocates began to stress the virtue of contact tracing and isolation.[43] But this vision of public health was never uncontested.[44] Even in the heyday of the public health movement, some adherents stressed education over coercion, arguing for the need to obtain a patient's cooperation.[45] Other public health notables argued that public health had to focus less on identifying and treating individuals and more on what we today would call the social conditions for health. In 1904, for example, Herman Biggs claimed that the time had come for public health to emphasize the occupational conditions that give rise to morbidity.[46] Less than two decades later, C.E.A. Winslow, noted that while "[s]anitation, isolation, vaccine and serum therapy, provided the complete machinery necessary for controlling many of the acute communicable diseases; . . . it became clear that the major problem of tuberculosis required other methods for its solution."[47] He described these methods as including the organization of sanatoriums and dispensaries, the development of ambulatory care and home visits, and most especially a campaign of public education.[48] It might also include, he suggested, the establishment of some system of health care financing to permit the poor to pay for the kind of medical care that public health advocated.[49]

. . .

All of this is not to deny a role, even a vital one, for the restriction of individual liberty in times of public health crisis. But it is to question the claims . . . that such restraints are core to public health powers. Rather, other forms of government activity, including especially the regulation of goods and services and the formation of government services, such as the provision of clean water and the inspection of food supplies, are far more apt candidates for the title of core public health powers (even if some of these activities are no longer carried out by boards of health).

This suggests that the assumption of the drafters of the Model Act that updating and expanding the government's ability to coerce individuals is central to confronting bioterrorism may well be misplaced. There is no evidence to conclude that public health in the past has been most successful when it has relied primarily upon individual coercion and there is little reason to believe that such a policy would be the most effective approach were we faced with another bioterrorist incident.[50] Indeed, if history teaches us anything about the use of such "traditional powers" it is that they are often, especially in crises, misused, sacrificing the rights of especially vulnerable individuals often for little or no public health benefit.[51]

. . .

The reliance upon courts to mediate the tensions between public health and individual rights also derives in part from the AIDS epidemic. Although courts reviewed public health actions prior to HIV, the AIDS epidemic was certainly the first fully litigated public health crisis. Space here precludes a full discussion of the important role that courts played in the HIV epidemic, but there can be no doubt that they played a critical role in signaling the inappropriateness of discrimination against people who are HIV positive.[52] Indeed, looking at the role that courts played during the HIV epidemic, Professor Gostin was able to write confidently about the courts' insistence that infringements on civil liberties can be undertaken only after careful consideration and when no less restrictive alternative is available.[53] This substantive standard has been incorporated, with modification, into the Model Act.[54]

Without denying the critical role legal standards and judicial process played with respect to HIV, there are serious reasons to examine whether they can be expected to play as constructive a role in the event of a bioterrorist event. Indeed, it may be that the judiciary's initial response to HIV, not public health's rejection of coercion, is what made AIDS policy truly exceptional: In other times, judges have been far less apt to protect the rights of individuals subject to public health orders.[55]

Generally limitations on individual liberty made in the name of public health are imposed by public health officials. In the case of HIV, in contrast, limitations upon an individual's freedom, or discrimination, usually came not from a public health official, but from a private citizen or another governmental agency not charged with or particularly expert in public health.[56] In those cases, more often than not, public health officials sided with the individual and argued that the restriction upon the individual's rights would not advance any public health goal.[57] Thus when the courts in those cases safe-guarded individual rights, they did it in a context in which public health authorities supported those rights. We cannot derive from those cases the lesson that courts can be trusted to engage in a meaningful review of public health powers, especially when those powers are exercised during an emergency.

. . .

V. Rethinking Therole Of quarantine and Isolation

There is no magic bullet for bioterrorism, just as there isn't one for most public health threats. Unfortunately, protection of the public health usually requires a complex array of strategies, from public education to surveillance, from vaccine development to market controls. Most or all of them will involve law. Only a few of them will require the curtailment of individual liberties.

The sponsors and drafters of the Model Act are acutely aware of the need for a sophisticated, multi-prong approach to bioterrorism. They have never advocated that restrictions on individual rights should play the sole or even leading role in that struggle. Instead they rightly see the Model Act and the coercive powers it would provide as but a single element in a multi-tiered process. And, they have attempted to construct that process while providing for significant judicial protections for individual rights.

Nevertheless, there is a danger that the dissemination of the Model Act may be construed by political leaders and others as "solving" the problem of legal preparedness. Today when our public health infrastructure is sorely tattered,[58] and when "solutions" seem hard to envision, the clarification of coercive powers may provide an easy and relatively inexpensive fix.[59]

The danger brought by such a balm is not merely the illusion of false comfort. It is the potential for distraction and misdirection of priorities. By focusing on how we can update the law to do a better job of isolating and quarantining individuals, or vaccinating them without their consent, we risk overlooking the other ways that we can and should use law proactively to help prevent and prepare for bioterrorism.

One obvious candidate for legal attention is the international development and transport of dangerous pathogens and other ingredients of biological weapons. Last year, a few weeks after the unveiling of the Model Act, the Bush administration announced its rejection of international talks aimed at strengthening the 1972 Biological Weapons Convention.[60] More recently, the Administration has stated that it is abandoning efforts to strengthen the Convention.[61] While a full analysis of that particular international effort is beyond the purview of this paper, the point remains that there is a critical need for legal efforts to curtail the creation and shipment of biological weapons. Emergency powers designed to contain a bioterrorist outbreak by isolating individuals can never be a substitute for legal efforts designed to prevent one in the first place.

Domestically, last spring's Public Health Security and Bioterrorism Preparedness and Response Act ("PHSBPRA") undertook many important steps, greatly increasing federal funding for state and local preparedness and tightening the regulation of laboratories that use dangerous pathogens.[62] Nevertheless, if we focus upon law's ability to regulate and structure markets, as opposed to its ability to restrain individuals, gaps appear. For example, although the PHSBPRA gives the Secretary of Agriculture authority to expand the capacity of the Food Inspection Service to protect against bioterrorism, the Act does not provide anything close to a comprehensive approach for inspection and protection of the food supply. In a recent report,[63] the National Academy of Science warned that inadequate attention has been given to this issue and the nation remains vulnerable to a bioterrorist attack on the food supply.[64] Likewise, the PHSBPRA does not require states to rebuild their broken public health systems to ensure the "dual-use" capacity that is so clearly needed.[65] While the PHSBPRA authorizes grants to help states address bioterrorism,[66] the danger remains that states will remain unprepared as their public health systems as a whole remain unsupported.[67]

. . .

In developing quarantine strategies, a state may want to go beyond enhancing its powers to impose detention orders and providing legal process for those who are detained involuntarily. Instead, a state may want to give thought to how *voluntary* quarantine and/or isolation recommendations may be more tolerable and acceptable to the population. In other words, the state may want to think about how it can promote voluntary compliance. After all, the state will never have sufficient resources to "round up" and involuntarily detail large numbers of people. But in order to obtain voluntary compliance, states may need to move beyond a police power model, and think not only about how they can enforce laws and protect legal rights of those detained, but also how they can make quarantine less frightening and more palatable. The

Model Act moves in that direction by requiring that states provide for the needs of those involuntarily detained, but as noted above, it does not specifically address the economic consequences of quarantine, nor does it ensure that dependents will be care for.[68] In addition, the Model Act does not provide for the care or compensation of individuals who stay put without the imposition of a public health order. But, if quarantine is critical to the public good, then perhaps like jury duty or reserve duty, those who serve (voluntarily or involuntarily) should be provided with job protection and compensation.

When health threats appear, as in times of war, there is an inevitable tendency to focus on the need for efficient power and the virtues of a powerful executive. But just as our framers taught us that the preservation of peace requires a far more complex and less tidy political state than is needed to win a war, so too, we may recall that the protection of public health whether from bioterrorism or natural causes ultimately requires complex and multifaceted laws. There is a lot of work for lawyers yet to do.

Notes

[t] Professor of Law, Northeastern University School of Law. Many thanks to Anthony Robbins, M.D. and Anthony Moulton, Ph.D., for their comments on an earlier version of the paper, to Daniel McCabe, Jennifer Hoenig, Jamie Quigley, Kevin Pechulis, David Roberts and Jason Smith for their wonderful help researching this paper, and to Jan McNew for her terrific secretarial assistance. All opinions and errors are my own.

[!] This paper was written in September 2002 and does not discuss developments in the field subsequent to that date.

1 The literature from that time is extensive. For a few examples, *see* RONALD BAYER, PRIVATE ACTS, SOCIAL CONSEQUENCES: AIDS AND THE POLITICS OF PUBLIC HEALTH (1989); *see also* Scott Burris, *Fear Itself: AIDS, Herpes, and Public Health Decisions*, 3 YALE L. & PoL'Y REV. 479 (1985) (discussing the role of health law as related to individual rights against the public good).

2 *The Report on the Global HIV/AIDS Epidemic: The Barcelona Report*, UNAIDS, XIV International Conference on AIDS (July 2002) (reporting the latest global HIV/AIDS statistics and putting forth new suggestions on how to better deal with the crisis), *available at* http://www.unaids.org/barcelona/presskit/report.html.

3 THE MODEL STATE EMERGENCY HEALTH POWERS ACT (Center for Law and the Public

Health at Georgetown and John Hopkins Universities, Draft for Discussion 2001), *at* http://www.publichealthlaw.net/msehpa/msehpa2.pdf (Dec. 21, 2001) [hereinafter MODEL ACT].

4 *See* The Model State Emergency Health Powers Act: State Legislative Activity (as of Oct. 1, 2002) (compiling all 50 states activity relating to the Model State Emergency Health Powers Act), *available at* http://www.pubichealthlaw.net/MSEHPA_Leg_Activity_050102.pdf.

5 *See* text accompanying notes 27-54, *infra*.

6 MODEL ACT, *supra* note 3, at Preamble.

7 *See* JUDITH MILLER ET AL., GERMS: BIOLOGICAL WEAPONS AND AMERICA'S SECRET WAR, 37-38 (2001) (explaining several uses of disease to harm opponents during warfare throughout history).

8 *Id.*

9 *Id.* at 38.

10 Justin Gillis, *States Weighing Laws to Fight Bioterrorism*, WASH. POST, Nov. 19, 2001, *at* A-1.

11 Matt Mientka, *CDC Releases Model Bioterrorism Law*, U.S. MEDICINE INFORMATION CENTER (Dec. 2001), *at* http://www.usmedicine.com/article.cfm?articleID=314&issueID=33 (last visited Oct. 24, 2002).

12 MODEL ACT, *supra*, note 3, at § 102(a).

13 *Id.* at § 401.

14 *Id.* at § 403(a), Article V. The Model Act also has provisions that apply prior to an emergency. For example, Article II of the Act requires the Governor to appoint a commission charged with developing a "public health emergency plan." *Id.* at §§ 201, 202 (emphasis omitted). The Act, however, does not require the state to actually implement any elements of the plan. In addition, Article II of the Act requires health care providers, coroners, and medical examiners to report "any illness or health condition that may be potential causes of a public health emergency." *Id.* at § 301(a). Pharmacists are also required to "report any unusual or increased prescription rates, unusual types of prescriptions, or unusual trends in pharmacy visits that may be potential causes of a public health emergency." *Id.* at § 301(b). *But see* Annas, *supra* note 25, at 1340 (criticizing what the Model Act actually requires and the potential privacy implications of the requirement). The uncertainty as to what that actually requires, and the potential privacy implications of the requirement, have elicited significant criticism.

15 MODEL ACT, *supra* note 3, at § 104(m) (emphasis omitted). The sections in brackets are meant to offer states the choice to expand the category of public health emergencies beyond bioterrorism, if they desire. *See* Letter of Lawrence O. Gostin, December 21, 2001 (on file with author).

16 MODEL ACT, *supra* note 3, at § 401.

17 *Id.* at § 405(b).

18 *Id.* at §§ 405(b), (c). It is an interesting question whether such a legislative veto is constitutional under all state constitutions. *Cf*, INS v. Chadha, 462 U.S. 919 (1983) (holding that federal legislative veto violates U.S. Constitution).

19 The Model Act is unclear as to whether the declaration or its repeal is reviewable by a court. Although the Act provides for immunity for the state and its officials for injuries or damages caused by the declaration (except when there is gross negligence or willful misconduct), it says absolutely nothing about reviewability and the possibility of prospective injunctive relief. Presumably many state courts would find that they have the power to review such orders. Indeed, they may find that the denial of any possibility of review raises grave questions under the due process clause of the 14th amendment as well as state constitutional provisions guaranteeing access to the courts. *See, e.g.,* Heather Brann, *Utah's Medical Malpractice Prelitigation Panel: Exploring State Constitutional Arguments Against a Nonbinding Inadmissible Procedure*, 2000 UTAH L. REV. 359, 365-67 (2001) (applying due process clause and state open courts provision to pre-litigation panels in medical malpractice cases).

20 *See* Annas, *supra* note 25, at 1338, 1340. *See also* Jennifer King, *Power Grab: The States in a State of Emergency. The Model Emergency Health Powers Act,* American Legislative Exchange Council Issue Analysis (Jan. 2002) (discussing the key points of the Model Emergency Health Powers Act), *at* http://www.alec.org/meSWFiles/pdf/0202.pdf.

21 MODEL ACT, *supra* note 3, at § 403(a)(l).

22 *Id.* at § 403(a)(4).

23 *Id.* at § 50l(a).

24 *Id.* at § 502(b).

25 *See id.* at §§ 503(b), (c) (noting that the services must be "reasonable and necessary to respond to the public health emergency").

26 MODEL ACT, *supra* note 3, at § 602.

27 *Id.* at § 602(c). Although the Act would seem to permit the public health authority to conduct almost any kind of diagnostic test or examination, quarantine or isolation is only permitted if there is uncertainty as to whether the

individual has been exposed to a contagious disease. *Id.* Generally, a contagious disease is one that can be transmitted by casual contact. *See* MERRIAM-WEBSTER'S COLLEGIATE DICTIONARY 249 (10th ed. 1998). However, the Act defines a contagious disease more broadly to include any "infectious disease that can be transmitted from person to person." MODEL ACT, *supra* note 3, at § 104 (c). Hence while HIV is not typically considered a "contagious disease," it would appear to be so within the literal meaning of the Act.

28 *Id.* at § 603.

29 *Id.* §§ 603(a)(3), (b)(3).

30 Isolation, as the term is defined by the Model Act

[I]s the physical separation and confinement of an individual or groups of individuals who are Infected or reasonably believed to be infected with a contagious or possibly contagious disease from non-isolated individuals, to prevent or limit the transmission of the disease to non-isolated individuals. *Id.* at § 104(h). Furthermore, the Model Act defines "quarantine" as: The physical separation and confinement of an individual or groups of individuals, who are or may have been exposed to a contagious or possible contagious disease and who do not show signs or symptoms of a contagious disease, from non-quarantined individuals, to prevent or limit the transmission of the disease to non-quarantined individuals. *Id.* at § 104(0).

31 *See* MODEL ACT, *supra* note 3, at § 604(b)(l)-(15) (listing the components of such an emergency plan).

32 *Id.* at § 604(b)(6).

33 *Id.* at § 804(a).

34 Parmet, *supra* note 55, at 55.

35 *Id.* at 56.

36 *Id.* at 59-66.

37 For arguments that quarantine and isolation would likely be fairly useless under most bioterrorism scenarios, see Joseph Barbera et al., *Large-Scale Quarantine Following Biological Terrorism in the United States, Scientific Examination, Logistic and Legal Limits, and Possible Consequences*, 286 JAMA 2711 (Dec. 2001).

38 *See* WILLIAM J. NOVAK, THE PEOPLE'S WELFARE: LAW AND REGULATION IN NINETEENTH-CENTURY AMERICA 204-05 (1996) (explaining the frequent use of maritime quarantines on vessels arriving on American shores). *See also* Sylvia N. Tesh, *Miasma and "Social Factors" in Disease Causality: Lessons from the Nineteenth Century*, 20 J. HEALTH POL. PoL'Y

& L. 1001, 1005 (1995) (discussing how quarantines not only interfered with commerce but the interest of the people).

39 Wendy E. Parmet, *After September 11, Rethinking Public Health Federalism* 30 J.L. MED. & ETHICS 201, 202-03 (2002).

40 NOVAK, *supra* note 82, at 209. On the other hand, business interests also sometimes favored public health regulations, for example a historian of food inspection laws claims that the livestock and packing industries pressed for regulations so that European countries would open their markets to American meat. VIVIAN WISER, U.S. DEP'T OF AGRIC, MEAT AND POULTRY INSPECTION IN THE UNITED STATES DEPARTMENT OF AGRICULTURE.

41 *See* GEORGE ROSEN, A HISTORY OF PUBLIC HEALTH 216-16 (expanded ed., The Johns Hopkins Univ. Press 1993) (1958) (discussing the causes of public health reform in the 19th century). *See also* Wendy E. Parmet, *From Slaughter-House to Lochner: The Rise and Fall of the Constitutionalization of Public Health*, 40 AM. J. LEGAL HIST. 476, 489 (1996) (stating the importance of clean water and pure food).

42 Parmet, *supra* note 85, at 491. Scott Burris has noted that the so-called traditional public health powers have been used only infrequently and have "deep roots in a medicalized approach to public health." Burris, *supra* note 8, at 257.

43 *E.g.,* George H. Rohe, *Recent Advances in Preventive Medicine*, 9 JAMA 1, 10-11 (1887) (arguing that the first requirement for dealing with an infectious disease from a "State Medicine Point of View" is notification and the second is segregation. The third requirement according to Rohe was disinfection).

44 Burris, *supra* note 8, at 256 (noting that the process of identifying and treating at-risk individuals had the effect of separating social reform from medical treatment in the field of public health). *See also,* Barbara Gutmann Rosenkrantz, *Cart Before Horse: Theory, Practice and Professional Image in American Public Health, 1870-1920*, J. HIST. MED. & ALLIED Sci. 55, 66-68 (1974) (discussing problems associated with registration and tracing of tuberculosis patients as prevention of spreading the disease).

45 *See* Rosenkrantz, *supra* note 88, at 63-64 (emphasizing the importance of education the public to increase health improvements and battle diseases).

46 Herman M. Biggs, *Preventive Medicine: Its Achievements, Scope, and Possibilities*, 65 MED. RED, 956 (1904).

47 C.E.A. Winslow, *The Evolution and Significance of the Modern Public Health Campaign*, J. PUB. HEALTH PoL'Y, at 50 (3d printing 1984).

48 *Id.* at 52.

49 *Id.* at 61-62.

50 Barbera et al., *supra* note 81, at 2713-14. This is not to question the appropriateness of applying the coercive authority of the criminal law to the perpetrators of bioterrorism. My focus here is on the application of coercion to *victims* of bioterrorism.

51 For a discussion of how public health officials in San Francisco in the early 1900s came to equate bubonic plague with race and as a result imposed a quarantine on Chinatown, see NAYAN SHAH, CONTAGIOUS DIVIDES: EPIDEMICS AND RACE JN SAN FRANCISCO'S CHINATOWN 120-57 (2001).

52 *See, e.g.,* Bragdon v. Abbott, 524 U.S. 624, 641 (1998) (ruling in favor of a plaintiff seeking anti-discrimination protection on the basis of disability under the ADA due to her HIV infection).

53 Lawrence O. Gostin, *Public Health Theory and Practice in the Constitutional Design*, 11 HEALTH MATRIX 265, 306-08 (2001).

54 More specifically the Model Act uses the language of "least restrictive means" to limit the methods of isolation employed, not the actually determination of whether or not isolation or quarantine is required. Sec. 604(b)(l) states:

> Isolation and quarantine must be by the least restrictive means necessary to prevent the spread of a contagious or possibly contagious disease to others and may include, but are not limited to, confinement to private homes or other private and public premises.

When reviewing whether to grant a petition to isolate or quarantine an individual, the Model Act requires that the court determine whether the isolation or quarantine is "reasonably necessary" to prevent or limit the transmission of a contagious disease. *Id.* at § 605(b)(5).

55 Gostin, *supra* note 107, at 295.

56 Thus several school boards voted to exclude children who were HIV positive. *See* Parmet & Jackson, *supra* note 57, at 16-20 (discussing various courts' treatment of school boards' discrimination against HIV positive students).

57 *See* Wendy E. Parmet, *The Supreme Court Confronts HIV: Reflections on Bragdon v. Abbott*, 26 J.L. MED. & ETHICS, 225, 226 (1998) (changing the role of public health from restricting to protecting individual rights).

58 COMMIITEE FOR THE STUDY OF THE FUTURE OF PUBLIC HEALTH, THE FUTURE OF PUBLIC HEALTH 73-106 (1988).

59 For example, last fall Governor Jane Swift of Massachusetts supported the Model Act and promised to push for its passage in her state. Justin Gills, *States Weighing Laws to Fight Bioterrorism*, THE WASH. POST, November 19, 2001, at AOL Only a few days later the state passed a budget that slashed public health programs and the Governor vetoed part of that program, imposing further cuts on public health. *See* Rick Klein, *Legislators are Likely to Restore Social Funding*, BOSTON GLOBE, Dec. 5, 2001, at B-4.

60 Steven Erlanger, *Bush's Move on ABM Pact Gives Pause to Europeans*, N.Y. TIMES, Dec. 13, 2001, at A-19.

61 Peter Slevin, *U.S. Drops Bid to Strengthen Germ Warfare Accord*, WASH. POST, Sept. 19, 2002, at AOL

62 Pub. L. No. l 07-188, §§ 131 et seq; 20 l et seq; 301, 116 Stat. 594 (2002) (codified at 42 U.S.C. §§ 243; 262 et seq.)

63 21 U.S.C. § 679(c) (2000).

64 National Academies, *Better Plan Needed to Protect U.S. Agriculture from Bioterror Attack*, at http://www4.nationalacademies.org (Sept. 19, 2002).

65 Experts agree that preparation for bioterrorism requires an overall enhancement of the public health infrastructure, which should be built upon and would expand public health's capacity to respond to naturally occurring disease outbreaks. *See* GENERAL ACCOUNTING OFFICE, BIOTERRORISM-FEDERAL RESEARCH AND PREPAREDNESS ACTIVITIES, GA0-01-915 (September 2001), at 6. A pressing problem today is that investments made for bioterrorism preparedness activities will not offset cuts made elsewhere in public health budgets, thereby weakening the overall public health infrastructure. *See* note 124, *supra*.

66 42 U.S.C. § 247d-3(a).

67 *See* Gostin et al., *supra* note 71, at 95-97 (discussing the decline in funding and support for state public health systems).

68 MODEL ACT, *supra* note 3, at § 604(b)(6).

WENDY E. PARMET is Matthews Distinguished University Professor of Law and Director of the Center for Health Policy and Law in the Law School of Northeastern University; she holds a joint appointment as Professor of Public Policy and Urban Affairs at Northeastern University School of Public Policy and Urban Affairs.

EXPLORING THE ISSUE

Is It Morally Permissible for Individuals to Break Quarantine?

Critical Thinking and Reflection

1. What action would you take if you were exposed to a deadly and contagious disease and quarantined alongside other people who were also exposed? How would you morally justify your action?
2. What actions would you take if you saw a person without obvious symptoms breaking quarantine and approaching your home? How would you morally justify your actions?
3. Suppose that you are a public health administrator and you learn that a deadly disease like anthrax or small-pox has been introduced by a terrorist into your community. Would you quarantine those who were exposed? What would you need to know in order to make that decision?

Is There Common Ground?

While Parmet appears more willing than the ACLU to admit that there are times when quarantine may be desirable, both agree that it is wrong to force people into quarantine in situations where quarantine is not efficacious in preventing the spread of disease. In such a situation, the loss of personal freedom and the other negative consequences of being involuntarily detained are not balanced by any public benefit, and are thus unacceptable.

In cases where quarantine would be effective in preventing the spread of disease, Parmet and the ACLU agree that safeguards should be in place to protect those who are placed in quarantine. For example, both argue that people who are quarantined need to be compensated for their time, their dependents must be provided with support, and their ability to return to their jobs afterward should be guaranteed.

Additional Resources

Becky Akers, "The Quarantine Quandary," The Independent Review, XII:4, Spring 2008.

Daniel Markovits, "Quarantines and Distributive Justice," The Journal of Law, Medicine, and Ethics, Summer 2005.

Mark A. Rothstein, "The Moral Challenge of Ebola," American Journal of Public Health, 105:1, January 2015.

Matthew K. Wynia, American Medical Association, "Ethics and Public Health Emergencies: Restrictions on Liberty," The American Journal of Bioethics, 7:2, February 2007.

Internet References . . .

Center for Disease Control and Prevention: Quarantine and Isolation

https://www.cdc.gov/quarantine/index.html

National Conference of State Legislatures: State Quarantine and Isolation Statutes

http://www.ncsl.org/research/health/state-quarantine-and-isolation-statutes.aspx

Podcast: What is the Moral Status of Quarantine?

http://www.peikoff.com/2009/12/07/what-is-the-moral-status-of-quarantine/

When is a quarantine justified? A group of philosophers offers an answer.

https://bigthink.com/when-is-a-quarantine-justified

Selected, Edited, and with Issue Framing Material by:
Owen M. Smith, *Stephen F. Austin State University*
and
Anne Collins Smith, *Stephen F. Austin State University*

ISSUE

Are Parents Morally Obligated to Vaccinate Their Children?

YES: Charlotte A. Moser, Dorit Reiss and Robert L. Schwartz, from "Funding the Costs of Disease Outbreaks Caused by Non-vaccination," *Journal of Law, Medicine & Ethics* (2015)

NO: Leonard F. Vernon and Christopher Kent, from "Chiropractors and Vaccinations: Ethics is the Real Issue," *Complementary Health Practice Review* (2009)

Learning Outcomes

After reading this issue, you will be able to:

- Explain the meaning of the expression "herd immunity" with regard to communicable diseases.
- Identify the conditions that typically exclude children from mandatory vaccination and explain the moral grounds for the exclusion of children with these conditions.
- State the Principle of Autonomy and the Principle of Welfare and then explain how the topic of mandatory vaccination embodies a conflict between these two moral principles.
- Formulate your own position on the morality of refusing to vaccinate children who do not have any of the conditions that would normally exclude them from vaccination.
- Identify the main objections to your position on the morality of refusing to vaccinate children who do not quality for exclusion from vaccination and formulate responses to these objections.

ISSUE SUMMARY

YES: Charlotte A. Moser et al. take the position that parents are responsible for vaccinating their children, and that parents who choose not to do so must take responsibility for the consequences, not only to their own children, but to others.

NO: Leonard F. Vernon and Christopher Kent claim that attempts to portray anti-vaccination proponents as unscientific extremists clouds important issues of informed consent and freedom of choice relating to health care that they espouse, rather than facing the ethical issues surrounding fully informed consent.

The world is a far different place in which to raise children than it was even a generation or two ago. Not merely have improvements in transportation, communication, and information technology transformed our society, but developments in health care have been stunning. In particular, the scourge of communicable diseases has been significantly reduced, and in some cases virtually eliminated.

As our parents and grandparents were growing up, it was common for them to lose classmates, friends, cousins, or even siblings to illnesses such as measles, mumps, pertussis ("whooping cough"), scarlet fever, or diphtheria. Many of those who were fortunate enough to survive a disease such as infantile paralysis ("polio") were forced to use iron lungs to breathe, crutches or braces to walk, or wheelchairs to travel. Expectant parents were terrified by rumors of an outbreak of rubella ("German measles") out of fear than their children would be born with severe disabilities. Faces covered with the horrible scars left by smallpox could still be encountered on a regular basis.

Fast-forward a few decades. Smallpox had been entirely eradicated. Once deadly diseases like scarlet fever were easily treated by antibiotics and no longer elicited the dread they once did. Epidemics of measles, mumps, pertussis, diphtheria, and polio were virtually unheard of, especially in industrialized countries like the United States. Once every corner of the world received the full benefits of modern medical care, these dangerous communicable diseases would at last be relegated to history.

Now read contemporary news accounts with an eye toward the names of these once dreaded illnesses. Epidemics of dangerous, communicable diseases are breaking out once again, infecting many and even killing a few before they are brought under control. The reason for this disturbing trend: a sufficient number of parents have chosen not to vaccinate their children against these diseases, damaging the herd immunity of our communities and endangering people who, for a variety of medical conditions are ineligible for vaccination themselves.

While there was understandable hesitancy to embrace vaccination when it was a revolutionary procedure in the late 18th and early 19th centuries, the publication of a single fraudulent article in a medical journal more than twenty years ago has laid the foundation for a growing anti-vaccination fervor. The author of this article was Andrew Wakefield, a medical researcher in the employ of a law firm that sought to win a massive monetary award by alleging significant negative side effects from vaccinations. Wakefield studied 12 children, gathered a rather limited set of data, and claimed to prove a causal connection between common childhood vaccines and autism. When later studies failed to replicate these conclusions, investigators examined the research used by Wakefield in the original article. To their dismay, they discovered that he had grossly misrepresented the data he had gathered and drew unjustified conclusions from these data. In an unusual move, the journal in which the article appeared formally retracted the article, and Wakefield was stripped of his credentials. Numerous studies conducted under rigorous scientific procedures have reexamined the purported link between childhood vaccination and autism and have found no evidence to support Wakefield's discredited claim. However, whenever a sensational claim is made, even with minimal or flawed evidence, conspiracy theories can arise, reasserting the original sensational claim, ignoring the flaws in the original research, and dismissing

any evidence to the contrary as manufactured by powerful interest groups seeking to suppress the truth. As a result, an increasing number of parents have decided against vaccinating their children based on the unfounded fear that the vaccinations might cause autism.

Unfortunately, the false dilemma between vaccination and autism has masked a real moral concern regarding the topic of mandatory vaccinations. Health-care professionals have always acknowledged the fact that every vaccination is accompanied by a risk of side effects, the vast majority mild and temporary, but a few serious or even fatal. These risks, while real, are nevertheless extremely small, far smaller in fact than the risks associated with abstaining from vaccination and contracting a communicable disease, with its attendant dangers of disability or death.

In addition to the direct risks to an unvaccinated individual, there are broader social implications of the decision not to vaccinate a child. Epidemiologists, who study the transmission of disease throughout a population, have observed that, when a high proportion of the individuals in a community has been vaccinated against a communicable disease, the entire community, including unvaccinated individuals, have a greater overall resistance to the spread of the disease. This resistance, which reflects the diminished ability of an infected individual to transmit disease organisms to vulnerable populations, is known as "herd immunity."

Herd immunity is critical to the safety of those individuals who are medically ineligible for vaccination. Conditions that make it medically unwise to vaccinate an individual include age (certain vaccinations are not recommended for extremely young children) and compromised immune systems, which can result from chemotherapy, radiation therapy, immunosuppressive drug therapy for transplant recipients, and autoimmune diseases. As long as a sufficiently high proportion of the population has been vaccinated, however, these individuals are protected by herd immunity. When parent choose not to vaccinate eligible children, they compromise the herd immunity of the community in which they reside, thus placing imperiling the welfare of vulnerable individuals.

A moral conflict thus arises between the good of an individual, represented by freedom from the negative side effects of vaccination, and the common good of a community, represented by herd immunity. Morally speaking, this conflict is just one aspect of a general tension between the Principle of Autonomy, which asserts that moral agents should be permitted to make decisions regarding their own interests and the interests of those entrusted to their care, and the Principle of Welfare, which asserts that it is morally permissible to restrict a person's autonomy to benefit others.

Charlotte A. Moser, Dorit Reiss, and Robert L. Schwartz argue that parents who make the decision not to vaccinate children need to be held financially responsible for the costs of their decision. They enumerate the costs generated by the loss of herd immunity in a community and, using classical predicaments such as the prisoner's dilemma and the tragedy of the commons, explore the moral dimensions of a decision not to vaccinate an eligible child.

Leonard Vernon and Christopher Kent provide a historical overview of objections to government-mandated vaccinations, beginning with the smallpox vaccinations of the early 19th century. They argue that there is nothing extremist about respecting the autonomy of parents to make fully informed decisions about the vaccination of their children. In reading this text, however, it is important to recognize that Vernon and Kent cite Wakefield's article in support of their position without mentioning the fact that it has been discredited and formally retracted.

YES ↵   Charlotte A. Moser, Dorit Reiss and Robert L. Schwartz

Funding the Costs of Disease Outbreaks Caused by Non-Vaccination

Introduction

Preventable diseases not only cause suffering and physical harm, they also impose financial costs on private individuals and public authorities. By disregarding evidence of the safety and effectiveness of vaccines and choosing not to vaccinate their children, some parents are increasing the risk of outbreaks and their attendant costs. In a very real sense, since those families are not currently required to cover the full costs of outbreaks, they are externalizing those costs onto others—individuals affected and society at large. Since non-vaccinating can directly lead to costly outbreaks, this paper argues that it is both fair and desirable to impose those costs upon those making the choice not to vaccinate. There are, in fact, strong policy reasons to support doing so regardless of whether we use an approach based on fault or a no-fault framework. Not only can the decision not to vaccinate be seen as culpable, aside from the culpability consideration, it is appropriate to compel those deciding not to vaccinate to internalize the costs in order to prevent free riding and to mitigate harms to others.

This article addresses the legal tools that can be used to manage the costs associated with outbreaks, focusing on those that do not require demonstrating fault. In particular, the article considers the imposition of a fee or a tax on non-vaccinators so that those who avoid immunization are required to internalize the costs associated with their decisions.

Costs Associated with Non-Vaccination

Widespread use of vaccines has transformed the landscape of medicine. Diseases that were once significant causes of morbidity and mortality are, in some cases, no longer suspected when patients report with symptoms characteristic of these diseases. (1) In fact, according to a recent study by William van Panhuis and colleagues, vaccines have prevented about 103 million cases of disease since 1924. (2) Despite the unquestionable effectiveness and proven safety of vaccines, some parents are concerned enough about the safety of vaccines that they choose not to have their children vaccinated. (3) While the number of completely unvaccinated children—those who received none of the recommended vaccines—remains low, pockets of unimmunized individuals make some communities particularly susceptible to outbreaks. (4) In recent years, outbreaks of the most contagious diseases, such as measles and pertussis, have started to reappear in communities throughout the country. (5) Recent examples include outbreaks of measles in New York, California, Washington, and Ohio; and one of mumps in Ohio. A recent press announcement by the Centers for Disease Control and Prevention (CDC) stated that the number of measles cases in the United States in the first half of 2014 was the highest since 1994. (6)

Outbreaks are more likely to occur where pockets of susceptible people cause a breakdown in herd immunity. Herd immunity results when enough individuals are immunized, so that the few who are not are still afforded protection. In fact, data have shown that it is better to be an unimmunized person in a highly vaccinated community than to be an immunized person in a community of susceptible people. (7) The disease is less likely to penetrate communities with high vaccination rates, so it is less likely that an unimmunized person will be infected. In contrast, an infectious agent will spread more readily through a lesser-vaccinated population resulting in infections in both unimmunized individuals as well as those for whom the vaccine was not effective. When families choose not to immunize themselves or their children, discussions often focus on the health consequences that the breakdown in herd immunity imposes on individuals and society. However, society must also absorb some of the financial burden related to cases of infectious diseases.

When an individual contracts a preventable disease, the costs are typically covered by the individual or family, their insurance company or, if they lack private insurance, a federally funded program, such as Medicare or Medicaid. Individual costs are incurred for medications (over-the-counter or prescription), co-pays and uncovered procedures or treatments, and loss of productivity (time at doctor visits or not at work). Several variables affect these costs, including who in the family is ill, which disease they have, the severity of illness, and the extent of their private or public medical coverage. Lee and Pichichero studied costs to families during a pertussis outbreak in New York during 1995-96 and found costs to families were $181 per ill adult, $254 per ill adolescent, $308 per ill child, or $2,822 per ill infant. (8) In 2014 USD, these costs would range from $278-$4,331. While these costs could seem exorbitant to individual families, they are minor when compared with the lifetime medical costs for an individual who is permanently harmed as well as the costs associated with stopping the spread of an infectious disease. Both of these are significantly higher and ultimately absorbed by society.

Costs Associated with Permanent Harm

While most infectious diseases can lead to permanent harm, rubella and meningococcal disease may cause the worst personal devastation. For example, a pregnant woman infected with rubella may miscarry, deliver early, suffer a spontaneous abortion or stillbirth, or have a child born with congenital rubella syndrome (CRS). Children affected by CRS can suffer deafness, heart or eye damage, mental retardation, skeletal damage, autism, or some combination of these. If the child survives, the cost to care for the child over his or her lifetime is estimated to be about $143,000. (9) Likewise, about 10-20 percent of the people who survive meningococcal infection, which can cause bloodstream infection (sepsis) or meningitis, will have permanent consequences such as deafness, limb amputations, or neurologic disabilities. Costs associated with acute disease and lifetime medical costs for these individuals have been estimated to range from $87,261 for deafness to $253,723 for someone with multiple amputations. (10) Most of the costs associated with permanent harm caused by an infectious disease are absorbed by the family and its insurer. Because private insurers base their fee structures on calculated risks, costs associated with permanent harm are passed on to insureds through premiums. For those insured through public programs, such as Medicare or Medicaid, costs associated with permanent harm are absorbed by tax payers.

Costs Associated with Containment Measures When an infectious disease is identified, one of the most pressing concerns becomes stopping the spread to others. Containment measures include limiting exposure of infected individuals to others who may be susceptible; identifying those who were exposed; monitoring for additional cases; establishing diagnostic testing and preventive or treatment measures, such as vaccination clinics; alerting and updating health care providers and the CDC; and addressing the public and the media. (11) A measles outbreak in 2005 showcases the complexities:

When an unvaccinated six year old was hospitalized with measles in Illinois, public health officials in that state traced the child's exposure to a church gathering of 500 people two weeks prior—in Indiana. When the Indiana health department began investigating, they identified the source case as an unvaccinated teenager who had returned from a church-mission trip. Despite symptoms of illness, she attended the church gathering where she not only directly infected the hospitalized child, but also seventeen others attending the gathering and one other person during a visit with a neighbor (19 first generation infections). In addition, thirteen additional people were infected by close (household) contact with the 19 directly infected individuals (second generation infections). Public health officials attempted to contact the 500 picnic attendees as well as anyone in contact with what ultimately became 34 people infected over three generations of spread. Workers had to ascertain vaccination status of attendees, attempt to identify additional cases, and try to get unvaccinated individuals vaccinated. Containment activities involved "ninety-nine public health officers and infection-control personnel working in 12 health departments and health care facilities . . ."(p.449). These personnel reported 3,650 hours of work, 4,800 telephone calls, 5,500 miles driven, and 550 lab samples to contain the outbreak started by a single unvaccinated teen returning from travel. (12)

The cost of containment for public health authorities was $62,216. The total cost of the outbreak was over two hundred thousand dollars. While the aforementioned outbreak started at a church gathering, outbreaks can begin anywhere that people gather. (13)

Because each situation is different, the extent of and need for containment measures varies. In addition, the responsibility for and distribution of the financial burden associated with containment may also vary. For example, in 2008 a measles-infected traveler visited a hospital resulting in an additional 13 cases, most of which were acquired by others in the hospital at that time or secondary cases related to those people. Costs to that hospital were estimated to be around $632,084 ($695,993 in 2014 U.S.);

most of which was related to wages and salaries of furloughed workers. (14) In contrast, when a refugee entered the U.S. while infected with measles in 2010, containment measures were spearheaded by the state public health department, but also involved personnel from the local public health and refugee departments, CDC, and hospital personnel. While the containment succeeded in stopping the spread of measles to others, the $25,000 ($26,818 in 2014 US dollars) costs associated with this single case fell completely to the government. (15)

Paying the Costs Associated with Infectious Diseases

While the government supports public health, the annual budget does not typically garner large percentages of the whole. For example, of the $969.8 billion health care dollars in the FY14 federal budget, only $4.7 billion were earmarked for public health, (16) and a recent report by Trust for America's Health called for increases in core funding at all levels of public health after presenting data showing that variability in health statistics between states was related to variation in funding. (17) In addition, public health departments are not funded for unexpected events, which means that during an outbreak caused by an infectious disease, departments may need to reassign staff and reallocate funds to complete containment measures in a timely manner. (18) A 1995 outbreak in Minnesota is instructive:

> Nine cases of invasive meningococcal disease with one death and seven cases of streptococcal disease with four deaths occurred over a one month period during the winter of 1995 in Minnesota. The cases occurred in two towns and were coincident with influenza season thereby complicating diagnoses in those presenting with respiratory symptoms.
>
> Containment measures included immunizing 30,000 residents; 26,000 of whom were vaccinated over a 4-day period. Public health staff worked 18-hour days for more than 23 days; in all, more than 600 people were involved in the public health response. Costs of vaccine alone were $1.2 million ($1.8 million 2014 US dollars). The state health department's budget for that year was $2.2 million ($3.4 million 2014 US dollars). While the state legislature provided an emergency appropriation for vaccine costs, the local hospital,

which had to set up a separate emergency area, was never reimbursed. (19)

Costs and Savings Associated with Vaccination

Recently, researchers at the CDC compared the costs of the vaccination program with the costs savings over the lifetime of a single birth cohort. (20) Using the 2009 U.S. recommended immunization schedule and a hypothetical U.S. birth cohort of more than 4.2 million children, the researchers calculated estimated cases of disease and deaths as well as the direct and societal costs associated with the diseases, immunizations, and net differences. Direct costs included inpatient and outpatient visits as well as outbreak control; indirect costs included loss of productivity and premature death. In addition to preventing about 42,000 deaths and 20 million cases of disease, vaccines were estimated to save about $14.7 billion (2014 U.S. dollars) in direct costs and $75 billion (2014 U.S. dollars) in societal costs over the lifetime of the cohort.

Costs of Outbreaks in the Eyes of the Law

The costs associated with outbreaks are unquestionably substantial and may constitute legally compensable damages. For example, direct costs of a tortious act are compensable and, in a case concerning a preventable infectious disease, may include the costs of treating current cases and preventing further ones. In addition, when an individual has been afflicted with an infectious disease, their costs may include lost earnings, future lost earnings (losing the ability to work generally or to work in specific types of jobs), physical and emotional pain and suffering (as allowed by the particular state), and subsequent decrease in life expectancy. Additional relevant costs are costs associated with inability to perform household tasks. If the afflicted individual dies as a result of the disease, relatives of the individual can sue for wrongful death, and for the harm they suffered as a result of the loss, including economic contributions that individual would have made, lost value of services, and loss of companionship. Individuals may also recover for pain and suffering, including physical pain and emotional harm accompanying a physical injury or illness (though some states limit pain and suffering awards in some or all contexts). In some rare cases, where behavior is especially culpable, for example, intentionally exposing a child to chickenpox, punitive damages may also be appropriate.

The Justification for Recouping Costs

Whether it is appropriate to compel an individual to bear the costs associated with the decision to not vaccinate is an important starting point to this discussion. It is especially important in terms of those costs generally imposed on the public purse and financed through taxation for the benefit of all. Sometimes, society does pay for problematic choices made by individuals. For example, individuals are generally not required to pay for police activity caused because they got into a dangerous situation. This is not always the case, however. For example, when individuals tortuously cause damages to public property, they are responsible for the damages even though the property has been purchased and maintained with public funds. (21)

Whether we use a fault or a no fault basis, there are powerful public policy reasons to compel those choosing not to vaccinate to bear the costs associated with their actions. (22) As demonstrated, imposing costs is justified whether we see the decision not to vaccinate as negligent or as blameless, since it is based on the costs the choice not to vaccinate imposes on society, costs those making the choice should internalize.

A Fault-Based Argument for Recouping Costs

Not vaccinating is, arguably, at least negligent. A detailed discussion of the beliefs that lead people to misestimate the risks of vaccinating and the risks of not vaccinating and why they are incorrect is beyond the scope of this paper and has already been done by others. (23) But while nothing is guaranteed safe, it is clear that serious harms from vaccines are extremely rare, and as pointed out in a recent article that reviewed a large number of studies, far outweighed by the benefits of vaccinating, even to the individual— and certainly for society collectively. (24) Because of this extensive evidence, vaccination is supported by the overwhelming majority of doctors, scientists, and policymakers. Both from a risk/benefit analysis and through a community norm lens, the failure to vaccinate is problematic. The justifications for not vaccinating are often based on information that is simply incorrect. (25) As a matter of fact, modern anti-vaccine arguments are surprisingly

similar to those used in the early days of vaccines, and are no better supported by evidence today than they were in the 19th or early 20th centuries. (26)

Unlike intentional torts, negligence does not require actual knowledge that one's understanding of the risks is wrong or that one is making a risky choice. As long as the decision maker should have known that the decision was unreasonable, then the decision is negligent. Given the scientific consensus supporting vaccines, the abundant information from reputable sources supporting immunization, and the problematic sources relied upon by those who choose not to vaccinate, it is easy to support the claim that those who choose not to vaccinate should know they are making an unreasonable choice. As is the case here, when an individual engages in behavior that free rides on others, puts others at risks, and is unreasonable or even reckless, there is strong justification to require the individual to internalize the costs of that behavior.

A No Fault-Based Argument for Recouping Costs

An argument can be made that the choice not to vaccinate is not always negligent. In reality, the reason for failing to vaccinate children is rarely the result of parents forgetting to bring children to the pediatrician or the pediatrician's failure to remember to provide the vaccination. Rather, failure to vaccinate is occasionally the result of intentional actions based on serious religious or philosophical principles or is the result of safety concerns. In most cases, we do not categorize principle-based decisions as "negligent," even when most of the society rejects the same principles. For example, the law does not characterize a woman's decision to carry a pregnancy to term and not to have an abortion following a negligently performed tuballigation as a negligent failure to mitigate damages. Because there is sufficiently widespread support for an individual woman's right to choose to have a baby or choose to have an abortion, no court has ever declared that choosing one option over the other is negligent. Similarly, Jehovah's Witnesses generally are not found to be negligent for refusing medically necessary blood transfusions on religious grounds, even though the vast majority of the society rejects their religiously based principle. One court has been willing to reduce damages for a plaintiff who agreed to forgo blood transfusions and subsequently suffered greater injury because she could not be provided blood, but that was justified by some version of the doctrine of assumption of the risk rather than contributory or comparative negligence. (27) Whether we are willing to declare a parent to be negligent for failing to vaccinate a child is a more difficult question, but it involves the same considerations, especially when it is done for religious reasons. A case can be made based in part on the reasoning in Prince v. Massachusetts that parents cannot use their religious principles to endanger a child's health. (28) In fact, some jurisdictions have applied a recklessness standard and convicted parents for manslaughter when the reasons underlying decisions that led to a child's death were religious. (29) This conclusion is not, however, obvious, nor is it consistent with the prevailing view of negligence in the tort context.

The second alternative, deciding not to vaccinate based upon ill-founded safety concerns, is more obviously akin to negligence. Acting according to your best judgment but choosing a larger risk can be negligent. (30) Sincere belief that your choice is the correct one does not make it any less negligent when it imposes risks on others. Even in those cases, however, a court may find for the defendant on the basis that an error of judgment is not always negligent. (31) Given the abundance of anti-vaccine misinformation on the Internet, (32) some judges or juries may find that the decision not to vaccinate was an error on judgment, rather than a negligent act.

However, even if the decision to forego vaccination is not regarded as negligent, imposing the cost on the decision maker is justified for a number of reasons. The most important reason is that the question of childhood vaccination imposes unusual pressures upon parents, which can be analogized to the prisoner's dilemma, whereby it is in the interest of each individual to make a decision that will undermine the social interest of all of the decision makers. Assuming that there is substantial value in herd immunity and that there are some adverse side effects of immunization that cannot be controlled, each individual child would be better off if that child were not vaccinated (so she would avoid any risk of side effects) and every other child were vaccinated (giving the one unvaccinated child the protection of herd immunity). In other words, there are some circumstances where virtually everyone else in the community is vaccinated—in which parents would be acting rationally in deciding not to vaccinate their children, as long as their only consideration is the health of that child. In these cases, people would rely—intentionally or not—on others to protect them or their children against diseases rather than take the small risk vaccines pose. In other words, they would be free riding on herd immunity. (33)

This situation can also be analogized to the tragedy of the commons, where a common good is put at risk by individuals acting in their own self-interest. Here the commons—the disease free state of an immunized community—is put at risk by people who depend upon that commons for their own benefit. The costs of the choice, rather than being borne by those making it, are then externalized to others, or to society at large. The effect can be even less just: since non-vaccination is more prevalent among the wealthy today, there is a distributional injustice, with wealthy individuals increasing the risk of disease to others who are less fortunate. (34)

While people sought to opt out of vaccination from the earliest days of immunization for the same reasons that are now advanced, this problem was not so severe when parents often saw children who were harmed by the diseases we vaccinate against and understood the risks facing their own children. Today, few parents have ever seen these conditions and, as a result, most do not fully understand the potentially terrible consequences of these preventable diseases. On the other hand, stories of vaccine injuries, most of which, like the claim that vaccines cause autism, are not based on credible medical evidence are advanced by anti-vaccine movements, and may easily scare parents.

Regardless of whether a parent's decision to forego vaccination is made as a conscious decision to "hide in the herd," or is based upon an incorrect belief that their children are not really at risk from preventable diseases or that the risks of vaccines are greater than those of the diseases, in all of these cases the parents' decisions not to immunize threaten both the social consensus on vaccination and the herd immunity on which they rely. We can justify imposing costs upon these parents both as a deterrence mechanism, which may force them to internalize the costs associated with their decisions, and as a matter of fairness, to prevent them from forcing others to pay for the risks created by their decisions.

From a public policy perspective, not vaccinating imposes avoidable costs on government which lead to decreased funding for other important public health programs. Not vaccinating also increases the risk of outbreak to the community by undermining herd immunity. Imposing costs upon those who choose not to vaccinate can help deter individuals from making such problematic choices without limiting their autonomy with a vaccination mandate.

One possible claim is that by allowing exemptions to school immunization requirements, the legislature had provided a right not to vaccinate and therefore imposing costs is inappropriate. Even if our proposal was focused on common law suits, we believe that claim unjustified: exemptions from school immunization requirements balance public health with parental rights in the context of the child's education, considering the importance of education for children. There is no indication that in passing them the legislature considered the question of the cost of harms from non-vaccination. Further, acting legally is not always acting reasonably, and costs are imposed, under our system, for acts that are legal but not reasonable when those acts harm others. For example, having a glass shower door that is not made of tempered glass may be legal, but not reasonable. Similarly, having a pile of hay in your yard may be legal, but not reasonable (in fact, many negligence cases are about acts that were completely legal but deemed unreasonable). (35) But since our remedy is a statutory one, this is not a problem: in the same way that the legislature can choose to provide or not provide an exemption, the legislature may impose costs on those using exemptions.

Legal Tools for Imposing Costs

There are four general types of mechanisms for imposing costs. While this article briefly mentions all of them, only the fourth will be explored in detail. The first and most coercive mechanism, is the use of criminal law. For example, in Jacobson v. Massachusetts, the United States Supreme Court recognized that a state can impose a fine for failure to obtain an immunization against a communicable disease that the state reasonably believes is threatening the community. (36) The criminal approach assumes that those who do not receive vaccinations have an even higher level of culpability than negligence. Because the possibility of imposing costs through criminal law liability is a subject that deserves its own treatment, it is not explored in this article.

The second mechanism is the use of the coercive power of the law to condition social activities on vaccination without formally invoking criminal law. Today we enforce mandatory vaccination policies primarily through attendance at school (or, in some states, only public school). It makes a great deal of sense to use school attendance as the conditioning factor because of the importance of immunizing children and the potential for contagion at schools. On the other hand, there are additional activities that could be dependent upon vaccination, too. For example, the use of public meeting places like amusement parks, pools and water parks, government buildings, theaters, sporting venues, shopping centers, and other public accommodations could each be conditioned on the vaccination of the people using it although, admittedly, enforcing these restrictions could prove challenging and people may resist the requirement to carry evidence of their vaccination status whenever they are in public. Like

mandatory vaccination for school attendance policies, these other vaccination requirements could allow for vaccination opt-outs or could be enforced only when particular legally-identified circumstances occur. For example, they could be enforced only when there is an outbreak of a disease or the vaccination level in the community falls below herd immunity levels.

The third mechanism is to allow suits in negligence for non-vaccination. This possibility, and its challenges, have been discussed elsewhere. (37) However, bringing a negligence case is not easy. Even meritorious cases may be difficult for plaintiffs to win because there may be substantial problems in proving causation and because they will need to overcome the duty hurdle. In addition, on a social level, negligence actions are a highly inefficient way to resolve disputes, in large part because the cost of enforcing an obligation through the use of negligence law is very high. So while this approach provides an option, it is likely that other more effective and efficient legal devices are available to encourage vaccination and properly distribute the cost of the failure to vaccinate.

The fourth alternative mechanism for imposing costs, and the one this article examines in depth, is a no-fault approach that seeks to force every person who opts out to internalize the cost of the failure to vaccinate so that the one who incurs the cost is the one who bears it. The no-fault approach would cause those who decide against vaccination to internalize the cost of that decision by imposing a tax, fee, premium, or other cost equal to the actuarially-based cost of avoiding the immunization. Like the Arizona Stupid Motorist Act, or similar statutes allowing for the collection of rescue costs for lost hikers and skiers, or like the federal Superfund administered by the EPA, which is based on ordinary principles of negligence, the justifications for putting such a scheme in place to impose costs associated with the failure to vaccinate may draw on the culpability of the action. Alternatively, efforts to impose costs may be more like governments' attempts to collect the direct costs of their services like city trash collection fees (where the fees collected must actually cover the costs of trash collection) or bridge tolls (where the toll is priced to cover bond payments on the bridge and operating expenses). Cost imposition may have some of the attributes of congestion pricing, like the costs being imposed on drivers of cars that enter central London or demand-based parking pricing in San Francisco, where the price goes up as the number of users (in our case, non-vaccinators) goes up, increasing the cost to society. Imposition of costs could also be analogous to the "headless motorcycle rider" statutes being suggested in some states where the fee to register a motorcycle that could be driven by someone without a helmet would reflect the additional costs to society of that risk (estimated to be between $600 and $1000 each year above the regular registration fee). While some of the costs of these actions are already internalized (after all, non-vaccinators' children may acquire these diseases) without an effective legal intervention, many of the costs associated with communicable diseases are imposed on vaccinated members of society or those who cannot be vaccinated.

The mechanisms discussed here all probably require a legislative change.

No-Fault Tools for Covering the Costs Associated with Non-Vaccinating

Ex Ante Tools: Taxes, Fees, or Costs

One way to manage the problem of the costs of non-vaccinating is to impose the costs of the choice not to vaccinate upfront, ex-ante (before the fact). In other words, we can make those who do not vaccinate pay a certain sum to the public purse or insurance companies to cover costs imposed by the outbreak they cause before an outbreak ever happens. This approach has the advantage of supplying the money in advance, of distributing the costs of the risk they create among the entire non-vaccinating population, and of absolving the government from showing causation. It can, however, run into implementation problems, including the difficulty of assessing an appropriate amount, of identifying non-vaccinating parents and of collecting the money. It also imposes costs on those who may never actually cause an outbreak. In a sense, this approach makes the non-vaccinating pay for the risk they create, not for costs they impose.

There are many ways in which such fees, taxes, or costs could be assessed and imposed. As noted earlier, currently the most common mechanism for assuring childhood immunization in the United States is the requirement that parents provide proof of vaccination at the time of their childrens school registration. Current law in all states allows parents to opt out of vaccination for their children when it is medically prudent to do so, and the law in all but three states permits parents to opt out for other reasons, including religious, philosophical, or personal objections. Thus, the least disruptive way to have parents internalize the cost of failing to vaccinate their children may be to impose an opt-out fee equal to the actual cost to all of society of having another child unvaccinated. This fee might vary by locality, by incidence of disease, or by the number of others who have opted out. As the number of whooping cough cases increases, for example, the opt-out fee could increase; as the number of people opting out of whooping cough immunization increases, the opt out fee could increase. The need for flexibility and the fact that fees will vary according to circumstances, suggests that the fee should be determined by an administrative agency rather than by legislation, potentially in a manner similar to the assessment of utilities rates. For example, states use Public Utility Commissions to periodically determine energy rates. While rate setting is complex, states are accustomed to grappling with this challenge and could apply their experience to non-vaccination as well. Furthermore, using commissioners appointed for fixed, lengthy terms, ideally with expertise in related fields, can help isolate the process from political pressures.

While Jacobson held that the right to opt out for medical reasons was constitutionally protected by the due process clause, all other opt outs could be assessed a consistent fee because, regardless of their different underlying reasons, these decisions impose the same cost on society. When transferring these costs to those who decide not to vaccinate, the state would be making a purely economic determination devoid of moral judgment and without evaluation of the sincerity or honesty of the parents. In fact, the statute creating the scheme would determine which opt-out factors may be considered.

Of course, an opt-out fee is not the only way that parents could be effectively required to internalize the costs they impose on others by failing to vaccinate their children. The cost could be assessed as a tax payable along with income or other taxes to the federal government or the state, or those who do vaccinate themselves and their children could be given tax credits. (38) Alternatively, cash grants or benefits could be provided to families in which everyone is vaccinated. Politically, it is easier to allow for tax credits and deductions than to impose penalties, although behavioral research suggests that the incentive value of a penalty is greater than the incentive value of a credit or deduction, even when the formal economic value of each is the same.

The actuarial work required to determine the appropriate cost of an opt-out and the collection of any such fees could be effectively delegated to private instead of public agencies, as well. For example, one of the primary costs of failure to vaccinate is the medical cost incurred by the unvaccinated person. Currently, the ACA allows for health coverage premiums to be rated on only four grounds: (1) age, (2) geography, (3) smoking status, and, sometimes, (4) participation in wellness programs. Vaccination status could be an additional rating factor used in policies recognized under the ACA (and, presumably, other policies as well). In fact, the decision to have a vaccination, like the decision to have a blood pressure measurement done, could be considered evidence of participation in a wellness program. Anyone can participate in a vaccination program, and anyone can succeed without reference to their health status; thus, a program offering vaccinations to those for whom vaccines are medically appropriate would seem to meet the requirements for ACA recognized wellness programs. Those who do not get recommended immunizations without a medically valid reason, though, would be subject to higher monthly insurance premiums and would be forced to internalize at least a part of the costs of the failure to vaccinate. (39)

The Public Use of Revenue Raised from Taxes and Fees Imposed on Non-Vaccination

A tax or fee might be used to raise general revenue for the government, but there may be far greater public support for a tax or fee that is designated for particular purposes related to the failure to vaccinate. For example, the revenue can be used to pay the cost of vaccinations, the cost of tracing the source of communicable diseases, the cost of caring for those who are injured by the failure to vaccinate, the cost of public and professional education about immunization, and the pain and suffering of those who could not protect themselves against the underlying diseases. If a state decides to use a no-fault mechanism to impose the cost of non-vaccination on those who should bear it, it would make political and economic sense to direct the resources to a fund to be used for that purpose.

Every tax, fee, or other incentive with regard to immunization will have to be consistent with the constitutional limitations of the due process clauses of the Fifth and Fourteenth Amendments, and with the religion clauses of the First Amendment. Since the United States Supreme Court approved the imposition of criminal penalties against those who refused locally mandated vaccinations for other than medical reasons a century ago, it is hard to question the general validity of such laws. Indeed, if criminal penalties intended to compel compliance are justifiable, then the imposition of other fees and taxes that are related to the actual cost of noncompliance seem likely to be Constitutionally sound.

Since the Supreme Court upheld the state use of mandatory school attendance law to enforce vaccination laws in Zucht v. King, it has been clear that a state can enforce its immunization requirements through school registration requirements. (40) Because Jacobson was decided before the First Amendment was applied against states, there may

still be a free exercise clause argument against requiring vaccinations that are contrary to religious principles. On the other hand, limitations put on free exercise claims to exemptions from generally applicable laws in the Smith case (1991) strongly suggest that such arguments will not be successful, at least under current law. The United States Constitution is unlikely to hinder any state action imposing a tax, fee, penalty, or any other cost on someone who does not arrange for vaccinations required by law without having a medical excuse.

Ex Post Tools: Billing by Public Health Authorities

An alternative to an ex-ante approach is to allow the public health authority to recoup their costs after the fact by sending a bill to a family whose decision not to vaccinate caused the outbreak. This approach has the advantage of adhering to traditional principles of causation, and prevents the problem of determining and implementing a fee or tax structure by connecting the amount collected to the harm caused. It has the disadvantages of requiring proof of causation—not always easy—and of placing the entire cost on one family or a few families rather than distributing it across all non-vaccinating individuals, making that family bear the costs associated with a choice made by many, regardless of their ability to bear the cost.

While this approach draws on tort principles of individual responsibility and causation, it creates a public law remedy.

Under the Free Public Services Doctrine, municipalities cannot recoup costs of services needed because of a citizen's negligence absent a statute. (41) The most compelling rationale for this controversial doctrine is that part of government's role is to provide services to the public financed via taxation that spreads the costs to all citizens. (42) Deciding how to allocate the costs of providing services should be left to the democratically elected legislature, as a matter of public policy, not to the courts. (43) We are unsure if this doctrine bars recovery in this instance; however, we believe that there is a case for allowing the courts to recoup these costs under a public nuisance doctrine, by analogy, especially since many states and municipalities have public nuisance statutes that can provide the statutory basis the Free Public Services Doctrine requires. (44)

But handling the problem via a statutory scheme of some kind has substantial advantages. For example, it would allow the polity to decide, via the democratic process, on the terms for imposing such liability and the process for handling it. In addition, it would offer the opportunity to create a more streamlined and efficient administrative process rather than requiring an adversarial one. For those reasons, we propose a statute that will create a mechanism for recouping the costs of outbreak caused by non-vaccinating.

Potential Models: Existing Statutes Imposing Costs

Statutes imposing costs of public services on citizens exist in a variety of contexts. (45) Several states have statutes allowing the state to recoup the costs of environmental hazards. For example, agencies may recoup the costs of handling fires (46) or hazardous spills. (47) States and municipalities also have statutes allowing recovery in damages for nuisance. Nuisance can be defined broadly-for example, California law defines it as "Anything which is injurious to health, including, but not limited to, the illegal sale of controlled substances, or is indecent or offensive to the senses, or an obstruction to the free use of property, so as to interfere with the comfortable enjoyment of life or property, or unlawfully obstructs the free passage or use, in the customary manner, of any navigable lake, or river, bay, stream, canal, or basin, or any public park, square, street, or highway, is a nuisance." (48) Most examples relate to inadequate property management that causes harm to others (49) though the principle can be seen as broad enough to encompass non-vaccination. While that is not the focus of this article, it is certainly a possibility.

In addition to requiring property owners and others causing environmental hazards to internalize the costs of their choices, these laws also reflect a value judgment. In particular, they support the idea that the public should not have to pay for the costs of those behaviors. They can also help deter such problematic behavior by imposing costs on the actors. This is the same logic we wish to apply to non-vaccination.

Finally, a small number of states have statutes addressing recovery of costs spent on rescuing an individual from a dangerous situation created by the individual's own negligence. For example, the Arizona Stupid Motorist Act allows non-profit and public entities to collect costs expended in rescuing a driver who, ignoring barricades (or otherwise behaving recklessly), drives a vehicle onto a public street or highway that is temporarily covered by floodwaters. (50) Similarly, North Carolina has a statute that allows government agencies to recover costs incurred in rescuing someone during an emergency if the person rescued ignored a warning. (51) The logic behind these statutes is that if the need for public assistance was brought about by an individual's highly culpable behavior, then the individual should reimburse the public purse.

Drawing on these existing models, we propose a statute that imposes the costs on those whose choice to not vaccinate created costs. (52) The statute follows the logic embodied in existing recovery statutes, and draws heavily on the Arizona statute for its specifics.

Bill Text

Title of Bill: Recovering Costs of Outbreaks Caused by Non-Vaccinating

SECTION 1: If a person does not vaccinate herself or a minor on whose behalf that person had legal authority to consent to vaccination, and that failure to vaccinate causes or contributes to an outbreak of an infectious disease, that person is liable for the costs incurred by any public agencies in containing and treating the outbreak if:

a. Vaccination against the disease is recommended by the Advisory Committee on Immunization Practices (ACIP).
b. There is no medically confirmed health reason not to administer the vaccination. Vaccination of the individual and minor would, more likely than not, have prevented the outbreak.

In considering which costs, if any, a public agency may impose on that person, the agency shall consider:

a. How contagious the disease is.
b. The rate of complications imposing long-term costs from the disease.
c. The difficulty of investigating and containing the disease.
d. Other equities, such as objective difficulties in obtaining a vaccine or getting a child vaccinated.

SECTION 2: It is a public nuisance for any person who may be liable to any agency under Section 1 to have failed to obtain a vaccination.

SECTION 3: Any agency responsible for containing and managing the outbreak will determine that the requirements above are fulfilled, assess the costs of investigation, containment and treatment and provide the person with a reasoned decision and an itemized bill. Once provided, the charge constitutes a debt of that person and may be collected by any process available to that agency to collect debts.

SECTION 4: A person determined by any agency to be liable for the payment of any amount under Section

1 or 2 may seek review of the decision to impose costs, and that review will be conducted by a hearing officer agency according to the procedures enumerated in the Administrative Procedures Act or the state equivalent. Judicial review of an agency's final decision is available in accord with the provisions of the Administrative Procedures Act.

SECTION 5: The appropriate state departments shall have the authority to promulgate rules to implement this statute.

SECTION 6: Qualifying for a religious or personal belief exemption under other provisions of state law is not a defense against liability to an agency under this statute.

SECTION 7: A summary of the provisions of this statute will be provided to patients and those who have authority to consent on their behalf at each medical visit in which vaccines should be offered according to the CDC's immunization schedule, and whenever there is a request for any form used to obtain an exemption from the states immunization requirements.

Discussion

The statute makes not vaccinating a public nuisance and forces individuals to internalize those costs. It thus fits comfortably within the ideas of personal responsibility embodied in our system: individuals are free (subject to other applicable rules, like school immunization requirements) not to vaccinate themselves or their children. If, however, an individual's choice creates risk, then the individual is required to pay for those risks if they materialize. The specific risk the statute enacts is the costs of outbreaks borne by those having to contain them. By using principles of nuisance, it justifies liability whether or not we view not vaccinating as negligent. By requiring causation, it keeps the principles of justice that justify compensation in other contexts.

The statute's remedy here is a public law remedy. That means that it needs to follow public law norms in substance and procedures. The decision must be based on the appropriate criteria. Procedurally, it must be reasoned and transparent. Once written and reasoned, allowing the entity seeking reimbursement to collect it as a debt—again, following the Arizona statute—makes the initial process of recouping costs more efficient and streamlined.

The statute offers the individual a process to challenge the decision via, in the first instance, an appeal to the public agency. In contrast to the simple, streamlined

initial billing, the appeal process includes full formal adjudicatory procedures as described in the Administrative Procedures Act (or the state equivalent—for the purposes of the statute, the Administrative Procedures serves as a model and source of procedures). This will provide the parties the right to bring witnesses and documents and rights of cross-examination, as far as feasible. By offering an adversarial process, the statute offers the non-vaccinating party ample opportunity to correct errors in the initial decision. But by making the first step administrative it assures that the decision will be heard by officials with expertise in administrative adjudications and prevents adding burden to the courts. Courts will judicially review the decision if there is further appeal, but will not have to undertake the initial fact-finding.

In section 5, the statute clarifies that the state's decision to allow unvaccinated children to attend school if they obtain an exemption does not relieve the parent making that problematic choice from having to bear the cost of that choice to the public.

Both fairness and deterrence support providing notice to the individual beforehand of the potential costs. While individuals are on constructive notice of the law—not knowing the law is not a defense—it would be more effective and fair to provide individuals with a direct warning, if possible. Of course, if an individual does not visit a doctor or apply for an exemption, it may be impossible to alert them, but if there is an opportunity, they should be put on notice. Section 6 enacts a requirement of notifying the individual in two circumstances: during a doctor visit where vaccines are discussed, and if an individual applies for an exemption.

Conclusion

Not vaccinating has direct costs: beyond a certain level, it can and does increase the incidence of preventable diseases. Outbreaks, in turn, lead to direct monetary costs that often cannot be anticipated in advance, both the costs of treating the disease and the costs of containing it. When those costs come out of the public purse, resources are diverted from other needs, and important public values can suffer. There is abundant data showing that modern vaccines are effective and safe, and their small risks are far outweighed by their tremendous benefits. From this perspective, it is appropriate to require those who choose not to vaccinate to internalize the costs of that choice, rather than imposing them on the public. There are several tools available to allow that. We should use them.

References

1. S. Y. Chen et al., "Health Care-associated Measles Outbreak in the United States after an Importation: Challenges and Economic Impact," Journal of Infectious Disease 203, no. 11 (2011): 1517-1525; D. Sugerman et al., "Measles Outbreak in a Highly Vaccinated Population, San Diego, 2008: Role of the Intentionally Undervaccinated," Pediatrics 125, no. 4 (2010): 747-755; A. Calugar et al., "Nosocomial Pertussis: Cost of an Outbreak and Benefits of Vaccinating Health Care Workers," Clinical Infectious Diseases 42, no. 7 (2006): 981-988; L. H. Lee and M. E. Pichichero, "Cost of Illness Due to Bordatella Pertussis in Families," Archives of Family Medicine 9, no. 10 (2000): 989-996.

2. W. G. Van Panhuis et al., "Contagious Diseases in the United States from 1888 to the Present," New England Journal of Medicine 369, no. 22 (2013): 2152-2158.

3. D. A. Salmon, L. H. Moulton, S. B. Omer, M. P. deHart, S. Stokley, and N. A. Halsey, "Factors Associated with Refusal of Childhood Vaccines among Parents of School-Aged Children," Archives of Pediatric and Adolescent Medicine 159 (2005): 470-476.

4. S. Omer et al., "Nonmedical Exemptions to School Immunization Requirements: Secular Trends and Association of State Policies with Pertussis Incidence," JAMA 296 (2006): 17571763; S. Omer et al., "Geographic Clustering of Nonmedical Exemptions to School Immunization Requirements and Associations with Geographic Clustering of Pertussis," American Journal of Epidemiology 168 (2008): 1389-1396.

5. Centers for Disease Control and Prevention, "Update: Measles—United States, January-July 2008," Morbidity and Mortality Weekly Report 57 (2008): 893-896; I. R. Ortega-Sanchez et al., "The Economic Burden of Sixteen Measles Outbreaks on United States Public Health Departments in 2011," Vaccine 32 (2014): 1311-1317; Centers for Disease Control and Prevention, "Pertussis Epidemic—Washington, 2012," Morbidity and Mortality Weekly Report 61 (2012): 517-522.

6. Centers for Disease Control and Prevention, "Measles Cases in the United States Reach 20-Year High," May 29, 2014, available at <http://www.cdc.gov/media/releases/2014/p0529-measles.html> (last visited September 15, 2015).

7. D. Feikin et al., "Individual and Community Risks of Measles and Pertussis Associated with Personal Exemptions to Immunization," JAMA 284 (2000): 3145-3150; S. Von den Hof et al., "Measles Epidemic in the Netherlands: 1999-2000 " Journal of Infectious Disease 186 (2002): 1483-1486.

8. Lee and Pichichero, supra note 1.

9. J. B. Babigumira et al., "Health Economics of Rubella: A Systematic Review to Assess the Value of Rubella Vaccination," BMC Public Health 13 (2013): 406-418 (represented in 2014 U.S. dollars).

10. C. W. Shepard et al., "Cost-Effectiveness of Conjugate Meningococcal Vaccination Strategies in the United States," Pediatrics 115 (2005): 1220-1232 (represented in 2014 U.S. dollars).

11. Ortega-Sanchez, supra note 5.

12. A. Parker et al., "Implications of a 2005 Measles Outbreak in Indiana for Sustained Elimination of Measles in the United States," New England Journal of Medicine 355 (2006): 447-455.

13. L. Lasher et al., "Contacting Passengers After Exposure to Measles on an International Flight: Implications for Responding to New Disease Threats and Bioterrorism," Public Health Reports 119 (2004): 458-463; T. Chen et al., "Measles Outbreak Associated with an International Youth Sporting Event in the United States, 2007," Pediatric Infectious Disease Journal 29 (2010): 794-800.

14. Chen, supra note 1.

15. M. S. Coleman et al., "Direct Costs of a Single Case of Refugee-Imported Measles in Kentucky," Vaccine 30 (2012): 317321. These numbers are available at: <http://www.usgovernment spending.eom/year_spending_2014USbt_15b s2n_10#usgs302> (last visited September 15, 2015).

16. U.S. Government Spending. 2014, available at <http://www.usgovernmentspending.com/year_spending_2014USbt_15bs2n_10#usgs302> (last visited September 15, 2015).

17. Trust for America's Health, Investing in America's Health: A State-by-State Look at Public Health Funding and Key Health Facts (April 2013), available at <http://healthyamericans.org/assets/files/TFAH2013InvstgAmrcsHlth05%20FINAL.pdf> (last visited September 15, 2015).

18. Ortega-Sanchez, supra note 5.

19. M. Osterholm et al., "Efficacy and Effectiveness of Influenza Vaccines: A Systematic Review and Meta-Analysis," The Lancet Infectious Diseases 12 (2001): 36-44.

20. F. Zhou et al., "Economic Evaluation of the Routine Childhood Immunization Program in the United States, 2009," Pediatrics 133 (2014): 1-9.

21. Pennsylvania v. Gen. Pub. Utils. Corp., 710 F.2d 117, 122-23 (3d Cir. 1983).

22. A. L. Caplan et al., "Free to Choose But Liable for the Consequences: Should Non-Vaccinators Be Penalized for the Harm They Do?" Journal of Law, Medicine & Ethics 40, no. 3 (2012): 606-611.

23. A. M. Kennedy et al., "Vaccine Beliefs of Parents Who Oppose Compulsory Vaccination," Public Health Reports 120 (2005): 252-258.

24. M. A. Maglione, et al., "Safety of Vaccines Used for Routine Immunization of US Children: A Systematic Review," Pediatrics (2014), available at <http://pediatrics.aappublications.org/content/early/2014/06/26/peds.2014-1079.abstract> (last visited September 15, 2015).

25. P. Offit and C. Moser, Vaccines and Your Child: Separating Fact from Fiction (New York: Columbia University Press, 2011); A. Kata, "A Postmodern Pandora's Box: Anti-vaccination Misinformation on the Internet," Vaccine 28(2010): 1709; V. Iannelli, "Anti Vaccine Myths and Misinformation," Pediatrics.About.Com, January 17, 2015, available at <http://pediatrics.about.com/od/immunizations/tp/Anti-Vaccine-Myths-and-Misinformation.htm> (last visited September 15, 2015); S. Calandrillo, "Vanishing Vaccinations: Why Are So Many Americans Opting Out of Vaccinating Their Children," University Michigan Journal of Law Reform 37 (2004): 353-440.

26. P. Offit, Deadly Choices: How the Anti-Vaccine Movement Threatens Us All (New York: Basic Books, 2010): at 111-123.

27. Shorter v. Drury, 695 P.2d 116 (1985), cert, denied, 474 U.S. 827 (1985)).

28. Prince v. Massachusetts, 321 U.S. 158,166-67 (1944).

29. Commonwealth v. Twitchell, 617 N.E.2d 609 (Mass. 1993); State v. Norman, 808 P.2d 1159 (Wash. App. 1991).

30. Vaughan v. Menlove, 132 Eng. Rep. 490 (C.P.) (1837) ("[W]hether the Defendant had acted honestly and bona fide to the best of his own judgment ... would leave so vague a line as to afford no rule at all ... [Because the judgments of individuals are ...] as variable as the length of the foot of each ... we ought rather to adhere to the rule which requires in all cases a regard to caution such as a man of ordinary prudence would observe").

31. Reed v. Tacoma Ry. Power Comp., 188 P. 409 (Wash. 1921).

32. R. Wolfe and L. Sharp, "Vaccination or Immunization? The Impact of Search Terms on the Internet," Journal of Health Communication 10 (2005): 537-551.

33. P. Fine et al., "Herd Immunity: A Rough Guide," Vaccines 52 (2011): 911-916.

34. E. Conis, "How the Poor Get Blamed for Disease," The Atlantic, November 9, 2014, available at <http://www.theatlantic.com/health/archive/2014/ll/how-the-poor-get-blamed-for-disease/382338> (last visited September 15, 2015).

35. D. R. Reiss, "Compensating the Victims of Failure to Vaccinate: What Are the Options?" Cornell Journal of Law and Public Policy 23 (2014): 595-633.

36. Jacobson v. Massachusetts, 197 U.S. 11, 25-27 (1905).

37. Caplan, supra note 22; Reiss, supra note 35.

38. C. Parkins, "Protecting the Herd: A Public Health, Economics and Legal Argument for Taxing Parents Who Opt-Out of Mandatory Childhood Vaccinations," Southern California Interdisciplinary Law Journal 21 (2012): 437-490.

39. O. Lobel and O. Amir, "Healthy Choices: Regulatory Design and Processing Modes of Health Decisions," Social Science Research Network (2011), available at <http://dx.doi.org/10.2139/ssrn,1876734> (last visited September 15, 2015).

40. Zucht v. King, 260 U.S. 174 (1922).

41. M. I. Krauss, "Public Services Meet Private Law," San Diego Law Review 44 (2005): 1-53; T. Lytton, "Should Government Be Allowed to Recover the Costs of Public Services from Tortfeasors?: Tort Subsidies, the Limits of Loss Spreading, and the Free Public Services Doctrine," Tulane Law Review 76 (2002): 727-781.

42. Lytton, supra note 41.

43. 32 American Law Reports 261 (6th ed.); Krauss, supra note 41.

44. See, e.g., Cincinnati v. Beretta U.S.A. Corp., 768 N.E.2d 1136 (Ohio 2002) (holding that a city's allegation that the negligent conduct of the handgun manufacturers, trade associations, and handgun distributor, relating to the manufacture and distribution of firearms, involved continuing misconduct and stated a claim for recoupment of costs of government services, such as police, emergency, health, corrections, and prosecution services under a public nuisance theory); California v.Atl. Richfield Co., 2014 WL 280526 (Cal. Super. 2014) (awarding damages in a lead paint case on a public nuisance theory).

45. E.g. Cal. Health & Saf. Code [section]13009 et seq., NRS 459-537 (2), (3) (Nevada), Alaska Stat. [section] 46.03.822.

46. Wash. Rev. Code Ann. [section] 76.04.495 (West 2014); Cal. Health & Saf. Code [section]13009 et seq. (West 2014); N.C. Gen. Stat. Ann. [section] 106-947 (West 2014).

47. Nev. Rev. Stat. Ann. [section] 459-537 (2), (3) (West 2014); Alaska Stat. Ann. [section] 46.03.822 (West 2014); N.C. Gen. Stat. Ann. [section] 166A-27 (West 2014).

48. Cal. Civ. Code [section] 3479 (West 2014).

49. See, e.g., Sacramento, Cal., Health & Safety Code [section] 8.04.100 (2014), available at <http://qcode.us/codes/sacramento/> (last visited September 15, 2015).

50. Ariz. Rev. Stat. Ann. [section] 28-910 (West 2014).

51. N.C. Gen. Stat. Ann. [section] 166A-19.62 (West 2014).

52. Caplan et al., supra note 22 and Reiss, supra note 35.

. . .

Charlotte A. Moser, BS, is the assistant director of the Vaccine Education Center and the creator of the Parents PACK program at The Children's Hospital of Philadelphia. She has extensively published in scientific journals on the topics of immunology and virology, and is the co-author of Vaccines and Your Child: Separating Fact from Fiction.

Dorit Reiss is Professor of Law at UC Hastings College of the Law in San Francisco. Her current research and publications are focused on legal issues related to vaccines, including exemption laws and tort liability related to non-vaccination.

Robert L. Schwartz, JD, is a Member and Domestic Relations & Family Law Practice Group Chair at Dickinson Wright PLLC in Phoenix. He. Schwartz has been practicing law for over 40 years, specializing in family law; he has testified as an expert in family law matters.

Leonard F. Vernon and Christopher Kent

 **NO**

Chiropractors and Vaccinations: Ethics is the Real Issue

Introduction

Despite survey results, which indicate an increase in parental vaccine safety concerns, routine coverage among US preschool children is at, or near, an all time high (Allred, Shaw, Santibanez, Rickert, & Santoli, 2005). There is, however, continued concern among public health officials that if the anti-vaccination movement were to gain considerable ground in this country, it could lead to a decrease in vaccination rates, as has occurred in other countries where the movement is larger (Gangarosa et al., 1998).

Among the sources that individuals rely on in making the decision not to vaccinate themselves or their children are the media, books, public health authorities, and health care providers (Meszaros et al., 1996). Increased use of the Internet, which now offers access to a great deal of vaccination information, has become a concern for public health officials as well (Schmidt & Ernst, 2003).

Historically, those groups listed as opponents to vaccination are religious organizations and citizens' groups. Campbell, Busse, and Injeyan (2000) add to this list "practitioners and followers of alternative health care systems," including chiropractors, whom the papers' authors (two of whom are chiropractors) describe as a "vocal element in minority." Other authors have described this segment of the profession as a "significant minority of American chiropractors" (Colley & Haas, 1994). This is a statement that on its surface appears as a contradiction.

Philosophical Issues

D. D. Palmer, who founded chiropractic in 1895, was profoundly influenced by the 19th century metaphysical movement. The chiropractic concept that the body is a self-healing mechanism possessing an innate intelligence led Palmer and other chiropractors to eschew drugs, vaccines, and other treatments. D. D. Palmer wrote, "Vaccination and inoculation are pathological; Chiropractic is physiological" (Palmer, 1910, p. 52). Yet, Palmer's criticisms of vaccination were not based solely on philosophical issues. He also made a health freedom argument: "Compulsory vaccination is an outrage and a gross interference with the liberty of the people in a land of freedom" (Palmer, 1910, p. 448).

To focus on the early philosophical background of chiropractic, in an attempt to explain chiropractics' cautionary vaccination position, while ignoring the fact that there is genuine disagreement within the scientific community as to the safety and effectiveness of vaccinations, is misleading at best, and borders on being disingenuous.

The origins and growth of chiropractic have been well documented and include an extensive history of intraprofessional leadership struggles leading to the development of multiple professional organizations, often presenting divergent philosophical views (Wardwell, 1992). The literature has attempted to simplify this division into two camps, "mixers" and "straights" (Phillips, 1995) with the "mixers" being portrayed as the group that is more progressive and change oriented, willing to give up the historical elements of the subluxation complex for an explanation that leans more toward joint dysfunction (Seaman, 1997), whereas the "straights" are described as practitioners who are soldiers in a holy war with a mission to provide a completely different form of health care (Anderson, 1990).

Vaccination Attitudes in the Chiropractic Profession

Attempts have been made to determine the prevalence of anti-vaccination attitudes within the chiropractic profession, and to link these results to a philosophical belief—this being determined by the professional organization in which the chiropractor held membership. One study that used this criterion found a strong anti-vaccination rate of approximately one-third of those surveyed, with the majority of this group holding membership in the

Vernon, Leonard F.; Kent, Christopher, "Chiropractors and Vaccinations: Ethics Is the Real Issue," Complementary *Health Practice Review*, vol. 14, no. 1, January 2009, 36–50. Copyright ©2009 Sage Publications, Inc. All rights reserved. Used with permission.

International Chiropractors Association (ICA; Colley & Haas, 1994). A survey of chiropractic students conducted at The Canadian Memorial Chiropractic College (CMCC), a school known more as a "mixer" school than a "straight" school in terms of philosophical leanings (Keating, 1995), indicated that more than 50% of the study respondents believed that the risks of the pertussis vaccination outweighed its benefits, whereas 81% felt that immunization should not be mandatory, but a voluntary decision, with only 39.5% of fourth-year students agreeing with vaccination. Most students (425 or 91.0%) felt that core CMCC lectures presented vaccination either positively or neutrally, further questioning the extent to which the schools' philosophical leanings played in the development of a student's belief system (Busse, Kulkarni, Campbell, & Injeyan, 2002). In a later study of Canadian chiropractors (Russell, Injeyan, Verhoef, & Eliasziw, 2003), the majority of whom were graduates of CMCC, it was shown that almost 60% of the respondents believed that immunizations were not safe. In this same study, almost 89% of the respondents stated that they believed that people are not adequately informed about the risks of immunization. These appear to indicate that at a minimum, chiropractic's concern regarding vaccines is safety and full disclosure, and that this attitude appears to be prevalent in a majority of the profession, and not, as some authors have written, isolated to a fringe element of the profession whose opposition is solely based on a philosophical background (Campbell et al., 2000; Colley & Haas, 1994).

The strongest belief among chiropractors regarding the issue of vaccinations appears to be freedom of choice in health care, and that adequate information regarding the risks involved with any medical procedure be provided to the patient (Russell et al., 2003). In fact, it is essentially these beliefs that form the basis for the established policy on vaccination of both the American Chiropractic Association (ACA) and the ICA. The World Chiropractic Alliance (WCA) also has a policy of freedom to choose; however, it goes one step further in stating that it is the obligation of medical professionals to advise the patient of the risks/benefits of vaccination. The ACA policy on vaccination reads as follows (ACA, 2008):

Resolved, that the ACA recognize and advise the public that

> Since the scientific community acknowledges that the use of vaccines is not without risk, the ACA supports each individual's right to freedom of choice in his/her own health care based on an informed awareness of the benefits and possible adverse effects of vaccination. The ACA is supportive of a conscience clause or waiver in

compulsory vaccination laws thereby maintaining an individual's right to freedom of choice in health care matters and providing an alternative elective course of action regarding vaccination (Ratified by the House of Delegates, July 1993, Revised and Ratified June 1998).

The ICA policy on vaccination reads as follows (ICA Policy Statements, 2008):

> ICA recognizes that vaccines are not without risk and supports freedom of choice in such matters. The use of vaccines is not without risk. The ICA supports each individual's right to select his or her own health care and to be made aware of the possible adverse effects of vaccines upon a human body. In accordance with such principles and based upon the individual's right to freedom of choice, the ICA is opposed to compulsory programs which infringe upon such rights (p. 19).

It is the position of the WCA, in its position statement entitled "Vaccinations and freedom of choice in health care" that

> No person should be forced by government regulation or societal pressure to receive any medication or treatment, including vaccines, against his or her will. This includes mandated vaccines as a requirement for public school admission or for employment eligibility.

> All medical practitioners and public health care officials should be obligated to provide full disclosure of the potential risks of vaccines, including those given to school children in mass vaccination programs. This disclosure should include the relevant facts about the growing concern about vaccines including, but not limited to, the following documented research and actions by health care advocates (WCA).

Historical Background

Many observers believe that the anti-vaccination and health freedom movements are a recent phenomenon, and a consequence of concerns arising from the large number of immunizations now given to children at a very early age; actually, concern over vaccination began shortly after the introduction of the smallpox vaccination and has continued ever since (Robert & Sharp, 2002).

Widespread vaccination began in the early 1800s following Edward Jenner's presentation of an article to the Royal Society of London in 1796 detailing his success in preventing smallpox in 13 people by inoculation with live infectious material from the pustules or scabs of people infected with cowpox. The process induced cowpox, a mild viral disease that conferred immunity to smallpox. Jenner called the cowpox material "vaccine" (from *vacca*, the Latin for cow), and the process "vaccination". Although Jenner did not discover vaccination, (Horton, 1995) he was the first person to confer scientific status on the procedure and was chiefly responsible for popularizing it (Barquet & Domingo, 1997).

Legal Issues

Mandatory Vaccination

By the mid-1800s, the United Kingdom had instituted various laws regarding vaccinations. The Vaccination Act of 1840 provided free vaccinations for the poor and outlawed "inoculation," which at that time meant "variolation," inoculation of smallpox material (usually at an unobtrusive site, to prevent later disfigurement by natural infection). The Vaccination Act of 1853 made vaccination compulsory for all infants in the first 3 months of life and made defaulting parents liable to a fine or imprisonment. In 1867, an Act of Parliament extended the compulsory vaccination requirement to age 14, with cumulative penalties for noncompliance. These laws were a political innovation that extended government powers into areas of traditional civil liberties in the name of public health (Porter & Porter, 1998).

Towards the end of the 19th century, anti-vaccination activity also began increasing in the United States. In the 1870s, smallpox became epidemic, and states attempted to enforce existing vaccination laws or pass new ones, in turn spawning a vigorous anti-vaccination movement. In 1879, after a visit to New York by William Tebb, the leading British anti-vaccinationist, the Anti-Vaccination Society of America was founded. Subsequently, the New England Anti-Compulsory Vaccination League was formed in 1882, and the Anti-Vaccination League of New York City in 1885. Using pamphlets, the courts, and vigorous fights on the floors of state legislatures, the anti-vaccinationists succeeded in repealing compulsory vaccination laws in California, Illinois, Indiana, Minnesota, Utah, West Virginia, and Wisconsin, while a continual battle was waged between public health authorities and anti-vaccinationists in the courts of others states (Williamson, 1984). In the historic case *Jacobson v. Massachusetts* (Supreme Court of the United States, 1905), the United States Supreme Court upheld the right of a state, under its police power, to enforce mandatory vaccination. As stated by the Court,

"The possession and enjoyment of all rights are subject to such reasonable conditions as may be deemed by the governing authority of the country essential to the safety, health, peace, good order and morals of the community . . . a community has the right to protect itself against an epidemic of disease which threatens the safety of its members . . . we do not perceive that this legislation has invaded by right secured by the Federal Constitution."

McCoy (2008) notes that measles outbreaks in the 1960s and 1970s led to an aggressive initiative to raise vaccination levels, and that by 2004, only four states did not have mandatory vaccination requirements for all grades through high school. Although there is no constitutional mandate to do so, 48 states provide for religious exemptions, and 20 have provisions for exemptions based on philosophical beliefs. Every state provides exemption for medical reasons, although the application of the law may be broadly or narrowly construed.

Oversight of Vaccine Manufacturing

Although attempts would be made to establish some form of governmental oversight of vaccine manufacturers, it would not be until 1902, in response to public outcry following the death of 13 children who had received injections of diphtheria antitoxin contaminated with tetanus toxin, that congress would pass the Biologics Control Act. This act required biologics to be manufactured in a manner that assured their safety, purity, and potency. Responsibility for these regulations was assigned originally to the Hygienic Laboratory of the Public Health Service, which evolved into the National Institutes of Health. The regulation of biologics, including vaccines, was eventually transferred to the Food and Drug Administration (FDA) in 1972 (Kaufman, 1967).

The Vaccine Safety Movement in the United States

Most medical historians agree that public concern for vaccine safety in the present era in the United States began following what has become known as "The Cutter Incident" (Offit, 2005a, 2005b). In 1955, Cutter Laboratories, one of several companies licensed by the US government to produce Salk polio vaccine, encountered a production error. The error caused certain lots of the Cutter vaccine to be tainted with live polio; this event has been called one of the worst pharmaceutical disasters in US history, and one that caused several thousand children to be exposed to live polio virus on vaccination (Offit, 2005a, 2005b). The production mistake resulted in 120,000 doses of polio vaccine that contained live polio virus. Of the children who received the vaccine, 40,000 developed abortive poliomyelitis (a form of the disease that does not involve the central nervous system), 56 developed paralytic polio-myelitis, and of these, 5 children died as a result of polio infection (Nathanson & Langmuir, 1963). Eventually, with the aid of Dr. Salk, a new set of safety standards was developed, and the wheels of the polio vaccination program slowly began to turn again; however, the credibility of the vaccine manufacturing industry remained suspect in the minds of a great deal of the public (Engel, 1955).

Problems remain in the manufacturing process of vaccines, even today. Recent vaccine recalls such as the one in December 2007 by Merck & Co. Inc., of about 1.2 million doses of its PedvaxHIB and Comvax immunizations (used to prevent pneumonia, meningitis, and hepatitis B) occurred when, during testing, Merck found certain bacteria in their vaccine manufacturing equipment at the plant where the vaccines are manufactured (MSNBC, 2008).

President Gerald Ford, confronted with a potential swine flu pandemic, urged that every person in the United States be vaccinated for the disease; eventually, almost 24% of the population was vaccinated. A halt to the program occurred, when, because of a reaction to the vaccine, about 500 cases of Guillain-Barré syndrome were found shortly after vaccination occurred (Schonberger, Bregman, & Sullivan-Bolyai, 1979). This resulted in death from severe pulmonary complications for 25 people. In the end, more people died from the vaccine than from the swine flu (Warner, 1999). Other cases of adverse vaccine reactions, and possible links to asthma, multiple sclerosis, and diabetes, have been widely reported in the literature (Classen & Classen, 1997; Gout & Lyon-Caen, 1998; Kemp, Pearce, & Fitzharris, 1997; Wakefield, Murch, & Anthony, 1998).

In February of 2007, reports in the United States of cases of infants suffering intussusception as a result of taking a new vaccine RotaTeq against the rotavirus, prompted the US FDA to issue a warning after 28 cases of the life-threatening condition were linked to the vaccine. The manufacturer, Merck, said RotaTeq was safe and was tested in trials involving 70,000 infants (Gillis, 2006). Herein lies another problem: How is safety determined?

In the United States, the postlicensure program for vaccine safety is a cooperative effort between the Centers for Disease Control and Prevention (CDC) and the FDA. The Vaccine Adverse Event Reporting System (VAERS) is a postmarketing safety surveillance program, which collects information about adverse events that occur after the administration of US licensed vaccines. VAERS consolidates these voluntarily submitted reports of suspected vaccine adverse effects from manufacturers, health care workers, and patients, looking for clues that might indicate a problem with a vaccine. The question is how reliable are the data? Although the National Childhood Vaccine Injury Act of 1986 (Pub L No 99-660) obliges physicians to submit certain reports, VAERS data are derived from what is best described as "a passive drug safety surveillance program with a highly variable fraction of actual event numbers" (Wise et al., 2000). The government, by its own estimates, agrees that adverse reporting to the system is low, with the FDA estimating that as few as 1% of serious adverse reactions to vaccines are ever reported, and the CDC admitting that only about 10% of such events are ever reported (Department of Health and Human Adverse Event Reporting System, 2007; Kessler, 1993).

Ethical Issues

Perle and Ferrance (2005) have raised the issue of ethics in the vaccination debate within the chiropractic community. The authors describe a segment of chiropractic as "zealously anti-vaccination" and then go on to compare the fanaticism of this movement and "their meetings" as "similar to the level of fanaticism one sees in some religious meetings." An extensive search of the professions' trade journals failed to yield advertisements for such chiropractic anti-vaccination events.

No one is denying that there are persons who could be described as zealots in the antivaccination movement, some of whom are chiropractors. An example of this can be seen in media reports of a New Jersey chiropractor who has started a church, The Congregation of Universal Wisdom, which does not require members to give up their current religion, and which was established for anyone who wishes to seek a religious exemption to mandatory vaccination laws. The tenets of the church consider "the injection into the body of medication or other matter of substances that defy natural law" as sacrilege (McNeil, 2003).

Although some may consider this group to be a fringe element, to describe it as such within chiropractic would not be fair. We would venture to say that a majority of the profession would support this groups' right to exist because it avails parents of an option for vaccine exemption.

Attack on the anti-vaccination chiropractors by Perle and Ferrances (2005) include statements, such as "some of them push the concept that vaccinations are the major contributor to the increases in certain diseases (e.g., asthma, autism, juvenile diabetes, learning disabilities and attention deficit hyperactivity disorder [ADHD])" (Jaroff, 2005), implying that any suggestion of these potential adverse effects to a patient is simply ludicrous and would place the practitioner outside the mainstream of chiropractic. The irony here is that experts outside of chiropractic believe that there may in fact be a link. Take, for example, the recent decision by the government's Division of Vaccine Injury Compensation, which concluded that five shots Hannah Poling received in July 2000, when she was 19 months old, "significantly aggravated an underlying mitochondrial disorder" and resulted in a brain disorder "with features of autism spectrum disorder." It should be noted here that Hannah Poling's father is a prominent Georgia neurologist, and her mother is a registered nurse and an attorney; both of whom helped convince the panel of the vaccination–autism link that led to the decision. The decision was the first time the government panel agreed that there was evidence of the link (Wallis, 2008).

Perle and Ferrance imply that chiropractors have abdicated their ethical responsibility to the patient when they talk about the negative aspects of vaccination. They cite as their reason "because most fail to include discussion as to their benefits." They note that by giving any anti-vaccination information, "It harms people by scaring them away from preventive treatments—vaccinations—that have been shown to be effective, with real but small risks comparable to chiropractic care itself" (Perle & Ferrance, 2005; Rome, 1999). Although the authors focus on extremely rare complications resulting from spinal manipulation, the data from insurance claims in the United States estimate that there is in fact only 1 stroke per 2 million after a chiropractic adjustment (Dabbs & Lauretti, 1995) and while also rare, the immediate adverse reactions associated with vaccinations are more common than serious manipulation-related complications, and the actual harm may not be known for decades because long-term adverse outcomes are biologically plausible and may be occurring, given findings from recent epidemiologic studies.

Two committees convened by the Institute of Medicine concluded that there are causal relationships of measles–mumps–rubella (MMR) and diphtheria–tetanus–pertussis (DTP) vaccines with anaphylaxis (Howson, Howe, & Fineberg, 1991; Stratton, Howe, & Johnston, 1994). The estimated rates of anaphylaxis range from 50 per million children for MMR to 60 per million children for three doses of DTP. The death rate from anaphylaxis is about 5% (Yocum & Khan, 1994); thus, for every million children given MMR or three doses of DTP, two to three children are expected to die. Of seven studies addressing the possible association of pertussis or DTP immunization with subsequent development of asthma or other allergies (Farooqi & Hopkin, 1998; Henderson, North, Griffiths, Harvey, & Golding, 1999; Hurwitz & Morgenstern, 2000; Kemp et al., 1997; Nilsson, Kjellman, & Bjorksten, 1998; Nilsson, Kjellman, Storsaeter, Gustafsson, & Olin, 1969; Odent, Culpin, & Kimmel, 1994), findings from four studies (Farooqi & Hopkin, 1998; Hurwitz & Morgenstern, 2000; Kemp et al., 1997; Odent et al., 1994) are suggestive of an increased risk of allergic disease with immunization. Evidence from animal and human studies support the hypothesis that vaccinations may be one of many genetic and environmental factors contributing to the increasing prevalence of atopic disease in recent years (Parronchi, Brugnolo, Sampognaro, & Maggi, 2000).

The position espoused by both Perle and Ferrance (2005) fails to address the ethical issue of one's obligation to one's fellow human beings. If one has information regarding a potential danger to a fellow human being, is there not a moral/ethical obligation to discuss this potential for harm with them? Does being a chiropractor exempt one from this obligation?

Perle and Ferrance (2005) fail to acknowledge that the use of some vaccines on a routine basis has become a contested issue within the community of medical ethicists. Both the varicella vaccine and the hepatitis B vaccine have come under question by this group, who argue that, for a prophylactic intervention to be performed in the interest of public health rather than in the best interest of the individual, there must be certain criteria met. This includes evidence that the disease must have serious consequences if transmitted (Hodges, Svoboda, & Van Howe, 2002). To qualify under this definition, the disease must carry a high rate of morbidity and mortality. Experts have argued that in light of the low mortality and morbidity associated with chicken pox, as well as the unknown long-term efficacy of the varicella vaccine, that it may fail the definition of "serious consequences if transmitted." The same argument is made by medical ethicists with regard to the routine immunization against hepatitis B. Because this is a disease that is spread through sexual contact and intravenous drug use, and has a potential for serious adverse reactions, some experts argue that this vaccine should be limited to high-risk populations and should not be given on a routine basis (Hodges et al., 2002; Van Damme, 2001). The fact is that what we may be witnessing is an attempt by would-be medical ethicists like Perle and Ferrance to promote their own political agenda.

Any discussion regarding professional ethics and vaccination cannot be limited to chiropractic, as medicine has similar ethical issues. The highly regarded international guidelines for research on human participants, the Declaration of Helsinki, states that "considerations related to the well-being of human subjects should take precedence over the interests of science and society" (World Medical Association, 2000). The authors argue that these guidelines are appropriate not only for participants in formal research programs but are applicable to all medical procedures.

The decision to refuse immunization has a societal consequence. In a community in which most people are vaccinated, the likelihood of members being exposed to the corresponding infection is quite low. As a result, it may be in an individual's best interest not to get vaccinated, as they may benefit from the high vaccination rate, reducing the likelihood of infection without exposing themselves to any vaccine-associated risks, however small. Consequently, is it not the ethical responsibility of the physician to discuss this concept with patients? The truth is that the participant is not discussed because of the fear that if too many individuals take this approach, the community's immunity will not be sufficient to prevent outbreaks of disease.

Another question that the physician must ask is, "Would I be so cavalier in the administration of vaccinations if I were not exempt from liability?" This is certainly an ethical issue that is not widely discussed. Because most vaccines are mandated by state law, the manufacturer and the physician administering the vaccine are substantially relieved of liability for adverse effects under federal law. The relationship of patient and physician is now conflicted, and in administering the vaccine, the physician is now serving as the agent of the state, applying the new population-based ethic in which the interests of the individual patient may be sacrificed to the "needs of society."

Ethical issues are not confined to health care practitioners. What about the person who has opted out of vaccination? Have they violated an ethical principle? Ethicists would argue that people who refuse vaccinations are taking advantage of everyone else who has been vaccinated. Epidemiologists believe that once the majority of a population is vaccinated, there are few susceptible people the disease can infect, thus lowering the odds of an outbreak. People who refuse to be vaccinated have been labeled "free riders" by ethicists, who claim that these objectors can afford to refuse the vaccine because they are surrounded by people who have fulfilled their obligations to the community (Lotte, 2008).

We fail to see how supplying vaccine risk information to patients is unethical, as has been suggested by Perle and Ferrance (2005). These two authors do, however, illustrate the complexities that are involved in examining the ethical issues of vaccination.

Conclusions

With mounting evidence that there may be a link between vaccines adverse reactions and certain illnesses (Wallis, 2008), and that the long-term consequences of vaccination practices remains largely unknown, why are certain members of the chiropractic profession encouraging us to run from the issue, continuing to portray this segment of the profession as a small minority or fringe element of the profession? Clearly, the belief that vaccinations carry risk and that patients/parents should be properly informed of these risks, permeates almost every segment of the chiropractic profession, regardless of school or philosophical affiliation. Any attempt to tie this position exclusively to philosophical beliefs is an oversimplification of the issue. The real reason may lie in acceptance, or the lack of it, by the medical community. Strauss has said "the profession continues to vacillate between attacking the medical establishment and craving acceptance from it. We attack medicine but we want to be accepted as equal to the medical doctor . . . " (Strauss, 1999).

It is more than likely that this craving for acceptance from the medical community has caused some in the profession to portray those chiropractors who disseminate vaccination information as zealots and a minority.

Further evidence of this can be seen in the recent attempts in the profession to establish cultural authority for chiropractic as the doctor of the spine. In their paper, *Chiropractic as spine care: A model for the profession*, Nelson et al. (2005) state that the chiropractic profession has failed to develop the legitimacy necessary to defend its autonomy and cultural authority. They go on to cite the following reasons for this saying: Three specific characteristics of the profession are identified as impediments to the creation of a credible definition of chiropractic: departures from accepted standards of professional ethics, reliance on obsolete principles of chiropractic philosophy, and the promotion of chiropractors as primary care providers.

If chiropractic is to establish itself as "the" spine doctor in society then, they suggest, the profession must abandon its philosophical tenets. What some are saying is that for the profession to succeed, it must abandon its vitalistic belief system and avoid issues such as vaccination. It must also convince the medical establishment that those chiropractors who are involved in issues such as vaccination are a small minority, an embarrassing fringe element within chiropractic. The irony of this is that while chiropractic as a profession is being encouraged to abandon its beliefs and to run from the controversial issue of vaccination, the medical research community has a different view. Chen (1999) of the CDC in Atlanta stated the following:

In this evolutionary process, we have been relatively slow in appreciating the importance that the public now places on vaccine safety. In fact, much of our resource allocations still unfortunately reflect safety last rather than safety first. This reflects in part an unfortunate legacy of us characterizing this arena for years in narrow, negative terms of adverse events, instead of the more broad and positive terms of safety. Furthermore, it shows that we have not been as interested in preventing vaccine-induced illnesses as we are with vaccine-preventable diseases.

We believe that Dr. Chen's statement is exactly the reason why the majority of chiropractors supply vaccine information to their patients, regardless of their philosophical affiliation. This is not an issue rooted in 19th century philosophy. It is however, an issue of trust, or better stated, a lack of trust. While this lack of trust usually does not extend to the individual physician, it does extend to organized medicine and large pharmaceutical companies, and the often alleged incestuous relationship the two have enjoyed (Zuger, 2004).

The reasons for this belief paradigm can be well substantiated. Over the years organized medicine has made multiple efforts to eliminate the chiropractic profession (Getzendanner, 1988), an effort that continues to this day (Devitt, 2006). At the same time, vaccine manufacturers have not always been forthcoming when it comes to the issue of vaccine safety (Mackenzie, 2008). Additionally, recent drug recalls amidst pharmaceutical companies' failure to release negative data about its drugs have all added to this distrust, leading to a perception among the public of *profit before safety* (Kaufman, 2005).

It is the lack of credibility among pharmaceutical companies, as well as the belief that organized medicine is too closely linked to pharmaceutical companies, that has, in essence, caused a crisis in confidence, both among chiropractors and the public. This attitude of mistrust has been confirmed in a study among parents who refused vaccinations for their children; the study found that health professionals are not perceived as providers of balanced information (Sporton & Francis, 2001).

Others studies have confirmed what these parents suspected. In a national survey of pediatricians, researchers found that while the majority of providers reported discussing some aspect of vaccine communication, 40% indicated that they did not mention risks. In the same study (despite the law that became effective in 1988 that requires physicians to supply those receiving a vaccination or the parent of a child receiving a vaccination with a discloser document known as the Vaccination Information Statement [VIS]), 31% of pediatricians and 28% of family physicians in private practice reported that their offices were not using the VIS at all, and 38% and 42%, respectively, were not giving the VIS at every visit. The authors of the study note that this noncompliance may be even greater than reported in the study because the findings are based on self-reporting (Davis et al., 2001).

Other studies have reported similar findings, including reports that physicians say little to parents about immunizations (Clayton, Hickson, & Miller, 1994; Cross, Davis, & Arnold, 1999; Fulginiti, 1982, 1984; Page, Eason, Humiston, & Barker, 2000). This, in spite of the fact that Stoto and colleagues of the Institute of Medicine's Vaccine Safety Forum have pointed out that "people appreciate receiving vaccine risk information; it is a fundamental form of respect and it indicates they are treated more equally in the decision-making process" (Stoto, Evans, & Bostrom, 1998, pp.237-239).

The call for full disclosure of potential adverse events from vaccinations has come from within the medical community itself. David C. Classen, an infectious disease physician at Latter Day Saints Hospital, in Salt Lake City, believes that there is a severe weakness in prelicensure testing and that

> . . . the public should be fully informed that vaccines, though effective in preventing infections, may have long term adverse effects. An educated public will probably increasingly demand proper safety studies before widespread immunization . . . (Classen & Classen, 1999, p. 193).

We conclude that it is this respect for the patient's need for balanced information, coupled with the growing distrust of pharmaceutical companies and the lack of confidence in government oversight (e.g., Furberg, Levin, Gross, Shapiro, & Strom, 2006) and not the dogmatic adherence to a philosophical belief system that has resulted in the majority of chiropractors' becoming the disseminators of vaccine information. We further conclude that a minority of the chiropractic profession would have this majority cease from offering information about the possible adverse effects of vaccination in its effort to gain cultural authority for the chiropractic profession (Nilsson et al., 1969). We also conclude that the chiropractic profession must stop this continued fleeing from the unpopular, such as the refusal to advocate vaccination, in the effort to gain "acceptance." Until the day comes when chiropractors begin to trust the messages from the health institutions, the profession should continue to inform and advise parents of the inherent risks as well as benefits associated with immunizations, in terms of their safety and effectiveness.

There are a number of ethicists in the medical community who argue against compulsory immunization; they believe that, "compulsory immunization infringes the autonomy of parents to make choices about child rearing, an autonomy which we generally respect unless doing so seriously endangers the child's health" (Isaacs, Kilham, & Marshall, 2004).

We argue that the complex clinical and ethical issues associated with vaccination need to be made on an individual basis, incorporating the principles of freedom of choice and informed consent.

References

Allred, N. J., Shaw, K. M., Santibanez, T. A., Rickert, D. L., & Santoli, J. M. (2005). Parental vaccine safety concerns. Results from the National Immunization Survey, 2001-2202. *American Journal of Preventive Medicine, 28*, 2.

American Chiropractic Association. (2008). ACA policies on public health and related matters. From http://www.amerchiro.org/level2_css.cfm?T1ID=10&T2ID=117#106

Anderson, R. (1990). Chiropractors for and against vaccines. *Medical Anthropology, 12*, 169-186.

Barquet, N., & Domingo, P. (1997). Smallpox: The triumph over the most terrible of the ministers of death. *Annals of Internal Medicine, 127*, 635-642.

Busse, J. W., Kulkarni, A. V., Campbell, J. B., & Injeyan, H. S. (2002). Attitudes toward vaccination: a survey of Canadian chiropractic students. *Canadian Medical Association Journal, 166*, 1544-1545.

Campbell, J. B., Busse, J. W., & Injeyan, H. S. (2000). Chiropractors and vaccination: a historical perspective. *Pediatrics, 105*, E43.

Chen, R. T. (1999). Vaccine risks: Real, perceived and unknown. *Vaccine, 17*(Suppl. 3), S41-S46.

Classen, D. C., & Classen, J. B. (1997). The timing of pediatric immunization and the risk of insulin-dependent diabetes mellitus. *Infectious Diseases in Clinical Practice, 6*, 449-454.

Classen, D. C., & Classen, J. B. (1999). Public should be told that vaccines may have long term adverse effects. *BMJ, 318*, 193.

Clayton, E., Hickson, G., & Miller, C. (1994). Parents' responses to vaccine information pamphlets. *Pediatrics, 93*, 369-372.

Colley, F., & Haas, M. (1994). Attitudes on immunization: A survey of American chiropractors. *Journal of Manipulative and Physiological Therapeutics, 17*, 584-590.

Cross, J., Davis, T. C., & Arnold, C. (1999). Physicians are from Pluto, nurses are from Jupiter, and parents are from Mercury: Focus group interviews on immunization practices. *Pediatric Research, 45*, 2.

Dabbs, V., & Lauretti, W. J. (1995). A risk assessment of cervical manipulation vs NSAIDs for the treatment of neck pain. *Journal of Manipulative and Physiological Therapeutics, 18*, 530-536.

Davis, T. C., Fredrickson, D. D., Arnold, C. L., Cross, J. T., Humiston, S. G., Green, K. W., et al. (2001). Childhood vaccine risk/benefit communication in private practice office settings: A national survey. *Pediatrics, 107*, E17.

Department of Health And Human Services Public Health Service Food And Drug Administration/ Centers For Disease Control Vaccine Adverse Event Reporting System (VAERS). Retrieved June 2007, from http://vaers.hhs.gov/search/README.txt

Devitt, M. (2006). AMA creates "Partnership" to limit other providers' scope of practice. The next attempt to "contain and eliminate" chiropractic? *Dynamic Chiropractic*. Retrieved June 6, 2006, from http:// www.chiroweb.com/mpacms/dc/article.php?id=51219

Engel, L. (1955, August). The Salk vaccine: What caused the mess? *Harpers Magazine*, 27-33.

Farooqi, I. S., & Hopkin, J. M. (1998). Early childhood infection and atopic disorder. *Thorax, 53*, 927-932.

Fulginiti, V. A. (1982). Informed consent in Immunization practice. *Immunization in Clinical Practice*, 29-47.

Fulginiti, V. A. (1984). Patient education for immunizations. *Pediatrics* (Suppl):961-963.

Furberg, C. D., Levin, A. A., Gross, P. A., Shapiro, R. S., & Strom, B. L. (2006). The FDA and drug safety: A proposal for sweeping changes. *Archives of Internal Medicine, 166*. Retreived October 9, 2006, from www.archinternmed.com

Gangarosa, E. J., Galazka, A. M., Wolf, C. R., Phillips, L. M., Gangarosa, R. E., & Chen, R. T. (1998). Impact of the anti-vaccine movements on pertussis control: the untold story. *Lancet, 351*, 356-361.

Getzendanner, S. (1988). Permanent injunction order against the AMA. *JAMA, 259*, 81.

Gillis, J. (2006, February 4). New vaccine against rotavirus approved. *The Washington Post*, p. D01.

Gout, O., & Lyon-Caen, O. (1998). Multiple sclerosis and hepatitis B vaccination. *Revue Neurologique, 154*, 205-207.

Henderson, J., North, K., Griffiths, M., Harvey, I., & Golding, J. (1999). Pertussis vaccination and wheezing illnesses in young children: prospective cohort study. *BMJ, 318,* 1173-1176.

Hodges, F. M., Svoboda, J. S., & Van Howe, R. S. (2002). Prophylactic interventions on children: balancing human rights with public health. *Journal of Medical Ethics, 28,* 10-16.

Horton, R. (1995). Myths in medicine: Jenner did not discover vaccination. *BMJ, 310,* 62.

Howson, C. P., Howe, C. J., & Fineberg, H. V. (1991). *Adverse effects of pertussis and rubella vaccines: A report of the Committee to review the adverse consequences of pertussis and rubella vaccines.* Washington, DC: National Academy Press.

Hurwitz, E. L., & Morgenstern, H. (2000). Effects of diphtheria-tetanus-pertussis or tetanus vaccination on allergies and allergy-related respiratory symptoms among children and adolescents in the United States. *Journal of Manipulative and Physiological Therapeutics, 23,* 81-90.

ICA Policy Statements. (2008). From http://www.chiropractic.org/index.php?p=ica/policies#immunization

Isaacs, D., Kilham, H. A., & Marshall, H. (2004). Should routine childhood immunizations be compulsory? *Journal of Paediatrics and Child Health, 40,* 392-396.

Jaroff, L. (2005, June 7) Chiropractors v. vaccination. *Time Magazine.* From http://www.time.com/time/columnist/jaroff/article/0,9565,1069538,00.html

Kaufman, M. (1967). The American anti-vaccinationists and their arguments. *Bulletin of the History of Medicine, 41,* 463-478.

Kaufman, M. (2005, February 26). Drugs get good ratings, but drugmakers less so; industry targets profit primarily, Americans think. Washington Post, p. A03.

Keating, J. (1995, December 4). Birth of the CMCC. *Dynamic Chiropractic,* p. 21.

Kemp, T., Pearce, N., & Fitzharris, P. (1997). Is infant immunization a risk factor for childhood asthma or allergy? *Epidemiology, 8,* 678-680.

Kessler, D. (1993). Introducing MedWatch: A new approach to reporting medication and device adverse effect and product problems. *JAMA, 269,* 2765-2768.

Lotte, A. (2008). Mass-vaccination programmes and the value of respect for autonomy bioethics. doi:10.1111/j.1467-8519.2008.00630.x.

Mackenzie, J. (2008). French judges probe firms over vaccinations. Retrieved February 1, 2008, from http://www.reuters.com/article/rbssHealthcareNews/idUSL0173467120080201

McCoy, M. (2008). Autonomy, consent, and medical paternalism: Legal issues in medical intervention. *Journal of Alternative and Complementary Medicine, 14,* 6.

McNeil, D. G. (2003, January 14). Congregation of Universal Wisdom. *The New York Times online.* From http://query.nytimes.com/gst/fullpage.html?res=9E01E5DA1531F937A25752C0A9659CB63&sec=health&spon=&scp=1&sq=Congregation%20of%20Universal%20Wisdom%20&st=cse

Meszaros, J. R., Asch, D. A., Baron, J., Hershey, J. C., Kunreuther, H., & Schwartz-Buzaglo, J. (1996). Cognitive processes and the decisions of some parents to forgo pertussis vaccination for their children. *Journal of Clinical Epidemiology, 49,* 697-703.

MSNBC. (2008). FDA found concerns at Merck vaccine plant. Retrieved April 24, 2008, from http://www.msnbc.msn.com/id/24301679/

Nathanson, N., & Langmuir, A. D. (1963). The cutter incident poliomyelitis following formaldehyde-inactivated poliovirus vaccination in the United States during the spring of 1955. II. Relationship of poliomyelitis to Cutter vaccine. *American Journal of Hygiene, 78,* 29-60.

Nelson, C. F., Lawrence, D. J., Triano, J. J., Bronfort, G., Perle, S. M., Metz, R. D., et al. (2005). Chiropractic as spine care: a model for the profession. *Chiropractic & Osteopathy, 13,* 9.

Nilsson, L., Kjellman, I. M., Storsaeter, J., Gustafsson, L., & Olin, P. (1969). Lack of association between pertussis vaccination and symptoms of asthma and allergy [letter]. *JAMA, 275,* 760.

Nilsson, L., Kjellman, N. I., & Bjorksten, B. (1998). A randomized controlled trial of the effect of pertussis vaccines on atopic disease. *Archives of Pediatrics & Adolescent Medicine, 152,* 734-738.

Odent, M. R., Culpin, E. E., & Kimmel, T. (1994). Pertussis vaccination and asthma: is there a link? *JAMA, 272,* 592-593.

Offit, P. A. (2005a). The Cutter incident, 50 years later. *The New England Journal of Medicine, 352,* 1411-1412.

Offit, P. A. (2005b). *The Cutter incident: How America's first polio vaccine led to the growing vaccine crisis.* New Haven, CT: Yale University Press.

Page, D., Eason, P., Humiston, S., & Barker, W. (2000). Notes from the Association of Teachers of Preventive Medicine: vaccine risk/benefit communication project. *Archives of Pediatrics & Adolescent Medicine, 18,* 47-50.

Palmer, D. D. (1910). *The Chiropractor's Adjuster.* Portland, OR: Portland Printing House.

Parronchi, P., Brugnolo, F., Sampognaro, S., & Maggi, E. (2000). Genetic and environmental factors contributing to the onset of allergic disorders. *International Archives of Allergy and Immunology, 121*, 2-9.

Perle, S. & Ferrance, R. (2005). What's good for the goose is ... Ethics and vaccinations. *Dynamic Chiropractic*. Retrieved February 12, 2005, from http://www.chiroweb.com/mpacms/dc/article.php?id=50074

Phillips, R. B. (1995). Philosophy and chiropractic: Divisions and directions. *Journal of Chiropractic Humanities, 5*, 2-7.

Porter, D., & Porter, R. (1998). The politics of prevention: anti-vaccinationism and public health in nineteenthcentury England. *Medical History, 32*, 231-252.

Robert, W. M., & Sharp, L. K. (2002). Anti-vaccinationists past and present. *British Medical Journal, 325*, 430-443.

Rome, P. (1999). Perspectives: An overview of comparative considerations of cerebrovascular accidents. *Chiropractic Journal of Australia, 29*, 87-102.

Russell, M. L., Injeyan, H. S., Verhoef, M. J., & Eliasziw, M. (2003). Beliefs and behaviors: understanding chiropractic and immunization. *Vaccine, 24*, 372-379.

Schmidt, K., & Ernst, E. (2003). MMR Vaccination advice over the Internet. *Vaccine, 21*, 1044-1047.

Schonberger, L. B., Bregman, D. J., & Sullivan-Bolyai, J. Z. (1979). Guillain–Barre´ syndrome following vaccination in the national influenza immunization program, United States, 1976–1977. *American Journal of Epidemiology, 110*, 105-123.

Seaman, D. R. (1997). Joint complex dysfunction, a novel term to replace subluxation complex: etiology and treatment considerations. *Journal of Manipulative and Physiological Therapeutics, 20*, 634 644.

Sporton, R. K., & Francis, S. A. (2001). Choosing not to immunize: are parents making informed decisions? *Family Practice, 18*, 181-188.

Stoto, M., Evans, G., & Bostrom, A. (1998). Vaccine risk communication. *American Journal of Preventive Medicine, 14*, 237-239.

Stratton, K. R., Howe, C. J., & Johnston, R. B. (1994). *Adverse events associated with childhood vaccines: Evidence bearing on causality*. Washington, DC: National Academy Press.

Strauss, J. (1999). Acceptance and chiropractic. *The Pivot Review* 15, 2. From http://www.f-a-c-e.com/v15n2.htm#acceptance

Jacobson v. Massachusetts, 25 S. Ct. 358, 197 U.S. 11 (1905).

Van Damme, P. (2001). Hepatitis B: Vaccination programs in Europe-an update. *Vaccine, 19*, 2375-2379.

Wakefield, A. J., Murch, S. H., & Anthony, A. (1998). Ileal lymphoid nodular hyperplasia, non-specific colitis and regressive developmental disorder in children. *Lancet, 351*, 637-641.

Wallis, C. (2008, March 10).Case study: Autism and vaccines. *Time Magazine*. From http://www.time.com/time/health/article/0,8599,1721109,00.html

Wardwell, W. I. (1992). *Chiropractic: History and evolution of a new profession*. St Louis, MO: Mosby–Year Book.

Warner, J. (1999). The sky is falling: An analysis of the Swine Flu affair of 1976. From http://www.haverford.edu/biology/edwards/disease/viral_essays/warnervirus.htm

Williamson, S. (1984). Anti-vaccination leagues. *Archives of Disease in Childhood, 59*, 1195-1196.

Wise, R. P., Salive, M. E., Braun, M. M., et al. (2000). Post-licensure safety surveillance for Varicella vaccine. *JAMA, 284*, 1271-1279.

World Medical Association. (2000). Declaration of Helsinki, as amended by the WMA 52nd General Assembly, Edinburgh, Scotland.

World Chiropractic Alliance. (2008). Vaccinations and freedom of choice in health care. Position statement. From http://worldchiropracticalliance.org/positions/vaccines.htm

Yocum, M. W., & Khan, D. A. (1994). Assessment of patients who have experienced anaphylaxis: a 3-year survey. *Mayo Clinic Proceedings. Mayo Clinic, 69*, 16-23.

Zuger, A. (2004, July 27). Commentary. How tightly do ties between doctors and drug company bind? *The New York Times*. From http://query.nytimes.com/gst/fullpage.html?res=9D07E6DD153DF934A15754C0A9629C8B63&sec=&spon=&pagewanted=2

LEONARD F. VERNON is a 1978 graduate of New York Chiropractic College, who has been in private practice for 30 years. He has served as the director of post graduate education for the University of Bridgeport College of Chiropractic as well as associate professor of clinical sciences at the same institution. He has published numerous papers in peer-reviewed journals including the Journal of Manipulative and Physiological Therapeutics, Clinical Rheumatology, The Delaware Medical Journal and the Journal of Addiction Medicine. He co authored the textbook Case Studies in Chiropractic MRI with Christopher Kent.

CHRISTOPHER KENT, co-founder of the Chiropractic Leadership Alliance, is a 1973 graduate of Palmer College of Chiropractic. He is former chair of the United Nations NGO Health Committee, the first chiropractor elected to that office. An attorney as well as a chiropractor, Dr. Kent is an active member of the California bar.

EXPLORING THE ISSUE

Are Parents Morally Obligated to Vaccinate Their Children?

Critical Thinking and Reflection

1. Do you think the common (public) good provided by the mandatory vaccination of eligible individuals, with its resultant herd immunity, supersedes the private good of avoiding the possible negative side effects of a vaccination? Why or why not?
2. All vaccinations pose a slight risk of negative side effects. In your opinion, how significant would these risks have to be in order to morally justify a parent's decision not to vaccinate a child? Explain your position.
3. Is it morally justified to exclude unvaccinated children from school or community activities? Why or why not? Is that fact that some children have medical conditions that prevent them from being vaccinated morally relevant to the decision to exclude unvaccinated children? If so, how?
4. Since most parents are not medical professionals or epidemiologists, what obligations do parents have to inform themselves about vaccinations in order for their decision not to vaccinate a child to be morally justified?
5. Are there any non-medical situations in which a parent's autonomy to make decisions about the welfare of their children might be superseded by a concern for the common good? If so, what morally relevant factors in these situations give the Principle of Welfare precedence over the Principle of Autonomy?

Is There Common Ground?

The authors of both articles concur that parents have an obligation to ensure the welfare of their children by making well-informed health-care decisions on their behalf, such as the decision whether or not to vaccinate against communicable diseases. Aside from this agreement, however, they have little in common.

Vernon and Kent emphasize the Principle of Autonomy, asserting that pediatricians who administer government-mandated vaccinations are violating their responsibility to act for the benefit of their patients and are instead acting as agents of the state. Thus, they emphasize the responsibility of parents to protect the welfare of their children when making decisions about vaccination. On the other hand, Moser, Reiss, and Schwartz emphasize the Principle of Welfare, noting that families are not isolated units, but parts of communities. Thus, when making decisions about vaccination, parents should consider the benefits of herd immunity, which protects the health of vulnerable members of society who cannot be vaccinated.

Additional Resources

Douglas S. Diekema, "Physician Dismissal of Families Who Refuse Vaccination: An Ethical Assessment," Journal of Law, Medicine & Ethics 43:3 (Fall 2015): 654.

Lawrence O. Gostin, "Law, Ethics, and Public Health in the Vaccination Debates: Politics of the Measles Outbreak," Journal of the American Medical Association 313:11 (March 2015): 1099–1100.

Jason L. Schwartz, "Evidence and Ethics in Mandatory Vaccination Policies," The American Journal of Bioethics 13:9 (September 2013).

Brian Martin, "On the Suppression of Vaccination Dissent," Science and Engineering Ethics 21:1 (2015): 43–157.

Internet References . . .

ProCon.org: Should Vaccines Be Required for Children?

> https://vaccines.procon.org

Scientific American blog: The Ethics of Opting out of Vaccination

> https://blogs.scientificamerican.com/doing-good-science/the-ethics-of-opting-out-of-vaccination/

The History of Vaccines: An Educational Resource by the College of Physicians of Philadephia

> https://www.historyofvaccines.org/

World Health Organization: Immunization

> http://www.who.int/topics/immunization/en/

Unit 4

UNIT

Humanity, Nature, and Technology

*W*hen we think about what it means to be human, we cannot help but recognize a paradox. Humans are part of nature, and as such we have certain natural tendencies. One of these natural tendencies is our drive to create technology, which is traditionally considered the opposite of nature. The issues in this unit raise questions about the relationship between humans and the natural world, the relationship between humans and technology, and the relationship between technology and the natural world.

Selected, Edited, and with Issue Framing Material by:
Owen M. Smith, *Stephen F. Austin State University*
and
Anne Collins Smith, *Stephen F. Austin State University*

ISSUE

Does Morality Require Vegetarianism?

YES: Nathan Nobis, from "Vegetarianism and Virtue: Does Consequentialism Demand Too Little?" *Social Theory & Practice* (2002)

NO: Beth K. Haile, from "Virtuous Meat Consumption: A Virtue Ethics Defense of an Omnivorous Way of Life," *Logos: A Journal of Catholic Thought and Culture* (2013)

Learning Outcomes

After reading this issue, you will be able to:

- Use utilitarianism to make a moral argument against the consumption of meat.
- Use virtue ethics to make a moral argument in favor of the consumption of meat.
- Explain how virtue ethics can be combined with utilitarianism to make a moral argument about the consumption of meat.
- Formulate your own position on the consumption of meat and identify evidence supporting your position.
- Identify the main objections to your position and formulate responses to these objections.

ISSUE SUMMARY

YES: Nathan Nobis argues that utilitarianism, an ethical theory in which the moral worth of an action is determined solely by its consequences, requires us to be vegetarians and avoid the consumption of meat. According to Nobis, meat and other animal products are produced under cruel conditions, and utilitarian principles require that we should not participate in or support activities that are cruel or inflict unnecessary pain on animals.

NO: Beth Haile argues that the consumption of meat can be part of a life that seeks to cultivate virtue and avoid vice. Although the way in which our society produces meat for consumption is morally unacceptable, there is nothing intrinsically wrong about the consumption of meat. Once meat is produced in a morally acceptable way, a virtuous life can include the consumption of meat.

Many living beings, especially animals, consume meat or animal products, often in a way that inflicts unnecessary pain and suffering on the animal being consumed. Indeed, some animals kill not only for sustenance, but for reproductive advantage or even as a form of entertainment. Human consumption of meat and animal products, even under cruel conditions, is often justified by terrible examples of "nature, red in tooth and claw."

However, many objections can be raised against the use of animal behavior as a basis for the human consumption of meat and animal products. First, unlike many animals, people do not need to consume meat in order to survive; vegetarianism is a viable method of meeting human nutritional requirements. In addition, humans have the capacity to change their behaviors profoundly in a short period of time. As various cultural practices, such as slavery, have come under rational scrutiny and moral critique, they have been abandoned in favor of less objectionable alternatives. Although human consumption of meat is currently widespread, it is possible for humans to eliminate the practice altogether and obtain the protein they need in other ways. Indeed, vegetarianism is found in most cultures, either as a common practice or as an individual choice. Finally, human beings have the rational capacity not only to choose their goals, but to choose the means by which they achieve these goals. Even if humans choose to continue consuming meat, there is usually no need for that meat to be produced in a way that treats animals cruelly. There exist more humane alternatives to the current methods of factory farming of meat and animal products, although these alternatives may decrease the availability of meat and animal products and increase their cost.

While some people object to the very practice of consuming meat and animal products, a more common objection focuses on the deplorable conditions under which some animals are currently raised and slaughtered. According to this objection, consumers of meat and animal products should be held morally responsible for these conditions because cruel, yet efficient methods are required to produce meat and animal products in the large quantities and at the low prices that consumers demand. Many consumers prefer to remain ignorant of the precise methods by which meat and animal products reach retail outlets so that these products can be enjoyed without the moral qualms that would be raised by their manner of production.

In the following selections, Nathan Nobis argues against the consumption of meat and animal products. He bases his argument on the ethical theory of utilitarianism, noting that it is an important moral principle not to participate in or support morally repugnant practices such as factory farming, regardless of whether our individual actions will bring an end to such practices. Thus, he concludes that a person is still morally obligated to become vegetarian, even if that person's individual choice to avoid the consumption of meat and animal products has no appreciable impact on factory farming.

Beth Haile, in contrast, bases her view on virtue ethics, an approach to ethics that focuses on the character of a moral agent, rather than the morality or immorality of particular actions. She argues that a moral agent must take a number of factors into consideration, including the compassionate treatment of farm animals, fairness toward agricultural workers, and the avoidance of waste. It is possible, she concludes, for a person to be a virtuous moral agent and, under certain circumstances, still consume meat and animal products.

YES ⤶

Nathan Nobis

Vegetarianism and Virtue: Does Consequentialism Demand Too Little?

I will argue that each of us personally ought to be a vegetarian.[1]

Actually, the conclusion I will attempt to defend concerns more than one's eating habits in that I will argue that we should be "vegans." Not only should we not buy and eat meat, but we should also not purchase fur coats, stoles, and hats, or leather shoes, belts, jackets, purses and wallets, furniture, car interiors, and other traditionally animal-based products for which there are readily available plant-based or synthetic alternatives. (Usually these are cheaper and work just as well, or better, anyway.) I will argue that buying and eating most eggs and dairy products are immoral as well. (Since it's much easier to avoid all fur, leather, and wool than all eggs and dairy products, I mention those first.) My conclusion might even imply that outfitting one's self in what has been, in recent history, the most "philosophical" of fabrics—tweed—is immoral too!

Many arguments defending the moral obligation to become vegetarian and, to a lesser extent, adopt a vegan lifestyle, have been given, especially in recent decades.[2] While these arguments have convinced many to become vegetarians or vegans, most are still not convinced. My discussion is directed towards those who have not been convinced, especially for these reasons: first, it is often unclear what the argument is for the exact conclusion that *"You, the reader, are morally obligated to be a vegetarian (or a vegan)."* Second, it is often unclear what moral premise is given to justify this conclusion. And, third, it is often especially unclear how this premise might be justified from a broadly consequentialist moral perspective.[3]

This final lack of clarity is somewhat surprising, since much of the contemporary vegetarian movement takes its inspiration from the work of Peter Singer, a self-professed utilitarian consequentialist.[4] He writes, "I am a utilitarian. I am also a vegetarian. I am a vegetarian *because* I am a utilitarian. I believe that applying the principle of utility to our present situation—especially the methods now used to rear animals for food and the variety of foods available to us—leads to the conclusion that we ought to be vegetarians."[5] While a number of non-consequentialist ethical theories can justify a vegetarian or vegan conclusion fairly easily, I will present some doubts that consequentialism can so easily do so. I will then attempt to cast doubts on these doubts.

So my target reader is a consequentialist who denies that she ought to become a vegetarian or vegan. As a consequentialist, she believes this, presumably, because she thinks that her making these changes in her eating habits and lifestyle would result in her bringing about less intrinsic goods into the world than were she to maintain her current omnivorous eating and consumer habits. In effect, she thinks that, in terms of doing what she can to increase the world's overall amount of goodness, there are ways for her to spend her time and resources that are, at least, morally equivalent to becoming a vegetarian, and so it is not obligatory. She must also think that her becoming a vegetarian will prevent her from achieving these other goals that she believes yield equal or, perhaps greater, goods. . . .

I will argue that if consequentialism does not imply or justify a moral principle that *we should not benefit from or (even symbolically) support very bad practices when we can easily avoid doing so*, then consequentialism is mistaken. . . .

This kind of consequentialism is unique in that it takes the instrumental value of having and acting from certain virtues seriously. Some might respond, "So much the worse for consequentialism," but this might be unwise, since, as Henry Sidgwick argued, the theory provides, "a principle of synthesis, and a method for binding the unconnected and occasionally conflicting principles of common moral reasoning into a complete and harmonious system."[6] My discussion is directed towards someone who thinks that consequentialism does this organizing and synthesizing job best, but is skeptical that her

Nobis, Nathan. From *Social Theory and Practice*, January 2002, pp. 135–137, 138–143, 149–156. Copyright ©2002 by Florida State University Dept. of Philosophy. Used with permission.

seemingly well-confirmed theory implies that she should be a vegetarian or vegan and do her best to develop and act from the virtues that are commonly said to motivate vegetarianism: compassion, caring, sensitivity to cruelty and suffering (both animal and human), resistance to injustice, and integrity, among others.[7]

Contemporary Animal Agriculture and Human Nutrition

First, I will briefly summarize some facts about modern animal agriculture and human nutrition. While this information is readily available, relatively few people are aware of it.

Many people become vegetarians or vegans when they learn about modern animal agriculture and slaughter techniques, especially "factory farming." In the U.S., each year around nine billion animals live in factory farms where most lead generally miserable lives. Newborns are separated from their mothers hours or days after birth; they are then kept in small cages or crates or confined for most of their lives in extremely cramped, overcrowded pens. Male chicks at egg farms are discarded by the tens of thousands each day into trash bins because their meat is deemed unsuitable for human consumption, or they are ground alive into feed for other animals. Male calves of dairy cows are fed liquid, iron-deficient diets and raised in crates that wholly restrict movement so that their muscles remain weak and tender.

Most animals are confined indoors: very few live "happy lives" in an outdoor barnyard. This confinement results in the animals' basic instinctual urges being frustrated. Many animals become psychotic and exhibit neurotic, repetitive behaviors: many become unnaturally cannibalistic. To ward off death and disease from the stressful and unsanitary conditions, a constant regimen of antibiotics and growth hormones is maintained. On both factory and non-intensive family farms animals are subject to surgical modifications such as beak, toe, and tail removal, ear tagging and clipping, teeth removal, branding, dehorning, castration, and ovary removal. In the interest of containing costs, all these procedures are performed without anesthesia.

Many animals die from starvation and exposure to cold in transport to the slaughterhouse. Those that are unable to walk to slaughter are labeled "downers" and are left to die lying in the yard. Those that remain are slaughtered in extremely painful and inhumane ways. Fur-bearing animals are either trapped in the wild and typically die a slow, painful death, or are raised in small cages, fed each others' remains, and killed by anal electrocution so their pelts are not marred.

Understanding these facts is a common motivation for ethical vegetarianism and adopting a vegan lifestyle: people learn of, especially by *seeing*, the pain, suffering, and death involved in these practices and, at least, simply do not want to be involved with or benefit from it anymore.

One might think that this suffering and death is justified because we need to eat meat and other animal products, but, clearly, nobody needs to eat meat to survive. In fact, the common diet in the U.S. and Europe, a meat-based diet, is strongly correlated with such health problems as heart disease, stroke, diabetes, obesity, stroke, and various cancers. Vegetarians are far less prone to these chronic diseases and they tend to outlive meat-eaters by seven years.[8] There is strong medical evidence that not eating meat is to one's health advantage: even conservative health organizations encourage people to cut back on their consumption of meat to reduce cholesterol and saturated fat intake; others encourage cutting it out completely.

The same things, in fact, can be said about all animal products: no one needs to eat eggs or milk or cheese. Progressive health organizations that advocate preventative medicine, such as the Physician's Committee for Responsible Medicine, advise eliminating them completely and adopting a vegan diet that contains a wide variety of foods solely from the four new food groups: vegetables, fruits, legumes (beans and nuts), and whole grains.[9] There is ample evidence that people not only survive on such a diet, but that they thrive.[10] The list of world-champion vegan athletes is impressive, so no one can honestly say that vegans can't achieve optimal health or nutrition.[11] And, of course, no one needs to wear fur, leather, or wool, or use products made from these materials.

Thus, no product of factory farming, non-intensive farming or animal slaughter is necessary for human health or survival. Animals' short and often miserable lives and cruel and painful deaths are not outweighed or justified by any human need. As for the aesthetic pleasures of taste and fashion, vegetarian cuisine and cruelty-free clothing and accessories can easily gratify those interests. But even if the pleasures of consuming animal-based dishes uniformly outweighed the pleasures of all vegan alternatives (which they don't), it is exceedingly unlikely that the difference in aesthetic pleasure for us outweighs the great pains, suffering, and death for the animals. Thus, it is quite unlikely that the status quo regarding the use and treatment of animals is justified from a consequentialist perspective.

The "Impotence of the Individual" Objection

. . . A critic might accept that it is likely that if *everyone* became a vegetarian (perhaps gradually, so the economy is not disturbed) utility would be maximized, but object that her *personally* becoming a vegetarian won't make any difference to the overall utility. Because the meat and animal products industry is so huge and markets are too insensitive, no consequence of her becoming a vegetarian, or even a vegan, would be that fewer animals would be raised and killed than if she were to continue in her omnivorous ways. While these industries do exist only because people buy their products, they don't exist because *she* buys their products, and they won't come tumbling down if she divests herself from them. If she is supposed to become a vegetarian or vegan *because* doing so will help the plight of animals, this seems to not be the case.

Call this the "impotence of the individual" objection. It obviously depends on an empirical assumption concerning the failure of an individual's consumer behavior to affect a huge industry. This claim seems plausible; it is even accepted by a number of philosophers who defend vegetarianism.[12] As far as I know, nobody has summoned the empirical data to show that it is false. I will presume it is true and so here's the rub: if an individual's refraining from purchasing animal-based products does not make a difference for the animals, then this critic might think that Singer's argument is sound, but that it just does not imply the relevant conclusion, namely that *she* should become a vegetarian. The conclusion seems to be that it ought to be the case that *we all* become vegetarians, which is importantly different from the conclusion that *she* ought to be vegetarian, irrespective of whether others do the same (for one difference, the critic can make it the case that *she* is vegetarian, but her powers over others are quite limited). A consequentialist case for *personal* vegetarianism or veganism, if it can be made, will thereby have to be made on the *actual* positive consequences of an individual's becoming a vegetarian, and it appears that less animals being raised and killed is, unfortunately, not one of the actual consequences. . . .

Vegetarianism and Virtue

One way . . . is to think of the vegetarian in terms of his or her virtues. While Tardiff does not present his case as a virtue-based one, he does describe the meat eater as "selfish," in that she accepts the system of killing animals for

her own pleasure; he also describes the ethical vegetarian as "generous," "compassionate," and "peace-loving."[13] Stephens suspects that a "compassionate person would feel moral discomfort, or even revulsion, enjoying something made possible only by the suffering of another."[14] Dixon argues that an individual who thinks it is wrong to cause animals to suffer and be killed for food yet continues to eat meat "seems to be guilty of a lack of integrity."[15]

The common suggestion is that one should be a vegetarian or a vegan because, given an understanding of the relevant facts about both animal and human suffering, this is just how a virtuous, good person would respond. Since people should be virtuous, and being virtuous entails being caring and compassionate (among having other traits), and these traits entail disassociation from the animal-products industry *even if* doing so won't result in less harm to animals, virtuous people should be vegetarian.

In exploring a virtue-based defense of vegetarianism, Russ Shafer-Landau suggests that meat-eaters may be "condemnable to the extent that they display an indifference to the cruelty that went into the 'production' of their 'goods'," and that "they demonstrate a disregard for the suffering experienced by the animals whose remains one is wearing or eating." He describes fur-wearers as "callous." He writes that "[s]eeking and deriving satisfaction from 'products' that are known to result from cruel practices diminishes one's admirability. This is so even if the practical impact of one's indulgence is nonexistent or negligible." Similar judgments are made outside of the vegetarian context: there is "something morally repugnant about a willingness to utilize or purchase soap made from the bodies of concentration camp victims," even if doing so won't prevent any future harms. Also, voicing one's support for a racist dictator or wearing a fur coat received as a gift both seem objectionable.[16]

From these intuitions, Shafer-Landau formulates a moral principle similar to Curnutt's: "One must refuse (even symbolic) support of essentially cruel practices, if a comparably costly alternative that is not tied to essentially cruel practices is readily available."[17] He suspects that something like this principle offers the best hope for those concerned to defend the existence of an obligation to refrain from animal consumption. The problem here, as he notes, is that it's not easy "to identify the sorts of considerations that can ground such a principle," or to find a general moral theory that would justify such a principle.[18]

One approach would be to go the route of a rule-based non-consequentialist or deontological ethic, and hold that this is one of the rules. However, this probably wouldn't be wise, since an ethic of rules is often thought to be "fundamentally non-explanatory" and "anti-theoretical."[19] Presumably, there is a unifying principle that makes these rules the right rules: if there is such a principle, then this is what justifies the rule and makes it the case that the rule should be followed. This fundamental principle is thereby of theoretical interest, not the mid-level rule.

Another route would be virtue ethics. Virtue ethics says, roughly, that evaluations of character and motive are primary in ethics and that other ethical evaluations—say of actions—are derivative from considerations of character and motive: for example, that an action is right if, and only if, a virtuous person would do it. The morality of an action is to be explained by the character of the agent. If one is interested in defending vegetarianism or veganism (and other intuitions about concerned and responsible consumer behavior in general), and one suspects that non-virtue-based theories have a hard time generating the correct judgments about these cases, then one might have a good reason to take more interest in virtue-based ethical theory. It just seems that a virtuous person would not, in response to an understanding of the facts about animal agriculture and nutrition, think that even though animals suffer greatly and die for these products that she does not need (and, in fact, are sometimes harmful to her) and thus only fulfill aesthetic preferences for her, she is nevertheless justified in consuming and using them, even though she could easily refrain from doing so. Thus, virtue theory seems to provide a ready defense for a general principle, similar to Curnutt's and Shafer-Landau's, that *we shouldn't (even symbolically) support bad practices when good alternatives are readily available,* which we might call the "vegetarian justifying principle."

Virtue theory's greatest "vice," however, is that it simply does not seem to provide much of an explanation for why it's good to be virtuous, for example, why it's good (or virtuous) to be compassionate or why a virtuous person would accept the vegetarian justifying principle. Consequentialists can plausibly argue that it's good to be compassionate because compassionate people tend to bring more happiness into the world. They see the virtues as instrumentally valuable: virtue ethics, at least in its bolder varieties (and the non-bold varieties seem to just be theories *of* the virtues, which don't imply anything about ethical theory), holds that the virtues are intrinsically valuable.

In taking a consequentialist view on the virtues, one attempts to give more basic reasons why someone should be compassionate (assuming compassion is a virtue), not merely asserting, as virtue ethics does, that it's just a brute, unexplained fact that compassion is good. The consequentialist critic, of course, will be more attracted to the option that it's a brute fact that, say, happiness or pleasure is good and that virtues are means to those ends. This seems more likely than the idea that the virtues are ends in themselves or are intrinsically good.

If this criticism of virtue ethics is compelling, then while virtue ethics does readily support vegetarianism, it lacks explanatory power. The theory-minded ethical vegetarian seems to be faced with a dilemma: *either* accept a generally plausible ethical theory (e.g., consequentialism) that gets a broad range of cases right (and for seemingly good reasons) but doesn't seem to do as well with personal vegetarianism or veganism in that it seems to lack a place for concerns about animals to provide reasons for action, *or* adopt a virtue ethics or other non-consequentialist, rule-based perspective that readily supports vegetarianism or veganism but, unfortunately, doesn't amount to much of a general moral theory because it lacks explanatory power.

I suspect that there may be a compromise here, one that will be amenable to consequentialists and help them defend the vegetarian justifying principle. There already are reasons to believe that the locus of evaluation for consequentialism should be broadened beyond individual actions to include the "life histories" of a person. One proposal is to hold that an individual action is right for a person just in case it is part of one of that person's optimal life histories, that is, a life history in which value is maximized over the span of the life.

And here we have a natural place to merge the plausible insights of virtue ethics with consequentialist ethical theory. Pre-theoretically, it seems that, all else equal, a person will bring about more goodness if she has the virtue of compassion, cares about and is sensitive to unnecessary cruelty and suffering (wherever it is found, in humans or animals), opposes injustice and unfairness, and, in general, attempts to have an integrated, coherent moral outlook. These seem to be virtues that we try to instill in our children. And earlier we saw that these virtues (and others) readily support vegetarianism and veganism, as well as a general moral outlook typically associated with them (e.g., deep concerns about human health and the recognition that the most effective ways to promote this are through simple dietary changes and non-animal based medical research,[20] disappointments that people are starving to death while cattle are well-fed, environmental concerns, concern for public health and safety, concerns for the safety of slaughterhouse workers, and so on).

These virtues have deep implications for how one lives one's life and how one affects others' lives. For each person, it is unclear how their characters would not be improved and how they would fail to bring about more goodness were they to adopt the virtues that commonly motivate vegetarian or veganism. What other better character traits would preclude doing this? Becoming caring and compassionate about animals invariably seems to have "trickle down" positive effects for the rest of one's life. It seems exceedingly unlikely that anyone would, in general, come to treat other humans worse were she to become a vegetarian or vegan out of compassion or sympathy for animals. In fact, the opposite seems likely. One common motive for telling others about the plight of animals, and attempting to persuade them to be vegetarian or vegan, is that others' lives will improve and they will develop these virtues.

One could practice these virtues selectively and not have them affect one's views about animals, or allow one's self to occasionally eat, but probably not buy, meat (whatever amount won't have negative consequences for health, which is unknown). In doing so, however, it seems not unlikely that one would be taking oneself down a life history that would be, on balance, worse than the vegan one. This is because, first, a thoughtful humanist should probably come to conclusions about how to behave that would be very similar to the vegan's (since all their prescriptions promote human well-being anyway) and, second, personal consistency, integrity and commitment typically contribute to better character anyway. It might be difficult to be selectively caring and compassionate: if this would lead one down a slippery slope, the better strategy for doing the best one can with one's life might be to consistently hold these virtues and act in accordance with them. If this is the case, this bridges the gap between the consequentialist case for near-vegetarianism or veganism articulated above and the more consistent outlook, character, and behavior that many vegetarian and vegan philosophers advocate.

Singer states that "becoming a vegetarian [or a vegan, I think he'd agree] is a way of attesting to the depth and sincerity of one's belief in the wrongness of what we are doing to animals."[21] He probably would agree that veganism also is a way to attest to the sincerity of one's belief in the wrongness of what happens to *humans* as a result of how animals are used. I suspect that, in general, a person who has these beliefs and attests to them by becoming a vegetarian or vegan brings more goodness into the world than her non-vegetarian counterpart: some of these ways are more obvious (e.g., health, comparative ability to make financial contributions to good causes), others are less obvious and, of course, harder to evaluate (e.g., consequences of character). If a switch to a vegetarian or vegan lifestyle results in a life history that brings about greater overall value than an omnivorous life history, then this is what consequentialism demands, and, therefore, consequentialism does not demand "too little" because it will require that one conform one's behavior to the "vegetarian justifying principle" (which has implications beyond vegetarianism).

In conclusion, my discussion can be presented as this argument:

1. If consequentialism is true, then S ought to live an optimal life history.
2. If S ought to live an optimal life history, then S ought to have the virtues entailed by an optimal life history.
3. If S ought to have the virtues entailed by an optimal life history, then S ought to be compassionate, sensitive to cruelty (wherever it is found), resist injustice, have moral integrity, etc.
4. If S ought to be compassionate, sensitive to cruelty (wherever it is found), resist injustice, and be morally integrated, etc., then S ought to be a vegetarian or vegan.
5. Therefore, if consequentialism is true, then S ought to be a vegetarian or vegan.

Consequentialists readily accept premise (1) and should accept premise (2) as well, since it explains why it's good to be virtuous. Premise (3) is defended by the quasi-empirical observation that people with these and related virtues tend to, in general and all else being equal, bring about more good in the world than people who lack these virtues. Were major lifestyle changes not at stake, many would probably readily accept this premise: it is difficult to see how people who *lack* compassion, caring, and sensitivity would bring about *more* goods than those who have these traits, or have them to a greater degree.

Premise (4) is obviously difficult, since it concerns empirical matters. It is the claim that people who become vegetarians or vegans in order to more consistently practice virtue produce more overall good than those who dabble in virtue or practice it selectively. Admittedly, this is an exceedingly difficult premise to defend. The data regarding the positive consequences of changing one's character by becoming vegetarian are, for the most part, anecdotal and speculative. However, this is a problem in general for trying to defend any view about personal morality from a consequentialist perspective, since it is very difficult to find any hard data on the consequences of character and lifestyle. Intuitions and impressions are often all we have to go on for such matters, especially those concerning personal choice. But that does not leave us in the dark, since one impression that most of us have is that it is better to be more compassionate and caring, compared to less, unless doing so would be emotionally draining, which being a vegetarian typically isn't (in fact, many find it quite uplifting). Furthermore, whatever other projects we have, it is unclear exactly how becoming a vegetarian could preclude our efforts with them: if our other projects are noble, it is likely that our reasons for doing them would support being a vegetarian as well.

So, while (4) is not easy to defend on consequentialist grounds, it is not easy to deny either. The vegetarian consequentialist typically has some personal experience to justify her sense that her becoming a vegetarian or vegan has resulted in her bringing about better consequences, while the critic typically has little personal experience to think that her being an omnivore has had the best consequences. If this consequentialist strategy for defending personal vegetarianism has promise, further research into the actual consequences of having the kind of character that is receptive to concerns about animal suffering will be necessary. Until then, I hope that some burden has been shifted to those who hold that their becoming vegetarians or vegans would not maximize intrinsic value to explain why this is so and why their characters, and the consequences of their characters, would become worse for their making this change.[22]

Notes

1. My argument is restricted to apply only to people with nutritious and readily available alternatives to meat. I will say nothing about the morality of meat-eating among the relatively few people who, due to insufficient vegetable-food sources, literally *must* eat meat to survive.

2. The recent literature on ethical issues concerning non-human animals is immense, but the writings of Peter Singer and Tom Regan have been most influential. See, e.g., Peter Singer, *Animal Liberation,* 3rd ed. (New York: Ecco Press, 2001), and *Practical Ethics,* 2nd ed. (Cambridge: Cambridge University Press, 1993); Tom Regan, *The Case for Animal Rights* (Berkeley: University of California Press, 1983), *Defending Animal Rights* (Urbana: University of Illinois Press, 2001), and (with Carl Cohen) *Animal Rights: A Debate* (Lanham, Md.: Rowman & Littlefield, 2001). Singer's and Regan's articles are widely reprinted, especially in introductory moral problems texts.

3. Consequentialism is, very roughly, the ethical theory that says the morality of a token action is determined solely by the value of the consequences in terms of the overall balance of intrinsic goods versus evils produced by that action. . . .

4. Utilitarianism is a species of consequentialism that says, roughly, that the only morally relevant consequence is the overall balance of pleasures and pains (or preference satisfactions and dissatisfactions) that come about as a result of the action.

5. Peter Singer, "Utilitarianism and Vegetarianism," *Philosophy and Public Affairs* 9 (1980): 325–37, p. 325 (my emphasis).

6. Henry Sidgwick, *The Methods of Ethics,* 7th ed. (London: Macmillan, 1907), p. 422.

7. For discussion of vegetarianism and these and other virtues, see Nicholas Dixon, "A Utilitarian Argument for Vegetarianism," *Between the Species* 11 (1995): 90–97, p. 96; Steve Sapontzis, "Everyday Morality and Animal Rights," *Between the Species* 3 (1987): 107–27; Russ Shafer-Landau, "Vegetarianism, Causation and Ethical Theory," *Public Affairs Quarterly* 8 (1994): 85–100, pp. 97–98; William Stephens, "Five Arguments for Vegetarianism," *Philosophy in the Contemporary World* 1 (1994): 25–39, p. 33; and Andrew Tardiff, "Simplifying the Case for Vegetarianism," *Social Theory and Practice* 22 (1996): 299–314, pp. 307, 312.

8. See, e.g., the position paper, "Position of the American Dietetic Association: Vegetarian Diets," *Journal of the American Dietetic Association* 97 (November 1997): 1317–21, p. 1317, where the ADA reports: "Scientific data suggest positive relationships between a vegetarian diet and reduced risk for several chronic degenerative diseases and conditions, including obesity, coronary artery disease, hypertension, diabetes mellitus, and some types of cancer. . . . It is the position of The American Dietetic Association (ADA) that appropriately planned vegetarian diets are healthful, are nutritionally adequate, and provide health benefits in the prevention and treatment of certain diseases." Mylan Engel, in "The Immorality of Eating Meat," summarizes the *extensive* medical literature on the health benefits of vegan and vegetarian diets. See also Mark and Virginia Messina, *The Dietician's Guide to Vegetarian Diets: Issues and Applications,* 2nd ed. (Gaithersburg, Md.: Aspen Publications, 2001); John Robbins, *The Food Revolution* (Berkeley: Conari Press, 2001); and Brenda Davis and Vesanto Melina, *Becoming Vegan: The Complete Guide to Adopting a Healthy Plant-Based Diet* (Summertown, Tenn.: Book Publishing Co., 2000).

9. Available at http://www.pcrm.org/health/VSKN SK9.htrnl

10. See the references to the nutrition literature above. For a brief review of the medical literature on the benefits of eliminating dairy products, see Robert Cohen, *Milk A-Z* (Englewood Cliffs, N.J.: Argus Publishing, 2001).

11. See Robbins, *The Food Revolution,* pp. 78–79.

12. Hud Hudson, in "Collective Responsbility," writes that he "is persuaded that the [meat] industry is not fine-tuned enough to be affected at all by [his] becoming a [strict] vegetarian," much less be affected by his purchasing a "large basket of extra-hot chicken wings" every two weeks at his favorite restaurant (p. 94). James Rachels, in "The Moral Argument for Vegetarianism," in his *Can Ethics Provide Answers?* (Lanham, Md.: Rowman & Littlefield, 1997), pp. 99–107, notes: "It is discouraging to realize that no animals will actually be helped simply by one person ceasing to eat meat. One consumer's behavior, by itself, cannot have a noticeable impact on an industry as vast as the meat industry" (p. 106). Bart Gruzalki discusses this objection in his 'The Case Against Raising and Killing Animals for Food," in Harlan Miller and William Williams (eds.), *Ethics and Animals* (Clifton, N.J.: Humana Press, 1983), pp. 251–66, p. 265. His reply focuses on dubious estimations of the probable positive consequences for animals that an individual's becoming a vegetarian would have. In "Opportunistic Carnivorism," *Journal of Applied Philosophy* 17 (2000): 205–11, p. 205, Michael Almeida and Mark Bernstein argue that "insensitivity of the market notwithstanding, consistent consequentialists are morally prohibited from each additional purchase and consumption of meat" because of the very small probability that any individual will purchase the "threshold chicken" (or other animal) that will result in the "increased terror, slaughter, and death of more chickens" (or other animals). The argument is troubled by the dubious empirical assumption that there is such a "threshold chicken" and a wavering back and forth between a subjective or probabilistic consequentialism that judges acts by their expected or probable consequences and an "objective" consequentialism that judges acts by their actual consequences. R.G. Frey raised this objection in his *Rights, Killing, and Suffering: Moral Vegetarianism and Applied Ethics* (Oxford: Basil Blackwell, 1983); Michael Martin raises it in "A Critique of Moral Vegetarianism," *Reason Papers,* No. 3, Fall 1976, pp. 13–43, and his "Vegetarianism, the Right to Life and Fellow Creaturehood," *Animal Regulation Studies* 2 (1979-80): 205–14. This objection is not new. Unfortunately, it seems little has been said to respond to it.

13. Tardiff, "A Catholic Case for Vegetarianism," pp. 307, 312.

14. Stephens, "Five Arguments for Vegetarianism," p. 33.

15. Dixon, "A Utilitarian Argument for Vegetarianism," p. 97.

16. Shafer-Landau, "Vegetarianism, Causation and Ethical Theory," pp. 96–98.

17. Ibid., p. 95. DeGrazia, in *Taking Animals Seriously,* pp. 262, 285.

18. Shafer-Landau, "Vegetarianism, Causation and Ethical Theory," p. 96.

19. See David McNaughton, "Intuitionism," in Hugh LaFollette (ed.), *The Blackwell Guide to Ethical Theory* (Oxford: Blackwell, 2000), pp. 268–87, at pp. 270–71.

20. See Hugh Lafollette and Niall Shanks, *Brute Science: Dilemmas of Animal Experimentation* (London: Routledge, 1997), and Ray and Jean Greek, *Sacred Cows and Golden Geese: The Human Cost of Experiments on Animals* (New York: Continuum, 2001).

21. Singer, "Utilitarianism and Vegetarianism," p. 337.

22. For critical comments that greatly improved this paper, I am grateful to an anonymous referee and, especially, Christian Basil Mitchell. I am also grateful for comments and discussion from Michael Almeida, Trulie Ankerberg-Nobis, Mark Bernstein, David DeGrazia, Mylan Engel, Bob Holmes, Joel Marks, Gwen Olton, Louis Pojman, Russ Shafer-Landau, Ted Stolze, and Linda Zagzebski. A version of this paper was presented at the Society for the Study of Ethics and Animals at the 2001 meeting of the American Philosophical Association, Pacific Division.

NATHAN NOBIS is an Assistant Professor of Philosophy at Morehouse College. His publications include articles on bioethics, animal rights, and ethical theory.

Beth K. Haile  **NO**

Virtuous Meat Consumption: A Virtue Ethics Defense of an Omnivorous Way of Life

Contemporary Christian ethicists and moral theologians have not, for the most part, attempted a serious ethical defense of an omnivorous way of life. Those who take the question of eating meat seriously from both an ethical and theological perspective usually do so in order to either oppose eating meat as totally unethical or to defend a vegetarian way of life as more morally sound than an omnivorous way of life. . . .

What does not exist in the literature, however, are any moral theologians offering a moral defense of eating meat, despite the fact that most do. The question of eating meat is an important issue for moral theologians to address, not just in order to defend a vegetarian way of life, but in order to defend an omnivorous one, especially in light of all the moral arguments against eating meat. Working within the Roman Catholic tradition, this paper will attempt to provide a moral defense of an omnivorous way of life by following the principles of virtue ethics. This tradition, as Romano Guardini writes, "seeks to do justice to the living majesty, nobility, and beauty of the good."[1]

The Questionable Ethics of Eating Meat

Many people realize the questionable ethics of eating meat when they learn about modern husbandry and slaughtering techniques.[2] In 2008, 17,328,000 cattle, 4,590,314,000 chickens, and 57,542,000 hogs were slaughtered for food. The factory farm industry uses selective breeding and growth-promoting antibiotics to unnaturally and painfully produce animals ready for slaughter as quickly as possible. Most factory farms house their animals in small, overcrowded confinements, prohibiting the animals from engaging in their natural habits like foraging, nesting, roaming, and running. The slaughtering processes themselves are also quite atrocious, with practices like cutting the beaks off of chickens and the tails off of cows preslaughter commonly utilized. As slaughter lines run at rapid speeds, mistakes are recurrent, with many animals left suffering for long periods of time before slaughter.[3]

The ethical status of factory farms is starting to receive greater media coverage following public health scares such as mad cow disease and more recently, [E.] coli outbreaks from consuming factory farm-produced ground beef.[9] This, along with a greater understanding of the negative impact factory farms have on the environment as major contributors of greenhouse gases and fertilizer runoff, has led many people to forgo eating meat as part of adopting a more environmentally friendly lifestyle.[5] In the midst of all this, those still choosing to practice an omnivorous way of life have been silent about the moral justification for their choice. . . .

There have been few contributions among virtue ethicists on the questionable ethics of eating meat, despite the growing prominence of virtue ethicists in the field. Rosalind Hursthouse briefly defends vegetarianism as a practice of temperance in her book *On Virtue Ethics*.[6] In her book entitled *Ethics: Humans and Other Animals*, Hursthouse illustrates how virtue-based arguments can be used to oppose certain ways of treating animals such as using animals for scientific experiments and fox-hunting for sport.[7]

Despite the relative silence among virtue ethicists on the issue, I argue that virtue ethics is well suited to addressing the ethical concerns of meat consumption. Virtue ethics moves beyond a focus on discrete acts toward a morality concerned rather with a unified life, both personal and communal. From the perspective of virtue ethics, the question is not about whether any specific act of consuming meat is ethical or not, but rather about how meat consumption may or may not fit into a life oriented toward the good.

A Virtue Ethics Approach to an Omnivorous Way of Life

Virtue is a quality of character inclining a person toward the good, or as Aquinas says, "a good quality of the mind, by which we live righteously, of which no one can make bad use" (I-II, Q, *55*, art. 4). A virtuous person does not have to think in every discrete circumstance what a good action would be, but rather spontaneously and naturally desires and acts in such a way that is in accordance with the truly good life she is trying to lead. As Jean Porter notes, the human good is attained "by sustaining a life-long course of activity that is determined by our rational grasp of that in which the truly human good consists."[8]

The classical division of the moral virtues that Aquinas adopts identifies four cardinal virtues, which represent four modes of pursuing the good according to the natural inclinations of the human being. Prudence directs the intellect toward the good as the virtue concerning the right choice about things to be done. Justice directs the will toward the good as the virtue concerning right relations with others. Fortitude directs·the irascible appetite toward the good as the virtue concerning the pursuit of the arduous good. Temperance directs the concupiscible appetite toward the good as the virtue concerning the pursuit of the simple sensual good.

The virtues are open-ended in the sense that there is no one correct way to exercise them. Through the operation of prudence, a virtuous person is able to discern how to be virtuous given a specific moral context with specific circumstances. In light of the infinite number of contexts and circumstances that can exist "the virtues allow a person to pursue the good in a way that is uniquely suited to her. From the perspective of virtue, the primary question is not whether eating meat is immoral, but rather, how eating meat might be incorporated into a life directed toward the good.

One way to approach this question is to identify individuals who make the conscious choice to consume meat, and yet still seem to lead lives oriented toward the good. One such person is chef, farmer, and writer Hugh Fearnley-Whittingstall, author of *The River Cottage Meat Book*, who is widely known for his commitment to seasonal, sustainable, and ethically produced food. In 2006, Fearnley-Whittingstall organized the "Chicken Out Campaign," producing a series of television shows detailing how commercial breeds of chickens are raised in an effort to encourage people to buy more humanely treated free-range chickens. As part of this campaign, he encouraged activists to purchase shares of Tesco, a major chicken retailer, so they could participate in shareholder meetings encouraging the company to adopt more humane practices toward their chickens, consistent with the Farm Animal Welfare Council's "Five Freedoms."[9] Though unsuccessful at changing Tesco's farming practices, Fearnley-Whittingstall continues to campaign for more responsible and humane farming and consumption practices.

In the introduction to his *The River Cottage Meat Book*, Fearnley-Whittingstall offers a thorough explanation of the morality of eating meat rather than adopting what he calls a "vegetarian utopian" view:

> [The dependency of animals on humans] would not be suspended if we all became vegetarians. If we ceased to kill the domesticated meat species *for* food, then these animals would not revert to the wild. The nature of our relationship would change, but the relationship would not end. We would remain their custodians, with full moral responsibility for their welfare. . . . If we are not to be guilty of great cruelty, we would still have to manage the populations, by veterinary means for their good health and by culling to avoid population booms and consequent starvation. And wouldn't [we] want to minimize the suffering of old and diseased animals by "putting them down" humanely? Then what happens to the corpses of the deceased? Do we bury them? Are we allowed to feed them to our cats and dogs, or have they become vegetarian too? Or should they just be composted to produce fertilizer for the vegetarian agriculture that is now feeding us? But then wouldn't we sort of end up eating them anyway?[10]

Fearnley-Whittingstall clearly takes the moral implications of meat-eating seriously, yet he has not chosen a vegetarian lifestyle. For meat-eaters looking for ways in which meat consumption can be integrated into a life oriented toward the good, turning to such a person might be a good place to begin, in order to identify specific virtues related to eating meat. Although Fearnley-Whittingstall does not mention virtue ethics specifically in his writing, his book is nevertheless filled with virtue language that virtue ethicists can appropriate into a virtue-based defense of eating meat.

Identifying Virtues for an Omnivorous Way of Life

Although the cardinal virtues give general qualities of character necessary for living a good life, virtues are also context-bound, and for specific questions such as how eating meat may fit into a good life, we need to identify more specific subvirtues that address the question at hand, namely, virtuous consumption of meat. Jean Porter suggests four considerations in the identification of any specific virtue:

> (1) A notion of a particular kind of action that is characteristic 'of the virtue (although not necessarily linked with it in every instance), which will include some idea of the kind of context in which the sort of action would be appropriate; (2) some idea of kinds of actions that are characteristically failures to act well, in the context that provides the setting for the virtue in question; (3) some idea of what it would mean, concretely, for a person to display this virtue through his actions and reactions over a substantial period of time; and finally, (4) some guidelines for distinguishing true from false exemplifications of the virtue in question, guidelines derived from a higher principle that will enable us to say whether in a particular instance this putative virtue is truly being exercised in such a way as to promote the true good of the human person.[11]

Based on these criteria, we can develop a virtue-based approach to the question of meat consumption by examining the example of specific virtuous individuals, in this case, the example set by Fearnley-Whittingstall. We will discuss three specific virtues—responsibility, temperance, and thrift. In each case, we will follow Porter's guidelines, identifying actions constitutive of the virtue, actions that are antithetical to the virtue, how these actions may be manifest over time, and how acts constitutive of the virtue may be distinguished from false manifestations of the virtue.

One virtue identified by Fearnley-Whittingstall is responsibility both in husbandry and in purchasing. Responsible husbandry means "that we embrace, not reject, the moral status of the animals we farm for food. . . . This means among other things, better health, better survival rates, less pain, less stress, more comfort, suitable food and plenty of it."[12] Consumers can practice responsibility by supporting farmers engaged in practices characteristic of this virtue. This means that consumers must research where their meat is coming from, what the animals were fed, how the animals lived and were killed, how their flesh was processed, stored, and shipped: "It's the answers to these questions that tell us whether what we have in front of us is worth taking back to the kitchen. And all too often it's those answers, not the price, that should really make us flinch."[13]

However, if responsibility is a virtue of meat consumption, we must still distinguish true versus false manifestations of this virtue by identifying the end, the *telos*, to which the actions constitutive of this virtue are directed. It is not enough for virtue to simply farm responsibly by avoiding intensive farming practices, nor is it enough for virtue to only buy meat from local farms that practice humane and responsible husbandry. A farmer could engage in humane husbandry because then she may be able to charge more for her meat and bring in a greater profit than if she did not practice humane husbandry. A consumer may buy meat from farms practicing humane husbandry because all her friends buy such meat, and she does not want to be shamed in front of her peers.

Fearnley-Whittingstall says that the end of responsibility, what all the actions constitutive of the virtue of responsibility are directed to, is care for the animals' welfare and recognition that domestic animals raised for meat are still living creatures that need to be cared for, valued, and respected:

> The adjective "happy" is more than a little anthropomorphically loaded. But I don't think it's too much to say that a good extensive livestock system aims to keep its animals at least contented. However, my point is not that the sun always shines as cockerels crow from the gatepost, lambs skip through the meadow, cows called Buttercup mellifluously chew the cud, and pigs romp and root through leafy Arcadian glades. Extensively farmed animals will, from time to time, get cold, muddy, sore, and sick. Occasionally, they will get pushed around and prodded, by the farmer or the vet, and then they may get confused and stressed, for a while. But they will nonetheless spend almost all of their time—with a bit of luck, day after unmolested day—doing what cows, sheep, pigs, and chickens freely choose to do.[14]

Another virtue Fearnley-Whittingstall identifies is good, or what I will call temperate, meat eating. Temperance is typically used to refer to moderate meat eating, meaning not eating too much (gluttony) or too little (insensibility). Moderation is certainly important in identifying temperance as virtue of meat consumption. However, Fearnley-Whittingstall's virtuous example presents us with a more specific understanding of how moderation in the context of eating meat may be manifested.

Fearnley-Whittingstall points out that temperate meat eating must include eating fat.[15] He notes that although fat gets bad press, the threads of fat running through meat known as "marbling" are a clear indicator that the animal was raised properly. Lean meat comes from animals raised quickly for slaughter that do not have time to develop a stage of maturity in which fat can develop. Marbled meat, on the other hand, comes from animals grown slowly, and generally killed at a proper age and stage of development:

> It is fair to say that a generous layer of external fat, as well as good marbling, occurs in meat that grows naturally, slowly, and predominantly out of doors (the primary function of subcutaneous fat being to insulate the animal against the cold weather). It follows naturally (or unnaturally) enough, that the industrial production of meat, in intensive indoor systems at a speeded-up rate, is well suited to production of lean meat. Certain feeds, and feed additives such as antibiotics, steroids, and hormones, are routinely used in intensive systems, both to speed up the development of muscled (lean meat) and to inhibit the development of fat.[16]

Properly marbled meat not only indicates that an animal was raised correctly, it also makes meat taste better, and makes it more filling, resulting in the need to eat less meat in order to achieve satiation. Fearnley-Whittingstall argues that eating lean meat is not necessarily a way to practice moderation in meat consumption because it takes more lean meat to achieve satiation, and the experience of eating lean meat is less satisfying, leading it to be eaten more quickly rather than savored:

> The critical thing is that many flavor-bearing molecules are soluble in fat but not in water. In addition the flavorful substances incorporated into otherwise dry foods are far more effectively absorbed by the taste buds when combined with or accompanied by fat. It's more or less a straight function of time. Fat effectively slows down the progress of the aromatics over the tongue and across the palate—a sensation you may even be conscious of when you are eating chocolate, for example—giving us more time to appreciate and enjoy the taste experience.[17]

Temperate—that is, good—meat eating means more than just eating the proper amount of meat from the proper source; it also means deriving the proper pleasure from the experience. It is the job of temperance to regulate this.

Another virtue Fearnley-Whittingstall identifies is thrift. This may come as a surprise to those who are used to the argument for purchasing more organic and humanely raised meat—that it is worth the higher cost. Thrift, as Fearnley-Whittingstall sees it, is just as much about kitchen creativity as it is about economic purchasing. Thrift is more properly understood as "resourcefulness" and "thoroughness," "adjectives that best describe the outlook of the complete meat cook, as he or she assesses the full spectrum of available meat cuts and the endless possibilities they present."[18] Thrift means refusing to waste the animal, as much as is possible. For the home cook, this means using the bones to make stock, and recycling leftover meats in soups and stews and casseroles.

> [Thrift means making] an active commitment to explore those thrifty dishes that have served the "peasants" of the world so well. These are invariably among the most delicious dishes of any food culture—necessity being the mother of invention and all that. Of course, knowledge of such dishes is indispensable to those on a tight budget—it always has been. But these days it is clear that there are two ways of saving money when it comes to buying meat. The modern way is to head straight for the section of the supermarket where low prices reflect low standards and a complete lack of concern for welfare. The old-fashioned approach is to know what to do with certain cuts of meat that are inexpensive even when taken from the best possible carcass. . . . Such thrifty practice has always been in the best interests of good farming, good cooking, and good conscience.[19]

An action not constitutive of thrift is simply buying the cheapest cut of meat available. The way to distinguish true manifestations of thrift from false again resides in the *telos* or purpose to which a person's thrifty actions are directed. The *telos* Fearnley-Whittingstall identifies as critical for truly virtuous thrift is respect for the animals that have died to feed us: "Respect for the farmers who have (assuming you've chosen your meat well) worked tirelessly to keep those animals healthy and contented, so their meat is as good as it can be. And respect for the whole history of animal husbandry and meat gastronomy—endeavors that until recently scorned any practice that was wasteful of the livestock on which they depended."[20]

Thrift also means cooking and eating as much of the animal as possible. Fearnley-Whittingstall dedicates an entire chapter of his book to "offal," known in the United States as variety meats, but meaning essentially the nonmuscle parts of the animals that are frequently discarded as unfit for consumption. This includes organ meat like liver, kidney, spleen, and lights (lungs), as well as tail, trotters (hooves), ear, and tongue.

Offal offers us a chance to pay our respects, in a full and holistic manner, to the animals we've raised for meat. The nose-to-tail approach to using the animals we kill for food must be a central tenet of the contract of domestication and good husbandry. Waste is not acceptable. It's all or nothing. These are sentiments that have long been readily embraced by cultures more in tune with their environments, and more fully and mutually engaged with their livestock than ours. Sacrifice and libation at the time of slaughter, of an animal's heart, say, or a little of its spilled blood, are not only about thanking your god, they are about thanking an individual animal, by ritually acknowledging the passing of its life.[21] . . .

Conclusion

My goal in writing this article is twofold. First, I want to argue that the decision to eat meat should not be considered a foregone moral choice, simply because it is the norm. In light of all the evidence that an omnivorous way of life is bad for the environment, bad for health, and bad for animals, those who choose to continue eating meat must provide sufficient reasons for their choice. Second, I want to illustrate that one can provide a moral defense of an omnivorous way of life, a task that virtue ethics is particularly suited for, because virtue ethics is not primarily concerned with the intrinsic rightness or wrongness of eating meat, but rather, with how eating meat may be incorporated in a life oriented toward the good.

From the perspective of virtue, both a vegetarian and omnivorous way of life can be oriented toward the good through the cultivation of the appropriate virtues. A vegetarian who cares profoundly for animal welfare but is dismissive of agricultural workers' rights or other aspects of human welfare is not leading a virtuous life. An omnivore who does volunteer social justice work in Latin America but who buys only the cheapest cuts of meat from animals aised intensively on factory farms is also not leading a virtuous life. The virtues I identified in this essay—responsibility, temperance, and thrift (certainly not an exhaustive list)—are not just virtues for an omnivorous way of life, but virtues for consumption in general. As the U.S. bishops wrote in *Renewing the Earth*, human beings are not justified in using any created thing capriciously. Just as Christian charity and justice make a special claim on followers of Christ to care for the poor, so too do these virtues make a claim not just on Christians but on all people of good will to exercise a stewardship

that "places upon us responsibility for the well-being of all God's creatures," whether we fulfill that responsibility as a vegetarian or as an omnivore.

Notes

1. Romano Guardini, *The Virtues: On Forms of Moral Life* (Chicago: Henry Regenery Company, 1963), vi.

2. Gail A. Eisnitz, *Slaughterhouse* (Prometheus Books, 1997); Paula Young Lee, *Meat, Modernity, and the Rise of the Slaughterhouse* (UPNE, 2008); Participant Productions and Karl Weber, *Food Inc.: A Participant Guide: How Industrial Food is Making Us Sicker, Fatter, and Poorer—And What You Can Do About It*, 1st ed. (Public Affairs, 2009); Eric Schlosser, *Fast Food Nation: The Dark Side of the All-American Meal*, 1st ed. (Harper Perennial, 2002).

3. "An HSUS Report: The Welfare of Animals in the Meat, Egg, and Dairy Industries," The Humane Society of America, http://www.hsus.org/farm/resources/research/welfare/welfare_overview.html. See also U.S. Department of Agriculture National Agricultural Statistics Service. 2006. Livestock slaughter: 2005 summary. usda. mannlib. cornell. edu I usda/ current/ LiveSlauSu I LiveSlau Su-o3-06-2006_revision. pdf."

4. See Michael Moss, "E. Coli Path Shows Flaws in Beef Inspection," *The New York Times*, October 4, 2009, sec. Health, http://www.nytimes.com/2009/10/04/health/04meat.html.

5. Ezra Klein, "The Meat of the Problem," *Washington Post*, July 29, 2009. A 2006 UN Report notes that livestock accounts for 18 percent of greenhouse gas emissions across. the globe. The *National Catholic Reporter* has done much to raise awareness among Catholics about the moral implications of their food choices. See Colman McCarthy, "USDA and the Unhealthy Status of Meat," *National Catholic Reporter* 32, issue 27 January 19, 1996); Rich Heffern, "The Ethics of Eating," *National Catholic Reporter* (May 24, 2002); Colman McCarthy, "Think Twice Before Asking 'Where's the Beef?': Amid Mad Cow Disease Alarms We Ignore the Greater Health Dangers Linking Meat to Top Three Killers of Americans," *National Catholic Reporter* 40, issue 23 (April 9, 2004). See also "Catholic Reflections on Food, Farmers, and Farmworkers," United States Catholic Bishops Conference (2003 Statement) http://www.ncrlc.com/Catholic-Reflections-Food.html.

6. Rosalind Hursthouse, *On Virtue Ethics* (Oxford: Oxford University Press, 2002), 2 27.

7. Rosalind Hursthouse, *Ethics, Humans and Other Animals: An Introduction with Readings* (Routledge, 2000).

8. Jean Porter, *Recovery of Virtue* (Presbyterian Publishing Corporation, 1990), 67.

9. See http://www.chickenout.tv I, Steve Hawkes, "Hugh Fearnley-Whittingstall Lobbies Tesco Investors Over Chicken," *The Times*, June 18, 2008; "Five Freedoms," Farm Animal Welfare Council, http://www.fawc.org.uk/freedoms.htm. See also Fearnley-Whittingstall, *The River Cottage Meat Book* (Berkeley, CA: Ten Speed Press, 2004), 54. The five freedoms Fearnley-Whittingstall identifies for domestic animals are (1) freedom from hunger and thirst, (2) freedom from discomfort, (3) freedom from pain, injury, or disease, (4) freedom to perform normal patterns of behavior, and (5) freedom from fear or distress.

10. Fearnley-Whittingstall, *The River Cottage Meat Book*, 17.

11. Porter, *Recovery of Virtue*, 109.

12. Fearnley-Whittingstall, *The River Cottage Meat Book*, 24.

13. Ibid., 28.

14. Ibid., 33.

15. For more on how eating fat from meat is an action constitutive of temperate meat consumption, see Jennifer McLagan, *Fat: An Appreciation of Misunderstood Ingredient, with Recipes* (Ten Speed Press, 2008).

16. Fearnley-Whittingstall, *The River Cottage Meat Book*, 37.

17. Ibid., 36.

18. Ibid., 462.

19. Ibid., 463.

20. Ibid., 462.

21. Ibid., 182.

22. *Renewing the Earth: An Invitation to Reflection and Action on Environment in Light of Catholic Social Teaching*, United States Catholic Conference (November 14, 1991).

BETH K. HAILE is an Assistant Professor of Moral Theology at Carroll College. Her research interests include fundamental moral theology, bioethics, moral psychology, and social ethics.

EXPLORING THE ISSUE

Does Morality Require Vegetarianism?

Critical Thinking and Reflection

1. What role should the suffering of animals play in human moral decision making?
2. Is it consistent for a person to be a vegetarian and still permit animals to inflict pain and suffering on each other? Why or why not?
3. Should people be made more aware of the morally objectionable practices of factory farming? If so, how?
4. How might current practices of factory farming be changed to become more humane and still provide meat and animal products in sufficient quantity and at a sufficiently low price?
5. If animals are processed in a human manner, would there still be good reasons to pursue a vegetarian lifestyle? If so, what are they?

Is There Common Ground?

The authors appear to be coming from incompatible theoretical backgrounds, since utilitarianism and virtue ethics are radically different approaches to moral decision making. However both authors acknowledge the role that virtue can play in this moral issue. Haile's entire argument focuses on becoming a moral agent by cultivating virtues. Nobis also argues for the consideration of virtue, since the inclusion of virtues within utilitarianism can be considered a way to ensure choices have the right moral consequences.

The two authors also share a sense of moral horror at the current practices of the meat industry, and both argue that people should not participate in, or support, such abhorrent practices. Nobis argues that the correct response to the meat industry is not to participate in the consumption of meat at all, while Haile argues that the correct response is to support farmers who raise and slaughter animals under humane conditions.

Additional Resources

Josephine Donovan and Carol Adams, eds., *The Feminist Care Tradition in Animal Ethics* (Columbia University Press, 2007)

Michael A. Fox, "Why We Should Be Vegetarians," *International Journal of Applied Philosophy* (vol. 20, no. 2, 2006)

Steve F. Sapontzis, *Food For Thought: The Debate over Eating Meat* (Prometheus Books, 2004)

Matthew Scully, *Dominion: The Power of Man, the Suffering of Animals, and the Call to Mercy* (St. Martin's Press, 2002)

Internet References . . .

Animal Rights and Vegan Ethics

http://ar.vegnews.org/Animal_Rights.html

The Ethical Omnivore Movement

www.go-eo.org/GoEO/Welcome.html

The Vegetarian Resource Group

www.vrg.org/

Selected, Edited, and with Issue Framing Material by:
Owen M. Smith, *Stephen F. Austin State University*
and
Anne Collins Smith, *Stephen F. Austin State University*

ISSUE

Is It Right to Produce Genetically Modified Food?

YES: **Ronald Bailey**, from "Dr. Strangelunch—Or: Why We Should Learn to Stop Worrying and Love Genetically Modified Food," *Reason* (2001)

NO: **Michael W. Fox**, from "Killer Foods: When Scientists Manipulate Genes, Better Is Not Always Best," *Lyons Press* (2004)

Learning Outcomes
After reading this issue, you will be able to:
• Describe the benefits that could result from the production of genetically modified foods.
• Describe the dangers that could result from the production of genetically modified foods.
• Describe the relationship between biotechnology and economics.
• Formulate your own position on genetically modified food and identify evidence supporting your position.
• Identify the main objections to your position and formulate responses to these objections.

ISSUE SUMMARY

YES: Ronald Bailey is a strong supporter of genetically modified food (GMF). He argues that it is feared by many activists, but there is no strong proof that there are any problems with it. In fact, he suggests that there are great benefits that can be provided by GMFs, especially to the world's poor and to those suffering from natural calamities.

NO: Michael Fox is cautious about the spread of *scientism* and the morally blind push for technological development. This scientism, when combined with an aggressive spirit of enterprise, threatens to upset the balance of nature. We may try to rearrange natural things (including plants and animals) to serve our own purposes, but Fox believes that in this way we end up alienating ourselves from the natural world.

Is it right to produce genetically modified foods (GMFs)? The technology that produces GMFs is a powerful technology that can have effects that are very good and also effects that are very bad. There are two mail sorts of problems here. First, there are the problems that we know about or can reasonably anticipate. Second, there are unanticipated problems that may arise. By way of illustration, consider the idea of environmental impact. We can anticipate certain concerns and make efforts to control them. For example, we may be worried about the cross-pollination of some GMFs with cultivated crops or wild plants. This sort of thing is easily anticipated and maybe controlled or taken into account. On the other hand, the second kind of problem is one that we cannot anticipate. Suppose, for example, that some genetic modification will make an important crop resistant to certain pests. So far, so good. But if the pests don't destroy the genetically modified plants, they may end up as pests of other plants, plants that were until then relatively safe. In this case, we may have a serious problem on our hands; and it may be too late to do much about it.

Consider an analogous case. There have been problems in the past when a non-native animal was induced into a new environment in order to deal with some problem there. But this non-native species may cause widespread and unanticipated damage. This is exactly what happened with the introduction of European rabbits into Australia. A small group of 12 rabbits were released by an Englishman living in Australia, who thought that he could use them to hunt (as he was used to doing in England) and that in any case 12 rabbits would have no great impact on the land. But these rabbits proliferated at an enormous rate and became pests, eating the very crops that the European settlers were trying to grow in Australia. In addition, the rabbits consumed much of the ground cover and ate the bark around the bases of trees that the settlers tried to plant. The erosion and environmental damage that resulted was huge. Throughout the 1800s, the rabbits continued to spread across Australia. In the early 1900s, a rabbit-proof fence was built, and further fencing was added until the whole fence extended over 2,000 miles. Today, there are hundreds of millions of rabbits in Australia. Estimates of annual damage caused by them in recent times range from $200,000,000 to $600,000,000.

So, a wise choice would be to proceed with caution—perhaps with utmost caution—when it comes to GMF. Supporters of GMF tend to be optimistic, as if the only problems are the kind that we can anticipate. But even if the optimists are correct that these concerns can be addressed, there are still the unanticipated problems. There are really two reasons for proceeding slowly and carefully. One has to do with the unanticipated problems that I have mentioned, but another has to do with people and their having to get used to new ideas—especially when the new ideas have to do with what sort of food they will consume. The problems are connected in this way: if there should arise one of these unanticipated problems, people will be *very* resistant to GMF. Hence, it is in the interest of the optimists themselves to be cautious.

Some critics of GMFs are worried about the powerful connection of capitalism and biological technology. Genetically modified organisms are developed for profit; they are patented. Individuals tend to do what is best for themselves and not necessarily what is best for other people, animals, or the environment. We have already seen how the "family farm" has given way to the "factory farm," in which huge numbers of animals are kept in close quarters, given hormones, and raised and slaughtered as quickly as possible. Some critics worry that the changes made possible by genetic modification would only exacerbate this sort of problem.

In the following readings, we can regard Ronald Bailey as an optimist. He foresees only good results from GMFs. And he is surely correct that there are many good results. But in the next piece, Michael Fox warns us of the dangers of GMFs. These, he would say, are not only of a physical kind, but also spiritual.

YES ⮐

Ronald Bailey

Dr. Strangelunch—Or: Why We Should Learn to Stop Worrying and Love Genetically Modified Food

Ten thousand people were killed and 10 to 15 million left homeless when a cyclone slammed into India's eastern coastal state of Orissa in October 1999. In the aftermath, CARE and the Catholic Relief Society distributed a high-nutrition mixture of corn and soy meal provided by the U.S. Agency for International Development to thousands of hungry storm victims. Oddly, this humanitarian act elicited cries of outrage.

"We call on the government of India and the state government of Orissa to immediately withdraw the corn-soya blend from distribution," said Vandana Shiva, director of the New Delhi–based Research Foundation for Science, Technology, and Ecology. "The U.S. has been using the Orissa victims as guinea pigs for GM [genetically modified] products which have been rejected by consumers in the North, especially Europe." Shiva's organization had sent a sample of the food to a lab in the U.S. for testing to see if it contained any of the genetically improved corn and soybean varieties grown by tens of thousands of farmers in the United States. Not surprisingly, it did.

"Vandana Shiva would rather have her people in India starve than eat bioengineered food," says C.S. Prakash, a professor of plant molecular genetics at Tuskegee University in Alabama. Per Pinstrup-Andersen, director general of the International Food Policy Research Institute, observes: "To accuse the U.S. of sending genetically modified food to Orissa in order to use the people there as guinea pigs is not only wrong; it is stupid. Worse than rhetoric, it's false. After all, the U.S. doesn't need to use Indians as guinea pigs, since millions of Americans have been eating genetically modified food for years now with no ill effects."

Shiva not only opposes the food aid but is also against "golden rice," a crop that could prevent blindness in half a million to 3 million poor children a year and alleviate vitamin A deficiency in some 250 million people in the developing world. By inserting three genes, two from daffodils and one from a bacterium, scientists at the Swiss Federal Institute of Technology created a variety of rice that produces the nutrient beta-carotene, the precursor to vitamin A. Agronomists at the International Rice Research Institute in the Philippines plan to crossbreed the variety, called "golden rice" because of the color produced by the beta-carotene, with well-adapted local varieties and distribute the resulting plants to farmers all over the developing world.

Last June, at a Capitol Hill seminar on biotechnology sponsored by the Congressional Hunger Center, Shiva airily dismissed golden rice by claiming that "just in the state of Bengal 150 greens which are rich in vitamin A are eaten and grown by the women." A visibly angry Martina McGloughlin, director of the biotechnology program at the University of California at Davis, said "Dr. Shiva's response reminds me of . . . Marie Antoinette, [who] suggested the peasants eat cake if they didn't have access to bread." Alexander Avery of the Hudson Institute's Center for Global Food Issues noted that nutritionists at UNICEF doubted it was physically possible to get enough vitamin A from the greens Shiva was recommending. Furthermore, it seems unlikely that poor women living in shanties in the heart of Calcutta could grow greens to feed their children.

The apparent willingness of biotechnology's opponents to sacrifice people for their cause disturbs scientists who are trying to help the world's poor. At the annual meeting of the American Association for the Advancement of Science last February, Ismail Serageldin, the director of the Consultative Group on International Agricultural Research, posed a challenge: "I ask opponents of biotechnology, do you want 2 to 3 million children a year to go blind and 1 million to die of vitamin A deficiency, just because you object to the way golden rice was created?"

Vandana Shiva is not alone in her disdain for biotechnology's potential to help the poor. Mae-Wan Ho, a reader in biology at London's Open University who advises another activist group, the Third World Network, also opposes golden rice. And according to a *New York Times* report on a biotechnology meeting held last March by the Organization for Economic Cooperation and Development, Benedikt Haerlin, head of Greenpeace's European anti-biotech campaign, "dismissed the importance of saving African and Asian lives at the risk of spreading a new science that he considered untested."

Shiva, Ho, and Haerlin are leaders in a growing global war against crop biotechnology, sometimes called "green biotech" (to distinguish it from medical biotechnology, known as "red biotech"). Gangs of anti-biotech vandals with cute monikers such as Cropatistas and Seeds of Resistance have ripped up scores of research plots in Europe and the U.S. The so-called Earth Liberation Front burned down a crop biotech lab at Michigan State University on New Year's Eve in 1999, destroying years of work and causing $400,000 in property damage. . . . Anti-biotech lobbying groups have proliferated faster than bacteria in an agar-filled petri dish: In addition to Shiva's organization, the Third World Network, and Greenpeace, they include the Union of Concerned Scientists, the Institute for Agriculture and Trade Policy, the Institute of Science in Society, the Rural Advancement Foundation International, the Ralph Nader–founded Public Citizen, the Council for Responsible Genetics, the Institute for Food and Development Policy, and that venerable fount of biotech misinformation, Jeremy Rifkin's Foundation on Economic Trends. The left hasn't been this energized since the Vietnam War. But if the anti-biotech movement is successful, its victims will include the downtrodden people on whose behalf it claims to speak.

"We're in a war," said an activist at a protesters' gathering during the November 1999 World Trade Organization meeting in Seattle. "We're going to bury this first wave of biotech." He summed up the basic strategy pretty clearly: "The first battle is labeling. The second battle is banning it."

Later that week, during a standing-room-only "biosafety seminar" in the basement of a Seattle Methodist church, the ubiquitous Mae-Wan Ho declared, "This warfare against nature must end once and for all." Michael Fox, a vegetarian "bioethicist" from the Humane Society of the United States, sneered: "We are very clever little simians, aren't we? Manipulating the bases of life and thinking we're little gods." He added, "The only acceptable application of genetic engineering is to develop a genetically engineered form of birth control for our own species." This creepy declaration garnered rapturous applause from the assembled activists.

Despite its unattractive side, the global campaign against green biotech has had notable successes in recent years. Several leading food companies, including Gerber and Frito-Lay, have been cowed into declaring that they will not use genetically improved crops to make their products. Since 1997, the European Union has all but outlawed the growing and importing of biotech crops and food. Last May some 60 countries signed the Biosafety Protocol, which mandates special labels for biotech foods and requires strict notification, documentation, and risk assessment procedures for biotech crops. Activists have launched a "Five-Year Freeze" campaign that calls for a worldwide moratorium on planting genetically enhanced crops. . . .

To decide whether the uproar over green biotech is justified, you need to know a bit about how it works. Biologists and crop breeders can now select a specific useful gene from one species and splice it into an unrelated species. Previously plant breeders were limited to introducing new genes through the time-consuming and inexact art of crossbreeding species that were fairly close relatives. For each cross, thousands of unwanted genes would be introduced into a crop species. Years of "backcrossing"—breeding each new generation of hybrids with the original commercial variety over several generations—were needed to eliminate these unwanted genes so that only the useful genes and characteristics remained. The new methods are far more precise and efficient. The plants they produce are variously described as "transgenic," "genetically modified," or "genetically engineered."

Plant breeders using biotechnology have accomplished a great deal in only a few years. For example, they have created a class of highly successful insect-resistant crops by incorporating toxin genes from the soil bacterium *Bacillus thuringiensis*. Farmers have sprayed *B.t.* spores on crops as an effective insecticide for decades. Now, thanks to some clever biotechnology, breeders have produced varieties of corn, cotton, and potatoes that make their own insecticide. *B.t.* is toxic largely to destructive caterpillars such as the European corn borer and the cotton bollworm; it is not harmful to birds, fish, mammals, or people.

Another popular class of biotech crops incorporates an herbicide resistance gene, a technology that has been especially useful in soybeans. Farmers can spray herbicide on their fields to kill weeds without harming the crop plants. The most widely used herbicide is Monsanto's

Roundup (glyphosate), which toxicologists regard as an environmentally benign chemical that degrades rapidly, days after being applied. Farmers who use "Roundup Ready" crops don't have to plow for weed control, which means there is far less soil erosion.

Biotech is the most rapidly adopted new farming technology in history. The first generation of biotech crops was approved by the EPA, the FDA, and the U.S. Department of Agriculture in 1995, and by 1999 transgenic varieties accounted for 33 percent of corn acreage, 50 percent of soybean acreage, and 55 percent of cotton acreage in the U.S. Worldwide, nearly 90 million acres of biotech crops were planted in 1999. With biotech corn, U.S. farmers have saved an estimated $200 million by avoiding extra cultivation and reducing insecticide spraying. U.S. cotton farmers have saved a similar amount and avoided spraying 2 million pounds of insecticides by switching to biotech varieties. Potato farmers, by one estimate, could avoid spraying nearly 3 million pounds of insecticides by adopting *B.t.* potatoes. Researchers estimate that *B.t.* corn has spared 33 million to 300 million bushels from voracious insects.

One scientific panel after another has concluded that biotech foods are safe to eat, and so has the FDA. Since 1995, tens of millions of Americans have been eating biotech crops. Today it is estimated that 60 percent of the foods on U.S. grocery shelves are produced using ingredients from transgenic crops. In April a National Research Council panel issued a report that emphasized it could not find "any evidence suggesting that foods on the market today are unsafe to eat as a result of genetic modification." *Transgenic Plants and World Agriculture*, a report issued in July that was prepared under the auspices of seven scientific academies in the U.S. and other countries, strongly endorsed crop biotechnology, especially for poor farmers in the developing world. "To date," the report concluded, "over 30 million hectares of transgenic crops have been grown and no human health problems associated specifically with the ingestion of transgenic crops or their products have been identified." Both reports concurred that genetic engineering poses no more risks to human health or to the natural environment than does conventional plant breeding.

As U.C.-Davis biologist Martina McGloughlin remarked at last June's Congressional Hunger Center seminar, the biotech foods "on our plates have been put through more thorough testing than conventional food ever has been subjected to." According to a report issued in April by the House Subcommittee on Basic Research, "No product of conventional plant breeding . . . could meet the data requirements imposed on biotechnology products by U.S. regulatory agencies. . . . Yet, these foods are widely and properly regarded as safe and beneficial by plant developers, regulators, and consumers." The report concluded that biotech crops are "at least as safe [as] and probably safer" than conventionally bred crops. . . .

Activists are also fond of noting that the seed company Pioneer Hi-Bred produced a soybean variety that incorporated a gene—for a protein from Brazil nuts—that causes reactions in people who are allergic to nuts. The activists fail to mention that the soybean never got close to commercial release because Pioneer Hi-Bred checked it for allergenicity as part of its regular safety testing and immediately dropped the variety. The other side of the allergy coin is that biotech can remove allergens that naturally occur in foods such as nuts, potatoes, and tomatoes, making these foods safer.

Even if no hazards from genetically improved crops have been demonstrated, don't consumers have a right to know what they're eating? This seductive appeal to consumer rights has been a very effective public relations gambit for anti-biotech activists. If there's nothing wrong with biotech products, they ask, why don't seed companies, farmers, and food manufacturers agree to label them?

The activists are being more than a bit disingenuous here. Their scare tactics, including the use of ominous words such as *frankenfoods*, have created a climate in which many consumers would interpret labels on biotech products to mean that they were somehow more dangerous or less healthy than old-style foods. Biotech opponents hope labels would drive frightened consumers away from genetically modified foods and thus doom them. Then the activists could sit back and smugly declare that biotech products had failed the market test. . . .

It is interesting to note that several crop varieties popular with organic growers were created through mutations deliberately induced by breeders using radiation or chemicals. This method of modifying plant genomes is obviously a far cruder and more imprecise way of creating new varieties. Radiation and chemical mutagenesis is like using a sledgehammer instead of the scalpel of biotechnology. Incidentally, the FDA doesn't review these crop varieties produced by radiation or chemicals for safety, yet no one has dropped dead from eating them.

Labeling nonbiotech foods as such will not satisfy the activists whose goal is to force farmers, grain companies, and food manufacturers to segregate biotech crops from conventional crops. Such segregation would require a great deal of duplication in infrastructure, including separate grain silos, rail cars, ships, and production lines at factories and mills. The StarLink corn problem is just a small taste of how costly and troublesome segregating conventional from biotech crops would be. Some analysts estimate that segregation would add 10 percent to 30 percent to the prices of food without any increase in safety. Activists are fervently hoping that mandatory crop segregation will also lead to novel legal nightmares: If a soybean shipment is inadvertently "contaminated" with biotech soybeans, who is liable? If biotech corn pollen falls on an organic cornfield, can the organic farmer sue the biotech farmer? Trial lawyers must be salivating over the possibilities.

The activists' "pro-consumer" arguments can be turned back on them. Why should the majority of consumers pay for expensive crop segregation that they don't want? It seems reasonable that if some consumers want to avoid biotech crops, they should pay a premium, including the costs of segregation. . . .

Under the "precautionary principle," regulators do not need to show scientifically that a biotech crop is unsafe before banning it; they need only assert that it has not been proved harmless. Enshrining the precautionary principle into international law is a major victory for biotech opponents. "They want to err on the side of caution not only when the evidence is not conclusive but when no evidence exists that would indicate harm is possible," observes Frances Smith, executive director of Consumer Alert.

Model biosafety legislation proposed by the Third World Network goes even further than the Biosafety Protocol, covering all biotech organisms and requiring authorization "for all activities and for all GMOs [genetically modified organisms] and derived products." Under the model legislation, "the absence of scientific evidence or certainty does not preclude the decision makers from denying approval of the introduction of the GMO or derived products." Worse, under the model regulations "any adverse socio-economic effects must also be considered." If this provision is adopted, it would give traditional producers a veto over innovative competitors, the moral equivalent of letting candlemakers prevent the introduction of electric lighting.

Concerns about competition are one reason European governments have been so quick to oppose crop biotechnology. "EU countries, with their heavily subsidized farming, view foreign agribusinesses as a competitive threat," Frances Smith writes. "With heavy subsidies and price supports, EU farmers see no need to improve productivity." In fact, biotech-boosted European agricultural productivity would be a fiscal disaster for the E.U., since it would increase already astronomical subsidy payments to European farmers.

The global campaign against green biotech received a public relations windfall on May 20, 1999, when *Nature* published a study by Cornell University researcher John Losey that found that Monarch butterfly caterpillars died when force-fed milkweed dusted with pollen from *B.t.* corn. Since then, at every anti-biotech demonstration, the public has been treated to flocks of activist women dressed fetchingly as Monarch butterflies. But when more-realistic field studies were conducted, researchers found that the alleged danger to Monarch caterpillars had been greatly exaggerated. Corn pollen is heavy and doesn't spread very far, and milkweed grows in many places aside from the margins of cornfields. In the wild, Monarch caterpillars apparently know better than to eat corn pollen on milkweed leaves.

Furthermore, *B.t.* crops mean that farmers don't have to indiscriminately spray their fields with insecticides, which kill beneficial as well as harmful insects. In fact, studies show that *B.t.* cornfields harbor higher numbers of beneficial insects such as lacewings and ladybugs than do conventional cornfields. James Cook, a biologist at Washington State University, points out that the population of Monarch butterflies has been increasing in recent years, precisely the time period in which *B.t.* corn has been widely planted. The fact is that pest-resistant crops are harmful mainly to target species—that is, exactly those insects that insist on eating them.

Never mind; we will see Monarchs on parade for a long time to come. Meanwhile, a spooked EPA has changed its rules governing the planting of *B.t.* corn, requiring farmers to plant non-*B.t.* corn near the borders of their fields so that *B.t.* pollen doesn't fall on any milkweed growing there. But even the EPA firmly rejects activist claims about the alleged harms caused by *B.t.* crops. "Prior to registration of the first *B.t.* plant pesticides in 1995," it said in response to a Greenpeace lawsuit, "EPA evaluated studies of potential effects on a wide variety of non-target organisms that might be exposed to the *B.t.* toxin, e.g., birds, fish, honeybees, ladybugs, lacewings, and earthworms. EPA concluded that these species were not harmed."

Another danger highlighted by anti-biotech activists is the possibility that transgenic crops will crossbreed with other plants. At the Congressional Hunger Center seminar, Mae-Wan Ho claimed that "GM-constructs are designed to invade genomes and to overcome natural species barriers." And that's not all. "Because of their highly mixed origins," she added, "GM-constructs tend to be unstable as well as invasive, and may be more likely to spread by horizontal gene transfer."

"Nonsense," says Tuskegee University biologist C.S. Prakash. "There is no scientific evidence at all for Ho's claims." Prakash points out that plant breeders specifically choose transgenic varieties that are highly stable since they want the genes that they've gone to the trouble and expense of introducing into a crop to stay there and do their work.

Ho also suggests that "GM genetic material" when eaten is far more likely to be taken up by human cells and bacteria than is "natural genetic material." Again, there is no scientific evidence for this claim. All genes from whatever source are made up of the same four DNA bases, and all undergo digestive degradation when eaten. . . .

The environmentalist case against biotech crops includes a lot of innuendo. "After GM sugar beet was harvested," Ho claimed at the Congressional Hunger Center seminar, "the GM genetic material persisted in the soil for at least two years and was taken up by soil bacteria." Recall that the *Bacillus thuringiensis* is a *soil bacterium*—its habitat is the soil. Organic farmers broadcast *B.t.* spores freely over their fields, hitting both target and nontarget species. If organic farms were tested, it's likely that *B.t.* residues would be found there as well; they apparently have not had any ill effects. Even the EPA has conceded, in its response to Greenpeace's lawsuit, that "there are no reports of any detrimental effects on the soil ecosystems from the use of *B.t.* crops."

Given their concerns about the spread of transgenes, you might think biotech opponents would welcome innovations designed to keep them confined. Yet they became apoplectic when Delta Pine Land Co. and the U.S. Department of Agriculture announced the development of the Technology Protection System, a complex of three genes that makes seeds sterile by interfering with the development of plant embryos. TPS also gives biotech developers a way to protect their intellectual property: Since farmers couldn't save seeds for replanting, they would have to buy new seeds each year.

Because high-yielding hybrid seeds don't breed true, corn growers in the U.S. and Western Europe have been buying seed annually for decades. Thus TPS seeds wouldn't represent a big change in the way many American and European farmers do business. If farmers didn't want the advantages offered in the enhanced crops protected by TPS, they would be free to buy seeds without TPS. Similarly, seed companies could offer crops with transgenic traits that would be expressed only in the presence of chemical activators that farmers could choose to buy if they thought they were worth the extra money. Ultimately, the market would decide whether these innovations were valuable.

If anti-biotech activists really are concerned about gene flow, they should welcome such technologies. The pollen from crop plants incorporating TPS would create sterile seeds in any weed that it happened to crossbreed with, so that genes for traits such as herbicide resistance or drought tolerance couldn't be passed on.

This point escapes some biotech opponents. "The possibility that [TPS] may spread to surrounding food crops or to the natural environment is a serious one," writes Vandana Shiva in her recent book *Stolen Harvest.* "The gradual spread of sterility in seeding plants would result in a global catastrophe that could eventually wipe out higher life forms, including humans, from the planet." This dire scenario is not just implausible but biologically impossible: *TPS is a gene technology that causes sterility; that means, by definition, that it can't spread. . . .*

As one tracks the war against green biotech, it becomes ever clearer that its leaders are not primarily concerned about safety. What they really hate is capitalism and globalization. "It is not inevitable that corporations will control our lives and rule the world," writes Shiva in *Stolen Harvest.* In *Genetic Engineering: Dream or Nightmare?* (1999), Ho warns, "Genetic engineering biotechnology is an unprecedented intimate alliance between bad science and big business which will spell the end of humanity as we know it, and the world at large." The first nefarious step, according to Ho, will occur when the "food giants of the North" gain "control of the food supply of the South through exclusive rights to genetically engineered seeds."

Accordingly, anti-biotech activists oppose genetic patents. Greenpeace is running a "No Patents on Life" campaign that appeals to inchoate notions about the sacredness of life. Knowing that no patents means no investment, biotech opponents declare that corporations should not be able to "own" genes, since they are created by nature.

The exact rules for patenting biotechnology are still being worked out by international negotiators and the U.S. Patent and Trademark Office. But without getting into the arcane details, the fact is that discoverers and inventors don't "own" genes. A patent is a license granted for a limited time to encourage inventors and discoverers to disclose publicly their methods and findings. In exchange for disclosure, they get the right to exploit their discoveries for 20 years, after which anyone may use the knowledge and techniques they have produced. Patents aim to encourage an open system of technical knowledge.

"Biopiracy" is another charge that activists level at biotech seed companies. After prospecting for useful genes in indigenous crop varieties from developing countries, says Shiva, companies want to sell seeds incorporating those genes back to poor farmers. Never mind that the useful genes are stuck in inferior crop varieties, which means that poor farmers have no way of optimizing their benefits. Seed companies liberate the useful genes and put them into high-yielding varieties that can boost poor farmers' productivity.

Amusingly, the same woman who inveighs against "biopiracy" proudly claimed at the Congressional Hunger Center seminar that 160 varieties of kidney beans are grown in India. Shiva is obviously unaware that farmers in India are themselves "biopirates." Kidney beans were domesticated by the Aztecs and Incas in the Americas and brought to the Old World via the Spanish explorers. In response to Shiva, C.S. Prakash pointed out that very few of the crops grown in India today are indigenous. "Wheat, peanuts, and apples and everything else—the chiles that the Indians are so proud of," he noted, "came from outside. I say, thank God for the biopirates." Prakash condemned Shiva's efforts to create "a xenophobic type of mentality within our culture" based on the fear that "everybody is stealing all of our genetic material."

If the activists are successful in their war against green biotech, it's the world's poor who will suffer most. The International Food Policy Research Institute estimates that global food production must increase by 40 percent in the next 20 years to meet the goal of a better and more varied diet for a world population of some 8 billion people. As biologist Richard Flavell concluded in a 1999 report to the IFPRI, "It would be unethical to condemn future generations to hunger by refusing to develop and apply a technology that can build on what our forefathers provided and can help produce adequate food for a world with almost 2 billion more people by 2020."

One way biotech crops can help poor farmers grow more food is by controlling parasitic weeds, an enormous problem in tropical countries. Cultivation cannot get rid of them, and farmers must abandon fields infested with them after a few growing seasons. Herbicide-resistant crops, which would make it possible to kill the weeds without damaging the cultivated plants, would be a great boon to such farmers.

By incorporating genes for proteins from viruses and bacteria, crops can be immunized against infectious diseases. The papaya mosaic virus had wiped out papaya farmers in Hawaii, but a new biotech variety of papaya incorporating a protein from the virus is immune to the disease. As a result, Hawaiian papaya orchards are producing again, and the virus-resistant variety is being made available to developing countries. Similarly, scientists at the Donald Danforth Plant Science Center in St. Louis are at work on a cassava variety that is immune to cassava mosaic virus, which killed half of Africa's cassava crop two years ago. . . .

Biotech crops can provide medicine as well as food. Biologists at the Boyce Thompson Institute for Plant Research at Cornell University recently reported success in preliminary tests with biotech potatoes that would immunize people against diseases. One protects against Norwalk virus, which causes diarrhea, and another might protect against the hepatitis B virus which afflicts 2 billion people. Plant-based vaccines would be especially useful for poor countries, which could manufacture and distribute medicines simply by having local farmers grow them. . . .

[O]pponents of crop biotechnology can't stand the fact that it will help developed countries first. New technologies, whether reaping machines in the 19th century or computers today, are always adopted by the rich before they become available to the poor. The fastest way to get a new technology to poor people is to speed up the product cycle so the technology can spread quickly. Slowing it down only means the poor will have to wait longer. If biotech crops catch on in the developed countries, the techniques to make them will become available throughout the world, and more researchers and companies will offer crops that appeal to farmers in developing countries.

Activists like Shiva subscribe to the candlemaker fallacy: If people begin to use electric lights, the candlemakers will go out of business, and they and their families will starve. This is a supremely condescending view of poor people. In order not to exacerbate inequality, Shiva and her allies want to stop technological progress. They romanticize the backbreaking lives that hundreds of millions of people are forced to live as they eke out a meager living off the land.

Per Pinstrup-Andersen of the International Food Policy Research Institute asked participants in the Congressional Hunger Center seminar to think about biotechnology from the perspective of people in developing countries: "We need to talk about the low-income farmer in West Africa who, on half an acre, maybe an acre of land, is trying to feed her five children in the face of recurrent droughts, recurrent insect attacks, recurrent plant diseases. For her, losing a crop may mean losing a child. Now, how can we sit here debating whether she should have access to a drought-tolerant crop variety? None of us at this table or in this room [has] the ethical right to force a particular technology upon anybody, but neither do we have the ethical right to block access to it. The poor farmer in West Africa doesn't have any time for philosophical arguments as to whether it should be organic farming or fertilizers or GM food. She is trying to feed her children. Let's help her by giving her access to all of the options. Let's make the choices available to the people who have to take the consequences."

RONALD BAILEY is science editor of *Reason* magazine. He has published articles in *The Washington Post, The Wall Street Journal, Commentary,* and *Forbes.* He has given lectures at many institutions, including Harvard University, Rutgers University, the Cato Institute, and the American Enterprise Institute.

Michael W. Fox   → **NO**

Killer Foods: When Scientists Manipulate Genes, Better Is Not Always Best

Scientific and Bioethical Issues in Genetic-Engineering Biotechnology

> Every creature has its own reason to be. All its parts have a direct effect on one another, a relationship to one another, thereby constantly renewing the circle of life.
>
> —Johann Wolfgang von Goethe

Through genetic-engineering technology, we now have the power to profoundly alter all life forms and the very nature of nature—the natural world, or earth's creation. What are the short- and long-term consequences for humanity, animals, and nature, and what are the ethical principles and boundaries? What risks are justified by what benefits?

This new technology is complex, with many risks, costs, and benefits that need careful consideration because it could permanently and irreversibly alter the biology of life forms, the ecology, and natural evolution.

Through various techniques, the genetic composition of animals, plants, and microorganisms can be altered in ways radically different from those achieved by traditional selective breeding. Genes can be deleted, duplicated, and switched among species. Animal and human genes have been incorporated or "spliced" into the genetic structure or germ plasm of other animals, plants, bacteria, and other microorganisms. Human genes are now present in the genetic makeup of some mice, sheep, pigs, cattle, fish, and other animals.

The creation of transgenic plants, animals, and microorganisms, along with a host of other developments in genetice-ngineering biotechnology, are touted as progressive, if not necessary, and as promising great benefits to society (and investors). Although I have found

no coherent argument based on reason, science, or ethics to support any of these claims unconditionally, the biotechnology life-science industry and its supporters, just like the supporters of factory farming and vivisection, give enthusiastic and unconditional endorsement to new developments in biogenetic manipulation and to the industrialization and patent protection of its processes and products. The hyperbole employed on behalf of such new developments, coupled with a highly competitive and volatile world market, is driven by risk-taking venture capitalists whose cavalier attitude toward such significant risks as socioeconomic inequity, ecological damage, and animal suffering is neither progressive nor visionary. Unfortunately, this attitude is understandably often shared and rarely challenged by bioengineering scientists and academics in their employ, and by politicians and policy makers, who are generally scientifically illiterate.

This is not a good foundation for any new technology, least of all for such a profound and complex one as bioengineering. It is incumbent upon all who do not feel so sanguine about the directions this new technology is taking to challenge its assumptions and presumptions.[1] The doublethink and newspeak logic* of the biotechnocracy evidences some disturbing warning signs, notably of historical amnesia, ecological and biological illiteracy, ethical and moral dyslexia, blind faith, and ideological rigidity.

An international bioethics council within the United Nations would be a beginning to help ensure that this technology is applied with the minimum of harm to further the good of society and the integrity and future of the planetary biosphere. Insofar as its applicability to organic agriculture, biogenetic engineering is, from a philosophical perspective, anathema. It is mechanistic, deterministic, and reductionistic, while organic agriculture is seen as emulating nature—i.e., ecologistic, dynamically indeterminate,

*E.g.: *Knowledge is Power and Science is Truth.* From *1984* by George Orwell.

holistic, and regenerative. There is also an inimical difference in attitude that separates these two worldviews and in the kinds of medicine, industry, and market economy they aspire to. It has to do with reverential respect for the sanctity and intrinsic value of life, which is more evident on a well-operated (and well-loved) organic farm than in a biotech laboratory or on an industrial farm.

The ideal of value-free objectivity in the method of scientific investigation provides no ethical basis for determining the risks, costs, and benefits in the technology transfer of biotechnical discoveries from the laboratory setting to the real world. A technocratic society runs the risk of serious error in believing that the "truth" of the scientific method is an ethically objective yardstick. This belief system of *scientism,* which is like a religion in the late twentieth century, accounts for the rigid "science-based" criteria and policies that corporations and governments—the entwined limbs of the technocracy—so adamantly adhere to. Yet this yardstick is as linear as it is simplistic. A broader bioethical framework is urgently needed in order for society to transcend technological enchantment, so that the fruits of scientific research may be realized for the benefit of the entire life community of the planet. . . .

Two contexts of particular interest to me are agriculture and the use of animals for biomedical research and biopharmaceutical industrial purposes. I am especially concerned about applications of genetic-engineering biotechnology in agriculture, because it is being applied primarily to maintain a dysfunctional system. We have an animal- rather than a plant-based agriculture in the industrial world, which causes much animal suffering and isn't good for the environment, for consumers, or for the social economy of rural communities. And it is now well documented that conventional agricultural practices are ecologically unsound, inhumane, and in the long term unsustainable, even with ever more costly corrective inputs. Some of these are being developed and misapplied by agricultural biotechnologists, who endeavor to maintain and expand globally a bioindustrialized food and drug industry that must be opposed by all because it fails to meet any of the following bioethical criteria of acceptability: that it be humane, ecologically sound, socially just, equitable, and sustainable. Rather, it is a major threat to biodiversity and to the social economies of many more sustainable farming communities.

Now, via GATT, the World Trade Organization, and Codex Alimentarius, the life-science industry, with its new varieties of patented seeds and other bioengineered products and processes, is moving rapidly to a global agricultural and market monopoly.

With regard to the patenting of animals, plants, and other life forms, I believe that it is demeaning to refer to them as "intellectual property" and that there are unresolved questions of ethics and equity over the patenting of life.

The spirit of enterprise and state of mind behind genetic engineering evidences an ethical blindness to the natural integrity, purity, and sanctity of being. Otherwise, how would we ever consider inserting our own and other alien genes into other species, drastically altering their nature and future to make them more useful to us rather than fulfilling their biologically ordained ecological, evolutionary, and spiritual purposes?

The domestication of plants and animals and the transformation of their habitats and ecosystems to serve human ends have had profound consequences on their nature and on the entire natural world. But do thousands of years of domestication and ecosystem alteration provide a historically valid and ethically acceptable precedent for even more profoundly altering the intrinsic nature of other living beings through genetic engineering?

We must ask: Is it necessary? Who are the primary beneficiaries? What are the direct and indirect costs and risks? Are there safer, less invasive and enduring alternatives? Does a cultural history of exploiting life justify its continuation and intensification through genetic-engineering biotechnology?

"Hard" and "Soft" Paths

There are two basic paths that this new technology can take, and I have designated them as "hard" and "soft." The hard path results in permanent physical changes that may be transmissible to subsequent generations. These changes in animals' physiology or anatomy may result in their suffering. For purely ethical, humanitarian reasons, I am opposed to all hard-path applications of genetic-engineering biotechnology of which there is no demonstrable benefit to the animals themselves.

Where such benefits can be demonstrated, as in efforts to conserve endangered species and to prevent or treat various animal diseases of genetic origin, and there are no alternative strategies to achieve the same ends,

---

*Utilitarian ends such as to increase appetite, growth, muscle mass, leanness, fertility, or milk or egg production or to deliberately create developmental abnormalities and genetic disorders.

then I would accept on a case-by-case basis some hard-path applications. But those applications that design animals for purely utilitarian ends should be questioned and opposed in the absence of demonstrable animal benefit.*

Likewise, any nontherapeutic product of genetic-engineering biotechnology, such as recombinant (synthetic) bovine growth hormone (rBGH), that is used to increase animals' utility and can result in animal sickness and suffering, or increase the risk thereof, is not ethically acceptable.

The creation of transgenic plants that are resistant to herbicides and virus infections, or that produce their own insecticides, belong in the hard-path category. They do not accord with accepted standards and principles of organic and sustainable agriculture and are a potential threat to wildlife and nonharmful insects, microorganisms, and biodiversity.

Soft-path developments with this technology include the creation of new-generation vaccines, veterinary pharmaceuticals and diagnostic tests, and genetic screening to identify defective genes and those that convey disease resistance and other beneficial traits. The most promising of these soft-path developments that I would endorse are immunocontraceptives, new-generation contraceptive implants for humans and other mammals.

Soft-path genetically engineered products are acceptable, provided they are safe and effective without side-effects that could cause animal suffering; provided they cannot be transmitted to or harm nontarget species (as with modified live virus vaccines); and provided they are not used to help prevent diseases in animals kept under stressful, inhumane conditions (as on factory farms), rather than changing the conditions that contribute to increased susceptibility to disease. A full socioeconomic and environmental impact assessment is needed prior to approving these soft-path products for animal use. For example, a new vaccine for cattle to combat trypanosomiasis (to which wild ruminants are immune) could result in an unacceptable loss of biodiversity and an ecologically harmful expansion of livestock numbers. . . .

Genetic Determinism

The broad range of potentially beneficial applications of genetic-engineering biotechnology in agriculture and in veterinary and human medicine are being overshadowed and undermined by an overarching narrowmindedness. This is the reductionist view that since there is a genetic basis to disease, then genetic engineering is the answer to preventing and treating various human, crop, and farm-animal health problems. And that along the way we may even discover ways to genetically engineer (and patent) life forms to enhance their usefulness and "improve" their nature, be it the stature and intelligence of our own species, the growth rates of chickens and pigs, or the herbicide and pest resistance of corn and beans. This simplistic view of genetic determinism is a potentially harmful one because even though it claims to be scientific and objective, i.e., value free, it is extremely subjective and biased since it puts so much value (and faith) in the genetic approach to improving the human condition and the disease resistance and productivity of crops and farm animals.[2]

A more interdisciplinary and holistic approach to human, animal, and crop health and disease prevention is urgently needed. Seeking purely genetic solutions is too narrow and reductionistic, and because of the uncertainty principle inherent in the genotype-environment interface, genetic determinism is unlikely to bring the benefits that its proponents and investors hope and believe are possible.

In its unsubstantiated promises to feed the hungry world, and its promises of great profits for investors, genetic-engineering technology drains human resources from funding more sustainable, eco-friendly, and socially just ways of producing food. It likewise impedes the medical sciences from breaking free of a reductionistic and mechanistic paradigm of human health that blames either nature or our genes for most of our ills. Once people blamed the gods, but as Hippocrates advised, "Physician, do no harm." Conventional medicine has yet to realize this wisdom and put it into practice.

Had the dominant Western culture based its foundation on the worldview of Pythagoras or Plato, rather than that of Aristotle, with his hierarchical, linear thinking, and not on interpreting the book of Genesis as giving man unconditional dominion over God's creation, then our powers over the atoms of matter and the genes of life would probably be applied to very different ends: wholeness and healing, rather than commodification, monopoly, and selfish exploitation.

The original meaning of *dominion* in the book of Genesis does not rest in the Latin *domino*, to rule over, but in the root Hebrew verb *yorade*. *Yorade* means to come down to, to have humility, compassion, and communion with all of God's creation. It is an injunction of reverential care, of humane stewardship. Hence, genetic engineering is antithetical to Judeo-Christian tradition and ethics. It also violates the precept of Islam, where it is regarded as a sin to willfully interfere with God's creation, and would be considered a blasphemy of hubris to engage in creating transgenic life forms and then to go and patent them.

Genetic engineering is anathema to Buddhists, Hindus, and Jains, since it is a direct violation of the doctrine of *ahimsa,* of noninterference and nonharming. It is also a fundamental biological interference with the earth's creative process of natural unfoldment and thus a disruption in the spiritual process of incarnation.

One would think that an enlightened biotechnology industry would make every effort to protect the remaining integrity and biodiversity of genetic resources of the first creation—the last of the wild. Future generations, with a more sophisticated understanding of genetic engineering, will need wild places as a source of uncontaminated genetic resources. This "biobank" must be protected now and not ransacked by the industries of timber, mining, real estate, and other business enterprises, and by the millions of poor people who are malnourished and either landless or without sustainable agriculture or way of life. I have seen them in India and Africa leaving an imprint similar to that left by the clear-cutting of old-growth forests and totally obliterated prairies that the U.S. government still permits. To this destruction by the rural poor—especially from grazing too many livestock, plowing marginal land that erodes easily, and killing trees for firewood—we must add industrial and agrochemical pollution in both the "first" and "third" worlds.

An important step to protect the biobank is to eliminate all possibilities of genetic pollution from transgenic crops, bacteria, insects, oysters and other mollusks, shrimp, and other genetically engineered seafoods, which will be the first foods of animal origin on the market.[3] The second step must be to label all foods to indicate whether any product or ingredient has been genetically engineered. To have this information is a consumer's right, on religious and ethical grounds, since many, regardless of assurances as to food quality and safety, would prefer not to unknowingly purchase genetically modified foods. The public has a right to be informed and a right to be able to choose natural foods if they prefer, especially since genetically altered foods violate many people's religious principles.

The third step entails international cooperation on the scale of a United Nations environmental paramilitary police force to help countries protect their wildlife preserves and biodiversity, both aquatic and terrestrial, from further human encroachment, wholesale exploitation, and genetic piracy.

There is no way to collect all potentially useful life forms and store them in culture media, or in seed, sperm, embryo, and cell banks. Many seeds lose their vitality when stored and need to be frequently germinated and harvested, genetic changes due to local environmental influences notwithstanding. They must be protected *in situ* and *in toto.*

The late Professor René Dubos, a renowned biologist from Rockefeller University, said, "An ethical attitude to the scientific study of nature readily leads to a theology of the earth." His concerns, expressed in 1972 in his book *A God Within,* are extremely relevant today with the advent of genetic engineering.[4] He cautioned, "A relationship to the earth based only on its use for economic enrichment is bound to result not only in its degradation but also in the devaluation of human life. This is a perversion which, if not corrected, will become a fatal disease of technological societies." Without an "ethical attitude," beginning with a reverential respect for all life and based on internationally accepted bioethical principles and values, . . . this disease is very likely to be fatal to the dominant culture.

The ethics of preserving the earth's bio-integrity must serve to direct and constrain the emerging biotechnocracy. The biotechnology industry must adopt these ethics; otherwise, the costs and risks to future generations will far outweigh the short-term profits of the present.

Obedience to natural law, which is based on the bioethics of sound science and moral philosophy, must be absolute, like compassion, or else it is not at all. Through science, reason, and reverence, we learn the wisdom of obedience. Industry and commerce must conform to natural law and, like human society, do nothing to jeopardize natural biodiversity, bio-integrity, or the future of earth's creation. The first task of science and of biotechnology is to begin the healing of humanity, which is biologically, economically, and spiritually dependent on the protection and restoration of what is left of the natural world: first creation first!

The application of bioethics, which is the foundation of natural law, to establishing the necessary limits and boundaries of new technologies like genetic engineering is long overdue. Every nation-state needs to have a bioethics council that would function to maximize the benefits and minimize the risks and costs of all new technologies and related commercial activities, and to ensure international harmonization of their policies and guidelines with all countries via the United Nations Council on Sustainable Development.

Beyond Genetic Determinism and Reductionism

Genes "intelligently" organize structural proteins into myriad environmentally co-evolved, living forms. These life forms are variously self-healing, self-replicating, even marginally self-conscious to varying degrees; and they form mutually enhancing or symbiotic communities.

Collectively, for example, they help create and maintain the soil and the atmosphere that sustains the body-earth and life community; much like our digestive, circulatory, and respiratory systems are cellular communities that sustain the body-human. We find phenomenological parallels between the ecological roles of a living forest or a watershed of streams and swamps, and the functions of our own lungs, circulatory system, and kidneys.

In order to know, therefore, *how* genes, organs, and forests function, we must understand their purpose within the larger functional systems in which they participate. Therefore, we must seek to understand the *contexts* in which genes operate, their history (or evolution and development), and their consequences. Such knowledge of temporal and spatial relationships within the intersecting biofields of organisms and their environments is lacking in the reductionistic paradigm of conventional scientific inquiry, and in conventional medical practice, which has been so reticent to recognize the myriad connections between healthy forests and a healthy people. Hence, most of our agricultural, medical, and technological inventions and interventions have caused more harm than good.[5]

The direction being taken by the life-science industrial biotechnocracy today, especially its investment in creating and patenting transgenic life forms that have been engineered to serve narrow human ends, is cause for concern, as the science base is unsound and there is no ethical or ecological framework. . . .

It is unlikely that genetically engineered crops will ever help compensate for nutrient-deficient soils, polluted water, or a contaminated food chain. Using biotechnology to make farm animals more productive and efficient in the context of intensive industrial agriculture will only extend the animals' suffering and prolong the adverse environmental, economic, and consumer health consequences of this kind of agriculture.

Genetic-engineering reductionists might find it advantageous to further reduce life conceptually to its next level—primordial energy, vital force, or chi—and then reflect upon the possibility that the final frontier of materialistic and mechanistic science, molecular genetics, is a grand illusion, a mirage created by a defective worldview and a misconception of human purpose and significance. The antidote is a paradigm shift that broadens our understanding of life by fostering a sense of reverence and awe and a feeling for the spirit or essence of life that is omnipresent in all matter and manifest in all sentient beings.

Ecological and Social Concerns

In relation to ecological concerns, I would concur with Mario Giampietro that:

> Current research on agricultural applications of genetic engineering seems to be heading exactly in the same direction as the green revolution. The main goal is to provide yet another short-term remedy to sustain, if not increase, the scale of human activity. . . . Genetic engineering aimed only at increasing economic return and technological efficiency is likely to further lower the compatibility of human activity and natural ecosystem processes. . . . Before introducing a massive flow of new transgenic organisms into the biosphere, a better understanding of the endangered equilibrium of the biosphere should be achieved.[6]

Philosopher, scientist, and activist Vandana Shiva eloquently expresses my concerns over the harmful consequences of this new technology and the need for public input to minimize potential harm:

> My major concern these days is with the protection of cultural and biological diversity. I am preoccupied with the ecological and social impacts of globalization of the economy through free trade on the one hand and the colonization of life through genetic engineering and patents on life forms on the other hand. My sense is that unless we can put limits and boundaries on commercial activity and on new technologies, the violence against nature and against people will become uncontrollable. The question I constantly ask myself is, What are the creative catalytic linkages that strengthen community and enable communities of people to exercise social and ecological control of economic and technological processes?[7]

One of the major risks of genetic-engineering biotechnology has a conceptual basis that Craig Holdrege thoroughly dissects in his book *Genetics and the Manipulation of Life*.[8] It stems from scientific reductionism, objectivism, and the mechanomorphizing and reification of genetic and developmental processes and shows no concern and responsibility for effects on the organism and the environment. The belief in genetic determinism is as dangerous ethically as it is flawed scientifically because it is based on the central dogma that genes alone determine how an organism develops and functions.[9] The antidote that Holdrege offers is in seeking an understanding of relationships via contextual thinking, based in part on regarding heredity as potential or plasticity complemented by heredity as limitation or specificity. *Genetics and the Manipulation of Life* is an important book for all students of the biological sciences and for those proponents and critics of biotechnology in particular.

We must be mindful of the fact that nothing that exists originated independently. Therefore, all existences are ultimately interconnected, co-evolved, and interdependent. Genes are not the sole or even the primary controllers and regulators of life processes. It is a product of hubris and reductionism that in isolating and manipulating DNA, we believe we can gain control over life. If we do not act quickly to address all the factors that are leading to the death of nature, then the virtual reality that the global life-science industrial biotechnocracy is fabricating will collapse. We have neither the wisdom nor the resources to develop a viable analog of the earth's atmosphere, or of an old-growth forest, a mountain stream, or a coral reef. . . .

How then can we expect unnatural, genetically engineered life forms to do any better in the virtual world of global industrialization, even when we too are engineered to withstand the harmful, somatic effects of chemicals, pathogens, and radiation?

Some Bioethical Concerns and Solutions

I am deeply concerned by what I see as a lack of vision in the agricultural biotechnology. industry, which is limiting its benefits to humanity and its potential for profitability and sustainability. The cavalier attitude of corporations, governments, and much of academia toward the release and commercialization of transgenic crops is especially troubling. A related concern is over the fact that agricultural biotechnology is focused primarily on major commodity crops and not linked in any significant way with ecologically sound and sustainable crop and livestock husbandry. It therefore cannot play any significant role in helping relieve world hunger or, especially, in implementing appropriate practices and inputs to restore agricultural and rangelands now sorely degraded worldwide.

Lester Brown writes in *State of the World 1994* that University of Minnesota agricultural economist Vernon Ruttan summarized the feeling of a forum of the world's leading agricultural scientists when he said, "Advances in conventional technology will remain the primary source of growth in crop and animal production over the next quarter century." Biotechnology should not be seen as a panacea, or as a substitute for conventional technologies, the most basic of which are good farming practices in accordance with the land ethic and the principles of humane sustainable agriculture. My opposition to conventional agricultural biotechnology is based on its evident band-aid and high-input roles in conventional, nonsustainable agriculture. As such, it represents a major obstacle to the research, development, and adoption of more sustainable, ecologically sound, and in the long-term more profitable farming practices. . . .

The conservative Hastings Center has published a report that details the complexity of bioethics, especially the creation of genetically engineered animals.[10] This report emphasizes the difficulties of developing a "grand monistic scheme" that "establishes a hierarchy of values and obligations under the hegemony of one ultimate value." Such an approach to dealing with contemporary ethical concerns is dismissed by the authors because, while it "may serve the peace of the soul by reducing internal moral conflict," it would, they believe, work only in relatively small and homogeneous communities. It "invariably is bought at the price of the variety and richness of human experience and significant cultural activity. In this sense it impoverishes the human soul."

I would argue to the contrary. There are moral absolutes such as reverence for life, compassion, and *ahimsa* (nonharmfulness) that can provide both a goal and a common ground for a reasoned and scientific approach to resolving ethical issues. These absolutes are the cornerstones of a monistic hierarchy of human values that could effectively incorporate the plurality of interests of various segments of society and of different cultures. . . .

References

1. *Cancer Weekly Plus,* via News Edge Corp., April 8, 1998.
2. C. McKee et al., "Production of biologically active salmon calcitonin in the milk of transgenic rabbits," *Nature Biotechnology* 16 (1998): 647–49.
3. P. B. Thompson, *Food Biotechnology in Ethical Perspective,* London, England: Chapman Hall, 1997.
4. R. Goldburg, "Something Fishy," *Gene Exchange* (Union of Concerned Scientists), Summer 1998, p. 6.
5. Genetic engineering news email: rwoifson@concentric.net (November 14, 1998).
6. *Eurobarometer Survey,* London, 46.1.

7. See: M. W. Fox, *Eating with Conscience: The Bioethics of Food,* Troutdale, OR: NewSage Press, 1997.
8. V. Shiva, *Biopiracy: The Plunder of Nature and Knowledge,* Boston, MA: South End Press, 1997.
9. *New Scientist,* February 14, 1998, pp. 14–15.
10. S. Nec and R. May, "Extinction and the loss of evolutionary history," *Science* 278 (1997): 692–94.

MICHAEL W. FOX is a well-known veterinarian, the author of over 40 adult and children's books about animal care, animal behavior, and issues in bioethics. He is a long-time activist involved in issues such as the ethical treatment of animals and the protection of the environment.

EXPLORING THE ISSUE

Is It Right to Produce Genetically Modified Food?

Critical Thinking and Reflection

1. How should competing interests related to genetically modified food, such as protecting the environment and providing resources for the poor, be balanced?
2. Are there any possible alternative approaches to solve diseases that afflict food crops, farm animals, and human beings other than genetic modification? What moral problems might arise with these alternative solutions?
3. How are genetically modified organisms similar to and different from those produced naturally? How are they similar to and different from those produced by breeding programs? Do these similarities and differences have any moral relevance? Explain your answer.

Is There Common Ground?

At first sight this dispute might seem hopeless. Ronald Bailey can hardly find a problem with GMF and Michael Fox can hardly find anything good about it. But this conclusion is too strong. Bailey is right that GMFs are widely used and there haven't been the kinds of dire problems that some critics have predicted. In fact, some of the objections of the critics have been shown by Bailey to be based on groundless misunderstandings.

Fox, for all his criticism of GMF, is dismayed that what he calls a "lack of vision" limits the benefits that are possible through genetic modification. We could benefit from genetic modification of living things if, for example, this modification were focused on restoring damaged ecologies, bringing back degraded rangelands, etc. But instead, because of what Fox describes as the "cavalier attitude of corporations, governments, and much of academia," biotechnology is focused on major commodity crops. If the genetic modification of plants leads only to more crowded factory farming conditions, then we are going in the wrong direction. What we really need, in his view, is not a technological fix at all, but a change in attitude.

Additional Resources

Paul Lurquin, High Tech Harvest: Understanding Genetically Modified Food Plants (Basic Books, 2004)

Michael Ruse and David Castle, eds., Genetically Modified Foods (Prometheus, 2002)

Lisa H. Weasel, Food Fray: Inside the Controversy over Genetically Modified Food (AMACOM, 2009)

Internet References . . .

Genetically Modified Foods: Harmful or Helpful?

www.csa.com/discoveryguides/gmfood/overview.php

Pew Initiative on Food and Biotechnology

www.pewhealth.org/projects/pew-initiative-on-food-and-biotechnology-85899367237

World Health Organization: 20 Questions on Genetically Modified Foods

www.who.int/foodsafety/publications/biotech/20questions/en/

Selected, Edited, and with Issue Framing Material by:
Owen M. Smith, *Stephen F. Austin State University*
and
Anne Collins Smith, *Stephen F. Austin State University*

ISSUE

Is It Morally Necessary for Autonomous Vehicles to be Programmed to Kill their Drivers?

YES: MIT Technology Review, from "Why Self-Driving Cars Must Be Programmed to Kill," *MIT Technology Review* (2015)

NO: Jesse Kirkpatrick, from "The Ethical Quandary of Self-Driving Cars," *Slate* (2016)

Learning Outcomes

After reading this issue, you will be able to:

- Explain the meaning of the expression "moral algorithm" with regard to autonomous vehicles.
- Distinguish between an altruistic moral algorithm and an egoistic moral algorithm, and explain the different ways they maximize the outcomes of using autonomous vehicles.
- Define the expression "experimental ethics" and explain the role of experimental ethics in formulating moral algorithms for autonomous vehicles.
- Formulate your own position on the type(s) of moral algorithm that should be used in autonomous vehicles and identify evidence supporting your position.
- Identify the main objections to your position on the type(s) of moral algorithm that should be used in autonomous vehicles and formulate responses to these objections.

ISSUE SUMMARY

YES: MIT Technology Review argues that applying a utilitarian analysis makes it clear that there will be times when the best outcome of a possible crash will involve injury or even death to the occupants of the car. Studies show that people want other people's cars to be programmed in this way, although they are unwilling to ride in such cars themselves.

NO: Jesse Kirkpatrick argues that crash optimization is a complex and subtle task, and that what is most important is transparency: drivers need to know in advance how their car is programmed.

Impairment by alcohol, impairment by psychoactive substances, fatigue, distraction, impatience, and inexperience—the litany of causes for vehicular accidents is staggering, as is their cost in lives lost, injuries sustained, and property damaged. What can be done? Drivers are human, and humans are fallible. By all means, let us train drivers more effectively and enforce traffic regulations more efficiently. Let us reward the good drivers and punish the

bad. Yet, the single most important element in vehicular accidents has been the one element that seemed impossible to eliminate: the human factor. Until now.

With the advent of advanced computer technology, it is now within our grasp to develop autonomous vehicles—vehicles that drive themselves and therefore have no need for human guidance. Autonomous vehicles, however, must be directed by a preprogrammed operating system that assesses road conditions and traffic regulations to guide the occupants safely and efficiently to their destinations. It is a daunting task, to be sure, to design an operating system that is sufficiently complex to handle the wide range of driving situations a vehicle can encounter and yet sufficiently reliable to entrust with human lives. The market for autonomous vehicles is so lucrative, however, that a wide variety of automobile manufacturers have not merely begun to design autonomous vehicles but are now actually testing them on public roadways. It is therefore no longer a question of whether autonomous vehicles will be available for public use, but when, and the answer to this question is soon—very soon.

An urgent task, therefore, faces the developers of autonomous vehicles: when an accident is unavoidable, what course of action should the operating system choose? The component of the operating system that makes this decision is known as its moral algorithm. There is general consensus that the hierarchy of values that form the parameters of an operating system's moral algorithm should be the same as those that guide human drivers: whenever possible, preference should be given to persons rather than objects, just as lesser harm (injury, damage) should be preferred to greater harm (death, destruction). In fact, given the superior reaction times of computerized operating systems over their human counterparts as well as the greater accuracy of their sensors, the developers of autonomous vehicles are confident that both the number and the severity of accidents will decrease as the number of autonomous vehicles in operation grows.

The complexity of the task increases, however, when the moral algorithm must choose which persons should be injured or killed and whose property should be damaged or destroyed. What decision-making procedure should be programmed into the moral algorithms of autonomous vehicles? The people who design the moral algorithms are not primarily ethicists or philosophers, but software engineers. Therefore, it should not be surprising that they initially demur when addressing this issue: Are there truly any "right" answers to moral dilemmas? Yet, this appeal to ethical relativism is only a feint; for autonomous vehicles to succeed, their operating systems must contain a moral algorithm of some kind, and therefore this issue must be resolved.

The dominant theoretical foundation adopted by software engineers in devising their moral algorithms is consequentialism: the moral algorithm must choose to optimize the outcomes of using an autonomous vehicle. The precise implementation of this consequentialist approach, however, is more difficult than it may initially appear. The dominant issue seems to be one of focus: Should the moral algorithm adopt a narrow focus, optimizing the outcomes of a specific accident involving an autonomous vehicle, or should the moral algorithm adopt a broad focus, optimizing the outcomes of all accidents in which autonomous vehicles play a role?

If software engineers adopt a narrow focus, they should design altruistic moral algorithms: when faced with an inevitable accident, the optimal outcome would be the one in which the fewest persons are injured or killed. Accordingly, the moral algorithm should show no preference to the occupants of its own vehicle, but should consider the welfare of all persons affected by the accident equally. An autonomous vehicle might well then choose an outcome that inflicts greater harm on its own passengers than on pedestrians or the passengers of other vehicles.

While an altruistic moral algorithm accords well with the views of Jeremy Bentham and John Stuart Mill, the authors of classic Utilitarianism, it appears that most potential consumers of autonomous vehicles beg to differ. According to them, it is all well and good for other autonomous vehicles to be programmed with altruistic moral algorithms; they strongly prefer an autonomous vehicle that protects its own occupants in an unavoidable accident, even at the expense of causing greater harm to the other persons involved. In order to maximize the outcomes of using an autonomous vehicle, therefore, software engineers should adopt a broad focus on increasing the number of autonomous vehicles in use, thereby decreasing the number and seriousness of accidents. They should design the operating systems of their autonomous vehicles with egoistic moral algorithms: when faced with an inevitable accident, the optimal outcome would be the one that best serves the occupants of the vehicle.

So, how should the moral algorithms of autonomous vehicles be designed? One set of authors, who comprise the Physics ArXiv staff, use a method they call "experimental ethics" to reach their conclusion. Rather than providing a theoretical defense for their choice of a moral algorithm, they prefer to "crowd source" the issue, using the work of Jean-François Bonnefon of the Toulouse School of Economics to determine the most popular form of moral algorithm for autonomous vehicles.

In contrast, Jesse Kirkpatrick appears to favor allowing individuals a variety of options with regard to the moral algorithms in their autonomous vehicles. He is most concerned with holding consumers responsible, both morally and legally, for the choices made by the operating systems of their autonomous vehicles. He thus emphasizes the requirement that owners of autonomous vehicles explicitly provide voluntary informed consent to their choice of moral algorithm.

YES ↵

MIT Technology Review

Why Self-Driving Cars Must Be Programmed to Kill

Self-Driving Cars are Already Cruising the Streets. But before they can become Widespread, Carmakers must Solve an Impossible Ethical Dilemma of Algorithmic Morality

When it comes to automotive technology, self-driving cars are all the rage. Standard features on many ordinary cars include intelligent cruise control, parallel parking programs, and even automatic overtaking—features that allow you to sit back, albeit a little uneasily, and let a computer do the driving.

So it'll come as no surprise that many car manufacturers are beginning to think about cars that take the driving out of your hands altogether. These cars will be safer, cleaner, and more fuel-efficient than their manual counterparts. And yet they can never be perfectly safe.

And that raises some difficult issues. How should the car be programmed to act in the event of an unavoidable accident? Should it minimize the loss of life, even if it means sacrificing the occupants, or should it protect the occupants at all costs? Should it choose between these extremes at random?

The answers to these ethical questions are important because they could have a big impact on the way self-driving cars are accepted in society. Who would buy a car programmed to sacrifice the owner?

So can science help? Today, we get an answer of sorts thanks to the work of Jean-Francois Bonnefon at the Toulouse School of Economics in France and a couple of pals. These guys say that even though there is no right or wrong answer to these questions, public opinion will play a strong role in how, or even whether, self-driving cars become widely accepted.

So they set out to discover the public's opinion using the new science of experimental ethics. This involves posing ethical dilemmas to a large number of people to see how they respond. And the results make for interesting, if somewhat predictable, reading. "Our results provide but a first foray into the thorny issues raised by moral algorithms for autonomous vehicles," they say.

Here is the nature of the dilemma. Imagine that in the not-too-distant future, you own a self-driving car. One day, while you are driving along, an unfortunate set of events causes the car to head toward a crowd of 10 people crossing the road. It cannot stop in time but it can avoid killing 10 people by steering into a wall. However, this collision would kill you, the owner and occupant. What should it do?

One way to approach this kind of problem is to act in a way that minimizes the loss of life. By this way of thinking, killing one person is better than killing 10.

But that approach may have other consequences. If fewer people buy self-driving cars because they are programmed to sacrifice their owners, then more people are likely to die because ordinary cars are involved in so many more accidents. The result is a Catch-22 situation.

Bonnefon and co are seeking to find a way through this ethical dilemma by gauging public opinion. Their idea is that the public is much more likely to go along with a scenario that aligns with their own views.

So these guys posed these kinds of ethical dilemmas to several hundred workers on Amazon's Mechanical Turk to find out what they thought. The participants were given scenarios in which one or more pedestrians could be saved if a car were to swerve into a barrier, killing its occupant or a pedestrian.

At the same time, the researchers varied some of the details such as the actual number of pedestrians that could be saved, whether the driver or an on-board computer made the decision to swerve and whether the participants were asked to imagine themselves as the occupant or an anonymous person.

The results are interesting, if predictable. In general, people are comfortable with the idea that self-driving vehicles should be programmed to minimize the death toll.

This utilitarian approach is certainly laudable but the participants were willing to go only so far. "[Participants] were not as confident that autonomous vehicles would be programmed that way in reality—and for a good reason: they actually wished others to cruise in utilitarian autonomous vehicles, more than they wanted to buy utilitarian autonomous vehicles themselves," conclude Bonnefon and co.

And therein lies the paradox. People are in favor of cars that sacrifice the occupant to save other lives—as long they don't have to drive one themselves.

Bonnefon and co are quick to point out that their work represents the first few steps into what is likely to be a fiendishly complex moral maze. Other issues that will need to be factored into future thinking are the nature of uncertainty and the assignment of blame.

Bonnefon and co say these issues raise many important questions: "Is it acceptable for an autonomous vehicle to avoid a motorcycle by swerving into a wall, considering that the probability of survival is greater for the passenger of the car, than for the rider of the motorcycle? Should different decisions be made when children are on board, since they both have a longer time ahead of them than adults, and had less agency in being in the car in the first place? If a manufacturer offers different versions of its moral algorithm, and a buyer knowingly chose one of them, is the buyer to blame for the harmful consequences of the algorithm's decisions?"

These problems cannot be ignored, say the team: "As we are about to endow millions of vehicles with autonomy, taking algorithmic morality seriously has never been more urgent."

MIT Technology Review is a magazine owned by the Massachusetts Institute of Technology.

Jesse Kirkpatrick   → **NO**

The Ethical Quandary of Self-Driving Cars

When a Crash is Inevitable, Autonomous Vehicles will have to Decide whom to Collide with

Imagine the beginning of what promises to be an awesome afternoon: You're cruising along in your car and the sun is shining. The windows are down, and your favorite song is playing on the radio. Suddenly, the truck in front of you stops without warning. As a result, you are faced with three, and only three, zero-sum options.

In your first option, you can rear-end the truck. You're driving a big car with high safety ratings so you'll only be slightly injured, and the truck's driver will be fine. Alternatively, you can swerve to your left, striking a motorcyclist wearing a helmet. Or you can swerve to your right, again striking a motorcyclist who *isn't* wearing a helmet. You'll be fine whichever of these two options you choose, but the motorcyclist with the helmet will be badly hurt, and the helmetless rider's injuries will be even more severe. What do you do? Now imagine your car is autonomous. What should *it* be programmed to choose?

Although research indicates that self-driving cars will crash at rates far lower than automobiles operated by humans, accidents will remain inevitable, they will be unavoidable, and their outcomes will have important ethical consequences. That's why people in the business of designing and producing self-driving cars have begun considering the ethics of so-called crash-optimization algorithms. These algorithms take the inevitability of crashes as their point of departure and seek to "optimize" the crash. In other words, a crash-optimization algorithm enables a self-driving car to "choose" the crash that would cause the least amount of harm or damage.

In some ways, the idea of crash optimization is old wine in new bottles. As long as there have been cars, there have been crashes. But self-driving cars move to the proverbial ethicist's armchair what used to be decisions made exclusively from the driver's seat. Those of us considering crash optimization options have the advantage of engaging in reflection on ethical quandaries with cool, deliberative remove. In contrast, the view from the driver's seat is much different—it is one of reaction, not reflection.

Get Future Tense In Your Inbox

Does this mean that you need to cancel your subscription to *Car and Driver* and dust off your copy of Kant's *Critique of Pure Reason*? Probably not. But it does require that individuals involved in the design, production, purchase, and use of self-driving automobiles take the view from both the armchair and driver's seat. And as potential consumers and users of this emerging technology, we need to consider how we want these cars to be programmed, what the ethical implications of this programing may be, and how we will be assured access to this information.

Returning to the motorcycle scenario, developed by Noah Goodall of the Virginia Transportation Research Council, we can see the ethics of crash optimization at work. Recall that we limited ourselves to three available options: The car can be programmed to "decide" between rear-ending the truck, injuring you the owner/driver; striking a helmeted motorcyclist; or hitting one who is helmetless. At first it may seem that autonomous cars should privilege owners and occupants of the vehicles. But what about the fact that research indicates 80 percent of motorcycle crashes injure or kill a motorcyclist, while only 20 percent of passenger car crashes injure or kill an occupant? Although crashing into the truck will injure you, you have a much higher probability of survival and reduced injury in the crash compared to the motorcyclists.

So perhaps self-driving cars should be programmed to choose crashes where the occupants will probabilistically suffer the least amount of harm. Maybe in this scenario you should just take one for the team and rear-end the truck. But it's worth considering that many individuals, including me, would probably be reluctant to purchase self-driving cars that are programmed to sacrifice their owners in situations like the one we're considering. If this is true, the result will be fewer self-driving cars on the road. And since self-driving cars will probably crash less, this would result in more traffic fatalities than if self-driving cars were adopted.

Consumers have a right to know how their cars will be programmed.

What about striking the motorcyclists? Remember that one rider is wearing a helmet, whereas the other is not. As a matter of probability, the rider with the helmet has a greater chance of survival if your car hits her. But here we can see that crash optimization isn't only about probabilistic harm reduction. For example, it seems unfair to penalize motorcyclists who wear helmets by programming cars to strike them over non-helmet wearers, particularly in cases where helmet use is a matter of law. Furthermore, it is good public policy to encourage helmet use; they reduce fatalities by 22-42 percent, according to a National Highway Traffic Safety Administration report. As a motorcyclist myself, I may decide not to wear a helmet if I know that crash-optimization algorithms are programmed to hit me when wearing my helmet. We certainly wouldn't want to create such perverse incentives.

Scenarios like these make clear that crash-optimization algorithms will need to be designed to assess numerous ethical factors when arriving at a decision for how to reduce harm in a given crash. This short scenario offers a representative sample of such considerations as safety, harm, fairness, law, and policy. It's encouraging that automakers have been considering the ethics of self-driving car for some time, and many are seeking the aid of philosophers involved in the business of thinking about ethics for a living. Automakers have the luxury of the philosopher's armchair when designing crash-optimization algorithms, and although the seat is not always comfortable it's one that they must take.

As crash-optimization algorithms plumb some of our deepest ethical intuitions, different people will have different judgments about what the correct course of action should be; reasonable people can deeply disagree on the proper answers to ethical dilemmas like the ones posed. That's why transparency will be crucial as this technology develops: Consumers have a right to know how their cars will be programmed. What's less clear is how this will be achieved.

One avenue toward increasing transparency may be by offering consumers nontechnical, plain-language descriptions of the algorithms programmed into their autonomous vehicles. Perhaps in the future this information will be present in owner manuals—instead of thumbing through a user's guide trying to figure out how to connect your phone to the car's Bluetooth system, you'll be checking to see what the ethical algorithm is. But this assumes people will actually be motivated to read the owner's manual.

Instead, maybe before using a self-driving car for the first time, drivers will be required to consent to having knowledge of its algorithmic programming. This could be achieved by way of a user's agreement. Of course the risk here is that such an approach to transparency and informed consent will take the shape of a lengthy and inscrutable iTunes-style agreement. And if you're like most people, you scroll to the end and click the "I agree" button without reading a word of it.

Finally, even if we can achieve meaningful transparency, it's unclear how it will impact our notions of moral and legal responsibility. If you buy a car with the knowledge that it is programmed to privilege your life—the owner's—over the lives of other motorists, how does this purchase impact your moral responsibility in an accident where the car follows this crash-optimization algorithm? What are the moral implications of purchasing a car and consenting to an algorithm that hits the helmetless motorcyclist? Or what do you do when you realize you are riding in a self-driving car that has algorithms with which you morally disagree?

These are complex issues that touch on our basic ideas of distribution of harm and injury, fairness, moral responsibility and obligation, and corporate transparency. It's clear the relationship between ethics and self-driving cars will endure. The challenge as we move ahead is to ensure that consumers are made aware of this relationship in accessible and meaningful ways and are given appropriate avenues to be co-creators of the solutions—*before* self-driving cars are brought to market. Even though we probably won't be doing the driving in the future, we shouldn't be just along for the ride.

Jesse Kirkpatrick is the assistant director of the Institute for Philosophy and Public Policy at George Mason University and also works as a Research Consultant at Johns Hopkins University's Applied Physics Lab. He specializes in political and moral philosophy, with an emphasis on the just war tradition, emerging technologies, and human rights.

EXPLORING THE ISSUE

Is It Morally Necessary for Autonomous Vehicles to be Programmed to Kill Their Drivers?

Critical Thinking and Reflection

1. Do you think that consumers should be offered the opportunity to choose among different moral algorithms when purchasing an autonomous vehicle? Why or why not?
2. If you purchased an autonomous vehicle, would you prefer its operating system to have an altruistic moral algorithm or an egoistic moral algorithm? Explain your answer.
3. Should drivers who choose an egoistic moral algorithm for their autonomous vehicle be held to a greater level of moral (and legal) responsibility for the harm caused by their vehicle? Why or why not?
4. If consumers are forced to purchase an autonomous vehicle containing a moral algorithm with which they disagree, would it be moral for them to "hack" their vehicle's operating system and change the algorithm? Why or why not?
5. Do you think "experimental ethics" is an appropriate tool for solving moral dilemmas? Is the most popular solution always the best solution? Why or why not?

Is There Common Ground?

There is no dispute among the authors that autonomous vehicles will soon be available for purchase, and therefore a resolution of the moral dilemmas associated with their use is urgently needed. They acknowledge the research demonstrating that the operating systems of autonomous vehicles will cause fewer and less serious accidents than human drivers, and they use consequentialist ethics to frame their respective analyses of the moral algorithms in these operating systems. They also acknowledge that the choice of focus for their consequentialist analysis will determine whether an altruistic moral algorithm or an egoistic moral altruism should be included in the operating systems of autonomous vehicles.

The staff at Physics ArXiv is more sympathetic to moral relativism than Jesse Kirkpatrick, although they all acknowledge the lack of a moral consensus on the moral issues associated with autonomous vehicles. Kirkpatrick seems more open to the possibility of offering different moral algorithms to consumers, thus allowing them to choose between the common good and their own welfare,

while the Physics ArXiv staff seems more interested in maximizing the sale of autonomous vehicles by determining the most popular attitude toward moral algorithms among potential consumers.

Additional Resources

Michael Anderson and Susan Leigh Anderson, "Robot Be Good: A Call for Ethical Autonomous Machines," Scientific American, October 2010.

Noah Goodall, "Ethical Decision Making During Automated Vehicle Crashes," Transportation Research Record: Journal of the Transportation Research Board, 2014.

Patrick Lin, "The Ethics of Autonomous Cars," The Atlantic Monthly, October 2013.

Gary Marcus, "Moral Machines," The New Yorker, November 2012.

John Villasenor, "Products Liability and Driverless Cars: Issues and Guiding Principles for Legislation," Brookings Center for Technology Innovation: The Project on Civilian Robotics, April 2014.

Internet References . . .

AI Topics: Ethics & Social Issues

http://aitopics.org/topic/ethics-social-issues

The Center for Ethics in Science and Technology

http://www.ethicscenter.net/

The Research Center on Computing and Society

http://ares.southernct.edu/organizations/rccs/category/home/

Selected, Edited, and with Issue Framing Material by:
Owen M. Smith, *Stephen F. Austin State University*
and
Anne Collins Smith, *Stephen F. Austin State University*

ISSUE

Is It Moral to Engage in Relations with Sex Robots?

YES: Elizabeth Nolan Brown, from "Sex, Love, and Robots," *Reason* (2015)

NO: Kathleen Richardson, from "The Asymmetrical 'Relationship': Parallels Between Prostitution and the Development of Sex Robots," *SIGCAS Computers & Society* (2015)

Learning Outcomes

After reading this issue, you will be able to:

- Identify and explain the concept of "anthropomorphism" and explain how it applies to pets and robots, including nonsexual robots.
- Identify and explain the concept of "empathy" and explain its importance in sexual relationships and in society.
- Formulate your own position on the morality of sex with robots and identify evidence supporting your position.
- Identify the main objections to your position on the morality of sex with robots and formulate responses to these objections.

ISSUE SUMMARY

YES: Elizabeth Nolan Brown predicts that people will never lose their preference for actual human companionship, and will enjoy sex with robots primarily as a harmless diversion.

NO: Kathleen Richardson argues that the ability to treat sex robots as things rather than people, without regard for their feelings or dignity, will increase and worsen the lack of empathy already felt by those who treat prostitutes as things rather than people.

Recent advances in robotics, materials science, and artificial intelligence are enabling researchers at several different organizations to work toward building life-like, responsive, people-shaped sex robots. As yet, these robots are not self-aware, which would raise a plethora of concerns about the exploitation of human-equivalent beings. While such concerns are currently being explored in works such as the television program Westworld, they are still confined to the world of fiction. When considering the moral implications of having sex with a robot in the present day, we do not yet need to ascribe human moral agency to the robot. Instead, we need to consider the moral implications for the human involved.

It is difficult to categorize sex with robots according to the labels that we now possess. Businesses that purchase sex robots and rent them on-premises to customers by the hour are nicknamed "robot brothels," which would suggest that sex with robots is analogous to sex with prostitutes. Indeed, both authors of the following selections base their arguments on precisely this analogy. Furthermore, the city council of Houston, Texas, was recently disturbed by the resemblance of sex with robots to prostitution. In October 2018, the council voted to update a city ordinance to make it illegal for businesses to rent human-like devices to customers for the purpose of having sex. The measure was taken to prevent the KinkySdolls company from building and running a robot sex establishment within the city.

On the other hand, since sex robots are simply objects without consciousness, others have suggested that sex with a sex robot is simply a case of self-pleasuring with a fancier sex toy than previously available. In that case, the morality of using a sex robot might be seen as equivalent to the morality of masturbation.

More complex moral concerns arise from the use of sex robots, however, other than simply the act of sex itself. For example, there are concerns that the way people treat sex robots will affect the way they treat human sex partners. Since robots really are merely objects, people who routinely have sex with robots may come to objectify sex partners in general, thus dehumanizing the actual humans with whom they have relationships. In addition, there are concerns that people will come to prefer having sex with robots to having sex with human sex partners, increasing the kind of social detachment currently ascribed to the overuse of cell phones, and ultimately leading to a decline in the human population.

Elizabeth Brown describes recent technological advances and limitations in the production of realistic sex robots. While hobbyists who are interested in such robots still say that they are not yet satisfactory, there is a drive for constant improvement. Furthermore, the human tendency to anthropomorphize nonhuman entities with which they interact, including robots, contributes to a sense of humanlike mutuality in relationships with robots. Brown reports that some researchers express concern that the availability of sex with robots will reduce the incidence of actual human sex, as people will prefer the idealized appearance of the robots as well as the freedom of sex without commitment. Brown claims, however, that for most people, a substantial part of their enjoyment of sex is specifically the encounter with another human being.

Drawing on interviews with customers of prostitutes, she notes that they prefer to have a sense that the prostitute enjoys having sex with them. Thus, while robot sex may provide an entertaining supplement, sex with robots will never replace sex with actual humans. Indeed, she comments, prostitution may be one of the few professions that is especially resistant to being replaced by robots. Therefore, while there may need to be regulations of certain aspects of robot sex, such as the use of sex robots that mimic the appearance of young children, on the whole Brown asserts that it is best to remain open-minded.

Richardson, on the other hand, is opposed to sex with robots. She compares using robots for sex to prostitution, and discusses in detail the ways in which prostitution degrades the dignity of the prostitute as well as the empathy of the customer. While some argue that the availability of sex robots will bring about a decrease in prostitution, she states that this is unlikely. Increased sex-related technology, such as the availability of pornography on the Internet, has not decreased the practice of prostitution, but rather increased it. What is especially pernicious about prostitution, Richardson argues, is that it frames a sexual encounter as an inherently unequal situation, in which the buyer alone is a subject, while the seller is considered merely as an object. In sharp contrast to Brown's findings, Richardson cites examples of interviews in which male customers speak about female prostitutes in ways that demonstrate that they are aware that prostitutes are people whose feelings are being disregarded, but the customers don't care. This lack of empathy on the part of sex customers can only be exacerbated by sex robots, which are literally objects which are easily substituted for female prostitutes, who are human beings treated as objects. The more the customers anthropomorphize such robots, the more they become accustomed to treating female sex partners as objects. Sex robots, therefore, will contribute to, rather than alleviate, gender inequalities.

YES ←

Elizabeth Nolan Brown

Sex, Love, and Robots

Will Sexbots Make Human Life Better, Creepier, Or Both?

HER JOINTS ARE "a bit tight and creaky." Her head circumference is smaller than expected, and there's "a slight chemical smell again." But "Mr-Smith" is mostly proud to introduce Page to other members of the message boards at DollForum.com. And they are happy to meet her, too: "Glad to see such an awesome lady of mystery!" one responds. "Have a fantastic honeymoon," types another. "Congratulations, she is a beauty," posts a third. "When you get around to completely introducing yourself to her, you will find that her softness will blow your mind."

Page is what's known as a "love doll" or "sex doll." She is "anatomically correct"–that is, built so people can penetrate her–but she doesn't move on her own or speak. There are at least a dozen high-end doll makers globally, and many more making cheaper models. "Even China is getting into it . . . in a year's time China has gone from being non-existent in the doll market to having like 15 different manufacturers," artist Stacy Leigh, who styles and photographs these dolls, told Acclaim magazine in 2013. "The world better be prepared, because love dolls are coming."

Katie Aquino, a futurist and self-proclaimed techno-optimist who goes by the name "Miss Metaverse" online, agrees that sex dolls and sex robots are poised to go big. But Aquino doesn't think improved industrial tech will be the main force driving the growth. Instead, she thinks hobbyists are the future: "I believe that the first truly life-like sex dolls won't be made in factories, they'll be made in people's garages. Sex robots will be made by makers," she says, using a catchall term for the growing do-it-yourself subculture in everything from 3D printing to mead brewing. And she's mostly on board with this: "New sexual technologies will liberate us, allowing us humans to freely express our desires and fantasies while remaining safe and healthy from the comfort of our homes."

But Aquino also worries about possibilities like "a population decline because more people will choose synthetic relationships over 'organic' human relationships"

and human women "comparing themselves to synthetics and therefore choosing to modify themselves, just as we see how Photoshopped models and celebrities affect women today." Some men are already predicting this day with glee, crowing on blogs and Reddit boards that human women will have to lower their expectations, step up their beauty rituals, or face the fact that many men will find sex robots a "better option."

On the other end of the spectrum, you have people like Sinziana Gutiu, whose presentation at the 2012 We Robot conference focused on how artificially intelligent sexbots could "foster antisocial behavior in users and promote the idea that women are ever-consenting beings, leading to diminished consent in male-female sexual interaction." In other words, she thinks sex robots may lead to more rape.

By promoting "lies about women's humanity," sexbots present "a danger that builds on and surpasses the harms attributed to pornography," Gutiu wrote in her conference paper. In this she joined the laments of social conservatives. "Sodom and Gomorrah never dreamed of sexual immorality like this," Jennifer LeClaire wrote last year in the Christian magazine Charisma. Dave Swindle, an associate editor at the conservative/libertarian site PJ Media, asked, "What happens when a bunch of teenage boys pool their money to buy a robot prostitute they can gang rape? . . . What will our world be when people lose their virginity to a machine?"

Is that last option even possible? Virginity is more a social construct than a physical state; we don't say someone whose hymen breaks using a Tampax or whose penis enters a Flesh-light have "lost their virginity" to tampons and sex toys. But it's this rather outlandish hypothetical that gets us to the crux of the issue: Will sex robots be more like vibrators, pets, partners, or slaves?

That question–and how technologists, potential customers, ethicists, and legislators will answer it–is mostly the concern of a few academics at this point. But in the not-too-distant future it will become much less hypothetical for billions of people. We are drawing ever closer to the era of realistic, affordable, emotionally intelligent robots, including sex robots. These have the potential to change not just how we relate to technology but how we relate to one another. The challenge: How can we make robots part of our social/sexual fabric without letting them remake us?

Meet the Sexbots

Contemporary commercial sex dolls can appear quite lifelike, but they're mostly non-robotic. The dolls, produced by companies such as California-based RealDoll and Japan's Orient Industry, tend to be made from silicone and a metal skeleton and weigh as much as 120 pounds. Depending on the company, dolls can be customized in a variety of ways, from hair and eye color to pubic hair style, plus the addition of features like artificial milk glands. Some offer simulated breathing, pulse, and heartbeat.

One of the few existing robotic sex dolls appears to be Roxxxy, from New Jersey-based TrueCompanion. With an appearance akin to an especially lifelike (yet not especially attractive) store mannequin, Roxxxy is in no danger of being mistaken for human. But she has three "inputs" (mouth, vagina, and anus), according to TrueCompanion's website, and the deluxe model boasts five programmable personalities, including Young Yoko, described on the company's website as "oh so young and waiting for you to teach her," and S&M Susan, "ready to provide your pain/pleasure fantasies." Roxxxy and her male counterpart, Rocky, are billed as responsive companions able to "listen, talk, carry on a conversation, and feel your touch." Owners can purportedly program them with likes, dislikes, and foreign languages, as well as upload their "personalities" to the cloud.

Roxxxy's renown has been wide since her debut at a 2010 adult-entertainment expo, garnering mentions everywhere from tech blogs to the BBC. But many in the love-doll community are skeptical that TrueCompanion has ever sold any robots.

Davecat, 41, is one such person. A "Synthetik advocate," Davecat is part of a group known as the iDollators, who say they prefer sex dolls and robots to intimacy with "Organiks," a.k.a. human beings. Davecat lives with three dolls, whom he has named Sidore, Elena, and Muriel. He has made up personalities and created Twitter accounts for each of them.

Davecat was there for Roxxxy's debut, and he was not impressed. The product "fell far short of everyone's expectations," he says. "Robots by definition are capable of movement, which Roxxxy was incapable of." He

and fellow iDollators found Roxxxy too heavy and visually unappealing, with "the guts of a laptop." And though advertised as the "first" sex doll responsive to stimulus, the Japanese doll company Axis Japan was already using the same sort of technology–sensors that trigger various MP3S to play when a doll is touched in different places.

"Essentially, Hines had his prototype and was attempting to catch the eye of potential investors, so he could build more and cash in on the perceived trend of robosexuality," Davecat says. "None have been sold, TrueCompanion haven't really existed since roughly 2011, and Hines is a charlatan. The contemporary media picked up on the story, but it was much ado about nothing." Hines did not respond to requests for comment.

"Today's sex robot industry is underwhelming," agrees Aquino. "A new techno-sexual revolution is upon us," she explains, but it's currently focused on technologies like teledildonics and virtual reality, which are "converging to bring sexual fantasies to life while allowing users to participate in sexual activities safely and without risk of STDs."

The main thrust of "teledildonics" has been to combine things we conventionally think of as sex toys with haptic interfaces that allow users to "touch" and be touched remotely. Long-distance lovers, for instance, could use teledildonics to have robot-mediated sex, in combination with such technologies as shared virtual reality, webcams, or even old-fashioned phone calls. Users hooked up to virtual-reality headsets such as Oculus Rift could "participate" in porn or virtual erotic worlds. Simple teledildonics include things like Mojowijo, a set of paired vibrator attachments for the Wii, and OhMiBod, a vibrator that can be controlled remotely via an iPhone app. A website called Kiiroo allows teledildonics users to hook up with other users (known or unknown) from around the world, the ultimate fulfillment of the ancient promise of the AOL chatroom.

Meanwhile, those whose tastes are more technologically advanced must make do. Aquino says "a significant number of robosexuals, those who are attracted to robots, choose to partner with love dolls like RealDolls because they are limited by today's embryonic sex robot industry."

Count Davecat among that cohort. "All told, I'd rather have a Gynoid than a Doll," he says in an email, using the technical term for a female humanoid robot. "Dolls are fantastic, but realistically speaking, they can only do so much, and with a completely Synthetik lover, I'd have all the opportunities that are afforded in relationships with Organiks, but without all the drama."

The sex doll company Orient Industry announced in 2014 that it has developed skin "not distinguishable from the real thing." Sex robots could eventually be imbued with an almost real-time capability to "respond" to touch. Gerhard Fettweis, a professor of communications technology at Dresden University, believes that within 20 years wireless technology will match the speed of the human neural system. Some have proposed the idea of sex-bots that mimic humans' biochemical signaling system, releasing pheromones corresponding to arousal and love at the appropriate times.

At the start of 2015, however, roboticists are still struggling with problems like making autonomous humanoid robots that can walk and move their faces realistically. Last summer, the National Museum of Emerging Science and Innovation in Tokyo debuted a girl and woman android, Kodomoroid and Otonaroid, to much fanfare. The robots are used to greet and read news to museum visitors and hold press conferences announcing new robots. They can make facial expressions and move their upper bodies, but they can't walk and can only lip-sync recorded speech. Convincingly human, emotionally intelligent androids of the kind seen in sci-fi are, for now, far more fantasy than reality.

How Much is that Robot in the Window?

In a 2014 paper, the Brown University psychologist Bertram Malle and Matthias Scheutz, director of the Human-Robot Interaction Laboratory at Tufts University, defined social robots as "any robots that collaborate with, look after, or help humans." Kate Darling, a robot ethics researcher with the Massachusetts Institute of Technology (MIT), prefers the wordier "a physically embodied, autonomous agent that communicates and interacts with humans on an emotional level." Social robots, according to Darling, can also "follow social behavior patterns, have various 'states of mind' and adapt to what they learn through their interactions." Sexbots, of course, would fall squarely in this category. So would robots designed to interact with nursing home patients and robot pets.

Early examples of social robo-pets include Furbies and Tamagotchi, which lived on tiny screens on key rings and alerted owners when they needed food or bathing. The Roomba, an autonomous robot vacuum cleaner that has sold millions since 2002, is considered a primitive social robot. Robotic puppies, seals, and other animals are now being tested to interact with nursing home residents and autistic children, with promising anecdotal results.

Human beings love their pets, in large part, because of our deep tendency toward anthropomorphism: the imputation of human-like qualities onto animals and non-living things. Anthropomorphizing a pet doesn't require believing the pet is fundamentally human, it just means its personality and behavior inspires humans to treat it like a person with complex desires, motivations, or memories. It is a near certainty that we will do the same with social robots as they become increasingly commonplace.

The human inclination to anthropomorphize animals "translates remarkably well to autonomous robots," Darling noted in her 2012 paper, "Extending Legal Rights to Social Robots." A robot that can mimic human behavior, social gestures, and facial expressions "targets our involuntary biological responses."

In 2013 Julie Carpenter, a psychology researcher at the University of Washington, interviewed 23 U.S. soldiers working with bomb-disarming robots. While the troops defined the robots as technological tools, they were still given to naming them, gendering them, and talking about them with empathy. "They would say they were angry when a robot became disabled because it is an important tool, but then they would add 'poor little guy,' or they'd say they had a funeral for it," Carpenter explained in a statement about her work.

In a 2007 study from the University of California, San Diego, toddlers introduced to the humanoid robot QRIO quickly lost interest when the robot merely danced continually. But when dancing and giggling were triggered by their touch–when the robot was responsive in a humanlike way–"that completely changed everything," study leader Javier Movellan said in a press release.

It is this illusion of agency that helps endear social bots to human beings. Social robots are designed to elicit anthropomorphic reactions. "There are many of us in the robotics community that study not just robots but human psychology," says Ron Arkin, an American roboticist and roboethicist who teaches at the Georgia Institute of Technology. To Arkin, the central question is: "Can we effectively design robots to interact with people in the way that people want to be interacted with? And that involves understanding the human mind as well as the robotic mind."

People bond with pets in part because we like things that seem to need us. This trait transcends flesh and blood. "Nurturing a machine that presents itself as dependent creates significant social attachments," wrote the MIT scholar Sherry Turkle in her 2006 paper "A Nascent Robotics Culture." Turkle found people are prone both to nurturing feelings toward autonomous robots and to believing, at least on some level, that robots reciprocate these feelings.

So is this something we should worry about? Projection onto traditional objects can be ignored and revived at will, noted Darling. But an artificially intelligent robot "that demands attention by playing off of our natural responses may cause a subconscious engagement that is less voluntary." Scientists and ethicists alike are exploring where to draw lines. Is it wrong, for instance, to "trick" dementia patients into caring for robo-pets?

Right now, social robots' potential benefits for everything from elder care to education seem to outweigh ethical concerns. But right now, intelligent and autonomous robots don't exist. In "The Inherent Dangers of Unidirectional Emotional Bonds Between Humans and Robots," Matthias Scheutz raises concerns that robot companions will have the ability to "exploit human innate emotional mechanisms that have evolved in the context of mutual reciprocity . . . which robots will (not have to) meet."

What are the potential repercussions of this? "Unfortunately, there is currently very little work aimed at trying to minimize the natural human tendency to anthropomorphize," Scheutz tells me. "The key question is how to walk the fine line between making robots useful to people without having them fall for robots."

Before Roomba and Roxxxy

While coverage of Roxxxy and her sisters tends to focus on the unprecedented nature of "lifesized robot girlfriends," creating convincing facsimiles of human beings in order to masturbate into them is actually an ancient pursuit. A Japanese anthology published in the late 1600s refers to Koshoku Tabimakura, a "traveling pillow," with an azumagata ("woman substitute") made from thin layers of tortoiseshell lined with velvet, silk, or leather. The dolls were also known as tahi-joro, or "traveling whores." In the 1904 book Les Detraques de Paris (which loosely translates as The Paris Crazies), Rene Schwaeble quotes "Dr. P," who sold "fornicatory dolls" (though he had to pretend to police he made balloon animals) for around 3,000 francs apiece in French catalogues. "Every one of them takes at least three months of my work!" said Dr. P. "There's the interior framework which is carefully articulated, there's the hair on the head, the body hair, the teeth, the nails! There's the skin, which has to be given a certain tint, certain contours, a particular pattern of veins. . . . The only thing these haven't got is the power of speech!"

In 1908, the German doctor Iwan Bloch wrote of "hommes or dames de voyage," the "artificial imitations of the human body, or of individual parts of the body" sold in France with "genital organs represented in a manner true to nature." Dames were equipped with oil-filled pneumatic tubes, the hommes an apparatus by which "the ejaculation of the semen is imitated." By the 1920s,

customizable sex dolls were advertised "fitted with a phonographic attachment, recording and speaking at will."

Though perhaps some were attracted to the dolls, these were largely considered masturbatory devices, or in some cases a tribute to a dead loved one. Will sex robots be similarly functional, or will they provoke desire in their own right?

"Right now, we're at an inflection point on the meaning of sexbot," Kyle Machulis, a systems engineer with Mozilla, told Aeon magazine last summer. "Tracing the history of the term will lead you to a fork: robots for sex (idealized version: Jude Law in the movie At), and people that fetishize being robots (clockworks, etc.). There was a crossover in the days of alt. sex.fetish.robots, but I see less and less people fetishizing the media/aesthetics, and more talking about actually having sex with robots."

In a survey of 61 DollForum.com members—75 percent men who own dolls, 10 percent women who own dolls, and 15 percent men thinking about purchasing a doll—the psychology researcher Sarah Valverde asked owners what motivated their purchase. Not-mutually-exclusive answers included sexual stimulation (70 percent), companionship (30 percent), and using the doll in sex with a human partner (17 percent). About a third of male owners reported some issues with sexual functioning. Most rated their sex with dolls as "above average" to "excellent."

None of the respondents were in therapy related to their relationship with the sex dolls. Most were employed, educated, and reported similar anxiety and depression levels as the general population. While the use of sex dolls is often seen as pathological, Valverde makes the case that "a diagnosis of paraphilia would be unwarranted, without significant distress or impairment in functioning. Provided a doll-owner doesn't need the sex doll in order to achieve sexual satisfaction, a diagnosis of a fetish would not be appropriate" either. "Anecdotal evidence suggests these dolls have brought relief, security, and happiness to their owners," she concluded.

In his 2007 book Love + Sex with Robots, the artificial intelligence specialist David Levy—a former professional chess player and now president of the International Computer Games Association—pinpoints II major triggers that inspire emotions humans recognize as love. Many of these factors could presumably be inspired by social robots, including proximity, reciprocal liking (liking things that like us), need-fulfillment, a sense of mystery, and the presence of certain desired characteristics (like red hair or a deep voice). To Levy, it's not a stretch to imagine some humans falling in love with and even marrying robots within a few decades.

First, Do No Harm

One result of this influx of robots into our bedrooms is that it may "trigger a broader role for the concept of moral harm in law," suggests University of Washington law professor Ryan Calo in a 2014 paper, "Robotics and the Lessons of Cyberlaw." Certain uses of robots may be deemed undesirable because they compromise the actor, rather than a specific victim or society. The fact that a robot itself can't feel pain or be exploited may not stop pushes to prohibit particular uses of or behavior toward social robots.

"The Kantian philosophical argument for preventing cruelty to animals is that our actions towards non-humans reflect our morality–if we treat animals in inhumane ways, we become inhumane persons," noted Darling in her paper "The Rights of Social Robots." "This logically extends to robot companions. Granting them protection may encourage us and our children to behave in a way that we generally regard as morally correct."

In her We Robot conference paper, Gutiu suggests that, "if regulated," we may be able to use sex robots "to correct violent and demeaning attitudes toward women." But this sort of large-scale social-engineering-through-sexbot could quash the potential for their more individualized use in rehabilitation.

Levy imagines a role for sex robots similar to sex surrogates, therapists who use actual sexual intimacy to address clients' issues. "All of the most common sexual dysfunctions and their cases can be treated by surrogate-partner therapy, including premature ejaculation, non-consummation of a relationship, erection difficulties, performance anxiety, and fear of intimacy," he explains in Sex + Love With Robots. The book cites the California sex therapist Barbara Roberts, who laments that "we have no traditional rite of passage nor meaningful ceremonies to initiate young people into informed adult sexuality"–a role Levy also envisions for sexbots.

And then there's the inevitable question of kiddie sexbots.

Last summer, at a Berkeley Law School panel on ethical and legal challenges in robotics, Arkin spawned a flurry of sensational headlines by suggesting that "childlike robots could be used for pedophiles the way methadone is used to treat drug addicts," potentially reducing recidivism rates for sex offenders. Many people find this idea immediately distasteful. Arkin empathizes with them, he tells me, but he thinks it's better to investigate the therapeutic potential of such robots "in a controlled way" rather than simply avoiding research because it makes us squeamish. While no U.S. companies are publicly selling them, childlike sex dolls are already available online from foreign makers.

In Canada, child sex robots are illegal, but there are no U.S. laws yet specifically criminalizing them. In fact, there is reason to think the U.S. courts might carve out some legal space for them, as unlikely as that might seem: In 2002, the U.S. Supreme Court struck down parts of a federal law criminalizing "virtual" child pornography, described as either digitally created images or those featuring young-looking adults pretending to be younger. "I could see that extending to embodied [robotic] children," said Calo, the law professor, at the panel, "but I can also see courts and regulators getting really upset about that."

Regulatory concerns notwithstanding, "it's coming to the time when we start talking about these things," Arkin argues. "Should the design of [sex robots] be informed by science? Yes. Is anyone doing true scientific study on intimate robots at this time? Not to my knowledge. I would encourage that line of research to be undertaken if we can get past our Victorian taboos."

One area where academics and journalists seem enthusiastic about the possibilities for sexbots concerns robot prostitution. Love doll brothels can already be found in Japan. In a 2012 paper, "Robots, Men and Sex Tourism," the New Zealand researchers Ian Yeoman and Michelle Mars enthusiastically predict that robot prostitutes will overtake human sex workers by 2050. Yeoman and Mars paint an elaborate portrait of a posh Amsterdam robot brothel catering to a high-end clientele and niche sexual preferences–a situation the writers see largely as a social good, capable of invalidating all the messy moral concerns that human sex workers present.

Prostitution is illegal in the U.S. and many other countries, and various nations have previously criminalized everything from vibrators to adultery, so lawmakers may well move to block robot brothels also. But should robot prostitution be legalized, would "the oldest profession" find itself, like so many others, vulnerable to technological disruption?

In his 2014 paper "Sex Work, Technological Unemployment, and the Basic Income Guarantee," John Danaher, a law lecturer with The National University of Ireland, Galway, rejected the idea that sex workers and clients will all go quietly into the good robot night. This is largely due to the fact that people like having sex with other people; even in the presence of a robust robot sex trade, those inclined to pay for sex will still sometimes want to do so with a human being. But we also shouldn't discount sex-worker resiliency–like the move from streetwalking to advertising on Backpage, those in the sex trade will adjust to suit the times. "Prostitution could well be one of the few forms of human labour that is likely to remain resilient in the face of technological unemployment," posits Danaher.

Research on why men pay for sex has found, more than any other common denominator (variety, convenience, etc.), a desire for mutuality. Clients want to feel, at minimum, like a sex worker somewhat enjoys her time with them. In a 1997 study of male prostitution clients ages 27 to 52–nearly half of whom were married–a desire for sex was frequently met with "social, courting behaviors that were often flavored with varying degrees of romance." Interviewing clients at a New Zealand massage parlor, researcher Elizabeth Plumridge found they "all wanted a responsive embodied woman to have sex with. This they secured by ascribing desires, response and sexuality to prostitute women. They did not know the true 'selves' of these women, but constructed them strategically in a way that forwarded their own pleasures."

Read one way, this research could support the future popularity of robot prostitutes, which could theoretically be programmed to portray care and lust sufficiently well that we fall for it. This, of course, depends in part on how effectively artificial emotional intelligence and sociability is developed. But even if we grant that realistically emo sexbots are possible, will they be "real" enough to afford mutuality? Whether we're talking orgasms or affection, convincing oneself that a human sex worker isn't faking it rests on the fact that, technically, she may not be. With robot companions, the fakery is inherent. It's a given. How much that actually matters remains to be seen.

Everyday Ethics

Giving sex toys and sex dolls the illusion of agency will attract new users, Arkin suspects. "Not for everybody–it may go from one-tenth of a percent to I percent–but it would grow the demographic exponentially."

In a June 2014 YouGov poll, Americans were split on whether using a sexbot is moral. Forty-three percent of those surveyed said using sex robots is wrong, and 39 percent said it's acceptable. Only 10 percent said they would use a sex robot themselves.

Should sexbot use reach the mainstream, couples will have to wrestle with questions like how to handle jealousy over robot companions and whether robot sex counts as cheating. Is having sex with a robot more like using a vibrator or having a fling? Is it uncouth for friends to share a sexbot? What if someone creates a sexbot in your likeness?

Sex robots also present ethical issues for academics. "From a researcher's point of view, what is appropriate?"

asks Arkin. "There are no guidelines for researchers in this particular space."

The goal of many roboticists is to get to a point where robots can successfully manipulate our emotions. To make robots more like socio-paths, able to recognize and use social cues, create an illusion of empathy, and gain trust and intimacy without reciprocity.

Osaka University's Hiroshi Ishiguro, who supervised last summer's "Android: What Is Human?" exhibition in Tokyo, has said that "the process of understanding (human) nature is the most interesting part of androids." And for some, a faith in a quintessential humanness–something even the most sophisticated and intelligent robots can't approximate–is one way to mitigate worry over the future of social robots. If human beings bond with robots not for what they are but what they inspire in us, perhaps our insurance lies in what they can't inspire: a sense of mutuality, reciprocity, and genuine agency. To paraphrase David Levy, people don't fall in love with an algorithm but a convincing simulation of a human being. Yet can any simulation really be convincing enough ? Enough to have mass appeal? Enough to significantly change the social fabric?

Near the end of Sex + Love with Robots–a techno-utopian volume if there ever was one–Levy writes that he does not believe for one moment that sex between two people will become outmoded. "What I am convinced of," he declares, "is that robot sex will become the only sexual outlet for a few sectors of the population–the misfits, the very shy, the very sexually inadequate and uneducable–and that for some other sectors of the population robot sex will vary between something to be indulged in occasionally . . . to an activity that supplements one's regular sex life."

On the margins, sexbots could dissuade some individuals from pursuing human-to-human intimacy and relationships, just as pornography, sex toys, and everything from alcohol to work are also sometimes used to avoid attachments. But it has become clear through countless bouts of cultural and technological change that, for the most part, people see no substitute for knowing and loving another person. To predict sexbots as even moderately widespread stand-ins for sex and relationships reveals a not-insignificant misanthropism.

That isn't to say that individual use of sex robots is misanthropic. For many men and women, they will remain ancillary to interhuman relationships, more like sex toys than humanity surrogates. For a subset, social robots may provide opportunities for companionship and sexual satisfaction that otherwise wouldn't exist. When this occurs, we'd all do well to remember that having faith in human institutions and relationships means not panicking over new possibilities. Staying conscientious but open-mined toward the use of social robots, including sex robots, can only enhance our understanding of what it means to be–and to fall for–human beings.

ELIZABETH NOLAN BROWN is an award-winning associate editor at Reason, where she covers criminal justice, politics, and policy with a special focus on the intersection of sex, speech, technology, and law. Her work has appeared in numerous publications, including The New York Times, the Los Angeles Times, and Buzzfeed.

Kathleen Richardson

The Asymmetrical 'Relationship': Parallels Between Prostitution and the Development of Sex Robots

1. Introduction

A number of initiatives are now in place to incorporate the development of sex robots into mainstream robotic activity. For example, in November 2015, roboticists interested in developing the area of sex robots can participate in the Second International Conference on Love and Sex with Robots to be held in Malaysia. The conference will explore topics such robot emotions, humanoid robots, teledildonics, and intelligent electronic sex hardware. In his book, *Sex, Love and Robots* [1] David Levy proposes a future of human-robot relations based on the kinds of exchanges that take place in the prostitution industry. Levy explicitly creates' 'parallels between paying human prostitutes and purchasing sex robots' [1 p.194] . I want to argue that Levy's proposal shows a number of problems, firstly his understanding of what prostitution is and secondly, by drawing on prostitution as the model for human-robot sexual relations, Levy shows that the sellers of sex are seen by the buyers of sex as *things* and not recognised as human subjects. This legitimates a dangerous mode of existence where humans can move about in relations with other humans but not recognise them as human subjects in their own right.

What are the ethics of extending robots into new fields such as sex and what model of sexual relationship is invoked in the transference to robots? Ethically, there is a strong reaction to the use of robots in the military, and as such a well established organisation The Campaign to Stop Killer Robots (http://www.stopkillerrobots.org/) is devoted to preventing automated and robotic warfare developments that further take humans out of the loop. Should we as a robotic community also reflect on implementing a similar response to the development of sex robots? Could the development of sex robots also mark a disturbing trend in robotics? I will propose at the end of this article the urgent need to establish a Campaign Against Sex Robots.

2. Consumption of Intimate Bodies as 'Goods'

Prostitution is the practice of selling a sex for monetary payment. In recent years those who work in the prostitution industry (particularly in Europe and North America) have promoted the term 'sex-work' over prostitution as a way to show how it is similar to other kinds of service labour. A term like prostitution implies that the provider is in a subservient position. *Third Wave Feminism* proposes that women are not subservient but are making conscious choices to choose work that is influenced by their sex [2]. By contrast, the term 'sex-worker' extends the framework of labour to include sexual work. This redefinition of prostitution to sex-work (and therefore framed as a service) has been challenged by a number of campaigners and scholars [3, 4, 5]. While those in favour of the sex industry describe it as an extension of free sexual relations, campaigners against prostitution point to the fact that in the absence of consent, prostitution cannot be reframed as positive. The facts of prostitution are disturbing where violence and human trafficking are frequently interconnected [3, 4]. Moreover the industry is extensive and a recent European Union Survey found:

- prostitution revenue can be estimated at around $186.00 billion per year worldwide.
- prostitution has a global dimension, involving around 40-42 million people worldwide, of
- which 90% are dependent on a procurer. 75% of them are between 13 and 25 years old.

When robots are introduced as possible alternatives to women (or children), some, like Levy ask 'what's the harm? It's only a machine?' The same views are also proposed by some towards those who sell sex.

Levy also proposes that sex robots could help to reduce prostitution. However, studies have found that the introduction of new technology supports and contributes to the expansion of the sex industry. There are more women are employed by the sex industry than any other time in history [5]. Prostitution and pornography production also rises with the growth of the internet. In 1990, 5.6 per cent of men reported paying for sex in their lifetime, by 2000, this had increased to 8.8 per cent. These figures are likely to be even higher due to the reluctance of people admitting to paying for sex [6]. As the buying of sex relies on only acknowledging the needs of the buyer, it is no surprise that children also suffer as a consequence. The National Crime Agency in the UK has identified the web as a new source of threat to children including the proliferation of indecent images of children and online child sexual exploitation [7].

The arguments that sex robots will provide artificial sexual substitutes and reduce the purchase of sex by buyers is not borne out by evidence. There are numerous sexual artificial substitutes already available, RealDolls, vibrators, blow-up dolls etc., If an artificial substitute reduced the need to buy sex, there would be a reduction in prostitution but no such correlation is found. To understand why males buy sex it is important to understand what happens in an exchange and how males describe what is happening. The following are statements from males who buy sex:

'Prostitution is like masturbating without having to use your hand',
'It's like renting a girlfriend or wife. You get to choose like a catalogue',
'I feel sorry for these girls but this is what I want' [3 p.8].

While males are the chief buyer of human sex, females are more likely to purchase artificial nonhuman substitutes such as vibrators [1] that stimulate a discrete part of the body rather than purchase an adult or child for sex. Take a look again at the above– 'renting a girlfriend' or 'feeling sorry for the girls' these and many more indicate that the buyer of sex is putting his needs over and above the other person. In the prostitution/client exchange both enter the encounter in specific ways. A study by Coy [3 p. 18] found the asymmetrical form of encounter between buyers and sellers of sex. As modern subjects, male and females have equal rights under the law, and these rights recognise them as human agents. In prostitution, only the buyer of sex is attributed subjectivity, the seller of sex is reduced to a *thing*. This is played out in multiple ways where . . .

. . . a denial of subjectivity occurs when the experiences and feelings of the "object" are not recognised. This denial of women's subjectivity can also be understood as sexual objectification. Both were evident in these men's lack of empathy with the feelings of women in prostitution. They constructed her in their own minds, according to their own masturbatory fantasies, as opposed to recognising the reality of the woman's feelings. It is also telling that often the men switched from understanding the woman's situation and feelings to attributing to her what they wanted her to feel during or after sex [3 p. 18].

In the sex exchange in prostitution, the subjectivity of the seller of sex is diminished and the subjectivity of the buyer is the only privileged perspective and viewpoint. As robots are programmable entities with no autonomous (or very limited) capabilities, it seems logical then that prostitution becomes the model for Levy's human-robot sex relations.

A key factor that is missing is the inability of the buyer of sex to have empathy with the seller of sex. Expert of autism, Simon Baron-Cohen [8] in his book *Zero Degrees of Empathy* proposes a gendered basis to empathy as a normative category. Baron-Cohen has this to say about empathy:

Empathy is without question an important ability. It allows us to tune into how someone else is feeling, or what they might be thinking. Empathy allows us to understand the intentions of others, predict their behavior, and experience an emotion triggered by their emotion. In short, empathy allows us to interact effectively in the social world. It is also the "glue" of the social world, drawing us to help others and stopping us from hurting others [9 p.163].

Baron-Cohen suggests that the higher prevalence in crime, sexual abuse, the use of prostitutes and murder are disproportionately committed by men and show that men lack empathy in comparison to females [8]. By proposing that empathy is an ability to recognise, take into account and respond to another person's genuine thoughts and feelings is something that is absent in the buying of sex. The buyer of sex is at liberty to ignore the state of the other person as a human subject who is turned into a thing.

3. 'Downloading' Human Lifeworlds into Things

The use of robots for sex (adults and children) are justified on the basis that robots are not real entities, they are things. This narrative is also replayed in the production of video nasties, sexual abuse images of children in virtual reality settings [11] and the sexual and racial violence seen in some video games such as Grand Theft Auto where gamers are rewarded for killing prostitutes [12]. The transference of humanlike qualities to things has provoked extensive discussion in the robotics community. Is it possible to transfer human constructs of gender, class, race or sexuality to a robot or nonhuman? Anthropologically speaking the answer is yes. This theme has been replaced in a discussion of robots as slaves. Bryson [10] has railed against arguments associating robots with slaves because, she argues, they are nothing more than mechanical appliances –do to robots what you wish. But is it only possible to have an either or position? Is it possible then to propose that sex robots are harmful, knowing they are not human? While Bryson has important arguments, the way that human attribute meanings to robots, nature and animals reflect back to us what is of value.

But where do the fantasy images and products come from? Is fantasy just a neutral domain that is a sphere separated off from the 'real' and therefore unproblematic? I propose that fantasy, and the ways that robots are seen show human relations at work. The question is not do humans extend their lifeworlds into robots but what is being transferred to the robot? Anthropologists have developed an extensive literature on the anthropomorphism of things, framing it within the context of 'animism' as the attribution of a spirit to nonhuman animals [13, 14]. Moreover, the anthropology of technology explores how gender, class, sexuality and race is inflected in the cultural production of technological artefacts [15, 16, 17]. In a forthcoming paper I propose that technological-animism is at work in the sphere of robotics, but rather than come from spirit or religion as in classical studies, technological-animism comes from a lack of awareness and attention given to how cultural models of race, class and gender are inflected in the design of robots [18]. The issue then becomes not a why question (that is still open for debate), but a how question. In what ways are robots made and what uses are they put to and what can these practices tell us about gender, power, inequalities, race and class? Campaigns to extend rights to robots without due attention paid to humans are problematic. Robertson [19] notes that campaigns to extend rights to robots are done in contexts where the campaigners do not simultaneously campaign for the extension of rights to all human beings. When this happens it is important to explore the ethics of the human that is reproduced in robotics. In some cases, such as sex-robots it will rest on a disturbing vision of a seller of sex as a thing.

In a recent article on gender and robots, Watercutter [20] highlighted the recurring imagery in fictions and robotic labs which overly presented female robots as young, attractive and focused on performing roles in the service industry as receptionists or waitresses. When it come to the explicit design of sex robots, Roxxxy designed by New Jersey-based company TrueCompanion shows a male view of a sexually attractive adult female complete with three points of entry in the body, the mouth, the anus and the vagina. But the development of sex robots is not confined to adult females, adult males are also a potential market for homosexual males. But the potential for a market in sex robots will be extended to child sex robots. Some researchers such as Ronald Arkin, professor of mobile robotics at Georgia Institute of Technology proposed that child robots could also be used in the treatment of paedophilia [21].

4. Campaigns and Robots

In this paper I have tried to show the explicit connections between prostitution and the development and imagination of human-sex robot relations. I propose that extending relations of prostitution into machines is neither ethical, nor is it safe. If anything the development of sex robots will further reinforce relations of power that do not recognise both parties as human subjects. Only the buyer of sex is recognised as a subject, the seller of sex (and by virtue the sex-robot) is merely *a thing* to have sex with. As Baron-Cohen shows, empathy is an important human quality. The structure of prostitution encourages empathy to be effectively 'turned-off'. Following in the footsteps of ethical robot campaigns, I propose to launch a campaign against sex robots, so that issues in prostitution can be discussed more widely in the field of robotics. I have to tried to show how human lifeworlds of gender and sexuality are inflected in making of sex robots, and that these robots will contribute to gendered inequalities found in the sex industry. I did not create these parallels between prostitution and the making of sex robots, these have been cultivated and explicitly promoted by Levy [1]. By campaigning against sex robots, we will also promote a discussion about the ethics of gender and sex in robotics and help to draw attention to the serious issues faced by those in prostitution.

6. References

Levy, D. 2009. Love and sex with robots: The evolution of human-robot relationships. New York.

Synder-Hall, C. 2010 'Third-Wave Feminism and the Defense of "Choice"' Perspectives on Politics, Vol. 8, No. 1 (March 2010), pp. 255–261.

Farley, M., Bindel, J., & Golding, J. M. 2009. Men who buy sex: Who they buy and what they know (pp. 15–17). London: Eaves.

Schulze, E., Novo, S.I., Mason, P., and Skalin, M. 2014 Research Assistant Gender Exploitation and Prostitution and its impact on Gender Equality. Directorate General for Internal Policies. http://www.europarl.europa.eu/RegData/etudes/etudes/join/2014/493040/IPOL-FEMM_ET(2014)493040_EN.pdf

Barton, B. 2006. Stripped: Inside the lives of exotic dancers. NYU Press.

Balfour, R., and Allen, J. 2014. A Review of the Literature on Sex Workers and Social Exclusion. By the UCL Institute of Health Equity for Inclusion Health, Department of Health. https://www.gov.uk/government/uploads/system/uploads/attachment_data/file/303927/A_Review_of_the_Literature_on_sex_workers_and_social_exclusion.pdf

National Crime Agency, *Child Exploitation* http://www.nationalcrimeagency.gov.uk/crime-threats/child-exploitation

Baron-Cohen, S. 2011. Zero degrees of empathy: A new theory of human cruelty. Penguin UK.

Baron-Cohen, S., & Wheelwright, S. (2004). The empathy quotient: an investigation of adults with Asperger syndrome or high functioning autism, and normal sex differences. Journal of autism and developmental disorders, 34(2), 163–175.

Bryson, J. B. 2010. Close Engagements with Artificial Companions: Key social, psychological, ethical and design issue, Yorick Wilks (ed.), John Benjamins (chapter 11, pp 63–74) 2010.

Eneman, M., Gillespie, A. A., & Stahl, B. C. Criminalising fantasies: The regulation of virtual child pornography. In Proceedings of the 17th European Conference on Information Systems (pp. 8–10). Tavel, P. 2007. *Modeling and Simulation Design*. AK Peters Ltd., Natick, MA.

DeVane, B., & Squire, K. D. 2008. The meaning of race and violence in Grand Theft Auto San Andreas. Games and Culture, 3(3–4), 264–285.

Swancutt, K., and Mazard, M (eds.) forthcoming 2016. Special Issue: The Anthropology of Anthropology in Animistic Ontologies. *Social Analysis.*

Boyer, P. 1996. What makes anthropomorphism natural: Intuitive ontology and cultural representations. Journal of the Royal Anthropological Institute, 83-97.

Helmreich, S. 1998. Silicon second nature: Culturing artificial life in a digital world. Univ of California Press.

Martin, E. 2001. The woman in the body: A cultural analysis of reproduction. Beacon Press.

Richardson, K. 2015. An Anthropology of Robots and AI: Annihilation Anxiety and Machines. Routledge, New York.

Richardson, K. Forthcoming 2016. Technological Animism: The Uncanny Personhood of Humanoid Machines. In Swancutt, K and Mazard, M (eds.) forthcoming 2016. Special Issue: The Anthropology of Anthropology in Animistic Ontologies. Social Analysis.

Robertson, J. 2014. Human rights vs. robot rights: Forecasts from Japan. Critical Asian Studies, 46(4), 571-598.

Watercutter, A. 2015. Ex Machina has a serious Fembot problem. Wired. 9th April 2015. http://www.wired.com/2015/04/ex-machina-turing-bechdel-test/

Robertson, J. 2010. Gendering humanoid robots: robo-sexism in Japan. Body & Society, 16(2), 1–36.

Hill, K. 2014. Are Child Sex Robots Inevitable? Forbes Magazine. http://www.forbes.com/sites/kashmirhill/2014/07/14/are-child-sex-robots-inevitable/

KATHLEEN RICHARDSON is a professor of Ethics and Culture of Robots and AI in the School of Computer Science and Informatics at De Montfort University. She is the Director of the Campaign Against Sex Robots and also part of the Europe-wide DREAM project (Development of Robot-Enhance Therapy for Children with AutisM). Her publications include the book *An Anthropology of Robots* and *AI: Annihilation Anxiety and Machines.*

EXPLORING THE ISSUE

Is It Moral to Engage in Relations with Sex Robots?

Critical Thinking and Reflection

1. Suppose a married person visits a robot brothel and has sex with a robot. Has that person committed adultery? Why or why not?
2. In what way is our behavior toward animals related to our behavior toward people? Be sure to provide justification for your position.
3. In what way is our behavior toward machines such as computers and cell phones related to our behavior toward people? Be sure to provide justification for your position.

Is There Common Ground?

Brown and Richardson agree that having sex with a robot is very similar to having sex with a prostitute. Their differing views on the acceptability of sex with robots can be traced in part to their differing views on prostitution.

Brown uses the more positive term "sex workers" to describe prostitutes and appears primarily concerned with the economic impact of the availability of sex with robots on the business of sex work. Richardson rejects the term "sex workers" and makes it clear that prostitution reinforces unhealthy gender inequalities. It is not surprising, therefore, that their views on sex with robots are similarly opposed.

Additional Resources

Facchin, Federica, et al. "Sex robots: the irreplaceable value of humanity," BMJ 358 (August 2017).

"Let's talk about sex robots." Nature 547:7662 (2017).

Mariano Gomes, Leonardo and Rita Wu, "User evaluation of the Neurodildo: A mind-controlled sex toy for people with disabilities and an exploration of its applications to sex robots," Robotics 7:3 (August 2018), p. 46.

Internet References . . .

Amnesty International: Sex Workers' Rights Are Human Rights

https://www.amnesty.org/en/latest/news/2015/08/sex-workers-rights-are-human-rights/

Health 24: Are Sex Robots Healthy for Humans?

https://www.health24.com/Sex/News/are-sex-robots-healthy-for-humans-20180624-3

Nordic Model Now: Facts About Prostitution

https://nordicmodelnow.org/facts-about-prostitution/

Selected, Edited, and with Issue Framing Material by:
Owen M. Smith, *Stephen F. Austin State University*
and
Anne Collins Smith, *Stephen F. Austin State University*

ISSUE

Is It Ethical to Employ Service Animals?

YES: **Nora Wenthold and Teresa A. Savage**, from "Ethical Issues with Service Animals," *Topics in Stroke Rehabilitation* (2007)

NO: **Randy Malamud**, from "Service Animals: Serve Us Animals: Serve Us, Animals," *Social Alternatives* (2013)

Learning Outcomes

After reading this issue, you will be able to:

- Understand the role of service and therapy animals in assisting humans with disabilities.
- Describe specific issues involved in the ethical treatment of such animals.
- Understand the concept of speciesism and speciesist objections to employing service and therapy animals.
- Formulate your own position on employing service and therapy animals and identify evidence supporting your position.
- Identify the main objections to your position and formulate responses to these objections.

ISSUE SUMMARY

YES: Nora Wenthold and Teresa A. Savage consider the overall use of service animals to be justified. They describe, however, a number of situations in which ethical treatment of service animals requires careful consideration of the animal's strengths, limitations, and well-being. Understanding and respecting the animal's nature is a crucial and sometimes overlooked ethical requirement.

NO: Randy Malamud argues that our current attitudes toward service animals spring from speciesism, an attitude that members of certain species (such as humans) have greater value or more rights than certain other species (such as nonhumans). He is especially concerned about the extension of the practice to animals such as monkeys, parrots, and dolphins, who may derive little benefit to themselves from their association with humans.

Human beings, as Aristotle noted, are social animals, and therefore it is no surprise that most of the contemporary moral problems that occupy our attention involve interactions between humans, whether individually or collectively. This focus, however, should not blind us to the recognition that human beings exist in a much wider context than human society, and thus contemporary moral problems arise as a result of interactions with other beings in our environment, such as plants and animals.

The manifold interactions between human beings and animals, especially domesticated animals, gives rise to a number of ethical issues, especially when these interactions involve inflicting injury on an animal or deliberately causing its death. Yet, even apparently mutually beneficial interactions between animals and humans have recently come under ethical scrutiny, as in the case of employment of service animals.

In order to frame this moral issue, it will be necessary to clarify the notion of a service animal. For millennia, humans have used domesticated animals for a variety of purposes, including providing meat, milk, and fiber for human consumption, assisting humans in the performance of tasks such as hunting and drawing loads, and providing comfort and companionship as pets. It was not until recently, however, that humans began systematically using animals to assist them in overcoming disabilities. The first school devoted to this purpose in the United States was the Seeing Eye, which was established in 1929 to train large dogs such as German shepherds or Labrador retrievers to assist people with visual disabilities. Over the past several decades, similar training regimens have been developed for a wide variety of animals to assist humans in a diverse set of ways. In fact, it may be helpful to distinguish animals that provide assistance to human beings into two groups.

The first group, service animals, are defined under the Americans with Disabilities Act of 1990 as "any guide dog, signal dog, or other animal individually trained to do work or perform tasks for the benefit of an individual with a disability, including but not limited to, guiding individuals with impaired vision, alerting individuals with impaired hearing to intruders or sounds, providing minimal protection or rescue work, pulling a wheelchair, or fetching dropped items." As indicated by this definition, dogs are the most common type of service animal, although miniature horses and capuchin monkeys have also been trained as service animals.

The second group, therapy animals, is less rigorously defined. Any animal that is used to improve a person's quality of life by assisting that person to achieve a therapeutic goal may be considered a therapy animal. Thus, animals that provide a calming presence to patients suffering from stress-induced cardiac problems are therapy animals, as are animals that provide emotional support to individuals suffering from panic disorders and PTSD (posttraumatic stress disorder). The success of therapy animals in helping humans achieve therapeutic goals has led to their widespread utilization in a variety of institutional settings, including nursing homes, rehabilitation centers, and even prisons.

There is no doubt that service animals and therapy animals provide enormous benefit to humans. What basis could there be, then, for raising a moral objection against using animals in this way? The answer lies in the key word "using." In philosophical terms, service animals have instrumental value, rather than intrinsic value. This denial of intrinsic value to animals is at the heart of the moral objection to the use of service animals and therapy animals.

Philosophers have traditionally distinguished between two types of value: instrumental value and intrinsic value. Instrumental value is the value that a thing possesses as a means to an end, while intrinsic value is the value that a thing possesses in and of itself. Traditionally, human beings are regarded as having intrinsic value, and so it would be immoral to use a human being merely as a means to an end, even if that end is improving the life of another human being. Animals, however, are traditionally considered to have only instrumental value. Consequently, there would be no moral objection to using an animal to improve the life of a human being.

There are, however, contemporary challenges to this view of animals. These challenges are based on a principle of critical thinking known as the Universalization Principle. According to this principle, similar cases must be treated similarly. In order for two cases to be treated differently, there must be a morally relevant difference between them; if there is no such morally relevant difference, the two cases must be treated similarly. The Universalization Principle, however, does not tell us which differences are morally relevant and which are not; this determination must be based upon an inquiry into the specific cases under consideration.

The philosopher Peter Singer focuses on the capacity to suffer as the only relevant moral factor in applying the Universalization Principle to humans and animals. Since humans and animals both have the capacity to suffer, they should both be treated similarly; in particular, they both should be accorded intrinsic value. Consequently, assigning service/therapy animals merely instrumental value is a violation of the Universalization Principle, and hence is fundamentally wrong. Indeed, the claim that human beings have a moral status superior to animals is a form of discrimination described by Singer as "speciesism," which, like racism and sexism, would be repugnant because it favors one group over another without any objective, morally relevant justification.

Philosophers who wish to defend the use of service/therapy animals as moral also have recourse to the Universalization Principle. They agree with Singer that service/therapy animals and humans have a common capacity to suffer. Consequently, they propose stringent requirements for protecting the physical and psychological health of these animals, just as they advocate protecting the physical and psychological health of the humans they assist.

However, they defend assigning humans a moral status superior to service/therapy animals by asserting a morally relevant difference between them: the ability to reason. Since humans have this ability, and service/therapy animals do not, there is no moral objection to the instrumental use of these animals to assist humans.

In their article, Nora Wenthold and Teresa A. Savage do not question the morality of using service/therapy animals in general, but raise a number of particular issues that must be considered in the training and employing of these animals. The most important issue to be considered, they assert, is a balance between beneficence (providing benefits to human beings) and nonmaleficence (inflicting harm on the service/therapy animals). They describe a number of situations in which it is crucial to understand and respect the nature of a service/therapy animal in order to treat the animal in an ethical manner.

By describing the many layers of meaning inherent in the language we use to describe service/therapy animals, Randy Malamud points out troubling speciesist attitudes in the use of such animals to benefit humans. He is also concerned about our negative attitude toward animals that are not obedient and useful to us, emphasizing that all animals deserve value and respect. If we can come to understand each animal as it exists in nature, rather than as it can be exploited in our society, we can consider each animal's "service" as the role it plays in contributing to the natural world. Then we will be able to take the next step, which is determining the service that humans can provide to other animals.

YES ⬅

Nora Wenthold and Teresa A. Savage

Ethical Issues with Service Animals

Humans have used animals since the beginning of time—for food, clothing, and shelter, as beasts of burden and transportation, for amusement, for medical experimentation, and for companionship. Although their moral status is debated and some philosophers advocate for elevating nonhuman animals to a higher moral status than they currently occupy, animals are treated as property.[1,2] The role of service animal touches on a mutual need of both humans and animals, especially dogs, and that is the need for companionship. Although there are tasks and duties required of the service animal in rehabilitation health care, the service animal brings an acceptance and devotion to their human partners that can surpass a species difference. The bond is as strong as a family bond. Service animals display behaviors often interpreted as caring and loving, but it must be remembered that they are not there by their own volition; they are trained and carefully monitored for any deviations from their trained behavior. They are subject to stresses in their environment and can be harmed or can harm others if not properly managed and cared for. This article will address the ethical issues with service animals.

History

According to the Humane Society of the United States, there are approximately 66 million owned dogs in the United States.[3] A rough estimate is that there are 17,000 assistance dogs currently working in the United States.[4] It is unknown when a dog was used the first time to assist someone with a disability. However, there is evidence such as records of dogs being kept at healing temples in ancient Greece or an illustration on a wooden plaque from medieval times depicting a dog on a leash leading a blind man to suggest that we are simply rediscovering an ancient practice in our use of dogs in rehabilitation. However, more recent records can be found at Les Quinze-Bingts,

a Paris hospital for the blind, that has dated records from 1780 describing systematic attempts to train dogs to aid blind people. From 1788, there are records of a blind sieve-maker from Vienna who trained his spitz (a breed of dog like the husky, malamute, or chow chow) so well that many doubted his disability. A couple decades later, the founder of the Institute for the Education for the Blind in Vienna, Johann Wilhelm Klein, published a book that described his methods on training guide dogs for people with blindness. Unfortunately, there is no evidence of his ideas being realized.

The modern history of the assistance-dog movement began in 1929, with the first guide dog school, The Seeing Eye. This school was inspired by a partnership created between Dorothy Harrison Eustis and Morris Frank. While living in Switzerland, Ms. Eustis observed trained dogs guiding blind veterans. This inspired Ms. Eustis to write an article for the *Saturday Evening Post* describing what she had witnessed and offering to work with an interested blind American. Morris Frank, a young blind man living in Nashville, wrote to Ms. Eustis asking her to train a dog for him and, in return, he would teach others who were blind so that they too could become independent. Morris Frank became the first American to use a dog guide, and Buddy, a female German shepherd, became the pioneer dog guide in America. Morris Frank returned home to Nashville and honored his promise. With $10,000 from Ms. Eustis, he worked to establish the first dog guide school in America.

In contrast to the population of people with visual impairments, Americans with physical disabilities and members of the deaf community have had about 30 years of working with service and hearing dogs in a formalized setting. In the mid- 1970s, Bonnie Bergin pioneered the service dog movement and founded Canine Companions for Independence. Agnes McGrath, her contemporary, also pioneered a program to train dogs to assist the hearing impaired and inspired the development of a number of hearing impaired dog training centers.

Assistant Animal Terminology

Although the Americans with Disabilities Act (ADA) defines a service animal, there are many terms for assistant animals. There are three major categories: service animals, therapy animals, and companion animals. The ADA defines a *service animal* as any animal that has been "individually trained to perform tasks for people with disabilities such as guiding people who are blind, alerting people who are deaf, pulling wheelchairs, alerting and protecting a person who is having a seizure, or performing other special tasks."[5] This article will focus primarily on the service group. *Therapy animals* are animals that are used in the course of improving a person's quality of life or in helping the person achieve some therapeutic goal. The Delta Society describes the use of therapy animals in animal-assisted activities, which are opportunities for motivational, educational, recreational, and/or therapeutic benefits to enhance a person's quality of life.[6] Animal-assisted therapy is goal directed in which the animal meeting specific criteria is an integral part of the treatment process.[6] *Companion animal* is another term for a pet, and this animal is usually owned by the person.

Service animals are primarily dogs, so the term *service dog* will be used. Sometimes service dogs are also called assistance dogs. In one particular organization, Paws With a Cause, dogs are rescued from animal shelters, rigorously evaluated for physical attributes and temperament consistent with the duties of a service animal, and then undergo extensive training. The cost of preparing and placing a service or hearing dog with a client exceeds $18,000.[6] The agency will acquire and train the dog to suit the needs of a particular client. A client must be over 14 to get a service dog and over 18 to get a hearing dog.

Hearing dogs are trained to bring their owner (the client) to the source of a noise, such as a ringing doorbell, phone, or smoke alarm. Guide dogs, often bred for the purposes of being service animals, assist persons with blindness to navigate in their home and community.[7] Service dogs perform multiple tasks, such as opening doors, retrieving dropped objects, or turning switches off/on.

There have been studies demonstrating the usefulness of service dogs—the positive economic impact and the positive psychosocial aspects, both to adults and children with disabilities, in using service dogs.[8-11] Little has been written on the ethical issues with service animals. Managing expectations and the workload of the service dog, attending to the physical and psychological needs of the dog, and anticipating separation through retirement or death are all ethical issues to be addressed in this article. Before tackling the ethical issues, certain terminology needs explanation. There are many humans involved with a single service animal. There is the owner of the animal, the leader or handler, the human partner, and patients. Many service animals are trained and owned by an agency that provides the dog to an institution, such as a rehabilitation hospital, through a contractual arrangement. One or two people who undergo special training are designated as the service dog's facilitators. The service dog lives with them, is brought to work by them, and they are responsible for the dog's well-being. The facilitators also act as the service dog's advocate and are pivotal in facilitating communication between the agency that owns the dog, the dog handlers, and the institution where the dog works. Facilitators may or may not be directly involved in the service dog's daily work activities, such as working with the dog during a therapy session, but they are available to the dog or dog's handlers during the day and communicate with dog handlers daily to address pertinent issues. Facilitators provide the constant "behind-the-scenes" care, so the service dog is physically and psychologically ready for work. There are other humans, therapists or other clinicians, who also undergo special training to work with the dog during the day. These are the service dog's handlers. There is oversight of the dog's well-being by the agency owning the service dog. The owner of a service dog assumes ultimate responsibility for the dog. This is done by setting standard guidelines regarding care of the dog that the institute has agreed to uphold, such as the frequency of veterinary visits, the types of toys that the service dog can have, and the equipment that the dog is allowed to wear. This information is communicated to the service dog's owners through site visits, completion of annual progress reports, submission of medical records, and correspondence with the facilitators.

Guide dogs for people who are blind or hearing dogs for people with hearing impairment may be owned by the person with the disability or a service animal agency. Service dogs working in facilities are typically owned by an agency, live with one or two facilitators, and are led by a variety of trained handlers. Inconsistency between humans interacting with the service dog can be a source of ethical problems.

Ethical Issues

The primary ethical issue with service animals is the tension between using the dog to achieve patient or client goals (beneficence) and monitoring the welfare of the dog (nonmaleficence). As an animal, the dog does not have autonomy to choose to be a service animal, but the dog's temperament and response to situations belie the dog's choice. Clarity about who is representing and advocating for the dog's interests is also at issue.

Managing Expectations and the Workload

The role for a service dog in a health care setting is usually defined by patients' needs within the health care institution. This may include game playing, visiting, walking, or grooming activities. Typically, the service dog is asked to participate in activities that he/she enjoys. A select group of handlers, people within an institution who are specially trained to work with a specific service animal within specific guidelines, are the only ones who should direct the service dog's activities. Dogs, like most pack animals, rely on consistency and trust to complete requests made by people. The irregular dynamics of a health care environment can make a seemingly easy request a challenge for the dog. A service dog's performance is strongly impacted by an overstimulating health care environment, so to be successful it is vital that the service dog has complete confidence in his or her dog handler or is known to the dog as the leader. It is critical to have consistency in the people trained to handle the service dog and in the behaviors and signals used to communicate with the dog. Mixed messages, new untrained people, and general confusion can be very stressful for the dog and result in unreliable responses from the dog. The facilitators and handlers must communicate with each other so they know what can be expected from the dog, how to lead and respond to the dog, how to assess the dog for signs of stress, and how to manage the dog's stress.

One of the reasons that dogs have always worked so well with people is that both humans and dogs share a common fundamental need of companionship. However, the companionship that service dogs receive when they are "off-duty" is vastly different from the companionship they receive while "working." Both types of companionship are important to the dog as most service dogs are selected from working breeds that enjoy engaging in task-related duties. However, clear communication is required by the facilitator or handler to ensure the dog reacts appropriately in a given situation. An example of this is how service dogs are trained to greet people in different ways to accommodate various settings. People are always instructed to ask a dog handler if they may pet the dog or many people will ask the question, "Is your dog off duty?" If the dog's facilitator or handler is able to comply, they may look at the dog and give a command such as "release" or "play" and at that point the dog will stand from the seated position to greet the individual in a similar way that a dog may greet someone walking through the front door. Usually, this greeting includes a wagging tail, kisses, and maybe a small run. A much different reaction is seen from a service dog when the dog is working and the dog handler asks the dog to "visit" or "greet" a patient. When the dog is working, the dog will walk up quietly to a patient, gently rest his/her head on a patient's lap, and wait to receive a pet.

It is crucial that all demands made of a service dog are considered reasonable and appropriate. Failure to do so can result in injury to the dog or to people near the dog. For example, even though a service dog working in a health care setting may be physically able to and enjoy pulling people in a wheelchair, it may not always be appropriate. The tile floors can cause the dog and wheelchair to gain speed quickly and newly waxed floors can prove to be slippery, which can lead to accidents. There are service dogs that pull their human companions in wheelchairs. Typically, these dogs have been trained and conditioned for this specific task and wear proper equipment such as a harness to accomplish this task safely. Most important, these dogs have developed a long-term relationship and trust with the individual using the wheelchair.

Other tasks may be physically appropriate for a service dog but may cause psychological stress. The best way to eliminate psychological stress on a service dog is to provide consistent leadership. Because service dogs are expected to ignore specific survival instincts such as their "flight-or-fight" response, trust in their facilitators and handlers is crucial. Most service dogs only have one or two people that they look to for leadership, and most service dogs have only one home with one set of family dynamics to interpret. However, service dogs working in large facilities may have as many as seven leaders at any given time. In addition, they may live in multiple homes, which require them to adapt to various family dynamics. How can a service dog adapt to this lifestyle successfully and fulfill countless requests from dozens of individuals daily?

The key is consistent leadership. All individuals who handle the service dog must be trained, certified, and have adequate bonding time with the dog. The training and certification process educates the facilitators and handlers on the dog's basic physical and psychological needs. Facilitators and handlers also learn the meaning of all the commands and how to help the service dog to be successful. They learn to interpret the dog's body language and how to lead the dog during situations of unpredictability. All of the facilitators and handlers for the same dog need to work together to mimic each other's behavior. The more similar the leaders' interactions and expectations, the easier the requested tasks are for the dog to understand and perform.

The most important requirement that each facilitator or handler must undergo is to spend bonding time with the service dog. This can be done through the practice of commands, grooming, and spending time "off-duty" together. This helps to build trust between a facilitator or handler and a service dog. If a service dog does not trust his or her facilitator/handler, then it is a set-up for disaster; it will cause psychological stress in the dog, which may lead to injury of the dog or a person.

Addressing the Physical and Psychological Needs of the Dog

Whether a service dog works in a large or small facility, there always needs to be coordination between units and staff to ensure that a dog is not overtaxed. This can be done by setting a schedule for the dog allowing for ample times for breaks between activities and recognizing what a dog would consider a break as opposed to what a person considers a break. For example, being told to sit in a corner of a room while a therapist finishes working with a patient is not a break to a dog as the dog is still "on command" and watching his or her leader for the next command. However, having a dog go into a crate for 15 to 30 minutes in a quiet office gives the dog a clear signal that they are not being expected to respond to commands at the moment and can relax.

In addition to short breaks between tasks at work, service dogs also need breaks on a larger scale. This may include weekend hikes or long walks or breaks from being on a leash. Many service dogs spend a lot of their time active on a leash and following commands; even though they enjoy their work and love being around people, all dogs benefit from time "off leash" and interacting with other dogs. Some service dogs may not be able to fully enjoy this with some of their facilitators or handlers they work with in the health care setting as they are always waiting for the next command. However, these dogs seem to do fine if taken to a dog park with other dogs by a family member of a facilitator or handler. Any facilitator or handler can help his or her service dog enjoy relaxation time in his or her presence by participating in "off-duty" activities, such as taking their service dog to a dog park, on a consistent basis. However, it is important for a facilitator or handler to practice work commands before they reenter the work environment. This provides the service dog with a clear signal that it is time to be "on-duty" and to wait for the next command.

The most important element to remember when working with a service dog is that they are in fact dogs. It sounds silly, but because these dogs perform on a consistent basis and are so well trained it is easy to forget that they can be inconsistent. It is a leader's role to try and interpret the cause of the inconsistency and act appropriately. For example, if a service dog is shying away from a patient who is trying to pet behind the dog's ear, then the leader needs to recognize that behavior and request that the patient refrain from petting the dog behind the ear. Next the leader needs to determine what has caused the dog's resistance. This is usually done by noting the dog's reaction and discussing it with other leaders for the dog. Then it is determined if the problem is physical or psychological. A veterinarian can treat a physical problem, such as an ear infection, and the service dog will refrain from working until the infection is gone. However, the problem may be psychological, such as the previous day a patient grabbed the dog's ear too tightly while petting and now the dog has developed a negative association with having his or her ears petted. This type of problem takes more time to work through as the facilitators and handlers will need to help the service dog develop more positive associations to having his or her ears petted. The facilitators and handlers will need to spend extra time to bond with the dog to reassure him or her that no discomfort will come to the dog while the facilitators and handlers are present. In addition, the facilitators and handlers will advise all patients and staff to refrain from petting the dog's ears until the service dog is comfortable having his or her ears petted by strangers.

Physical and mental capabilities of a service dog are decided by the dog's owners, facilitators, handlers, and veterinarians. Sometimes these decisions are made collectively as a group and sometimes they are individual judgments made as a result of a particular situation. This is why it is so important for each person who handles a service dog in a health care setting to be trained and maintain a certain level of expertise. The popularity of service animals can mean that any given facility may have a number of service animals at any given time. Occasionally, there are some dogs that do not do well around other animals. An important qualification of being a facilitator or handler of a service dog is to know how to lead dogs in an emergency situation, such as if another animal provokes them or is threatening to the facilitator or handler. A qualified facilitator or handler is required to direct the service animal through situations such as these to ensure safety is maintained.

It is ideal for a facilitator or handler to recognize and provide the service dog with a break before common stress signs are apparent. However, if a facilitator or handler notices panting, shedding, or hesitation, it is a sign that the service dog is experiencing stress and needs a break. This may necessitate shortening a session with a patient or moving up the dog's break time. Usually, the service dog will be ready to work again after a 30-minute break that allows for water and a nap in the dog's crate.

A service dog that displays signs of chronic stress such as digestive problems, lack of enthusiasm, or fearfulness/aggression requires more than a 30-minute break. These are signs that something is clearly not working, and a lifestyle change may be required. For a service dog working in a health care facility, chronic stress signs are most likely symptoms caused by a lack of consistency in the dog's lifestyle. Dogs rely on habits, and service dogs rely on the habits of their facilitator or handler to ensure their comfort level. Therefore, a change in the leader's behavior or a 2-week absence from a dog's facilitator or handler can be stress triggers. Stress can also be a sign that the way a facilitator or handler is acting in a situation needs to be changed. An example of the latter occurs frequently when a service dog hesitates. When the dog hesitates, the facilitator or handler will stop walking and face the service dog as if to ask the dog what is wrong. These actions indicate to the service dog that the facilitator or handler is relinquishing the leadership role and this encourages the dog's hesitation further. In a situation like this, the leadership style needs to be altered. The facilitator or handler needs to first identify if there are any obvious reasons for the dog's hesitation, then he or she needs to demonstrate leadership body language and redirect the service dog's focus through treats or additional commands to curb the service dog's hesitation. If these stress signs are not recognized or not properly managed, a service dog may experience chronic stress.

Since service dogs in health care facilities are accustomed to receiving lots of attention, sometimes the lack of attention from an absent leader can cause significant stress. Again, communication between leaders is vital to predict and recognize when a service dog is exhibiting stress signs. The other leaders may need to provide more attention to the service dog or adjust the dog's work schedule to ensure the dog's well-being and prevent the dog from experiencing unnecessary stress.

Facility service dogs are selected specifically because they have a high desire to interact with people. Therefore, many of these dogs are strongly impacted by separation from the facilitators or handlers. Being left alone in a dog crate at work for an afternoon can be just as stressful as working all afternoon without a break. Therefore,

scheduling the duration of break time is just as important as work time. During times when facilities are short staffed, such as over the holidays, it seems to be less stressful for a service dog to stay home in an off-duty mode than to come to work and sit alone for an extended period.

Anticipating Separation Through Retirement or Death

Each agency that owns service dogs has different parameters that address when a dog is ready for retirement. Most service dogs are from work breeds such as German shepherd, Labrador retriever, or golden retriever, which have life expectancies of 12–13 years.[12] Many of these agencies predict a 6–10 year work life for the dog and the majority of service dogs enter the work force around 2 years of age, so they are expected to work until the ages of 8–12 years. The number of years that a service dog is able to work is directly related to the physical and psychological well-being of the service dog. Physical aliments such as arthritis, hip dysplasia, and cataracts and psychological ailments in the form of gastrointestinal problems, hesitation, or fearfulness behavior can all contribute to an earlier retirement.

The agency that owns the service dog makes the final decision of when a service dog is ready to retire. This decision is based on veterinarian medical reports, annual reports submitted by facilitators and handlers, and site visits. The agency also decides the disposition of the dog when the dog retires. Recognizing that consistency is of vital importance in any dog's life, especially in a service dog's life, the facilitator has the first option to keep the retired service dog. Multiple handlers or facilitators may make this situation difficult, but the agency has final say as to who keeps the dog. If the facilitator is unable to take the dog, the dog is typically returned to the agency and an appropriate home for the dog's retirement is found. Usually the individual who raised the dog as a puppy has first option, and most of these agencies have long waiting lists for retired service dogs. If for some reason a home cannot be found, the dog is guaranteed a home at the agency.

When a loss occurs in the life of a service dog, a facilitator, a handler, a frequently seen patient, or another animal that lives with the service dog, the dog may exhibit signs of grief in the form of depression or withdrawal. As with humans, time and understanding may help the dog through this grieving process.[13] During this time, it is important for a service dog to feel secure and successful. This can be done by giving a dog easy commands and adequate praise before having the dog complete more complex commands. It is also always important to make commands and work fun from the dog's perspective. The more fun there is in a service dog and facilitator/handler partnership, the greater the potential for success. The effect of the death of the service animal should not be minimized. Often the service dog is thought of as a friend and companion whose loss is intensely felt.[14] The grief can be as acute as a loss of a family member or close friend. Although grief over the death of an animal is not often recognized in our society, people who work with service animals can appreciate the depth of grief that the animal facilitators, handlers, and patients experience.

Summary

Service animals can fulfill an important role in the lives of people with disabilities. The training, care, and supervision of the animal are extremely important to the animal's success as a service animal. The training and ongoing monitoring of the interactions of facilitators, handlers, and health care professionals with the service animal are also critical to the service animal's success. Managing expectations and the workload of the service dog, attending to the physical and psychological needs of the dog, and anticipating separation through retirement or death raise ethical issues. The ethical issues, from the perspective of the animal's welfare, have been presented with recommendations for resolving the issues.

References

1. Nussbaum MC. The moral status of animals. *Chron Higher Educ.* 2006;52(22): B6–8.
2. Singer P. *Animal Liberation: A New Ethics for Our Treatment of Animals.* New York: Random House; 1975.
3. Humane Society of the United States. Available at: www.hsus.org/pets/issues_affecting_our_ pets/pet_overpopulation_and_ownership_statis- tics/us_pet_ownership_statistics.html. Accessed December 12, 2006.
4. Eames E, Eames T. Bridging differences within the disability community: the assistance dog move- ment. *Dis Stud Q.* 2001;21(3):55–66.
5. ADA business brief: service animals. Available at: http://www.usdoj.gov/crt/ada/svcanimb.htm. Accessed December 12, 2006.
6. Delta Society. The human-animal health connection. Available at: www.deltasociety.org/ ServiceInformationBasic.htm. Accessed December 12, 2006.
7. Guide-dogs for the blind. Available at: www. guidedogs.com/site/PageServer. Accessed Decem- ber 13, 2006.
8. Mader B, Hart LA, Bergin B. Social acknowledg- ments for children with disabilities: effects of ser- vice dogs. *Child Dev.* 1989;60:1529–1534.
9. Allen K, Blascovich J. The value of service dogs for people with severe ambulatory dis- abilities: a randomized controlled trial. *JAMA.* 1996;275:1001–1006.
10. Duncan S. The 1997, 1998, 1999 APIC Guidelines Committees: APIC State-of-the-Art Report: the implications of service animals in health care set- tings. *AJIC.* 2000;28(2):170–180.
11. Eddy J, Hart LA, Boltz RP. The effects of service dogs on social acknowledgments of people in wheelchairs. *J Psych.* 2001;122(1):39–45.
12. Fogle B. *The New Encyclopedia of the Dog.* New York: Dorling Kindersley Publishing, Inc.; 2000.
13. K-State veterinarian says pets can grieve over a loss, too. Available at: http://www.mediarelations. kstate.edu/WEB/News/NewsReleases/listpetgrief. html. Accessed January 9, 2007.
14. Schneider KS. The winding valley of grief: when a dog guide retires or dies. *J Visual Impairment Blind- ness.* 2005;99(6):368–370.

Nora Wenthold is a research administrator at the Reha- bilitation Institute of Chicago and a Certified Canine Facilitator with Canine Companions for Independence, Chicago, Illinois.

Teresa A. Savage is a clinical assistant professor in the Department of Women, Children & Family Health Sci- ence at the University of Illinois College of Nursing. She has written and coauthored several articles as well as four books addressing ethical issues in nursing.

Randy Malamud

Service Animals: Serve Us Animals: Serve Us, Animals

The term "service animals" describes animals who render assistance of some sort to people with disabilities. I am interested in the boundaries of this concept of service animals, and also the blurriness around the edges; this blurriness surfaces when we consider service animals in relation to companion animals (the animals formerly known as "pets"), working animals, military animals, pack animals, harness animals, prison animals, comfort animals.

"Comfort animals" evokes the term "comfort women," who were forced into sexual slavery, raped and horribly abused by the Japanese military during World War II. Comfort animals are in fact not at all like comfort women—they may provide comfort, as we snuggle with them, to people who are for some reason uncomfortable, somehow afflicted. But the commonality is the idea of "comfort," that is, of course, our comfort—the human's comfort in relation to comfort animals, the man's comfort in relation to comfort women. The World War II term, with its insidiously exploitative, Orwellian connotations wrapped around the simple, pleasant word 'comfort', fuels my anthrozoological[1] cynicism; the idea of "service," too, carries a polyvalence that begs investigation.

Though my definition seems concisely focused—"service animals render assistance to people with disabilities"—consider the proposition that, in some sense, all people have disabilities: none of us is perfect. Everyone could be more *able*, more *enabled*, more fully *capable*, of doing something. Every person lacks, for example, a dog's keen senses of smell and hearing, or a bird's highly-refined sensitivity to a threatening predator, or a horse's bulk and strength, or a seal's ability to insulate against extreme cold. There are a range of 'animal powers' that people do not have as keenly as other animals do: sight, smell, speed—all the senses which facilitate a better attunement to one's environment and a better ability to prosper, safely and powerfully in that environment: flight, camouflage

and disguise, hibernation, toxic defense—powers of adaptation and survival.

In taking on animal strengths, can we take without taking? "Taking" the sightedness and instincts of a German Shepherd, training and transforming that animal into a guard dog, or a guide dog, is one way of appropriating animal powers. With comfort animals, people take the serenity of a cat or dog or gerbil (who seems unaware of how anxiety-filled the human world is) and harvest some of the animals' gentleness, their sanity, their happiness, their coping-skills. Do people "take" the serenity of these animals, or "share" their serenity? Probably it varies according to the specific situation, the specific person, and the specific animal.

This sense of the animal strengths that humans lack (the dog's powerful sense of smell, the horse's strength, and so on) combined with a sense of entitlement means that in our perennial disability we are inclined to harvest, or co-opt, or borrow, or steal some aspect of those abilities, that able-ness, from other creatures. This paradigm offers an interesting way to think about our own sense of limit, our own sense of inferiority to other animals; and it may suggest dynamics by which that able-ness may be shared between two species, between a human and another animal. It may suggest ecologically interesting moments of trans-species harmony, coexistence, mutual support. Or we may see the foundation of a relationship that, while predicated upon people's sense of inferiority to other animals' talents and abilities, manifests itself in a trope of jealousy, denial, and imperialism. That is, humans may decide to take, abrogate, exploit, animals' abilities for their own benefit, in which case the ecological equanimity described above would instead manifest as usurping and controlling whatever animal strengths we desire and need for our human progress.

"Service" is etymologically related to "subservience," calling attention to the dynamics and consequences of hierarchy. The *OED* defines "service" as the condition of being a servant; the fact of serving a master (as a servant or as a slave) ("service" *OED*). There's a religious sense of the word—one does God's service, one serves God, by obedience, piety, and good works. The ritual of public worship itself is called a service. A devout person's service denotes her service to God (so perhaps, by implication, an animal in service to people analogously evokes a person's service to God, suggesting that we are to service animals as God is to us).

A soldier is "in the service," as is a public employee—we speak of the diplomatic service, the civil service, Her Majesty's secret service—so by this association, the service animal may be regarded as a participant and supporter of some larger civic mission. Other civic services are provided not just by people but also by technology: telephone service, electric service, broadcasting service, internet service.

We fill cars with gas at service stations. There is a supra-human (posthuman) sense in which anything that adds to the benefit, the infrastructure, of our society comes under the heading of service. The designation of 'service animal' fits into this space, this custom, this ideology, of expecting support for our systems and pleasures and needs. We are used to being serviced.

Going back further into the word's history, "service" describes feudal allegiance, fealty, homage. We see a trace of this in the deference of the polite assistant or clerk who announces that she's "happy to be of service." The *OED* sends one off in myriad directions, stirring up a bundle of provocative associations, explicit and subliminal, lurking in the language. I want to unpack the word to reinforce the point of the pun, the echolalia, in my title: "Service animals; serve us animals; serve us, animals."

The first iteration of "service animals" is meant to be merely descriptive of this topic, this category, this class of animals, though at the same time, the category is not as simple and straightforward as it seems. We can detect and deconstruct a wealth of subtextually derogatory characterisations lurking here, and despite the seeming terminological precision, there's some fuzzy imprecision—therapy animals, harness animals, *et al.*: where do we draw the line? The second iteration conveys the demand of the imperial consumer (in which the empire is the dominion of humanity, and the subalterns are, as described in Genesis, the other animals who exist for people to use as we see fit). *Serve us animals.* We want animals . . . on platters, in cages, on leashes, wherever. And finally, the third iteration is meant as a direct address, a command, a fiat, from the oppressor to the oppressed: serve us, animals. Jump. Entertain. Guide. Protect. Carry. Die. Interestingly, people do not often actually verbalise this command to other animals: we don't have to, because it goes without saying that we expect animals' service, and in any case, they don't understand us: most of them don't speak English. We don't tell seals to serve us their pelts, or pigs to serve us their ribs, or elephants to serve us their tusks. We just take—perhaps the command would be superfluous, or perhaps the command is inherent in the taking. But we do, actually, tell dogs to serve us—Fetch! Heel! Come! Good dog! It is because dogs are so readily trainable to "serve us" in these ways that they have become the prototypical service animal, which is the guide dog.

The Animal as Guide

Today guide dogs are often called "seeing eye dogs," a phrase originating in a specific business, The Seeing Eye, the oldest extant dog training school. Located now in Morristown, NJ, it was founded in 1929 by Dorothy Harrison Eustis who had been a dog trainer in Switzerland, training police dogs, when she learned about a German school that was training dogs to help German soldiers blinded by mustard gas in the Great War. She wrote an article about it in the Saturday Evening Post, and was besieged by blind American soldiers who wanted her to create a similar facility for them (The Seeing Eye, Inc., n.d.).

Today, people who come to The Seeing Eye are assigned a dog and a trainer. Over a month-long course, they learn how to navigate the world around them with their dogs. The most common breeds are German Shepherds, Labrador Retrievers and Golden Retrievers, though other breeds include Poodles, Collies, Dobermans, Rottweilers, Boxers, and Airedale Terriers.

In the last few decades, the service animal rubric has expanded to include many other animals besides dogs for many other disabilities besides visual impairment. Miniature horses have been impounded into duty to perform services similar to guide dogs. Some people find them more trainable, more mild-mannered, and less threatening than large dogs—and they can live and serve for as long as 30 years, significantly longer than a guide dog. Monkeys are used by people who are quadriplegic or agoraphobic; goats by people with muscular dystrophy; and people with anxiety disorders have conscripted cats, ferrets, pigs, iguanas, and ducks as service animals. There are parrots for people with psychosis. It may seem counterintuitive to put a parrot on the shoulder of a psychotic person, but one such person profiled in the *New York Times* credited his parrot with helping him to keep from snapping, or exploding. Sadie the parrot accompanied him in a backpack-cage, and when she sensed him getting agitated, she would "talk him down," saying, "It's ok, Jim. Calm down, Jim. You're all right, Jim. I'm here, Jim" (Skloot 2008 n.p.).

When animals help us by doing things we cannot do for ourselves, this probably makes people appreciate more keenly the value of other animals, the importance of animals, and maybe even, in a larger sense, the ethical desirability of a more egalitarian, even-handed, respectful relationship with other animals. It seems likely that a person using a guide dog or a service parrot develops a profound appreciation for how smart, loyal, and supportive another animal can be. Certainly, the people who use these service animals are prone to this enlightenment, and possibly even those who simply see people using service animals develop a heightened respect for the animals' powers and their value.

But what is in it for the animals? Maybe the dogs and parrots come to appreciate the intense inter-species bond that they are involved in, and value the feelings of their human companion's dependence, and appreciation. Or perhaps parrots don't like zipping around town in a psychotic person's backpack. Included in the recent trend of more variegated service animals, we see comfort animals for old and disabled people; prison animals (a variant of comfort animals) who help mitigate the violent atmosphere of incarceration.

Military animals include bomb-sniffing dogs and patrol dogs. In the past, armies have used horses and mules in a variety of ways, as well as carrier pigeons. Hannibal used elephants to cross the Alps. It is not a stretch to regard such animals as service animals. News stories describe the bonds that form between soldiers and military dogs in Afghanistan and Iraq, recounting the intensely loving devotion that soldiers express, and the intense mourning on the soldiers' part if these animals die (and also on the animals' part if the soldiers die), and the services these dogs may render for soldiers with PTSD. This seems comparable to the relationship between blind people and guide dogs.

Other service animals include helper monkeys (capuchin monkeys, who often help paralysed people and others with mobility impairments: scratching an itch, picking up dropped objects, turning on a DVD player, turning the pages of a book) and dolphins (who are supposedly therapeutic for depressed and autistic children who swim with them to learn compassion, though Lori Marino and Scott Lilienfeld have done much work to debunk the myth of the supposed benefit to autistic children from swimming with dolphins, and also to expose the trauma that the dolphins themselves experience in this enterprise (2007). Cats are sometimes considered service animals: they can supposedly be trained (though this may seem unlikely) to alert people to danger by pawing at them, to notice in advance the onset of a seizure, and even to use the phone for help if a person is unable to. More credibly, cats are excellent comfort animals: often used in animal assisted therapy to improve a person's physical, social, emotional and cognitive condition. Monkeys, parrots, lizards, and other animals are also used in this capacity.

As guide dogs are joined by parrots and horses and ducks in the service animal cohort, I wonder what this profuse proliferation means. Are we somehow reverting to the ark-story, where people gather up tokens of every animal in existence and remove them from their natural habitats—enclosing them, capturing them, "saving" them, in a human structure? And then are these animals indebted to us because we have saved them from nature, bringing them into the promised land of human culture?

There is a sense of dominionism, manifest destiny, in our recent additions to the canon of service animals. We are expanding our service corps, expanding the range and realm of "services" they can provide us. As when Europeans began to expand the range of spices, gems, silks, furs that "serviced" their fashion and culinary cultures, to support the expansion of imperialist networks and markets, animals, too, figure as an unexploited resource: here are more services we can harvest from them, augmenting our own potential "wealth."

This profusion perhaps pathologises our socioecological isolation as a species: the loneliness, the inadequacy, of the human, the merely human. It is undesirable to be locked inside a bubble, a climate-controlled, pesticide-treated, hermetically sealed capsule designed to efface the outside world. We do need animals. We need comfort; we need to rub up against cats, and worms, and sheep. But balanced against this is the exploitative paradigm by which other animals' existence is appraised in terms of how they may assist us.

Service animals are fetishised: they are so valuable, so "smart," because they help us—because we can use them to remediate clearly-defined human deficiencies. We appreciate them. Does this make us appreciate other animals (those without training certificates) less? Are service animals the exceptions that prove the rule, that most animals do not seem to help us all that much? "The dogs go on with their doggy lives," as W. H. Auden (1989) wrote in Des "Musée de Beaux Arts." Note also that animals do help us in all kinds of ways that may not register in our consciousness: pollinating flowers, fertilising crops, sustaining the ecosystem . . . but in any case, who said it was their job to help us? Where did they sign up for that?. . .

Conclusions

Does the person who depends on a service animal have an admirable relationship to another member of another species, or is he weakened? Is the guide dog smart, useful, valuable, valued? These dogs are, clearly, very intelligent: do we understand that intelligence, do we appreciate it, do we perhaps even take the next step, and extend that insight that *this dog is intelligent* to the larger implication that lots of animals have intelligence that we are not aware of?

Service animals augment our own inadequacies—as do companion animals, military animals, work animals. Guide dogs amply and gloriously fulfil a rubric of value to their human users. But what about annoying animals, scary animals, stupid animals, useless animals? (The question is sarcastic—these are not judgements that are ecologically or ethically proper for people to make, though we make them anyway.)[3] They fare poorly in our rankings. They suffer by comparison to the exemplary animals that work so hard to help us, suggesting the negative repercussions of fetishising of service animals. The "good" animals make the others look lazy, hostile, useless. They set an impossible and ridiculous standard for animals: helping us. What have you done for me lately?! Are service animals the "Uncle Toms" of the animal kingdom? Unthreatening, servile, seemingly happy with their lot; they do not make trouble; they live to serve.

Human expectations of animals' services—our sense of entitlement to these services—exemplifies what Peter Singer (1975: 8–9) calls "speciesism," thus violating Jeremy Bentham's moral principle of equal consideration of interests: "each to count for one, and none for more than one." Just as racism and sexism violate the principles of equality, Singer writes, so too speciesism "allows the interests of [our] own species to override the greater interests of members of other species. The pattern is identical in each case." The discourse of anthrozoology invites the interrogation and deconstruction of even such an intimate human–animal interaction as service animals: one might even say, ". . . *especially* such an intimate human–animal interaction . . ."

As numerous artistic representations suggest, there is at least a subliminal tendency to conflate 'intimacy' and 'equality' when looking at the relationship between a person and a service animal. But this supposition sidesteps a vast tradition of speciesist exploitation in which we are prone to conflate an animal's intrinsic value with his or her usefulness to humans. It is tempting, and flattering, for people to imagine that other animals are eager to help us in our times of greatest need, and that they are gratified by our symbiotic or dependent relation with them.

In closing, there is an alternative perspective, an idealistic ecofantasy, suggesting one way we might problematise, unpack, and co-opt the idea of service animals. On the one hand, envision every animal you see as a service animal—and think about the services they're providing. The bright red cardinal bird is wearing a brilliant new outfit to remind you that it's March, and you should move out of your hibernating winter phase and step into your spring regeneration phase, along with the rest of the natural world. Time for you to put on a bright new outfit, too, and get with the game; be in the season. The elephants you see in a nature documentary service you by spreading seeds in their faeces to replenish the savannahs, by revitalising African grasslands. They dig water holes that assist the survival of other species, thus sustaining biodiversity in their habitats, thus preventing the ecosystemic degradations that lead to global warming, thus keeping our coastal cities from being flooded (for at least a few more years): a pretty vital service rendered.

And on the other hand, besides seeing every animal as a service animal, we may also learn to think of ourselves as service animals: turnabout is fair play. What kinds of services do we provide? What kind of services should we provide? Ecologically, it's symbiotic. Ethically, it's altruistic—but it can also be seen as self-interest (which is often an easier sell than altruism): Do unto others as you would have others do unto you. Think about the ecosocial onus of playing our part as good citizens and rendering services where we can, if only for the selfish reason that this would allow the other animals to continue more easily and more prosperously to render their services back to us.

Earlier I invoked a religious service, the civil service, telephone service: connoting service as a metaphysical calling, a civic mission, a foundation for a more desirable and more functional and durable community. Thinking about how much aid and ability a blind man gets from his guide dog, imagine how amazing it would be if people could render a comparable level of service, a comparable value of service, to some of the other animals who share our world.

Notes

1. Anthrozoology refers to the study of interaction between human beings and other animals.
2. See Nagy K and Johnson P 2013, *Trash Animals: How we live with nature's filthy, feral, invasive, and unwanted species*, University of Minnesota Press, Minneapolis.

References

Auden, W. H. 1989 *Selected Poems*, Vintage, London.

Marino, L. and Lilienfeld S. 2007 'Dolphin-Assisted Therapy: More Flawed Data and More Flawed Conclusions', *Anthrozoos*, vol. 20, no. 3: 239–49.

OED Online, 2004 Oxford University Press <http://dictionary.oed.com/>

The Seeing Eye, Inc. 'Guide Dogs for People Who Are Blind or Visually Impaired,' 20 March 2013 <http://www.seeingeye.org>

Singer, P. 1975, *Animal Liberation*, HarperCollins, New York.

Skloot, R. 2008, 'Creature Comforts,' *New York Times*, 31 December, <http://www.nytimes.com/2009/01/04/magazine/04Creatures-t.html?pagewanted=all>

Tucker, M. 1984, *The Eyes That Lead: The story of guide dogs for the blind*, Robert Hale, London.

RANDY MALAMUD is Regents' Professor and Chair of the English Department at Georgia State University. He has written six books and edited two others, along with 70 essays, book chapters and reviews. He is a Fellow of the Oxford Centre for Animal Ethics, a Patron of the Captive Animals' Protection Society, and an International Faculty affiliate of the New Zealand Centre for Human–Animal Studies at the University of Canterbury.

EXPLORING THE ISSUE

Is It Ethical to Employ Service Animals?

Critical Thinking and Reflection

1. Identify and reflect on the similarities between human beings and animals that you consider to be morally relevant. Why are these similarities morally relevant? How do these similarities affect the moral treatment of animals, especially service animals?

2. Identify and reflect on the differences between human beings and animals that you consider to be morally relevant. Why are these differences morally relevant? How do these differences affect the moral treatment of animals, especially service animals?

3. In addition to concerns about service animals, some philosophers object to the practice of keeping animals as pets (comfort animals). Have you ever had a relationship with a pet (or observed the relationship between another human being and his/her pet)? Do you consider pet ownership to be a moral practice? Why or why not?

4. If humans develop intelligent machines, would it be morally appropriate to use them in place of service/therapy animals? Why or why not?

5. What are the morally relevant similarities and differences between the use of service/therapy animals and the use of low-paid human attendants, such as nursing home attendants? How should these similarities and differences affect the treatment of service/therapy animals? How should they affect the treatment of the human attendants?

Is There Common Ground?

At first glance, the authors appear diametrically opposed. Wenthold and Savage do not question the moral acceptability of the use of animals to assist the disabled, while Malamud finds fundamental moral problems with this practice. If we read carefully, however, we can see subtle points of agreement.

Malamud suggests that humanity needs to rethink its relationship with animals. While he deplores the uncritical placement of animals in a subservient position to humans, he acknowledges the theoretical possibility of a morally acceptable relationship between a disabled person and an animal assistant. In such a relationship, "trans-species harmony, coexistence, mutual support" would predominate. Moreover, Malamud suggests that we can see all animals as service animals by coming to understand what each animal naturally does and recognizing how each animal contributes to the world we share. Meanwhile, Wenthold and Savage describe the ideal relationship between a service dog and the human whom the dog assists as a bond that can "surpass a species difference" and be "as strong as a family bond." They repeatedly emphasize that those who handle service animals must understand and respect how the animal naturally behaves, learning to work with the animal in the manner that the animal—not necessarily the handler—prefers. All three authors, then, discourage treating animals in a purely instrumental manner and express support for understanding and respecting animals by transcending the boundaries of species.

Additional Resources

Susan Armstrong and Richard Botzler, *The Animal Ethics Reader*, 2nd ed. (Routledge, 2008)

Rebecca Huss, "Why context matters: Defining service animals under federal law," *Pepperdine Law Review* 37:4 (2010)

Robert Garner, *Animal Ethics* (Polity, 2005)

Internet References . . .

Ethics Updates: The Moral Status of Animals

> http://ethics.sandiego.edu/Applied/Animals/
> index.asp

Ethical Considerations in Animal-Assisted Therapy

> http://suzanneclothier.com/the-articles/ethical-
> considerations-animal-assisted-therapy

Animal Welfare: The National Agricultural Law Center

> http://nationalaglawcenter.org/research-by-topic/
> animal-welfare/